48: *American Poets, 1880-1945*, Second Series, edited by Peter Quartermain (1986)

49: *American Literary Publishing Houses, 1638-1899*, 2 parts, edited by Peter Dzwonkoski (1986)

50: *Afro-American Writers Before the Harlem Renaissance*, edited by Trudier Harris (1986)

51: *Afro-American Writers from the Harlem Renaissance to 1940*, edited by Trudier Harris (1987)

52: *American Writers for Children Since 1960: Fiction*, edited by Glenn E. Estes (1986)

53: *Canadian Writers Since 1960*, First Series, edited by W. H. New (1986)

54: *American Poets, 1880-1945*, Third Series, 2 parts, edited by Peter Quartermain (1987)

55: *Victorian Prose Writers Before 1867*, edited by William B. Thesing (1987)

56: *German Fiction Writers, 1914-1945*, edited by James Hardin (1987)

57: *Victorian Prose Writers After 1867*, edited by William B. Thesing (1987)

58: *Jacobean and Caroline Dramatists*, edited by Fredson Bowers (1987)

59: *American Literary Critics and Scholars, 1800-1850*, edited by John W. Rathbun and Monica M. Grecu (1987)

60: *Canadian Writers Since 1960*, Second Series, edited by W. H. New (1987)

61: *American Writers for Children Since 1960: Poets, Illustrators, and Nonfiction Authors*, edited by Glenn E. Estes (1987)

62: *Elizabethan Dramatists*, edited by Fredson Bowers (1987)

63: *Modern American Critics, 1920-1955*, edited by Gregory S. Jay (1988)

64: *American Literary Critics and Scholars, 1850-1880*, edited by John W. Rathbun and Monica M. Grecu (1988)

65: *French Novelists, 1900-1930*, edited by Catharine Savage Brosman (1988)

66: *German Fiction Writers, 1885-1913*, 2 parts, edited by James Hardin (1988)

67: *Modern American Critics Since 1955*, edited by Gregory S. Jay (1988)

68: *Canadian Writers, 1920-1959*, First Series, edited by W. H. New (1988)

69: *Contemporary German Fiction Writers*, First Series, edited by Wolfgang D. Elfe and James Hardin (1988)

70: *British Mystery Writers, 1860-1919*, edited by Bernard Benstock and Thomas F. Staley (1988)

71: *American Literary Critics and Scholars, 1880-1900*, edited by John W. Rathbun and Monica M. Grecu (1988)

72: *French Novelists, 1930-1960*, edited by Catharine Savage Brosman (1988)

73: *American Magazine Journalists, 1741-1850*, edited by Sam G. Riley (1988)

74: *American Short-Story Writers Before 1880*, edited by Bobby Ellen Kimbel, with the assistance of William E. Grant (1988)

Documentary Series

1: *Sherwood Anderson, Willa Cather, John Dos Passos, Theodore Dreiser, F. Scott Fitzgerald, Ernest Hemingway, Sinclair Lewis*, edited by Margaret A. Van Antwerp (1982)

2: *James Gould Cozzens, James T. Farrell, William Faulkner, John O'Hara, John Steinbeck, Thomas Wolfe, Richard Wright*, edited by Margaret A. Van Antwerp (1982)

3: *Saul Bellow, Jack Kerouac, Norman Mailer, Vladimir Nabokov, John Updike, Kurt Vonnegut*, edited by Mary Bruccoli (1983)

4: *Tennessee Williams*, edited by Margaret A. Van Antwerp and Sally Johns (1984)

5: *American Transcendentalists*, edited by Joel Myerson (1988)

Yearbooks

1980, edited by Karen L. Rood, Jean W. Ross, and Richard Ziegfeld (1981)

1981, edited by Karen L. Rood, Jean W. Ross, and Richard Ziegfeld (1982)

1982, edited by Richard Ziegfeld; associate editors: Jean W. Ross and Lynne C. Zeigler (1983)

1983, edited by Mary Bruccoli and Jean W. Ross; associate editor: Richard Ziegfeld (1984)

1984, edited by Jean W. Ross (1985)

1985, edited by Jean W. Ross (1986)

1986, edited by J. M. Brook (1987)

1987, edited by J. M. Brook (1988)

Concise Series

The New Consciousness, 1941-1968 (1987)

Colonization to the American Renaissance, 1640-1865 (1988)

Realism, Naturalism, and Local Color, 1865-1917 (1988)

Dictionary of Literary Biography • Volume Seventy-four

American Short-Story Writers Before 1880

Dictionary of Literary Biography • Volume Seventy-four

American Short-Story Writers Before 1880

Edited by
Bobby Ellen Kimbel
Pennsylvania State University, Oguntz Campus

with the assistance of
William E. Grant
Bowling Green State University

A Bruccoli Clark Layman Book
Gale Research Inc. • Book Tower • Detroit, Michigan 48226

Manufactured by Edward Brothers, Inc.
Ann Arbor, Michigan
Printed in the United States of America

Library of Congress Cataloging-in-Publication Data

American short-story writers before 1880 / edited by Bobby Ellen Kimbel, with the assistance of William E. Grant.

p. cm.–(Dictionary of literary biography; v. 74)
"A Bruccoli Clark Layman book."
Includes index.
ISBN 0-8103-4552-8
1. Short stories, American–History and criticism. 2. Short stories, American–Bio-bibliography. 3. Authors, American–Biography–Dictionaries. I. Kimbel, Bobby Ellen. II. Grant, William E. (William Earl), 1933-   . III. Series.
PS374.S5A38 1988
813'.01'09–dc19   88-21462
                                                      CIP

for my husband, Philip

Contents

Plan of the Series

. . . Almost the most prodigious asset of a country, and perhaps its most precious possession, is its native literary product–when that product is fine and noble and enduring.

Mark Twain*

The advisory board, the editors, and the publisher of the *Dictionary of Literary Biography* are joined in endorsing Mark Twain's declaration. The literature of a nation provides an inexhaustible resource of permanent worth. We intend to make literature and its creators better understood and more accessible to students and the reading public, while satisfying the standards of teachers and scholars.

To meet these requirements, *literary biography* has been construed in terms of the author's achievement. The most important thing about a writer is his writing. Accordingly, the entries in *DLB* are career biographies, tracing the development of the author's canon and the evolution of his reputation.

The purpose of *DLB* is not only to provide reliable information in a convenient format but also to place the figures in the larger perspective of literary history and to offer appraisals of their accomplishments by qualified scholars.

The publication plan for *DLB* resulted from two years of preparation. The project was proposed to Bruccoli Clark by Frederick G. Ruffner, president of the Gale Research Company, in November 1975. After specimen entries were prepared and typeset, an advisory board was formed to refine the entry format and develop the series rationale. In meetings held during 1976, the publisher, series editors, and advisory board approved the scheme for a comprehensive biographical dictionary of persons who contributed to North American literature. Editorial work on the first volume began in January 1977, and it was published in 1978. In order to make *DLB* more than a reference tool and to compile volumes that individually have claim to status as literary history, it was decided to organize volumes by topic, period, or genre. Each of these freestanding volumes provides a biographical-bibliographical guide and overview for a particular area of literature. We are convinced that this organization–as opposed to a single alphabet method–constitutes a valuable innovation in the presentation of reference material. The volume plan necessarily requires many decisions for the placement and treatment of authors who might properly be included in two or three volumes. In some instances a major figure will be included in separate volumes, but with different entries emphasizing the aspect of his career appropriate to each volume. Ernest Hemingway, for example, is represented in *American Writers in Paris, 1920-1939* by an entry focusing on his expatriate apprenticeship; he is also in *American Novelists, 1910-1945* with an entry surveying his entire career. Each volume includes a cumulative index of subject authors and articles. Comprehensive indexes to the entire series are planned.

With volume ten in 1982 it was decided to enlarge the scope of *DLB*. By the end of 1986 twenty-one volumes treating British literature had been published, and volumes for Commonwealth and Modern European literature were in progress. The series has been further augmented by the *DLB Yearbooks* (since 1981) which update published entries and add new entries to keep the *DLB* current with contemporary activity. There have also been *DLB Documentary Series* volumes which provide biographical and critical source materials for figures whose work is judged to have particular interest for students. One of these companion volumes is entirely devoted to Tennessee Williams.

We define literature as the *intellectual commerce of a nation:* not merely as belles lettres but as that ample and complex process by which ideas are generated, shaped, and transmitted. *DLB* entries are not limited to "creative writers" but extend to other figures who in their time and in their way influenced the mind of a people. Thus the series encompasses historians, journalists, publishers, and screenwriters. By this means readers of *DLB* may be aided to perceive litera-

*From an unpublished section of Mark Twain's autobiography, copyright © by the Mark Twain Company.

ture not as cult scripture in the keeping of intellectual high priests but firmly positioned at the center of a nation's life.

DLB includes the major writers appropriate to each volume and those standing in the ranks immediately behind them. Scholarly and critical counsel has been sought in deciding which minor figures to include and how full their entries should be. Wherever possible, useful references are made to figures who do not warrant separate entries.

Each *DLB* volume has a volume editor responsible for planning the volume, selecting the figures for inclusion, and assigning the entries. Volume editors are also responsible for preparing, where appropriate, appendices surveying the major periodicals and literary and intellectual movements for their volumes, as well as lists of further readings. Work on the series as a whole is coordinated at the Bruccoli Clark Layman editorial center in Columbia, South Carolina, where the editorial staff is responsible for accuracy of the published volumes.

One feature that distinguishes *DLB* is the illustration policy—its concern with the iconography of literature. Just as an author is influenced by his surroundings, so is the reader's understanding of the author enhanced by a knowledge of his environment. Therefore *DLB* volumes include not only drawings, paintings, and photographs of authors, often depicting them at various stages in their careers, but also illustrations of their families and places where they lived. Title pages are regularly reproduced in facsimile along with dust jackets for modern authors. The dust jackets are a special feature of *DLB* because they often document better than anything else the way in which an author's work was perceived in its own time. Specimens of the writers' manuscripts are included when feasible.

Samuel Johnson rightly decreed that "The chief glory of every people arises from its authors." The purpose of the *Dictionary of Literary Biography* is to compile literary history in the surest way available to us—by accurate and comprehensive treatment of the lives and work of those who contributed to it.

The *DLB* Advisory Board

Foreword

This volume of the *Dictionary of Literary Biography*, the first of a subseries of volumes devoted to American short-story writers, focuses on those authors who began their careers before 1880. It is remarkable that against the background of the early American republic, characterized by the hardships of settlement life, the brutalizing effects of the Revolutionary War, and the repressiveness of Puritanism, there arose a vital new literary form: derivative and moralistic at first, but gradually emerging as an extraordinary and uniquely American contribution to the world of letters. When Washington Irving lifted the short story out of its wooden, imitative didacticism in his romantic and vividly descriptive *The Sketch Book of Geoffrey Crayon, Gent.* (1819-1820); and when Nathaniel Hawthorne in his *Twice-Told Tales* (1837) and Edgar Allan Poe in his *Tales of the Grotesque and Arabesque* (1840) explored with rich symbolic patterning the dark regions of the human soul, the short story as a native American art form was born.

The earliest examples of the short prose narrative appeared in the late-eighteenth century in the newly developing monthly periodicals. Often, these stories were adaptations of tales cavalierly and anonymously copied from British and Continental magazines and, like them, were designed to amuse and entertain readers while achieving their more deliberate aims of preaching and instructing. The satiric and pointedly moral essays of Joseph Addison and Sir Richard Steele were being published with regularity in the *Spectator* and the *Tatler* in England, and, doubtless, emulations of these models were thought to lend respectability to American periodical publications.

The readership of periodicals remained for many years hopelessly meager. Given the harsh conditions under which they lived, those colonists who had the skill to read had little time to practice it. In the 1790s, when the population of the colonies had reached four-and-one-half million, only *Pennsylvania Magazine* achieved a circulation of one thousand. The average life of a magazine was eighteen months, and many folded within the first year of publication.

There were, in the late 1700s, as yet no publishing houses—only small commercial printers, who acted also as editor, salesman, advertiser, adviser, solicitor, and publisher. These early publishers initiated those journals that first produced a native American literature. Even though the material of early periodicals was largely imitative of European and British models, the motivation to promote the image of the newly emerging Republic to the rest of the world led to the gradual evolution of a separate and distinct expressive form. In the preface to Hugh Henry Brackenridge's *United States Magazine,* one of only two periodicals published during the Revolution, the pride in this growing distinctiveness is made explicit: "We have fought them no less successfully with the pen than with the sword. We hope to convince them yet more fully that we are able to cultivate the belles lettres, even disconnected with Great Britain; and that liberty is of so noble and energetic a quality, as even from the bosom of a war to call forth the power of human genius in every course of literary fame and improvement."

These early short fiction pieces were primitive: characters were flat and stereotyped, and narrative and description were deployed in the service of the story's moral purpose. To counteract the resultant woodenness of the prose, lurid details were scattered throughout: depictions of gambling, drunkenness, seduction, suicide, and murder proliferated, demonstrating finally the penalty for wickedness and working toward the general improvement of character.

By 1740 the library societies of Philadelphia, Newport, New York, and Charleston had been founded; by 1764 seven colleges had been established, and although there was little study of English or modern literatures, the colleges functioned as meeting places for like-minded people and as such stimulated further learning. When the Peace of 1783 made the publication of native writing not just desirable but urgent, an intellectual climate existed, at least in some parts of the country, where such writing could flourish. At the same time, British prose, still the strongest single literary influence, was becoming increasingly romantic. The informal essays of Samuel Johnson, Addison, and Steele, the robust novels of Henry Fielding and Laurence Sterne, and the mystical, inward-turning poetry of William Blake, William Wordsworth, and Samuel Taylor Coleridge created bold new patterns whose emphasis lay on the primacy, complexity, and value of the individual. The revolt in Europe against political and religious authority and against reason itself found a responsive national consciousness in the United States that was expressed as a repudiation of the European cultural heritage. The grand, endless mysteries of nature on the unexplored western continent and a developing pride in exclusively American ideas and subjects led to the creation of a new American myth, given first articulation in the tales of Washington Irving. Born in New York City of British parents, he was beyond the bleak shadow cast by New England Puritanism; his early reading, before he came upon the work of Sir Walter Scott, taught him a classical grace and restraint, evident in his Jonathan Oldstyle papers and the *Salmagundi* papers of 1807. Irving's exposure to Scott and his knowledge of the German folktale tradition pervasive in New York State led to his creation of *The Sketch Book of Geoffrey Crayon, Gent.*, a remarkable blend of classical order and form and romantic thematic impulses. The immediate success of these tales, particularly "Rip Van Winkle" and "The Legend of Sleepy Hollow," encouraged a host of younger writers to attempt the short prose narrative. Literary annuals—including Christmas and New Year gift books—and other anthologies of verse and stories began to proliferate. These collections were the most widely distributed short-story publications in America before the rise of the magazine in the mid-nineteenth century. Contributors included James Kirke Paulding, Catharine Sedgwick, Lydia Maria Child, and Nathaniel Parker Willis, who were among the most significant short-story writers in the period before the work of Poe and Hawthorne appeared.

In the decades following the Revolutionary War reading habits across the continent changed. The increase in population, the development of urban centers, the rapid spread of literacy, and the enormous technical advances in printing, binding, and publishing led to a newly created audience hungry for both information and entertainment. By 1845 the combined college libraries in the country contained six hundred thousand volumes, and public collections totaled nearly one million. Many towns could boast some sort of public library or reading room with significant holdings. At the same time American publishers turned increasingly to American writers. In 1820 the ratio of British to American authors repre-

sented in public libraries was seventy to thirty percent; thirty years later the ratio had been reversed.

During the 1830s and 1840s extraordinary changes occurred on the American continent. Westward expansion led both to a sense of national invincibility and to a new political coalition of West and South; and the shift to urbanization, with concomitant growth in manufacture, finance, and investment, changed forever the texture of life in the new country. The radical transformation of the culture was recorded in the periodicals, which, with the newspapers, were the sole means of disseminating news and information. There were, in addition to the general periodicals, magazines directed to audiences with special needs and interests, and among these there flourished a number of publications designed specifically for women. The general magazines had counted among their contributors significant women writers and editors. With the advent of women's magazines came enhanced opportunities for women with literary skills. The first of these specialized periodicals to continue publication for more than five years was the *Ladies' Magazine* (1828), edited by Sara Josepha Hale in Boston. It was billed as "the first magazine edited by a woman for women." In 1837, at the insistence of Louis Godey, Hale moved to his *Lady's Book* in Philadelphia, where she remained as literary editor for several years. *Godey's Lady's Book* was the most successful and influential of the women's magazines: it was conspicuous alongside the general monthly periodicals and newspapers on virtually every newsstand in America. Godey, a clever entrepreneur and businessman, designed his magazine to meet the changing tastes of the public, and he understood the special requirements of his women readers, who were, in ever-growing numbers, eager to devour essays and fiction in which they could find useful patterns of personal and social behavior. In 1836 an editorial in *Godey's* boasted: "This magazine has a much larger circulation than any other monthly in the country." As its circulation grew, Godey relied increasingly on native material; in an 1834 issue all seven stories included were written by American authors, Poe among them. Editorial policy, strictly applied, determined the nature and length of Godey's stories, as indicated in these instructions to contributors provided after Mrs. Hale assumed editorship: "We want short, racy, spirited essays; stories and sketches that embody pages of narrative and sentiment in a single paragraph, and by a few, bold touches paint rather than describe the character they exhibit for the instruction and entertainment of our readers. Such stories may be called *too short,* but that usually implies they are very popular."

The importance of *Godey's Lady's Book* cannot be overstated: the carefully circumscribed limits set by this periodical helped determine the shape and direction of the American short story in its earliest phase of development. Further, the magazine functioned as a forum for the dissemination of fiction specifically addressed to women's issues: stories written by women, addressed to women and retelling, in one or another of its guises, the same tale. Nearly all of these short-fiction pieces chronicle the triumph of their young heroines–who possess enormous resources of independence, intelligence, and courage–over the most adverse and frequently harrowing circumstances. Whether or not they were understood as such, these stories, and many of the essays that accompanied them, were feminist in point of view. Sara Hale, who frequently exhorted her female readers to further their educations as teachers or physicians, said in her first editorial at *Godey's:* "We offer a field where female genius may find scope; where the female mind may engage in its appropriate work–that of benefiting the female sex. . . . It is our aim to prepare a work which, for our own sex, should be superior to every other periodical. To effect this, ours must differ in some important respects from the general mass of monthly literature. It must differ as do the minds of the sexes." These short-fiction works by women, and the novels they wrote as well, have often been dismissed as "sentimental." Modern scholarship has worked to reverse this view and has revealed the number of ways in which the literature of mid-nineteenth-century American women, while admittedly moralistic, excessively genteel, and often melodramatic, reflects the contemporary scene with an extraordinary fidelity to social customs, values, and behaviors and illuminates complex issues of social and marital injustice.

And so, the "damned mob of scribbling women," to use Hawthorne's by-now overly familiar phrase, was in fact writing out of a new tradition of realism, while its male counterparts were perpetuating the tradition of romanticism: the exploration of the dark, perverse, and demonic impulses in the human spirit established by those titans of the genre, Hawthorne and Poe. Clearly then, Catharine Sedgwick, Caroline Kirkland,

Elizabeth Stuart Phelps, Rose Terry Cooke, Fanny Fern (Sara Payson Willis Parton), and Harriet Prescott Spofford were, in a very real if limited sense, the literary progenitors of William Dean Howells and Henry James.

It is generally understood that the fundamental motivation of the magazine-story writer was commercial. Even though remuneration was pitifully inadequate (one dollar per page of prose was standard), authors capable of producing enough acceptable work could earn modest incomes. Still, the mercantile stigma attached to magazine writing worked against the acceptance of the short story as a serious literary form. At midcentury most critics regarded the genre as subliterary but necessary: an exercise in preparation for the more respectable novel; or a phenomenon of mass culture destined to wither and to have only historical significance. But the perceptive editor Rufus Griswold, who in *The Prose Writers of America* (1847) collected a number of tales by contemporary authors–among them Irving, Poe, Kirkland, Hawthorne, and Lydia Maria Child–said about the form: "Admitting very readily that it requires more application–more time and toil–to produce a three volume novel, it must not be supposed that the production of the tale is a very easy business. On the contrary, there is scarcely anything more difficult, or demanding the exercise of finer genius, in the whole domain of prose and composition."

The 1850s (derided by commentators as the "feminine fifties" due to the enormous number of women whose fiction pieces were published regularly in the weekly and monthly periodicals) were transitional years for the short-story form. The decade was dominated at first by stories–written in a deliberately inflated style–whose themes reaffirm ideals of Christian doctrine and American democracy. But increasingly, authors responded to growing changes in popular taste and to the negative reviews of critics who had long decried the moralizing impulse of short fictions. Utilizing their own expanding cultural experience and literary sophistication, they turned to prose forms now recognized as foundations of the modern short story. As fictional narrative relinquished the pieties, stereotypes, and remoteness of allegory, and as characters and settings became increasingly identifiable–especially as central characters possessed of an inner life were shown logically to change and grow–the short-story form attained a renewed aesthetic and thus, critical validity. The transformation of the form can be seen in Herman Melville's shift from "The Bell-Tower" with its poeticisms, exotic setting, and emphasis on the nature of original sin to "Bartleby the Scrivener," whose antiheroic narrator moves through a recognizable contemporary world, gradually revealing to the reader a complex consciousness wherein resides the significance of the story.

A literary bridge between romanticism and realism was effected by the writers of local color. In these works emphasis is on the setting–natural scenery as well as domestic details–and on the specifics of custom, dress, manners, and speech (usually dialect) so that the picturesque idiosyncrasies of a given region are revealed. The industrialization of the North and the great expansion of the South and West (those twin forces whose collision was in large measure responsible for the Civil War) led to distinctions readily transcribed in a fictional form which preserved the essence–the look and feel–of a given region. An American folk tradition resulted. Its seeds were in European folktales, traveling minstrel shows, tall tales and ballads of the South and Midwest, adventures of the prairies, and tales of Broadway "bohemians." Among its most successful expressions were Bret Harte's tales of the California gold mines, Joel Chandler Harris's Uncle Remus stories, George Washington Cable's New Orleans sketches, Fitz-James O'Brien's New York fictions, and the stories by Mark Twain, for whom all of America was source and subject. The voice of this fiction was impatient of hypocrisy; its cadences were no-nonsense, high-spirited, humorous, irreverent, and earthy. The absence of "masterpieces" in regionalist or local-color fiction (Mark Twain's fiction is the obvious exception) may have been in the tendency of these works to blur distinctions between fact and fiction, between reality and romance, and between robust humor and a deeply felt sense of social injustice. There appeared no critic to help codify the structure of the new fiction, no guide to assess its strengths and to help nudge it toward true artistic maturity and public acclaim–none, that is, until William Dean Howells, whose editorials and book reviews for the *Atlantic Monthly*, the *North American Review*, the *Nation*, and *Harper's Monthly* created an appreciative audience for local colorists and especially for Mark Twain.

But even Howells, as late as the 1880s, did not recognize the degree to which the short prose narrative (still indiscriminately referred to as story, sketch, or tale) was no longer an inferior apprentice exercise but had evolved into a rich, distinctive form from whose myriad expressions could be gathered the rudiments of literary theory. There had been, up to this time, only two notable short-story theorists: Poe, who in his 1847 review of Hawthorne's *Twice-Told Tales* argued for unity of effect, truth, and brevity (perhaps more important was his assertion that "stories belong to the highest regions of Art"); and Brander Matthews, who in a *Lippincott's* magazine essay of 1884 prescribed the following: originality, unity, compression, brilliancy of style, action, form, substance, and, if possible, fantasy. Short-story writers have long since abandoned such strictures (or found them too loose and impressionistic to be of value), but, nonetheless, the effect of carefully organized critical theory–that is, description, interpretation, assessment–was to bring validity and respectability to the new literary form. The advent of responsible criticism as a practiced discipline heralded a new age in American literature. It created an awareness, indeed, an acute self-consciousness in fiction writers about the requirements of their craft with the consequent elevation of the novel and short-story forms to the realms of high art.

If Howells was, as editor, critic, and reviewer, the spokesman for the modernist spirit, especially as he acknowledged and celebrated the shift from the excesses of romantic idealism to the solidity and "truth-telling" of realism, then Henry James was its most eloquent exemplar. In his writings many of the finest strains in the slowly evolving fictional prose forms were met; through his extraordinary sensibility–always at a remove from, but somehow understanding perfectly the essence of, the human dilemma–the short story as genre became the narrative voice of the age. Early in his career James had remarked, "To write a series of good little tales I deem ample work for a lifetime." By the end of his life he had written 112 short-fiction works. While precious few are little, most are indeed good, and many are the expression of extraordinary genius. In his early and middle phases James was drawn to subjects which allowed him a meticulous scrutiny of problems of conduct ("Daisy Miller," "Washington Square," "The Real Thing"). Whatever their final effect, the canvas is broad and sweeping, and character and setting are convincingly realized. By the turn of the century ("The Great Good Place," "The Beast in the Jungle," "The Jolly Corner") this richly textured social world and its interest in the subtleties of ethical behavior and the difficulties of interpersonal relations gave way to more philosophical considerations and to explorations of the conflicting currents of the inner life. But throughout his work, from the earliest experiments to the late fully mature expressions, one finds at the center a solitary soul, frequently an artist, dreamer, idealist, expatriate, or all of these, signifying, as agent or victim, missed opportunities, the inability to love, the failure somehow to have lived fully. In his unparalleled treatments of loneliness, James found the very hallmark of the American and indeed the modern experience. By way of his prodigious and profound contributions to the genre, the American literary community could claim, as it has since his death, the short-story form as its own.

—Bobby Ellen Kimbel

Acknowledgments

This book was produced by Bruccoli Clark Layman, Inc. Karen L. Rood, senior editor for the *Dictionary of Literary Biography* series, was the inhouse editor.

Production coordinator is Kimberly Casey. Art supervisor is Cheryl Crombie. Copyediting supervisor is Joan M. Prince. Typesetting supervisor is Kathleen M. Flanagan. Laura Ingram and Michael D. Senecal are editorial associates. The production staff includes Rowena Betts, Charles D. Brower, Joseph Matthew Bruccoli, Amanda Caulley, Patricia Coate, Mary Colborn, Holly Deal, Mary S. Dye, Sarah A. Estes, Eric Folley, Cynthia Hallman, Judith K. Ingle, Maria Ling, Warren McInnis, Kathy S. Merlette, Sheri Beckett Neal, Joycelyn R. Smith, Virginia Smith, Jack Turner, and Mark Van Gunten. Jean W. Ross is permissions editor. Joseph Caldwell, photography editor, and Penney Haughton did photographic copy work for the volume.

Walter W. Ross and Rhonda Marshall did the library research with the assistance of the reference staff at the Thomas Cooper Library of the University of South Carolina: Daniel Boice, Cathy Eckman, Gary Geer, Cathie Gottlieb, David L. Haggard, Jens Holley, Dennis Isbell, Jackie Kinder, Marcia Martin, Jean Rhyne, Beverly Steele, Ellen Tillett, Carol Tobin, and Virginia Weathers.

American Short-Story Writers
Before 1880

Dictionary of Literary Biography

Thomas Bailey Aldrich
(11 November 1836-19 March 1907)

Samuel I. Bellman
California State Polytechnic University, Pomona

See also the Aldrich entries in *DLB 42: American Writers for Children Before 1900* and *DLB 71: American Literary Critics and Scholars, 1880-1900.*

BOOKS: *The Bells: A Collection of Chimes* (New York: J. C. Derby/Boston: Phillips, Sampson/Cincinnati: H. W. Derby, 1855);

Daisy's Necklace: And What Came of It. (A Literary Episode.) (New York: Derby & Jackson/Cincinnati: H. W. Derby, 1856);

The Course of True Love Never Did Run Smooth (New York: Rudd & Carleton, 1858);

The Ballad of Babie Bell and Other Poems (New York: Rudd & Carleton, 1859);

Pampinea and Other Poems (New York: Rudd & Carleton, 1861);

Out of His Head, A Romance . . . Also, Paul Lynde's Sketch Book (New York: Carleton, 1862); republished in part as *Père Antoine's Date Palm* (Cambridge, U.K.: Printed by Welch, Bigelow, 1866);

Poems (New York: Carleton/London: Low, 1863);

Songs of War (Albany: Munsell, 1863);

The Poems of Thomas Bailey Aldrich (Boston: Ticknor & Fields, 1865);

The Story of a Bad Boy (Boston: Fields, Osgood, 1870; London: Low & Marston, 1870); republished as *Tom Bailey's Adventures; Or, The Story of a Bad Boy* (Boston: Osgood, 1877);

Pansy's Wish: A Christmas Fantasy, With a Moral (Boston: Marion, 1870);

Marjorie Daw and Other People (Boston: Osgood, 1873; London: Routledge, 1873); enlarged as *Marjorie Daw and Other Tales* (Leipzig: Tauchnitz, 1879); republished as *Marjorie*

Thomas Bailey Aldrich.

Daw and Other Stories (Boston: Houghton, Mifflin, 1885; Edinburgh: Douglas, 1885);

Prudence Palfrey: A Novel (Boston: Osgood, 1874; London: Routledge, 1874);

Cloth of Gold and Other Poems (Boston: Osgood, 1874; London: Routledge, 1874);

Flower and Thorn: Later Poems (Boston: Osgood, 1877; London: Routledge, 1877);

A Midnight Fantasy, and The Little Violinist (Boston: Osgood, 1877);

The Queen of Sheba (London: Routledge, 1877; Boston: Osgood, 1877; revised edition, Edinburgh: Douglas, 1885);

The Stillwater Tragedy (Boston: Houghton, Mifflin, 1880; London: Low, 1880);

XXXVI Lyrics and XII Sonnets, Selected from Cloth of Gold and Flower and Thorn (Boston: Houghton, Mifflin, 1881; London: Low, Marston, Searle & Rivington, 1881);

Friar Jerome's Beautiful Book . . . Selected from Cloth of Gold and Flower and Thorn (Boston: Houghton, Mifflin, 1881; London: Low, Marston, Searle & Rivington, 1881);

The Poems of Thomas Bailey Aldrich (Boston & New York: Houghton, Mifflin, 1882);

From Ponkapog to Pesth (Boston & New York: Houghton, Mifflin, 1883);

Mercedes, and Later Lyrics (Boston & New York: Houghton, Mifflin, 1884); revised in part as *Mercedes: A Drama in Two Acts* (Boston & New York: Houghton, Mifflin, 1894);

The Poems of Thomas Bailey Aldrich, Household Edition (Boston & New York: Houghton, Mifflin, 1885);

The Second Son: A Novel, by Aldrich and M. O. W. Oliphant (Boston & New York: Houghton, Mifflin, 1888);

Wyndham Towers (Boston & New York: Houghton, Mifflin, 1890);

The Sisters' Tragedy with Other Poems, Lyrical and Dramatic (Boston & New York: Houghton, Mifflin, 1891; enlarged edition, London: Macmillan, 1891);

An Old Town by the Sea (Boston & New York: Houghton, Mifflin, 1893);

Two Bites at a Cherry, with Other Tales (Boston & New York: Houghton, Mifflin, 1893; Edinburgh: Douglas, 1893);

Unguarded Gates and Other Poems (Boston & New York: Houghton, Mifflin, 1895);

Later Lyrics (Boston & New York: Houghton, Mifflin, 1896; London: John Lane, 1896);

Judith and Holofernes: A Poem (Boston & New York: Houghton, Mifflin, 1896);

A Sea Turn and Other Matters (Boston & New York: Houghton, Mifflin, 1902; Edinburgh: Douglas, 1902);

Ponkapog Papers (Boston & New York: Houghton, Mifflin, 1903);

Judith of Bethulïa: A Tragedy (Boston & New York: Houghton, Mifflin, 1904; revised, 1905).

Collections: *The Writings of Thomas Bailey Aldrich*, 8 volumes (Boston & New York: Houghton, Mifflin, 1897); enlarged as *The Writings of Thomas Bailey Aldrich*, Ponkapog Edition, 9 volumes (Boston & New York: Houghton, Mifflin, 1907).

PERIODICAL PUBLICATIONS: "What Jedd Pallfrey Found in the Coffin: A Christmas Story," *Knickerbocker, New-York Monthly Magazine*, 49 (January 1857): 21-30;

"All Sorts of A Paper: Being Stray Leaves From a Note-Book," *Atlantic Monthly*, 90 (December 1902): 735-740.

Thomas Bailey Aldrich, so closely identified with the Boston Brahmin-literati of the later nineteenth century, was *Boston plated* rather than the genuine article, to paraphrase his self-description, quoted in the official biography by Ferris Greenslet (1908). This extremely witty humorist, editor, and writer of popular verse, short stories, sketches, and novels–who remains best-known for his slightly fictionalized autobiography, *The Story of a Bad Boy* (1870), and his epistolary short story "Marjorie Daw" (1873)–was also intimately linked with three other locales: Portsmouth, New Hampshire; New York City; and the village of Ponkapog in Massachusetts.

The son of Elias Taft Aldrich and Sarah Abba Bailey Aldrich, Thomas Bailey Aldrich was born in Portsmouth, where he lived for the first five years of his life, until 1841 when the family moved to New York. In 1846 they went to live in New Orleans, but in 1849 Aldrich returned to Portsmouth, where he entered Samuel De Merritt's school to prepare for admission to Harvard. So deep an impression did this antique, decayed seaport make on the little boy–an only child, and much influenced by his strong-willed grandfather Thomas Darling Bailey–that the "old town by the sea" figured prominently in many of his writings and, as can be seen from *The Story of a Bad Boy* (where the town is called Rivermouth), helped shape his thinking. Aldrich was unable to attend Harvard College because of his widowed mother's relative poverty after his father's death in 1849. He had been much taken with Henry Wadsworth Longfellow's poetry, but he was obliged to abandon his plans to study literature under Longfellow at Harvard and to enter the world of commerce.

From 1852 until the end of 1865 he lived mostly in New York City, spending the first three years in the employ of his uncle Charles Frost, a well-to-do merchant. Then, yielding to his literary proclivities, he entered the world of journalism and popular literature. In 1855, the year his first book of verse was published, he became junior literary critic for the *Evening Mirror;* the next year he became subeditor of the *Home Journal,* and in 1858, while retaining this position, he accepted an associate editorship at the *Saturday Press.* Aldrich left the *Home Journal* in 1859 but retained his post at the *Saturday Press,* which ceased publication the following year. In the fall of 1861, with the Civil War getting under way, Aldrich was at the battlefront in the Virginia, Washington, D. C., and Maryland area, as a war correspondent for the *New York Tribune,* attached to the division of Gen. Louis Ludwig Blenker, of the Army of the Potomac. Finding frontline reporting not to his liking, he returned to Portsmouth in the early part of 1862, before going on to New York to resume his literary career. Congenial, and devoted to a life in letters, he benefited greatly from being part of the New York literary and artistic scene. The renowned beer cellar and restaurant, Pfaff's, where Aldrich might occasionally be found, was a meeting place for writers, artists, wits in general, and appreciators of those with creative imaginations. Fortunately for him, in his formative adult years he came to know a wide range of the famous and the near-famous: among them his employers (owners of the *Evening Mirror* N. P. Willis and George Pope Morris, author of "Woodman, Spare That Tree!"), Fitz-Greene Halleck, Bayard Taylor, Edwin Booth, E. C. Stedman, R. H. Stoddard, and Walt Whitman. (Aldrich and Whitman did not appreciate each other.)

Much as Aldrich enjoyed life in New York City, he was drawn back to an area closer to his origins and filled with stronger literary associations: Boston. Aldrich had never lost physical contact with his birthplace, since he frequently vacationed in Portsmouth, and over the years had made himself fairly familiar with Boston, whose *Atlantic Monthly* had begun publishing his verses in 1860. Too staid and conservative, finally, for the raffish high life of New York's bohemia, he sought to relocate. At the end of 1865, following his marriage to Lilian Woodman on 28 November, he took up residence in Boston, where he be-

Aldrich in 1855, the year he became junior literary critic for the New York Evening Mirror

came editor of *Every Saturday* for Ticknor and Fields, which that year had published a collection of his poems. For a number of years Aldrich, like his more illustrious friend William Dean Howells, would combine editorial duties with literary production. He continued as editor of *Every Saturday* until 1874 and took over the editorship of the *Atlantic Monthly* from Howells in 1881, retaining the post until 1890. Throughout these Boston years he published extensively: short stories, novels, articles, verses. After his retirement in 1890 he and his wife traveled abroad frequently, thanks to an inheritance from a friend, Henry L. Pierce, and he added travel sketches to his ample list of publications.

In his late years Aldrich and his wife spent a portion of their time at their estate on what had been an Indian reservation near Ponkapog, in the Blue Hills not far from Boston. Aldrich gave this quaint name to two collections of his sketches: *From Ponkapog to Pesth* (1883) and *Ponkapog Papers* (1903); the 1907 edition of Aldrich's collected works is called the Ponkapog Edition. In his 1903 introductory note to the

Ponkapog Papers Aldrich explained: "These miscellaneous notes and essays are called *Ponkapog Papers* not simply because they chanced, for the most part, to be written within the limits of the old Indian Reservation, but, rather, because there is something typical of their unpretentiousness in the modesty with which Ponkapog assumes to being even a village." In *The Autobiography of Mark Twain* Samuel Clemens told a lively anecdote about his relations with Aldrich and his wife and about his stay at Ponkapog in 1905, at the "urgent invitation" of the Aldriches. Describing their "cheap" but "showy" automobile, the "incompetent" attempt of Aldrich and his friends to play polo ("another symbol and advertisement of financial obesity" that proved "dangerous to everybody but the ball"), and the comfortable guest room to which he was shown, Clemens, who was seventy at the time, went on to tell how he was transferred to "the meanest cell . . . I had ever been in since I got out of jail" to make room for a twenty-year-old former governor's daughter, whom Mrs. Aldrich hoped to match with her thirty-seven-year-old, unmarried son.

In their anthology *American Short Stories* (1952) Eugene Current-García and Walton R. Patrick observe that at the height of the local-color movement of the 1880s "the short story was officially 'discovered' by writers and critics who now resurrected Poe's theories and reapplied them," adding that "Thomas Bailey Aldrich, H. C. Bunner, and Brander Matthews" in 1885 reformulated those principles of the form. Of greater significance "than the mere restating of the principles were the new technical effects" employed by these practitioners, whose " 'well-made' story was interesting chiefly for its emphasis on technique," rather than "for its subject matter, which was realistic only" insofar as characters representing a few "social groups could be identified in it." According to Current-García and Patrick, these stories ranged "in content and tone all the way from the light foolery of Frank Stockton's 'The Lady, or the Tiger?' to the tartly ironic cross purpose of Aldrich's 'Two Bites at a Cherry,' " but their authors shared a new "concern over the manner of presenting the story most effectively."

The so-called well-made story features ingeniously contrived plots, as well as lively, compact, and witty characterization. These stories emphasize, invariably with the aid of suspense, a painstakingly thorough sequence of occurrences, moving rapidly to a terse ending with abrupt climax and dénouement. Aldrich's clever tale "Marjorie Daw"

with its amusing surprise ending came to be a prototype for comparable short fiction by Bunner, Matthews, and Stockton.

However far short-story writers have moved since Aldrich–emphasizing social and psychological realism (as in the fiction of Howells and Henry James), naturalism (as in Frank Norris, Stephen Crane, and Theodore Dreiser), variants of expressionism within a modernist framework, and (since the 1960s) the antistory abolishing plot, character, mimesis, or other basic ingredients–much credit may still be accorded his essential storytelling skills. Although Aldrich never attended college, he read widely and displayed the literary sensitivity and erudition of a serious, academically minded individual. His writings, for example, are saturated with Shakespearean references, quotes, sidelights (as in his sketch "Poor Yorick"), and even parodies ("A Midnight Fantasy"). His head teemed with ideas for possible stories, and, as was the case with Nathaniel Hawthorne, Aldrich recorded in his notebooks and literary sketches examples of these flashes of inspiration. Yet he admitted in one notebook entry, "The instant I jot down an idea the desire to utilize it leaves me, and I turn away to do something unpremeditated." This statement may be a slight exaggeration. When he wrote short stories, he habitually began with the last paragraph and wrote his way up to it without going off on tangents. It is interesting to see just how his characters came to life in his mind and took over. They *talked* more than he felt they should: in another notebook entry he wrote, "I have to let them; but when the story is finished, I go over the dialogue and strike out four fifths of the long speeches. I fancy that makes my characters pretty mad."

Perhaps the most significant themes in Aldrich's short fiction are a fantasy-based misunderstanding (involving two people), sometimes one-sided, sometimes mutual, and a pure fantasy in which the individual momentarily escapes the everyday world. The pure fantasy is all too familiar in nineteenth-century American short fiction, especially in that of Hawthorne (whom Aldrich echoes occasionally). But contrived as they are, Aldrich's tales–with their improbable reversals of intention and their superficial character development–possess an engrossing charm just because their author is so direct, inventive, and expressive in his language. (According to Greenslet, Aldrich once objected to the long-drawn-out character analyses in James's fiction because James

The Nutter House, Aldrich's boyhood home in Portsmouth, New Hampshire

was concerned with people who were not doing anything.)

The great majority of Aldrich's short fictions–roughly twenty-two of twenty-eight stories–are structured around a character's fantasies. "What Jedd Pallfrey Found in the Coffin: A Christmas Story" (*Knickerbocker,* January 1857) is a painfully sentimental, totally improbable, reconciliation tale in the manner of Charles Dickens's *A Christmas Carol* (1843), with overtones of Hawthorne's marble-hearted Ethan Brand and that author's obsession with the Unpardonable Sin of pride and alienation from society. A misanthropic undertaker, having once rejected his daughter and her illegitimate son, is unexpectedly and unintentionally visited on Christmas Eve by her child, now destitute and near death. Finding no one in the undertaking establishment, the boy climbs into an empty coffin and falls asleep. On his return old Pallfrey finds the lad and realizes who he is; his hard heart melts. The curious skeleton that Pallfrey earlier saw in that coffin (a phantom of past misconduct, which troubled him every Christmas Eve) is presumably banished, and he is reunited with his grandson. This little fable is embellished with an appropriate moral about the dangers of harboring skeletons

(born of "evil deeds and malignant thoughts") in human hearts.

Aldrich's next short stories are, with one exception, of quite another order. In 1862 he collected five stories and one sketch in *Out of His Head, A Romance.* The title piece, a rambling novelette about a jilted lover who is mentally disturbed, a mad girl who drowns herself and turns into a water lily, and other absurdities of plot, is of interest only because of Aldrich's uncharacteristic use of jerky emotional outbursts, the mark of the so-called Spasmodic School, whose influence may be detected in the work of such diverse nineteenth-century writers as Percy Bysshe Shelley, Hawthorne, Alfred Tennyson, and John Neal. The only story in the collection that resembles "What Jedd Pallfrey Found in the Coffin" is a pious romantic legend, "Père Antoine's Date-Palm" (which appeared anonymously in the *Atlantic Monthly,* June 1862).

This syrupy tale, most of which is set in eighteenth-century New Orleans, deals with Antoine and Émile, two young candidates for the priesthood who are such fast friends that they do everything together. Anglice, a beautiful young orphan girl from an island in the Pacific, comes under their care. Both fall in love with her, but

Émile wins her affections, and the pair flees to a distant locale, leaving behind a shattered Antoine. Years later the widowed Anglice, dying of a fever, sends Antoine their little girl, a second Anglice, to raise. Antoine falls in love all over again with this Anglice–product of the two people he had loved most–but the child pines for her faraway home and soon dies. Father Antoine buries her in his garden, and a strange exotic date palm, like those in her island home, grows out of her grave.

This unsophisticated story–which greatly pleased Hawthorne's wife–seems far removed from much of the fiction the sophisticated Aldrich was to write. The three remaining short stories in *Out of His Head* are witty, light, and worldly by contrast with "Père Antoine's Date-Palm." Two embody Aldrich's theme of the fantasy-based misunderstanding. "Miss Hepzibah's Lover" is an amusing satire of an old maid, as cruel to its subject as Oliver Wendell Holmes's poem "My Aunt" (1831). Poor, ridiculous, fortyish Miss Hepzibah is "vestalizing" while waiting–hopelessly it seems–for her Beau Ideal to appear. When young, eligible (and ironically named) Philip Winter begins to pay court to her, it seems too good to be true. In fact, he is already engaged to be married, and he is a somnambulist, who has been courting Miss Hepzibah in his sleep. Miss Hepzibah comforts herself with the thought that he was not completely fast asleep when he wooed her so gallantly. "The Lady with the Balmoral: The Impressible Man's Story" clearly anticipates Aldrich's best-known short story, "Marjorie Daw," as Charles Samuels has pointed out. This pleasant story tells of a Mr. Tibbs, who becomes infatuated with someone he has never seen, an enchanting lady wearing a tantalizing Balmoral petticoat described to him by a fellow lodger, Frederick Markem, who saw her on the corner of Broadway and Thirteenth Street. The inconstant Tibbs loses his ardor for his fiancée, Clementina, and is determined to see this *belle inconnue* for himself. Tibbs and Markem manage to encounter her on Broadway, and she turns out to be Clementina.

The other short story in *Out of His Head* is "The Cup and the Lip: A Christmas Story." As with the two stories just discussed, particularly "The Lady with the Balmoral," it includes a trick ending, and its plot borders on the incredible. Yet these stories are funny and well told. If they lack the elaborate character analysis of a James story, they reflect the pure joy of a witty, urbane storyteller going enthusiastically about his business. The action of "The Cup and the Lip" takes place in the 1660s near Portsmouth. A "Heavy Father" and a "Mercenary Mother," the autocratic Jeffrey and Mehitable Langdon, are in reduced circumstances and want their daughter, Gervase (a "Heroine coming to grief"), to marry Squire Davie Howe's son Richard. She demurs, preferring a poor lad, Walter Brandt, who is forced to go abroad to make his fortune. After Richard dies unexpectedly, Jeffrey promotes a match between the widowed squire and Gervase. Before this misalliance can be solemnized, the now-wealthy Walter returns, and the cash-counting "Heavy Father" approves his marriage to Gervase.

One of Aldrich's best short fictions (justly praised by Samuels) is "A Struggle for Life" (*Atlantic Monthly*, July 1867; collected in *Marjorie Daw and Other People*, 1873), a suspenseful and powerfully narrated comic, horror tale. It is a story within a story, much in keeping with the mood if not the style of Edgar Allan Poe. The narrator is told an implausible story of a young man who was accidentally trapped in his fiancée's tomb in Montmartre. Thinking he would not be rescued before he died, he lost his sense of time. At this point the story takes a series of wild turns, each one more fascinating than the one before it. In that same year "A Young Desperado," one of the least engaging of Aldrich's short stories, appeared in the *Atlantic Monthly* (December 1867; collected in *Marjorie Daw and Other People*). A trivial piece about the narrator's cute and prankish six-year-old son Johnny, it was written before Aldrich's twin sons (and only children) were born.

Aldrich also wrote two amusing confidence-man narratives, "The Friend of My Youth" (*Atlantic Monthly*, February 1871; collected in *Marjorie Daw and Other People*) and "My Cousin the Colonel" (*Harper's New Monthly Magazine*, December 1891; collected in *Two Bites at a Cherry, with Other Tales*, 1893). The first story is about a Rivermouth (that is, Portsmouth) boy who supposedly made good in the outside world and, during the narrator's youth, returned home as the self-styled Governor Dorr. Charming and disarming, he first beguiled the narrator with his literary knowledge and his sweet talk. Over the years, however, the narrator discovers him to be a gambler, adventurer, fraud, burglar, and vandal. On a later return to Rivermouth the narrator chances to encounter Dorr's small, modest funeral pro-

Aldrich in 1880, the year before he took over editorship of the Atlantic Monthly *from William Dean Howells*

cession. "My Cousin the Colonel" suggestively echoes Hawthorne's "My Kinsman, Major Molineux." Not long after the close of the Civil War, the narrator encounters in Manhattan his cousin, George Washington Flagg, dressed in the uniform of a Confederate soldier. Flagg was ten years old when he went with his father to live in the South, and the narrator, who is three years older, has not seen him since twenty years before when they were on their grandfather's New Jersey farm. Now the pretentious moocher Flagg attaches himself to the narrator. He complains endlessly about the conduct of the North, exalts the lost cause of the South, and brags pathetically (as Governor Dorr had done) about his once-grand prospects and his powerful connections. Hoodwinked like his counterpart in "The Friend of My Youth," the narrator eventually learns of the Great Pretender's death and accepts the news with absolute equanimity.

In his Civil War tale "Quite So" (*Atlantic Monthly,* April 1872; collected in *Marjorie Daw and Other People*) Aldrich moved away temporarily from fantasies of time, of *belles inconnues,* and of predatory con artists, to a realm of sentiment and pathos. John Bladburn is a solitary, taciturn, self-sacrificing individual who bravely endures deprivation, rejection by the girl who earlier accepted his proposal of marriage, and the horrors unto death of the War Between the States. His re-

sponse "Quite So" to practically everything (until he divulges his story) expresses this humble creature's acceptance of all his losses, including finally his own life, on the field of battle. Aldrich's prototypical self-sacrificing victim of adversity suggests certain of Thomas Hardy's and William Faulkner's male suffering-servant characters.

There is a fantasy of sorts in "A Rivermouth Romance" (*Atlantic Monthly,* August 1872; collected in *Marjorie Daw and Other People*), a sad, hopeless account of an Irish maid named Margaret Callaghan, who is employed by a well-to-do Rivermouth family named Bilkins. She marries a twenty-two-year-old Irish seaman, Larry O'Rourke, eighteen years her junior, and through long, painful experience learns the truth of the "marry in haste" adage. An unstable, irresponsible drunkard, O'Rourke taps her modest savings, disappears for extended periods of time, and acts as a thoroughly unfit husband. Through all these misdeeds, Margaret continues to dote on him, apparently fantasizing some redeeming virtues for the lout. After years of uncertain "grass widowhood"–O'Rourke enlists in the Union navy, jumps ship just before his discharge and enlists in the army, is imprisoned for life and then granted amnesty, returns home only to vanish again–Margaret finally gives up on him. "She has had her romance," Aldrich concludes. Only two or three years earlier, in his semi-

Charles and Talbot, twin sons of Thomas and Lilian Aldrich, born 17 September 1868

autobiographical novel, *The Story of a Bad Boy*, Aldrich described a mirror-image relationship in which sailor Ben Watson of Nantucket is reunited after a long and excusable absence from his wife Kitty (maid to the Nutter family) and ever afterward is a model husband.

The next four stories Aldrich published are all fantasies of "dream people." The widely celebrated "Marjorie Daw" (*Atlantic Monthly*, April 1873; collected in *Marjorie Daw and Other People*) and the almost unknown but marvelously effective "Miss Mehetabel's Son" (*Atlantic Monthly*, June 1873; collected in *Marjorie Daw and Other People*) both deal with make-believe people created by story characters. In "Marjorie Daw" a young man, invalided and home-bound, falls in love with the imaginative description of a girl in the letters of a vacationing friend. Brought finally to a fever pitch of excitement by the news that this girl has developed a romantic interest in him through what the vacationing friend has been tell-

ing her, the recovered invalid goes to find her at the place where his friend has been staying. On his arrival he finds neither maiden nor friend, only a letter from that friend, who confesses that he has invented the girl and explains: "I tried to make a little romance to interest you, something soothing and idyllic, and, by Jove! I have done it only too well!" For all of Aldrich's doubts about the way James wrote fiction, "Marjorie Daw" reads very much like one of James's sophisticatedly entertaining epistolary fictions, such as "A Bundle of Letters" (1879) or "The Point of View" (1892). The playfully elegant style and the overall handling of subject mater in "Marjorie Daw" bring these two very disparate authors together, however momentarily.

"Miss Mehetabel's Son" is a witty and amusing account of a civil engineer's stay at a New Hampshire country hotel in October 1872, during which he is entertained by an old codger, the only other boarder, who gives him in installments an account of the life of the son he might have had, if he had married his longtime lady friend, Mehetabel Elkins. Samuels stresses the local-color aspect of this and other tales dealing with Aldrich's Portsmouth, but the story's strength lies not so much in its descriptions of regional characters or in its representation of local idioms, but rather in the enthralling quality of the entire narrative; it is *story* at its most delightful.

So are two other "fantasy" stories, "Mademoiselle Olympe Zabriski" (*Atlantic Monthly*, October 1873; collected in *Marjorie Daw and Other People*) and "A Midnight Fantasy" (*Atlantic Monthly*, April 1875; collected in *A Midnight Fantasy, and The Little Violinist*, 1877), wherein Aldrich was never surer in his handling of his material: that is, in finding a provocative, suspenseful story line and developing it with high (if comic) seriousness. "Mademoiselle Olympe Zabriski," a lighthearted treatment of New York's idle-rich playboys belonging to "Our Club," is also something of a satire on the old Dutch aristocracy, now run to seed. Ralph Van Twiller, a gentleman millionaire and good fellow ("the flower of Our Club"), becomes infatuated with a female trapeze artist at a downtown Manhattan theater. Much to their consternation, he forsakes his fellow club members and tries to attend as many of her stunning performances as he can. In his ardor Van Twiller presents this artist—another *belle inconnue*, who goes under the name of Mademoiselle Olympe Zabriski—with "the finest diamond bracelet procurable." To his amazement he receives only a courteous if semi-literate thank-you letter, in which the recipient of the bracelet reveals that he is a man, and, explaining that he cannot continue female impersonation any longer because his beard is becoming heavier, says that he plans to sell the bracelet.

This neatly worked-out tale, which in its sharp focus on setting and in its narrative roundness suggests what H. C. Bunner and O. Henry (though in different language and style) would do with their New York materials a few years later, ought not to be disparaged for its trick ending. Aldrich also cleverly inserts a reference to the hoax in "Marjorie Daw": clubman Edward Delaney was the letter writer who tricked his ailing friend—now his fellow-clubman—John Flemming, and in this story Delaney reminds Flemming that he had once fallen in love with a nonexistent girl.

In "A Midnight Fantasy" the narrator, after attending a performance of *Romeo and Juliet*, takes a late night stroll through the Boston Common to Cambridge and beyond. Thinking of other couples who, like Shakespeare's star-crossed lovers, have entered into misalliances, he finds his mind filled with a powerful dream vision: Prince Hamlet, angry and out of sorts over the murder of his father and his mother's marriage to his Uncle Claudius, leaves Denmark, and after many adventures, he arrives in Verona, Italy. There he falls in with gallants such as Mercutio, Benvolio, and Romeo Montague, who is in love with Juliet, the fair daughter of the Capulets; but she soon spurns him because their families are feuding.

Hamlet encounters Juliet at a masked ball and loses his heart to her. Because of his royal status, he easily obtains her hand quite honorably, since his disheartened friend Romeo has left town. The good Friar Laurence marries the happy pair, and at Hamlet's request the Montagues are invited to the nuptial banquet, where the feud between the two families is brought to an end. Then Horatio arrives from Denmark with the news that Ophelia has married Romeo. The narrator's vision ends with Hamlet's Juliet making a face at the thought of her discarded lover taking another, and with Hamlet wondering what the children of Romeo and Ophelia will be like, considering her thoughtful nature and his impetuosity.

"The Little Violinist" (written in 1874 and first published in *A Midnight Fantasy, and The Lit-*

tle Violinist) is a polemic in the guise of a fictional sketch about an overworked and ill-used violinist, James Speaight, who died at about age seven. Urging the formation of a Society for the Prevention of Cruelty to Little Children, Aldrich expresses his sadness at reading about Speaight's death, in contrast to his exultation over the condition of his own twin sons, Charley and Talbot, then about five and a half years old.

Aldrich's next story, "Two Bites at a Cherry" (*Atlantic Monthly*, January 1886; collected in *Two Bites at a Cherry, with Other Tales*), is perhaps his second-best-known work of short fiction and one of his very best creations. The protagonist, Marcus Whitelaw, is an unsubtle version of a James character, as Samuels observes in his provocative summary. In fact the entire story resembles a simplified version, a parody perhaps, of a James romance set in Italy. An American named Whitelaw, a wealthy and idle world traveler with a penchant for "missing the boat" in life, unexpectedly encounters in Naples the alluring heartbreaker Rose Jenness, whom he had loved but not won fifteen years earlier. Before long he is moved to try a "second bite at the cherry," but he is turned down once again.

Many of Aldrich's stories are not up to the level of "Two Bites at a Cherry." "A Christmas Fantasy, with a Moral" (*Century Illustrated Monthly Magazine*, December 1891; collected in *Two Bites at a Cherry, with Other Tales*) is a lame dream allegory about the common experience of pain caused by obtaining the object of one's misdirected desire and the subsequent pain and wasted time that result from trying to get rid of that object. In "A Christmas Fantasy" wealthy seven-year-old Mildred Wentworth quickly tires of the jumping jack toy she receives on Christmas day and wishes it might come to life, but when it does take on a life of its own, it horrifies her and she finds the change extremely regrettable.

A recurrent character in Aldrich's short fiction is the determined individualist, working against odds to pursue his own ends. The conservative, traditional Aldrich might have been expected to do some of his best writing on this subject, in line with his deep sympathy for self-determination within, or in opposition to, current social conventions; yet his stories about such individualists tend toward flatness of narrative and a dismaying evenness of tone.

" 'For Bravery on the Field of Battle' " (*Century Illustrated Monthly Magazine*, October 1892; collected in *Two Bites at a Cherry, with Other Tales*) con-

Aldrich's grave at Mount Auburn Cemetery, Cambridge, Massachusetts

cerns a poor, shy Rivermouth boy, James Dutton, a shoemaker. Enlisting in the unpopular war with Mexico, Dutton performs valiantly in battle, where he loses a leg, and he is awarded a medal, which he cherishes to the end. Returning home a hero, he receives the initial support of the townspeople, who patriotically give him their business for a while but finally neglect him. He steadfastly refuses to change his line of business or his methods of operation, however, and dies alone in his little apartment.

"Shaw's Folly" (*Harper's Monthly Magazine*, December 1900; collected in *A Sea Turn and Other Matters*, 1902) shows perhaps more clearly what a fiercely self-directed solid citizen doing his best as a member of society must put up with when contending with the moral weakness or character deficiency of "ornery" folk. A wealthy retired businessman, Augustus Shaw, prompted to use his money for some socially beneficial purpose, provides a properly outfitted apartment house for low-income, working-class tenants, on a nonprofit basis. The tenants, disinclined to apply the practical virtues he seeks to foster, all betray his trust, damaging both the building and his hopes. But

Aldrich, who touches on the essential socioeconomic dilemma of the unmet challenge of poverty, holds out hope for the eventual success of such a social-betterment scheme. Thus Shaw's "folly," based on his fantasy of human perfectibility, is not without merit and deserves another chance, sometime in the future, somewhere in the world, at the hands of someone with a better program.

"The Case of Thomas Phipps" (*Harper's Monthly Magazine*, June 1901; collected in *A Sea Turn and Other Matters*) deals with an amiable fool, poor and dependent on his rich uncle for support. Phipps, reminiscent in some ways of Twain's Pudd'nhead Wilson, seems to be the kind of incompetent of whom people expect little other than wrong guesses and faulty judgment. Through his fierce determination to do what he thinks is right he alienates his uncle, by refusing to take over the uncle's farm. At the time of his uncle's death Tom and his wife are extremely poor, but there is a thousand-dollar bequest for Tom from his uncle, payable only on condition that Tom does not attend the funeral. Upholding his principles, Tom—who in the last years of his uncle's life has tried unsuccessfully to be friendly with him–insists on going to the funeral anyway. But because of an obscure and complicated clause in the old man's will, Tom's having gone to the funeral makes him eligible for a much larger bequest, thirteen thousand dollars, and so he has the last laugh after all.

"The White Feather: The Major's Story" (*Atlantic Monthly*, September 1902; collected in *A Sea Turn and Other Matters*), in a way a sort of mirror image to "The Case of Thomas Phipps," is a sad account of a young Southern gentleman, Jefferson Kane, who defies tradition by joining the Union forces during the Civil War. At a crucial encounter with the enemy, the capable, highly respected Lieutenant Kane backs down, showing the "white feather" of cowardice, to the horror of his men and to his own disgrace. Within a short time he shoots himself. Later it is revealed that in the confrontation with the Rebel forces Kane actually came face to face with his own father, a Confederate captain, and was unable to press his attack. His father was killed at the battle of Gettysburg.

The mood of fantasy is strong in Aldrich's remaining stories, a few of which are distinguished by an engrossing narrative style and tight, suspenseful plots. "Goliath" (*Century Illustrated Monthly Magazine*, February 1893; collected in *Two Bites at a Cherry, with Other Tales*) is a clever tale of a dog-shy businessman, David Willis, who is invited to an acquaintance's country house, where–to his profound distress–he knows he will encounter the man's dog, Goliath. David's miseries before and during his meeting with the fearsome Goliath, which turns out to be a noisy but quite harmless little pup, make delightful reading.

"The Chevalier De Resseguier" (*Century Illustrated Monthly Magazine*, May 1893; collected in *Two Bites at a Cherry, with Other Tales*) recalls "A Christmas Fantasy, with a Moral." At once a dream fantasy, a commentary on writer's block, a "voice-from-the-dead" story, and a joking jeu d'esprit like Poe's "Some Words with a Mummy" (1845), it briefly brings to life the skull of a French adventurer and literary pretender who lived at the time of Louis XV.

"Her Dying Words" (*Scribner's Magazine*, August 1893; collected in *Two Bites at a Cherry, with Other Tales*)–like "Two Bites at a Cherry," suggesting a James story simplified almost to bare plot– is an entertaining account of a poor doctor, Newton Downs, the guest of a wealthy retired merchant and his wife, the Tredicks, who are trav-

eling with their beautiful daughter Louise to Europe on a freighter. Smitten with her charms but unwilling to declare himself to Louise Tredick because of his qualms about marrying for money, Dr. Downs suffers in silence. A storm at sea threatens to sink the freighter, and, when death seems imminent, Louise is moved to express her undying love for him. As another vessel approaches, and rescue is certain, Dr. Downs briskly reminds Louise of "her dying words."

In "His Grace the Duke" (*Century Illustrated Monthly Magazine*, May 1898; collected in *A Sea Turn and Other Matters*) the narrator (who appears to be Aldrich himself) is on a visit to London, where he views the skull of Henry Grey, Duke of Suffolk (father of Lady Jane Grey, England's "nine-day queen"), executed for treason in 1554. This setting affords Aldrich the opportunity to discuss English political history during the sixteenth century, to speculate on life after death, and to elaborate on his strange déjà vu sensation concerning the Duke of Suffolk's beheading.

"An Untold Story" (*Scribner's Magazine*, December 1900; collected in *A Sea Turn and Other Matters*), set in Budapest, presents a deliberately unexplained mystery filled with ambiguity. The narrator thinks he sees a beautiful young girl drown in the Danube, and, two years later, stopping again in Budapest, he has a feeling that the same thing will happen again. Suddenly he sees the same girl, very much alive and in a setting that suggests her state before the drowning. The reader is left to ponder, with the narrator, the tantalizing story sealed within "That shut book."

"A Sea Turn" (*Harper's Monthly Magazine*, June 1901; collected in *A Sea Turn and Other Matters*) is a light, amusing tale of domestic misunderstanding between Helen and Edward Brandon. Each, unknown to the other, stays out all night (quite innocently) on someone's yacht, and the next day, filled with guilt and embarrassment, they do not know how to handle their confused feelings. When each learns the truth from a different informant, there is a sweet and mutually forgiving reunion that evening and a promise of future bliss.

Aldrich's reputation as a short-story writer soared, according to Samuels, following the publication of his 1873 collection, *Marjorie Daw and Other People;* and he retained a lofty rank among American writers until the time of his death in 1907, after which his reputation declined. There was a popular and critical reaction against

Aldrich's simplified, Victorian view of life. His stories do not challenge social, moral, religious, or economic conventions, and they are characterized by gentility, rather than the dark, worrisome strains of realism or naturalism.

Though literary (and literary-political) fashions can be ephemeral and unfair, Aldrich did not, in fact, continue to develop steadily as a craftsman of the short story, from 1857 to 1901. Yet between 1862 and 1886 Aldrich produced at least five memorable short stories aside from "Marjorie Daw" (1873) that deserve to be anthologized and read in the 1980s: "The Lady with the Balmoral" (1862), "A Struggle for Life" (1867), "Miss Mehetabel's Son" (1873), "A Midnight Fantasy" (1875), and "Two Bites at a Cherry" (1886).

Letters:

Ferris Greenslet, "A Group of Aldrich Letters," *Century Illustrated Magazine*, new series 54 (August 1908): 495-505.

Bibliography:

Frederic Fairchild Sherman, *A Check List of First Editions of Thomas Bailey Aldrich* (New York: Privately printed, 1921).

Biography:

Ferris Greenslet, *The Life of Thomas Bailey Aldrich* (Boston & New York: Houghton Mifflin, 1908).

References:

Mrs. Thomas Bailey Aldrich, *Crowding Memories* (Boston & New York: Houghton Mifflin, 1920);

Charles E. Samuels, *Thomas Bailey Aldrich* (New York: Twayne, 1965).

Papers:

Aldrich's letters and manuscripts are scattered. Significant collections are located at the Houghton Library, Harvard University; Dartmouth College Library; the Huntington Library in San Marino, California; the Library of Congress; the Alderman Library, University of Virginia; the Berg Collection, New York Public Library; the Pierpont Morgan Library; and Princeton University.

William Austin
(2 March 1778-27 June 1841)

Dean G. Hall
Kansas State University

BOOKS: *Strictures on Harvard University.—Personal satire is worthy of little notice—It is seldom just. By a Senior* (Boston: Printed & sold by John W. Folsom, 1798);

An Oration, Pronounced at Charlestown, at the Request of the Artillery Company, on the Seventeenth of June; Being the Anniversary of the Battle of Bunker Hill, and of That Company (Charlestown, Mass.: Printed by Samuel Etheridge, 1801);

Letters from London: Written during the years 1802 & 1803 (Boston: Printed for W. Pelham, 1804);

An Essay on the Human Character of Jesus Christ (Boston: Printed for William Pelham, 1807);

Peter Rugg, The Missing Man (Worcester, Mass.: F. P. Rice, 1882);

Literary Papers of William Austin, With a Biographical Sketch by His Son, James Walker Austin (Boston: Little, Brown, 1890).

OTHER: "The Origin of Chemistry, a manuscript recently found in an old trunk," *New England Magazine*, 6 (January 1834): 13-18.

Portrait by Henry C. Pratt (Walter Austin, William Austin, The Creator of Peter Rugg, *1925)*

Although William Austin wrote only a handful of stories and devoted most of his life to the law and politics, he was quite a popular writer in his time. His best-known story, "Peter Rugg, or the Missing Man," was nearly continuously in print for a century after the appearance of the first part in the 10 September 1824 issue of the *New England Galaxy*. The early chroniclers of the American short story reserved Austin a small but important role. For example, Henry Seidel Canby, in *The Short Story in English* (1909), compared Austin's "Peter Rugg" favorably with the tales of Washington Irving, claiming it was "a striking exception, perhaps the only notable instance in America before 1830" in an otherwise undistinguished first decade of American short stories. Elias Lieberman, in *The American Short Story* (1912), calls Austin and Harriet Beecher Stowe the only two writers in the "pre-modern era" whose "work requires some mention because it shows the influence of older New England." Fred Lewis Pattee, in *Development of the American Short Story* (1923), listed "Peter Rugg" as one of "only three short stories produced in America before 1826 [which] have any merit as judged by modern standards," and Edward J. O'Brien, in *Advance of the American Short Story* (1923), claimed that "Peter Rugg" "has the same legendary value as Rip Van Winkle and The Legend of Sleepy Hollow" and that "in the psychological subtlety of its craftsmanship, it points the way to Hawthorne." Writing about this same story, Col. Thomas Wentworth Higginson, in his long review-essay for the 29 March 1888 issue of the *Independent,* had already named Austin "a precursor of Hawthorne" and noted that the "penumbra," the interplay of "light and shadow" in Austin's tales, is quite similar in technique to Hawthorne's. Nathaniel Hawthorne was himself aware of at least one of Austin's short-story characters, for he includes him in a brief episode in "A Virtuoso's Collection" (1842), where his virtuoso labels Peter Rugg "the most unfortunate man in the world." In recognizing Austin's influences one should not assume that his stories are inferior models for better works by later writers; though few, his stories are good, and, had Austin written more of them, he might be as important in the development of the American short story as Edgar Allan Poe or Hawthorne.

Austin was born in Lunenburg, Worcester County, Massachusetts, the only child of Nathaniel and Margaret Rand Austin not born in Charlestown. The Austin family could trace their lineage in Charlestown from 1651, and only the conflagration of the city and the destruction of the family home after the Battle of Bunker Hill in 1775 could cause their temporary removal. They returned to Charlestown in late 1778. Except for the years of his schooling, he spent nearly his entire life there and became one of Charlestown's best-recognized citizens. He attended the Reverend John Shaw's prep school in Haverhill, Massachusetts, and was known as an able student. On 13 July 1794 he was admitted to Harvard, where he was a member of the Porcellian and secretary and poet of the Hasty Pudding Club. He turned down an invitation to join Phi Beta Kappa because he refused "to belong to any secret society." Though Austin was later to recant his condemnations of Harvard, his first publication was his *Strictures on Harvard University* (1798), which he wrote as a senior. Austin's complaints were generally that the Harvard environment was too formalistic, strict, and impersonal. He believed that college laws "threw an Andes" between master and disciple because students were given no rights and their ideas no credence. He blamed Harvard's "strictures" for its failure to have yet produced a mathematician or historian of note, making the irreverent claim that the "college is the death-bed of genius."

Graduating with an A.B. when he was twenty, Austin disdained teaching as a way to earn the money needed to take up his preferred profession, the law. He chose rather to join the U.S. Navy (1799) and served on the *Constitution* as the first chaplain appointed in that service by government commission. Fortunately, Austin was aboard the famous ship when it captured the *Amelia,* and he received two hundred dollars as his share of the "salvage" money. In 1802, as soon as his term was finished, he left the navy and used his salvage money to finance his study of law in London at Lincoln's Inn (5 July 1802-November 1803). Probably realizing his countrymen's obvious interest in England in those years after the Revolutionary War, Austin gathered his observations and impressions in *Letters from London* (1804). Overtly democratic in point of view, the work, as expected, received scathing reviews from conservative presses and praise by journals with democratic leanings, though the *Boston Democrat* (13 March 1805) lauded the "American typography" as much as the author's "softened philosophy." The *Literary Magazine and American Register,* edited by Charles Brockden Brown in Philadelphia (1805), concluded that "this work abounds with amusing and instructive passages" and that "some eminent persons are described with considerable eloquence." The forty letters in the volume contain interesting anecdotes and sketches but primarily compare the English and American governmental systems, with Austin's pro-American prejudice quite apparent.

Between the Revolutionary War and the War of 1812, America was divided by political and church affiliations, and many times these differences resulted in violence. As an ardent democrat, Austin entered willingly into public debates, and he too was caught up by the overzealous spirit of the times. In an open letter addressed to Gen. Simon Elliot published in the *Independent Chronicle* (17 March 1806), Austin attacked the general for his role in the court-martial of Capt. Joseph Loring, an affair taken up in the newspapers, which divided the populace chiefly along party lines. Loring, a democrat, had been acquitted of all charges against him but was not released because his pleas fell on conspicuously deaf Federalist ears. The accusations in Austin's letter were primarily that General Elliot was responsible for "false imprisonment" and that he had refused Loring "the first duty of a gentleman." Austin signed the letter "Decius" but added that his real name was available from the publisher if the general asked for it in person; the general did so within the day and within twenty-four hours his son, James Henderson Elliot, sent representatives to Austin challenging him to a duel. At sunrise on 31 March 1806 Austin and James Elliot dueled with pistols in Cold Spring, Rhode Island. Austin was wounded twice; Elliot was unharmed, and both retired from the affair with their honor intact. Austin was not proud of the duel, suppressed the event in the local newspapers, and kept it from his children, who did not learn of it until after his death.

In addition to *Letters from London* and *Strictures on Harvard University* Austin wrote three other separately published nonfiction works. His oration on 17 June 1801, the anniversary of the Battle of Bunker Hill, was published in the same year. In *An Essay on the Human Character of Jesus Christ* (1807) he attempted to "explore a new but indirect source of argument in favor of the *Divinity of Jesus Christ*." The essay's arguments are certainly "indirect," as Austin tries to infer from Christ's action that because he was the epitome of perfect human action he must have been divine. Quoting no legitimate sources and sometimes ignoring scriptural accounts, Austin freely describes Christ's actions, motivations, and physical make-up to argue for Christ's strength of character and his authenticity as son of God. Obviously Unitarian in sympathy but illogically presented, the essay is difficult to follow and unimpressive except perhaps as a specimen of the sentimental "appreciations" so typical at that time. Years later Austin brought out "The Origin of Chemistry" (*New England Magazine*, January 1834) which is nearly indecipherable; it elicited no critical comment when published and was fortunately Austin's only sally in that direction.

When Austin returned from London in 1803, he immediately set up a law practice. For several years between 1814 and 1840 he was justice of the peace for the County of Middlesex and was intermittently state representative from Charlestown to the General Court of Massachusetts (1811, 1812, 1816, 1827, 1834) and a state senator (1821, 1822, 1823). He was never defeated for any public office for which he announced. In religion Austin was a liberal, attaching himself and his family to the Unitarian offshoot when they removed themselves from the

First Church of Charlestown in 1815 to form their own church in February of the next year. Austin was married to Charlotte Williams from 17 June 1806 until her death on 10 December 1820; nearly two years later, on 3 October 1822, he married Lucy Jones. He fathered a total of fourteen children, and five of his seven sons graduated from Harvard. Austin was elected to his last public office, representative to the General Court, in 1833. He was debilitated in his last years, suffering a lingering illness and weakness; in 1839 he was already complaining that he was too weak to hold a pen long enough to finish even a short letter. He died on 27 June 1841 at his home in Charlestown.

Austin was not a prolific fiction writer, publishing only five stories in his lifetime (all posthumously collected in *Literary Papers of William Austin*, 1890). Yet "Peter Rugg, or the Missing Man" (*New England Galaxy*, 10 September 1824, 1 September 1826, and 19 January 1827) alone should preserve for Austin at least a footnote in American literary history. That footnote, however, nearly went to someone else, for it was originally published under the pseudonym Mr. Jonathan or J. Dunwell, and many years elapsed and some misattribution took place before Austin was correctly identified as author. Combining the best elements of Washington Irving's "Rip Van Winkle" (1819) and the mysterious psychological hauntings of Hawthorne's stories, "Peter Rugg" concerns the title character's continual flight through New England in a desperate attempt to find his way to Boston. The story is presented as a letter, which recounts the narrator Dunwell's personal encounters with Rugg and research into Rugg's history. The story opens in 1820, by which time Rugg has become a fantastic figure, appearing in many locales at nearly the same time. Austin presents Rugg as a tortured creature suffering the consequences of an oath he uttered in anger at about the time of the Boston Massacre in 1770. Rugg was returning with his daughter, Jenny, from Concord to Boston when they were overtaken by a vicious storm. In other ways a normal and well-respected man, Rugg is sometimes carried away by fits of uncontrollable anger; such was the case during the storm when he cursed his fate and himself, saying he would either return home that night "in spite of the last tempest, or may I never see home again." Thereafter, Rugg and his daughter have been seen rushing hither and yon stopping only to ask directions to Boston.

Portrait of Gen. Simon Elliot and a Gilbert Stuart portrait of his son James. In a 17 March 1806 letter to the Independent Chronicle *Austin attacked General Elliot for his role in the court-martial of another officer, prompting James Elliot to challenge Austin to a duel in which Austin was wounded (Walter Austin,* William Austin, The Creator of Peter Rugg, *1925).*

Rugg's "chair" is drawn by a magnificent steed, who can bring the entire carriage off the ground to leap over toll rails or outdistance any followers. The carriage is constantly pursued by violent storms, and people learn to run for cover when they see Rugg rush by. Somehow Rugg, the horse, and Jenny slip out of time and space, never aging while the world changes around them. Rugg's plight is both humorous and pathetic. The toll takers' continual attempts to make Rugg pay when Rugg "knows" that the king's roads are "freeways" have comic overtones. Yet one cannot help but sympathize, for in one episode Rugg does return to his home only to discover the surroundings so changed that he believes he must be in some "new" Boston, and he hurries away from the very goal he still seeks. Those who see Rugg are never quite sure what they have seen—"the man's fancy was doubtless at fault. It is a very common thing for the imagination to paint for the senses, both the visible and invisible world." The story ends just as Rugg's estate is to be escheated for lack of heirs; in a poignant scene he returns home again and recognizes likenesses of his long dead friends in their offspring's faces, but because he "profanely defied" the tempest, he is "cut off from the last age" and "can never be fitted to the present."

Between the Rugg episodes, Austin published "Some Account of the Sufferings of a Country Schoolmaster" (*New England Galaxy,* 8 July 1825), an exaggerated tale of a Cambridge-educated youth who suffers for two months in the hinterland as a schoolmaster. The story was unattributed in its original appearance in the *Galaxy,* and another of Austin's stories was nearly miscredited, for it was mistakenly attributed to Leonard Apthorp when Joseph T. Buckingham, the editor of the *Galaxy,* wrote his *Personal Memoirs and Recollections of Editorial Life* (1852). The story relates the schoolmaster's near starvation, caused by citizens so penurious that they do not support him adequately. For example, the people who hire him begin by auctioning off his "keep" to the lowest bidder. As a consequence, his meager allotment of victuals forces him into catching rats, eating tallow candles, lying under neighbors' milk cows to steal fresh milk, and cutting steaks from live animals. He even considers cannibalism when he eyes one fat schoolboy, but fortunately

Lucy Jones Austin, whom Austin married on 3 October 1822 (Walter Austin, William Austin, The Creator of Peter Rugg, *1925)*

he happens upon a skunk which he skins, cooks, and devours in one sitting. The story is concerned less with his experiences as a teacher and more with exaggerating how communities expect too much of teachers (even after sending home the "half in less need" he still has fifty students) yet provide little in wages and other compensation. Perhaps anticipating some criticism for allowing the story to fill the entire front page, the editors follow the piece with a note: "The reader will find in the article which fills up the front page, descriptive passages, which are not inferior to any of the celebrated tales in Blackwood's Magazine. We offer no apology for excluding other matters, to give the story entire–if we had divided it, an apology might have been necessary."

The rest of Austin's small canon comprises chiefly parablelike tales which advocate the benefits of some particular virtue. Austin's "The Late Joseph Natterstrom" (*New England Magazine,* July 1831) makes clear that patience, honesty, and good reputation will be rewarded in the end. The title character is a meticulously honest

merchant-broker who refuses the temptation to use others' money and profits for his own benefit. The story begins in 1790 when, in an unusual beginning for an American story, two Arabs, Ebn Beg and Ibrahim Hamet, return from Mecca to their home village of Abou Jbee only to find that the town has been wiped out by Wheehabites. The wealthy Beg and Hamet study French and English in Smyrna, pick up local manners and speech during residences in Marseilles and London, and eventually travel to America with a Captain Dixon. Some flashes of humor occur when they encounter American government (they are amazed that it meets only once a year as if the government were some gigantic clock that needed only occasional winding) and the jury system (so inefficient that their cadis could have settled the whole affair in twenty minutes). Attracted by Natterstrom's reputation, Beg decides to test him by leaving five hundred guineas in his possession for investment. Beg returns to Smyrna to become a prosperous merchant while Natterstrom invests the guineas for "Eben Beck." During the next thirty years, Natterstrom's own fortunes suffer while Beck's money multiplies. The Beck enterprises are so successful and Natterstrom so involved as agent for the fortune that his own identity is gradually subsumed and people refer to him as Eben Beck. Eventually Beg is made aware of the status of his original investment when Captain Dixon returns to Smyrna in a ship laden with goods garnered by Natterstrom. Beg returns to America, where Natterstrom turns over the entire enterprise and all its fruits, and as a result is left personally penniless. Beg, in his will, leaves his entire estate to Natterstrom as a reward for his stalwart honesty.

In his "The Man With the Cloaks: A Vermont Legend" (*American Monthly Magazine,* January 1836) Austin tells of John Grindall, a miser who refuses to lend a poor traveler his old cloak even though Grindall has just bought a new and more-than-sufficient cloak. The traveler and Grindall exchange Franklinesque aphorisms with Grindall defending self-interest and the traveler selfless goodwill. As his parting volley, the traveler predicts that "you may want more than two cloaks to keep you warm when I perish with the cold." When Grindall hears that a traveler has died on the far side of the lake by which he lives, he feels "a sudden chillness shoot through his frame." The narrator cautions that "there was nothing supernatural in this; the body is often the plaything of the mind. The imagination can produce a fever; and why may it not turn the heart to an icicle . . . ?" Ironically Grindall borrows a cloak from his friend the innkeeper, the very man who had recommended Grindall as a possible source of generosity to the traveler. Although summer comes on, Grindall gets colder and colder and adds a cloak per day until he looks like a many-layered ball; consequently he becomes an outcast to all except the physicians, who can find no natural cause for his ailment. After some amusing incidents, such as Grindall's rolling down a hill like a snowball or chickens' roosting in his vast expanse of cloaks, the traveler appears again and suggests a cure. The solution, of course, is to give away a cloak to some needy person. After doing so, Grindall feels a bit warmer, and the story ends with Grindall's becoming satisfactorily warm without any extra cloaks. He has learned to "keep yourself constantly warm, you must have a constantly warm heart." Though the story's main thrust is this trite aphorism, it is told with vigor and humor, and Austin makes his point without cloying sentimentality.

Austin's last story, "Martha Gardner: or Moral Reaction" (*American Monthly Magazine*, December 1837), is set in Austin's native Charlestown and uses an old woman, Martha, to make some unsubtle political digs at self-serving city administrators who have little sense of conscience or charity. The city fathers covet Martha's real estate after the building of the Charles River Bridge in 1785 makes some of her property, a dock near the foot of the bridge, valuable; the city decides that Martha should give up her land for the corporate good, but Martha refuses, choosing instead litigation–her moral reaction. Austin symbolizes the selectmen's deceit and Martha's privilege with a dock post upon which Martha had played as a child; the post is cut down by the corporation and floats out to sea on the river, but it miraculously returns by floating back up the river two years later to represent her true claim. In the interim Martha is told in a dream that the deeds written by the original founder, Francis Willoughby, may be found in an old trunk. Martha's friends tell her not to lose heart as the city presses its claim again and again because "the whole Corporation in the eye of the

court weighs no more than Martha Gardner." Austin's presentation of the corporation is decidedly modern: "unhappily the animal and intellectual part of Corporations govern the body, and conscience is a non-corporate word." When a great storm attacks Charlestown and threatens Martha's home, she responds that nature is always God's handiwork and not to be feared while manmade institutions are sources of dread: "I had rather see this tempest with open eyes than the Great Corporation in my sleep." As the storm covers the bridge with water, Martha predicts that, though she will not be avenged in her day, no more traffic will cross the bridge in the future than at that present moment. History confirms Martha's curse, for a new toll-free bridge is built at Warren Street, and soon no one pays for the privilege of crossing the river. The bridge becomes desolate and decays, a symbol of Martha's vindication and the corporation's futile greed.

William Austin's place in American literary history is minor but revealing, for, earlier than others, he explained traditional supernatural events as possible imaginative products of the human mind. As Hawthorne does, Austin blurs the edges of his fictional reality so that facts are never certain, and the ambience is mystical, a place where psychological causes are as plausible as any. Austin's tales are delightful for their homespun humor, their consistently moral points of view, and their sometimes intriguing characterizations.

References:

James Walker Austin, "Biographical Sketch," in *Literary Papers of William Austin* (Boston: Little, Brown, 1890);

Walter Austin, *William Austin, The Creator of Peter Rugg* (Boston: Marshall Jones, 1925);

Thomas Wentworth Higginson, "A Precursor of Hawthorne," *Independent*, 40 (29 March 1888): 1-2.

Papers:

The Essex Institute has "William Austin's Occasional Diary or Journal at the Isle of France in 1817. Bombay in the Same Year, and at Mocha in 1818 & 1819."

Ambrose Bierce

(24 June 1842-January 1914?)

Cathy N. Davidson
Michigan State University

See also the Bierce entries in *DLB 11: American Humorists, 1800-1950; DLB 12: American Realists and Naturalists; DLB 23: American Newspaper Journalists, 1873-1900;* and *DLB 71: American Literary Critics and Scholars, 1880-1900.*

BOOKS: *The Fiend's Delight,* as Dod Grile (London: John Camden Hotten, 1873; New York: A. L. Luyster, 1873);

Nuggets and Dust Panned Out in California, as Dod Grile (London: Chatto & Windus, 1873);

Cobwebs from an Empty Skull, as Dod Grile (London & New York: Routledge, 1874);

The Dance of Death, by Bierce and Thomas A. Harcourt, as William Herman (San Francisco: Privately printed, 1877; corrected and enlarged edition, San Francisco: Henry Keller, 1877);

Tales of Soldiers and Civilians (San Francisco: E. L. G. Steele, 1891); also published as *In the Midst of Life* (London: Chatto & Windus, 1892; revised and enlarged edition, New York & London: Putnam's, 1898);

Black Beetles in Amber (San Francisco & New York: Western Authors Publishing, 1892);

Can Such Things Be? (New York: Cassell, 1893);

Fantastic Fables (New York & London: Putnam's, 1899);

Shapes of Clay (San Francisco: W. E. Wood, 1903);

The Cynic's Word Book (New York: Doubleday, Page, 1906); enlarged as *The Devil's Dictionary,* volume 7 of *The Collected Works of Ambrose Bierce* (New York & Washington: Neale, 1911);

The Shadow on the Dial and Other Essays, edited by S. O. Howes (San Francisco: A. M. Robertson, 1909); revised as *Antepenultimata,* vol. 11 of *The Collected Works of Ambrose Bierce* (New York & Washington: Neale, 1912);

Write It Right: A Little Blacklist of Literary Faults (New York & Washington: Neale, 1909);

The Collected Works of Ambrose Bierce, 12 volumes (New York & Washington: Neale, 1909-1912) —comprises 1) *Ashes of the Beacon, The Land Be-*

Ambrose Bierce

yond the Blow, For the Ahkoond, John Smith, Liberator, Bits of Autobiography; 2) *In the Midst of Life;* 3) *Can Such Things Be?, The Ways of Ghosts, Soldier-Folk, Some Haunted Houses;* 4) *Shapes of Clay, Some Antemortem Epitaphs, The Scrap Heap;* 5) *Black Beetles in Amber, The Mummery, On Stone;* 6) *The Monk and the Hangman's Daughter, Fantastic Fables, Aesopus Emendatus, Old Saws with New Teeth, Fables in Rhyme;* 7) *The Devil's Dictionary;* 8) *Negligible Tales, The Parenticide Club, The Fourth Estate, The Ocean Wave, "On with the Dance!," Epigrams;* 9) *Tangential Views;* 10) *The Opinionator, The Reviewer, The Controversialist, The Timorous Reporter, The March Hare;* 11) *Ante-*

21

penultimata; 12) *In Motley, Kings of Beasts, Two Administrations, Miscellaneous;*

Battlefields and Ghosts, edited by Hartley E. Jackson and James D. Hart (Palo Alto: Harvest Press, 1931);

Selection from Prattle by Ambrose Bierce, edited by Carroll D. Hall (San Francisco: Book Club of California, 1936);

Enlarged Devil's Dictionary, edited by Ernest J. Hopkins (Garden City, N. Y.: Doubleday, 1967);

The Ambrose Bierce Satanic Reader, edited by Hopkins (Garden City, N. Y.: Doubleday, 1968);

Ambrose Bierce: Skepticism and Dissent. Selected Journalism from 1898-1901, edited by Lawrence I. Berkove (Ann Arbor, Mich.: Delmas Books, 1980).

OTHER: "The Robin and the Woodpecker," "The Dog and the Bees," "The Ant and the Grain of Corn," "The Man and the Goose," "The Nobleman and the Oyster," "The Boy and the Tortoise," and "The Camel and the Zebra," in *Mark Twain's Library of Humor,* anonymously edited by William Dean Howells (New York: Webster, 1888), pp. 129-130, 196, 339-340, 348, 425-426, 542, 558;

Richard Voss, *The Monk and the Hangman's Daughter,* Gustav Adolf Danziger's translation, revised by Bierce (Chicago: Schulte, 1892).

In the more than seventy years since his mysterious disappearance in Mexico, Ambrose Gwinnett Bierce has been known almost as much for his colorful life as for his experimental fiction. Well over six feet tall, a muscular and handsome man who, in later years, had a thick crop of pure white hair, Bierce was an imposing figure, quick witted and equally quick tempered. He left a mark as one of the most effective and vituperative journalists of his day, but his most important contribution to American literary history is in the area of the short story. "Chickamauga" (*San Francisco Examiner,* 20 January 1889) and "An Occurrence at Owl Creek Bridge" (*San Francisco Examiner,* 13 July 1890), both collected in *Tales of Soldiers and Civilians* (1891), are standard entries in contemporary anthologies. Powerful evocations of war, these stories, like all his fiction, expanded the boundaries of American fiction and remain notable today for their surrealistic and even "postmodern" literary techniques.

Little in Bierce's childhood indicated that he would one day be a major American short-story writer. His family was poor. His father, like many pioneers in the middle decades of the nineteenth century, headed west and settled in Meigs County, Ohio, where he hoped America's dreams of westward expansion might finally come true. Ambrose, the tenth of thirteen children, was born in 1842, by which time his parents, Marcus Aurelius and Laura Sherwood Bierce, had come to realize that fortune would not come easily on the Western Reserve. In 1846 they moved again, this time to Warsaw, in northern Indiana, where Bierce lived until 1859, when he entered the Kentucky Military Institute in Franklin Springs, Kentucky.

Despite this seemingly inauspicious upbringing, there were some early signs of imagination. At ten Bierce read and studied Pope's translation of the *Iliad.* During his high-school days in Warsaw he worked on an antislavery paper, the *Northern Indianan,* gaining experience as a newspaper man. His schooling was rudimentary, but the young man did have some literary guidance from his father, who was well read for his time and place and even possessed a rudimentary library. He also must have possessed a quirkish wit: he gave each of his thirteen children a name beginning with the letter *A.* Perhaps a more important influence on Ambrose's early life was his uncle, "General" Lucius Verus Bierce. A militant abolitionist, this uncle seemed to represent a more colorful life than Bierce knew from his immediate surroundings. Bierce was later to acknowledge that "General" Bierce had a formative influence on him, particularly on his early military career.

The military provided Bierce with his first escape from the unprofitable and unglorious farm life of his childhood. He enlisted with the Ninth Indiana Infantry in April 1861, in time to take part in the first "battle" of the Civil War, a skirmish at Philippi, West Virginia. Some three months later, Bierce carried a wounded soldier off a battlefield. The comrade died, and Bierce had his first taste of ambivalence toward heroism, enjoying the glory of recognition but feeling the tragedy of his friend's unheroic death.

By the beginning of 1862 the Civil War had become a full-fledged war, and Bierce's participation increased. In 1862 and 1863 his regiment engaged in major and bloody encounters at Shiloh, Chickamauga, Lookout Mountain, Missionary Ridge, and Kenesaw Mountain. By 1864 Bierce had performed several notable feats of bravery, had reenlisted with the Ninth Indiana regiment, and had achieved the rank of first lieutenant and

Bierce during his military service with the Ninth Indiana Infantry. By 1864 he achieved the rank of first lieutenant and became a topographical engineer.

position of topographical engineer. He also, on 23 June 1864, received a severe head wound and probably would have died were it not for the ministrations of his brother Albert, a soldier with the Seventh Battery of the Indiana Light Artillery. After another furlough, Bierce again reenlisted, this time with the Fourth Army Corps. He was not discharged until spring 1865.

Like many soldiers after the Civil War, Bierce felt restless in civilian life. For nearly seven years he worked at various odd jobs or simply traveled to such places as New Orleans, Panama, and Acapulco. In late September 1865, unsure of what he wanted to do next, he agreed to serve under General Hazen on a trip surveying military outposts in the West, from Omaha to San Francisco, for which he was promised a commission to the rank of captain in the regular army.

The expedition began in July 1866. It was arduous, including a particularly difficult foray into the Montana territory, where food, water, and other necessities were scarce and the physical demands imposed by mountains and raging rivers proved harrowing. Bierce kept a detailed notebook, supplemented by his landscape drawings and copies of Indian petroglyphs, labeled "A. G. Bierce, Route Maps of a Journey from Fort Laramie–Dakota Terr. to Fort Benton–Montana Territory 1866" and now part of the Barrett Collection at the University of Virginia.

Bierce reached San Francisco early in 1867. On 3 April he received a telegram informing him that he had not been commissioned as a captain after all but, rather, as a second lieutenant. Never one to accept such setbacks philosophically, he immediately declined the appointment and resigned from General Hazen's expedition. In need of income, Bierce settled in San Francisco, taking a job as a night watchman at the U.S. Sub-Treasury, a job that allowed him time to pursue his vocation as a journalist. With the help of James T. Watkins, a suave English writer and managing editor of the *San Francisco News Letter and California Advertiser,* Bierce set out to make himself into an educated man and a smooth literary stylist. Watkins enjoined him to read classic eighteenth- and nineteenth-century writers including Jonathan Swift, Voltaire, Honoré de Balzac, and William Makepeace Thackeray.

Bierce's work first appeared in print on 21 September 1867 when a derivative and metrically awkward poem, "Basilica," was published in the *Californian.* He then swiftly placed a number of essays and sketches in California publications, including the *News Letter,* the *Californian,* and the *Golden Era.* He joined the staff of the *News Letter* in summer 1868 and, by December of the same year, succeeded his friend Watkins as managing editor. He also produced the weekly "The Town Crier" column for the paper from 5 December 1868 to 9 March 1872.

Early in his journalistic career, Bierce published his first short story, "The Haunted Valley," which appeared in the July 1871 issue of the *Overland Monthly* (collected in *Can Such Things Be?,* 1893). On 25 December 1871 he married Mollie Day. They lived briefly in San Rafael, California, and then, in March 1872, they moved to England, where he wrote mostly satirical pieces for *Fun* and *Figaro.* The Bierces continued to live in England until 1875, first in London, then in Bristol (where their son Day was born in 1872), Bath, and Leamington (where their son Leigh was born in 1874).

During these years Bierce continued to work hard at the craft of writing. He read widely in literature and philosophy, partly for knowledge and partly to help himself improve his spelling, grammar, and basic infelicities of prose. He continued to read major and minor English writers and was deeply influenced by classical philosophy, particularly Plato, the Eleatics, the Cynics, and the later Stoics. Self-taught, he was impatient with others who through laziness, ignorance, indifference, or dishonesty wrote sloppily or inaccurately. His little handbook, *Write It Right* (1909), a prescriptive book of grammar and usage, emphasizes that there is a correct way to write and, most definitely, a wrong way.

While in England Bierce published his first three books (all collections of journalistic pieces): *The Fiend's Delight* (1873), *Nuggets and Dust Panned Out in California* (1873), and *Cobwebs from an Empty Skull* (1874). He loved England and later called his time there the happiest of his life. However, his wife Mollie returned to America with their two sons on 22 April 1875 and then later wrote to her husband to inform him that she was pregnant. Bierce left England for America that fall and joined his family in San Francisco in early October, in time for the birth of his first daughter, Helen, on 30 October. He settled permanently in America.

Back in California and faced with a family to support, Bierce decided to give up writing for mining and worked in the assay office of the U.S. Branch Mint for over a year. But in 1877 he was again presented with a journalistic opportunity, and he took it. A new political magazine, the *Argonaut*, first appeared on 25 March 1877 with Ambrose Bierce named as associate editor and author of an editorial column, "The Prattler." Bierce enjoyed success (and notoriety) as a muckraking journalist and satirist, but an economic depression in the late 1870s forced him to find another source of income, and once again he turned to mining. For nearly two years he acted as a manager-overseer of a gold-mining operation in the Black Hills of South Dakota, a venture which, like almost all of Bierce's forays into business, ended so disastrously that Bierce returned again to California in January 1881, this time to edit the weekly *Wasp* and to continue his column (now called "Prattle") there.

The years 1887 to 1899 saw the publication of Bierce's best journalism and short stories, but they were personally disastrous for him. Asthma and chronic insomnia left him physically debili-

tated. He separated from his wife in late 1888, and his sixteen-year-old son, Day, was killed in 1899 as a result of a duel over a girlfriend. Perhaps as a reaction to his ill health and emotional torment, Bierce wrote at a prodigious rate, producing his "Prattle" column for William Randolph Hearst's prestigious *San Francisco Examiner* (beginning in 1887), as well as the collections *Tales of Soldiers and Civilians*, *Black Beetles in Amber* (1892), *Can Such Things Be?*, *In the Midst of Life* (1892), and *Fantastic Fables* (1899). In addition, from 1895 to 1898 Bierce wrote an influential series of articles denouncing America's involvement in the Spanish-American War and became one of America's best-known journalists.

It was for his short stories that Bierce wanted to be remembered, and these stories constitute his most important contribution to American literature. He wrote primarily three types of short stories, all of which have important connections to his biography. His Gothic tales, for example, are American Gothic. He eschewed the elaborate castles and mansions of much Gothic fiction, setting many of his stories in dilapidated cabins on bare stretches of countryside. The cabins and rude country people who inhabit them are rooted in his own upbringing on the Western Reserve. The countryside is often the California of his adult life, a Gothic landscape of tangled manzanita and madrona that replaces Hawthorne's dark New England forests. Bierce's second kind of fiction, the war tales for which he is best known, directly derive from his war experiences. It is often said that he was the only major American writer to both fight in and write about the Civil War, and he certainly had more battlefield experience in that war than any writer, major or minor. Finally, there are the grotesque, absurdist tales that have been called "tall tales." In no way resembling Paul Bunyan yarns, these tall tales come directly from Bierce's peculiarly macabre sense of humor. He kept a skull on his desk and liked to insist it belonged to a rival critic; on the same desk he kept a cigar box filled with ashes. These too, he liked to say, belonged to a critic, and he liked to add to the box with ashes from his own cigars. Both his fiction and his actions earned him such appellations as "bitter Bierce" and "the wickedest man in San Francisco."

Bierce's best-known story, "An Occurrence at Owl Creek Bridge," combines elements of all three of the forms in which he worked. It is often reprinted in collections of war stories and in anthologies of fiction on the supernatural.

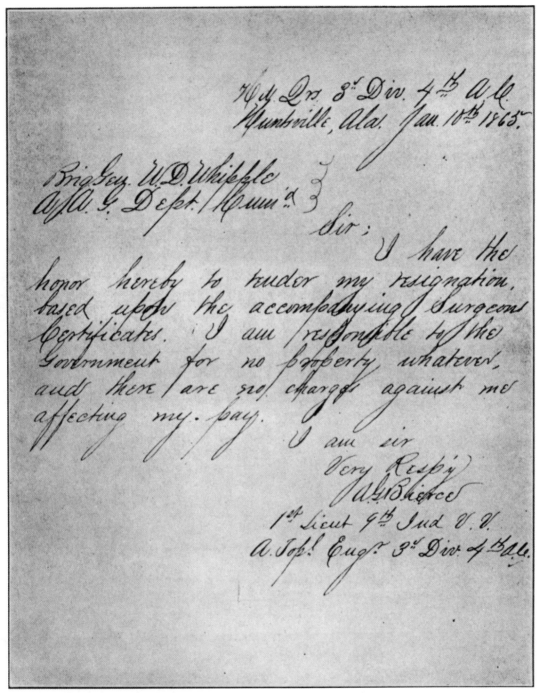

Bierce's letter of resignation from the Union army. He was formally discharged in spring 1865
(Adolphe de Castro, Portrait of Ambrose Bierce, *1929).*

Some of the details of the story, particularly the anatomical description (tinged with black humor) of Peyton Farquhar's hanging, recall the tall tales. But the story is most significant in its re-creation of subjective time and its alternating rhetorical stances and narrative points of view. Like nearly all of Bierce's fiction, "An Occurrence at Owl Creek Bridge" is short (Bierce hated novels and did not have much patience with long stories) and is divided into distinct parts. Each of the three brief sections is narrated in a different type of language: part 1 uses military terminology, objective and distant, and includes an almost handbook description of how to hang a man. Part 2 is Farquhar's flashback to his life as a southern plantation owner, a slaveowner, chafing under the "inglorious restraint" of his civilian life. The rhetoric here is jingoistic cant, deceiving and self-deceiving. In this portion of the story Farquhar recalls meeting a northern spy and being tricked into attempting a mission that, he believes, will win honor for the South and himself. He plans to burn down Owl Creek Bridge, a minor military crossing point. In part 3 Bierce documents Farquhar's fall from this bridge with a noose around his neck and his hallucinatory perception of escape from execution. The language is lush and sensuous. The story, of course, ends with Farquhar's body hanging, pendulumlike, beneath the timbers of the bridge.

It is not a trick ending. In part 1 Bierce differentiates between interior and exterior worlds and shows that the mind can create its own realities and its own escapes. This is a major theme in all of Bierce's fiction, and the technique Bierce uses in "An Occurrence at Owl Creek Bridge" is also typical. He does not tell the reader that Farquhar is hallucinating but expects that the careful reader will realize the impossibility of events described in the final portion of the story. The ending is a surprise only to the careless reader, a surprise that should force that reader to go back and reevaluate the events of the story.

With such literary techniques Bierce opposed the literary trends of his day. In both his journalism and his fiction, for example, he waged war against a simplistic notion of realism. He believed any view of life which ignored the unconscious processes of mind could not call itself realistic. Similarly, although many of his stories appear naturalistic in their bleak depiction of humans in hostile environments and in their meticulous description of violence, Bierce held humans more accountable for their actions than the naturalists. He also tended to interject his peculiar humor into the most gruesome of scenes, creating a tone more similar to Franz Kafka than to Frank Norris or Jack London.

Probably the best example of this tone is another of Bierce's well-known stories, "Chickamauga." Depicting a minor skirmish in a particularly bloody and pointless Civil War battle, the story centers on a small, deaf-and-dumb child who wanders off into the woods. Because his father has shown him pictures of militaristic glory, he is not afraid as he enters the woods: he is a tiny soldier, *homo absurdus* in miniature, brandishing a toy sword in the face of carnage. Soon he encounters the aftermath of a battle, and, in a particularly vivid scene, he assumes the position of

Bierce in 1871

commander over a parade of dying men crawling toward water. The scene is comically and pitifully grotesque. The small conqueror is oblivious to the pain and blood around him. Only when he returns to his home and finds the body of his mangled mother does he understand the meaning of all he has witnessed. His anguished howl of pain gives the lie to the picture-book view of the war with which the story began. "Chickamauga" remains one of the most powerful antiwar stories in American literature.

Bierce protested the insanity of war in other stories as well. In "One of the Missing" (*San Francisco Examiner*, 11 March 1888; collected in *Tales of Soldiers and Civilians*) a soldier finds himself trapped in debris, face to face with the barrel of his own rifle, which he had loaded a moment before the accident. The story is another allegory of the way men make war against themselves by believing patriotic cant and participating in battle. In "Parker Adderson, Philosopher" (originally published as "James Adderson, Philosopher and Wit," *San Francisco Examiner*, 22 February 1891; collected in *Tales of Soldiers and Civilians*) a spy bravely faces execution and delights himself with his own gallows humor. But as soon as the rituals of death are denied him, and he learns he will be "summarily shot," the pose of indifference collapses. Bierce suggests that human beings all have ways of dealing with their own mortality, but mostly these are self-deceptions.

War for Bierce becomes a metaphor for the kinds of deceptions and self-deceptions that pervade human life. In his well-known book of perceptive and cynical aphorisms, *The Devil's Dictionary* (originally published as *The Cynic's Word Book* in 1906), Bierce defined *war* as "a by-product of the arts of peace.... War loves to come like a thief in the night; professions of eternal amity provide the night." Politicians hypocritically foster war to aggrandize themselves, and the public contributes to the waste of human life by convincing themselves that a cause (whatever the cause) is worth dying for. Bierce also defined a *patriot* as "the dupe of statesmen and the tool of conquerors" and *patriotism* as "combustible rubbish ready to the torch of any one ambitious to illuminate his name."

Similarly, the best tales of the supernatural transcend the ghost story genre. Like the best Gothic fiction of Poe and Hawthorne, Bierce's ghost tales question the limits and nature of human perception. For example, in "The Suitable Surroundings" (*San Francisco Examiner*, 14 July 1889; collected in *Tales of Soldiers and Civilians*) Bierce questions the nature of the supernatural and of supernatural fiction. In this story James R. Colston, a Gothic writer, claims he can scare his friend, Mr. Marsh, literally to death, so long as his friend reads Colston's manuscript in a dilapidated and isolated cabin in the middle of the woods. Marsh *is* scared to death but by a pale face that appears in the window. The face belongs to a little boy who in turn is frightened out of his wits when he looks into the abandoned, "haunted" cabin and sees a stark white face illuminated by flickering candlelight. Again, the comic accumulation of errors leads to tragedy, a tragedy of misperception and self-deception. "The Death of Halpin Frayser" (*Wave*, 25 December 1891; collected in *Can Such Things Be?*), Bierce's most complicated narrative experiment, raises the process of misperception to its ultimate level. Near the end of the story two detectives try to solve the "rascally mystery" of Halpin Frayser's death on his mother's grave. Their explanation accounts for all the evidence but, at the same time, totally misses the point. Earlier sections depict Frayser's dream of being visited by his dead mother, his hallucination of writing a poem with

blood that dripped from the trees around him, and his final dream of his own death. Waking and dream consciousness are both called into question when the detectives do, in fact, discover a poem written by Frayser in what seems to be blood, and then the man who has dreamed his death *does* die, with the marks of bruising fingers on his throat. The meaning of the story is summarized by a final soulless laugh that reverberates in the fog, taunting detectives and readers who think they can make simple, logical sense out of a universe characterized by absurdity and meaninglessness.

The stories discussed in this entry represent Bierce at his best, his most innovative, and his most nihilistic. Although he stopped writing fiction by 1899 and although he produced fewer than a hundred short stories, he was an influential writer. Stephen Crane said of Bierce's "An Occurrence at Owl Creek Bridge," "Nothing better exists—the story has everything," and, as has been well documented, Crane consciously modeled his own impressionist tales of war on Bierce's. Bierce's vituperative journalism and his sardonic tall tales were greatly appreciated by H. L. Mencken, Carey McWilliams, and other writers of the post-World War I era. In fact, Bierce was almost a folk hero of the Roaring Twenties, as indicated even by the fact that one year, 1929, saw the publication of no fewer than four popular biographies of the author. The impetus for these mythmaking biographies was Bierce's unconventional life as much as his writing. The American public was especially intrigued by the end of that life, for Bierce, in 1913, over seventy years old, had crossed the Mexican border from El Paso to Juarez, in order to observe the Mexican Revolution and Pancho Villa firsthand. Although he was probably killed at the battle of Ojinaga on 11 January 1914, no one has ever succeeded in documenting, absolutely, the time, place, or manner of Bierce's death, and Mexican novelist Carlos Fuentes insists that one still hears tales of the "Old Gringo" roaming the Andes. It would be a strange ending for any writer but all the more so for a writer fascinated by disappearance and mysterious death.

While Bierce's short stories are widely anthologized, they have received relatively little critical attention. Yet in the past two decades this situation has begun to change. His surrealistic literary techniques and rhetorical presentations of subjective and objective time strike a contemporary note. Such modern masters of fiction as Jorge

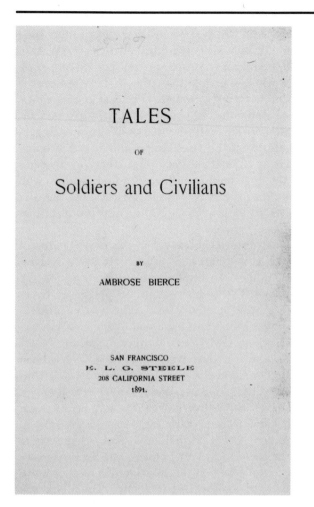

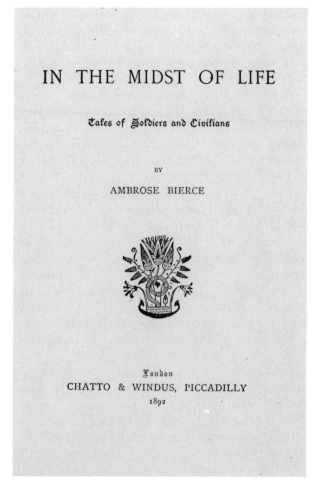

Title pages for the American and British editions of one of Bierce's short-story collections

Luis Borges, Julio Cortazar, and Fuentes have been influenced by Bierce's stories, particularly by his juxtaposition of multiple points of view and often contradictory perspectives and by his expositions of the deceptions that the mind plays upon itself. Increasingly Bierce is recognized as one of the masters of the short-story form and not just as that colorful Californian who disappeared into Mexico in 1914.

Letters:

The Letters of Ambrose Bierce, edited by Bertha Clark Pope (San Francisco: Book Club of California, 1922).

Bibliographies:

Vincent Starrett, *Ambrose Bierce, A Bibliography* (Philadelphia: Centaur Book Shop, 1929);

Joseph Gaer, ed., *Ambrose Gwinett* [sic] *Bierce, Bibliography and Biographical Data* (1935; republished, New York: Burt Franklin, 1968);

Paul Fatout, "Ambrose Bierce (1842-1914)," *American Literary Realism, 1870-1910*, 1 (Fall 1967): 13-19;

Philip M. Rubens and Robert Jones, "Ambrose Bierce: A Bibliographic Essay and a Bibliography," *American Literary Realism*, 16 (Spring 1983): 73-91.

Biographies:

Carey McWilliams, *Ambrose Bierce, A Biography* (New York: A. & C. Boni, 1929);

Paul Fatout, *Ambrose Bierce, the Devil's Lexicographer* (Norman: University of Oklahoma Press, 1951);

Fatout, *Ambrose Bierce and the Black Hills* (Norman: University of Oklahoma Press, 1956);

Richard O'Connor, *Ambrose Bierce, A Biography* (Boston: Little, Brown, 1967);

Richard Saunders, *Ambrose Bierce: The Making of a Misanthrope* (San Francisco: Chronicle Books, 1985).

References:

Lawrence I. Berkove, "The Man with the Burning Pen: Ambrose Bierce as Journalist," *Journal of Popular Culture*, 15 (Fall 1981): 34-40;

Berkove, " 'A Strange Adventure': The Story Behind a Bierce Tale," *American Literary Realism*, 14 (Spring 1981): 70-76;

Frederic Taber Cooper, "Ambrose Bierce," in *Some American Story Tellers* (New York: Holt, Rinehart & Winston, 1911);

Cathy N. Davidson, *The Experimental Fictions of Ambrose Bierce: Structuring the Ineffable* (Lincoln & London: University of Nebraska Press, 1984);

Davidson, ed., *Critical Essays on Ambrose Bierce* (Boston: G. K. Hall, 1982)—comprises H. L. Mencken, "Ambrose Bierce"; Van Wyck Brooks, "The Letters of Ambrose Bierce"; Carey McWilliams, "Ambrose Bierce"; Wilson Follett, "Ambrose, Son of Marcus Aurelius"; David D. Anderson, "The Old Northwest, the Midwest, and the Making of Three American Iconoclasts"; Jay Martin, "Ambrose Bierce"; James Milton Highsmith, "The Forms of Burlesque in *The Devil's Dictionary*"; Lawrence I. Berkove, "The Heart Has Its Reasons: Ambrose Bierce's Successful Failure at Philosophy"; Howard W. Bahr, "Ambrose Bierce and Realism"; Daniel Aaron, "Ambrose Bierce and the American Civil War"; Eric Solomon, "The Bitterness of Battle: Ambrose Bierce's War Fiction"; F. J. Logan, "The Wry Seriousness of 'Owl Creek Bridge' "; M. E. Grenander, "Bierce's Turn of the Screw: Tales of Ironical 'Terror'; and William Bysshe Stein, "Bierce's 'The Death of Halpin Frayser': The Poetics of Gothic Consciousness";

Howard M. Fraser, "Points South: Ambrose Bierce, Jorge Luis Borges, and the Fantastic," *Studies in Twentieth-Century Literature*, 1 (1977): 173-181;

Otto Friedrich, "The Passion of Death in Ambrose Bierce," *Zero*, 2 (Spring 1956): 72-94;

M. E. Grenander, *Ambrose Bierce* (New York: Twayne, 1971);

Grenander, " 'Five Blushes, Ten Shudders and a Vomit'; Mark Twain on Ambrose Bierce's *Nuggets and Dust*," *American Literary Realism*, 17 (Autumn 1984): 169-179;

Alfred Kazin, "On Ambrose Bierce and 'Parker Adderson, Philosopher,' " in *The American Short Story*, edited by Calvin Skaggs (New York: Dell, 1977), pp. 26-35;

Marcus Klein, "San Francisco and Her Hateful Ambrose Bierce," *Hudson Review*, 7 (Autumn 1954): 392-407;

Robert C. McLean, "The Deaths in Ambrose Bierce's 'Halpin Frayser,' " *Papers in Language and Literature*, 10 (1974): 394-402;

Arthur M. Miller, "The Influence of Edgar Allan Poe on Ambrose Bierce," *American Literature*, 4 (May 1932): 130-150;

Matthew C. O'Brien, "Ambrose Bierce and the Civil War: 1865," *American Literature*, 48 (November 1976): 377-381;

James G. Powers, "Freud and Farquhar: An Occurrence at Owl Creek Bridge?," *Studies in Short Fiction*, 19 (Summer 1982): 278-281;

Alfred C. Ward, "Ambrose Bierce: 'In the Midst of Life,' " in his *Aspects of the Modern Short Story, English and American* (London: University of London Press, 1924);

David R. Weimer, "Ambrose Bierce and the Art of War," in *Essays in Literary History*, edited by Rudolph Kirk and C. F. Main (New York: Russell & Russell, 1964), pp. 229-238;

Robert A. Wiggins, *Ambrose Bierce*, University of Minnesota Pamphlets on American Writers, no. 37 (Minneapolis: University of Minnesota Press, 1964);

Edmund Wilson, "Ambrose Bierce on the Owl Creek Bridge," *New Yorker*, 27 (8 December 1951): 159-170;

Napier Wilt, "Ambrose Bierce and the Civil War," *American Literature*, 1 (November 1929): 260-285;

Stuart C. Woodruff, *The Short Stories of Ambrose Bierce: A Study in Polarity* (Pittsburgh: University of Pittsburgh Press, 1964).

Papers:
The most important holdings of Bierce's papers are in the Bancroft Library of the University of California at Berkeley; the Clifton Waller Barrett Collection at the University of Virginia; the University of Cincinnati; the Huntington Library in San Marino, California; the Berg Collection of the New York Public Library; the Division of Special Collections at Stanford University; the George Arents Research Library at Syracuse University; and the Beinecke Library of Yale University.

George Washington Cable

(12 October 1844-31 January 1925)

George C. Longest
Virginia Commonwealth University

See also the Cable entry in *DLB 12: American Realists and Naturalists.*

BOOKS: *Old Creole Days* (New York: Scribners, 1879; Edinburgh: Douglas, 1883; enlarged edition, 2 volumes, New York: Scribners, 1883);

The Grandissimes: A Story of Creole Life (New York: Scribners, 1880; London: Hodder & Stoughton, 1898);

Madame Delphine: A Novelette and Other Tales (London: Warne, 1881);

Madame Delphine (New York: Scribners, 1881);

An Address . . . At the Commencement Exercises of the Academical Department, of the University of Louisiana, June 15th, 1883 (New Orleans: Printed by W. Harry Seymour, 1883);

The Creoles of Louisiana (New York: Scribners, 1884; London: Hamilton, 1884);

Dr. Sevier (1 volume, Boston: Osgood, 1884; 2 volumes, Edinburgh: Douglas, 1884);

The Silent South, Together with The Freeman's Case in Equity and The Convict Lease System (New York: Scribners, 1885; enlarged, 1889);

Madame Delphine, Carancro . . . Grande Pointe (Edinburgh: Douglas, 1887);

Bonaventure: A Prose Pastoral of Acadian Louisiana (New York: Scribners, 1888; London: Low, 1888);

The Negro Question [single essay] (New York: American Missionary Association, 1888);

Strange True Stories of Louisiana (New York: Scribners, 1889; London: Trübner, 1889);

The Southern Struggle for Pure Government. An Address . . . Delivered before the Massachusetts Club, Boston, on Washington's Birthday, 1890 (Boston: Press of Samuel Usher, 1890);

The Negro Question [six essays] (New York: Scribners, 1890);

What the Negro Must Learn. Address . . . at the Annual Meeting of the American Missionary Association, Held in Northampton, October, 21-23, 1890 (New York: American Missionary Society, 1890?);

The Busy Man's Bible and How to Study and Teach It (Meadville, Pa.: Flood & Vincent, Chautauqua-Century Press, 1891);

A Memory of Roswell Smith, Born March 30, 1829, Died April 19, 1892 (New York: Privately printed, 1892);

John March, Southerner (New York: Scribners, 1894; London: Low, 1895);

Strong Hearts (New York: Scribners, 1899; London: Hodder & Stoughton, 1899);

The Cavalier (New York: Scribners, 1901; London: Murray, 1901);

Père Raphaël (New York: Privately printed, 1901);

Bylow Hill (New York: Scribners, 1902; London: Hodder & Stoughton, 1902);

Kincaid's Battery (New York: Scribners, 1908; London: Hodder & Stoughton, 1909);

"Posson Jone'" and Père Raphaël, with a New Word Setting Forth How and Why the Two Tales Are One (New York: Scribners, 1909);

Gideon's Band: A Tale of the Mississippi (New York: Scribners, 1914);

The Amateur Garden (New York: Scribners, 1914);

The Flower of the Chapdelaines (New York: Scribners, 1918; London: Collins, 1919);

Lovers of Louisiana (To-Day) (New York: Scribners, 1918).

OTHER: *Tenth Census of the United States. Francis A. Walker, Superintendent. Social Statistics of Cities. History and Present Condition of New Orleans, Louisiana, and Report on the City of Austin, Texas,* includes a historical sketch of New Orleans by Cable and information about the city compiled by George E. Waring, Jr., with Cable's assistance (Washington, D.C.: U.S. Government Printing Office, 1881);

"New Orleans Before the Capture," in *Battles and Leaders of the Civil War,* edited by Robert Underwood Johnson and Clarence Clough Buel, volume 2, part 9 (New York: Century, 1888), pp. 14-21;

Famous Adventures and Prison Escapes of the Civil War, edited, with a contribution, by Cable (New York: Century, 1893);

"The Angel of the Lord," in *A House Party: An Account of the Stories Told at a Gathering of Famous American Authors, The Stories Being Introduced by Paul Leicester Ford* (Boston: Small, Maynard, 1901), pp. 340-386.

George Washington Cable's antecedents were not typical for a southern writer born prior to the Civil War. His father, George Washington Cable, Sr., came from an established Virginia line, while his mother, Rebecca Boardman Cable, was from a Calvinistic family that had settled in New England during the seventeenth century. In 1837, after residency in Indiana, both parents settled in New Orleans, where their fifth child, George Washington Cable, Jr., was born in 1844. The differing backgrounds of Cable's parents

Cable in 1863, the year he joined the Confederate army

were further enhanced by the diversity of the New Orleans population–genteel "yankee" Americans (the descendants of Americans who settled there after the Louisiana Purchase), Kentucky and Tennessee boatmen, Creoles (the descendants of the original French and Spanish settlers), Acadians, and free and enslaved blacks.

After his father's death in 1859 Cable left school to help support the family by taking a clerkship at the customhouse where his father had been employed. About two years later he took a job as a clerk and cashier for a wholesale grocer. In spring 1863, nearly a year after the Union army had begun its occupation of New Orleans, he and other family members crossed over to unoccupied Mississippi, where on 9 October 1863 Cable enlisted in the Confederate cavalry. Wounded twice during the war, Cable returned to New Orleans in May 1865 and worked at a series of clerkships until taking a job with a surveying party in July 1866. Several weeks later Cable became ill with malaria and was unable to work steadily for two years. First taking a job with a commission merchant, he then worked for two cotton businesses, and, when he married Louise Stewart Bartlett on 7 December 1869, he was secretary to the New Orleans Oil Works Company. The Cables' first child, Louise, was born the following November, to be followed by Mary in 1872, Lucy (1875), Margaret (1877), George (1878), Isabel (1883), William (1885), and Dorothea (1889).

By then Cable's literary career had begun with the first appearance of his "Drop Shot" column in the 27 February 1870 issue of the *New Orleans Picayune*. The early poems and sketches appearing in the column suggest the strengths that he was to demonstrate in writing the best of his short stories: sensitivity to the natural scene and to peculiar aspects of the life and history of the region.

By early 1871 Cable had become a full-time reporter for the *New Orleans Picayune*, but later that year he angered the paper's proprietor when he refused to join other newspapermen in denouncing the Republican-appointed superintendent of schools for calling an integrated teachers' meeting. As Cable recalled later, "Then and there I permanently lost grace with my employer," and that summer he was fired for refusing an assignment to report on a play because attending the theater violated the Calvinist principles instilled in him by his mother.

Cable took a job as a bookkeeper for William C. Black and Company, cotton factors, and continued to work there until December 1881. Soon after he was fired from the *Picayune*, however, the newspaper came under new ownership, and Cable was rehired to write his "Drop Shot" column as well as articles and reviews.

In early 1872 Cable agreed to write a series of sketches of New Orleans churches and charities for the *Picayune*. Availing himself of the archives at the Cabildo (the seat of the French colonial government) and at the St. Louis Cathedral, Cable discovered a rich deposit of historical documents which contained the raw material for his future fiction. Dating back as far as the New Orleans of 1718, these records of nations, cultures, races, and families in conflict–as they were filtered through Cable's perception–gave him the basis for writing a body of fiction with themes, conflicts, and ambiguities establishing his kinship with a much later generation of southern writers represented by William Faulkner, Ellen Glasgow, and Thomas Wolfe.

During Mardi Gras in 1873 a young journalist, Edward King, toured New Orleans in search of materials for the series on the South after the Civil War that he was writing for *Scribner's Monthly Magazine*. He and Cable met, and, recognizing his opportunity, Cable showed several of his stories to King, who took Cable's manuscripts

to *Scribner's Monthly* for consideration. In December 1871 Charles Scribner and Company had rejected a book of prose and verse, material from the "Drop Shot" column that Cable had reworked as a single narrative. One of the stories that King took back to New York–"Bibi," which Louis D. Rubin, Jr., calls Cable's first mature short story–was also rejected not only by Richard Watson Gilder at *Scribner's* but later by George Parsons Lathrop, an editor at the *Atlantic Monthly*, who returned it to Cable because of its "unmitigatedly distressful effect" on the reader. Another of the stories that Cable had shown to King met with success, however, and the appearance of " 'Sieur George" in the October 1873 issue of *Scribner's Monthly* marked the first publication of his fiction in a national magazine. By autumn 1875 seven of his stories had been accepted, six by *Scribner's Monthly* and a seventh by *Appletons' Journal*.

The ingredients of " 'Sieur George" are the hallmark of *Old Creole Days* (1879), the book in which it was later collected, and the story found Cable the audience he needed. The nostalgic charm of a rapidly disintegrating Creole culture was apparent in the story, and the author's sentimentality, didacticism, and romantic scene painting appealed to a late-nineteenth-century, middle-class audience already disposed, from having read the period's popular fiction romanticizing the antebellum South, to read of another fallen order. The timing was propitious, for " 'Sieur George" not only inaugurated Cable's career, it also began the vogue for southern local color.

'Sieur George, something of a stock villain from early-nineteenth-century melodrama, is a Gothic character. Living in two shabby rooms in a once fashionable neighborhood, he owns a mysterious trunk, which generates curiosity in his landlord and in the reader. It symbolizes his secret guilt, for it stores the thousands of worthless lottery tickets on which he has squandered his fortune. Taking in the orphaned infant daughter of a friend, he raises her to the age of sixteen while proceeding to spend the fortune she has inherited from her mother on still more lottery tickets.

What would have been pure melodrama, however, is saved from sheer sentimentality, Rubin suggests, when 'Sieur George informs his ward not only that he has been gambling with her money, but that, since they are not blood relatives, she must either leave the flat for the sake of propriety or marry him. This shocking pronouncement creates what Rubin calls a "savage depiction of human degradation." At the end of the story 'Sieur George is still trying to talk to the girl, who has entered a convent, so that he can ask her to lend him money for another lottery ticket.

The story is one of Cable's best, Philip Butcher, for example, judging it a "masterpiece of local color." On accepting it for *Scribner's*, Gilder wrote to Cable, "You have the makings of one of the best story-writers of the day," and readers have generally admired its beauty of setting, tone, and atmosphere. Arlin Turner, moreover, notes a powerful illumination in Cable's use in " 'Sieur George" of symbols, "not subtle in themselves, but subtle in the handling and in the way their meanings enter the reader's awareness."

By 1879 Cable was ready to gather " 'Sieur George" and six other stories into what would prove to be one of the most important collections of local-color fiction in American literature, *Old Creole Days*. The volume, as Fred Lewis Pattee early observed, is created from materials which are innately rich in romantic diversity: "It seemed hardly possible that the new world possessed such a Bagdad of wonder: old Spanish aristocracy, French chivalry of a forgotten *ancien régime*, Creoles, Acadians from the Grand Pré dispersion, adventurers from all the picturesque ports of the earth, slavery with its barbaric atmosphere and its shuddery background of dread, and behind it all and around it all like a mighty moat shutting it close in upon itself and rendering all else in the world a mere hearsay and dream, the swamps and lagoons of the great river."

The leading characters of the stories in this volume are among the best Cable ever created. His forte is depicting the Creole, the black, the American Yankee, and the curious and often star-crossed social intermixture of the three. Mostly, however, as Shirley Ann Grau has pointed out, it is Cable's portraits of the Creoles that are absorbing, especially his depiction of these aristocrats in the period near the "end of their social and political supremacy. . . . "

The stories in *Old Creole Days* are classics of the local-color genre in their use of dialect, setting, and regional eccentricity, and—as Alice Hall Petry has noted—they exhibit the values of nineteenth-century America: honor, heroism, stoicism, adaptability, brotherhood, and religious faith. Such pieties are readily apparent in "Belles Demoiselles Plantation" (first published in *Scribner's Monthly*, April 1874). Making a profound statement on the human condition, the story con-

Cable in 1868

tains two of Cable's most memorable characters– Injin Charlie and his distant relative Colonel De Charleu, the master of Belles Demoiselles Plantation. In the relationship between the proud Creole De Charleu and his humble half-caste relative– each of whom owns a portion of their illustrious ancestor's original land grant–is the narrative of human suffering and dignity.

"Belles Demoiselles" is set in both town and country. The colonel, knowing that his plantation house will soon be swept away by the river, seeks to trade it to Charlie for Charlie's humble, but well-located, place in town, where the colonel hopes to build an urban mansion worthy of his daughters. Charlie, though puzzled by the offer, finally agrees. As the two survey the great plantation prior to closing the deal, the colonel becomes conscience-stricken and abruptly changes his mind. At that moment the river erodes away the point of land upon which the mansion rests, consuming the mansion and taking the lives of his seven beautiful daughters. Injin Charlie, displaying the loyalty demanded by nineteenth-century audiences, nurses his pure-blood Creole relative until the colonel dies from grief.

The extent to which Cable was able to give mythic proportion to such a sentimental and moral narrative is admirable. The two lines of the family–created when the first De Charleu to settle in the New World married a white woman in France while his Choctaw wife and children waited for his return to Louisiana–are symbolized by the plantation house, an impressive edifice established on unstable ground. Like the house, both branches of the family are clearly doomed to extinction by the errors of the past, like the house and family in Edgar Allan Poe's "The Fall of the House of Usher."

The polarization of the two branches is apparent in the characters' use of language. English, rather than French, is the chosen medium of communication between the colonel and Injin Charlie, since, Cable observes, it answers, "better than French could, a similar purpose to that of the stick which we fasten to the bit of one horse and the breast-gear of another, whereby each keeps his distance" while the two pull together. Also the seven sisters, who usually speak French, speak only English when the half-caste Charlie is about to have business with their father.

The plantation by the river is the Eden of Creole order; there, all is, superficially at least, placid, harmonious, secure. Town life, the New American dream, appears postlapsarian. Yet the colonel's earthly Eden is an illusion, impossible to maintain. Only when he recognizes his consanguinity of blood with Charlie by negating their business deal can he attain a true Eden: in his dying hour he sees himself in paradise with his seven beautiful daughters.

First published in the October 1874 issue of *Scribner's*, " 'Tite Poulette," as Arlin Turner notes, is a "moving plea for the quadroon caste." The flowering of all that is graceful in human beauty, 'Tite Poulette is the illegitimate daughter of a quadroon dancer called Madame John or Zalli and a Creole gentleman whose first name is John. Because she is an octoroon, 'Tite Poulette is forbidden by law to marry a white man. Yet the still-beautiful Zalli, who supports herself and her daughter by dancing at the Salle de Condé, believes that she can save her daughter from the same fate only by arranging such a marriage. After Kristian Koppig, a recently arrived, well-to-do neighbor, strikes the manager of the Salle de Condé to prevent him from coercing Madame John into allowing him to hire her daughter, Koppig is severely beaten by the manager and his henchmen. Nursed back to health by mother

and daughter, he falls in love with 'Tite Poulette and marries her after Zalli denies that this much-loved daughter is her child. The villain in the story, as Philip Butcher observes, is not the manager of the Salle de Condé but the society practicing a double standard, and William Bedford Clark notes the irony of a law that "forbids legitimate intimacies between the races but does nothing to prevent them on an illicit basis."

"Jean-ah Poquelin" (first published in *Scribner's*, May 1875) is Cable's most poignant story of Creole life. In the best Southern Gothic fashion Jean spends his life hiding away and caring for his leprous brother in the family mansion, which has become "the object of a thousand superstitions." New Orleans begins to change under American dominion, and the land upon which the Poquelin mansion stands is needed for municipal expansion. Hoping to preserve his brother's privacy, Jean fights the condemnation of part of his land; but he fails, and a new street is built close to his house. He dies after a suspicious crowd storms his mansion, and his secret is finally exposed.

The Gothic line of the story is simple enough, and it is similar, as Edward Stone asserts, to William Faulkner's "A Rose for Emily" (1930). Of much greater importance is what the story says about the conflict between two cultures. As the city encroaches on the mansion's country setting, new, "American" ways encroach upon Creole tradition and, in the crowd's shivaree outside the mansion, defeat it.

Few characters in late-nineteenth-century American literature surpass Jean-ah Poquelin. In his stubborn insistence–at all cost–on caring for his leprous brother and in his quiet defiance of outside authority, Poquelin attains mythic proportions as the last hero of a disintegrating culture. Furthermore, as Joseph J. Egan has said, Poquelin's heroism suggests that the "measure of a civilization depends upon the value it assigns to the feelings of the heart."

"Madame Délicieuse" (first published in *Scribner's*, August 1875) depicts a far happier moment in Creole life. Perhaps because Cable's overall view of life is tragic, the story is one of the least successful in the collection. The plot centers upon Madame Délicieuse's successful attempts to reunite her gentle lover, Dr. Mossy, and his proud, authoritarian father, Gen. Hercule Mossy de Villivicencio, who loves her even after she has rejected his marriage proposal. The separation between father and son is the consequence of cul-

Pencil drawing that Cable enclosed in a letter written to his wife while he was in the Cascade Mountains. He captioned it: "We understand that Mr. Cable is deep in the study of glaciers" (Lucy Leffingwell Cable Biklé, George W. Cable: His Life and Letters, *1928).*

ture change, for the son has rejected his father's military way of life for one of quiet scholarship and has been, to his father's outrage, "Americanized," dropping "de Villivicencio" from his name. Beyond the picturesque setting, there is little to recommend the work save for its occasional satire on Creole life and Cable's portrait of General Villivicencio–a hot-tempered anachronism–and Madame Délicieuse–a beautiful, enterprising, and highly romantic lady.

"Café des Exilés" (first published in *Scribner's,* March 1876) lacks the psychological depth and the intense conflict of Cable's best fiction.

Within the political intrigue of an exiled Caribbean community, a love story develops rapidly and concludes with an outsider, Irishman Galahad Shaughnessy, marrying the daughter of the café proprietor. Cable's deft description is everywhere apparent, but he is obviously a local colorist in this story and not a skillful examiner of civilizations in conflict.

"Posson Jone' " represents Cable's most successful use of humor. Because Cable chose to picture a naive Protestant minister who is tricked into drinking and gambling in New Orleans, however, he had considerable difficulty selling the story. *Scribner's,* which was geared to genteel readers, turned it down. *Harper's* editor Henry Mills Alden rejected it because, he said, "the story leaves an unpleasant impression on the mind of the reader." The story finally appeared in the 1 April 1876 issue of *Appletons' Journal.*

The comedy approaches caricature if not stereotyping. In its best moments the narrative is Plautine. Jules St. Ange, for example, is a spoiled Creole who must depend upon his wits to supplement his allowance (a classic situation in Plautus); and he is, in his meandering intrigues, assisted by his clever, worldly servant Baptiste. A brawny, innocent preacher from rural Florida, Posson Jone' is accompanied (indeed, protected) by his faithful, perceptive black servant Colossus of Rhodes.

Cable carefully develops the sets of humorous contrasts–St. Ange and Baptiste versus Jone' and Colossus–implying in the process that neither approach to life is wholly satisfactory. Protestant self-denial cannot withstand the temptations of a New Orleans Vanity Fair, but Old World decadence can no longer sustain itself in face of New World innocence. Each pair finds redemption in what is learned from the other. Posson Jone' returns to Florida with his church funds restored (thanks to Colossus of Rhodes) and presumably with a healthier world view. Jules St. Ange reforms as a result of his encounter with the innocent.

"Bras-Coupé" has the most contemporary appeal of all Cable's stories. A slightly revised version of "Bibi," the story rejected in 1873 by Richard Watson Gilder of *Scribner's Monthly* and by George Parsons Lathrop of the *Atlantic Monthly,* it serves as chapters 28 and 29 of Cable's first novel, *The Grandissimes* (1880).

"Bras-Coupé" is the darkest of Cable's stories in the Southern Gothic mode, and the hero, in his dignity and his profound suffering, is one of the author's most intriguing characters. As Richard B. Eaton suggests, Bras-Coupé is the "Black Prince" of virtue, a tragic figure violated by the chains of life. Bras-Coupé is an African chieftain who has been transported to New Orleans on the slave ship *Egalité* and sold into bondage in an alien culture.

The story is derived from a legend told to Cable by old French-speaking blacks, and its plot hinges in part on the *Code Noir* or Black Code of Louisiana. Cable carefully developed contrasts. Two worlds (black and white) and two codes of law coexist. Two weddings and two pairs of lovers are juxtaposed. When Bras-Coupé leaves his own wedding in a drunken state, enters his master's wedding party, and strikes him, he commits an act that under the Black Code is punishable by death. He flees, placing a voodoo curse on the land as well as his owner and his male heirs, and by the time he is captured the master is dying while the land is fallow. While his life is spared, he is returned to his quarters with "a cloth thrown over his galled back, his ears shorn from his head, and the tendons behind his knees severed"–the prescribed punishment for a runaway slave. As he lies dying, Bras-Coupé lifts the curse out of compassion for his master's widow and her infant son.

The protagonist's unshakable dignity, courage, and humanity make him one of Cable's best characters. When a priest asks the dying Bras-Coupé if he knows where he is going, the hero replies, "To Africa."

"Madame Delphine" first appeared in *Scribner's Monthly* (May-June 1881) and was published as a separate volume the same year. It was subsequently added to the 1883 edition of *Old Creole Days* and was included in all succeeding editions of that collection. Cable believed the story to be his best work because of its forthright and powerful treatment of the quadroon's situation.

In "Madame Delphine" Cable achieves a beauty of setting unrivaled by other local colorists of the day. In describing the shabby, once elegant neighborhood where the quadroon Madame Delphine lives, the narrator reflects, "Yet beauty lingers here. To say nothing of the picturesque, sometimes you get sight of comfort, sometimes of opulence, through the unlatched wicket in some *porte-cochère*–red-painted brick pavement, foliage of dark palm or pale banana, marble or granite masonry and blooming parterres; or through a chink between some pair of heavy batten window-shutters, opened with an almost reptile weariness, your eye gets a glimpse of lace and brocade upholstery, silver and bronze, and much similar rich antiquity." This setting symbolizes in the most concrete manner the luxurious but fallen existence of the characters.

According to the Black Code of Louisiana, it is illegal for Madame Delphine's daughter, Olive, to marry Ursin Lemaitre-Vignevielle, a Creole privateer-turned-banker. Yet, like Zalli in "'Tite Poulette," Madame Delphine is willing to lie to assure a future for her daughter. The conflict between love and law reaches a climax in the dramatic scene where Madame Delphine asks the

Samuel Clemens and Cable during their 1884-1885 reading tour
(courtesy of the New-York Historical Society)

Creole priest Père Jerome why the state created the Black Code. Père Jerome replies: "Why did they make that law? Well, they made it to keep the two races separate." Madame Delphine rejoins tragically: "They do not want to keep us separated; no, no! But they *do* want to keep us despised!"

The story delivers Cable's strongest message concerning racial relations in the South. Robert O. Stephens has argued convincingly that the story is an indictment not so much of New Orleans in the 1820s but of the nation in the 1870s, with its willingness to abandon Reconstruction by passing Jim Crow laws.

By the time *Madame Delphine* appeared, Cable's first novel, *The Grandissimes* (1880), had established his reputation as a writer, and in Novem-

ber 1884, when he and Samuel Clemens began a five-month reading tour of eastern and midwestern states, the tour's promoter billed the two as "Twins of Genius." Audiences responded favorably to the readings, but in the South Cable was under fire not only for his condemnation of slavery and racism in his fiction but also for his essays and speeches calling for full civil rights for blacks. He and his family had come to feel unwelcome in New Orleans, and, having spent summers in New England, they decided to move there permanently, settling in Northampton, Massachusetts, in autumn 1885.

Cable continued to write about the South. His next collection of short fiction, *Bonaventure* (1888), gathered two stories written before his move north, "Carancro" (*Century,* January-Feb-

37

Louise Cable and the Cable children, 1889: Margaret, Lucy, Dorothea, Isabel, Louise, Mary, and William

ruary 1877) and "Grande Pointe" (*Century*, March 1881), with a more recent story, "Au Large" (*Century*, November 1887-1888), to form a trilogy set in Acadian Louisiana. Although Cable's sympathy for the Acadians, or Cajuns, was genuine and although he had visited Acadian communities to observe their lives firsthand, these stories are less realistic than his stories of Creole life.

Exiled from Nova Scotia by the British, persecuted and exploited, the Acadians are simple, humble, devout Catholics, bound together by their common heritage. Bonaventure, the Creole hero of the first two stories and an important character in the third, grew up among the Acadians, and "Carancro" chronicles his unsuccessful efforts to win the hand of Zoséphine Gradnego. In "Grande Pointe" he is a schoolteacher, devoting himself to improving the Cajun lot culturally and educationally, and the story ends with the beautiful Sidonie Le Blanc accepting his proposal of marriage. "Au Large" ends with the marriages of the widowed Zoséphine and her daughter to their respective suitors and with Bonaventure shedding

"the deepest, gladdest tears at those nuptials."

The stories collected in *Strange True Stories of Louisiana* (1889) are Cable's retelling of accounts drawn from old manuscripts, newspapers, and archival records or told to him by living witnesses. In the introduction to the book publication of the stories, all of which had first appeared in *Century* magazine, Cable said he had changed the original stories very little, but some of them have been reshaped more than others, and some of the stories have been discussed as fiction. According to Butcher, the stories–ranging in time from 1782 to the end of the nineteenth century–are "recounted with such skill that they have an impressive excellence." The three best stories in the collection–and the only ones which have received significant discussion–are "Salome Müller, the White Slave" (*Century*, May 1889), "The 'Haunted House' in Royal Street" (*Century*, August 1889), and "Attalie Brouillard" (*Century*, September 1889).

The daughter of German immigrants to Louisiana, Salome Müller is separated from her parents and later sold into slavery. Years later, when her family seeks her return, they find that because of her status she is considered to be of mixed blood and, hence, not to be freed. Only when a birthmark proves her to be the Müllers' child is Salome ruled to be white and legally free. As Butcher notes, Cable included this story of a case decided in the Louisiana Supreme Court during 1844-1845 "to flout Southern doctrines about race and to attack slavery."

"The 'Haunted House' in Royal Street" is one of Cable's strongest short stories. As Turner points out, the story is drawn in part from Harriet Martineau's account of her visit to New Orleans in her *Retrospect of Western Travel* (1838).

On 30 August 1831 Madame Lalaurie bought the house in Royal Street and with her husband began keeping an elegant establishment, one supported by house slaves, many of whom were kept in chains and tortured. At least one of the slaves died as a result of Madame Lalaurie's cruelty, and an angry mob stormed the mansion and chased Madame Lalaurie from town. In 1874 when the house was used as an integrated girls' school, an angry mob stormed the house once again and expelled all nonwhites. The story is Cable's strongest fictionalized attack on both slavery and segregation. Clark has observed that it is a "synoptic view of the whole Southern experience with regard to race."

"Attalie Brouillard" is based upon information Cable received from a New Orleans judge, but, as Rubin notes, it is closer to "pure fiction" than the other stories in the book. When an Englishman, who promised his quadroon landlady that he would leave her his estate, dies intestate, a scheming quadroon, Camille Ducour, persuades Attalie Brouillard to let him disguise himself as the dead man and dictate a "will" from which he would reap sizable profits as well. Friends of the deceased, because they know of Attalie's loyalty, validate the forged will but force Ducour to pay the estate's expenses from his share. The story marks, rather clearly, Cable's decline as a short-story writer. His move to Northampton had ended his firsthand observation of Creole life, the inspiration for his best fiction, and involvement in both civil-rights advocacy and community projects lowered his literary productivity. No longer the strict Calvinist who lost his job rather than accept an assignment to review a play, Cable had become a devout, liberal Presbyterian. His Sunday school classes for adults at Edwards Congregational Church attracted so

many nonmembers of the church that they were moved to Sunday afternoons at the local opera house. In 1887 he conducted Bible-study classes in Boston as well. Also concerned with cultural improvement, Cable formed the first Home Culture Club–for factory girls–in October 1886. By 1894 there were fifty-four clubs, mostly in Massachusetts but ten in other states and Canada. In 1892, however, he made his final public appeal on behalf of equal rights for blacks. His side of the civil-rights question had been losing support nationwide, and he had become aware, as Rubin points out, that he had "failed utterly . . . to arouse the conscience of the South" and that to northern "leaders of literary and cultural opinion in the genteel establishment, he was coming increasingly to be regarded as a crank."

He had, however, established an international reputation as a writer. In spring 1898 he made a lecture tour of England, where he was entertained by James M. Barrie (who had visited Cable two years earlier), Arthur Conan Doyle, Rudyard Kipling, and Henry James and introduced to other literary people, including George Meredith, George Gissing, Leslie Stephen, and Mrs. Humphry Ward.

Cable's last two collections of short stories, *Strong Hearts* (1899) and *The Flower of the Chapdelaines* (1918), have not received favorable critical estimates, nor do they merit praise.

"The Solitary" (first published as "Gregory's Island" in the August 1896 issue of *Scribner's*) is the best of the three stories in *Strong Hearts* because of its probing character analysis. The hero cures himself of alcoholism and finds strength of character by deliberately marooning himself for a month on a desert island in the Gulf of Mexico. Strongly moralistic, the tale is virtually a religious tract, but it is so skillfully written that Butcher has compared it to Stephen Crane's "The Open Boat" (1898).

"The Solitary" is followed by "The Taxidermist" (first published in *Scribner's*, May 1893), which concerns P. T. B. Manouvrier, a self-deprecating Creole taxidermist who calls himself "Pas-Trop-Bon" (not too good). After winning seventy-five thousand dollars in the lottery, he builds a mansion, but–without ever living in it– he gives it to house the children of an orphanage which has been destroyed by fire. Manouvrier's humility and benevolence suggest that the artist is interested not in material gain but in capturing the "soul" of his subject in his work.

James M. Barrie, Cable, and W. Robertson Nicoll at Cable's home in Northampton, Massachusetts, 1896

The third story in *Strong Hearts*, "The Entomologist" (first published in *Scribner's*, January-March 1899), is flawed by melodramatic moralizing. A married German entomologist and the English wife of a Creole develop an intimacy that could lead to adultery. A yellow-fever epidemic strikes the city, however, and both die after repenting their selfish infatuation. As Butcher has said, the tale extols the "superiority of feeling to intellect, of morality to science. . . . "

The Flower of the Chapdelaines employs a frame narrative to weave together three previously published short stories–"The Clock in the Sky" (*Scribner's*, September 1901), "A West Indian Slave Insurrection" (*Scribner's*, December 1892), and "The Angel of the Lord" (first published anonymously in the anthology *A House Party*, 1901). The twentieth-century frame is longer than the three stories and focuses on a young attorney who has been hired by three Creole ladies, a young woman and her spinster aunts, to advise them on selling an old manuscript written by a friend of the aunts'. The young lawyer soon discovers that the young lady's Vermont grandmother once published a magazine story about her visit to a southern plantation, and after reading it he realizes that an old family manuscript passed on to him by a lawyer uncle contains a related story. These three tales are the three previously published short stories, all of which deal with slavery.

The New England grandmother's story, set in 1860, is "The Clock in the Sky." The daughter of an Abolitionist, the narrator visits her uncle's plantation, and, through an astronomy lesson about the constellations that appear, as the night passes, to be revolving around the North Star (the clock in the sky), she teaches a family of slaves how to follow the North Star to freedom. "The Angel of the Lord" is presented as the lawyer uncle's story of how he aided the same family during their northward flight. "A West Indian Slave Insurrection," described in *The Flower of the Chapdelaines* as a friend's story bought from her drunken son for a dollar, is a reworked version of a true story that Cable purchased from Dora Richards Miller, who had been living on Santa Cruz during the uprising of the island's slaves in 1848.

Though Cable's 1901 novel, *The Cavalier*, was a best-seller, scholars now tend to see a decline in the quality of his fiction after the publication of *John March, Southerner* in 1894. He continued to be held in high regard by his contemporaries, and in 1909–for the first time in twenty years–he visited New Orleans, where he had become a celebrity. By then, his first wife having died on 27 February 1904, he had married forty-eight-year-old Eva Colegate Stevenson on 24 November 1906. After her death on 7 June 1923 he married Hanna Cowing, a Northampton widow, on 6 December of the same year. Cable died on 31 January 1925 in St. Petersburg, Florida, where he had gone to spend the winter.

Cable's career as a writer of short fiction was essentially over with the publication of *The Flower of the Chapdelaines*, and he wrote only one more novel, *Lovers of Louisiana (To-day)* (1918). Early in his career he was often compared favorably to Nathaniel Hawthorne. While his reputation later went into eclipse, he introduced Creoles and Acadians to American readers, and he probed the psychology of slavery and racial discrimination with dexterity, achieving a degree of realism unmatched by other local-color writers.

Most important, Cable rejected the role of racial apologist that had been adopted by Southerners such as Irwin Russell or Thomas Nelson Page. Rejecting Page's concept of the "good old days" before the Civil War, he refused to gloss over racial and class injustice. Like Faulkner, Cable found that he must write of things which "touch the heart," believing, as he wrote in "The Haunted House," that "Some day–some day/Eyes clearer grown the truth may see."

Biographies:
Lucy Leffingwell Cable Biklé, *George W. Cable: His Life and Letters* (New York: Scribners, 1928);

Kjell Ekström, *George Washington Cable: A Study of His Early Life and Work* (Uppsala: Lundequistska Bokhandeln/Cambridge, Mass.: Harvard University Press, 1950);

Arlin Turner, *George W. Cable: A Biography* (Durham: Duke University Press, 1956);

Philip Butcher, *George W. Cable: The Northampton Years* (New York: Columbia University Press, 1959);

Louis D. Rubin, *George W. Cable: The Life and Times of a Southern Heretic* (New York: Pegasus, 1969).

References:
Newton Arvin, Introduction to *Old Creole Days* (New York: Sagamore Press, 1957);

Alfred Bendixen, "*The Grandissimes*: A Literary Pioneer Confronts the Southern Tradition," *Southern Quarterly*, 18 (Summer 1980): 23-33;

Lawrence I. Berkove, "The Free Man of Color in *The Grandissimes* and Works by Harris and Mark Twain," *Southern Quarterly*, 18 (Summer 1980): 60-73;

Warner Berthoff, *The Ferment of Realism: American Literature, 1884-1919* (New York: Free Press, 1965);

Judith R. Berzon, *Neither White Nor Black: The Mulatto Character in American Fiction* (New York: New York University Press, 1978);

Philip Butcher, *George W. Cable* (New York: Twayne, 1962);

Butcher, "Two Early Southern Realists in Revival," *CLA Journal*, 14 (September 1970): 91-95;

Michael L. Campbell, "The Negro in Cable's *The Grandissimes*," *Mississippi Quarterly*, 27 (Spring 1974): 165-178;

Guy A. Cardwell, *Twins of Genius* (East Lansing: Michigan State University Press, 1953);

Richard Chase, "Cable and His Grandissimes," *Kenyon Review*, 18 (Summer 1956): 373-383; republished in his *The American Novel and Its Tradition* (Garden City, N.Y.: Doubleday, 1957);

William Bedford Clark, "Cable and the Theme of Miscegenation in *Old Creole Days* and *The Grandissimes*," *Mississippi Quarterly*, 30 (Fall 1977): 597-609;

Clark, "Humor in Cable's *The Grandissimes*," *Southern Quarterly*, 18 (Summer 1980): 51-59;

Richard B. Eaton, "George W. Cable and the Historical Romance," *Southern Literary Journal*, 8 (Fall 1975): 82-94;

Joseph J. Egan, " 'Jean-ah Poquelin': George Washington Cable as Social Critic and Mythic Artist," *Markham Review*, 3 (May 1970): 6-7;

Egan, "Lions Rampant: Agricola Fusilier and Bras-Coupé as Antithetical Doubles in *The Grandissimes*," *Southern Quarterly*, 18 (Summer 1980): 74-80;

Benjamin W. Farley, "George W. Cable: Presbyterian Romancer, Reformer, Bible Teacher," *Journal of Presbyterian History*, 58 (Summer 1980): 166-181;

Shirley Ann Grau, Foreword to *Old Creole Days* (New York: Signet, 1961);

W. Kenneth Holditch, "The Grandissimes and the French Quarter," *Southern Quarterly*, 18 (Summer 1980): 34-50;

Elmo Howell, "Cable and the Creoles: A Note on 'Jean-ah Poquelin,' " *Xavier University Studies*, 9 (Winter 1970): 9-15;

Howell, "George Washington Cable's Creoles: Art and Reform in *The Grandissimes*," *Mississippi Quarterly*, 26 (Winter 1972-1973): 43-53;

Jay Martin, *Harvests of Change: American Literature, 1865-1914* (Englewood Cliffs, N.J.: Prentice-Hall, 1967), pp. 85, 100, 102, 111;

Wayne Mixon, *Southern Writers and the New South Movement, 1865-1913* (Chapel Hill: University of North Carolina Press, 1980), pp. 98-109;

Fred Lewis Pattee, *The Development of the American Short Story: An Historical Survey* (New York: Harper, 1923), pp. 256-259;

Pattee, *A History of American Literature Since 1870* (New York: Century, 1915), pp. 246-253;

Alice Hall Petry, "Universal and Particular: The Local Color Phenomenon Reconsidered," *American Literary Realism,* 12 (Spring 1979): 111-126;

Griffith T. Pugh, "George Washington Cable," *Mississippi Quarterly,* 20 (1967): 69-76;

Thomas J. Richardson, "Honoré Grandissime's Southern Dilemma: Introduction," *Southern Quarterly,* 18 (Summer 1980): 1-12;

Donald A. Ringe, "The Double Center: Character and Meaning in Cable's Early Novels," *Studies in the Novel,* 5 (Spring 1973): 52-62;

Ringe, "Narrative Voice in Cable's *The Grandissimes,*" *Southern Quarterly,* 18 (Summer 1980): 13-22;

Louis D. Rubin, Jr., "The Division of the Heart: Cable's *The Grandissimes,*" *Southern Literary Journal,* 1 (Spring 1969): 27-47;

Robert O. Stephens, "Cable's 'Madame Delphine' and the Compromise of 1877," *Southern Literary Journal,* 12 (Fall 1979): 79-91;

Stephens, "Cable's The Grandissimes and the Comedy of Manners," *American Literature,* 51 (January 1980): 507-519;

Edward Stone, "Usher, Poquelin, and Miss Emily: The Progress of Southern Gothic," *Georgia Review,* 16 (Winter 1960): 433-443;

Edward Larocque Tinker, "Cable and the Creoles," *American Literature,* 5 (January 1934): 313-326;

Arlin Turner, *Critical Essays on George W. Cable* (Boston: G. K. Hall, 1980);

Turner, *George W. Cable,* Southern Writers Series (Austin: Steck-Vaughn, 1969);

Turner, Introduction to *Creoles and Cajuns: Stories of Old Louisiana,* edited by Turner (Gloucester, Mass.: Peter Smith, 1965);

Turner, Introduction to *The Negro Question: A Selection of Writings on Civil Rights in the South by George W. Cable* (Garden City, N.Y.: Norton, 1968);

Edmund Wilson, "The Ordeal of George Washington Cable," *New Yorker,* 33 (9 November 1957): 172, 174-184, 189-196, 199-206, 209-216; republished in his *Patriotic Gore* (New York: Oxford University Press, 1962), pp. 548-587.

Papers:

The bulk of Cable's papers (including both letters and manuscripts) are at Tulane University. His letters to his editors and publishers are in the Scribner archives. Other collections are at Columbia University Libraries, the New York Public Library, American Academy of Arts and Letters, People's Institute of Northampton, Berea College, Duke University, Fisk University, Harvard University, Huntington Library, Joint University Libraries of Nashville, Library of Congress, University of Virginia, Louisiana Historical Association, Louisiana State Museum, Xavier University, and Yale University.

Lydia Maria Child

(11 February 1802-20 October 1880)

Carolyn L. Karcher
Temple University

See also the Child entry in *DLB 1: The American Renaissance in New England.*

BOOKS: *Hobomok, A Tale of Early Times,* as "An American" (Boston: Cummings, Hilliard, 1824);

Evenings in New England. Intended for Juvenile Amusement and Instruction, as "An American Lady" (Boston: Cummings, Hilliard, 1824);

The Rebels, or Boston before the Revolution (Boston: Cummings, Hilliard, 1825; revised edition, Boston: Phillips, Sampson, 1850);

Emily Parker, or Impulse, Not Principle. Intended for Young Persons (Boston: Bowles & Dearborn, 1827);

Biographical Sketches of Great and Good Men. Designed for the Amusement and Instruction of Young Persons (Boston: Putnam & Hunt/ Philadelphia: Thomas T. Ash, 1828);

The First Settlers of New-England: or, Conquest of the Pequods, Narragansets and Pokanokets: As Related by a Mother to Her Children, and Designed for the Instruction of Youth. By a Lady of Massachusetts (Boston: Munroe & Francis/New York: Charles S. Francis, 1829);

The Frugal Housewife (Boston: Marsh & Capen/ Carter & Hendee, 1829; revised and enlarged, 1830); republished, from the eighth edition on, as *The American Frugal Housewife* (Boston: Carter & Hendee, 1832);

The Little Girl's Own Book (Boston: Carter, Hendee & Babcock, 1831; London: Tegg, 1832; enlarged edition, Boston: Carter, Hendee, 1834);

The Mother's Book (Boston: Carter, Hendee & Babcock/Baltimore: Charles Carter, 1831; Glasgow: Griffin/London: Tegg, 1832; revised and enlarged edition, New York: C. S. Francis/Boston: Joseph H. Francis, 1844);

The Coronal. A Collection of Miscellaneous Pieces, Written at Various Times (Boston: Carter & Hendee, 1832); slightly enlarged as *The Mother's Story Book; or, Western Coronal. A Collection of Miscellaneous Pieces. By Mrs. Child . . .*

Lydia Maria Child, 1856

To which are added, a few tales, by Mary Howitt, and Caroline Fry (London, Edinburgh, Dublin & Glasgow: Printed for T. T. & J. Tegg, 1833);

The Biographies of Madame de Staël, and Madame Roland (Boston: Carter & Hendee, 1832); republished in part as *The Biography of Madame de Staël* (Edinburgh: Thomas Clark, 1836); 1832 edition revised and enlarged as *Memoirs of Madame de Staël, and of Madame Roland* (New York: C. S. Francis/Boston: J. H. Francis, 1847);

The Biographies of Lady Russell, and Madame Guyon (Boston: Carter, Hendee, 1832); republished in part as *The Biography of Lady Russell* (Edinburgh: Thomas Clark, 1836);

Good Wives (Boston: Carter, Hendee, 1833); republished as *Biographies of Good Wives* (New York: C. S. Francis/Boston: J. H. Francis, 1846; London: Griffin, 1849); republished again as *Celebrated Women; Or, Biographies of Good Wives* (New York: Charles S. Francis, 1861); republished again as *Married Women: Biographies of Good Wives* (New York: Charles S. Francis, 1871);

An Appeal in Favor of That Class of Americans Called Africans (Boston: Allen & Ticknor, 1833);

The History of the Condition of Women, in Various Ages and Nations, 2 volumes (Boston: John Allen, 1835; London, 1835); revised and corrected as *Brief History of the Condition of Women, in Various Ages and Nations*, 2 volumes (New York: C. S. Francis/Boston: J. H. Francis, 1845);

No. 1. Authentic Anecdotes of American Slavery . . . Aged Slaves, anonymous, attributed to Child (Newburyport, Mass.: Charles Whipple, 1835);

No. 2. Authentic Anecdotes of American Slavery, anonymous, attributed to Child (Newburyport, Mass.: Charles Whipple, 1835);

The Happy Grandmother. By Mrs. Child. To Which Is Added, The White Palfrey (London: Darton & Clark, circa 1835);

Anti-Slavery Catechism (Newburyport, Mass.: Charles Whipple, 1836);

Philothea. A Romance (Boston: Otis, Broaders/New York: George Dearborn, 1836); republished as *Philothea: A Grecian Romance* (New York: C. S. Francis, 1845);

The Evils of Slavery, and The Cure of Slavery. The First Proved by the Opinions of Southerners Themselves, The Last Shown by Historical Evidence (Newburyport, Mass.: Charles Whipple, 1836);

The Family Nurse; or Companion of The Frugal Housewife (Boston: Charles J. Hendee, 1837);

No. 3. Authentic Anecdotes of American Slavery, anonymous, attributed to Child (Newburyport, Mass.: Charles Whipple, 1838);

Letters from New-York [First Series] (New York: Charles S. Francis/Boston: James Munroe, 1843; London: Bentley, 1843; extended edition, New York: C. S. Francis/Boston: Joseph H. Francis, 1844);

Flowers for Children, 3 volumes (New York: C. S. Francis/Boston: J. H. Francis, 1844, 1845, 1847); volume 1 republished as *The Christ-*

Child, and Other Stories (Boston: D. Lothrop/Dover, N.H.: G. T. Day, 1869); volume 2 republished as *Good Little Mitty, and Other Stories* (Boston: D. Lothrop/Dover, N.H.: G. T. Day, 1869); volume 3 republished as *Making Something, and Other Stories* (Boston: D. Lothrop/Dover, N.H.: G. T. Day, 1869);

Letters from New York. Second Series (New York: C. S. Francis/Boston: J. H. Francis, 1845);

Fact and Fiction: A Collection of Stories (New York: C. S. Francis/Boston: J. H. Francis, 1846; London: William Smith, 1847); republished as *The Children of Mt. Ida, and Other Stories* (New York: Charles S. Francis, 1871);

Sketches from Real Life. I. The Power of Kindness. II. Home and Politics (Philadelphia: Hazard & Mitchell, 1850; London: Collins, 1850); republished as *The Power of Kindness; and Other Stories* (Philadelphia: Willis P. Hazard, 1853);

The Childrens' [sic] Gems. The Brother and Sister: And Other Stories, anonymous, attributed to Child (Philadelphia: New Church Book Store, 1852);

Isaac T. Hopper: A True Life (Boston: John P. Jewett/Cleveland: Jewett, Proctor & Worthington/London: Sampson Low, 1853);

The Progress of Religious Ideas, through Successive Ages, 3 volumes (New York: C. S. Francis/London: S. Low, 1855);

A New Flower for Children (New York: C. S. Francis, 1856);

Autumnal Leaves: Tales and Sketches in Prose and Rhyme (New York & Boston: C. S. Francis, 1857);

Correspondence between Lydia Maria Child and Gov. Wise and Mrs. Mason, of Virginia (Boston: American Anti-Slavery Society, 1860);

The Right Way the Safe Way, Proved by Emancipation in the British West Indies, and Elsewhere (New York, 1860; enlarged, 1862);

The Duty of Disobedience to the Fugitive Slave Act: An Appeal to the Legislators of Massachusetts (Boston: American Anti-Slavery Society, 1860);

A Romance of the Republic (Boston: Ticknor & Fields, 1867); republished as *Rose and Flora*, 2 volumes (London: Routledge, 1867);

An Appeal for the Indians (New York: Wm. P. Tomlinson, 1868).

OTHER: *The Juvenile Souvenir*, edited, with many unsigned contributions, by Child (Boston: Marsh & Capen/John Putnam, 1827);

"The Church in the Wilderness," in *The Legendary*, edited by Nathaniel P. Willis (Boston: Samuel G. Goodrich, 1828);

The Oasis, edited, with contributions, by Child (Boston: Allen & Ticknor, 1834);

Memoir of Benjamin Lay: Compiled from Various Sources, edited by Child (New York: American Anti-Slavery Society, 1842);

American Anti-Slavery Almanac [for 1843], edited by Child (New York: American Anti-Slavery Society, 1843);

"Slavery's Pleasant Homes. A Faithful Sketch," in *The Liberty Bell* (Boston: Massachusetts Anti-Slavery Fair, 1843), pp. 147-160;

The Patriarchal Institution, As Described by Members of Its Own Family, compiled by Child (New York: American Anti-Slavery Society, 1860);

Linda Brent (Harriet A. Jacobs), *Incidents in the Life of a Slave Girl*, edited, with a preface, by Child (Boston: Privately printed, 1861); republished as *The Deeper Wrong; or Incidents in the Life of a Slave Girl* (London: Tweedie, 1862);

Looking Toward Sunset. From Sources Old and New, Original and Selected, edited, with contributions, by Child (Boston: Ticknor & Fields, 1865);

The Freedmen's Book, edited, with contributions, by Child (Boston: Ticknor & Fields, 1865);

Aspirations of the World. A Chain of Opals, collected, with an introduction, by Child (Boston: Roberts, 1878).

PERIODICAL PUBLICATIONS: "Loo Loo. A Few Scenes from a True History," *Atlantic Monthly*, 1 (May 1858): 801-812; (June 1858): 32-42;

"Willie Wharton," *Atlantic Monthly*, 11 (March 1863): 324-345;

"Poor Chloe. A True Story of Massachusetts in the Olden Time," *Atlantic Monthly*, 17 (March 1866): 352-364.

Child in 1865

For half a century, from 1824, when Lydia Maria Child's daring novel of interracial marriage, *Hobomok, A Tale of Early Times*, greeted a shocked public, to the turbulent Reconstruction era, which found her articles in the *National Anti-Slavery Standard* still calling for justice toward the beleaguered Plains Indians, advocating the extension of voting rights to blacks and women, and denouncing American imperialism in the Caribbean, Child's name was a household word in America. To retrace her career is to recapitulate the key struggles over the young Republic's political and cultural destiny–struggles over Indian policy, slavery, and woman's rights, and concomitantly, over the creation of a literature that would represent America to the world–for Child played an influential role in all these arenas.

Born in Medford, Massachusetts, the youngest of six children, Lydia Francis grew up in a milieu of "hard-working people, who had had small opportunity for culture," as she recalled in a letter to her brother's biographer, John Weiss (15 April 1863). Her father, Convers Francis, owned a bakery that enlisted the labor of his wife, Susannah Rand Francis, and of their children. Though viewing intellectual pursuits as "out of the line of himself or his family," Mr. Francis yielded to the advice of village notables and sent his promising son and namesake, Convers, to Harvard. In contrast, he became "alarmed" at his daughter's "increasing fondness for books," according to a lost letter quoted in Anna D. Hallowell's biographical reminiscences of Child. As a result, after his wife died of tuberculosis in 1814, Mr. Francis confided twelve-year-old Lydia to the care of her newly married sister, Mary Preston, in Norridgewock, Maine, so that she could be initiated into the domestic avocations befitting a woman. This early experience of the nineteenth-century woman's constricted lot sowed the seeds of a feminist consciousness in Child. She defiantly continued to read, encouraged by her brother Convers, and began equipping herself to teach school, taking her first job in Gardiner, Maine, in 1820. Maine could not offer Child the cultural stimulation available in the Boston area, however. Thus in 1822 she joined Convers's household in Watertown, Massachusetts, where he had acceded to the Unitarian pulpit. As if deliberately assuming a new identity, Child now had herself rebaptized Lydia Maria and subsequently dropped the use of her first name. The move also marked her induction into a new milieu, in which Convers had assumed a central place. The intellectuals congregating in the Francis parlor for animated philosophical discussions would eventually number among them such luminaries as Ralph Waldo Emerson; Bronson Alcott and his wife, Abba May Alcott; Theodore Parker; John Greenleaf Whittier; and Margaret Fuller.

It was in her brother's study that Child began her first novel, inspired by a review of James Wallis Eastburn and Robert Sands's narrative poem *Yamoyden* (*North American Review*, April 1821). The reviewer, John Gorham Palfrey, called on American romancers to take their cue from *Yamoyden* by laying their scene in their native land and exploiting its exotic history of Indian conquest. "I know not what impelled me," Child later claimed in a letter to the critic Rufus Wilmot Griswold (circa 1846), reconstructing the circumstances that had catapulted her into authorship; "I had never dreamed of such a thing as turning author; but I siezed [*sic*] a pen, and before the bell rang for afternoon meeting I had written the first chapter, exactly as it now stands."

Child was only twenty-two when she published *Hobomok;* yet the novel presaged the causes she would espouse and the literature of social protest she would develop into a fine art in her short stories. Appearing just as proslavery forces, fresh from their victorious campaign against Florida's Seminoles, were poising to confiscate the prosperous farms of Georgia's Cherokees, *Hobomok* implicitly offered intermarriage and assimilation as alternatives to these policies, which

many other novels of the period were endorsing. Its heroine, Mary Conant, rebels against the religious and racial bigotry of her Puritan father by successively marrying two men his ideology brands as outcasts—the Indian Hobomok and the Episcopalian Charles Brown. In an even more subversive departure from literary convention, Mary pays no price for violating the taboo against interracial marriage. Although she elopes with Hobomok on hearing the erroneous news that her Episcopalian fiancé has perished in a shipwreck, not only does the Indian restore her to her first love when he miraculously returns, but Brown takes her back and agrees to bring up her half-Indian son as his own. Indeed the promise of assimilation with which the novel ends, as it chronicles the metamorphosis of "little Hobomok" into an Englishman, permeates its entire plot, which symbolically fuses Mary's Indian and Episcopalian lovers.

"Unnatural," "in very bad taste, to say the least," "revolting . . . to every feeling of delicacy in man or woman," raged the critics in the *North American Review* (July 1824 and July 1825). Nevertheless, *Hobomok* achieved a succès de scandale that won Child entrée into Boston's most exclusive literary salons. Within the next decade, as publishers and editors of literary annuals vied for her favor, Child produced another historical novel, *The Rebels, or Boston before the Revolution* (1825), and a collection of miscellaneous pieces, *The Coronal* (1832); founded and edited the nation's first successful children's magazine, the popular and influential *Juvenile Miscellany* (1826-1834); published two best-selling domestic advice books, *The Frugal Housewife* (1829), the earliest housekeeping manual to address the needs of women who could not afford servants, and *The Mother's Book* (1831), notable for urging women to be self-supporting and to prepare their daughters for careers besides marriage; and launched the *Ladies' Family Library* (1832-1835), comprising her biographies of model women and her ambitious two-volume *The History of the Condition of Women, in Various Ages and Nations* (1835), which Sarah Grimké, Margaret Fuller, Elizabeth Cady Stanton, Susan B. Anthony, and Matilda Joslyn Gage all mined extensively, with Gage hailing it in the *History of Woman Suffrage* as "the first American storehouse of information" on the woman question. Despite her prolific output, Child had to supplement her income by teaching school in Watertown (1826-1827) and later in Dorchester Heights (1830).

Meanwhile, the radicalism Child had betrayed in *Hobomok* had already led her to embark on the crusade against racism for which she would shortly be ostracized–though this fact was not yet apparent to the arbiters of taste who were promoting her works through such organs as the *Ladies' Magazine,* the *American Monthly Magazine,* the *American Monthly Review,* and the *North American Review.* By 1828 she and David Lee Child, whom she married on 19 October of that year, were actively campaigning against Andrew Jackson and his Cherokee removal policy. By 1830 or 1831 the militant Abolitionist William Lloyd Garrison had recruited her into his ranks. And in 1833, the very year the prestigious *North American* opined in its July issue that "few female writers, if any, have done more or better things for our literature" than "Mrs. Child," pronouncing her "just the woman we want for the mothers and daughters of the present generation," she published the book that destroyed her literary popularity but propelled her to the forefront of the Abolitionist movement: *An Appeal in Favor of That Class of Americans Called Africans.*

What most scandalized Child's public in this monumental indictment of slavery–the first major study of the institution to advocate immediate emancipation and an end to all forms of racial discrimination–was its argument for racial equality and integration, which culminated in an attack on antimiscegenation laws. The public reaction to *An Appeal* was ironic because Child had been infiltrating the same ideas into her fiction ever since *Hobomok.* In fact, she had actually written antislavery stories for the *Juvenile Miscellany,* although her antiracist fiction for adults during this period focuses on Indians.

Three of the stories collected in *The Coronal*– "The Lone Indian," "The Indian Wife," and "Chocorua's Curse" (first published in *The Token* for 1828, *The Legendary* for 1828, and *The Token* for 1830, respectively)–seek to mobilize public opinion against the theft of Indian lands. Remarkable for the Indian point of view it assumes, "The Lone Indian" bitterly details the "ravages of the civilized destroyer," castigating the "insolence" of the white man who seizes the Indian's domains and then accuses him of trespassing on them. "The Indian Wife" uses the metaphors of seduction and violation of domestic sanctity to symbolize the white man's treachery; like Child's antislavery stories of the 1840s, it also exposes the hypocrisy of the double standard that prohibits interracial marriage, while allowing white men to treat women of color as fair game. Perhaps the most haunting of the three tales, "Chocorua's Curse," presents its white and Indian protagonists as mirror images of each other, inextricably bound together, and warns of the blight that threatens the nation if it persists in warring against nature, the Indian's birthright.

When these stories first appeared in the annual gift books that provided American writers with their main outlet for short fiction during the late 1820s and early 1830s, Indian themes enjoyed great appeal as materials for an indigenous national literature. Child's contribution to the genre of Indian fiction was to sever it from its origins in the Puritan narratives of captivity and Indian war that justified white conquest, and to turn it instead into a medium for dramatizing the wrongs committed against the Indian.

Her treatment of the decade's other favorite theme, the American Revolution, was equally distinctive. Collected in *The Coronal* but originally published in *The Atlantic Souvenir* for 1827, the year after that first American annual gift book had made its debut, Child's "The Rival Brothers" offers a woman's perspective on the Revolution. It is, of course, natural that a woman writer should stress an aspect of the war often neglected by her male peers: "the fortitude of our mothers" in sending their menfolk off to battle while braving hunger and the threat of rape at home. What is extraordinary about "The Rival Brothers," however, is the feature it shares with *Hobomok:* its exploration of women's secret sexual desires. The story intertwines the fratricidal strife of Tory and Revolutionary with the "contending passions" that its heroine, Frances, projects onto the two brothers who love her: the Tory Joseph, "fierce and ungovernable" but "tumultuous and exciting," and the Revolutionary William, tender, devoted, and "a thousand times more fitted to make her happy." Although Frances ends up choosing William when he enlists on the right side in the war, the outcome of the story suggests either that she may in reality have unconsciously chosen Joseph, or else that the two men may be psychological doubles; for Joseph intercepts her letter to William, replies in William's name with a letter decoying her to a clandestine rendezvous in the woods, and murders her when she resists rape.

Like Child's Indian tales, "The Rival Brothers" also invites a political interpretation. The death of William "in the very centre of the British army" and the survival of Joseph, who bursts

Wayland, July 28th 1867.

Dear Friend,

I thank you for your affectionate letter. It did my heart good. I was glad to find that you were more interested in my book, than Sarah seemed to be. I have never cared so much about the success of any of my books; for it is the Benjamin of my family, the child of my old age. It is refreshing to know that you think the plot ingenious and the characters lively. I thought them so myself, or I should not have dedicated the volume to you; but then I remembered how prone we poor humans are to deceive ourselves about our own performances, and I felt a nervous anxiety to know how my friends would view it. Dear Sarah objects to the word "respectfully" in the dedication; but I inscribed it to you, not as my personal friends, but as the friends of freedom. and if you do not deserve respect in that view, I should like to know who does.

mentioned it to Sarah, who asked me to write it on a handsome writing-desk she gave me. But after writing three or four chapters, a feeling of discouragement came over me; and I probably should never have finished it, if Mr. Fields had not earnestly importuned me to write a continuous story for the Atlantic. When it was done, he was so much taken with it, that he wanted to bring it out at once as a new novel; very kindly saying that I should make more by it in that way. Few echoes about it reach me in my solitude. I hope it will have an extensive circulation; for I had a good object in writing it. Having fought against slavery till I saw it go down in the Red Sea, I wanted to do something to undermine prejudice, and there is such a universal passion for novels, that more can be done in that way, than by the ablest arguments, and the most serious exhortations.

I, too, am deeply thankful that such a salutary change has taken place in this country. I never wished to have Jeff Davis, or any of his accomplices hung, or harshly treated; but I am vexed with Greely and Gerrit Smith. They confound all distinctions of right and wrong by their sickly sentimentality. I hope they will have to pay the whole of the bond. Here am I taxed to pay $100,000 for catching Jeff. For what? To have him feast on champagne & canvass-back ducks at the expense of the U.S. and then set out on his travels,

Child's letter to Francis George Shaw, in which she discusses her 1867 novel, A Romance of the Republic

The publishers promised that you should have the book a week sooner than you did; but I am glad it was delayed, so as to reach you on the 18th. It pleases me greatly that it happened so.   To work out all the details of that intricate plot was a labor, I tell you. It gave me many a hard head-ache, but digging in my garden, and watching my flowers has rested the old brain. A good many real incidents are woven into the fiction. There _was_ a police-officer in Boston, who used to go to Father Snowdon and tell him he was in search of a fugitive slave, and that if he should get sight of him he hoped he would keep hold of him till _he_ came along again.

There _was_ a fugitive slave huddled away and hidden in the islands of Boston Harbor. My dear friend Ellis Gray Loring went with Francis Jackson to plead with the merchant in whose vessel the poor fugitive was concealed. His stern, unfeeling manner affected Ellis so deeply, that when he returned home he bowed his head on the table and wept. The merchant's name was _not_ Bell, and he is dead.

I thought Sarah would smile at the use I made of her pretty shell-basket from Nassau. I was venturesome, was I not? to set forth my imaginary travels in Italy? But some how it seems to me as if I had _seen_ all these scenes. Sometimes I am in the mood to think it hard that I have seen so very little of God's beautiful world; but in general, it seems to me as if I _had_ seen the things I most _want_ to see. They rise up before my imagination almost like objective realities.

Some call the plot of the story very romantic, but there is nothing imagined that might not very naturally have happened, under the laws, custom, and opinions then existing. Those Quadroon connexions have actually given rise to incidents as startling as any I have described. I have _known_ of two cases, where elegant and accomplished girls were claimed as property by creditors. In one case, they were sold; in the other, they escaped, and married well at the North, where their secret remains unsuspected.   The nucleus of my plot came to my mind four or five years ago, and I then upon the narrator years later as she is wandering in the woods meditating on "those venerable heralds of our freedom," New England's Puritan forefathers, hint that America may not have won its revolution against Toryism after all–a possibility Child would entertain less tentatively once she found herself grappling with proslavery forces.

Appropriately, Child's next foray into short fiction took the form of adapting both the genre and its chief vehicle, the annual gift book, to furthering the antislavery cause she had recently embraced. When Child compiled *The Oasis* in 1834, gift books themselves had only existed in the United States for eight years, and the most famous of antislavery gift books, *The Liberty Bell*, would not appear until 1839.

The principal story she published in *The Oasis*, "Malem-Boo. The Brazilian Slave," was almost as innovative in form as in content. Combating the stereotypes of African savagery that served to justify slavery, the story draws an idyllic picture of life in the African village where Malem-Boo and his wife, Yarrima, live with Yazoo, her infant son by an earlier marriage. An important element of that idyllism is sexual freedom–a recurrent theme in Child's fiction, which frequently uses "primitive" peoples as vehicles for protesting against the sexual repressiveness of "civilized" society. "The rules of civilized life," she comments about the brief courtship of Malem-Boo and Yarrima, had "not as yet taught them to divorce their words and actions from the true affections of the heart." Only the shadow of the slave trade mars the family's bliss. Contrasting African probity with "Christian avarice, and civilized cruelty," Child spares no details in describing the kidnapping of Yazoo and Malem-Boo and the gruesome horrors of the "Middle Passage" across the Atlantic. Throughout the story she also emphasizes the strength of African family ties, which impel Malem-Boo to threaten suicide until his kidnappers, and later his owners in Brazil, restore his stepson to him. The unresolved ending, striking for its time, leaves Malem-Boo frantically working to purchase freedom and return passage to Africa for himself and his stepson–a goal the narrator pointedly characterizes as unrealistic: "should Malem-Boo regain his freedom, there is great danger that the avarice of white men will again enslave him, before he can reach his native shores."

A panoply of abolitionist tracts, *The History of the Condition of Women*, and a third novel, *Philothea* (1836), intervened before Child re-

turned to short fiction in 1841, the year she took on the editorship of the *National Anti-Slavery Standard* in New York. The three antislavery stories she published in *The Liberty Bell* during this period once again broke new ground. "The Black Saxons" (1841; collected in *Fact and Fiction*, 1846) furnishes an unusual glimpse of a slave-revolt conspiracy, as observed by an eavesdropping slaveholder who comes to recognize the parallel between his slaves and his own Saxon ancestors, likewise held in thrall by a race of conquerors. "The Quadroons" (1842; collected in *Fact and Fiction*) introduces into American literature the archetype of the tragic near-white heroine, whose tinge of black blood condemns her to slavery and bars her from marrying the white gentleman she loves. Through this archetype, which inspired a long series of works beginning with Harriet Beecher Stowe's *Uncle Tom's Cabin* (1852) and William Wells Brown's *Clotel* (1853), Child made it possible for a genteel public, otherwise hostile to blacks and Abolitionist agitation, to sympathize with the plight of slave women. "Slavery's Pleasant Homes" (*The Liberty Bell*, 1843), the boldest of her antislavery stories, depicts the plantation as a harem in which the white wife and a black slave woman both fall victim to the master's sexual promiscuity. At the same time, it highlights the dilemma of the black male slave, unable to protect his own wife from rape, and it defends his right to rebel.

In May 1843, embittered by disputes with the Garrisonians over her editorial policy and alienated by the factionalism that was splintering the Abolitionist camp, Child resigned from the *National Anti-Slavery Standard*. "I mean to devote the remainder of my life to the attainment of literary excellence," she wrote to her friend Francis Shaw (18 July 1844). For her reintroduction to a literary establishment that had turned its back on her in 1833 when she published her Abolitionist *Appeal*, Child decided to republish the popular column she had contributed to the *Standard*, "Letters from New-York," in book form. The venture proved so successful that the first and second series of *Letters from New-York*, first published in 1843 and 1845 respectively, went through eleven editions by 1851. Even today critics consider these freewheeling journalistic sketches, which launched a genre many women writers would adopt, to be Child's finest work.

The short stories Child began publishing regularly in the *Columbian Lady's and Gentleman's Magazine* are equally pioneering. Collected in her second volume of stories, *Fact and Fiction,* which also includes "The Black Saxons," "The Quadroons," and "The Falls of St. Anthony" (a revised version of "The Indian Wife"), their keynote is their daring treatment of sexuality.

The issue of sexual freedom had long engaged Child's imagination, but several factors combined to give it special urgency during her New York years. Informally separated from her husband, whom she had left on his failing Northampton, Massachusetts, beet farm when she moved to New York to edit the *Standard,* Child formed deep, though unconsummated, attachments to two other men: the young lawyer John Hopper, son of the Quaker Abolitionist Isaac Hopper, at whose home Child was boarding; and the Norwegian violinist Ole Bull, whose concerts she reviewed in "Letters from New-York." Apparently the sense of having violated nineteenth-century moral sanctions, at least in spirit, led her to identify passionately with the "fallen women" she encountered so frequently in the streets and prisons of New York. Casualties of urban poverty, limited employment opportunities for women, and a sexual double standard, these delinquents typically began their illicit careers when seduced and abandoned by unscrupulous employers. Their plight had prompted the growth of a female moral reform movement in the mid 1830s and was continuing to receive much sympathetic attention in the 1840s. Like the more radical moral reformers, and like her friend Margaret Fuller in *Woman in the Nineteenth Century* (1845), Child emphasized the hypocrisy of a social code that allowed "magistrates . . . [to] practise the same things for which they send women to Blackwell's Island," as she put it in "Rosenglory." The theory of "Woman's Rights," she asserted, furnished an explanation: "men made all the laws, and elected all the magistrates."

In stories such as "Elizabeth Wilson" (*Columbian,* February 1845), "Rosenglory" (*Columbian,* October 1846), and "Hilda Silfverling" (*Columbian,* October 1845), however, Child goes beyond other writers. In "Elizabeth Wilson," for example, Child defends the " 'strong necessity of loving,' which so pervades the nature of woman." Similarly in "Rosenglory"–the story of an orphaned servant girl whose need for love leads her to reciprocate the attentions of her employer's son, with predictable results–Child argues: "Society reflects its own pollution on feelings which nature made beautiful." Illustrating the point by contrast, her Indian tale "She Waits in

the Spirit Land" (*Columbian,* March 1846) conjures up an erotic picture of sexual relations in a less repressive culture. There "nature, subjected to no false restraints, manifests her innate modesty, and even in her child-like abandonment to impulse, rebukes by her innocence the unclean self-consciousness of artificial society." Most innovative is Child's brilliant science fiction story, "Hilda Silfverling. A Fantasy," in which an unwed mother, wrongly accused of having murdered her infant (whom she has given away for adoption), is condemned to be frozen for a century by an artificial process, for the sake of conducting a scientific experiment. On her reanimation, the heroine marries her own great-grandson, the very image of the lover who had perished at sea after impregnating her. Flouting all patriarchal taboos, the bawdily incestuous ending foreshadows a future that will give free play to sexual pleasure.

Child also experimented with science fiction in one of her last stories for the *Columbian Magazine,* "The Rival Mechanicians" (January 1847), later collected in *Autumnal Leaves* (1857). This eerie tale explores the relationship between sexuality and creativity, nature and art, through two gifted watchmaker's apprentices who vie with each other to contrive "the most perfect piece of mechanism," so as to inherit the business of their renowned master and win the love of his beautiful granddaughter. Their competition perverts "a genuine love of beauty, for its own sake, . . . the only healthy stimulus to produce the beautiful," into a soul-destroying psychosexual contest that ends in the murder of one, the death of the grief-stricken granddaughter, and the obsessive drive of the "machine-mad" survivor to "reproduce" his beloved in an image he comes to love "almost as much as he had loved the maiden herself."

Shortly after writing "The Rival Mechanicians," Child abandoned fiction for nearly a decade while she worked on a monumental three-volume comparative history of the world's religions, *The Progress of Religious Ideas, through Successive Ages* (1855). The project spanned a period of inward-turning in Child's life, apparently triggered by John Hopper's marriage. Ending her eight years of independence, Child reunited with her husband. In June 1850 they moved to the village of West Newton, outside of Boston, and in 1853 they went to live in nearby Wayland with her ailing father, whom she nursed until his death in 1856.

That year, galvanized by the civil war in Kansas into resuming an active role in the struggle against slavery, Child published her finest story, "The Kansas Emigrants." It was serialized in Horace Greeley's *New York Tribune* (October 23 through November 4 in the daily edition and October 25 and November 1 in the weekly) and collected in *Autumnal Leaves*. Powerfully dramatizing the political issues at stake in the bloody conflict between pro- and antislavery settlers seeking to determine the fate of Kansas, and ultimately of the nation, the story's vein of factual reportage represents a new departure in Child's fiction. For the first time it captures the force of her journalism and political tracts. The characters, too, stand out as the most realistic she ever created. Particularly interesting is the contrast Child draws between two feminine types–the helpless, clinging Alice, who, when she can no longer be sheltered from the brutal facts of Kansas politics, dies begging to "go home to my *mother*," and the self-reliant, adaptable Kate, who learns to tote a gun and participates actively in the crusade to make Kansas a free state. The task of rebuilding American society on a foundation of true liberty, Child implies, requires a new woman, ready to take her place in the political arena.

Child herself returned to that arena as the crisis over slavery intensified. Beginning with her stirring letters in defense of John Brown, which reached a circulation of three hundred thousand when published as a pamphlet in 1860 (*Correspondence between Lydia Maria Child and Gov. Wise and Mrs. Mason, of Virginia*), she produced countless books, tracts, newspaper articles, and letters to editors and politicians, molding the opinion of a broad public throughout the Civil War and much of the Reconstruction era. The writings of her last years include some of her most prescient contributions to shaping the nation's future: an anthology of selections presenting positive images of old age, *Looking Toward Sunset* (1865); a reader for the newly emancipated slaves, *The Freedmen's Book* (1865), designed with the threefold aim of teaching literacy, inculcating pride in the black heritage, and promoting black suffrage; and her eloquent *An Appeal for the Indians* (1868). They also include three remarkable short stories published in the *Atlantic Monthly* (1858, 1863, 1866) and her best novel, *A Romance of the Republic* (1867).

Collectively, these works articulate an ideal of national reconciliation that squarely faces the responsibility northern and southern whites share for slavery and that advocates interracial marriage as the means of integrating both blacks and Indians into white society. "Poor Chloe" (*Atlantic Monthly*, March 1866) reminds a northern population savoring its hard-fought victory over the Confederacy that New Englanders, too, had once owned slaves and mouthed biblical precepts to justify forcing unwanted marriages on their chattels and selling children away from their parents. "Willie Wharton" (*Atlantic Monthly*, March 1863), anticipating Child's arguments in *An Appeal for the Indians*, dramatizes a culturally sensitive process of guiding Indians "into increasing conformity with civilized habits" and shows how white culture might be enriched by an infusion of Indian elements. At the same time, it boldly revises the concept of assimilation projected in *Hobomok*; for Willie Wharton, adopted by Indians at the age of six, does not abandon his Indian bride A-lee-lah when he finally returns home to his white family–indeed his white family's acceptance of the marriage is what encourages both Willie and A-lee-lah to adapt to "civilized habits" now as alien to him as to her. *A Romance of the Republic*, which develops and extends Child's *Atlantic* story "Loo Loo" (May-June 1858) and its 1842 predecessor in *The Liberty Bell*, "The Quadroons," forecasts a republic literally and figuratively regenerated through interracial marriage.

On her death in Wayland, Massachusetts, in 1880, Child left a legacy that few writers of her generation could rival. Besides playing a key role in the most important reform movements of her epoch, she had pioneered almost every genre of nineteenth-century American letters, from the historical novel and the science fiction tale to children's fiction and the domestic advice book; founded an alternative literary tradition committed to racial and sexual equality; heralded the free exploration of sexual themes in literature; and blazed a broad path for other women writers to follow.

Letters:

Letters of Lydia Maria Child with a Biographical Introduction by John G. Whittier and an Appendix by Wendell Phillips (Boston & New York: Houghton, Mifflin, 1882);

The Collected Correspondence of Lydia Maria Child, 1817-1880, edited by Patricia G. Holland, Milton Meltzer, and Francine Krasno (New York: Kraus Microform, 1980);

Lydia Maria Child: Selected Letters, 1817-1880, edited by Meltzer, Holland, and Krasno (Amherst: University of Massachusetts Press, 1982).

Biographies:

Anna D. Hallowell, "Lydia Maria Child," *Medford Historical Register*, 3 (July 1900): 95-117;

Helene G. Baer, *The Heart Is Like Heaven: The Life of Lydia Maria Child* (Philadelphia: University of Pennsylvania Press, 1964);

Milton Meltzer, *Tongue of Flame: The Life of Lydia Maria Child* (New York: Crowell, 1965);

Kirk Jeffrey, "Marriage, Career, and Feminine Ideology in Nineteenth-Century America: Reconstructing the Marital Experience of Lydia Maria Child, 1828-1874," *Feminist Studies*, 2, no. 2/3 (1975): 113-130.

References:

Susan Phinney Conrad, *Perish the Thought: Intellectual Women in Romantic America, 1830-1860* (New York: Oxford University Press, 1976), pp. 104-116, 199-200, 218-220;

Alexander Cowie, *The Rise of the American Novel* (New York: American Book Co., 1948), pp. 177-184;

Patricia G. Holland, "Lydia Maria Child as a Nineteenth-Century Professional Author," in *Studies in the American Renaissance* (Boston: Twayne, 1981), pp. 157-167;

Carolyn L. Karcher, "Censorship, American Style: The Case of Lydia Maria Child," *Studies in the American Renaissance* (Charlottesville: University Press of Virginia, 1986), pp. 283-303;

Karcher, Introduction and headnotes to *Hobomok and Other Writings on Indians* (New Brunswick, N.J.: Rutgers University Press, 1986);

Karcher, "Patriarchal Society and Matriarchal Family in Irving's 'Rip Van Winkle' and Child's 'Hilda Silfverling,'" *Legacy*, 2 (Fall 1985): 31-44;

Karcher, "Rape, Murder, and Revenge in 'Slavery's Pleasant Homes': Lydia Maria Child's Antislavery Fiction and the Limits of Genre," *Women's Studies International Forum*, 9, no. 4 (1986): 323-332;

William S. Osborne, *Lydia Maria Child* (Boston: Twayne, 1980).

Papers:

The three main repositories of Child's papers are Cornell University, the Schlesinger Library at Radcliffe, and the Houghton Library at Harvard, but significant collections can be found at a number of other libraries. The bulk of her papers are reproduced in the microfiche edition of her *Collected Correspondence*.

Samuel Langhorne Clemens
(Mark Twain)
(30 November 1835-21 April 1910)

Alan Gribben
University of Texas at Austin

See also the Clemens entries in *DLB 11: American Humorists, 1800-1950; DLB 12: American Realists and Naturalists; DLB 23: American Newspaper Journalists, 1873-1900*; and *DLB 64: American Literary Critics and Scholars, 1850-1880.*

SELECTED BOOKS: *The Celebrated Jumping Frog of Calaveras County, and Other Sketches* (New York: C. H. Webb, 1867; London: Routledge, 1867);

The Innocents Abroad, or the New Pilgrims' Progress (Hartford, Conn.: American Publishing Company, 1869); republished in 2 volumes as *The Innocents Abroad* and *The New Pilgrims' Progress* (London: Hotten, 1870);

Mark Twain's (Burlesque) Autobiography and First Romance (New York: Sheldon, 1871; London: Hotten, 1871);

"Roughing It" (London: Routledge, 1872);

The Innocents at Home (London: Routledge, 1872);

Roughing It, augmented edition (Hartford, Conn.: American Publishing Company, 1872)–comprises *"Roughing It"* and *The Innocents at Home;*

A Curious Dream; and Other Sketches (London: Routledge, 1872);

The Gilded Age: A Tale of Today, by Twain and Charles Dudley Warner (Hartford, Conn.: American Publishing Company, 1873; 3 volumes, London: Routledge, 1874);

Mark Twain's Sketches, New and Old (Hartford, Conn.: American Publishing Company, 1875);

Old Times on the Mississippi, pirated edition (Toronto: Belford, 1876); republished as *The Mississippi Pilot* (London: Ward, Lock & Tyler, 1877); expanded as *Life on the Mississippi*, authorized edition (London: Chatto & Windus, 1883; Boston: Osgood, 1883);

The Adventures of Tom Sawyer (London: Chatto & Windus, 1876; Hartford, Conn.: American Publishing Company, 1876);

A True Story, and The Recent Carnival of Crime (Boston: Osgood, 1877);

An Idle Excursion (Toronto: Rose-Belford, 1878); expanded as *Punch, Brothers, Punch! and Other Sketches* (New York: Slote, Woodman, 1878);

A Tramp Abroad (London: Chatto & Windus/ Hartford, Conn.: American Publishing Company, 1880);

"1601" Conversation, As It Was by the Social Fireside, in the Time of the Tudors (Cleveland, 1880);

The Prince and the Pauper (London: Chatto & Windus, 1881; Boston: Osgood, 1882);

54

The Stolen White Elephant (London: Chatto & Windus, 1882); republished as *The Stolen White Elephant, Etc.* (Boston: Osgood, 1882);

The Adventures of Huckleberry Finn (London: Chatto & Windus, 1884); republished as *Adventures of Huckleberry Finn* (New York: Webster, 1885);

A Connecticut Yankee in King Arthur's Court (New York: Webster, 1889); republished as *A Yankee at the Court of King Arthur* (London: Chatto & Windus, 1889);

The American Claimant (New York: Webster, 1892; London: Chatto & Windus, 1892);

Merry Tales (New York: Webster, 1892);

The £1,000,000 Bank-Note and Other New Stories (New York: Webster, 1893; London: Chatto & Windus, 1893);

Tom Sawyer Abroad by Huck Finn (New York: Webster, 1894; London: Chatto & Windus, 1894);

Pudd'nhead Wilson, A Tale (London: Chatto & Windus, 1894); augmented as *The Tragedy of Pudd'nhead Wilson and the Comedy of Those Extraordinary Twins* (Hartford, Conn.: American Publishing Company, 1894);

Personal Recollections of Joan of Arc by the Sieur Louis de Conte (New York: Harper, 1896; London: Chatto & Windus, 1896);

Tom Sawyer Abroad, Tom Sawyer, Detective, and Other Tales (New York: Harper, 1896);

Tom Sawyer, Detective, as told by Huck Finn, and Other Stories (London: Chatto & Windus, 1896);

How to Tell a Story and Other Essays (New York: Harper, 1897);

Following the Equator (Hartford, Conn.: American Publishing Company, 1897); republished as *More Tramps Abroad* (London: Chatto & Windus, 1897);

The Man That Corrupted Hadleyburg and Other Stories and Essays (New York & London: Harper, 1900); enlarged as *The Man That Corrupted Hadleyburg and Other Stories and Sketches* (London: Chatto & Windus, 1900);

A Double Barrelled Detective Story (New York & London: Harper, 1902);

My Début as a Literary Person, with Other Essays and Stories, volume 23 of *The Writings of Mark Twain,* Autograph Edition (Hartford: American Publishing Company, 1903);

A Dog's Tale (New York & London: Harper, 1904);

Extracts from Adam's Diary Translated from the Original MS. (New York & London: Harper, 1904);

King Leopold's Soliloquy: A Defense of His Congo Rule (Boston: P. R. Warren, 1905);

Eve's Diary Translated from the Original MS. (London & New York: Harper, 1906);

What Is Man? (New York: De Vinne Press, 1906); enlarged as *What Is Man? and Other Essays* (New York & London: Harper, 1917);

The $30,000 Bequest and Other Stories (New York & London: Harper, 1906);

Christian Science with Notes Containing Corrections to Date (New York & London: Harper, 1907);

A Horse's Tale (New York & London: Harper, 1907);

Is Shakespeare Dead? (New York & London: Harper, 1909);

Extract from Captain Stormfield's Visit to Heaven (New York & London: Harper, 1909);

Mark Twain's Speeches, compiled by F. A. Nast (New York & London: Harper, 1910);

The Mysterious Stranger, a Romance, edited by Albert Bigelow Paine and Frederick A. Duneka (New York & London: Harper, 1916); enlarged as *The Mysterious Stranger and Other Stories,* edited by Paine (New York & London: Harper, 1922);

The Curious Republic of Gondour and Other Whimsical Sketches (New York: Boni & Liveright, 1919);

Mark Twain's Speeches, edited by Paine (New York & London: Harper, 1923);

Europe and Elsewhere, edited by Paine (New York & London: Harper, 1923);

Mark Twain's Autobiography, 2 volumes, edited by Paine (New York & London: Harper, 1924);

Sketches of the Sixties, by Twain and Bret Harte (San Francisco: Howell, 1926);

The Adventures of Thomas Jefferson Snodgrass, edited by Charles Honce (Chicago: Pascal Covici, 1928);

Mark Twain's Notebook, edited by Paine (New York & London: Harper, 1935);

Letters from the Sandwich Islands Written for the Sacramento Union, edited by G. Ezra Dane (San Francisco: Grabhorn, 1937);

The Washoe Giant in San Francisco, edited by Franklin Walker (San Francisco: Fields, 1938);

Mark Twain's Travels With Mr. Brown, edited by Walker and Dane (New York: Knopf, 1940);

Mark Twain in Eruption, edited by Bernard DeVoto (New York & London: Harper, 1940);

Mark Twain at Work, edited by DeVoto (Cambridge: Harvard University Press, 1942);

Mark Twain, Business Man, edited by Samuel Charles Webster (Boston: Little, Brown, 1946);

Mark Twain of the ENTERPRISE, edited by Henry Nash Smith (Berkeley: University of California Press, 1957);

Traveling with the Innocents Abroad: Mark Twain's Original Reports from Europe and the Holy Land, edited by Daniel Morley McKeithan (Norman: University of Oklahoma Press, 1958);

Contributions to The Galaxy, 1868-1871, by Mark Twain, edited by Bruce R. McElderry, Jr. (Gainesville, Fla.: Scholars' Facsimiles & Reprints, 1961);

Letters from the Earth, edited by DeVoto (New York: Harper & Row, 1962);

Mark Twain's "Which was the Dream" and Other Symbolic Writings of the Later Years, edited by John S. Tuckey (Berkeley: University of California Press, 1967);

Mark Twain's Satires and Burlesques, edited by Franklin R. Rogers (Berkeley: University of California Press, 1967);

Clemens of the "Call": Mark Twain in San Francisco, edited by Edgar M. Branch (Berkeley: University of California Press, 1969);

Mark Twain's "Mysterious Stranger" Manuscripts, edited by William M. Gibson (Berkeley: University of California Press, 1969);

Mark Twain's Hannibal, Huck, & Tom, edited by Walter Blair (Berkeley: University of California Press, 1969);

Mark Twain's Fables of Man, edited by Tuckey (Berkeley: University of California Press, 1972);

Mark Twain's Notebooks & Journals, volume 1, 1855-1873, edited by Frederick Anderson, Michael B. Frank, and Kenneth M. Sanderson; volume 2, 1877-1883, edited by Anderson, Lin Salamo, and Bernard L. Stein; volume 3, 1883-1891, edited by Robert Pack Browning, Frank, and Salamo (Berkeley: University of California Press, 1975, 1979);

Mark Twain Speaking, edited by Paul Fatout (Iowa City: University of Iowa Press, 1976);

Mark Twain Speaks for Himself, edited by Fatout (West Lafayette: Purdue University Press, 1978);

The Devil's Race-Track: Mark Twain's "Great Dark" Writings, edited by Tuckey (Berkeley: University of California Press, 1980);

Wapping Alice, Printed for the First Time, edited by Hamlin Hill (Berkeley: Bancroft Library, University of California, 1981);

The Adventures of Tom Sawyer by Mark Twain: A Facsimile of the Author's Holograph Manuscript, 2 volumes (Frederick, Md.: University Publications of America/Washington, D.C.: Georgetown University Library, 1982);

Adventures of Huckleberry Finn (Tom Sawyer's Comrade) by Mark Twain: A Facsimile of the Manuscript, 2 volumes (Detroit: Gale Research, 1983).

Collections: *The Writings of Mark Twain*, Autograph Edition, 25 volumes (Hartford, Conn.: American Publishing Company, 1899-1907);

The Writings of Mark Twain, Author's National Edition, 25 volumes (New York & London: Harper, 1899-1917);

The Writings of Mark Twain, Definitive Edition, 37 volumes, edited by Paine (New York: Wells, 1922-1925).

Editions prepared by the University of California Press for the Iowa Center for Textual Studies: *Roughing It*, edited by Franklin R. Rogers and Paul Baender (Berkeley: University of California Press, 1972);

What Is Man? and Other Philosophical Writings, edited by Baender (Berkeley: University of California Press, 1973);

A Connecticut Yankee in King Arthur's Court, edited by Bernard L. Stein (Berkeley: University of California Press, 1979);

The Prince and the Pauper, edited by Victor Fischer and Lin Salamo (Berkeley: University of California Press, 1979);

Early Tales & Sketches, volume 1 (1851-1864), volume 2 (1864-1865), edited by Edgar M. Branch and Robert H. Hirst (Berkeley: University of California Press, 1979, 1981);

The Adventures of Tom Sawyer; Tom Sawyer Abroad; Tom Sawyer, Detective, edited by John C. Gerber, Baender, and Terry Firkins (Berkeley: University of California Press, 1980).

OTHER: "An Encounter with an Interviewer," in *Lotus Leaves*, edited by John Brougham and

John Elderkin (Boston: Gill, 1875), pp. 27-32;

Mark Twain's Library of Humor, compiled by Twain, edited by William Dean Howells (New York: Webster, 1888);

"The Earliest Authentic Mention of Niagara Falls ... Extracts from Adam's Diary," in *The Niagara Book* (Buffalo: Underhill & Nichols, 1893), pp. 93-109;

"The Californian's Tale," in *The First Book of the Authors Club, Liber Scriptorum* (New York: Authors Club, 1893), pp. 154-161;

"A Cat Tale," in *Concerning Cats,* edited by Frederick Anderson (San Francisco: Book Club of California, 1959), pp. 1-19.

An author and platform entertainer who became tremendously popular in his own day, Samuel Clemens participated in the major literary movements of the century and knew virtually every one of his distinguished contemporaries. Biographers have emphasized the incredibly opposed forces that characterized his temperament and his literary works. Capable of gentle affection and great sacrifices, Clemens nevertheless antagonized or deserted numerous business and personal acquaintances. Suspicious of others' motives, he often terminated a relationship upon discerning a hint that the person was taking advantage of his trust; in other instances, however, he remained loyal to certain individuals in the face of evidence that he was being damaged monetarily by these erstwhile friends. Bret Harte, Edward H. House, and Charles L. Webster were among the many men and women Clemens came to detest; Joseph H. Twichell, William Dean Howells, and Henry H. Rogers were among the few who retained his long-term regard.

As both writer and personality, he perfectly illustrated his times. A flamboyant publicist, he directed the public eye upon himself at the outset of the period he helped to name "The Gilded Age." His intermittent lecture tours took him to numerous towns and cities, where his face became as familiar as his famous pen name. Initially he wrote in the vein of the humorous tales and sketches that were appearing in newspapers and magazines during and after the Civil War, and in 1867 Charles Henry Webb published Mark Twain's first book, *The Celebrated Jumping Frog of Calaveras County, and Other Sketches.* Subsequently he traveled as a columnist for both West Coast and East Coast newspapers, and eventually collected and revised a portion of this correspon-

Clemens in Constantinople, 1867, during the trip that served as the basis for his 1869 travel narrative, The Innocents Abroad *(photograph by Abdulah Frères; courtesy of the Mark Twain Papers, Bancroft Library, University of California, Berkeley)*

dence as a travel narrative of his journey to the Holy Land, *The Innocents Abroad* (1869). After producing another travel narrative about his sojourn in the Far West, *Roughing It* (1872), Twain turned to novel writing. His first effort, *The Gilded Age* (1873), written in collaboration with Charles Dudley Warner, is mainly read today as a period piece commentary on postwar American society. But around the time of his marriage to Olivia L. Langdon (whom he called "Livy") on 2 February 1870, Twain had begun to rehearse his memories of his days as a boy in Hannibal (1839-1853) and as a pilot on the Mississippi River steamboats (1857-1861), and these vivid recollections burst forth in a series of lyrically evocative manuscripts: *Old Times on the Mississippi* (serialized in the *Atlantic Monthly,* January-June and August 1875; published as a book in 1876); then a boy book accurately named *The Adventures of Tom Sawyer* (1876); next a collection of river lore titled *Life on the Mississippi* (1883); and, as culmination, his greatest achievement, *The Adventures of Huckle-*

berry Finn (1884). These books, together with his romance of medieval England, *A Connecticut Yankee in King Arthur's Court* (1889), and a postscript story of life in a small Mississippi River town, *Pudd'nhead Wilson* (1894), are considered by most critics to constitute his major literary works. In recent years greater notice has been accorded Twain's post-1900 efforts, particularly *The Mysterious Stranger* (1916) manuscripts. At intervals throughout his career Twain collected his shorter pieces in book form; the most notable are *Mark Twain's Sketches, New and Old* (1875), exuberant and infectiously comic; *The Stolen White Elephant* (1882), containing several fine stories; *The Man That Corrupted Hadleyburg and Other Stories and Essays* (1900); and *The $30,000 Bequest and Other Stories* (1906), characteristic in mixing marginal and previous work with superlative and fresh material.

It has become routine to view Samuel Clemens's life as tormented and tragic, and to consider his artistry as essentially dark and brooding. Primarily this perspective has resulted from relatively recent discoveries about the events and trials that marred the final portion of his life, but one should remember that his public generally perceived him as a jovial, contented platform artist and man of letters. Indeed, there was much about his existence that promoted a certain measure of happiness. For example, he left behind ample letters and other evidence to support his lifelong contention that he had found in Livy Clemens a wife whom he admired and who brought him much delight. Then, too, because he commenced his literary career in Nevada and California, he had been uninhibited about choosing his publisher and method of marketing when the moment arrived, in 1868, to sign his first contract for a travel book; as a consequence, he selected the American Publishing Company, which employed the subscription system of canvassing working-class neighborhoods, isolated farms, and rural hamlets, a potentially lucrative approach to authorship disdained by most New England literati. When the profits rolled in from his successful books, Clemens was able in 1874 to build his family an ornate nineteen-room mansion in the intellectual atmosphere of Nook Farm, an exclusive suburb of Hartford, Connecticut. Although it is true that his infant son, Langdon (1870-1872), died just eighteen months after his birth, such a loss was an accepted risk of parenthood in the nineteenth century, and he and his wife reared three daughters—Olivia Susan ("Susy") (1872-1896),

Clara (1874-1962), Jean (1880-1909)—who lived into or beyond their twenties. Clemens himself had a long and prosperous existence, traveling at will and being waited upon by servants, and he was increasingly recognized and venerated by multitudes of readers. Most summers were spent idyllically at Quarry Farm, the hillside home near Elmira, New York, built by Livy Clemens's father, Jervis Langdon, and resided in by her sister Susan Crane. There were periodic sojourns in the fashionable resorts and cities of England and Europe. When his daring financial investments finally brought him to the low point of bankruptcy in 1894, he promptly gained the benefit of millionaire Henry H. Rogers's financial wizardry in disentangling his business affairs, and Clemens even had to discourage a movement among newspaper editors and readers to raise a subscription fund for his relief from creditors.

There is no doubt that Clemens suffered painfully from successive bereavements over the deaths of his oldest daughter, Susy (in 1896), his wife Livy (in 1904), and his youngest daughter, Jean (in 1909). These blows, however, came upon him at a time when his own fortunes and reputation were again on the rise; indeed, he had more than recouped his former financial standing by the end of his life. The public adulation of his persona and his unpredictable quips reached a crescendo in 1900, when he returned triumphantly from a self-decreed exile in England, where the family had gone to live in 1891. He never could bear to resume his life in the Hartford house on Farmington Avenue that had sheltered his family in their halcyon years (1874-1891), but he ultimately constructed for himself (in 1908) a large house in Redding, Connecticut, that was modeled on Italianate villas, and he passed the last decade of his life writing fiction and autobiography, visiting friends, attending plays, delivering speeches, and granting interviews. He died on 21 April 1910 in Redding. The journals of his secretary Isabel Lyon record the hurried pace of his final years. Despite the unassuaged tribulations, this note of agony in Clemens's life has been overstressed by twentieth-century writers. The Lear-like rages of his later days should be weighed against the contentment and affluence of preceding decades. Moreover, he was one of the fortunate citizens of his epoch who perfectly achieved his specific American dream: he became wealthy and famous as an esteemed author. The honorary degree he received from Oxford University in 1907 symbolized for Samuel Clemens the transatlantic recognition of his place among the writers and intellectuals of his century.

A large number of Mark Twain's best tales did not originally appear as separate short stories; he embedded them instead in the long travel narratives or novels he was constantly preparing for publication by the efficient subscription system, which employed trained "canvassers" to market books to households that normally purchased few if any books. Like "Baker's Bluejay Yarn" in *A Tramp Abroad* (1880), these fictional stories have an integrity and completeness of their own, yet their incorporation into longer works generally seems serendipitous and suitable. Introducing "The Professor's Yarn" at the end of chapter 35 in *Life on the Mississippi,* Twain breezily announces: "Here is a story which I picked up on board the boat [the *Gold Dust,* heading down from Vicksburg] that night. I insert it in this place merely because it is a good story, not because it belongs here–for it doesn't." Since Twain was an episodic writer, many of his finest feats in short fiction appear within these longer books; moreover, his method of composition and his dedication to subscription publishing made him eager to use every available scrap of manuscript in compiling the desirably large-sized volumes. It therefore appears reasonable and appropriate to treat as significant short stories "Grandfather's Old Ram" and other contextual tales. Placement of these stories actually involved considerably more artistic craft–or at least inspiration–than Twain would have his readers believe. Just as Howells struggled to fathom the purpose of Twain's apparently haphazard arrangement of their selections for an anthology titled *Mark Twain's Library of Humor* (1888) (Howells testified that after "I had done my work according to tradition, with authors, times, and topics carefully studied in due sequence, he tore it all apart, and 'chucked' the pieces in wherever the fancy for them took him at the moment"), so readers must penetrate Twain's putative artlessness in introducing the many brief tales that alter the pace and vary the tone of his longer narratives; and the gems that stud these large books also merit study and appreciation for their own literary merits.

In the remarkable tale in chapter 36 of *Life on the Mississippi,* "The Professor's Yarn," for instance, a college professor relates an incident that took place at sea in the days when he was a young land surveyor. (The basic conflict–urban sophistication in advantageous opposition against

hapless provincialism–had animated Clemens's first juvenile sketch to find national publication, "The Dandy Frightening the Squatter" in the 1 May 1852 issue of the *Boston Carpet Bag.*) On shipboard en route to California, the professor notices three professional gamblers, "rough, repulsive fellows." They have set their sights on friendly John Backus, a farmer from the backwoods of Ohio, and the surveyor watches with alarm as they maneuver gullible Backus into risking his ten-thousand-dollar savings in a card game. The young narrator agonizes as the ship sails through the Golden Gate at San Francisco with Backus, deceived into drunkenness, deeply involved in a high-stakes game. But the peeping narrator and the calculating gamblers are astonished alike when Backus wins the bettors' pot with a hand of four aces, then draws a revolver and announces himself to be " 'a professional gambler myself, and I've been laying for you duffers all this voyage!' Down went the anchor, rumbledy-dum-dum! and the long trip was ended."

Two brief variants of this poker-table tale, unpublished during Clemens's lifetime, end in bloodshed. Both involve male Jewish characters who intervene to save the lives, fortunes, and servants of an unwary plantation owner. In "Newhouse's Jew Story" (first published in *Mark Twain's Fables of Man,* 1972), a river pilot named George Newhouse recounts an incident of 1845, when an unsavory steamboat gambler named Jackson gambled with a wealthy Louisiana planter and won his money and slaves; about to add a lovely mulatto girl to his winnings (and hoping to goad the planter into a duel), Jackson is foiled when a young Jewish man challenges Jackson, chooses pistols rather than the bowie knives that Jackson always favored, and kills the arrogant cardsharp. In "Randall's Jew Story" (also written in the 1890s and first published in *Mark Twain's Fables of Man*), a bank president tells a similar story, this time set in 1850, of a slave trader named Hackett who was gambling aboard a steamboat with a Virginia plantation owner named Fairfax. Hackett wins the pretty mulatto servant of Fairfax's daughter, but a Jewish man named Rosenthal interferes, compelling Hackett to fight him with pistols and killing the gambler in a duel on the riverbank. In both instances the mysterious-stranger benefactors, alien because of their cultural and religious backgrounds, have previous knowledge of the gambler's motives and character; they only decide to intercede when innocent people are obviously going to suffer irreparable harm. This situation of a trained and superior individual vanquishing his villainous opponents, often concluding with the character's casting aside an efficacious disguise, held a continual fascination for Twain. Karl Ritter in chapter 31 of *Life on the Mississippi* takes revenge on the murderers of his wife and daughter by fingerprinting the suspects while disguised as a fortuneteller. The moral righteousness of such men's missions endows them with overpowering fury, and their Poe-like worship of the human intellect enables them to plan strategies that place their quarry within their powers. In this sense Twain's fiction is closer to romantic literature, with its superheroes, than to American realism with its picture of the ordinary possibilities of common life.

Twain's fascination with themes of doubleness, twins, and switched identities has many manifestations in his novels, and these motifs are also evident in his short fiction. A pair of burlesque Sunday-school stories, for instance, poke fun at the invariable formulas that operated within writings for young churchgoers. "The Story of the Bad Little Boy Who Didn't Come to Grief " (*Californian*, 23 December 1865; collected in *The Celebrated Jumping Frog of Calaveras County, and Other Sketches*) presents the anomalous case of an unrepentant little knave named Jim who grows rich and marries well despite his notorious behavior. Conversely, "The story of the Good Little Boy Who Did Not Prosper" (*Galaxy*, May 1870; collected in *Mark Twain's Sketches, New and Old*) reports the sad tale of little Jacob Blivens, who always minded his parents, never gave hot pennies to the organ-grinder's monkey, and studied his lessons assiduously, but nevertheless died without being able to deliver his deathbed speech or enjoy the comfort of sorrowful relatives and classmates. A later short work, "About Magnanimous-Incident Literature" (*Atlantic*, May 1878; collected in *The Stolen White Elephant*), teaches the same rueful lesson about discrepancies between the fate of people who perform noble deeds in storybooks and what happens to do-gooders in real life. Another variation on this theme, "Edward Mills and George Benton: A Tale" (*Atlantic*, August 1880; collected in *The $30,000 Bequest and Other Stories*), follows the story of two distantly related cousins adopted by the same childless couple. Edward is a selfless, striving, helpful child; George gets his way by being disobedient, obnoxious, and evasive. Yet George is left a half ownership in Edward's business firm by provisions in their stepparents' will, and, in spite of

George's heavy drinking, he manages to steal Edward's fiancée, who has hopes of reforming George. Pampered by temperance societies, George lectures as a reformed drunkard and finds sympathetic friends even when he is convicted of forgery. One evening George and some companions rob Edward's bank and kill him; although George is eventually tried and hanged for the murder, Edward's wife and children are left destitute. The two men's epitaphs ironically reflect the meager reward for the "pure, honest, sober, industrious, considerate" life that Edward tried to lead.

Twain's best-known story of interlocked contrasts, of course, is "Those Extraordinary Twins," apparently the germ for *Pudd'nhead Wilson* and often appended to that novel about Dawson's Landing. First published in the 1894 American edition of the novel, the bizarre short story centers on Siamese twins from Italy, Luigi (who smokes and drinks) and Angelo (who is fastidious, religious, and polite). These comical oppositions had been adumbrated in an earlier, nonsensical story, "Personal Habits of the Siamese Twins" (*Packard's Monthly*, August 1869; collected in *Mark Twain's Sketches, New and Old*), which recounted the canceling-out tendencies of Chang and Eng. In "Those Extraordinary Twins," Rowena Cooper finds herself drawn to Angelo, but the twins exercise an inflexible system by which one or the other of them is alternately in charge of their single body and pair of legs. Their adventures in Dawson's Landing include a much-publicized court trial, a duel in which Luigi is the participant but Angelo the wounded victim, and a religious baptism (of Angelo) in the Mississippi River. The twins run on opposing slates endorsed by different parties in a local election; Luigi wins the alderman post but cannot be officially seated because his accompanying brother was a loser in the same election. The townspeople, tired of the inconvenience of the twins and wanting to break the deadlock in voting by their board of aldermen, simplify matters by hanging Luigi. What Twain termed an "extravagant sort of tale" obviously suffered from its forcible removal from the larger story, although Twain was correct in sensing the disparity in moods that was developing. But "Those Extraordinary Twins" remains a piece of unfinished farce, skeletal in outline and execution, allowed by Twain to survive merely to illustrate the complexity and whimsicality of his creative processes. The freak of nature becomes a freak of fiction, more often alluded to as a curiosity than read by modern audiences.

Though Twain's long western sojourn (1861-1866, with another visit to California in 1868) fostered his lifelong aptitude for constructing literary hoaxes such as "The Petrified Man" (*Virginia City Territorial Enterprise,* 4 October 1862), Edgar Allan Poe and other eastern authors had left him numerous models, and he had experimented with hoaxlike elements in sketches written in Hannibal and during his piloting period. In "A Medieval Romance" (*Buffalo Express,* 1 January 1870; collected in *Mark Twain's Sketches, New and Old*) Twain constructed a brief five-part spoof of the Gothic thriller; two brothers ruling apart in their feudal castles in Klugenstein and Brandenburgh, vie for their progeny's succession to the duchy's throne. This relatively early tale contains several situations and themes that Twain would develop more seriously in subsequent fiction such as *The Prince and the Pauper* (1881): an impostor (in this case, a girl impersonating a boy heir) ably rules over the royal palace; the girl must pass excruciating tests of her ability to play this role, including a comic interview with a lovesick princess who flirts with the comely ruler; a huge, ceremonious public trial resembles Guinevere's; a scandalous incident of adultery must be revealed in public. But suddenly the authorial narrator intrudes and, presaging Twain's subsequent difficulties with the twists and turns of plot for his novels, abruptly concedes that "the truth is, I have got my hero (or heroine) into such a particularly close place that I do not see how I am ever going to get him (or her) out of it again, and therefore I will wash my hands of the whole business"–abandoning the story at the climactic moment. This notion of screwing the reader's suspense tighter and tighter, and then simply breaking off the story at its most frantic and pulsing moment, would amuse Twain again and again. By that means, the author jarringly reminds his reader of the spellbinding power of his fiction and the extent of the reader's dependence upon his invention; he shatters the illusion for the moment in order to prove that he can restore it yet once more in another story with the barest effort.

Twain based the incident in the balloon story, first published in the Heritage Press edition of *Life on the Mississippi* (edited by Willis Wager, 1944), on the disappearance during the 1870s of several balloonists who drifted over Lake Michigan. Mr. Harvey tells about a horrifying experience when his airborne balloon reached a stagnant strata of the atmosphere where he could see the corpses of other unfortunate sky voyagers. Before he can relate his presumably miraculous release from this peril, however, the steamboat *Gold Dust* reaches his landing and he departs without enlightening the awed passengers. Likewise, in "A Story Without an End" (first published in *Following the Equator,* 1897) one passenger on an ocean steamer entertains the men in the smoking room with the story of a complicated dilemma involving a shy young man named John Brown who must make a moral decision with social consequences. "We worked at the troublesome problem until three in the morning," adds the narrator. "Meantime Mary was still reaching for the lap-robe. . . . It is the reader's privilege to determine for himself how the thing came out."

More frequently, however, Mark Twain's stories reach their conclusions. His extravagant humor showed to good advantage in "The Great Landslide Case," part of chapter 34 of *Roughing It.* (Earlier versions had appeared in a 30 August 1863 letter to the *San Francisco Morning Call* in 1863 and the *Buffalo Express,* 2 April 1870.) There Twain recounted a hoax played on a self-important, newly arrived United States attorney for the Territory of Nevada, General Buncombe. Dick Hyde retains this lawyer to represent his interests in a preposterous real-estate case, claiming that Tom Morgan's "ranch, fences, cabins, cattle, barns and everything" had been shoved by a landslide "down on top of *his* ranch and exactly covered up every single vestige of his property, to a depth of about thirty-eight feet. Morgan was in possession and refused to vacate the premises." Arguing persuasively on the basis of "law-books" and "history" and "eternal justice," Buncombe nonetheless loses the case when the referee, former Governor Roop, concludes that "Heaven, in its inscrutable wisdom, has seen fit to move this defendant's ranch for a purpose. . . . It ill becomes us, insects as we are, to question the legality of the act or inquire into the reasons that prompted it." Roop can only suggest that perhaps Hyde has the right to dig his ranch out from under Morgan's. Buncombe grows better acquainted with the territory and its citizens, and "at the end of two months the fact that he had been played upon with a joke had managed to bore . . . through the solid adamant of his understanding."

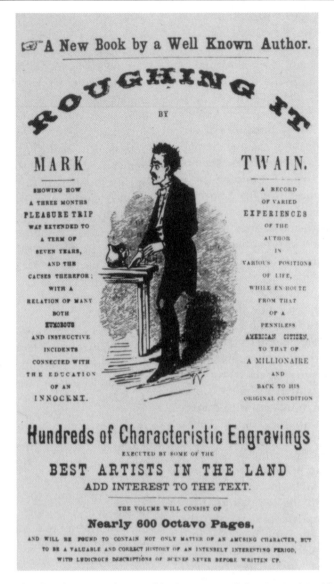

Prepublication advertising circular for Clemens's 1872 travel book (courtesy of the New York Public Library, Astor, Lenox and Tilden Foundations)

Another practical joke, sometimes titled "The Petrified Man" or "A Washoe Joke," appeared in the *Virginia City Territorial Enterprise,* the *San Francisco Daily Evening Bulletin,* and other newspapers in 1862. It has been collected in volume 1 of *Early Tales & Sketches* (1979). Taking recent paleontological discoveries in the western desert for its point of departure, Twain's straightfaced news item reports the finding of a wellpreserved "petrified man" at a place known as Gravelly Ford in the mountains. Describing the mummy's features in careful detail, the reporter ludicrously reveals that the position of the body's right hand resembles a gesture of sarcastic defiance (the equivalent of "thumbing his nose"),

that a coroner's verdict declared that "the deceased came to his death from protracted exposure," and that he cannot be moved because of "a limestone sediment under him which had glued him to the bed rock upon which he sat." Among other things, this hoax demonstrates Twain's ability to reproduce the standard form of journalistic writing in his day; it also mingles his intense interest in scientific investigations with his low opinion of human credulity. At least ten newspapers throughout California reprinted the piece, but only a few shrewdly detected the joke and labeled it as such. Burlesques such as this one were as much a testimony to the lure of the western tall-tale tradition as they were a tribute to the earlier examples produced by Poe and others.

Still another hoax by Mark Twain, "A Bloody Massacre Near Carson," published in the 28 October 1863 issue of the *Virginia City Territorial Enterprise* and collected in volume 1 of *Early Tales & Sketches*, included such gory details of a father's murder of his entire family and his suicide that the editors who copied the story in Nevada and California newspapers were scarcely amused when Twain's satirical intentions were revealed. Here again he had proved his adeptness at burlesquing the sensational tone of journalism in the mid nineteenth century. Twain relied on absurd details as clues to his intention–he locates a "great pine forest" in the desert by Dutch Nick's, for example, and the mother's premonitions were ignored by her neighbors because "it was Mrs. Hopkins' misfortune to be given to exaggeration." The grisly scene that Sheriff Gasherie finds is not much worse than the one Poe pictures in "The Murders in the Rue Morgue" (1841), but the unelaborated newspaper "report" of course lacks Poe's mood and denouement. Actually Twain had wanted to draw attention to crooked practices in various mining and water companies, and he had not sought in this instance to create the indignant furor that his piece provoked.

Twain's penchant for clever burlesque carried over into much of his later work, including stories such as "The Facts in the Case of the Great Beef Contract" (*Galaxy*, May 1870; collected in *Mark Twain's Sketches, New and Old*). A succession of thirteen family members tries to collect money owed by the Federal government for thirty barrels of beef that a New Jersey man agreed in 1861 to deliver to General Sherman (he was never able to catch up to Sherman's forces and died, "tomahawked and scalped" by Indians, trying to find Sherman on the Great Plains after the Civil War was over). A malevolent relative ("he had had a grudge against me for a long time"), one of those plotting mysterious strangers like Tilbury Foster in "The $30,000 Bequest" (*Harper's Weekly*, 10 December 1904; collected in *The $30,000 Bequest and Other Stories*), places the long-overdue bill in the hands of the narrator, who attempts to find someone in the U.S. government willing to pay the seventeen thousand dollars owed for the beef and the transportation costs. "I said I would haunt them. . . . I would collect the bill, or fall, as fell my predecessors, trying." The piece reminds one of Charles Dickens's

sketch of the Circumlocution Office presided over by Sir Tite Barnacle in *Little Dorrit* (1855-1857): "Unfortunates with wrongs, or with projects for the general welfare . . . , who in slow lapse of time and agony had passed safely through other public departments, . . . got referred at last to the Circumlocution Office, and never re-appeared in the light of day." The narrator of Twain's tale finds himself mired in the multiple levels of the U.S. Treasury Department, always being passed on to still more specialized auditors, until at last he reaches "the Commissioner of Odds and Ends." But a government bureaucrat refuses to pay the claim until the Indian (and tomahawk) who murdered the original claimant are produced ("we must have proofs"). Even if this condition is met, the government is willing to pay only for the single barrel of beef that Sherman's men found untouched; "it will not pay for the twenty-nine barrels the Indians ate"). After all the narrator's effort, he learns that the most he could collect would be one hundred dollars. "We do things by routine here," explains the smug young clerk. . . . It is very regular, and very slow, but it is very certain."

In a similar line of exaggeration contrasted with understatement, "Journalism in Tennessee" (*Buffalo Express*, 4 September 1869; collected in *Mark Twain's Sketches, New and Old*), the narrator ridicules the verbal mayhem that southern newspaper editors inflict upon one another. As the assistant editor of the *Morning Glory and Johnson County War-Whoop*, he suffers virtual dismemberment merely from sitting in the office while a series of libeled citizens and competing newspaper editors drop by to pay their respects to the editor for his "peppery and to the point" editorials. Aghast at the "fervent spirit of Tennesseean journalism," the narrator takes his leave of the newspaper. "The Southern heart is too impulsive; Southern hospitality is too lavish with the stranger. . . . I decline to be present at these festivities." In another exuberant sketch, "How I Edited an Agricultural Paper" (*Galaxy*, July 1870; collected in *Mark Twain's Sketches, New and Old*), the narrator accepts a guest editorship and awakens the subscribers of the journal with farcical advice: "Turnips should never be pulled, it injures them. It is much better to send a boy up and let him shake the tree." The chagrined editor returns to find that his replacement has been "discussing oysterbeds under the head of 'Landscape Gardening.' " "I want you to go," implores the editor. "Nothing on earth could persuade me to take another holiday. Oh! why didn't you *tell* me you didn't know anything about agriculture?" But his guest-editor is nonchalant: "I have done my duty. I said I could make your paper of interest to all classes—and I have." It seems relevant that George Horatio Derby (whose pen name was John Phoenix) had chronicled what happened when the editor of the *San Diego Herald*, deciding to travel, left Phoenix in charge of the newspaper; his substitute took the liberty of altering its political position from that of the Democratic party to that of the Whig party. Such similarities remind us of Twain's genius for reworking the techniques and forms of literary comedians who were his predecessors or his rivals.

A short satiric tale, "The Great Revolution in Pitcairn" (*Atlantic*, March 1879; collected in *The Stolen White Elephant*), pretends to review the history of the tiny colony established by the *Bounty* mutineers; all is harmonious for nearly a hundred years until a stranger, an American, arrives; as one visiting admiral notes, he is "*a doubtful acquisition.*" Before long this person foments an insurrection, gains absolute power, severs the island's ties with Britain, levies heavy taxes, and extends the powers of the church. At last the people arise to unseat this tyrant and return to their peaceful, simple existence under the British flag. There are strains of Clemens's conflicting political views in evidence in this early obverse of the *Connecticut Yankee* plot, and the story is not the compelling dystopian parable he evidently intended. Even more odd is another political satire written in the 1870s, "The Curious Republic of Gondour" (*Atlantic*, October 1875; collected in *The Curious Republic of Gondour and Other Whimsical Sketches*, 1919). Bearing certain affinities to Samuel Butler's satirical romance *Erewhon* (1872), Twain's brief tale describes a previously undiscovered society whose citizens have adopted drastic solutions to problems that trouble many civilizations: people with education and wealth are entitled to extra votes in this republic, and therefore voting privileges are a sign of status; government officials' salaries are so generous that they are not tempted to steal or to tolerate corruption; the Grand Caliph (sometimes a woman) has a twenty-year term. The narrator implies that most of these reforms are desirable, but a few of the customs—especially the constant singing of the national anthem—irritate him. Commentators have wondered just how serious Twain intended to be in this little romance, and whether his social and political views at the time were accu-

rately reflected in Gondour's system of government.

A number of Twain's stories relate events that depend for their effect, like the balloon hoax, on the narrator's sense of being stranded or isolated, frozen passively in an eternity of hopeless watching for deliverance. "The Enchanted Sea-Wilderness" (first published in *Mark Twain's "Which was the Dream" and Other Symbolic Writings of the Later Years*, 1967), one of Twain's late pieces, posits a deathly calm place in the sea where circular winds trap unwary vessels. The region is known as "The Everlasting Sunday." In this prose version of Samuel Taylor Coleridge's "The Rime of the Ancient Mariner" (1798) Capt. Elliot Cable drifts for seven dreadful months to atone for killing a St. Bernard dog that was the pet of his crew on the *Mabel Thorpe*.

Increasingly in Clemens's later years the motif of delirious, reality-distorting dreams took prominence in his fiction. Representative of these rehearsals of family or personal tragedy is the suggestively named "Which Was the Dream?" (first published in *Mark Twain's "Which was the Dream"*) written in 1897. In that feverish story, a narrator named Thomas endures financial disaster and humiliation, then awakens with a new name to learn that eighteen months have passed and that his family has moved from Washington, D.C., to Hell's Delight, California. Similarly, in "The Great Dark" (also first published in *Mark Twain's "Which was the Dream"*), a fragment of the same period, the Superintendent of Dreams places the Edwards family in a whaling vessel trapped for twelve years (possibly in a drop of moisture beneath a microscope) on a never-ending voyage; Henry Edwards begins to have doubts about whether this terrifying experience is the true reality, and his earlier domestic bliss a cruel dream.

Other tales, less obviously linked with dreams, nevertheless depict a future or present state that gravely alters normalcy. "The Secret History of Eddypus, the World-Empire" (first published in *Mark Twain's Fables of Man*, 1972), written in 1901 and 1902, proposes a world in which Mary Baker Eddy's theology has taken control of the religious and educational institutions as effectively as the Roman Catholic faith did in the Middle Ages; the sad consequences of this theocracy are detailed, relieved only by the narrator's amusing attempts to reconstruct the now-lost history of the nineteenth century, comically misidentifying Mark Twain as a bishop of New Jersey and a historian, and likewise mistaking the accomplishments of other eminent personages.

A large proportion of Mark Twain's writings during the last fifteen years of his life belongs to this "what if ?" vein of philosophical musing; nearly all of these dreams turn out badly for the participants. This sort of fiction is also marked by a vast diminishment of Twain's penchant for realistic details of cultural region–the telling signs of speech, dress, and custom drop away, leaving only the starkest elements of human existence and frustration at the fore. Although "The $30,000 Bequest" supplies a few more regional distinctions than many such stories, it simply begins: "Lakeside was a pleasant little town of five or six thousand inhabitants, and a rather pretty one, too, as towns go in the Far West.... Everybody knew everybody and his dog, and a sociable friendliness was the prevailing atmosphere." The Foster family in that short story exemplifies the fatal error of characters in Twain's late fiction: the husband and wife amuse themselves each night when they "put the plodding world away, and lived in another and a fairer, reading romances to each other, dreaming dreams, comrading with kings and princes and stately lords and ladies in the ... splendor of noble palaces." For this seemingly innocuous pastime, they must pay a great penalty. Transferring their wishes to the tangible fortune of Tilbury Foster, who promises to bequeath them $30,000, they foolishly daydream of plans for spending the wealth until their vastly inflated but still imaginary money is lost in stock-market speculations; they then learn that Tilbury had no money to leave them in the first place. Heartbroken, they die after two agonizing years of appreciating the cunning trap that their impoverished relative laid for them.

Another, better-known tale, "The Man That Corrupted Hadleyburg" (*Harper's Magazine*, December 1899; collected in *The Man That Corrupted Hadleyburg and Other Stories and Essays*, 1900), has been among the most frequently anthologized American works of fiction during the past two decades, despite its fairy-tale introduction: "It was many years ago. Hadleyburg was the most honest and upright town in all the region round about it .... But at last, in the drift of time, Hadleyburg had the ill luck to offend a passing stranger.... What he wanted was a plan which would comprehend the entire town, and not let so much as one person escape unhurt." Readers are so engrossed in the stranger's chosen

David Ross Locke (Petroleum Vesuvius Nasby), Clemens, and Henry Wheeler Shaw (Josh Billings) during their lecture tour of 1869-1870

retribution–to corrupt the whole town–that they accept the sweeping premises of this plot and willingly forego the enriching details that distinguished Twain's earlier depictions of small-town life. This story portrays only the private soul-searching of Edward and Mary Richards and the public humiliation–staged at the town hall–of eighteen esteemed citizens of Hadleyburg. It is as though Twain has reached an agreement with his audience: what I wish to say here pertains to universal greed and hypocrisy among humans; for the setting and all quaint local-color touches, see my previous works. The resulting grim tale, perhaps overlong in chronicling tediously intricate maneuvers of the prevaricating citizens and the inventive stranger, has little in common with Twain's strongly crafted fiction from other periods. The tidy, postmark ending and the absence of regional, identifying details qualify it as one of the stories that John S. Tuckey groups together as "fantasy pieces or fables: ... events that he saw as representative or symbolic of the nature and condition of man, past, present, or yet to be." Again in this narrative, readers encounter a devotedly married couple who alternate between dreaming of material goods and pleasures deriving from a sack of "gold coin weighing a hundred and sixty pounds four ounces," and grappling with a consciousness of their not deserving so much reward in this world–indeed, of meriting rather the strange illness and sudden death that follow their receipt of forty thousand dollars in checks. The superior stranger who devises the plan that entraps a town belongs, as others have pointed out, to the extensive procession of "mysterious strangers" who stride into many of Twain's narratives, emboldened by wider experience and greater knowledge than that possessed by the villagers whom they manipulate; often scoffed at upon their arrival by the townspeople, they eventually select a few malleable souls to whom they impart bits and pieces of awesome philosophic wisdom, sometimes punishing or destroying other citizens. This pattern of what Paul Baender and Henry Nash Smith have called "transcendent figures" culminated, of course, in Twain's repeatedly attempted narrative generally referred to as "The Mysterious Stranger."

"The Man That Corrupted Hadleyburg" also incorporated one of Twain's most effective devices: the obtaining of revenge by slow and pleasurable degrees. In such stories a victim, almost invariably a culprit who committed an offense resulting in an injustice, is persecuted by an avenging angel who cannot be given the slip, who has already foreseen every action the person can possibly take, and who has countered it with the skill of a practiced chess player (Clemens's first personal notebook recorded a series of strategic chess moves in 1855). In a manifestation of this pattern in "A Double Barrelled Detective Story" (*Harper's Magazine*, January and February 1902; published as a book in April of the same year) the indefatigable Archy Stillman, gifted with a bloodhound's ability to follow scents, inadvertently takes up the trail of the wrong man, and thereby pursues and ruins (at his mother's instructions) Jacob Fuller; but at least the reader learns that Flint Buckner, the miscreant who had disgraced Archy Stillman's mother, is killed by a mining explosion. Chapter 31 of *Life on the Mississippi* is Karl Ritter's narrative of the revenge he effected on the men who robbed him and murdered his wife and daughter; stalking one of them, Franz Adler, he accidentally stabs Adler's accomplice in the heart; then–more than fifteen years later–he at last gets Adler in his clutches

when the criminal lies shivering in a Bavarian morgue, mistakenly declared dead by a physician. Adler's only possible savior is the night watchman, who happens to be Karl Ritter. The result is worthy of one of Poe's obsessively mad narrators: "He was a satisfactory long time dying. . . . Yes, he was a pleasant long time at it. I got a chair and a newspaper, and sat down by him and read. . . . I read aloud: mainly imaginary accounts of people snatched from the grave's threshold and restored to life and vigor by a few spoonsful of liquor and a warm bath."

In many of these stories besides "A Doubled Barrelled Detective Story" there is a figure, sometimes comic, sometimes cunning, who qualifies as a criminal detective. During the town-hall scene in "The Man That Corrupted Hadleyburg," "a stranger, who looked like an amateur detective gotten up as an impossible English earl, had been watching the evening's proceedings with manifest interest"; he is the mysterious stranger who has arranged these proceedings; now he prompts a frantic bidding war for the sack of lead disks. In various guises this type of detective enters other stories under different circumstances. Sherlock Holmes himself is bumptiously ineffectual at grasping the circumstances of "A Double Barrelled Detective Story" and must be rescued from lynching by the disgruntled miners of Hope Canyon, California. (Twain was parodying Arthur Conan Doyle's *A Study in Scarlet*, 1888.) "Simon Wheeler, Detective" (first published in *Mark Twain's Satires and Burlesques*, 1967), a fragmentary story written sporadically between 1877 and 1898, ends shortly after the title character is introduced as "a born detective" in his self-appreciation, obtuseness, and veneration for a book titled *Tales of a Detective*. In "The Stolen White Elephant" (first published in *The Stolen White Elephant*), the incompetent police detectives play cards and sleep in the basement of the police station, where lies the "rotting carcass" of the missing white Siamese elephant Hassan (a fact that does not stop Inspector Blunt and his New York detectives from dividing up the fifty-thousand-dollar reward).

The commandant of Fort Trumbull in Connecticut plays detective in "A Curious Experience" (*Century*, November 1881; collected in *The Stolen White Elephant*), and the results are exciting but ultimately farcical. A boy of fourteen or fifteen who joins the company as a drummer is suspected of laying plans for an invasion of the fort by Confederate sympathizers; the major arrests a number of people seen talking with the boy, telegraphs the war department, and attempts to decode a series of cryptic notes the boy leaves in hiding places around the fort and city. When the soldiers track him to the home of his parents, the adults learn that he had dreamed up the entire adventure as a prank–another one of Twain's hoaxes.

Tom Sawyer and David Wilson are more successful as detectives in "Tom Sawyer, Detective" (*Harper's Magazine*, August and September 1896; collected in *Tom Sawyer Abroad, Tom Sawyer, Detective, and Other Stories*, 1896) and *Pudd'nhead Wilson*. In "Tom Sawyer, Detective," virtually a novelette in length, Tom Sawyer and Huck Finn return to the Phelps farm in Arkansas, where they come to the assistance of a downcast Silas Phelps, arrested for murdering one of the Dunlap twin brothers, Jubiter. Only a few passages in this story evoke the magic of a boy's life along the Mississippi River that Twain had conjured up in *Huckleberry Finn*, even though Huck Finn gamely narrates this tale in his familiar vernacular voice: " 'Tom Sawyer,' I says, 'I'll say it again as I've said it a many a time before: I ain't fitten to black your boots' " (chapter 6). When Huck and Tom are moseying about in the woods, the story shows flashes of Twain's artistry ("we talked and smoked and stuffed watermelon as much as two hours"), but on the Phelps farm and in the town the boys settle down to the sort of overblown antics that critics have long faulted in the concluding episodes of Twain's most famous novel. In this instance, as in most of his other detective tales, Twain's urge to burlesque sleuth-heroes did not serve him well. Here he also seems hampered by adherence to his literary source for the framework of this story, whether that source was an oral rendition of the plot of Steen S. Blicher's *The Minister of Veilby* (1829) or, more likely, Samuel M. Phillipps's summary of the same story in *Famous Cases of Circumstantial Evidence* (revised edition, 1879). Tom Sawyer is allowed another melodramatic courtroom scene, this time revealing that Jubiter Dunlap is still alive and is seated in the audience; recovering the stolen diamonds, Tom divides a two-thousand-dollar reward with Huck. The mixture of Sherlock Holmesian deductions and rustic Arkansas farm folk is not successful for Twain, and the burlesque never finds its true focus. The briefly sketched cast of characters, moreover, becomes confusing because of the proliferation of disguises and lies. Perhaps detective fiction rightfully belongs in the setting of a large city or an English country house rather than a small American farm.

Had Mark Twain never written *Tom Sawyer* or *Huckleberry Finn*, then perhaps a minor work like "Tom Sawyer Abroad" (*St. Nicholas,* November 1893-April 1894; published as a book in April 1894) would attract more notice as a tour de force in the direction of Jules Verne's science fiction (and as one of the few nineteenth-century narratives that incorporate balloon ascensions and voyages). Again in this tale Tom Sawyer enlists Huck and Jim in the sorts of escapades he tried to instigate in the horseplay ending to *Huckleberry Finn*. This time Tom, Huck, and Jim travel to St. Louis, Missouri, where they are examining the gondola of a balloon when it suddenly begins to ascend with them and its professor-inventor, a ravingly mad genius, aboard. The professor falls overboard and the three passengers then have a series of African adventures with lions, robbers, caravans, and sandstorms. They land on top of the Sphinx, tell tales from *The Arabian Nights*, visit Cairo. In a ludicrous ending, they return to Missouri, planning a brief stop before further travels, but Aunt Polly catches Jim trying to sneak into her house to fetch Tom's pipe and leave a note for her, and she orders the boys home. The story is entertaining only in places, despite Huck's colorful dialect, but it graphically attests to Twain's yearning to write fantasy as well as realistic fiction. It also reminds his readers how much he was fascinated by early inquiries into aviation, and how avidly he followed trends in scientific discoveries.

In a story mainly notable for its early employment of the telephone as an instrument of long-distance communication, "The Loves of Alonzo Fitz Clarence and Rosannah Ethelton" (*Atlantic*, March 1878; collected in *An Idle Excursion*, 1878, and *Punch Brothers, Punch! and Other Sketches*, 1878), Twain spoofs romantic melodrama with a downright silly tale of a wealthy young bachelor in Eastport, Maine, who falls in love with the lovely Rosannah Ethelton of San Francisco. A conniving rival gains access to Alonzo's telephone, mimics his voice, and insults Rosannah so that she breaks off her engagement to Alonzo. Her despairing lover wanders about the country, listening to telephones in hopes of hearing Rosannah singing her favorite song, "The Sweet By-and-By." The lovers reunite and the trickster-suitor is foiled. The ending includes what is surely the first marriage-ceremony-by-telephone recorded in fiction.

Mark Twain was also amused by the difficulties of grasping nuances in the idiom of a foreign language, and he produced a number of sketches and spoofs dedicated to these problems. In a pretended playlet titled "Meisterschaft: In Three Acts" (*Century*, January 1888; collected in *Merry Tales*, 1892), his characters employ Meisterschaft German grammars, speaking the inane model sentences proposed by such textbooks, while overcoming trivial obstacles to the happy courtships of two couples who are trying to learn the German language.

The domestic woes of the married spouse formed the pretext for several stories, beginning with jokes about Brigham Young's numerous wives and children in chapter 15 of *Roughing It*. These domestic tribulations link this yarn with several tales that Twain set down about the sorely tried Mr. Mortimer McWilliams, who in "Mrs. McWilliams and the Lightning" (*Atlantic*, September 1880; collected in *The Stolen White Elephant*) describes his wife's intense fear of thunderstorms and the absurd precautions she obliges him to take (he must put on a metal fireman's hat and stand on a chair). Having related his trials, McWilliams departs from the train. "The Experience of the McWilliamses with the Membranous Croup" (first published in *Mark Twain's Sketches, New and Old*) is related because "very few married men have such an experience, . . . and so . . . maybe the novelty of it would give a passing interest to the reader." Here are found the further trials of domestic life borne by a man "whose strength is all gone and whose soul is worn out." (His child really has no croup at all, but simply has been chewing on a piece of pine wood.) Still another tale of this couple, "The McWilliamses and the Burglar Alarm" (*Harper's Christmas*, 1882; collected in *The Mysterious Stranger and Other Stories*, 1922), tells of one more train ride with Mr. McWilliams, who takes that opportunity "to unload his heart" with "ill-controlled emotion." At his wife's behest he installed a burglar alarm, but the contraption went off on every occasion except a burglar's entrance. The burglars came at will, in fact, eventually even stealing the alarm system itself; meantime, the repair bills mounted. Then "the burglars moved in" for an entire summer. With his wife's consent, Mr. McWilliams "took the whole thing out and traded it off for a dog, and shot the dog."

Mark Twain never quite achieved the drollery of James Thurber's stories in these efforts to sketch the trying aspects of the married state. But he did at least, here and in "Playing Courier" (*Illustrated London News*, 19 and 26 December 1891; collected in *The £1,000,000 Bank-Note and Other New Stories*, 1893), contribute to the tradition of the downtrodden "little man" that would later find its master artist in Robert Benchley. In attempting to prove that he can take his party of five people from Geneva to Bayreuth without hiring a courier to attend to the details, Twain's persona reveals himself to be dense, vain, officious, foolish–and ineffectual. He purchases two-year-old lottery tickets instead of railway tickets, misplaces the baggage, and loses his family's accommodations; but there is something rather heroic, as well, in his refusal to show himself as perturbed, even under the threats of henpecking and heckling.

Another narrator afflicted with great troubles, but enduring them with Job-like suffering equanimity, is encountered in an earlier story, "Punch, Brothers, Punch" (first published as "Literary Nightmare," *Atlantic*, February 1876; collected in *Punch, Brothers, Punch! and Other Sketches*). Possessed by an infectious little rhyming jingle that he noticed in a newspaper–"Punch, brothers! punch with care!/Punch in the presence of the passenjare!"–Mark Twain is unable to complete any writing or behave normally until he has exorcised "those heartless rhymes" by passing them on to a friend, who in turn can only escape their curse by quoting the words to a group of unsuspecting college students. A Poe-like ending ("I was almost a lunatic when I got to Boston") dwells on the madness, hysteria, and grief engendered by this jingle.

Indeed, the affliction of human insanity recurs throughout Twain's fiction, generally for purposes of humor but sometimes otherwise. In chapter 70 of *Roughing It*, the narrator hears the sad tale of a Michigan preacher, driven mad by his correspondence with Horace Greeley and now living in the Sandwich Islands for his health. "It was easy to see that he was a gentle creature and that his madness had nothing vicious in it . . . . He was lost in his thought, or in his memories." His memories are of attempting to correspond with Greeley about the subject of turnips; the preacher had received a written reply that was so illegible as to offer a different interpretation each time it was perused–but none of them concerned turnips. Although Greeley finally sends a legible translation of his note, it arrives too late to alleviate "mental and bodily suffering and misunderstanding." Likewise, "Cannibalism in the Cars" (*Broadway* [London], November 1868; collected in *Mark Twain's Sketches, New and Old*) reports the tale of a man who lost his mind after being snowbound in a railroad car. His account of the episode claims that the passengers politely nominated and elected victims to serve as their food, but the conductor assures Twain that these horridly comic parliamentary procedures are merely figments of the man's deranged imagination.

Chapter 19 of *A Tramp Abroad*, chapter 53 of *Life on the Mississippi*, and "Doughface" (written in 1897 or 1902; published in *Mark Twain's Hannibal, Huck, and Tom*, 1969) all recount the terrible results of lighthearted practical jokes. In the *Life on the Mississippi* chapter and "Doughface," giddy people startle a friend with false-face masks and madness follows. In the story from *A Tramp Abroad*, "The Legend of Dilsberg Castle," Conrad von Geisberg's friends jestingly disguise themselves and convince him that he has slept, in the manner of Rip Van Winkle, in the haunted chamber of a castle while nearly half a century has passed; when they throw aside their disguises they find that Conrad has permanently become a "harmless madman." Twice Twain associated such sad transformations with the mining district of California. In "A Double Barrelled Detective Story" Jacob Fuller loses his grip on reality after being wrongly accused of mistreating Archy Stillman's mother. And in "The Californian's Tale" (*The First Book of the Author's Club*, 1893; collected in *The $30,000 Bequest and Other Stories*) Mark Twain's narrator is taken in by a madman's insistence that his beautiful young wife will soon return to their cabin on the Stanislaus River; only when other miners arrive to explain the circumstances does the narrator learn that the woman was captured by Indians who attacked her stagecoach: the afflicted Henry has buried his grief in the delusion that she will arrive home momentarily. Though written long after the vogue of Bret Harte's tales about California Forty-niners, Twain's story owes much to the sentimental tradition that "The Luck of Roaring Camp" and "How Santa Claus Came to Simpson's Bar" had explored. Twain's tale, however, is set in the twilight of these miners' lives; only a few die-hard inhabitants still reside in the Mother Lode cabins, and all about them the echoes of that pandemonium have long ago died away. This should be a bet-

ter story than it is. Twain unreels the tale with verve and every remnant of local-color features that he could recall, but the sentimentality of the miner's mournful existence and the melodramatic deed of the Indians spoils the mood for many modern readers.

Equally emotional but less troublesome for critics is the marvelous short work of fiction that first introduced Mark Twain to the audience of the *Atlantic Monthly*, "A True Story Repeated Word for Word as I Heard It" (November 1874; collected in *Mark Twain's Sketches, New and Old*), chosen by Twain's friend and supporter, editor William Dean Howells, as the ideal piece by which a more elite audience might make its acquaintance with Twain's talent. Aunt Rachel's tale of her slavery and woe, of her loss of husband and children, of her years of grief and hope, and, at last, of her reunion with her son Henry, is heavy with melodramatic and sentimental elements, but nevertheless it succeeds for readers willing to remember that these traits were considered marks of taste and refinement in nineteenth-century fiction. The evident artistry in the progressive physical elevation of Aunt Rachel ("now she towered above us, black against the stars") on the front porch of the farmhouse, the tag line ("I's one o' de old Blue Hen's Chickens, *I* is!"), and the repetition of identifying scars on Henry's forehead and wrist bear comparison with the stage-blocked scene of dramatic confrontation between Mrs. Slade and Mrs. Ansley in Edith Wharton's near-perfect "Roman Fever." Perhaps these stage movements in Twain's "A True Story" helped win the favor of Howells, who always had an interest in private theatricals and published plays himself. Twain's story, inspired by Aunty Cord, a black cook Clemens knew in Elmira, New York, ranks with his finest shorter compositions. Among other achievements "A True Story" demonstrates Twain's mastery of experimental techniques for reproducing southern black dialect as early as 1874, placing him midway in the evolution of this form that began with (among others) William Tappan Thompson in *Major Jones's Sketches of Travel* (1847), flourished with Irwin Russell, George Washington Cable, Joel Chandler Harris (especially in *Uncle Remus: His Songs and His Sayings*, 1880), and Mark Twain (in the speech of Jim and other black figures in *Huckleberry Finn*), and culminated in the short stories and novels of William Faulkner and various modern southern authors.

Clemens (left) and George Washington Cable (right) in Quincy, Illinois, 12 January 1885, visiting Lizzie Moffett, Mrs. Erasmus Mason Moffett, Ella Moffett, and Valentine Surghor (Clemens's relatives by marriage) during Clemens and Cable's lecture tour of 1884-1885 (collection of Samuel C. Webster, New York)

The unknowledgeable, inquiring narrator who opens "A True Story" belongs as well to a longstanding literary tradition employed by A. B. Longstreet and other southern frontier humorists and brought to a point of delicate refinement by Bret Harte, whose mincing, genteel personae fastidiously record the life and poker slang of brawling, earthy California mining camps in tales such as "The Iliad of Sandy Bar" (1870). Like his predecessors, Twain employed such a "frame" narrator to open and close what proved to be his most famous short story, "The Celebrated Jumping Frog of Calaveras County" (as "Jim Smiley and His Jumping Frog," *New York Saturday Press*, 18 November 1865; collected in *The Celebrated Jumping Frog of Calaveras County, and Other Sketches*). But there he wrought a rewarding innovation; instead of merely eliciting a sense of comic irony from the sharp cultural contrast between the arch, nettled, effete rhetoric of the easterner and the uneducated, meandering, folksy talk of Simon Wheeler, Twain injected a tone of indignant outrage into the unnamed narrator's introduction and conclusion. He does not wish to hear the interlinked chain of anecdotes to which

he is obliged to listen, and he takes the opportunity of the earliest interruption of Wheeler's monologue to make his escape. Thus the story works against itself from the inside out, and this tension partly accounts for its long popularity. Yet many first-time readers are vaguely disappointed in this frequently anthologized story about which they have heard so much. Its effects are subtle rather than rib tickling, and it hardly relies on any one line for its chief note of humor (although the stranger's observation that he "don't see no p'ints about that frog that's any better'n any other frog" carries the quail-shot weight in the latter section of the tale). But the fact is that an abundance of skillfully delivered touches informs the piece throughout–naming the animals Andrew Jackson and Dan'l Webster, recording a dog's discouraged demise after being pitted against another dog with no hind legs, inventing incongruous language and similes (the frog "hysted up his shoulders–so–like a Frenchman"). The story remains a dividing line for readers: either one sees the smiling humor behind it, or one misses it every time.

Appreciating "The Celebrated Jumping Frog" is crucial to fathoming much of Twain's fiction, because in general his introductory narrators belong to one of two types–men who eventually reveal themselves as capable and aggressive, as with the persona in "The Facts Concerning the Recent Carnival of Crime in Connecticut" (*Atlantic*, June 1876; collected in *A True Story, and The Recent Carnival of Crime*, 1877), and the increasingly appalled and incredulous but helpless variety, as in "A True Story." The second type of narrator often yields "his" control of the story to another person, someone who seems practically obsessed by the tale he will relate so earnestly (as in "Cannabilism in the Cars" and "The McWilliamses and the Burglar Alarm"). To this sort of tale Twain frequently added this hilarious ingredient: his frame narrator is a trapped listener, compelled to endure what gives the teller immense pleasure–and to him, commensurate anguish. "About Barbers" (*Galaxy*, August 1871; collected in *Mark Twain's Sketches, New and Old*) conveys an idea of this charade: Mark Twain fails to get the barber he wants, writhes under the painful scraping of a failure in the trade, and in the bargain must listen to the man brag about a little terrier that he owns. In an anecdote known as "The Man Who Put Up at Gadsby's" (chapter 26 of *A Tramp Abroad*), the victim is not Twain but instead Mr. Lykins, an office seeker in Washington, D.C. The newspaperman Riley "backed Mr. Lykins against an iron fence, buttonholed him, fastened him with his eye, like the Ancient Mariner, and proceeded to unfold his narrative . . . in . . . a wintry midnight tempest." This Simon Wheeler pattern of a caught-and-pinioned hearer would seem amusing to Mark Twain to the end of his writing career. A door-to-door salesman bends his ear in "The Canvasser's Tale" (*Atlantic*, December 1876; collected in *Punch, Brothers, Punch! and Other Sketches*): "Before I well knew how it came about, this one was telling me his history, and I was all attention and sympathy." The salesman's story concerns his wealthy uncle's peculiar taste in collecting "echoes" (a pastime that left his nephew penniless except for scattered echo ranges). A tale borrowed from the repertoire of southern frontier humorists somewhat jarringly interrupts chapter 36 in book 2 of Twain's exalted *Personal Recollections of Joan of Arc* (1896). The narrator fumes as "that simple old Laxalt sat up there and droned out the most tedious and empty tale one ever heard. . . . It was about old

Laxalt going to a funeral there at Domremy two or three weeks back." Laxalt tried to ride a young black bull to the Sunday funeral, but the bull "bellowed and reared and pranced," knocking over some beehives. Laxalt, the bull, and the bees "came roaring through the village like a hurricane, and took the funeral procession right in the centre, . . . every person with a layer of bees on him, and not a rag of that funeral left but the corpse." The disgusted narrator is nonplussed by Joan's amusement at Laxalt's straightforward account of the successive mishaps.

In 1867 Twain returned with Simon Wheeler as narrator of another tale, "Jim Wolfe and the Tom-cats" (*Californian*, 21 September 1867; collected in *Mark Twain's Speeches*, 1910); here again the hapless narrator "prepared to leave," recognizing "signs that he [Wheeler] was going to be delivered of another of his tiresome personal experiences–but I was too slow." The ensuing story recounts bashful Jim Wolfe's interruption of a girls' candy-pulling party when he slips off a roof in his nightshirt and lands "in them two dozen sassers of red-hot candy, and let off a howl that was hark f 'm the tomb!" Based on an actual incident when Jim Wolfe had been Sam Clemens's roommate, its telling also owes much to the patterns of southern frontier humor.

Now and then these great talkers are defeated in Mark Twain's short stories. Chapter 62 of *Roughing It*, for example, tells of the contest between "the old Admiral," a retired whaleman who "was a roaring, terrific combination of wind and lightning and thunder, and earnest, wholesouled profanity," and "a cheerful soul by the name of Williams." The admiral has an annoying habit of winning arguments by "inventing history, names, dates, and everything else necessary to make his point good," but Williams vanquishes him by resorting to the same methods of argumentation while pretending to flatter the admiral's memory; Williams "flooded him with invented history so sugar-coated with flattery and deference that there was no rejecting him. . . . From that time forward there was entire peace and serenity in the ship."

There are instances, however, where the introducing speaker has actually sought an opportunity to hear the narrative of a person renowned for fabricating a tale filled with lies and illogical half-truths. In chapter 53 of *Roughing It* Mark Twain and his Virginia City acquaintances watch solicitously whenever Jim Blaine drinks whiskey, always hoping that he will reach that perfect condition–"tranquilly, serenely, symmetrically drunk–not a hiccup to mar his voice, not a cloud upon his brain"–in which he sets out to tell the story of his grandfather's old ram but never reaches the point of his tale. Between Blaine's energetic launching ("I don't reckon them times will ever come again. There never was a more bullier old ram than what he was") and his drowsy slide into sleep while talking of William Wheeler (a name recalling Simon Wheeler) occurs deadpan artistry in a train of associative recollections about Miss Wagner's glass eye, undertaker Jacops's coffin, the Irishman's fall onto Uncle Lem, and the victim of a carpet factory. As in "The Celebrated Jumping Frog," the punch line of this series of absurdities never becomes clear, and the framing narrator realizes that he has been "sold" because his friends were well aware that Blaine was incapable of steering a direct course toward the objective of his story.

Sometimes, on the other hand, Mark Twain's narrators take the stance of active participants in their own stories, stepping aside for no one else and relishing the opportunity to relate their narrative. "The Facts Concerning the Recent Carnival of Crime in Connecticut" is one of the most entertaining in this line. Partaking of the Doppelgänger motif that shapes a dozen excellent short stories in English–Poe's "William Wilson" (1849), Robert Louis Stevenson's "Markheim" (1885), and Joseph Conrad's "The Secret Sharer" (1912)–Twain's droll tale matches an incorrigible hedonist against his dormant conscience, an abused alter ego whom he has reduced to the size and appearance of "a shrivelled, shabby dwarf," and whom he (with the timely arrival of his Aunt Mary) annihilates after a Socratic dialogue of the sort Twain favored in writings ranging from *Huckleberry Finn* to *What Is Man?* (1906).

Frequently the narrator figures in Twain's fiction find themselves disillusioned by the reality they encounter, especially in cases where they have imbibed heavily beforehand from the liquor of romance. In "A Day at Niagara" (*Buffalo Express*, 21 August 1869; collected in *Mark Twain's Sketches, New and Old*) the tourist-speaker extols the "dainty Indian beadwork" that can be purchased along its banks, then runs afoul of these merchants by trying to talk to them in the grandiloquent rhythms of Cooper's and Longfellow's Indians and the *ubi sunt* rhetoric common in the mid nineteenth century: "The paleface from beyond the great waters greets you all! War and pesti-

lence have thinned your ranks and destroyed your once proud nation. . . . Remember Uncas!" Disgusted, the Indians (who turn out to be Irish immigrants dressed in blankets) hurl the innocent narrator over the falls. The narrator is educated with similarly abrupt consequences in chapter 34 of *The Innocents Abroad*, in which, after dreaming "for years and years . . . of the wonders of the Turkish bath" and "the world-renowned Turkish coffee," Twain's persona is disillusioned when "a copper-colored skeleton" polishes him "with a coarse mitten" and invites him to drink coffee that is "black, thick, unsavory of smell, and execrable in taste." The best-known example of this pattern in Twain's fiction is chapter 24 of *Roughing It*, where the greenhorn Mark Twain makes a firm decision in Carson City: "I had quickly learned to tell a horse from a cow, and was full of anxiety to learn more. I was resolved to buy a horse." Acting on the tip of a man who is in fact the horse auctioneer's brother, the tenderfoot pays good money for a nag guaranteed to represent the species known locally as "a Genuine Mexican Plug." Finding to his dismay that the animal simply cannot be ridden, and only gobbles up costly hay, the narrator learns the truth from old Abe Curry: "Stranger, you've been taken in. Everybody in this camp knows that horse. Any child, any Injun, could have told you that he'd buck. . . . Why, you turnip, if you had laid low and kept dark, there's chances to buy an *American* horse for mighty little more than you paid for that bloody old foreign relic." Chagrined, the tenderfoot "made up my mind that if the auctioneer's brother's funeral took place while I was in the Territory I would postpone all other recreations and attend it."

On some occasions, to be sure, the traveler-victim is capable of retribution–particularly if he has help from his companions. Compelled to listen to smug descriptions of Italian antiquities delivered by smirking hired guides in chapter 27 of *The Innocents Abroad*, Mark Twain and his friends retaliate with absurd questions whose humor is lost on the baffled guides. The tourists criticize Christopher Columbus's penmanship in a letter from the explorer that is on display in Genoa. In Rome they take great amusement in inquiring, of every significant artifact, even of an Egyptian mummy, "Is–is he dead?"–a ridiculous refrain that became celebrated in Clemens's lifetime.

More often, however, the Mark Twain figure is the loser in these skirmishes with bitter experience. "Lost in the Snow," a self-contained story in chapters 31, 32, and 33 of *Roughing It,* chronicles the author's trip to Carson City in a snow-storm with Mr. Ballou and Mr. Ollendorff. Following Ollendorff's "instinct" rather than a compass, the party ends up making a huge circle in their own tracks. Attempting to light a fire without matches, "we broke more sticks and piled them, and once more the Prussian shot them into annihilation. Plainly, to light a fire with a pistol was an art requiring practice and experience, and the middle of a desert at midnight in a snow-storm was not a good place or time for the acquiring of the accomplishment." Convinced that they will perish, they apologize for their misdeeds and promise to give up their vices should they survive; the narrator lies down after "a last farewell" while "snow-flakes wove a winding sheet about my conquered body. Oblivion came. The battle of life was done." The sequel to these mock-heroic sentiments arrives in the concluding chapter, in which the inept travelers awaken to discover that they have camped only "fifteen steps" from a stagecoach station; disgusted and embarrassed, they surreptitiously return to their disowned vices of drinking, smoking, and playing cards. Twain's rendition of this humiliation stands among his superior stories dealing with the Far West. A less grandiose story in chapter 13 of *A Tramp Abroad* involves the same situation of being lost and circling throughout the night, but on a more modest scale. Ensconced at an old inn in Heilbronn, Germany, Mark Twain passes a restless night in his room: the soft noise of a mouse's gnawing disturbs him, a striking clock haunts him, and insomnia settles in upon him. Deciding to go for a walk, he stumbles about the room in vain efforts to locate his clothing. "I could not remember that there was much furniture in the room when I went to bed, but the place was alive with it now,—especially chairs,—chairs everywhere, —had a couple of families moved in, in the meantime?" After circling the room in total blackness for what seems hours, he finally knocks over a water pitcher, awakens his roommate (who shouts "murder" and "thieves"), and brings the landlord and his German guests running in their nightgowns. "I glanced furtively at my pedometer, and found I had made 47 miles," Twain adds.

The humor inherent in such vast exaggerations also fills chapter 37 of *A Tramp Abroad,* where, inspired by books recounting the exploits of fearless Alpine mountain climbers, Twain announces: "I WILL ASCEND THE RIFFEL-BERG." Forming a gigantic expedition of 198 people, the narrator hyperbolically recounts the supposed hardships he endures, once even stopping overnight because he lost his umbrella; at last, in chapter 38, he and his men complete the trek from Zermatt to the Riffelberg Hotel, taking seven days instead of the three hours normally estimated for tourists. "There were but seventy-five tourists at the hotel,—mainly ladies and little children,—and they gave us an admiring welcome which paid us for all our privations and sufferings."

This idea of "lying" for the sake of entertainment, together with questions about the morality of telling lies for any purpose whatever, had been staple topics for humorists earlier than and contemporary with Twain, but his writings focused on the subject more pervasively. When accused of lying about his bravery after being chased up a tree by a buffalo near the South Platte River, Twain's fellow stagecoach passenger George Bemis grows wrathful at the other men's "making themselves so facetious over it." Bemis proceeds to give his tall-tale version of the incident, averring that his horse outran dogs, jackrabbits, coyotes, and was "gaining on an antelope" when its saddle girth broke, throwing Bemis and his saddle toward "the only solitary tree there was in nine counties adjacent." Claiming that he was pursued thirty feet up the tree by the climbing buffalo bull, "his eyes hot, and his tongue hanging out," Bemis vows that he lassoed the bull, shot him in the face, and hung him from a limb. "I made up my mind," remarks Twain, "that if this man was not a liar he only missed it by the skin of his teeth." As he does with Markiss, king of the liars in the Sandwich Islands (chapter 77, *Roughing It*), Twain pretends that he truly wants to give this yarn spinner the benefit of the doubt but is troubled by a few inconsistencies. In "Travelling with a Reformer" (*Cosmopolitan,* December 1893; collected in *How to Tell a Story and Other Essays,* 1897), however, Twain broods about the ethics of a man who glibly tells lies in situations where the result will improve the conduct of public servants (the man threatens impertinent telegraph clerks and streetcar and railway conductors and brakemen that he will report their rudeness to his highly placed but nonexistent friends and relatives). This theme grows less lighthearted, indeed becomes burdensome, in a story resembling O. Henry's "The Last Leaf," titled "Was It Heaven? Or Hell?" (*Harper's Magazine,* December 1902; collected in *The*

Clemens in 1885 (courtesy of the Morse Collection, Yale University)

$30,000 Bequest and Other Stories). Two old-maid aunts fret about the morality of lying to the widow Margaret Lester and her sixteen-year-old daughter Helen, both lying near death with typhoid. But after a doctor called Christian convinces them that in some cases truth can be harmful and deceit beneficial, the aunts dutifully lie to each patient, assuring the one that the other is well, even forging notes from the dying mother to the dying daughter. Both women expire in peace, assured that their cherished relative is safe, but that night an angel visits the lying aunts, saying that he must report their misconduct to heaven, and leaving the reader to ponder whether the verdict will consign them to paradise or perdition.

Such unearthly visitants appear increasingly in Mark Twain's later fiction. In "The War Prayer" (first published in *Europe and Elsewhere*,

1923), accorded its first popularity by college-campus opposition to the Vietnam War, a white-haired stranger ascends to the pulpit, motions the minister aside, and lectures a startled congregation about the ulterior meaning of their prayer that their military forces shall be victorious in combat. In reality, he tells them, they are asking that God destroy the opposing troops and thereby "wring the hearts of their unoffending widows with unavailing grief" and cause "their little children to wander unfriended the wastes of their desolated land in rags and hunger and thirst." Ending on a note appropriate to warfare stories by Ambrose Bierce or Stephen Crane, "The War Prayer" concludes, "It was believed afterward that the man was lunatic, because there was no sense in what he said."

The story published as *The Mysterious Stranger* in 1916 (first as a serial in the May through November issues of *Harper's Monthly* and then as a Christmas gift book) has been revealed by John S. Tuckey and William M. Gibson to have been Albert Bigelow Paine's pastiche of four distinct manuscript versions, which naturally represent Mark Twain's most complete exploration of this situation. Three complete manuscript versions and the existing notes for a fourth were published for the first time in *Mark Twain's "Mysterious Stranger" Manuscripts* (1969). In the manuscript variant favored by many critics and teachers, "No. 44, The Mysterious Stranger," sixteen-year-old August Feldner, an apprentice printer in Eseldorf, Austria, befriends an arriving stranger who calls himself "Number 44, New Series 864,962." The historical setting (the date is 1490), the plot elements, and the character development work clumsily against one another in many portions of the story, but No. 44's supernatural wisdom and powers have an eerie fascination. He is a Tom Sawyer with genuine abilities of enchantment, and the scene in which he commands the great events of history to unreel themselves before August Feldner in reverse, culminating with an Assembly of the Dead, has undeniable force. In the "St. Petersburg Fragment" and "Schoolhouse Hill" Twain experimented with limning similar characters and incidents in the Hannibal-St. Petersburg of his boyhood; there are schoolyard bullies and classroom lessons. "The Chronicle of Young Satan" was an early effort to set the tale in Austria, this time in 1702; it concentrates on the church's brutal methods of enforcing thought control and conformist behavior, and on the foreordination of human actions. Owing to the wide availability of the posthumous pastiche now known as "The Mysterious Stranger" that Albert Bigelow Paine stitched together from these manuscripts, a version still widely reprinted and admired despite Twain's nonparticipation in its editing, this occult tale has drawn much attention during recent decades. It constitutes the major creative undertaking that survives from the irascible last years of Mark Twain.

This same Twain, who had once praised "the Arch-Fiend's terrible energy" after reading *Paradise Lost,* was capable of imagining the Satan figure's sarcasm in other circumstances than those depicted in "The Mysterious Stranger" variants. Satan tempts Adam and Eve in "That Day in Eden" and "Eve Speaks" (both first published in *Europe and Elsewhere*) and procures Mark Twain's soul—in exchange for investment advice—in "Sold to Satan" (first published in *Europe and Elsewhere*). In "Letters from the Earth" (first published in *Letters from the Earth,* 1962) an exiled Satan visits our world to study the human species, writing back a series of eleven letters to his former fellow archangels Michael and Gabriel. Mainly these missives trace the illogic apparent in a literal interpretation of the Bible, sifting through events surrounding the creation, the fall of Adam and Eve, Noah's ark (his family carried microbes, for "enough microbes had to be saved to supply the future races of men with desolating diseases"), the prophecies of Moses, and other incidents. Satan turns his scorn on man as well as God; all of the things that delight people on earth, including sexual intercourse, seem to be omitted from the human concept of eternal heaven, whereas loud singing and harp playing, not normally regarded as pleasant, are assuredly part of the regimen in the Christian hereafter. These salvos are often witty enough, and, although the epistles lack the plot structure ordinarily expected in a short story—relying instead on a chronological survey of Old Testament history—it is one of Twain's most diverting ventures into religious philosophy.

These mysterious-stranger figures inhabit much of Twain's fiction, and they do not always take the malevolent form of Satan. In "Appendix E" of *A Tramp Abroad,* "Legend of the Castles," two (mortal) twin brothers (another manifestation of Twain's character pairing) intervene benevolently to rescue the library of "the most renowned scholar in Europe," Franz Reikmann of Heidelberg. The scholar's daughter mistakenly in-

fers that one of the brothers is "Our Lady's Angel," one of "them that dwell above." Just as Hank Morgan becomes an interloper in Camelot in *A Connecticut Yankee,* so comparable mysterious strangers intercede in Twain's shorter fiction. In "You've Been a Dam Fool, Mary. You Always Was!" (first published in *Mark Twain's Fables of Man*) a millionaire cotton broker arrives in Rocky Hill, Wisconsin, just in time to save the reputation and blacksmith shop of his former partner, whose belongings are being auctioned off to pay his debts—and then astonishes the crowd by presenting the blacksmith with six hundred thousand dollars, his half of the assets of the firm they once owned jointly.

This notion of suddenly acquired wealth had a strong attraction for Mark Twain, in composition as in life. Two anecdotes in *Following the Equator* (1897), "Cecil Rhodes' Shark and His First Fortune" (chapter 13) and "The Joke That Made Ed's Fortune" (chapter 28), recount success stories: the former tells of Rhodes's advance notice that wool prices would climb, and the efficient use he made of this tip; the latter reports a practical joke that backfires when the victim unsuspectingly employs the forged introduction to Commodore Vanderbilt, an advantage that ultimately enables him to offer jobs to the wharfboat clerks in Memphis who dreamed up the prank. A short story, "The £1,000,000 Bank-Note" (*Century,* January 1893; collected in *The £1,000,000 Bank-Note and Other New Stories*), is equally optimistic. Henry Adams meets a pair of Twain's benevolent, mysterious strangers (brothers, it is worth noting) in London and accepts their challenge to survive in society with only a million-pound note, so large as to be virtually uncashable, in his possession. He not only dines and finds accommodations and clothes on the basis of merely appearing wealthy, but he also saves his friend Lloyd Hastings from financial ruin and woos and wins Portia Langham (whose name echoes Olivia Langdon's), a lovely English woman of twenty-two. The bank note becomes his wedding present from the eccentric brothers. In the same year, 1893, Mark Twain published another rags-to-riches fantasy, "Is He Living or Is He Dead?" (*Cosmopolitan,* September 1893; collected in *The Man That Corrupted Hadleyburg and Other Stories and Essays*). Its basic idea resembles a tale Twain published in 1869, "The Legend of the Capitoline Venus" (*Buffalo Express,* 23 October 1869; collected in *A Curious Dream, and Other Sketches,* 1872, and *Mark Twain's Sketches, New and Old*).

Four starving artists in Breton draw straws to select one of them who shall willingly pretend to die, so that the other three can market his paintings and fragmentary works for the inflated prices that posthumous fame invariably confers upon artists who have labored in poverty for a lifetime. François Millet is elected. He assumes the identity of Théophile Magnan, a silk manufacturer, while his fellow artists harvest the proceeds that predictably accrue after his "demise." All become wealthy from the enterprise.

In Twain's stories of the final decades there is a perceptible drift toward the forms of the fairy tale and the fable. The tendency toward fable is evident as early as "The Esquimau Maiden's Romance" (*Cosmopolitan*, November 1893; collected in *The Man That Corrupted Hadleyburg and Other Stories and Essays*), wherein Kalula, accused of stealing his prospective father-in-law's costly fish hook, is cast adrift on an iceberg, doomed; nine months later his beloved Lasca finds the fish hook in her hair, where it had landed when her father tossed it about in prideful display. In "Two Little Tales" (*Century*, November 1901; collected in *My Début as a Literary Person, with Other Essays and Stories*, 1903) a man learns that the way to deliver information to people in high places is simply to tell a close friend, who will tell a friend, and so on. When the emperor is cured of an illness, he traces the efficacious prescription to, a chimneysweep named Jimmy and rewards him. "The Death Disk" (*Harper's Magazine*, December 1901; collected in *My Début as a Literary Person*), set in Oliver Cromwell's England and indebted to Thomas Carlyle's historical narrative, concerns a military prisoner condemned to death. In Twain's story one of three prisoners will lose his life; the seven-year-old daughter of one of them, Colonel Mayfair, is told to give each man a disk—not knowing that the red one will signify immediate execution. The adoring daughter reserves the red one for her father, since it seems the prettiest; but at the conclusion she gains her father's release, for Cromwell, studying her, remembers his own daughter. A grimmer fable, "The Five Boons of Life" (*Harper's Weekly*, 5 July 1902; collected in *The $30,000 Bequest and Other Stories*), presents a fairy who offers a youth the choice of fame, love, riches, pleasure, or death, admonishing him that only one of the gifts has true value. The young man selects pleasure, then love, then fame, then riches—but all disappoint him. When he returns to beg for the last boon, the fairy has already given death away to a young child; conse-

quently the man must bear the agonies of old age.

Twain's "Extract from Captain Stormfield's Visit to Heaven" (*Harper's Magazine*, December 1907 and January 1908; collected in *The Mysterious Stranger and Other Stories*) contains parallels with these stories, though he worked at this tale in earlier decades. Stormfield, flying through space on a final cruise to heaven, meets friends and acquaintances as he goes, races a hell-bound comet, and enjoys the thirty-year trip. After difficulties with the head clerk in identifying his home port (earth is known as "The Wart" in the celestial realm), the captain provides a detailed vision of heaven, which seems to be organized along rational principles. For example, an unknown veterinarian from Tennessee is acclaimed there by adoring multitudes as the greatest poet in the universe–he merely lacked the circumstances necessary for realizing his potential. "Extract from Captain Stormfield's Visit to Heaven" exhibits such engaging candor and hearty gusto in the colorful central character, and such amusing twists on conventional Christian expectations regarding immortality, that it remains perennially popular. Fragmentary and diarylike, the satire resembles Twain's comic versions of certain Genesis events: "Extracts from Adam's Diary" (*Niagara Book*, 1893; separately published in 1904) and "Eve's Diary" (*Harper's Magazine*, December 1905; separately published in 1906). Two of Mark Twain's most underrated stories, these diaries record the innocent thoughts of the first humans as they get acquainted with their new world and each other. By turns domestic comedy and sentimental fantasy (Adam and Eve voice complaints about each other's habits but soon discover that they cannot bear to be parted), the stories follow the couple through their fall and into an existence of hunger, fear, and death that is made endurable only by each other's comforting presence. Various commentators have noted parallels between this Eden and Twain's fond remembrances of his family's halcyon Hartford years, and they have emphasized that in Twain's version of the banishment from paradise, Adam obviously benefits from abandoning his solitary existence and acknowledging, in a postscript to "Eve's Diary," that "wheresoever she was, *there* was Eden." While Twain's final moods could qualify him as an agnostic or occasionally even an atheist, his absorption with the Bible and its mythology was never ending, as this deft, affectionate burlesque illustrates; his blasphemy, if any, was his urge to rewrite biblical history and conceptualize Christian beliefs in less solemn, more charitable (and more commonsensical) terms.

The order of the universe that Mark Twain preferred would, among other things, endow with more dignity and reward with more mercy the nonhuman species of animal life. One of the earliest adumbrations of this theme, "Some Learned Fables for Good Old Boys and Girls" (first published in *Mark Twain's Sketches, New and Old*), registers the puzzlement of certain forest creatures who try to comprehend human civilization. (In their tendency to jump to conclusions on the basis of every individual piece of evidence, Twain seems to be spoofing the more excitable scientists of his day.) Twain published so many brief, perceptive sketches of animal behavior that within recent decades three anthologies have been compiled strictly from these writings. Because he was first and foremost a humorist, Twain generally employed anthropomorphism in these evocative delineations–unlike D. H. Lawrence, a poet who could seemingly penetrate an animal's scales or shell or feathers and imagine what its existence would be like on its own terms; for Twain the simile was generally mankind, but the results were empathetic.

Among the finest of Twain's contributions along this line was his vignette of the town dog pursuing the coyote in chapter 5 of *Roughing It*. A fuller tale, Twain's best-known venture into ornithology, begins by describing the ravens he encounters in the woods near Heidelberg on the Neckar River (chapter 2, *A Tramp Abroad*) and then swings into a recollection of Jim Baker's bluejay yarn, told in the next chapter of the travel narrative. The lead-in section is generally omitted from anthology versions, which is a pity, since it possesses a gentle charm of its own. The narrator wanders "down the columned aisles of the forest" near his hotel, meditating on the soothing effects of the "deep and mellow twilight [that] reigned in there, and also a silence so profound that I seemed to hear my own breathings." But this reverie amid natural scenes hardly resembles a poem by William Wordsworth or William Cullen Bryant, for after the speaker "stood ten minutes, thinking and imagining, and getting my spirit in tune with the place," a raven appears on a limb above him and proceeds to interrogate and scold the intruder into his woods. When another raven arrives, "the thing became more and more embarrassing. . . . They were nothing but ravens–I knew that . . . –and yet when even a

raven shouts after you, 'What a hat!' 'Oh, pull down your vest!' and that sort of thing, it hurts you and humiliates you, and there is no getting around it." This anecdote serves to introduce Jim Baker's views on the speech of "the beasts and the birds," together with Baker's opinion that "there's more *to* a bluejay than any other creature. He has got more moods, and more different kinds of feelings than other creatures. . . . Why *you* never see a bluejay get stuck for a word. No man ever did. They just boil out of him!" Following an energetic disquisition on the traits of bluejays, Baker tells as "a perfectly true fact about some bluejays" a splendidly contrived animal fable. Like the later "Californian's Tale" (1893), Baker's oral yarn is set in a mining camp long after the gold has played out and human society has moved away. In this relative isolation the bluejay who sets about the task of filling up a deserted log cabin with acorns assumes the proportions of a heroic protagonist; his speech and deeds become an absorbing source of entertainment and edification for the sole remaining miner. Gradually the jay's vernacular slang ("oh, no, this ain't no fat thing, I reckon!") competes with Baker's own talk for our attention. "The way he hove acorns into that hole for about two hours and a half was one of the most exciting and astonishing spectacles I ever struck," Baker declares admiringly. As in the tale of "The Celebrated Jumping Frog," there is no single hilarious punch line here–though there is a "nub," or "snapper," as Twain might say, in the Nova Scotia owl's laconic observation that "he couldn't see anything funny" about the bluejay's impossible mission, and Baker's quickly added aside that the same owl was "a good deal disappointed about Yo Semite, too"–but the humor quotient enlarges with every line for readers who can inwardly hear Baker's frivolous story.

Mark Twain set down dozens of memorable impressions of animal behavior, but most examples, like "Hunting the Deceitful Turkey" (*Harper's Magazine*, December 1906; collected in *The Mysterious Stranger and Other Stories*), lack essential features of short stories and remain sketches instead. One exception is the tall tale about Dick Baker's cat, Tom Quartz, as told in chapter 61 of *Roughing It*. Long after the cat's death, pocket miner Baker eulogizes its business and mining acumen: "He had more hard, natchral sense than any man in this camp." If the cat approved of the prospects of a quartz site, "he would lay down on our coats and snore like a steamboat till we'd struck the pocket, an' then get up 'n' superintend. He was nearly lightnin' on superintending." But when the miners turn to blasting powder in place of the old-fashioned pick and shovel, "he was down on it powerful–'n' always appeared to consider it the cussedest foolishness out. But that cat, you know, was *always* agin new fangled arrangements." His skepticism proves well-founded, because the careless Baker accidentally blows up a shaft where Tom Quartz is sleeping. After that "you might a blowed him up as much as three million times 'n' you'd never a broken him of his cussed prejudice agin quartz mining," says the slow-witted Dick Baker. A genteel narrator then concludes the narration, remarking on "the affection and the pride that lit up Baker's face when he delivered this tribute to the firmness of his humble friend of other days," and gratuitously adding that the touching story "will always be a vivid memory with me." The parallels with Twain's classic western yarning about the frog, the ram, and the bluejay are evident here–an initially rapt listener; a deadpan, masterful, but maundering talker; a disturbing sense of incredulity that overtakes the fictional hearer; a concluding effort by the first narrator to disclaim the tale and its teller.

One other animal narrative is closer in its tone and spirit to those of T. S. Eliot's *Old Possum's Book of Practical Cats* (1939) than to Twain's other animal writings. Around 1880 Mark Twain wrote "A Cat-Tale" (*Concerning Cats*, 1959; collected in *Letters from the Earth*), purportedly a juvenile story about cats once told to Susy and Clara Clemens, but mainly an exercise in finding words in the dictionary that begin with, or are puns on, the letters c-a-t. The mother cat is named Catasauqua ("because she lived in that region") and her "catlings" are called Cattaraugus and Catiline, and every word such as "caterwaul" and "cataract" and "catcall" duly makes its appearance in the course of this charming little tale, influenced by Jacob Abbott's Rollo books (1803-1879) and their demonstration of "how harmoniously gigantic language and microscopic topic go together." The persona's witty verbal sparring with his precocious children is exceptionally droll.

Two of Mark Twain's late efforts, now no longer preferred by either critics or readers, employed animals as narrators and dwelt on the cruelties of human attitudes and acts. "A Dog's Tale" (*Harper's Magazine*, December 1903; separate trade publication, 1904), inspired by Dr. John Brown's *Rab and His Friends* (1859), which Twain

referred to as a "pathetic and beautiful masterpiece," tells the story of an uncomplaining half-collie named Aileen Mavourneen that saves Mr. and Mrs. Gray's baby from a nursery fire and is rewarded by having her puppy used as the subject of painful vivisection investigating the causes of blindness. Soldier Boy, Buffalo Bill's horse, relates part of "A Horse's Tale" (*Harper's Magazine*, August and September 1906; separately published in 1907), which largely concerns General Alison's niece, Cathy, who frolics about as a nine-year-old tomboy at Fort Paxton. When Cathy falls off Soldier Boy and breaks her arm, he guards her from wolves until she is rescued by soldiers. After the general retires, he takes his niece and her horse to Spain, where Soldier Boy is stolen. Finally Cathy recognizes him in a bull-ring, where he has been gored fatally by a bull; as Cathy tries to comfort her beloved horse, the bull charges them and kills her. Neither of these saccharine stories was likely to enlarge Twain's reputation even in his own day; yet their publication satisfied urges within him that he no longer needed to repress after his literary standing finally seemed solid.

A great many of Twain's stories were immensely different from these tame tales; his training in writing journalistic sketches for audiences affected by the flush times of Mississippi steamboat travel and by the gold and silver fever left its mark in the form of stereotypical characters, melodramatic situations, casual violence, vulgar sights and odors. One situation, for example, recurrently came to his mind in various circumstances, and though he shaped it only a few times into a rounded short story, it evidently held a powerful grip on his memory and his imagination. In a life-threatening emergency a tight-lipped hero or heroine suddenly arises and takes charge of a milling crowd of people, singling out a ringleader and restoring order; this deed saves lives, rescues honor, and brings back a sense of normalcy to a scene of confusion. Sheriff Jack Fairfax faces down an unruly California mob in "A Double Barrelled Detective Story" (1902), for instance, saving the inept Sherlock Holmes from being burned alive. "Drop your hand, you parlor desperado," Fairfax commands the mob's leader, Shadbelly Higgins. Echoing the sentiments of Colonel Sherburn's speech in *Huckleberry Finn*, Fairfax disperses the crowd with sneering remarks: "If there's anything I do particularly despise, it's a lynching mob; I've never seen one that had a man in it . . . . Hunt your holes, you

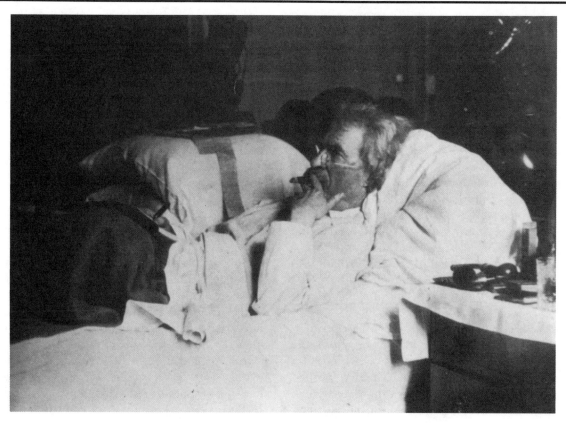

Clemens in 1904, photographed by his authorized biographer, Albert Bigelow Paine

scum!" This figure of moral strength and physical courage can be a woman as well as a man. In chapter 31 of *Roughing It*, stranded in an isolated log-cabin inn because of the flooded Carson River, the narrator and his companions are terrorized by a swaggering ruffian known as Arkansas, "who carried two revolvers in his belt and a bowie knife projecting from his boot, and who was always drunk." But when he begins shooting at the meek landlord, "the landlord's wife suddenly appeared in the doorway and confronted the desperado with a pair of scissors! Her fury was magnificent. . . . While the wondering crowd closed up and gazed, she gave him such another tongue-lashing as never a cowed and shamefaced braggart got before, perhaps!" The relieved narrator reports: "The lesson was entirely sufficient. The reign of terror was over, and the Arkansas domination broken for good." The manner in which this incident is told recalls the anecdote Mark Twain would include in an autobiographical recollection set down in 1890: the way his mother, Jane Lampton Clemens, confronted and vanquished a vicious Hannibal bully who was "chasing his grown daughter past cautious male citizens with a heavy rope in his hand."

In still another story that proves how powerfully Twain's imagination was stirred by this situation of a strong figure of lawful authority asserting himself against prevailing anarchy, Capt. Ned Blakely (another name for the perennial Captain Stormfield-Wakeman characters who populated Twain's notebooks and stories), his ship anchored in the Chincha Islands, learns that a bully named Bill Noakes has murdered Blakely's black mate. Even though Noakes has retreated to his own ship in the company of several other toughs, and despite the fact that "there were no courts and no officers; there was no government; the islands belonged to Peru, and Peru was far away," Blakely calmly readies the instruments of justice. "At nine o'clock at night he loaded a double-barreled gun with slugs, fished out a pair of handcuffs, got a ship's lantern, summoned his quartermaster, and went," merely explaining, "I'm going to march in on Noakes–and take him–and jug the other chaps." Boldly facing the gang, Blakely issues quiet instructions: "I'm Ned Blakely. I've got you under fire. Don't you move without orders–any of you. You two kneel down in the corner; faces to the wall–now. Bill Noakes, put these handcuffs on; now come up close." The next morning (after a pro forma trial) he hangs the ruffian from a tree in a nearby canyon, reading him four chapters of the Bible and saying, "There's few that would have took the pains with you that I have" (*Roughing It,* chapter 50).

At times Mark Twain indulged himself in producing stories with other themes that one seldom associates with his name. "The Belated Russian Passport" (*Harper's Weekly,* 6 December 1902; collected in *My Début as a Literary Person, with Other Essays and Stories*), in some respects merely another complaint about the slow-moving bureaucracy of governmental business, also emphasizes a curious feature about Alfred Parrish, a Yale student: "They used to call me Miss Nancy when I was a small chap, and I reckon I'm that yet—girlish and timorous, and all that. I ought to have *been* a girl!" Major Jackson talks the youth into an adventurous visit to Russia that risks Parrish's freedom and his life, since Jackson depends upon Parrish's passport catching up with them. A deus ex machina ending places Parrish in the office of a sympathetic secretary in the American legation who identifies the house Parrish once lived in by means of the painting that hung in the living room (although the reader can question whether the secretary is stretching the truth in claiming that he was the artist of that painting). One can see that Twain is preparing the reader for Parrish's helpless predicament by stressing, in turn-of-the-century fashion, Parrish's lack of masculinity, but when one recalls Huck Finn's adoption of the Sarah Mary Williams disguise in chapter 11 of *Huckleberry Finn,* this confusion of sexes here and elsewhere in his writings becomes intriguing. In "The $30,000 Bequest" (1904) there is a complete role reversal of the husband and wife; even their names are the opposite of what is expected: "It was an affectionate family, hence all four of its members had pet names. Saladin's was a curious and unsexing one—Sally; and so was Electra's—Aleck." Moreover, believing that they have inherited a large sum of money, the wife aggressively speculates in the stock market while the husband urges caution and patience. Only after she has lost the imaginary amount on Wall Street does Electra-Aleck resume her conventional sexual identity: "Then, and not till then, the man in her was vanquished, and the woman in her resumed sway." This teasing approach to the norms of human sexuality culminates in *Wapping Alice,* which was first published in 1981, as a limited-edition pamphlet. There a woman from the Wapping district of Lon-

don confesses to her employer, Mr. Jackson, that she has been disguising herself in men's clothing in order to go abroad with a young Swedish carpenter whom she has been hiding in the house. Mr. Jackson summons a minister and compels the young man to marry Wapping Alice forthwith; after the groom has reluctantly said his vows and kissed the bride, Mr. Jackson finds out from another servant that Wapping Alice is in fact a male, who has arranged the mock ceremony for the fun of it.

Even more daring (for their time) than these liberties with gender divisions were Twain's several excursions into the field of mildly scatological or lewd literature. His compositions in this realm seem inoffensively off-color to most readers today. Twain's *"1601" Conversation, As It Was by the Social Fireside, in the Time of the Tudors* (privately printed as a pamphlet in 1880) goes further toward being a bonafide short tale than his other sketches of this sort. Queen Elizabeth's cupbearer keeps a journal like Samuel Pepys's, and in this "1601" excerpt he records the conversation of five authors—William Shakespeare, Francis Bacon, Ben Jonson, Francis Beaumont, and Sir Walter Raleigh—with five ladies, in the presence of the queen. As in *A Connecticut Yankee,* Twain is intent upon reminding his readers that surviving records suggest that during the reigns of early monarchs, even the Tudors, people in the royal court talked very little like the prim, sexless shadows whom later schoolteachers made them out to be. In this story the guffaws, lusty and loud, are apt to be provoked by flatulence or sexual innuendos. The humor derives largely from the erotic language emanating from this esteemed company, and from the cupbearer's disgust at having to listen to such bawdy rubbish.

Among the stories that fully display the rawness of Twain's western concepts of comedy might be mentioned "The Invalid's Story" (first published in *The Stolen White Elephant* as part of "Some Rambling Notes of an Idle Excursion"), a recital by a man who is only forty-one but who appears to be sixty. Two years before he was asked to take the body of his deceased friend John B. Hackett to Wisconsin; on the journey the pinebox coffin was accidentally switched with a box of rifles, and someone placed a package of ripe Limburger cheese on the top of the shipment of guns. The coarser elements of frontier humor come to the fore: Twain's narrator smells the cheese ("a most evil and searching odor") in the express car where he is riding with a freight dispatcher and attributes the malodorousness to "my poor departed friend." In stories like this one, modern readers can begin to fathom why a few of Twain's contemporary critics regarded his literature as hopelessly unrefined. The baggageman's comments—"the Governor wants to travel alone, and he's fixed so he can out-vote us"—grow increasingly explicit as the two men vacate the interior of the car in favor of an exposed platform. In view of the unsavory premise for this tall tale, it is a tribute to the redeeming qualities of Twain's vernacular genius that some faint humor actually emerges from the conclusion, in which the narrator explains how he found out about the presence of the cheese. "Frozen and insensible" from riding in a winter storm on the open platform, however, he sinks into a comatose lethargy: "The news was too late to save *me;* imagination had done its work, and my health was permanently shattered."

Nearly as comic ad nauseam is Twain's "A Curious Dream, Containing a Moral" (*Buffalo Express*, 30 April and 7 May 1870; collected in *A Curious Dream; and Other Sketches* and *Mark Twain's Sketches, New and Old*), in which the narrator dreams of encountering a parade of moldy skeletons; they are evacuating a dilapidated cemetery, dismayed that their descendants should permit the burial plots to grow so unkempt, the monuments so tottering. Ghostly visions also appear to people in Twain's "The Golden Arm," his version of a black folktale included in "How to Tell a Story" (*Youth's Companion*, 3 October 1895; collected in *How to Tell a Story and Other Essays*); "A Ghost Story" (*Buffalo Express*, 15 January 1870; collected in *Mark Twain's Sketches, New and Old*); and "Ghost Life on the Mississippi" (*Pacific Coast Spectator*, Autumn 1948). The most memorable of Twain's supernatural tales is overheard by Huck Finn when he visits a raft to find out whether Cairo is nearby (the passage eventually omitted from *Huckleberry Finn* and published instead in chapter 3 of *Life on the Mississippi*.) Huck listens breathlessly as a keelboatman named Ed recounts the story of Dick Allbright, a river rafter who was pursued by a barrel containing the body of a baby he had murdered. The chaffing that Ed receives from his friends at the conclusion of his tale is testimony to the chilling efficacy of his rendition: " 'Say, boys,' says Bill, 'less divide it up. Thar's thirteen of us. I can swaller a thirteenth of the yarn, if you can worry down the rest.' "

The absurdities foisted off on the befuddled newspaperman in "An Encounter with an In-

terviewer" (*Lotus Leaves*, 1875; collected in *Punch, Brothers, Punch! and Other Sketches*) include assertions that the narrator is 183 years old, that he is actually dead, and that he attended Aaron Burr's funeral. "Aurelia's Unfortunate Young Man" (*Californian*, 22 October 1864; collected in *The Celebrated Jumping Frog*) emphasizes the disfigurations suffered by Williamson Caruthers of New Jersey. Whether in all such stories Mark Twain was being unnecessarily vulgar or was acting as an advance guard for the realism movement that ultimately won for American literature the freedom from restraint and decorum that writers enjoyed thereafter, at least one of Twain's jokes about deaths and burial—Buck Fanshaw's funeral in chapter 47 of *Roughing It*—strikes almost every reader as unequivocally funny. "A committee of one was deputed to call on the minister, a fragile, gentle, spirituel new fledgling from an Eastern theological seminary, and as yet unacquainted with the ways of the [Nevada] mines." The dialogue between Scotty Briggs, "a stalwart rough," and the "pale theological student" has long been cited as an epitome of the clash of cultural modes. Indeed, the slang-talking Scotty can barely make himself understood to the baffled minister. Asking for "the head clerk of the doxology-works next door," Scotty merely receives the reply: "I am the shepherd in charge of the flock whose fold is next door.... The spiritual adviser of the little company of believers whose sanctuary adjoins these premises." Taken aback, Scotty says, "You rather hold over me, pard. I reckon I can't call that hand. Ante and pass the buck." Not even Bret Harte, with his poker slang in "Tennessee's Partner" (1869) and other mining-camp stories, had the inspiration of depicting the comic misunderstandings that could result from a forced conversation of two men accustomed to different rhetorical levels. They cannot even agree on the terminology for what the minister will perform; Scotty asks him "to help plant" Buck Fanshaw; the startled young minister guesses, "Preach the funeral discourse? Assist at the obsequies?" The narrator of this yarn carefully remains in the background, taking neither man's side, but the proportion of paragraphs given over to Scotty's speech, "riddled with slang," indicates that his sympathies lie with the more colorful speaker.

Although a large number of Twain's short stories were based partially on incidents in his personal life, some are more explicitly autobiographical than most. Indeed, the wavering line between fact and fiction is hard to discern in "The Private History of a Campaign That Failed" (*Century*, December 1885; collected in *Merry Tales*), a serio-comic piece in which Twain claims that the Confederate militia band he joined in 1861 killed a stranger who "was not in uniform, and was not armed," and that they were frightened into the dissolution of their volunteer group by the approach of Ulysses S. Grant and his Union force. Exhorted by the "gunpowder and glory" speech of Colonel Ralls, a veteran of the Mexican War, the youths undergo a series of discouraging and demeaning setbacks that "took the romance all out of the campaign, and turned our dreams of glory into a repulsive nightmare." The narrator resolves to leave the war behind, "but there were those among us who afterward learned the grim trade; learned to obey like machines; became valuable soldiers." Anticipating Amborse Bierce, Stephen Crane, Thomas Hardy, and twentieth-century commentators, Twain concludes that "all war must be just that—the killing of strangers against whom you feel no personal animosity; strangers whom, in other circumstances, you would help if you found them in trouble."

Since the majority of literary critics still values the longer narrative form of the novel in preference to any writer's ventures in the field of short fiction, even Mark Twain's best stories are likely to remain in the shadow of his successful novels. Yet the variety and finesse in his stories ensure their continuing popularity among those readers willing to approach nineteenth-century short works, and literary historians and critics will discover and rediscover in these works many sources for, and echoes of, the finest passages in *Huckleberry Finn* and his other novels. Indeed, in his novels as in his travel narratives, Twain reveals himself as brilliant chiefly when composing episodically, in the manner of the short story. While he eventually learned the craft of connecting these discrete units into a larger narrative, he will always be, because of his predilection and his talent, a writer whose masterly achievements can be adequately appreciated on the basis of tales and excerpts collected in anthologies. It is rare for an author's works to show to advantage in that miscellaneous format, devoid of their surrounding original context, but Twain's short pieces shine there unclouded.

Letters:

Mark Twain's Letters, 2 volumes, edited by Albert Bigelow Paine (New York: Harper, 1917);

Mark Twain-Howells Letters, 2 volumes, edited by Henry Nash Smith and William M. Gibson (Cambridge: Harvard University Press, 1960);

Mark Twain's Letters to His Publishers, edited by Hamlin Hill (Berkeley: University of California Press, 1967);

Mark Twain's Correspondence with Henry Huttleston Rogers, 1893-1909, edited by Lewis Leary (Berkeley: University of California Press, 1969);

Mark Twain's Letters, Volume 1, 1853-1866, edited by Edgar M. Franch, Michael B. Frank, and Kenneth M. Sanderson (Berkeley: University of California Press, 1988).

Bibliographies:

Merle Johnson, *A Bibliography of the Works of Mark Twain, Samuel Langhorne Clemens: A List of First Editions in Book Form and of First Printings in Periodicals and Occasional Publications of His Varied Literary Activities*, revised and enlarged edition (New York & London: Harper, 1935);

Thomas A. Tenney, *Mark Twain: A Reference Guide* (Boston: G. K. Hall, 1977);

Alan Gribben, "Removing Mark Twain's Mask: A Decade of Criticism and Scholarship," *ESQ: Journal of the American Renaissance*, 26 (1980): 100-108, 149-171;

William M. McBride, *Mark Twain: A Bibliography of the Collections of the Mark Twain Memorial and the Stowe-Day Foundation* (Hartford, Conn.: McBride/Publisher, 1984).

Biographies:

Albert Bigelow Paine, *Mark Twain: A Biography*, 3 volumes (New York & London: Harper, 1912);

Justin Kaplan, *Mr. Clemens and Mark Twain* (New York: Simon & Schuster, 1966);

Hamlin Hill, *Mark Twain: God's Fool* (New York: Harper & Row, 1973);

Everett Emerson, *The Authentic Mark Twain: A Literary Biography of Samuel L. Clemens* (Philadelphia: University of Pennsylvania Press, 1984).

References:

Frederick Anderson, ed., *Mark Twain: The Critical Heritage* (Boston: Routledge & Kegan Paul, 1971);

Howard G. Baetzhold, *Mark Twain and John Bull: The British Connection* (Bloomington: Indiana University Press, 1970);

Gladys Bellamy, *Mark Twain as a Literary Artist* (Norman: University of Oklahoma Press, 1950);

Edgar M. Branch, *The Literary Apprenticeship of Mark Twain* (Urbana: University of Illinois Press, 1950);

Louis J. Budd, *Mark Twain: Social Philosopher* (Bloomington: Indiana University Press, 1962);

Pascal Covici, Jr., *Mark Twain's Humor: The Image of a World* (Dallas: Southern Methodist University Press, 1962);

James M. Cox, *Mark Twain: The Fate of Humor* (Princeton: Princeton University Press, 1966);

Beverly R. David, *Mark Twain and His Illustrators*, volume 1 (Troy, N.Y.: Whitston, 1986);

Robert L. Gale, *Plots and Characters in the Works of Mark Twain*, 2 volumes (Hamden, Conn.: Archon, 1973);

William M. Gibson, *The Art of Mark Twain* (New York: Oxford University Press, 1976);

Alan Gribben, *Mark Twain's Library: A Reconstruction*, 2 volumes (Boston: G. K. Hall, 1980);

Susan K. Harris, *Mark Twain's Escape from Time: A Study of Patterns and Images* (Columbia: University of Missouri Press, 1982);

Sholom J. Kahn, *Mark Twain's Mysterious Stranger: A Study of the Manuscript Texts* (Columbia: University of Missouri Press, 1978);

Sydney J. Krause, *Mark Twain as Critic* (Baltimore: Johns Hopkins University Press, 1967);

E. Hudson Long and J. R. LeMaster, *The New Mark Twain Handbook* (New York: Garland, 1985);

Kenneth S. Lynn, *Mark Twain and the Southwestern Humorists* (Boston: Little, Brown, 1959);

William R. Macnaughton, *Mark Twain's Last Years as a Writer* (Columbia: University of Missouri Press, 1979);

Elizabeth McMahan, ed., *Critical Approaches to Mark Twain's Short Stories*, National University Publication Series (Port Washington, N.Y.: Kennikat Press, 1981);

Robert Regan, *Unpromising Heroes: Mark Twain and His Characters* (Berkeley: University of California Press, 1966);

Forrest G. Robinson, *In Bad Faith: The Dynamics of Deception in Mark Twain's America* (Cam-

bridge: Harvard University Press, 1986);

Franklin R. Rogers, *Mark Twain's Burlesque Patterns* (Dallas: Southern Methodist University Press, 1960);

David R. Sewell, *Mark Twain's Languages: Discourse, Dialogue, and Linguistic Variety* (Berkeley: University of California Press, 1987);

David E. E. Sloane, *Mark Twain as a Literary Comedian*, Southern Literary Studies Series (Baton Rouge: Louisiana State University Press, 1979);

Henry Nash Smith, *Mark Twain: The Development of a Writer* (Cambridge: Belknap Press of Harvard University Press, 1962);

William C. Spengemann, *Mark Twain and the Backwoods Angel: The Matter of Innocence in the Works of Samuel L. Clemens* (Kent, Ohio: Kent State University Press, 1966);

Albert E. Stone, Jr., *The Innocent Eye: Childhood in Mark Twain's Imagination* (New Haven: Yale University Press, 1961);

John S. Tuckey, *Mark Twain and Little Satan: The Writing of "The Mysterious Stranger"* (West Lafayette: Purdue University Press, 1963);

Tuckey, ed., *Mark Twain's "The Mysterious Stranger" and the Critics* (Belmont, Cal.: Wadsworth, 1968);

Edward Wagenknecht, *Mark Twain: The Man and His Work*, revised and enlarged edition (Norman: University of Oklahoma Press, 1967);

Dennis Welland, *Mark Twain in England* (Atlantic Highlands, N.J.: Humanities Press, 1978);

James D. Wilson, *A Reader's Guide to the Short Stories of Mark Twain* (Boston: G. K. Hall, 1987).

Papers:

The major collections of Clemens's papers are at the Bancroft Library, University of California, Berkeley; the Beinecke Library, Yale University; the New York Public Library; the Mark Twain Memorial and the Stowe-Day Foundation, Hartford, Connecticut; the Library of Congress; the Houghton Library, Harvard University; the Buffalo and Erie County Public Library; the Harry Ransom Humanities Research Center, University of Texas at Austin; the Mark Twain Museum, Hannibal, Missouri; the Vassar College Library; and the Alderman Library, University of Virginia. A research facility was established in 1983: the Center for Mark Twain Studies at Quarry Farm, Elmira College.

Rose Terry Cooke

(17 February 1827-18 July 1892)

Josephine Donovan
University of Maine

See also the Cooke entry in *DLB 12: American Realists and Naturalists.*

BOOKS: *Poems by Rose Terry* (Boston: Ticknor & Fields, 1861);

Happy Dodd; Or, "She Hath Done What She Could" (Boston: Hoyt, 1878);

Somebody's Neighbors (Boston: Osgood, 1881);

A Lay Preacher (Boston: Congregational Sunday-School and Publishing Society, 1884);

The Deacon's Week (New York & London: Putnam's, 1885);

Root-Bound and Other Sketches (Boston: Congregational Sunday-School and Publishing Society, 1885);

The Sphinx's Children and Other People's (Boston: Ticknor, 1886);

No (New York: Phillips & Hunt/Cincinnati: Cranston & Stowe, 1886);

Poems (New York: Gottsberger, 1888);

The Old Garden (Boston: Prang, 1888);

Steadfast: The Story of a Saint and a Sinner (Boston: Ticknor, 1889; London: Trübner, 1889);

Huckleberries Gathered from New England Hills (Boston & New York: Houghton, Mifflin, 1891);

Little Foxes (Philadelphia: Altemus, 1904).

Collection: *How Celia Changed Her Mind and Selected Stories,* edited by Elizabeth Ammons (New Brunswick, N.J.: Rutgers University Press, 1986).

OTHER: "Harriet Prescott Spofford" and "Harriet Beecher Stowe," in *Our Famous Women. An Authorized Record of the Lives and Deeds of Distinguished American Women of Our Times* (Hartford: A. D. Worthington/Chicago: A. G. Nettleton, 1884), pp. 521-538, 581-601.

PERIODICAL PUBLICATIONS:
FICTION
"The Mormon's Wife," *Putnam's Monthly,* 5 (June 1855): 641-649;

Rose Terry Cooke

"Parson Field's Experience," *Putnam's Monthly,* 7 (April 1856): 420-427;

"Betsey Clark," *Putnam's Monthly,* 8 (August 1856): 124-133;

"Peter Flint's Story," *Putnam's Monthly,* 9 (January 1857): 44-48;

"Joe's Courtship," *Putnam's Monthly,* 9 (May 1857): 484-494;

"My Visitation," *Harper's Monthly,* 17 (July 1858): 232-239;

"Three of Us," *Atlantic Monthly,* 2 (July 1858): 139-150;

"Lizzie Griswold's Thanksgiving," *Atlantic Monthly,* 3 (March 1859): 282-289;

"The Ring Fetter: A New England Tragedy," *Atlantic Monthly,* 4 (August 1859): 154-170;

"Tenty Scran'," sometimes attributed to Elizabeth Stuart Phelps, *Atlantic Monthly,* 6 (November 1860): 587-601;

"A Woman," *Atlantic Monthly,* 10 (December 1862): 694-707;

"The West Shetucket Railroad," *Independent,* 24 (12 September 1872): 2;

"Number Two," *Harper's Monthly,* 47 (September 1873): 571-578;

"A Lay Preacher," *Independent,* 26 (24 September 1874): 1-4;

"Knoware," as B. Munn Chowson, *Harper's Monthly,* 58 (December 1878): 37-47;

"One of Them," *Independent,* 31 (20 November 1879): 3-5.

NONFICTION

"A Letter to Mary Ann," *Sunday Afternoon,* 3 (January 1879): 79-83;

"One More Letter to Mary Ann," *Sunday Afternoon,* 3 (August 1879): 752-755;

"Women's Views of Divorce," *North American Review,* 150 (January 1890): 123-128.

Rose Terry Cooke, together with her sister Connecticut writer Harriet Beecher Stowe, was a pioneer in the genre of the New England local-color short story, writing some of the earliest examples of American realistic fiction. While her overall achievement is uneven, her best stories rank among the finest short fiction.

Born to a distinguished Connecticut family, Rose Terry enjoyed a relatively privileged childhood. Her mother, Anne Wright Hurlbut, was the daughter of John Hurlbut, a shipbuilder who sailed on the first New England ship to circumnavigate the globe. Rose's father, Henry Wadsworth Terry, was on his maternal side a descendant of the New England Wadsworth family to which poet Henry Wadsworth Longfellow also belonged. Her paternal grandfather, Nathaniel Terry, was president of a Hartford bank and a member of the U.S. Congress. Cooke dedicated her novel *Happy Dodd* (1878) to her mother for encouraging her to write and in recognition of the hardships her mother endured–which suggests that her mother may have been a model for the many oppressed women characters that appear in Cooke's stories. Harriet Prescott Spofford says that Cooke's mother was "delicate" and "suffered from a morbid conscience," while her father was "generous . . . and open-hearted."

Rose was born on 17 February 1827 on a farm near Hartford. When she was six the family moved into the Wadsworth mansion in Hartford. Never in robust health, she, nevertheless, under her father's tutelage, developed an extensive knowledge of and love for nature, which she was to use effectively in her fiction. Cooke's precise and realistic description of local vegetation became a hallmark of the local-color school. Beyond realistic description Cooke forged strikingly original metaphors from these materials. In "Love," an 1857 story, for example, the narrator describes the psychic recovery of one defeated character as follows: "But now she acted for all the world like my scarlet runner that Old Red trod acrost one day . . . and crushed . . . into the mud; and there it lay . . . till one of the feelers got blowed against the pickets, and cotched hold, and lifted itself up, ring by ring, till the whole fence post was red with its blows, and covered with green leaves." The sophistication of Cooke's figurative language is one of her great contributions to local-color literature; she helped to establish the literary integrity of the genre.

In 1843 Rose Terry graduated from the Hartford Female Seminary, a school founded in 1823 by Catharine Beecher, who was its director until 1831. Like Harriet Beecher Stowe, who had attended and taught at the seminary from 1824 to 1832, Rose Terry studied under the influential John Pierce Brace, who in keeping with the seminary's philosophy advocated a liberal "feminized" kind of Christianity, undoubtedly nurturing her anti-Calvinism, which became a central theme in her fiction. She joined the Congregational church in 1843.

For a while after her graduation Terry taught school, first in Connecticut and then in Burlington, New Jersey, where she also worked as a governess in the family of William Van Rensselaer, a Presbyterian minister. In 1848 an inheritance from a great uncle allowed her to give up teaching and devote her time to writing poetry and fiction, a practice begun in childhood, and to keeping house in Hartford. Her first publication, a poem called "Trailing Arbutus," appeared 26 April 1851 in the *New York Daily Tribune* under the initials A. W. H. (her mother's).

According to Spofford, Terry published her first story in 1845 in *Graham's Magazine.* There are no stories attributed to Rose Terry in that volume of the magazine; however, "Cousin Matthew" by "Enna Duval" is a possible candidate. *Graham's Magazine* from 1845 to 1855 contains several stories by Enna, Edna, or Emma Duval, with the minor variation in the first name suggesting that it is a pseudonym. The name is not listed in any standard bibliographies of American literature. While these stories are not conclusively in the style or format of the mature Rose Terry Cooke, they do bear some traces that are characteristic–notably a tendency to begin *ab ovo* and an interest in "wild, passionate" feeling (to quote from "Cousin Matthew"). It seems possible, if not probable, that Terry published fiction under this pseudonym at least a decade before her first acknowledged story appeared.

"The Mormon's Wife," which Jean Downey, Cooke's bibliographer, lists as Cooke's first story, appeared in the June 1855 issue of *Putnam's Monthly*. Rose Terry was then twenty-eight. The following year her younger sister, Alice, married, and because she remained in ill health after the birth of two children, Rose Terry took over the responsibility of rearing them. Alice later died.

Another of her early stories, "Sally Parson's Duty," was accepted by editor James Russell Lowell for the first issue of the *Atlantic Monthly* (November 1857). The *Atlantic* was to become a major force in the growth of local-color realism, and Cooke was encouraged by a series of *Atlantic* editors to cultivate her realistic bent. The central character of "Sally Parson's Duty" (collected in *The Sphinx's Children and Other People's*, 1886), for example, is depicted weeding onions in the garden, something no "heroine" of then-popular romantic fiction would do, as Cooke herself noted.

Lowell's successor, James T. Fields, who edited the *Atlantic* from July 1861 to July 1871, became a personal friend and adviser to the young writer. Yet perhaps even greater was the connection between Terry and Fields's wife, Annie Adams Fields. The Fieldses' Charles Street townhouse in Boston had already become a gathering place for literary people by the time Cooke met them, and she visited the Fieldses often, corresponding with them regularly. Eventually Annie Fields's circle included most of the major women writers of the day, and it is probably through her that Cooke came to know and to influence Sarah Orne Jewett, now considered the greatest of the New England local colorists.

On 16 April 1873 Rose Terry married Rollin H. Cooke, an iron manufacturer in Litchfield County, Connecticut, who was a widower with two daughters. After her marriage Rose resided in Winsted, Connecticut, where her husband worked as a bank clerk. They had no children.

It appears that Rollin Cooke was either incompetent or ill-starred. In 1885 Rose Cooke wrote her editor Benjamin Ticknor that they were in desperate financial straits because of her father-in-law's business failure, which absorbed all of Rollin's (and some of her) assets. In 1887 the couple moved to Pittsfield, Massachusetts, where Rollin had found work, but by 1889 Rose was again writing Ticknor that Rollin had failed in his business venture, that all her property was gone, and that she would do any kind of hackwork to bring in money. Weakened, undoubtedly, by these stresses, Rose Terry Cooke became ill with pneumonia, which left her an invalid, and died on 18 July 1892 after a series of bouts with influenza.

Cooke produced nearly two hundred stories, more than two hundred poems, and two novels. Her realistic style was undoubtedly shaped by the literary winds of the time, but it was also rooted in her character. Of a down-to-earth, practical bent, she–like Stowe–strongly rejected the artificiality of the sentimental romance and in particular condemned its insipid, angelic heroines. In a pointed preface to an early story, "Miss Lucinda" (*Atlantic Monthly*, August 1861; collected in *Somebody's Neighbors*, 1881), Cooke wrote: "So forgive me once more, patient reader, if I offer to you no tragedy in high life, no sentimental history of fashion and wealth, but only a little story about a woman who could not be a heroine." True to her principles, Cooke created some of the first realistic women characters in American literature and was perhaps the first writer to depict New England life as it was–bleak, deprived, and difficult. Cooke's realistic fiction has an air of grim authenticity, and at times her view of New England anticipates that of a later local colorist, Mary E. Wilkins Freeman, or that of Edith Wharton in her tragedy of New England life *Ethan Frome* (1911). On the other hand Cooke also displayed a wry humor. Her use of authentic New England dialect, which heralded a local-color trademark, often created humorous effects. Her letters also reveal a sardonic wit.

Cooke's development as a writer was uneven. Many of her early stories err in the direction of sentimental moralism and have not withstood the test of time. Nevertheless, even as early as the 1850s, Cooke produced several stories that stand among the first examples of local-color realism in American literature. They depict authentically local characters with characteristically local names (Aunt Huldah Goodwin, Alonzo Masters, Achsah Root), who speak in dialect and live in realistic New England settings. Four of these stories are set in a mythical but realistic Connecticut village named Cranberry and include some of the same characters. "The Mormon's Wife" is narrated by a Parson Field, who tells his own story in "Parson Field's Experience" (*Putnam's Monthly*, April 1856), "Love" (*Putnam's Monthly*, March 1857), and "Joe's Courtship" (*Putnam's Monthly*, May 1857). In "Love," the only one of these stories to be collected in one of her books (*Huckleberries Gathered from New England Hills*, 1891), Cooke developed what became a standard local-color narrative structure; several local characters sit around reminiscing as they perform a chore together, in this case sorting apples. After initial chitchat one of the characters is sparked to narrate the central story. Many such local-color stories have provided valuable historical documentation of regional customs.

Cooke's early stories set forth two of her central themes: the oppression of wives by their husbands and the generally deleterious effect of Calvinism on human relations. "The Mormon's Wife" recounts the alienation and death of a woman whose husband converted to Mormonism. "The Ring Fetter: A New England Tragedy," an early *Atlantic Monthly* story (August 1859), is a grim indictment of child and wife abuse in which the female character is driven to commit suicide. The story includes a lengthy and angry aside in which Cooke castigates the authors of sentimentalist novels for "happily" ending their works at the moment of the wedding when the real stories begin after the vows are taken—another of Cooke's early calls for realism in fiction.

"Parson Field's Experience" criticizes a rigid and unreasonable adherence to Calvinist doctrine, which in this case destroys the possibility of love when a woman rejects a suitor because he has not professed the faith. "Uncle Josh" (*Putnam's Monthly*, September 1857; collected in *Somebody's Neighbors*) includes two women characters whose deaths are attributable to emotional starvation. Living by strictly puritanical standards, they have repressed their own desires and receive little sustenance from their husbands.

"Tenty Scran'" (*Atlantic Monthly*, November 1860), a work sometimes attributed to Elizabeth Stuart Phelps (though Phelps denied authorship), is undoubtedly a Cooke story. An early adumbration of Mary E. Wilkins Freeman's classic "A

New England Nun," it is set in Deerfield, Connecticut, and concerns Content Scranton, who waits twenty years for her lover to return from sea. When he does, she finds he has become repugnant (he is a "coarse, red-faced" man who swears "like a pirate," chews tobacco, and drinks to excess). One of the first of Cooke's many strong spinster figures, she gratefully chooses to remain single. The narrator comments on the plight of many New England wives: "Their lives are hard, their husbands are harder and stonier than the fields they half-reclaim to raise their daily bread from. . . ." This theme is developed even further in "The West Shetucket Railroad" (*Independent*, 12 September 1872), which Jay Martin has called a "brilliant analysis of the tragedy of New England character." In this story Cooke's narrator bitterly remarks: "When you bring to bear the daily dullness of work, the brutality, stupidness, small craft, and boorish tyranny of husbands to whom they are tied beyond escape, what wonder is it that a third of all the female lunatics in our asylums are farmers' wives?"

Cooke's finest stories are to be found in *Somebody's Neighbors*, *The Sphinx's Children and Other People's*, and *Huckleberries Gathered from New England Hills*. These collections comprise a total of forty-one stories, which were written over a period of more than thirty years.

Like many of Cooke's early stories, "Eben Jackson" (*Atlantic Monthly*, March 1858; collected in *Somebody's Neighbors*) contains elements of both New England realism and the romance. The title character is a seaman who left New England to make his fortune abroad. Twenty years later, after many adventures (including fifteen years on a tropical island where he had taken a wife), he dies in a Gulf town hospital after asking the attending physician to return a ring to Hetty Buel in Connecticut. The doctor, who narrates the story, takes the ring to Hetty, who is still waiting faithfully for her fiancé. Employing a classic local-color plot of wasted lives, this story is rendered less effective by Cooke's exotic and unrealistic descriptions of unfamiliar regions, in particular the Gulf area. Nevertheless, it still has an emotional impact on most readers.

In "Ann Potter's Lesson" (*Atlantic Monthly*, September 1858; collected in *The Sphinx's Children and Other People's*) Polly Mariner, perhaps Cooke's best character, appears for the first time, though briefly. The story's theme, common in the dominant sentimentalist fiction of the day, is the domestication of an unsubmissive housewife.

Yet the story also includes bleakly realistic descriptions of Ann Potter's impoverished and lonely life. Before her marriage she, her mother, and her sister barely manage to eke out a living on their farm in western Connecticut. After her marriage she accompanies her husband to Indiana, where she is discontent and homesick. When a tornado strikes and she is pinned in the wreckage of her house for fourteen hours, she decides that the storm is an expression of God's wrath. Repenting her "rebellious" attitude, she vows to become "pious," cheerful, and loyal to her husband.

One of Cooke's most forceful indictments of Calvinism appears in "Alcedama Sparks; Or, Old and New" (*Harper's Monthly*, July 1859; collected in *The Sphinx's Children and Other People's*), the story of a generational transition from a strict and inhuman Calvinism to a more humane, compassionate, and "feminized" religion. Deacon Sparks is the upholder of the older, patriarchal religion, while his wife exhibits a more liberal, tolerant philosophy, rejecting the deacon's Calvinist belief in infant damnation and human depravity. Mrs. Sparks is an early example of the strong, hardheaded but compassionate matriarchs that populate New England local-color literature. She was, Cooke wrote, "no heroine of novel or story. . . . Not a particle of sentimentality tinged her nature. She neither screamed nor shrunk at a hoptoad. . . . She never cried all night over her own troubles or anybody else's. . . ."

The story reaches a climax when Mrs. Sparks's bankrupt and destitute parents come to the area with their granddaughter Hannah. After Deacon Sparks refuses to take them in, they are designated "town poor" and "bound out" to the lowest bidder–a New England custom for dealing with welfare cases that Cooke appropriately compares to the auctioning of black slaves in the South. Hannah is bound out to the Sparkses themselves. Eventually she and Alcedama, their son, fall in love and marry. At the end of the story a "new school" liberal minister takes over the local church. The old patriarchal regime has been defeated.

"Miss Lucinda," a humorous portrayal of an eccentric spinster, includes asides to the reader that debunk aspects of the romance–yet another expression of Cooke's opposition to that popular genre. Instead of insipid "heroines" Cooke vows to depict "commonplace" figures. She also burlesques euphemistic romantic diction: Miss Lucinda, she notes, "lived by the aid of 'means,' which in the vernacular is money."

Lucinda's quaint outfits and habits are realistically, if comically, described. The central episode involves the escape of a pig from her farm and its recovery by a French dancing master whom Lucinda later marries. The viewpoint of the narrator throughout the story is one of comic irony.

Women's attachment to animals is an important theme in much New England local-color literature. In Cooke's stories it is best exemplified in the rather touching, if minor, story, "Dely's Cow" (*Atlantic Monthly*, June 1865; collected in *Somebody's Neighbors*). After Dely's mother marries an abusive drunkard, Dely escapes by marrying George Adams, who is soon called off to the Civil War, leaving Dely with no companion but her cow. Due to financial pressure Dely is forced to sell her, but the buyer is a kindly man who agrees to hold the cow until Dely can repurchase her. Her husband returns from the war, and all ends happily.

"Polly Mariner, Tailoress" (*Galaxy*, February 1870; collected in *Somebody's Neighbors*) introduces one of Cooke's most powerful characters and perhaps the most appealing of her self-reliant spinsters. After her parents die, Polly determines to learn a trade so that she can support herself and not become dependent on relatives. Neighbors urge upon her the impropriety of such a move, but she emphatically asserts her needs for freedom and independence: "Whilst I live by myself an' take care of myself, I a'n't beholden to nobody; and I know when my work's done, and what's to pay for't. I kin sing, or laugh, or cry, or fix my hair into a cocked hat, and nobody's got right or reason to say, 'Why do ye do so?' Fact *is*, I've got my liberty, 'n' I'm goin' to keep it. . . ." Because of her forthright ways and because her occupation brings her for extended stays into people's homes, she becomes a powerful member of the community. Polly, "a woman of strong character and great courage," expresses a belief in free will and salvation by works, clearly rejecting the Calvinist notion of preordination. "Folks's luck," she announces succinctly, "is generally their own makin'." Her own fate is decidedly her own choosing; even late in life she refuses to become a housekeeper for a neighboring widower. Cooke does impose a deathbed repentance on her spirited character, however. Polly claims to regret not having had a family, but her late conversion to the "cult of true womanhood" is belied by the rest of the story, which depicts the happy life she has led as a single woman.

"Too Late" (*Galaxy*, January 1875; collected in *The Sphinx's Children and Other People's*) is a strong indictment of the emotional repression effected by strict adherence to Calvinist tenets. As a child, Hannah Blair has been denied affection by her Calvinist mother, who feared making an idol of her daughter. Hannah later falls in love with Charley Mahew but learns of "certain lapses from virtue" he has committed. Even though she loves him passionately, Hannah refuses to marry him or even to see him again. Many years later on her deathbed Hannah remembers how she had resisted Charley's calls from her bedroom window: "I was upon the floor, with my arms wound about the bed-rail and my teeth shut like a vice, lest I should listen to the voice of nature. . . ." The story clearly condemns the destructive Calvinist denial of intense passion. Another character in this story is an eccentric Indian woman, Moll Thunder, who is given to drink and has the power of prophesy. She appears in several Cooke stories.

One of Cooke's best-known stories, "Freedom Wheeler's Controversy with Providence: A Story of Old New England" (*Atlantic Monthly*, July 1877; collected in *Somebody's Neighbors*), restates Cooke's concern about the oppression of wives, condemning Freedom Wheeler's exercise of stubborn willfulness toward his wife, Lowly. After having neglected to name his first son after himself, Freedom seeks to have another son. Providence decrees, however, that his son be followed by a long line of girls. When Lowly finally bears a son, whom he names Freedom, the infant dies. In the next childbirth Lowly and the baby die as well. The narrator comments: "This was the life that was once the doom of all New-England farmers' wives; the life that sent them to early graves, to mad-houses, to suicide; the life that is so beautiful in the poet's numbers, so terrible in its stony, bloomless, oppressive reality." Freedom's second wife and two spinster relatives manage to wear Freedom down by refusing to capitulate to his commands. When he accidentally kills another newborn son by stumbling and falling on the infant, Freedom finally submits to fate. In an 1877 letter to William Dean Howells, Samuel Clemens called "Freedom Wheeler" a "ten-strike. I wish she would write twelve old-time New England tales a year."

"Squire Paine's Conversion" (*Harper's Monthly*, March 1878; collected in *Somebody's Neighbors*) also concerns the chastisement of a tyrannical patriarch. Squire Paine has relentlessly dominated his family and systematically cheated the customers at his store for years. Finally, his daughter runs off with her lover, whom the squire has forbidden her to marry, and he receives word that the two have been killed in a train accident. This news precipitates the squire's repentance, and even though he later learns that the news is false, his "conversion" is permanent.

One of Cooke's most successful comic stories, "Cal Culver and the Devil" (*Harper's Monthly*, September 1878; collected in *Somebody's Neighbors*), is, like many of Cooke's tales, set in the town of Bassett, Connecticut. Having married Pollythi Bangs, a local harpy, Calvary Culver, the village do-nothing, finds life with her impossible. One day he tells the local minister that he has signed his name in blood on a contract given to him by a wayfarer. The minister assumes that this traveler was the devil and performs an exorcism. Soon after, Cal disappears, leaving the reader to wonder if the devil got him or if he concocted the whole story to escape from his wife.

Also set in Basset and including some of the characters from "Cal Culver and the Devil," "Mrs Flint's Married Experience" (*Harper's Monthly*, December 1880; collected in *Somebody's Neighbors*) is a culmination of Cooke's concern about wife oppression and Calvinist tyrannies. After mourning the death of her husband for fifteen years the widow Gold marries Deacon Flint, who turns out to be a parsimonious hypocrite. Her life becomes unmitigated misery: "She toiled on dumbly from day to day, half fed, overworked, desperately lonely. . . ." With the encouragement of two local spinsters Mrs. Flint leaves her husband, but the community strongly condemns this "rebellion" and forces her to recant her charges against him. One of the spinsters forcefully accuses the deacon: "you starve and browbeat and torment her," but community standards enforce "conjugal subjection." Mrs. Flint dies, however, before she must return to her husband.

In one of Cooke's most engaging stories, "Clary's Trial" (*Atlantic Monthly*, April 1880; collected in *Huckleberries Gathered from New England Hills*), Polly Mariner takes on the role of amateur detective. The plot is typical of a "seduced-and-abandoned" sentimentalist novel–until Polly intervenes. Clary Kent, an orphan who has worked as a bound servant at Goody Jakeway's tavern, nearly becomes the victim of Goody's son Alonzo, a rake, who returns from sea and attempts to seduce and then to marry her. Learning that Alonzo has deserted a wife in England,

Polly obtains a copy of the marriage license, thus thwarting Alonzo's plans. In retaliation Alonzo plants some stolen property in Clary's trunk. The defenseless Clary is convicted and sentenced to a one-hundred-dollar fine or thirty lashes. Just as the lashes are about to fall, Polly comes to the rescue with the one hundred dollars.

Sarah Orne Jewett singled out "Some Account of Thomas Tucker" (*Atlantic Monthly*, August 1882; collected in *The Sphinx's Children and Other People's*) for special praise in an 1884 letter to Cooke, which expressed her admiration for Cooke's work. This excellent and amusing story concerns a young minister who constantly shocks the community with his "ghastly honesty." In a funeral oration for a rich hypocrite he delivers a homily on "What shall it profit a man if he gain the whole world, and lose his own soul?" At the wedding of a ne'er-do-well and an innocent orphan, he preaches about the seriousness of marriage; the would-be bride faints, and the wedding is canceled. At the death of a drunken wife beater, whose wife is pretending to mourn, the Reverend Tucker consoles her by reminding her that she is better off without him.

"Odd Miss Todd" (*Harper's Monthly*, October 1882; collected in *Huckleberries Gathered from New England Hills*) is another of Cooke's fine stories about a spinster who becomes a community power. Jilted by a younger man, she is deeply wounded but continues her community work and is mourned by many at her death.

Also set in Bassett, "How Celia Changed Her Mind" (first published in *Huckleberries Gathered from New England Hills*) is one of Cooke's last published stories and the last to include Polly Mariner, this time as a minor character. In this strong story, one of Cooke's best, Celia Barnes, an orphan, has been bound out as "a white slave" until at age eighteen she apprentices herself to the elderly Polly Mariner. When Polly dies, Celia succeeds to her tailoring business and to her role in the community. Celia laments her single status and marries, but she soon realizes that she has made a mistake: "As her husband's mean, querulous, loveless character unveiled itself . . . she began to look woefully back to the freedom and peace of her maiden days." When her husband finally dies, Celia can barely keep from celebrating, and each year thereafter she holds a Thanksgiving dinner for all the town's old maids. She also adopts two girls, vowing to bring them up spinsters.

In addition to her local-color short fiction, Cooke produced many stories that preach Christian morals. Some of these tales, including those collected in *No* (1886) and *Little Foxes* (1904), were designed for children. Her adult religious fiction was collected in *Root-Bound and Other Sketches* (1885). Cooke's two novels also veer in the direction of sentimental moralism. *Happy Dodd*, however, includes interesting and realistic minor characters and affords insights into the brutal hardships endured by rural New Englanders. *Steadfast* (1889) is a moralistic story about a wife's adjustment in a marriage to a man she must learn to love. It has a realistic Connecticut setting, but the plot derives from the sentimentalist tradition. Cooke's strengths were not as a novelist, but as a writer of short stories.

As such, she received modest recognition in her own day. Lowell early singled her out as "one of the most successful sketchers of New England character, abounding in humor and pathos" (*Atlantic Monthly*, March 1861). Fields, Howells, John Greenleaf Whittier, Thomas Wentworth Higginson, Jewett, and Clemens were all enthusiastic about her local-color works. Contemporary reviews, however, were few and mixed. A February 1892 *Atlantic Monthly* review of *Huckleberries Gathered from New England Hills* said that while Cooke "draws her lives sharply, and succeeds with plain, strong characters . . . the attempt to deal with subtlety or complexity of any kind is apt to result in a rather hard inadequacy." A reviewer of the same book in the *Nation* (31 December 1891) commended Cooke for her realistic depiction of "the full-flavored human fruit of New England soil."

By 1907, however, *Atlantic Monthly* editor Bliss Perry, looking back on one hundred years of the magazine, recognized that Cooke had been one of its most important, if most neglected, contributors, stating that her achievement "as a pioneer in the field" of local color "still awaits due recognition by the critics." Perry's statement is still valid today, although important critics over the years have praised her sophistication, her intelligence, and her art. Fred Lewis Pattee, in his *A History of American Literature since 1870* (1915), noted: "None other has shown the whole of New England with the sympathy and comprehension and the delicacy of Rose Terry Cooke." In *The Development of the American Short Story* (1923) Pattee assigns Cooke a central role in the emergence of American local-color realism.

In *New England: Indian Summer, 1865-1915* (1940) Van Wyck Brooks singled out "Too Late" and "Some Account of Thomas Tucker" as especially significant and called Cooke the founder of the New England local-color school. Perry D. Westbrook's analysis of the local-color school, *Acres of Flint* (1951; revised edition, 1981), credits Cooke with having produced several stories "which rank with the best of American local color realism." Most recently Josephine Donovan's *New England Local Color Literature: A Women's Tradition* (1983) assigns Cooke a central role in the development of realism in American women's literature.

Cooke's accomplishment appears especially remarkable when viewed in the context of the popular sentimentalist fiction that was being produced by many women writers of her day. Much of that literature today seems moralistic, fraudulently sentimental, and marred by rhetorical hyperbole. Cooke, by contrast, produced a great many stories that are still distinctive for their psychological acuity, their focused sense of realistic detail, and the wit and clarity of their style.

Bibliography:

Jean Downey, "Rose Terry Cooke: A Bibliography," *Bulletin of Bibliography*, 21 (May-August 1955): 159-163; (September-December 1955): 191-192.

References:

Elizabeth Ammons, Introduction to *How Celia Changed Her Mind and Selected Stories* (New Brunswick, N.J.: Rutgers University Press, 1986), pp. ix-xxxviii;

Van Wyck Brooks, *New England: Indian Summer, 1865-1915* (New York: Dutton, 1940), pp. 85-88;

Josephine Donovan, *New England Local Color Literature: A Women's Tradition* (New York: Ungar, 1983);

Jean Downey, "A Biographical and Critical Study of Rose Terry Cooke," Ph.D. dissertation, University of Ottawa, 1956;

Katherine Kleitz, "Essence of New England: The Portraits of Rose Terry Cooke," *American Transcendental Quarterly*, 47-48 (Summer-Fall 1980): 127-139;

Babette Levy, "Mutations in New England Local Color," *New England Quarterly*, 19 (September 1946): 338-358;

Jay Martin, *Harvests of Change: American Literature 1865-1914* (Englewood Cliffs, N.J.: Prentice-Hall, 1967), pp. 139-142;

Evelyn Newlyn, "Rose Terry Cooke and the Children of the Sphinx," *Regionalism and the Female Imagination*, 4 (Winter 1979): 49-57;

Fred Lewis Pattee, *The Development of the American Short Story* (New York: Harper, 1923);

Harriet Prescott Spofford, *A Little Book of Friends* (Boston: Little, Brown, 1916), pp. 143-156;

Spofford, "Rose Terry Cooke," in *Our Famous Women. An Authorized Record of the Lives and Deeds of Distinguished American Women of Our Times* (Hartford: A. D. Worthington/Chicago: A. G. Nettleton, 1884), pp. 174-206;

Susan Allen Toth, "Character Studies in Rose Terry Cooke: New Faces for the Short Story," *Kate Chopin Newsletter*, 2, no. 1 (1976): 19-26;

Toth, "Rose Terry Cooke (1827-1892)," *American Literary Realism 1870-1910*, 4 (Spring 1971): 170-176;

Perry D. Westbrook, *Acres of Flint, Sarah Orne Jewett and Her Contemporaries*, revised edition (Metuchen, N.J.: Scarecrow Press, 1981), pp. 78-85;

Ann Douglas Wood, "The Literature of Impoverishment: The Women Local Colorists in America 1865-1914," *Women's Studies*, 1 (1972): 3-46.

Papers:

There are no major collections of Cooke's manuscripts and letters. Some of her papers are held by the Alderman Library, University of Virginia; the Beinecke Library, Yale University; the Berkshire Athenaeum, Pittsfield, Massachusetts; the Connecticut Historical Society; the Houghton Library, Harvard University; the Huntington Library, San Marino, California; and the Library of Congress.

Rebecca Harding Davis

(24 June 1831-29 September 1910)

Laurie Buchanan
and
Laura Ingram

BOOKS: *Margret Howth: A Story of To-Day* (Boston: Ticknor & Fields, 1862);
Dallas Galbraith (Philadelphia: Lippincott, 1868);
Waiting for the Verdict (New York: Sheldon, 1868);
Pro Aris et Focis: A Plea for Our Altars and Hearths (New York: Virtue & Yorston, 1870);
John Andross (New York: Orange Judd, 1874);
Kitty's Choice: A Story of Berrytown (Philadelphia: Lippincott, 1874);
A Law unto Herself (Philadelphia: Lippincott, 1878);
Natasqua (New York: Cassell, 1887);
Silhouettes of American Life (New York: Scribners, 1892; London: Osgood, McIlvaine, 1892);
Kent Hampden (New York: Scribners, 1892);
Doctor Warwick's Daughters (New York: Harper, 1896);
Frances Waldeaux (New York: Harper, 1897; London: Osgood, McIlvaine, 1897);
Bits of Gossip (Boston & New York: Houghton, Mifflin, 1904; London: Constable, 1905).

PERIODICAL PUBLICATIONS: "Life in the Iron Mills," *Atlantic Monthly,* 7 (April 1861): 430-451;
"John Lamar," *Atlantic Monthly,* 9 (April 1862): 411-423;
"David Gaunt," *Atlantic Monthly,* 10 (September 1862): 257-271; (October 1862): 403-421;
"Paul Blecker," *Atlantic Monthly,* 11 (May 1863): 580-598; (June 1863): 677-691;
"The Wife's Story," *Atlantic Monthly,* 14 (July 1864): 1-19;
"The Pearl of a Great Price," *Lippincott's,* 2 (December 1868): 606-617; 3 (January 1869): 74-83;
"Earthen Pitchers," *Scribner's Monthly,* 7 (November 1873): 73-81; (December 1873): 199-207; 8 (January 1874): 275-281; (February 1874): 490-494; (March 1874): 595-600; (April 1874): 714-721;

Rebecca Harding Davis (courtesy of Mrs. Hope Davis Kehrig)

"The Doctor's Wife," *Scribner's Monthly,* 8 (May 1874): 108-110;
"The Pepper-Pot Woman," *Scribner's Monthly,* 8 (September 1874): 541-543;
"The Rose of Carolina," *Scribner's Monthly,* 8 (October 1874): 723-726;
"Dolly," *Scribner's Monthly,* 9 (November 1874): 89-92;
"The Poetess of Clap City," *Scribner's Monthly,* 9 (March 1875): 612-615.

Rebecca Harding Davis, who came to maturity during the Civil War, wrote about the effects of that war on those who awaited its outcome at home. An astute and imaginative observer, she is noted for her skill in developing character and motivation, but she is most often remembered as the author of "Life in the Iron Mills" (*Atlantic Monthly*, April 1861), a story whose exposure of inhumane factory-working conditions made her one of the first American realists.

The eldest of five children, Rebecca Blaine Harding was born on 24 June 1831 to Richard and Rachel Leet Wilson Harding in Washington, Pennsylvania. Her mother's Irish grandfather has the distinction of being the first white settler in Washington County, Pennsylvania. Her mother had returned to her family home from Big Spring (now Huntsville), Alabama, where Richard Harding was in business, to give birth to her first child. The Hardings lived in Huntsville until Rebecca was five or six, when the family moved to Wheeling, Virginia (now West Virginia), where her father eventually became city treasurer. Educated at home, first by her mother and then by private tutors, she read John Bunyan, Maria Edgeworth, Sir Walter Scott, Charles Dickens, and Nathaniel Hawthorne. She completed her formal education at the Washington Female Seminary, which she attended from 1845 to 1848 while living with an aunt in Washington, Pennsylvania. After her graduation with highest honors, she returned to Wheeling, where she helped her mother manage the household and teach the younger children.

Her writing career began with the publication of her story "Life in the Iron Mills" in the April 1861 issue of the *Atlantic Monthly*. Taken from her experiences working among immigrant laborers and their families in Wheeling, this story introduced the labor question into American fiction. Its theme of environmental determinism made her a naturalist ten years before the first novel in Emile Zola's naturalistic series, *Les Rougen-Macquart* (1871-1893), and more than thirty years before Stephen Crane's *Maggie* (1893) marked the rise of naturalism in America. "Life in the Iron Mills" describes the deplorably harsh surroundings in which two mill workers struggle for day-to-day survival, with no hope for a better future. A sensitive young man who has the capacity to become an artist, Hugh Wolfe is fated to a life of work in an iron mill, and his hunchbacked cousin Deb works in a cotton mill, but the low sum of even their combined salaries forces her to

steal. These earnest and hardworking protagonists are morally superior to the unconcerned and self-centered mill owner and his dilettante friends, and contrasting the sincere poor and the careless rich became a recurrent theme in Davis's work. "Life in the Iron Mills," following the tradition of Dickens and Harriet Beecher Stowe in its attempt to make a statement about the so-called vulgar side of life, was her response to sentimental fiction of her day.

After the success of "Life in the Iron Mills," James T. Fields, editor of the *Atlantic Monthly*, asked Davis to send him more fiction. Fields rejected the original version of "A Story of Today," but he accepted a revised version, which was well received when it was serialized in the magazine (October 1861-March 1862) and was published in book form as *Margret Howth: A Story of To-Day* (1862). The success of this novel brought her an invitation to visit Fields and his wife, Annie Adams Fields, in Boston in summer 1862. There she met Hawthorne, Oliver Wendell Holmes, Emerson, Louisa May Alcott, and Bronson Alcott. She felt drawn to Hawthorne and Holmes but decided that Emerson and Bronson Alcott were too impractical, especially in their idealism about the Civil War.

On her way home from Boston, Rebecca visited Philadelphia to meet Lemuel Clarke Davis, an apprentice lawyer who had initiated a correspondence with her after being profoundly moved by "Life in the Iron Mills." L. Clarke Davis was three years her junior and was smaller in build than she, but the two fell in love and became engaged during this visit. They were married on 5 March 1863. Throughout their life together they lived for most of each year in Philadelphia, while spending summers in Point Pleasant, New Jersey, and later in Marion, Massachusetts.

Because West Virginia was on the border between North and South, Davis had experienced the Civil War at firsthand, and her own feelings about the war that raged during the early years of her career and marriage were far different from those she had encountered in Bronson Alcott and Emerson. In *Bits of Gossip* (1904) she described "the actual war; the filthy spewings of it; the political jobbery in Union and Confederate camps; the malignant and personal hatreds wearing patriotic masks, and glutted by burning homes and outraged women; the chances in it, on both sides, for brutish men to grow more brut-

Rebecca Harding and Lemuel Clarke Davis at the time of their marriage (courtesy of Mrs. Hope Davis Kehrig)

ish, and for honorable men to degenerate into thieves and sots."

Davis's Civil War stories, such as "John Lamar" (*Atlantic Monthly,* April 1862), "David Gaunt" (*Atlantic Monthly,* September and October 1862), and "Paul Blecker" (*Atlantic Monthly,* May and June 1863), are among the first realistic stories inspired by the war. Even so, these stories focus more upon the inner lives of the characters than upon the war itself. Davis's Civil War stories also are unusual for their time in that they reflect her awareness of the personal conflicts the war evoked and address some of the social problems that would result from it.

"John Lamar" depicts the confusion of a Negro slave, Ben, who–in that period before the Emancipation Proclamation (1 January 1863)– realizes that the future for blacks will be filled with hardship in the North as well as the South. Despite what appears to be a genuine affection between master and slave, the speech of a Bible-quoting abolitionist incites Ben to murder his master, Lamar, who is about to escape from the shed where he is being held prisoner by his cousin's hus-

band, a captain in the Union army. As he dies, Lamar seems bewildered that Ben has betrayed him in order to gain his freedom. "David Gaunt" explores the effect of the Civil War on a young woman, Dode Scofield, and the two men who love her. David Gaunt, a clergyman, enlists in the Union army despite the conflict between his role as a man of God and the demands that will be placed upon him as a soldier. Douglas Palmer, also a Union soldier, is plagued by religious doubt, and for this reason the devout Dode rejects him, although he is the only man she loves. The war provides a vehicle for self-realization for Gaunt, who discovers the horrors of warfare when he is forced to shoot Dode's father, a rebel spy, and for Dode, who risks her life–and, she is convinced, her immortal soul–to save the wounded Palmer. "Paul Blecker" also depicts the conflict between love and duty against the backdrop of the Civil War. The story concerns two lovers, Blecker, an army surgeon, and Lizzy Gurney, a young woman who believes herself to be permanently defiled by an early marriage to a distant cousin, now presumed dead, whom she did not love. After Blecker is finally able to convince Lizzy that she deserves a chance for happiness with him, her rogue husband reappears as a patient in the hospital over which Blecker presides. Despite Blecker's efforts to prevent Lizzy from discovering that her estranged husband is alive, the two meet, and, even though he leaves her once more, the knowledge that he is not dead crushes Lizzy's hopes for a new life with the man she loves.

In 1864 Davis bore her first child, Richard Harding Davis, whose career as a journalist and popular author now overshadows his mother's. She also had two other children, a second son, Charles Belmont, born in 1866, and a daughter, Nora, who was born in 1872. The family is said to have been close and admiring of one another's accomplishments. In 1870 L. Clarke Davis gave up the legal profession and became managing editor of the *Philadelphia Inquirer*. In 1893 he became editor of the *Philadelphia Public Ledger*, a position he held until his death in 1904. A devoted mother and wife, Davis also continued writing. In 1869 she became a contributing editor to the *New York Tribune*, for which she wrote articles on issues of the day.

During the later years of the Civil War, although still concerned with the effects of that war on individuals, Davis began writing fiction that focuses on women's problems and the expectations imposed upon them by others, as well as differences in personality and manners that seemed typical of specific regions of the country. In "The Wife's Story" (*Atlantic Monthly*, July 1864), for example, she portrays a Concord woman who analyzes all her emotions and becomes a victim of her unfavorable self-image. Her tortured conscience forces her into depression and paranoia, and she is contrasted to members of her husband's midwestern family, who are physically and mentally robust.

Most of the pieces Davis contributed to *Scribner's Monthly* in 1874 and 1875 also deal with women but could more aptly be classified as sketches than stories. In "The Doctor's Wife" (May 1874) a narrow-minded observer criticizes a young wife who refuses to play the role expected of an up-and-coming doctor's wife. Her unconventional behavior is not the product of a rebellious spirit, but rather of her obliviousness and total unconcern for social appearances. Davis's September 1874 character sketch, "The Pepper-Pot Woman," describes Sarah, a woman who has raised five children not her own because, as she explains, "somebody had to take 'em." Like the behavior of the doctor's young wife, Sarah's actions rise out of what seems natural and right to her rather than out of concern for the praise or condemnation of others.

"Dolly" (November 1874) is the story of a young convent orphan whose resemblance to Renaissance paintings of the Madonna inspires unrealistic expectations in a man who is infatuated by her. The girl knows nothing of his plans to return for her, presumably with the intent of marriage, and is taken by relatives to live in Pennsylvania and work as a chambermaid in their country inn. Several years later, while she is performing as a circus rider to earn money so that she and her husband will be able to buy land in Nevada, the man encounters her again and decides that she is an "unrepentant Magdalene." He is unable to accept that she is merely an ordinary woman who "only felt she was doing the natural and right thing for her to do"; he compares her to a musical instrument that has "died with all its music in it." "The Poetess of Clap City" (March 1875) concerns a woman who postpones a promising career as a poet to support her drunken but good-hearted husband and their children. "Let me keep to my cabbages and potatoes as long as I want to turn a penny," she tells the editor who encourages her to write for publication. After fifteen years, her hard work and industriousness have left her wealthy, but when she finally writes a single poem, it is wretched and unpublishable. Davis once again uses the metaphor of unplayed music as the narrator laments the would-be poet's failure and asks, "Were there ever 'voiceless singers' since time began? Would it be possible for them to 'die, with all their music in them'— even in Clap City?"

"Marcia," the only story from this period that was collected in *Silhouettes of American Life* (1892), is a vivid picture of an uneducated southern girl who comes to Philadelphia to write. Too proud to accept help, she supplements her modest income by stealing. After she is jailed and unsuccessfully tries to commit suicide, she allows the man who loves her to take her back home as his wife.

Also collected in *Silhouettes of American Life* is "At the Station" (*Scribner's Magazine*, December 1888), which portrays a woman waiting for the brother she has not seen in many years. One night she speaks of him to a sick prisoner whom she is nursing, and the man encourages her to retain her faith until her brother returns. When the brother reappears two years later, the reader suspects that he and the sick man are the same person. "Mademoiselle Joan" (*Atlantic Monthly*, September 1886) suggests that a pure and unselfish soul may have the supernatural power to overcome wickedness when a mysterious woman sacrifices her life to protect two children from the ill will of an evil stepmother.

Davis's heroines are often idealized by other characters who mistakenly view them as geniuses or saints when in reality they are ordinary women. Many of them embody traditional female traits such as nurturing and self-sacrifice. Homespun virtues, such as a sense of duty and the work ethic, frequently shape their behavior and, as often as not, hamper their chances for happiness and success. In many of the stories women are able to circumvent the constraints imposed upon them, but they are not feminists. In fact, although Davis continued to write throughout her life, she considered marriage and childbearing a woman's true vocation, writing in *Pro Aris et Focis: A Plea for Our Altars and Hearths* (1870) that women should work outside the home only if they were unmarried and had no other means of support.

Other stories in *Silhouettes of American Life* examine the role of heroism and nobility in everyday life. Set in Louisiana, "Tirar y Soult" (*Scribner's Magazine*, December 1888) portrays a Creole who risks his own life to save that of a rival whom he believes his beloved prefers. His unselfish concern for her happiness is rewarded when she recognizes his heroism and declares her love for him. "Walhalla" (*Scribner's Monthly*, May 1880), set in South Carolina among the German-Swiss immigrants, uses the devices of a carving competition, a runaway train, and a pair of rival suitors to examine the nature of true heroism. "Across the Gulf" (*Lippincott's*, July 1881) explores the feelings of a clergyman who discovers that the woman he has fallen in love with is an actress and the difficulties the two have in interacting because of their different temperaments and backgrounds. Although some critics have found the fiction Davis wrote after her Civil War stories too sentimental, these works reflect not only a powerful realistic vision but an understanding of human motivations.

After her husband's death in 1904, Davis went to live with her daughter, Nora. Her autobiography, *Bits of Gossip*, appeared in the same year. She later went to live with Richard Harding Davis at his home in Mount Kisco, New York, and she died there on 29 September 1910 from edema of the lungs induced by heart disease. Although her work covers a much broader range of subjects, Rebecca Harding Davis will continue to be remembered for her fiction portraying the realities of war and the hardships of the humble. It is these writings that put her in the vanguard of American realism.

References:

Fairfax Downey, "Portrait of a Pioneer," *Colophon*, 3 (December 1932): n. pag.;

Gerald Langford, *The Richard Harding Davis Years: A Biography of a Mother and Son* (New York: Holt, Rinehart & Winston, 1961);

Arthur Hobson Quinn, *American Fiction: An Historical and Critical Survey* (New York: Appleton-Century, 1936).

Philander Deming

(6 February 1829-9 February 1915)

Philip G. Terrie
Bowling Green State University

BOOKS: *The Court Stenographer: Containing Hints and Practical Suggestions in Regard to Court Reporting* (Albany: Munsell, 1879);
Adirondack Stories (Boston: Houghton, Osgood, 1880);
Tompkins, and Other Folks: Stories of the Hudson and the Adirondacks (Boston & New York: Houghton, Mifflin, 1885);
The Story of a Pathfinder (Boston & New York: Houghton, Mifflin, 1907).

In the 1870s and 1880s Philander Deming published a series of short stories about the Adirondack region of upstate New York. His best work places him among the major local-color writers: what rural Massachusetts was for Mary Wilkins Freeman or Down-East Maine was for Sarah Orne Jewett the Adirondacks were for Deming. Working with the lives of ordinary people he knew well, Deming portrayed local life while aiming at universal truths. Yet, perhaps because he published only sixteen stories and several brief autobiographical sketches and because his later stories failed to live up to his early promise, Deming is almost wholly forgotten today. This neglect is unfortunate, for his best stories are evidence of the vigor of early realistic fiction. William Dean Howells thought highly of Deming's work and accepted several of his stories for the *Atlantic Monthly*. Of the tales in Deming's first collection, *Adirondack Stories* (1880), Howells observed in "Recollections of an Atlantic Editorship" (*Atlantic Monthly*, November 1907), "They were, whether instinctively or consciously, in the right manner, and of a simplicity in motive, material, and imagination as fine as something Norse, or Slavic, or Italian, or Spanish." Howells went on to add that "such dear and true, and rare creatures" were the products of a truly "sympathetic mind" and, although the stories were then nearly forgotten, they would be honored in "some brighter and clearer future."

Born in Carlisle, a village in rural Schoharie County, New York, to Rufus Romeo and Julia Ann Porter Deming, Philander Deming spent his childhood in a series of small towns in the foothills of the Adirondacks while his father, a minister in the Champlain Presbytery, moved from one congregation to another. His early education came from his father's library, where he pored over works by Henry Wadsworth Longfellow, Ralph Waldo Emerson, James Russell Lowell, and other lights of the New England Renaissance. At Burke, a hamlet near the St. Lawrence Valley, he taught school from 1852 to 1854 while running a sawmill with two of his brothers. He then decided to work toward a college degree and prepared at the Whitestown Seminary in Whitesboro, New York, before entering the University of Vermont, from which he graduated in 1861, having been elected to Phi Beta Kappa. Settling in Albany, New York, he began a career as a journalist; within three years he was the legislative reporter for the *New York Times*. As a child Deming had mastered shorthand, and in 1865 he presented a dramatic demonstration in an Albany courtroom of the importance of the verbatim recording of testimony. He was immediately made official stenographer for the Albany District Supreme Court, where he worked until his retirement in 1882. He pioneered the technique of court reporting and published a handbook, *The Court Stenographer*, in 1879.

Throughout the time that Deming worked as journalist and court reporter he hoped to publish what he called "original literature." To the *Atlantic Monthly*, which he considered the "greatest magazine of the day," he mailed essay after essay, and each was returned. But in 1871, according to "Story Writing" in his *The Story of a Pathfinder* (1907), Deming experienced a "vision" of his true literary destiny, and after two days of inspired writing he produced his first short story. Like all his best stories, "Lost" is based on events and people he had personally known. This story was also submitted to the *Atlantic*, then edited by William Dean Howells, who accepted it for the February 1873 issue.

"Lost" displays the attributes of Deming's best fiction. It achieves deft characterization with a minimum of description, evokes the frontier setting effectively, and, most important, establishes the grim interaction between the natural environment and people's lives. The story opens with dramatic yet economical power: "He was lost in the edge of the Adirondack wilderness. It must have been the sound of the flail. 'Thud, thud, thud,' came the beat of the dull, thumping strokes through the thick, opaque, gray fog." Willie, a child of four, wanders away from his father's farm on a cold April day. A search party gathers but wastes time poking about the house and barn and waiting for the arrival of the neighborhood "fortune-woman," who finally appears but offers the searchers only the ambiguous pronouncements typical of oracles. Finally, the village colonel organizes the searchers into a company, which makes a "grand charge upon the wilderness." Despite a "magnificent tramp through the wild, wet woods," the boy is not found. Frustrated by their failure, some of the men begin to mutter that the boy could not have wandered so far, that he was probably murdered by his father. The father catches wind of these suspicions and stoutly denies them, but his innocence remains in doubt until the boy's frozen body is carried back to the farm by a trapper, who has come upon it deep in the woods.

From the start the dark Adirondack wilderness is seen as a brooding and antagonistic force, first swallowing and confusing the boy, then resisting and even mocking the efforts of the searchers. Once Willie has crossed the border between field and forest, the sound of the flail echoes deceptively in the woods and leads him deeper into the wilderness, where he becomes surrounded by "the same narrow dome of watery gray . . . everywhere shutting close down around him." While the colonel's searchers are combing the woods, a partridge flutters out of the underbrush and skips along for a few steps, with "her sharp, coquettish 'quit, quit, quit,'" admonishing the searchers that their quest is futile.

The primitive, uncooperative forest encourages the superstitions of the searchers. Deming suggests that the men's faith in the divining powers of the fortune-woman derives from their sense of hopelessness when confronted by the ostensibly endless wilderness. He paints a scene wherein the background of the "vast descending plain of evergreen forest, sloping away from the Adirondack highlands to the dim distance of the St. Lawrence Valley," hovers over the figure of the "vulgar old woman waddling along, and snatching here and there a teacupful of water from the puddles formed by the melting snow." The men's hope that she, at least, can interpret the ominous signs of the wilderness leads them, "awe-struck," to follow her about; but nature turns out to be as unfathomable to her as it is to them, and the old woman departs, no progress having been made in the search.

The men themselves are as cruel as the wilderness; the growth of their suspicions about the boy's father and their plans to search the farm buildings for the damning corpse suggest the lynch mentality of William Faulkner's "Dry September." The appearance of the boy's body in the arms of the trapper changes their sense of self-righteousness to a prurient fascination with the grief of the parents and finally to a detached speculation on how the boy could have strayed so far from home. With the exception of Willie's father and a few of his friends, human nature is as uncaring as the wilderness; but whereas the wilderness is grand in its demand for sacrifice, the men of this village are petty gossips, small in mind and vicious in their inclination to presume that everyone is as culpable as themselves.

In his next stories Deming continued to recall the people and events of his youth in the Adirondack foothills. "Lost" was followed by "Lida Ann" (*Atlantic Monthly*, January 1874), "John's Trial" (*Atlantic Monthly*, March 1874), "Willie" (*Atlantic Monthly*, July 1874), and "Benjamin Jacques" (*Atlantic Monthly*, June 1875); all these stories passed under the editorial scrutiny of Howells. With two stories not published elsewhere–"Joe Baldwin" and "Ike's Wife"–these tales from the *Atlantic* appeared in book form as *Adirondack Stories* (1880), a volume popular enough to be republished in 1902 and 1907. These Adirondack stories are Deming's best. They address themes of isolation, disappointment, misunderstanding, and violence. Their characterizations depend on direct, simple diction, their setting on the author's obvious respect for, and personal familiarity with, the Adirondack wilderness and the villages around it.

The characters in *Adirondack Stories* live in taciturn isolation, while a brutal environment enforces their loneliness and tests their fortitude. "Willie" involves the discovery of another child's body–a child with the same name as the boy in "Lost." This time the corpse, bloody and mangled, is found by three boys on the edge of a pasture. The boys decide that a horse must have kicked and killed the child. After several men, including Willie's father, have arrived on the scene, a dispute arises as to whether a horse could actually have killed the boy, but they finally discover that an old ram was seen knocking the boy down. The ram is caught, and blood is detected on his horns. In a passage of characteristic understatement Deming describes the ritual slaying of the ram: "In a moment a glittering keen knife flashed from somebody's keeping into the bright sunshine, and in a moment more a purple stream dyed the white wool around Buck's throat, and there was a red pool upon the grass, and a little later . . . 'some tough mutton.'" After the child's funeral the parents abandon their Adirondack farm and return to New England, sending Willie's remains ahead to their family plot.

The whole story is a triumph of understatement. Against the many nineteenth-century tales about the deaths of children–tales which shamelessly invited their readers to collapse in weepy sentimentality–"Willie" stands out in its refusal to become just another maudlin tearjerker. Instead, the story is about a bleak land where some people simply cannot adapt. Willie's parents are such people; even the boys who find the corpse know or suspect more about the ways of their world than these adults do. Willie's parents retreat to a safer, more intelligible New England because they cannot withstand the hostility of the Adirondacks.

Lucy, the main character in "Ike's Wife," who is introduced as a "subdued, sad-faced English woman, with deep-set, mournful eyes," cannot endure in the foothills either. Married to a lumberjack, Lucy has been brought to the wilderness, where, childless, she takes into her home one of the many daughters of a nearby family. One night, in a desperate rage, Lucy nearly beats this girl to death. Before she can be tried for assault, a group of men from the village sets out to give her a beating of her own. They find Lucy hanging from a rafter. Like the mob in "Lost," the men see nothing wrong in their own behavior but condemn Ike for leaving Lucy alone and chastise the neighborhood women for not paying more attention to this unstable woman. Lucy is yet another person who cannot endure the isolation of life in or near the wilderness. As an old woman says on the day of Lucy's funeral, "This lonely place had no rest for her." Ironically, the wilderness, which had been dark and forbidding while Lucy lived, becomes pleasant and accepting at her death: "Upon a sandy knoll, where brier-bushes grew, and where the wild birds sang, and the music of the flowing creek was near, they buried Ike's wife."

Despite its many virtues *Adirondack Stories* also contained hints that Deming might fall into just the sentimental trap his best stories avoided. In "Lida Ann" and "Joe Baldwin" Deming composed tales of unrequited or painfully delayed love. He handled this potentially dangerous theme well in these stories, but in later efforts Deming dwelt more and more on romance–usually love affairs frustrated by circumstance or coincidence. It is significant that these stories also largely abandoned the Adirondack setting and that they did not benefit from the criticism of William Dean Howells, who left the *Atlantic* in 1881.

Deming's susceptibility to sentimental themes is apparent in "Tompkins" (*Atlantic Monthly*, July 1883), where the story is told to a disinterested listener by a participant in the action. Deming's increasingly frequent use of the frame tale with a passive listener reflects his career as court recorder: as the stenographer in the District Supreme Court, he must have heard story after story of domestic strife and suffering–but he was never himself personally involved in such affairs. The passive listener of his frame stories seems to represent Deming himself, who never married, who lived quietly in boarding houses, and who eventually became known for a nearly obsessive shyness. His life contained neither adventure, tragedy, nor overt romance, but he listened to and wrote tales of intense experience.

In "Tompkins" the title character tells an old college friend (the college is the University of Vermont) about a girl from his hometown who arrived in Burlington, Vermont, at the same time he did, although she came not to be a student but to work in a mill. Tompkins recalls that he always liked Lucy but once in Burlington felt himself socially superior–he a college man with high hopes, she a mere mill girl. While working his way through college, he often received much-needed money from an uncle, but he eventually learned that Lucy was actually the source of this assistance but was too shy to let Tompkins know she wanted to help him. Years later, when Tompkins discovers this fact, he sets out for Burlington to find Lucy and declare the love for her he has kept secret, but he finds that Lucy has died. Thus summarized, the story seems more banal than it really is. Deming manages to handle this tale of sacrifice and disappointment in a manner emphasizing the sadness and ultimate isolation of the human spirit. Tompkins's disappointments involve more than his failure to overcome adolescent snobbery; he has also to accept his failure to fulfill his ambition to be a poet. He has made a modest life for himself as a pork dealer in Chicago and has only gradually adjusted to a rather ordinary reality. "Tompkins" is more than a sentimental tale of unrequited love–though the revelation of Lucy's death crosses the line separating the tragic from the mawkish; the story also suggests the diminishing role of the arts in a commercial nation and convincingly portrays the sense of regret through which most adults pass before reconciling themselves to the impossibility of fulfilling their youthful dreams.

This story was collected in *Tompkins, and Other Folks*, where other tales employ the frame device and pursue the theme of unfulfilled romance. Usually the romance leans toward the trite, but the disappointment of the lovers often reflects some inchoate, inarticulate disappointment with the direction of American life. In "Rube Jones" (*Atlantic Monthly*, November 1882) the title character contrasts the Albany of his youth, when he was optimistic about his career and his hopes for love, with the industrial city he sees at the time he relates his tale: "Albany was just a neat, queer Dutch place then.... All along the river were stately elms and lines of willows, and there was the greenest grass in the world. There were no railroads, or excavations, or dumping grounds, or decayed cabbages on the island, or dead cats in the river. Everything was just as neat and smooth and pretty as a picture on an old fashioned piece of china ware." As Rube elaborates the circumstances of his aborted romance, he also outlines a parable about the shift from rural, village culture to a nation of cities, where industry and science define life. Nor does Deming merely pander to the pastoral nostalgia of the late nineteenth century; he implies that Rube Jones has been something of a nostalgic fool for misconstruing the events of his life and allowing his true love to slip away. Rube has indulged in decades of emotional self-flagellation, and Deming suggests that those to whom the past is a dream of innocence and rural purity are equally deluded.

The adult lives of both Tompkins and Rube Jones are significantly different from what had once seemed possible. Deming criticizes each character for not seizing opportunity, for not involving himself directly in the determination of his own destiny. Tompkins is guilty of a false sense of self-importance, and Jones allows himself to wile away decades in an absurd, pathetic reverie of emotional masochism. These two men anticipate Henry James's Lambert Strether and John Marcher, in whom James offered pictures of himself as a man regretfully recalling chances not seized, a life not truly lived. That Deming had himself in mind in Tompkins and Jones seems clear. His own life was empty of most of the human relationships that supply warmth and meaning; his literary career, though he produced a few stories of the first order, fell short of the grand scale that he had contemplated as a young man. In "An Adirondack Home," an autobiographical vignette published in *Tompkins, and Other Folks*, Deming mentions "my own burden–the knowledge that life is so far advanced with me and I have accomplished so little."

After *Tompkins, and Other Folks* Deming published two more stories in the *Atlantic*: "A Stranger in the City" (August 1885) and "A Lover's Conscience" (November 1888). These tales, which display Deming's decline into the sentimental, were virtually his last efforts at writing fiction. With one previously unpublished story they were included in Deming's last book, *The Story of a Pathfinder* (1907). This book appeared just as Howells was noting regretfully that Deming had been nearly forgotten by the current generation of readers, whose tastes ran to the "human-nature fakirs of our latter-day fiction." Yet *The Story of a Pathfinder* seems an appeal to just the readership Howells scorned.

Like Bret Harte, another New Yorker who achieved fame as a writer of local-color fiction, Deming produced a handful of first-rate stories, though he hardly became a cult figure like Harte. Also like Harte, Deming was unable to sustain the high artistry of his earliest efforts. The element present in his best fiction and missing from his less successful stories is a focus on the environment and people of the Adirondacks. As long as Deming wrote about events he had witnessed or participated in during his youth, his stories evinced the simplicity, verisimilitude, and convincing diction found in the best of realism. When he departed from the Adirondack setting and tried to apply his talents to popular sentimental themes, his writing deteriorated, though even in some of his sentimental stories there is evidence of genuine strength. Howells was right in lamenting the neglect of Deming; his best stories truly deserve our attention. In 1915 Fred Lewis Pattee put Deming in the same class with Mark Twain, George Washington Cable, Sarah Orne Jewett, and many other of the best American writers; and in 1923 Pattee praised Deming as a "pioneer force in the gathering realistic movement" but observed, "to-day he is almost totally unread." It was Deming's fate to shine briefly, to help prepare the way for later exponents of realism, and then to slip into obscurity.

References:
Fred Lewis Pattee, *Development of the American*

Short Story (New York & London: Harper, 1923), pp. 269-271;

Pattee, *A History of American Literature Since 1870* (New York: Century, 1915), p. 24;

Abe C. Ravitz, "Philander Deming: Howells' Adirondack Prodigy," *New York History*, 36 (October 1955): 404-412;

Kate H. Winter, "North Country Voices," in *Upstate Literature: Essays in Memory of Thomas F. O'Donnell*, edited by Frank Bergmann (Syracuse: Syracuse University Press, 1985), pp. 143-164.

Alice French
(Octave Thanet)
(19 March 1850-9 January 1934)

Nancy Huse
Augustana College, Rock Island, Illinois

BOOKS: *Knitters in the Sun* (Boston & New York: Houghton, Mifflin, 1887);

Expiation (New York: Scribners, 1890; London: Warne, 1890);

Otto the Knight, and Other Trans-Mississippi Stories (Boston & New York: Houghton, Mifflin, 1891; London: Cassell, 1891);

We All (New York: Appleton, 1891);

An Adventure in Photography (New York: Scribners, 1893);

Stories of a Western Town (New York: Scribners, 1893; London: Low, 1893);

The Missionary Sheriff, Being Incidents in the Life of a Plain Man Who Tried to Do His Duty (New York & London: Harper, 1897);

A Book of True Lovers (Chicago: Way & Williams, 1897);

A Slave to Duty & Other Women (Chicago & New York: Stone, 1898);

The Heart of Toil (New York & London: Scribners, 1898);

The Captured Dream, and Other Stories (New York & London: Harper, 1899);

The Man of the Hour (Indianapolis: Bobbs-Merrill, 1905);

The Lion's Share (Indianapolis: Bobbs-Merrill, 1907);

By Inheritance (Indianapolis: Bobbs-Merrill, 1910);

Stories That End Well (Indianapolis: Bobbs-Merrill, 1911);

A Step on the Stair (Indianapolis: Bobbs-Merrill, 1913);

And the Captain Answered (Indianapolis: Bobbs-Merrill, 1917).

OTHER: *The Best Letters of Lady Mary Wortley Montagu*, edited, with a dedicatory letter, by French (Chicago: McClurg, 1890).

PERIODICAL PUBLICATIONS:
FICTION
"Hugo's Waiting," as Frances Essex, *Davenport Gazette*, 19 February 1871;

"My Lorelei: A Heidelberg Romance–From the Diary of Mrs. Louis Danton Lynde," *Western*, 6 (January 1880): 1-22;

"Under Five Shillings," *Scribner's Magazine*, 8 (July 1880): 68-80;

"A Spectre of Folly," *Scribner's Magazine*, 9 (May 1891): 563-568;

Alice French

"A Recognition," *Scribner's Magazine*, 10 (November 1891): 612-619;

"The Return of the Rejected," *Lippincott's Magazine*, 48 (November 1891): 593-611;

"The Proud Pynsents," *Scribner's Magazine*, 14 (November 1893): 549-560;

"The Merry Thanksgiving of the Burglar and the Plumber," *McClure's*, 5 (November 1895): 515-522.

NONFICTION

"The Tramp in Four Centuries," *Lippincott's Magazine*, 23 (May 1879): 565-574;

"The Indoor Pauper: A Study," *Atlantic Monthly*, 47 (June 1881): 749-764; 48 (August 1881): 241-252;

"Plantation Life in Arkansas," *Atlantic Monthly*, 48 (July 1891): 332-340;

"Folk Lore in Arkansas," *Journal of American Folklore*, 5 (April-June 1892): 121-125;

"Sketches of American Types," *Scribner's Magazine*, 15 (March 1894): 323-332; (April 1894): 399-409; (May 1894): 565-572; 16

(July 1894): 100-107; (August 1894): 190-198; (September 1894): 328-338;

"The Trans-Mississippi Exposition," *Cosmopolitan*, 25 (October 1898): 599-614.

Nine collections of Alice French's short fiction, published between 1887 and 1911 and gleaned from the larger body of work she began publishing in leading periodicals in 1878, suggest what a popular and prolific writer she was. Published under the pseudonym Octave Thanet, the stories detail records of life in Iowa towns and an Arkansas plantation as perceived by an intelligent and conservative woman; they are in the local-color tradition, their realism tailored by a genteel mind usually too alert and critical to be sentimental.

In 1856 Alice French moved with her family from her birthplace, Andover, Massachusetts, to Davenport, Iowa. Her father, George Henry French, prospered as a manufacturer and civic leader while his oldest child played with younger brothers, observed her father's businesses, and read history, theology, and conservative economics in the library of her uncle, the Episcopal bishop of Davenport. Her mother, Frances Morton French, was the daughter of a Massachusetts governor, Marcus Morton (1784-1864), and wanted her daughter educated in the East. After an unpleasant year at Vassar in 1866, where French liked to shock the eastern students by asserting that her father was a carpenter, she attended Abbott Academy, Andover, in 1867 and 1868. There she met Octavia Putnam, whose name she would adapt for the pseudonym Octave Thanet. (The origin of "Thanet" is less certain. The author's most frequent explanation was that she had seen the word on a boxcar.)

During the next ten years at home, French had many responsibilities in the household, including the care of a brother, Robert, born when she was twenty-one. She read European literature between social engagements in Davenport, Rock Island, and Chicago (where her friends included the Marshall Fields) and published a short story, "Hugo's Waiting," in the *Davenport Gazette* in 1871. That same year she went to Europe with her father and cousins and returned there in 1881 as the guest of Andrew Carnegie, whose attention she had attracted through an essay, "The Tramp in Four Centuries," in *Lippincott's Magazine* (May 1879).

After 1884 French concentrated on writing short fiction, following a suggestion of Richard Watson Gilder, editor of *Century Magazine*. Her life settled into an upper-class pattern. Uninterested in marriage, she spent winters from 1885 to 1909 at Clover Bend, a plantation near Walnut Ridge, Arkansas, that was owned in part by her friend Jane Allen Crawford. There, in 1897, the two women built a house, which they named Thanford, and in 1905 they merged their Davenport households permanently. Jane Crawford was the model for a few of the writer's characters, including the heroine of the uncollected story "My Lorelei" (*Western*, January 1880). Winters in Arkansas seemed to inspire some of Alice French's best writing. During French's later years she did Red Cross work and was interested in the antisuffrage campaign, though she actively promoted women's cultural groups. An inheritance from Jane Crawford eased the poverty of her last days, after the Wall Street crash of 1929 had depleted her own fortune and diabetes had ruined her eyesight and caused amputation of her right

foot. Members of the Allen and the French families cared for the aging writer until her death.

Energetic and exuberant, French described herself as a "carpenter" rather than an "architect" of literature. In the early 1890s she was paid five cents a word for her fiction, in contrast to the half cent Hamlin Garland was getting then. She acted as a mentor to Garland and idolized William Dean Howells because she thought of herself as a realist, though she might more properly be called a local colorist rather than a realist in the Jamesian sense. Her stories reflect the hours she spent recording dialect and observing distinct social groups in Iowa and Arkansas. Unlike other realists who were progressives, French was a social Darwinist who described domestic life, industrial tensions, and the effects of slavery, Reconstruction, and immigration within a framework that stressed the inherent superiority of the upper classes. She was one of the first American fiction writers to write tales of industrialists, plantation dwellers, and women of the upper and lower classes, shaping her stories according to the same sensibility which made her write to William Ernest Henley after her brother died in 1897 to thank the poet for having written "Invictus." Disagreeing with Garland's bleak view of midwestern farm life, she wrote stories emphasizing family bonds and individual responsibility. Often humorous or mildly satirical, the tales usually present midwestern and southern customs as seen through the eyes of narrators identified in some way with New England. Her plots frequently deal with marriage, friendships (especially those of women), relationships between employers and employees, and relationships with in-laws. Men are sometimes shown tending children, women managing money. In many stories upper-class characters display the decisiveness and foresight that lead to happy endings.

The title of *Knitters in the Sun* (1887), a collection of tales written after 1878, expresses the author's conviction that Americans are optimists working out a fortunate destiny. The earliest story, "A Communist's Wife," which was first published as "Communists and Capitalists" in the October 1878 issue of *Lippincott's Magazine*, is typical of much of French's work. It depicts the conflict between a striker and a former countess, who tries to help the man's suffering family. After she enables him to take his family away from the river town where "rats ate a little of the children now and then" in the strikers' shanties, the worker's wife is killed in a Chicago street riot, which the countess happens to witness.

The eight other tales in *Knitters in the Sun* indicate the range of French's work. Philosophical stories such as "The Ogre of Ha Ha Bay" (*Atlantic Monthly*, October 1885) and "Schopenhauer on Lake Pepin" (*Good Company*, 4, no. 2, 1879), drawn from her travels and reading, contrast with the domestic realism of "Mrs. Finlay's Elizabethan Chair" (*Century Magazine*, March 1884) and "Father Quinnailon's Convert" (*Good Company*, 5, no. 1, 1880). In the latter story a British-educated midwesterner's newly learned religious and social tolerance help him to reconcile his differences with his suffragist fiancée; both decide they have been foolish to part over principle. The catalyst is a humble Roman Catholic priest who becomes the new bishop of the region. This story strikes a more convincing note than do the longer philosophical tales.

Two of the four southern stories in this first collection, "Ma' Bowlin' " (*Harper's Weekly*, 15 January 1887) and "Whitsun Harp, Regulator" (*Century Magazine*, May 1887), demonstrate Alice French's skill at using dialect, her empathy for white rural southerners, and her ability to construct suspenseful plots around domestic incidents. In "Ma' Bowlin' " a father must search a cypress swamp for the little daughter he has rejected; his finding the eight-year-old, still in the clean dress her mother told her not to soil, ends suspicions that he murdered her. Somewhat more humorous and less moralistic is the tale of Whitsun Harp, who deputizes himself to "regulate" the morals of his Arkansas community. A rather careless young man upholds his own honor when the self-appointed regulator threatens to kill him and finds that his quiet wife has preferred him to the misguided Harp all along, despite his jealous forebodings. The complex plot, with its resolution hinging on conversation in dialect, caused Howells to write an unfavorable review in his "Editor's Study" column (*Harper's Magazine*, January 1888). A witty letter from Alice French pointed out that he had made an error about the resolution of the story and evoked an apology in a subsequent column (March 1888).

By 1891 French had published a novel, *Expiation* (1890; serialized in *Scribner's Magazine*, January-April 1890), and was producing about seven stories a year for leading periodicals such as *Scribner's Magazine* and *Atlantic Monthly*. In that year she accepted an offer from Horace Scudder of Houghton, Mifflin to bring out a second collec-

tion, *Otto the Knight, and Other Trans-Mississippi Stories* (1891). Of the book's ten tales, six deal with Arkansas, four with Iowa. Only the title story (*Scribner's Magazine*, August 1888) develops a didactic labor theme, demonstrating an immigrant laborer's reform from trade-union sympathizer to conservative. The Arkansas stories use humor, pathos, and vivid description to portray the social structure of the region. "Sist' Chaney's Black Silk" (*Harper's Bazar*, 4 May 1889) tells of a black woman's love for her invalid sister Chaney, which causes three white women from different backgrounds to defend an emphasis on life over death. Love for the invalid gives emotional meaning to the hard work of the protagonist Dosier, while her economic and physical sacrifices allow the invalid to die in peace. As a contrast to the somber theme, a middle-class southerner smacks her gum as she ponders–her name is Mrs. Ponder–the common experiences of white and black women. Another Arkansas story, "The Mortgage on Jeffy" (*Scribner's Magazine*, October 1887), uses the King Solomon theme. A migrant mother abandons her baby boy, who is then adopted by "Cap'n Bula," a young widow who runs her late husband's boating business. The natural mother returns to claim her child, working desperately to save money to repay the widow for his room and board. The melodramatic ending involves the migrant's death, after the two women reach an understanding about the child's welfare. The characteristic onlooker point of view, this time from the perspectives of an older woman and Bula's long-suffering suitor, prevents the story as a whole from becoming melodramatic.

A third Arkansas story, "Trusty, no. 49" (*Century Magazine*, June 1890), describes the harsh treatment of prisoners in rural work camps. French had to persuade a hesitant Gilder to publish her graphic account of beatings, exploitation, and degradation in *Century* because the editor feared that his genteel readers would be offended. The story is one of French's best treatments of a southern community.

Throughout the 1890s French enjoyed popular and critical success, ranking high as a chronicler of the West and the South. Her stories of Arkansas continue to seem authentic today, though her economic convictions are seen as a limitation to her credibility. The Iowa tales of *Otto the Knight, and Other Trans-Mississippi Stories* emphasize the sort of plain life-style, economic constraints, and triumphant personal relationships that French's later Davenport stories place in more detailed context. Remarkably unsentimental about the landscape of her native region, she concentrated on upper-class values practiced with humor and common sense for the general good. Two collections published by Scribners–after the loss of Horace Scudder's approval–display her economic theories against the background of the town she called Fairport. As he explained when he reviewed her next book (*Atlantic Monthly*, November 1893), Scudder believed that French needed to distill and revise her stories.

Stories of a Western Town (1893) offers a humorous representation of the foibles of the humble in their contacts with wiser, wealthier folk. Despite this class bias, the tales also depict successful social leveling, as well as the test of a young heir's values. Most characters seem based on family and friends, and their realistic presentation was praised by Marie Therese Blanc, a Parisian critic who compared French to Guy de Maupassant. The young model factory owner in several stories, Harry Lossing, was based on Robert French and was also, according to a letter French wrote in 1893 to Robert Bridges, associate editor of *Scribner's Magazine*, in response to Bridges's call for a hero, who, as French put it, "is doing his best for his community and country." This opening story, "The Besetment of Kurt Lieders" (*Scribner's Magazine*, August 1892), is a good example of the writer's notion that links between social classes in the Midwest were essentially beneficial to all. Lieders, a crusty old German carpenter, quits Lossing Manufacturing when Harry inherits the firm and changes production schedules. His depression then becomes the torment of his wife, who interrupts Lieders's several suicide attempts and finally gets his job back after explaining "Pappa" to the efficient, yet humane young Lossing. Another woman character comes to the rescue of the socialistic farmer Nelson in "The Face of Failure" (*Scribner's Magazine*, September 1892). The title character of the fourth story, "Mother Emeritus" (*Scribner's Magazine*, September 1892), is nearly forced by her well-meaning working daughter to leave her familiar city home for the restricted life of the suburbs. Her urban tenement and its neighborly community win her daughter's approval after the mother shows her independence and the Lossings intervene on her behalf.

The town's caste system receives a jolt when the hero of "Tommy and Thomas" (*Scribner's Magazine*, October 1892), the scrappy son of an Irish saloon keeper, rises to the status of congressman and relative by marriage to the story's narrator, genteel and satiric Mrs. Catherwood, who had tutored the boy for his first speech contest. To the relief of this snobbish narrator, the congressman proves to be the son of a formerly aristocratic family. Tommy's friend Harry Lossing is the protagonist of two of these tales, exercising small virtues in "An Assisted Providence" (*Scribner's Magazine*, December 1892) and using tact and cunning in "Harry Lossing" (*Scribner's Magazine*, February 1893) to win the wife of his choice. As the Lossing heir, Harry's intelligence and morality benefited the town and guaranteed his own success. These stories contain strains of sentimentality and melodrama, which may also be found in later works.

The second collection of Iowa stories, *The Missionary Sheriff* (1897), received favorable reviews in a year during which Henry James received poor ones. Readers were pleased that Octave Thanet had finally created a "real hero." That hero, Amos Wickliff, is depicted, in the book's six tales (republished from *Harper's Monthly*), as a homely, brave adventurer-moralist. The final story, "The Defeat of Amos Wickliff" (April 1896), wryly celebrates the bashful marriage proposal that now-prosperous Wickliff makes to the former fiancée of a dead man he had once rescued. In other stories the sheriff is a supporting character. Humorous satire of the lower middle class, such as that in "The Cabinet Organ" (July 1896), is mixed with admiration for middle-class values. In contrast to the unrelenting sadness with which Edith Wharton, for example, dealt with themes of fading gentility and female economic dependence, French depicts her middle-class characters as happy, thrifty, and wholesome. Young Pauline's noisy neighbors prove a source of new values, economic security, and love itself; she will bring them her exquisite taste and refinement, glad enough of solid domestic comforts to "marry down." This serious theme is presented farcically and melodramatically, an outgrowth of the hardheaded optimism the writer insisted on bringing to her craft. Though her diary reveals that she had doubts, fears, and disappointments–especially about money, since she outspent her considerable income regularly– it also shows that her feelings toward family and friends remained positive. A younger Davenport writer, Arthur Davison Ficke, presented French, in his poem about her decline ("My Princess," *Scribner's Magazine*, December 1922), as saying, "I will deny while I have living breath/All that is

Alice French

lonely, bitter, blind." As family members died, Alice French became curious about spiritualism and treated it skeptically in two stories in this collection, "The Next Room" (*Harper's Monthly*, November 1896) and "The Hypnotist" (*Harper's Monthly*, October 1896); in each case Wickliff is the sensible voice of practicality; yet the loneliness of the female protagonists, who have turned to spiritualism, is treated sympathetically.

From 1896 through 1900 editors of leading periodicals published fifty of Alice French's stories. Though her work does not show philosophical change, these late stories move away from dialect and regional description in favor of presenting domestic scenes which center on conflicts between personal and social responsibility. These tales, generally, have received less critical attention than those more squarely in the local-color or regional tradition. They do show the interaction of social groups, with more emphasis than in

previous tales on brief presentations of economic or social realities.

Almost immediately after the publication of *The Missionary Sheriff*, Alice French accepted an offer from Way and Williams to collect seven of her stories in a volume called *A Book of True Lovers* (1897), which increased her income from writing to $5,390 for that year. Her preface states that the lovers in these tales are tried by the "fire or . . . ireful acid" of marriage and left with the "pure gold" of the heart. In "The Dilemma of Sir Guy the Neuter" (*Scribner's Magazine*, May 1889) a couple is nearly pulled apart by the Reformation. In several of the other tales married women struggle to retain intellectual independence, women friends, and even–in the case of the black protagonist of "The Court of Last Resort" (*New Peterson's Magazine*, January 1893)–conjugal rights. One story, "The Strike at Glasscock's" (*Northwestern Miller*, Holiday Number, December 1893), seems derived from Mary Wilkins Freeman's "The Revolt of Mother" (1891), with the addition of an aristocratic arbitrator. Others in the collection–"Why Abbylonia Surrendered" (1897 is the presumed composition date of this tale) and "The Judgement on Mrs. Swift" (*New Peterson's Magazine*, November 1893)–are interesting treatments of mother-daughter themes.

In 1898, pressed by the desire to furnish Thanford, Alice French accepted two more offers for collections of stories she had published in magazines, while increasing her current output. The stories in *The Heart of Toil* and *A Slave to Duty & Other Women* (both published in 1898) show French, like other market-conscious contemporaries, following the trend away from regionalism; she turned more to comic and moralistic treatment of labor and domestic topics. *The Heart of Toil* includes six tales about workers. Reflecting the era's bias against immigrant laborers and their union movements, stories such as "Johnny's Job" (*Scribner's Magazine*, October 1898) and "The Scab" (*Scribner's Magazine*, August 1895) depict the wisdom of management. The positive reception of these tales, the thesis of which Alice French later developed into a novel, *The Man of the Hour* (1905), contrasted with the reviews of *A Slave to Duty & Other Women*. Labeled trivial because they deal with "unimportant" subjects, the tales concern women's dilemmas. The title story (*Woman's Home Companion*, January-March 1898) shows a brother-in-law refusing to allow his wife's sister to sacrifice her remaining resources and the good of the whole family by returning to an abusive husband. Despite the stereotypical situation (virgin bride and dissolute artist) the tale captures the tensions within the family quite well. Other stories in this volume, such as "A Colonial Dame" (*Woman's Home Companion*, August 1896) and "A Jealous Woman" (*Independent*, 29 July 1897), treat female friendships.

The Captured Dream, and Other Stories (1899) contains three tales on similar subjects–the title story, previously collected in *A Book of True Lovers*, "His Duty" from *The Missionary Sheriff*, and "The Stout Miss Hopkins' Bicycle" (*Harper's Monthly*, February 1897), a wry self-portrait. During the next decade the writer shifted her interests away from short fiction to novel writing and civic activities in favor of conservative issues. A potboiler, *The Lion's Share* (1907), evoked a rebuke from Sarah Orne Jewett, a friend, who in a 1907 letter to French called the book a waste of the author's "great heart . . . clear discernment of

character, [and] . . . knowledge of values." *By Inheritance* (1910), a novel about race relations in the South, earned high praise from Thomas Wentworth Higginson, and Booker T. Washington commented that the book told the unfortunate truth about education for blacks in the South.

A last collection of short fiction, *Stories That End Well* (1911), marks the end of Alice French's writing with any degree of distinction, though she published two other short works in book form, *A Step on the Stair* (1913) and *And the Captain Answered* (1917), a prowar tract. The 1911 collection was dismissed by her contemporaries, but these tales have consistently interested women reviewers and scholars. These stories reflect the writer's views on the woman-suffrage campaign, female friendships, the effects of slavery, the dangers of pacifism, the value of individual freedom, and the beneficent effects of land speculation in the Midwest. One story, "The Object of the Federation" (*Scribner's Magazine*, August 1901), shows how a couple renew their marriage when the woman discovers her leadership potential by working in a women's club. Most of these stories reflect French's opposition to the suffrage movement while she worked devotedly for various women's groups and engaged in other civic efforts.

During the last decades of her life, Alice French received significant honors. Theodore Roosevelt, who had carried *Knitters in the Sun* with him on a safari, entertained her at the White House in 1906 and visited her home in Davenport in 1910. She assisted Hamlin Garland–who always retained his respect for her–in the founding of the Society of Midland Authors in 1914; the Allied Arts Association honored her in November 1923 as the writer "who put the midland into midland literature." During the 1920s and 1930s an Octave Thanet Society thrived at the University of Iowa, which had given her an honorary doctorate in 1911; and she continued to encourage a group of Davenport writers which included Susan Glaspell. As a critic, she railed against naturalism, while praising Edna Ferber, Willa Cather, Sarah Orne Jewett, Mary Wilkins Freeman, and Margaret Deland as great writers. Her scorn for the work of Sinclair Lewis was unbounding because, she believed, Lewis made midwesterners look foolish. Recognizing her declining reputation, she said shortly before her death that she would "stand or fall" by the judgment of her generation, an opinion Henry Siedel Canby seemed to affirm by stating that she offered "an interesting and accurate picture of the thought and action of her time" (quoted by Rebecca Sewall, 1934).

Buried in the reaction against local color and regionalism, Alice French was treated somewhat negatively in George McMichael's 1965 biography, which is valuable for its extensive bibliographical information. Alice French must be recognized for her portraits of domestic relationships and social groups in Arkansas and Iowa. Two recent studies, Michael B. Dougan's 1976 article "When Fiction Is Reality: Arkansas Fiction of Octave Thanet" and Linda E. Rushton's 1982 dissertation, "The Arkansas Fiction of Alice French," indicate an interest in her southern tales. Sandra Ann Healey Tigges's 1981 American studies dissertation, "Alice French: A Noble Anachronism," discusses her work from an economic perspective. Though dismissed as unreadable in such reference sources as *Notable American Women*, the short fiction of Alice French invites study for the excellence of its plain diction, its complex but tidily resolved plots, its humor, and its energetic portrayal of two regions through the eyes of a transplanted New Englander. Her many literary friendships are also of interest, and feminist critics such as Lillian Faderman have already contributed toward a clearer understanding of her historical and literary contributions. Though McMichael's work emphasizes her decline, it might be more appropriate to recognize Ficke's view of the writer in "My Princess," which he ends by attributing to French a defiant response to pity or patronization: "Spare me your kindness:–For my pennon shall stream/Down to the place where the story's end is told."

Biography:
George McMichael, *Journey to Obscurity: The Life of Octave Thanet* (Lincoln: University of Nebraska Press, 1965).

References:
Th. Bentzon (Marie Therese Blanc), "In Arkansas Apropos of Octave Thanet's Romances," translated by Evelyn S. Schaeffer, *Midland Monthly*, 6 (July 1896): 37-47; (August 1896): 136-145;

Michael B. Dougan, "When Fiction Is Reality: Arkansas Fiction of Octave Thanet," *Arkansas Philological Association*, 2, no. 3 (1976): 29-36;

Lillian Faderman, *Surpassing the Love of Men: Romantic Friendship and Love Between Women from the Renaissance to the Present* (New York: Morrow, 1981);

Mary J. Reid, "The Theories of Octave Thanet and Other Western Realists," *Midland Monthly*, 9 (February 1898): 99-108;

Linda E. Rushton, "The Arkansas Fiction of Alice French," Ph.D. dissertation, University of Arkansas, 1982;

Rebecca Sewall, "Alice French: The Octave Thanet of Literature," M.A. thesis, Southern Methodist University, 1934;

Sandra Ann Healey Tigges, "Alice French: A Noble Anachronism," Ph.D. dissertation, University of Iowa, 1981.

Papers:
The Alice French Collection at the Newberry Library in Chicago includes diaries, letters, and some manuscripts, as well as an unpublished biography by Ruth Tucker, who knew Alice French at Clover Bend. Correspondence with other literary figures is in various other locations.

Edward Everett Hale

(3 April 1822-10 June 1909)

Samuel I. Bellman

California State Polytechnic University, Pomona

See also the Hale entry in *DLB 42: American Writers for Children Before 1900.*

BOOKS: *Jenny's Journey* (Boston: Carter, Hendee, 1840?);

A Tract for the Day; or, How to Conquer Texas before Texas Conquers Us (Boston: Redding, 1845);

"What Is the Worth of Doctrine?" A Sermon Preached at the Anniversary of the Charleston Unitarian Book and Tract Society (Charleston, S.C.: Printed by Walker & Burke, 1848);

Margaret Percival in America. Edited by a New England Minister, A.B., Being a Sequel to Margaret Percival: A Tale. Edited by Rev. William Sewell, B.A., by Hale and Lucretia Peabody Hale (Boston: Phillips, Sampson, 1850);

Sketches of Christian History (Boston, 1850); republished as *Scenes from Christian History* (Boston: Crosby, Nichols, 1852);

Christian Duty to Emigrants: A Sermon Delivered before the Boston Society for the Prevention of Pauperism at the Old South Church in Boston, May 9, 1852 (Boston: Printed by J. Wilson & Son, 1852);

The Lord Visits and Redeems His People. A Sermon Preached at the Installation of Rev. E. B. Wilson as Minister of the First Parish of West Roxbury, July 18, 1852 (Boston: Wilson, 1852);

Letters on Irish Emigration (Boston: Phillips, Sampson, 1852);

The Gospel of Freedom Extended by the Organization of Emigration, as F. I. (Boston, 1853);

Kanzas and Nebraska: The History, Geographical and Physical Characteristics, and Political Position of Those Territories; An Account of the Emigrant Aid Companies, and Directions to Emigrants (Boston: Phillips, Sampson/New York: J. C. Derby, 1854);

The Immaculate Conception: A Sermon Preached in the Church of the Unity, Worcester, and in the Second Congregational Church, Worcester, on the 14th and 21st of January, 1855 (Boston: Phillips, Sampson, 1855);

The Last Voyage of the Resolute (Boston, 1856);

The Relief of the Poor by Individuals, by the State, and by Benevolent Societies. A Discourse Delivered before the Howard Benevolent Society . . . Dec. 14, 1856 (Boston: Wilson, 1857);

Public Amusement for Poor and Rich. A Discourse Delivered before the Church of the Unity, Worcester, December 16, 1855 . . . (Boston: Phillips, Sampson, 1857);

How to Seek God. The Duties and the Dangers of a Revival: A Sermon Preached at the South Congregational Church, Boston, on the 14th of March, 1858 (Boston: Phillips, Sampson, 1858);

A Sermon Delivered before His Excellency Nathaniel P. Banks, Governor ... at the Annual Election, Wednesday, Jan. 5, 1859 (Boston: W. White, 1859);

The Elements of Christian Doctrine, and Its Development: Five Sermons Preached before the South Congregational Society, Boston, in January, February, and March 1860 (Boston: Walker, Wise, 1860);

Ninety Days' Worth of Europe (Boston: Walter, Wise, 1861);

Thirty Years of Boston: An Address Delivered at Hollis-street Church, Jan. 27, 1861 ... (Boston, 1861);

The Future Civilization of the South. A Sermon Preached on the 13th of April, 1862, at the South Congregational Church, Boston (Boston, 1862);

The Desert and the Promised Land. A Sermon (Boston: C. C. P. Moody, 1863);

The Emigration of Women to Oregon; A Report to the Directors of the New-England Emigrant Aid Co. (Boston, 1864);

Edward Everett in the Ministry of Reconciliation. A Sermon Preached in the South Congregational Church, Boston, Jan. 22, 1865 (Boston: Mudge, 1865);

The Man Without a Country (Boston: Ticknor & Fields, 1865);

The Public Duty of a Private Citizen: A Sermon Preached in the South Congregational Church, Boston, Sept. 3, 1865 ... (Cambridge, Mass.: J. Wilson & Sons, 1865);

The Christian Unity. A Sermon Preached at Boston, Nov. 11, 1866 (Boston: Mudge, 1866);

If, Yes, and Perhaps (Boston: Ticknor & Fields, 1868);

How They Live in Boston and How They Die There (N.p., 1869);

The Ingham Papers: Some Memorials of the Life of Capt. Frederic Ingham, U.S.N., Sometime Pastor of the First Sandemanian Church in Naguadavick, and Major General by Brevet in the Patriotic Service in Italy (Boston: Fields, Osgood, 1869);

Sybaris and Other Homes (Boston: Fields, Osgood, 1869);

People and Minister, An Anniversary Sermon, Preached at the South Congregational Church, Boston, January 9, 1870 (Boston, 1870);

How to Do It (Boston: Osgood, 1871);

Ten Times One Is Ten: The Possible Reformation, as Col. Frederic Ingham (Boston: Roberts, 1871);

Six of One by Half a Dozen of the Other: An Every Day Novel, by Hale, Harriet Beecher Stowe, Adeline D. T. Whitney, Lucretia P. Hale, Frederick W. Loring, and Frederic B. Perkins (Boston: Roberts, 1872);

His Level Best, and Other Stories (Boston: Roberts, 1872);

Christmas Eve and Christmas Day: Ten Christmas Stories (Boston: Roberts, 1873);

In His Name: A Christmas Story (Boston: Proprietors of Old and New, 1873);

Ups and Downs: An Every-day Novel (Boston: Roberts, 1873; London: Low, 1873);

A Summer Vacation. Four Sermons (Boston: Roberts, 1874);

Workingmen's Homes: Essays and Stories, by Edward E. Hale and Others, on the Homes of Men Who Work in Large Towns (Boston: Osgood, 1874);

One Hundred Years Ago. How the War Began (Boston: Lockwood, Brooks, 1875);

The Good Time Coming; or, Our New Crusade (Boston, 1875); republished as *Our New Crusade* (Boston: Roberts, 1894);

A Free-born Church. The Sermon Preached before the National Conference of Unitarian and Other Christian Churches, Sept. 12, 1876 (Boston, 1876);

Biographical Sketch of James Edward Root (Albany: Munsell, 1877);

G. T. T.; or, The Wonderful Adventures of a Pullman (Boston: Roberts, 1877);

Philip Nolan's Friends: A Story of the Change of Western Empire (New York: Scribner, Armstrong, 1877);

Salvation (Boston, 1877);

Wolf at the Door (Boston: Roberts, 1877);

Back to Back: A Story of To-day (New York: Harper, 1878);

Looking Back. A Sermon Preached at the South Congregational Church. Boston, Nov. 17, 1878 (Boston: Williams, 1878);

Mrs. Merriam's Scholars: A Story of the "Original Ten" (Boston: Roberts, 1878);

Sketches of the Lives of the Brothers Everett (Boston: Little, Brown, 1878);

What Career? Ten Papers on the Choice of a Vocation and the Use of Time (Boston: Roberts, 1878);

The Associated Charities. A Sermon Preached in the South Congregational Church, Boston, February 16, 1879 (Boston: A. Williams, 1879);

The Bible and Its Revisions: Three Addresses (Boston: A. Williams, 1879);

Blasphemy Against the Holy Ghost (Boston: A. Williams, 1879);

Candor in the Pulpit. A Sermon Preached at Boston, Sept. 7, 1879 (Boston, 1879);

Emigration to Kansas. An Address Delivered in Bismarck Grove, Lawrence, Kansas, on the 18th of September, 1879 (Boston: G. H. Ellis, 1879);

From Thanksgiving to Fast. Fifteen Sermons Preached at the South Congregational Church, Boston (Boston: Ellis, 1879);

The Future of New England. A Sermon Preached in the South Congregational Church, Boston, Fast Day, April 3, 1879 (Boston: A. Williams, 1879);

Stories of War, Told by Soldiers (Boston: Roberts, 1879);

Yourselves. A Sermon Preached at the South Congregational Church, Boston, Jan 12, 1879 (Boston: A. Williams, 1879);

The Channing Centennial. A Sermon Preached at the South Congregational Church, Boston, April 11, 1880 (Boston, 1880);

Crusoe in New York, and Other Tales (Boston: Roberts, 1880);

Exaggeration. A Sermon Preached at the South Congregational Church (Boston: G. H. Ellis, 1880);

Is Life Worth Living? A Sermon Preached at the South Congregational Church, Boston, April 25, 1880 (Boston, 1880);

The Kingdom of God, and Twenty Other Sermons Preached in the South Congregational Church, Boston (Boston: Roberts, 1880);

Life and Its Enemies. An Easter Sermon Preached at the South Congregational Church, Boston (Boston: G. H. Ellis, 1880);

The Life in Common, and Twenty Other Sermons Preached in the South Congregational Church, Boston (Boston: Roberts, 1880);

Purity and Temperance. Two Sermons Preached at the South Congregational Church, Boston (Boston: Ellis, 1880);

Stories of the Sea, Told by Sailors (Boston: Roberts, 1880);

Capt. Nathan Hale. An Address Delivered at Groton, Connecticut, on the Hale Memorial Day, September 7, 1881 (Boston: A. Williams, 1881);

A Family Flight through France, Germany, Norway and Switzerland, by Hale and Susan Hale (Boston: Lothrop, 1881);

June to May: The Sermons of a Year. Preached at the South Congregational Church in Boston, in 1880 and 1881 (Boston: Roberts, 1881);

Stories of Adventure, Told by Adventurers (Boston: Roberts, 1881);

A Congregational Church; A Sermon Preached in the South Congregational Church, Boston, on the Twentieth Anniversary of Its Dedication, January 8, 1882 (Boston: G. H. Ellis, 1882);

A Family Flight over Egypt and Syria, by Hale and Susan Hale (Boston: Lothrop, 1882);

Our Christmas in a Palace, A Traveller's Story (New York: Funk & Wagnalls, 1883);

Seven Spanish Cities and the Way to Them (Boston: Roberts, 1883);

Stories of Discovery, Told by Discoverers (Boston: Roberts, 1883);

A Family Flight around Home, by Hale and Susan Hale (Boston: Lothrop, 1884);

Christmas in Narragansett (New York & London: Funk & Wagnalls, 1884);

A Family Flight through Spain, by Hale and Susan Hale (Boston: Lothrop, 1884);

The Fortunes of Rachel (New York: Funk & Wagnalls, 1884; London: Funk & Wagnalls, 1884);

Stories of the Wadsworth Club (Boston: J. S. Smith, 1884);

Boys' Heroes (Boston: Lothrop, 1885);

The Joy of the Lord. A Sermon, June 21, 1885 (Boston: G. H. Ellis, 1885);

Stories of Invention, Told by Inventors and Their Friends (Boston: Roberts, 1885);

What Is the American People? An Address Delivered before the Phi Beta Kappa of Brown University . . . (Boston: J. S. Smith, 1885);

Easter, A Collection for a Hundred Friends (Boston: J. S. Smith, 1886);

A Family Flight through Mexico, by Hale and Susan Hale (Boston: Lothrop, 1886);

Red and White: A Christmas Story (Boston: J. S. Smith, 1887);

The Story of Spain, by Hale and Susan Hale (New York & London: Putnam's, 1887); republished as *Spain* (New York: Putnam's, 1899);

History of the United States. Written for the Chautauqua Reading Circles (New York: Chautauqua Press, 1887);

Franklin in France. From Original Documents, Most of Which Are Now Published for the First Time, by Hale and Edward Everett Hale, Jr., 2 volumes (Boston: Roberts, 1887, 1888);

Daily Bread: A Story of the Snow Blockade (Boston: J. S. Smith, 1888);

How They Lived in Hampton: A Study of Practical Christianity Applied in the Manufacture of Linens (Boston: J. S. Smith, 1888);

The Life of George Washington, Studied Anew (New York & London: Putnam's, 1888);

Mr. Tangier's Vacations, A Novel (Boston: Roberts, 1888);

My Friend the Boss: A Story of To-day (Boston: J. S. Smith, 1888);

The Ten Times One Is Ten and Lend a Hand Clubs (Boston: J. S. Smith, 1888);

Tom Torrey's Tariff Talks (Boston: J. Stilman, 1888);

The Temperance Puritan (Boston, 1890);

Four and Five: A Story of a Lend-a-Hand Club (Boston: Roberts, 1891);

The Life of Christopher Columbus, From His Own Letters and Journals and Other Documents of His Time (Chicago: G. L. Howe, 1891); republished as *The Story of Columbus as He Told It Himself* (Boston: J. S. Smith, 1893);

The Story of Massachusetts (Boston: Lothrop, 1891);

Afloat and Ashore (Chicago: Searle & Gorton, 1891);

The New Harry and Lucy: A Story of Boston in the Summer of 1891, by Hale and Lucretia P. Hale (Boston: Roberts, 1892);

The New Ohio: A Story of East and West (London: Cassell, 1892); also published as *East and West: A Story of New-Born Ohio* (New York: Cassell, 1892);

Every-day Sermons (Boston: J. S. Smith, 1892);

Sybil Knox; or, Home Again: A Story of To-day (New York: Cassell, 1892; London: Cassell, 1892);

For Fifty Years: Verses Written on Occasion, in the Nineteenth Century (Boston: Roberts, 1893);

A New England Boyhood (New York: Cassell, 1893); enlarged as *A New England Boyhood, and Other Bits of Autobiography,* volume 6 of *The Works of Edward Everett Hale* (Boston: Little, Brown, 1900);

One Good Turn, A Story (Boston: J. S. Smith, 1893);

Ralph Waldo Emerson. An Address Delivered before the Brooklyn Institute on the 24th of May, 1893 . . . (Boston: J. S. Smith, 1893);

Sermons of the Winter (Boston: J. S. Smith, 1893);

If Jesus Came to Boston (Boston: J. S. Smith, 1895);

Studies in American Colonial Life (Meadville, Pa.: Flood and Vincent, Chautauqua Century Press, 1895);

Susan's Escort (Boston: J. S. Smith, 1895);

Aunt Caroline's Present (Boston: J. S. Smith, 1895);

Col. Clipsham's Calendar (Boston: J. S. Smith, 1895);

Hands Off (Boston: J. S. Smith, 1895);

A Safe Deposit (Boston: J. S. Smith, 1895);

The Foundation of the Nation. Nov. 8, 1896 (Boston: J. S. Smith, 1896);

Independence Day. An Address (Philadelphia: Altemus, 1896);

Man and Beast (Boston: J. S. Smith, 1896);

The Contribution of Boston to American Independence. Oration delivered . . . July 5, 1897 (Boston: Printed by Order of the City Council, 1897);

Susan's Escort, and Others (New York: Harper, 1897);

Historic Boston and Its Neighborhood: An Historical Pilgrimage (New York: Appleton, 1898);

Personal Purity (Boston: Unitarian Temperance Society, 1898);

Young Americans Abroad, by Hale and Susan Hale (Boston: Lothrop, 1898);

The Brick Moon, and Other Stories, volume 4 of *The Works of Edward Everett Hale* (Boston: Little, Brown, 1899);

Comfort and Comforters. A Sermon Preached at the South Congregational Church, Boston, Sunday, January 8, 1899 (Boston: Rockwell & Churchill, 1899);

James Russell Lowell and His Friends (Boston & New York: Houghton, Mifflin, 1899);

The Old Diplomacy, Arbitration and the Permanent Tribunal (Boston: American Peace Society, 1899);

A Permanent Tribunal: The Emperor of Russia and His Circular Regarding Permanent Peace (Boston: G. H. Ellis, 1899);

Picturesque Massachusetts, volume 2 of *Picturesque and Architectural New England,* edited by D. H. Hurd (Boston: D. H. Hurd, 1899);

Ralph Waldo Emerson, by Edward Everett Hale, Together with Two Early Essays of Emerson (Boston: Little, Brown, 1899);

Addresses and Essays on Subjects of History, Education, and Government, volume 8 of *The Works of Edward Everett Hale* (Boston: Little, Brown, 1900);

How to Do It; To Which Is Added, How to Live, volume 7 of *The Works of Edward Everett Hale* (Boston: Little, Brown, 1900);

The Pilgrim Covenant of 1602, A Covenant for the Churches of To-day. A Sermon Preached before the Massachusetts Convention of Congregational Ministers at the South Congregational Church, Boston, on the 31st Day of May, A.D. 1900 (Cambridge, Mass.: Co-operative Press, 1900);

Young Americans in the Orient (Boston: Lothrop, 1900);

Hale's birthplace (far left), at the corner of Tremont and School Streets in Boston

Poems and Fancies, volume 10 of *The Works of Edward Everett Hale* (Boston: Little, Brown, 1901);

Sunday Afternoon Stories for Home and School. Written or Revised by E. E. Hale, 2 volumes (Boston: Office of Lend a Hand Record, 1901);

Memories of a Hundred Years, 2 volumes (New York & London: Macmillan, 1902; revised and enlarged, 1904);

How Shall Unitarianism Reach the People? A Plea for a Central Unitarian Temple in Boston. An Address . . . at the Hotel Vendome, Nov. 12, 1902 (Boston: Unitarian Club, 1903);

New England History in Ballads, By Edward E. Hale and His Children, with a Few Additions by Other People (Boston: Little, Brown, 1903);

"We, The People": A Series of Papers on Topics of Today (New York: Dodd, Mead, 1903);

The Ideas of the Founders: An Address Delivered before the Brooklyn Institute, November 4, 1903 (Boston: Lend a Hand Co., 1904);

Prayers in the Senate. Prayers Offered in the Senate of the United States in the Winter Session of 1904, by Edward E. Hale, Chaplain (Boston: Little, Brown, 1904);

The Real Presence of the Living God (Boston: American Unitarian Association, 1904);

The Foundations of the Republic (New York: Pott, 1906);

For Christmas and New Year: Dedicated to My Own Friends (Boston: Privately printed, 1906);

Tarry at Home Travels (New York & London: Macmillan, 1906);

Prospero's Island (New York: Printed for the Dramatic Museum of Columbia University, 1919).

Collection: *The Works of Edward Everett Hale*, 10 volumes (Boston: Little, Brown, 1898-1901).

Edward Everett Hale is best known for two short stories he collected in *If, Yes, and Perhaps* (1868): "The Man Without a Country" (first published in the *Atlantic Monthly*, December 1863) and a facetious account of a busy clergyman who attempted to employ a stand-in, "My Double and How He Undid Me" (*Atlantic Monthly*, September 1859). The son of Nathan and Sarah Preston Everett Hale, Edward Everett Hale counted among his ancestors some of the most illustrious Boston Brahmins. He was the grandnephew of Capt. Nathan Hale, the youthful Revolutionary War spy who–captured and about to be executed by the British–expressed his regret at having only one life to lose for his country. Edward Everett, Hale's maternal uncle, was a famous orator who became governor of Massachusetts, minister to England, secretary of state, and a U.S. senator. Hale's father was owner and editor of the *Boston Daily Advertiser*.

Having begun school, at his own request, when he was two, Hale later attended Boston Latin School and entered Harvard College at the age of thirteen. At times bored by the too-easy lessons, he received his A.B. in 1839, at seventeen, having been named class poet and elected to Phi Beta Kappa. Then followed a period of groping toward a career: teaching at Boston Latin School (1839-1841), writing for newspapers and magazines, and studying for the ministry on his own, rather than attending Harvard Divinity School, because he was tired of formal education and unwilling to ask his family to support him for three more years of school. Licensed to preach in 1842, he substituted in pulpits from Washington, D.C., to Boston and did not have his own church until 1846, when he was ordained minister to a Unitarian congregation, the Church of the Unity in Worcester, Massachusetts. On 13 October 1852 he married Emily Baldwin Perkins, granddaughter of Lyman Beecher and niece of Harriet Beecher Stowe and Henry Ward Beecher. The Hales had one daughter and seven sons in the course of their long, happy marriage.

In 1856 Hale left the Worcester pulpit to become minister of Boston's South Congregational Church, a post he held until 1899. His service in the Christian ministry was crowned by his tenure as chaplain of the U.S. Senate from December 1903 until his death on 10 June 1909. While fulfilling his clerical duties and participating in the activities of various societies and organizations, Hale–who clearly resented the claims on his time by assorted petitioners–was somehow able to turn out an endless flow of stories and novels, sketches, travel accounts, religious tracts, and journalistic pieces, in addition to his regular sermons. His first published short story, "The Tale of a Salamander," appeared in the January 1842 issue of the *Boston Miscellany*, a magazine edited by his brother Nathan. From 1857 to 1861 Hale and Frederic H. Hedge were coeditors of the *Christian Examiner*, and Hale served as associate editor of the *Army Navy Journal* in 1863, the first year of the magazine's existence. Hale's most significant venture was *Old and New*, which he founded in January 1870 and continued to edit until May 1875. Hale contributed heavily to his magazine (which was so much a reflection of its editor's personality that a competitor described it as "All-Hale") and to its special holiday number, or annual gift book, *The Christmas Locket*. *Old and New* was merged with *Scribner's Monthly* in mid 1875, but Hale went on to edit the *Lend a Hand Record*, a magazine for clubs inspired by his *Ten Times One Is Ten* (1871) and *Mrs. Merriam's Scholars* (1878), from 1886 to 1897; to edit *New England Magazine* in 1889; and–in 1899–to publish the *Peace Crusade*, a newspaper favoring the establishment of the Permanent Court of Arbitration at The Hague.

An important factor in Hale's development was his unusually happy and intellectually stimulating family circle. Through it and through his Harvard experience he was not only put on familiar terms with the great and the near-great, he was also made aware of many scientific and technological advances, knowledge of which he put to good use in his fiction. As complicated as Hale was in many ways, his religious faith remained unburdened by doctrinal distinctions or creeping doubts arising from theological dilemmas or logical impasses. His was a faith that fed on a disposition toward piety and the unwavering acceptance

of the Good News of the New Testament. Hale's biographer Jean Holloway attributes his simple outlook on religion to "the latitudinarianism of the 'Boston religion,' a healthy home life, and a native *joie de vivre*." Though few, if any, of the richly diversified cultural elements to which Hale was exposed were ever lost on him, he was not, for the most part, an original thinker. He was not the sort of person who synthesizes a bold new system of interpretation and belief, or develops a new technique for making his fictive fantasies come alive. Yet his best short fictions are excellent examples of what would later be called the "well-made short story."

This term dates from the 1880s when such writers as Thomas Bailey Aldrich, Brander Matthews, Frank Stockton, and H. C. Bunner were applying the techniques of French authors such as Alphonse Daudet and Guy de Maupassant to the same American subject matter drawn upon by the period's local-color writers for stories that tended to sacrifice plot to careful observation of language and setting. Though the carefully plotted fiction of the 1880s is directly derived from the French, it is rooted in the tales of Edgar Allan Poe, and some of Hale's short fiction may be seen as prototypical for these stories of ingenious situations reaching unexpected conclusions.

One of Hale's most effective contributions to the genre of the well-made story is his first important short story, "My Double and How He Undid Me," which concerns the vexations of a Protestant minister who cannot keep up with all of the social duties placed on him. (Hale whimsically made his narrator, Rev. Frederic Ingham, a Sandemanian minister, explaining much later in his career that this early Christian sect did not distinguish between laymen and the clergy.) In order to fulfill the demands for his presence at various organizations' meetings he enlists the aid of a dull-witted, shiftless person with a strikingly similar appearance, legally changes the man's name to his, and teaches him four stock responses sufficient for most occasions: "Very well, thank you. And you?"; "I am very glad you liked it"; "There has been so much said, and, on the whole, so well said, that I will not occupy the time"; and "I agree, in general, with my friend on the other side of the room." Instructing his double never to give speeches and always to vote with the minority, Ingham lets this simpleton alter ego serve as his stand-in whenever possible. Eventually this double finds himself in a situation where the four set responses will not serve, and the clergyman's deception is found out. Ingham is banished to a new parish, a remote tract in the state of Maine, where his only parishioners are his wife and little daughter.

Frederic Ingham became a sort of alter ego for Hale. Capt. Frederic Ingham is the pseudonymous author and narrator of "The Man Without a Country," Hale's classic of American patriotism. After its initial appearance in the *Atlantic* (December 1863), the story was separately published in 1865 and has had a continually successful publication history since that time. It has been the basis for a 1925 film and a 1973 television movie starring Cliff Robertson and Robert Ryan, and has also been adapted for stage and radio. The story began as a fictional response to Clement L. Vallandigham, a Peace Democrat (or Copperhead) candidate for governor of Ohio, who—as Hale explained in an article on the story's origins (*Outlook*, 5 May 1898)—said "he did not want to belong to a nation which would compel by arms the loyalty of any of its citizens; he did not want to belong to the United States." Hale hoped that his story would be published in time to influence the November election, but it did not appear in the *Atlantic* until the election was over. (Vallandigham was defeated, however, and banished to the Confederacy.) Hale set his story during the early 1800s and made his fictional protagonist, Philip Nolan, a young army officer who has taken part in Aaron Burr's attempts to seize southwestern territories for purposes that remain obscure. (Hale later discovered that there had been a real Philip Nolan, a horse trader killed on the Mexican border in 1801, and made him the subject of *Philip Nolan's Friends*, 1877.) Captured, brought to trial for his treasonous action, and found guilty—(Burr himself was found innocent)—Nolan is asked by the judge whether he wishes to say anything to indicate his loyalty to the United States. By way of reply the angered Nolan damns his country and states that he never wants to hear of it again. His punitive reward soon follows: eternal banishment from his native land and a lifetime of being kept at sea far from American shores, in custody on a succession of naval vessels. Nolan experiences something like twenty nautical transfers from the time of his sentencing in 1807 until his death in 1863. Yet, though he is never permitted to hear the name of the United States or to receive intelligence about what is happening there, he dies fully repentant, overflowing with belated loyalty toward, and love for, his once-rejected country.

In fact, early in his confinement Nolan becomes sorry for what he has done. One of his last requests is that he be buried at sea and that a memorial stone be erected for him, with an epitaph stating he loved his country as no other man has, but no other has deserved less from her.

These two "well-made" stories embody many of what John R. Adams calls the "recurrent themes and mannerisms that distinguished his work from that of other [contemporary] practicing writers . . . ," among which are "flights into pure whimsicality," "the framework device, including the creation of an alter ego," in his character Frederic Ingham, "a permanent campaign for the protection of privacy," and exemplifications of Hale's belief "that actions, trivial in themselves, initiate chain reactions of unpredictable complexity." Both "My Double and How He Undid Me" and "The Man Without a Country," which in most respects are so unlike, are in a sense "flights into pure whimsicality," in that the protagonist of each story has his improbable wish fulfilled. Moreover, his actions lead to consequences he has not predicted. The stories also share a narrator, Hale's alter ego Frederic Ingham, who in "My Double and How He Undid Me" creates his own alter ego when he "recreates" the simpleminded Daniel Shea in his own image. Finally, these stories deal with the individual's resistance to society's encroachments, which in its strongest form amounts to Nathaniel Hawthorne's unpardonable sin of pride, self-isolation from humanity.

The stories that present imaginative solutions give a rough idea of Hale's far-reaching inventiveness as a writer of short fiction. In "My Double and How He Undid Me" and in "The Man Without a Country," only if one suspended rational judgment could the workability of these solutions seem plausible. The more closely one examines Hale's other stories and fictional sketches, the more painfully unreal many of his solutions to his protagonists' problems seem. In comparison to Hale's contrived plots, O. Henry's story endings do not strike the reader now as such glaring departures from good sense. More to the point, the outrageously sentimental fiction of Horatio Alger, Jr.—with its themes of "luck and pluck" and the saving miracle—seems but a continuation of some of Hale's commonest fictional elements.

In "The Children of the Public" (*Frank Leslie's Illustrated Newspaper*, 24 and 31 January 1863; collected in *If, Yes, and Perhaps*) Hale develops a convoluted fable about two poor young

The Church of the Unity in Worcester, Massachusetts, where Hale preached from 1846 to 1856

waifs, Felix and Fausta, who meet by chance en route to New York City to attend a big lottery drawing. Each wins a large purse in the lottery; they marry and live "happily ever after." Years later, when they are temporarily low on funds, Fausta has her husband write the story of their coming together, which wins a prize in a story-writing contest held by *Frank Leslie's Illustrated Newspaper*. (Hale himself was to win such a prize with this story.) The point of Felix's long-winded narrative is that he and Fausta are "Children of the Public," the public representing the benevolent sovereign and father substitute on earth–faintly mirroring the heavenly one–who takes good care of his offspring, if they trust him, if they do honest work while seeking only their share of life's benefits, and if they never go to the pork-barrel (Hale's metaphor for applying to the public) before the moment of their need. Relying on such a parent, Felix and Fausta have up to

now surmounted all their obstacles and, the reader gathers, can look forward to a relatively trouble-free future so long as they continue to keep faith and follow the rules.

"The Rag-Man and the Rag-Woman" (*Atlantic Almanac*, 1868; collected in *The Ingham Papers*, 1869) is almost literally a rags-to-riches story. Lively and witty, full of amusing authorial intrusions, it treats the financial and domestic doings of George Haliburton, a friend of Frederic Ingham (once again Hale's fictional alter ego). Haliburton, a cashiered insurance salesman, begins collecting wastepaper for reclamation and profit. His venture succeeds, and he even starts a periodical, the *Unfortunates' Magazine*, so that submitted manuscripts can feed his paper mill. One day, while in the process of performing a good deed, he meets a beautiful and charming young woman, Anna Davenport, who is running a rag-picking and recycling operation with her much younger siblings. Soon taking to each other, she and Haliburton marry and pool their operations. With his rapidly increasing resources, Haliburton moves into lumbering and papermaking. Eventually he declines a bank presidency, on the plea that "though his fortune was made of rags, he preferred the crude to the manufactured article."

"Crusoe in New York" (*Frank Leslie's Illustrated Magazine*, date unknown; collected in *Crusoe in New York, and Other Tales*, 1880) is a lengthy tale of self-reliance and survivalism in the tradition of Daniel Defoe's *Robinson Crusoe* (1719-1720) and Thoreau's *Walden* (1854). The young protagonist, a skilled woodworker named Rob, erects a small dwelling for his widowed mother and himself on a lot owned by his employer. Here, unknown to the outside world, they live for many years, having solved their economic problems by an ingenious combination of parasitism and frugality, until the aptly named Rob gains his fortune and the hand of a beautiful young immigrant woman whom he rescues from a gang of villainous white slavers. Among the curious features of this flimsy story is Rob's unabashed "sweetheart" relationship with his mother, before he becomes involved with the angelic near victim of the flesh merchants.

"A Civil Servant" (*Old and New*, January 1874; collected in *Crusoe in New York, and Other Tales*) provides an ironically fitting solution to the economic problem of another kind of man. As Adams says, the story's "parasitic bureaucrat," John Sapp, having "been trained to do nothing in particular" and wanting "to do nothing, . . . is therefore fitted only for a job in which nothing is to be done." After applying for twenty such positions, Sapp is granted a post on an uninhabited Aleutian Island, where he goes mad but finds complete happiness.

"The Minister's Black Veil: With Full Particulars" (*Independent*, 21 February 1889; collected in *Susan's Escort, and Others*, 1897) purports to explain why Hawthorne's mysterious Reverend Hooper wears his black veil. According to Hale, Hooper, unable to concentrate on the preparation of his sermons and on the improvement of his inner life because of all the demands made on his time by the members of his flock, is given some useful advice by his sister Martha: he should wear a protective veil so that he will not be recognized when he strolls about on the outside. This expedient leads to beneficial results for Hooper and certain of his congregants, but the violence done to Hawthorne's theology and

the tenuous excuse for Hooper's self-imposed alienation (according to Hale "he could obey that great instruction of the Master to his disciples, that when they went on his imperial mission they should not stop on the way to salute vagrants") seem not to have bothered Hale at all.

"Susan's Escort" (*Harper's*, May 1890; collected in *Susan's Escort, and Others*) presents the ultimate solution to the problem of the proper female who must travel at night, unaccompanied, through the perilous city: one constructs a collapsible and easily held dummy in the form of a man, dresses it in man's attire, and opens it up for use when its "company" is needed. Susan's "escort," like Hawthorne's humanoid straw man Feathertop, comes to life after a fashion. When Susan no longer wants him they discuss his problematical future, and he ultimately becomes a tailor's dummy.

Other stories stressing the value of isolation from society's encroachments include "His Level Best" and "The Modern Psyche." In "His Level Best" (first published in *His Level Best, and Other Stories*, 1872) a good-hearted man and his wife, possessed of far more than average means, follow the admonitions of minister, family, and society in general and do all they can (their "level best") to meet the unceasing demands of the needy, the importunate, the petitioners. Thus victimized without respite or relief, they and their children end up in the poorhouse. In "The Modern Psyche" (*Harper's*, November 1875; collected in *Crusoe in New York, and Other Tales*) a newspaper editor deliberately conceals his occupation from his bride, lest her knowledge of his public position (in which he can somehow remain anonymous) cause all kinds of intruders to invade the privacy of their new home. Like "His Level Best," this deceptively lighthearted satire ends tragically. Once the wife's curious sisters manage to discover his secret, the world beats a path to their door, and in a sense his wife loses him forever. Fearing that, despite the title, his readers might miss the story's analogy to the classical tale of Cupid and Psyche, Hale summarizes it in a long footnote at the beginning.

"A New Arabian Night" (*Harper's*, March 1889; collected in *Susan's Escort, and Others*) once again invokes the notion of the double. The president of the United States encounters a club of "calenders," mendicants who stand in for wealthy or prominent people, and he obtains his own stand-in. When the president suffers an accident and dies, the crisis is self-correcting: "No public announcement of the President's death was thought necessary by the Secretary of State. Times were prosperous. As always, the country governed itself without much regard to Washington."

Hale's fictional other self, Frederic Ingham, appears so frequently throughout Hale's fiction (sometimes with his wife Polly and their friends the Carters, the Haliburtons, and the Hackmatacks) that he seems an authorial obsession. As Hale's son explained in his biography of his father, " 'My Double' and 'The Man Without a Country' were written in the days when magazines did not print the names of their authors, and came before the people as the work of Frederic Ingham. My father amused himself with the versatile Frederic Ingham. Sometimes he was Captain in the United States Navy, commanding the *Florida* captured from the Confederates; sometimes he was the Sandamanian [*sic*] minister at Naguadavick and later in the Third Range. . . . He was an all-around man, a man who could do anything that came up in the course of daily duty." Quoting from Hale's "Memoir of Captain Frederic Ingham," his somewhat idealized account of his other self, in the 1869 *Ingham Papers*, the younger Hale summed up Ingham's (and his father's) performing this *duty* wherever it lay with his "moral purpose entirely controlling such mental aptness or physical habits as he could bring to bear."

"Colonel Ingham's Journey" (*Harper's*, December 1883; collected in *Christmas in Narragansett*, 1884) has to do with Hale's familiar double, but this time he seeks out *his* other self by traveling to the North Pole, where he meets his opposite number: a Chinese man named Kan-schau. Hale explains soul sharing by antipodal opposites: one sleeps while the other is awake, and their one soul resides always in the waking body. At first Ingham and Kan-schau communicate beautifully, through written messages containing greetings and offers of food, but eventually the language barrier proves too much for them, and meaningful contact ceases.

Adams has also noted Hale's "fondness for Christmas tales." In fact, these stories are part of a larger group of tales concerned with Christian service and benevolence, which are returned in bountiful measure. These moralistic stories—often simplistic in the extreme—occupy a great part of Hale's short fiction and stand in marked contrast to his light, sophisticated, and funny stories, with their realistic appraisal of human nature and their clear focus on earthly doings. The stories collected in *Christmas Eve and Christmas Day* (1873)—taken from Hale's *Old and New* "and from such diverse sources as the *Christian Union, Galaxy,* and newspaper files"—will serve as examples.

"They Saw a Great Light" (*Old and New,* January 1872) and "The Same Christmas in Old England and New" (*Galaxy,* June 1868) also illustrate Hale's tendency to provide otherwise conventional story lines with historical or pseudo-historical settings. "They Saw a Great Light" traces a colonial family and their descendants through America's early wars and ends symbolically with the glorious illumination of a lighthouse at Christmastime leading home a loved one who was lost at sea. "The Same Christmas in Old England and New" extends the temporal view of the binding cultural influence of Christianity to the ancestral shores of England; thus Hale adds a geographical dimension to his treatment of the continuity of tradition. Deeply immersed in history and desirous of keeping America's national heritage alive, Hale frequently popularized history in his short fictions.

A different and more exotic historical narrative, which is a bit evocative of Saints' Lives, is "The Two Princes: A Story for Children" (*Old and New,* January 1870). Hale juxtaposes the reigns of two medieval kings—one Bohemian and the other Hungarian—working into the account the Crusades, the Black Death, and the building of a great cathedral. "See what faith hath wrought!" might serve as a motto for this pious little story.

It comes as no surprise that Hale on occasion used elements from Jesus' teachings to instruct his audience. "Love is the Whole: A Story for Children" (*Hearth and Home,* 2 December 1871) seems to be a secular application of Jesus' commands to his disciples, when he knew his last hour was drawing nigh: "This is my commandment, That ye love one another, as I have loved you" (John 15:12). Five motherless children living in a little house on the western prairie are urged by their dying father to love and be kind to one another, to stay together or at least love one another as though they were still together: "Love is the while." This parting message is not lost on his children.

"Alice Macneil's Christian Tree" (*Christian Union,* 25 December 1871) gives a lesson in moral redemption through properly handled chastisement. An early version of a "dead-end kid" from a slum misbehaves badly at a Christmas party for which the good-deed-doer Alice

Hale and his wife, Emily, with their daughter Ellen, daguerreotypes taken in 1855

Macneil has made a special Christmas tree. He is summarily and severely punished for his misconduct. Then he speedily reforms, goes to school so that he can learn to write, and in time becomes a respectable bookstore clerk. Alice is praised for her part in saving this lad, and she is described in a way that indicates Hale considers her a fisher of men (as Jesus called his first two disciples in Matthew 4:18-20).

Two variations on the motif of the immeasurable social benefits wrought by a "Good and Faithful Servant" are "Daily Bread" (*Boston Daily Advertiser*, 25 December 1869; collected first in *The Ingham Papers* before it appeared in *Christmas Eve and Christmas Day*) and "Stand and Wait" (*The Christmas Locket*, 1870). In "Daily Bread" the life of a gravely ill baby is saved because a dairyman's wife acts beyond the call of duty, milks some of her cows, and thus makes it possible for the much-needed milk to reach the baby–despite a formidable snow blockade–in the nick of time. The narrator's commentary on this social miracle story is emblematic and symptomatic of one essential facet of Hale's thinking: "And you and I, dear reader, if we can forget that always our daily bread comes to us, because a thousand brave men and a thousand brave women are at work in the world, praying to God and trying to serve him, we will not forget it as we meet at break-

fast on this blessed Christmas day!" "Stand and Wait" is a lengthy account of a worthy benefactor of society, Huldah Root, and other noble, self-sacrificing women, who wind up finally in a retirement home dedicated to the "Apotheosis of Noble Ministry." At a Christmas dinner the Order of Loving Service is created, and the six saintly women inducted into the order are each given a jeweled gold Maltese cross hanging from a blue-and-white ribbon. The title "Stand and Wait," evoking Milton's sonnet "On His Blindness"–in which Milton tells himself that those who *only* stand and wait also serve God–seems oddly chosen for a moral uplift piece about elderly women whose Christian service is characterized by both faith and good works.

Hale was not entirely humorless in the matter of religious concerns, nor was he naively unsophisticated, or sunk in closed-minded religiosity–despite his profound commitment to his pastoral duties and to conveying the Christian message through the medium of journalism. Occasionally he enlivened his subject matter with humor that seemed to come from a nontheological, sharply realistic appraisal of human nature. "Stand and Wait" contains–in one of those authorial intrusions that mitigate somewhat the banality of certain of Hale's short stories–a candid mockery or possibly a parody of the hack plots in the contemporary dime novels. Yet, ironically, Hale produced some of the most egregious hack story lines ever concocted, and he defended hack writing, when it was related to Christian duty, in "John Rich and Lucy Poor" (first published in *Susan's Escort, and Others*).

One of Hale's most amusing short fictions is "The Survivor's Story" (*The Christmas Locket*, 1870; collected in *Christmas Eve and Christmas Day*): a series of comic anecdotes told by eight travelers (four couples who happen to be close friends) stranded in a Springfield, Massachusetts, hotel over Christmas when a bad snowdrift interrupts their journey. Christmas here is treated in terms of adult, lighthearted holiday spirits, with none of the cloying pietistic constraints found in Hale's other Christmas stories. "Aunt Caroline's Present" (*Harper's*, February 1885; collected in *Susan's Escort, and Others*) is a rollicking yarn about a young married couple's dilemma: what are they to do with a most unsightly wedding gift from a kindly, generous, lovable aunt: "a thoroughly horrible picture from the parable of the Prodigal Son. It had escaped by misfortune from some 'chamber of horrors.'" However hard they try to escape from, or lose, this hideous reminder of one of Jesus' parables and of their aunt's love, it remains an irremovable albatross in their lives.

Hale's deep interest in history generally and American history in particular may be seen in stories other than the ones discussed earlier. Another Christmas story, "From Generation to Generation" (*New England Magazine*, December 1895; collected in *Susan's Escort, and Others*), describes the way Christmas was celebrated a few years after the arrival of the *Mayflower* in 1620, through the time of the great evangelist George Whitefield's visits to the New World in the 1740s, to about the end of the nineteenth century. Three short pseudohistorical tales—"From Making to Baking," "The First Grain Market," and "Pharaoh's Harvest" (all first published in *Susan's Escort, and Others*)—concern the production of grain and the making of bread. "The First Grain Market" is a fanciful piece about a Winnebago Indian boy and his sister inviting the great French explorer La Salle to their tribal feast celebrating the grain harvest. "Pharaoh's Harvest" concerns a Kentish family in the Massachusetts Bay Colony in 1630. Their saving and storing of their best grains ("Pharaoh's Wheat") yields, over a long span of generations, not only much good wheat but also other pleasant dividends for their descendants.

"The Story of Oello" (first published in *Christmas Eve and Christmas Day*) is a sentimental legend about a pious, prayerful couple–Oello and her husband Manco–who wandered south from their tropical home and encountered a tribe of savage Indians, whom they civilized by treating them kindly and teaching them agricultural techniques. On a more secular and less moralistic note, "Paul Jones and Denis Duval" (*Atlantic Monthly*, October 1864; collected in *The Ingham Papers*) is a fictional-historical extrapolation that places the hero of William Makepeace Thackeray's novel *Denis Duval* (1864) aboard the British ship *Serapis* during its Revolutionary War battle with the American *Bon Homme Richard*, captained by John Paul Jones.

In "The Old and the New, Face to Face" (*Sartain's*, 1852; collected in *If, Yes, and Perhaps*) the Apostle Paul confronts Emperor Nero and exerts his Christian superiority. "A Piece of Possible History" (*Monthly Religious Magazine*, October 1851; collected in *If, Yes, and Perhaps*) describes an accidental meeting of two harpists, David and Homer, at a summer bivouac of Philistines.

Hale's stories dealing with quasi-scientific or highly technical operations and procedures are among his most effective. Even his nonscientific stories demonstrate his interest in factual detail. For example, "The Rag-Man and the Rag-Woman" provides enough computational data to explain, on paper at least, how George Haliburton became wealthy, and "John Rich and Lucy Poor" includes a closely calculated account of the processes by which Rich's hack writing earned him, in one year, the sum of $351,234, which he augmented by extensive and lucrative investments. He seems to have had a special knack (thanks partly to his encyclopedic reading) for close calculations in certain business areas as well as in a variety of physical sciences, including physics, geography, and astronomy.

"The Tale of a Salamander" (collected in *His Level Best, and Other Stories*) details the flame-keeping experiments of a young student who wishes to determine whether a forty-day fire will actually bring forth a live salamander. His three attempts fail, for accidental and mostly amusing reasons. "The Good-natured Pendulum" (*Atlantic Monthly*, January 1869; collected in *The Ingham Papers*) is a droll tale about a schoolboy prank involving a clock tinkering and consequent time tampering: at Parson Whipple's Family Boarding School, back in 1826, Frederic Ingham and George Hackmatack cause the pendulum of the old school-

THE

ATLANTIC MONTHLY.

A MAGAZINE OF LITERATURE, ART, AND POLITICS.

VOL. XII.—DECEMBER, 1863.—NO. LXXIV.

THE MAN WITHOUT A COUNTRY.

I SUPPOSE that very few casual readers of the " New York Herald" of August 13th observed, in an obscure corner, among the " Deaths," the announcement,

" NOLAN. DIED, on board U. S. Corvette Levant, Lat. 2° 11′ S., Long. 131° W., on the 11th of May, PHILIP NOLAN."

I happened to observe it, because I was stranded at the old Mission-House in Mackinac, waiting for a Lake-Superior steamer which did not choose to come, and I was devouring, to the very stubble, all the current literature I could get hold of, even down to the deaths and marriages in the " Herald." My memory for names and people is good, and the reader will see, as he goes on, that I had reason enough to remember Philip Nolan. There are hundreds of readers who would have paused at that announcement, if the officer of the Levant who reported it had chosen to make it thus :— " Died, May 11th, THE MAN WITHOUT A COUNTRY." For it was as " The Man without a Country " that poor Philip Nolan had generally been known by the officers who had him in charge during

some fifty years, as, indeed, by all the men who sailed under them. I dare say there is many a man who has taken wine with him once a fortnight, in a three years' cruise, who never knew that his name was " Nolan," or whether the poor wretch had any name at all.

There can now be no possible harm in telling this poor creature's story. Reason enough there has been till now, ever since Madison's Administration went out in 1817, for very strict secrecy, the secrecy of honor itself, among the gentlemen of the navy who have had Nolan in successive charge. And certainly it speaks well for the *esprit de corps* of the profession and the personal honor of its members, that to the press this man's story has been wholly unknown,—and, I think, to the country at large also. I have reason to think, from some investigations I made in the Naval Archives when I was attached to the Bureau of Construction, that every official report relating to him was burned when Ross burned the public buildings at Washington. One of the Tuckers, or possibly one of the Watsons, had Nolan in charge at

VOL. XII.   44

Opening of the first publication of Hale's best-known story. Hale was disappointed that the Atlantic Monthly *published the story too late to influence the November 1863 elections. He had written the story as a response to the ultimately unsuccessful Ohio gubernatorial candidate on the Peace Democrat (or Copperhead) ticket, who proclaimed his unwillingness "to belong to a nation which would compel by arms the loyalty of any of its citizens."*

room to oscillate much faster than normal, making time fly "to accommodate a picnic they have planned." In "The Last of the Florida" (*Boatswain's Whistle*, 19 November 1864; collected in *If, Yes, and Perhaps*) a special dispatch from Frederic Ingham, captain of the *Florida*, sent from Bahia, Brazil, to his wife is "Received four years in advance of the mail by a lightning express, which has gained that time by running around the world 1,200 times in a spiral direction westward on its way from Brazil. . . ."

Yet another time-tampering story, "Colonel Clipsham's Calendar" (published as a pamphlet in 1895; collected in *Susan's Escort, and Others*), deals with a bachelor uncle, a princely gentleman of leisure whose every evening is taken up with speaking engagements at associations and societies. Unknown to him, his little niece fools with his cogwheel calendar, throwing off all the dates by one day, and each night he delivers the wrong speech to his host audience. The fantastic success which follows, not always through cause-and-effect, is too implausible for belief. Taking a trip west to recover from a worsening cold, he calls on a young lady (as his doctor had asked him to do), but he has misheard her name and visits the wrong young lady. Nevertheless, they hit it off instantly, she and her parents (who are at least as wealthy as Clipsham) accompany Clipsham to a western resort, near which they all have lucrative financial interests, and before long Clipsham and the young lady marry. Then he is elected governor, thanks to his enormous success at delivering the wrong speeches to his audiences, and things continue to improve. However effective other of Hale's quasi-scientific stories may be as entertaining fictions and flights of the imagination, this particular story seems preposterously contrived.

By far the most important of Hale's quasi-scientific stories is "The Brick Moon" (*Atlantic Monthly*, October-December 1869; collected in *His Level Best, and Other Stories*). Slowly gaining recognition–to the point where it may become almost as well known as "The Man Without a Country"–"The Brick Moon" is, according to John R. Adams, "the first story ever written about an artificial earth satellite" and "the longest one that deals mainly with this subject until 1953." Sam Moskowitz, in his *Explorers of the Infinite: Shapers of Science Fiction* (1963), calls the story prophetic. Replete with meticulous technical details drawn from the physical sciences, the story tells of a brick sphere, two hundred feet in diameter, constructed by Frederic Ingham and his associates to provide a reliable guiding star for mariners. Through a mischance the little satellite with thirty-seven of its workers trapped inside is launched prematurely by its gigantic flywheels. Scientific laws are left behind, so that the satellite prisoners still manage to communicate with Ingham and tell him how well they are getting on. (One message reads, "Write to Darwin that he is all right. We began with lichens and have come as far as palms and hemlocks.") The story is also part of Hale's permanent campaign for the protection of privacy. Narrator Ingham has time to discuss plans for the brick moon because his double is attending a "bored" meeting for him, and he wonders if everyone would not be better off living in small, self-contained worlds and just telegraphing kindly to the rest of the folks from time to time.

"The Lost Palace" (*Old and New*, October 1874; collected in *Crusoe in New York, and Other Tales*) also deals with the science of projectiles: this time, the mechanics of propelling a passen-

ger train at high speed over a deep ravine. In the course of the experiment the flying train loses its last car, the Palace Car. This story ends with the narrator mentioning that Jules Verne wants to go to the bottom of that ravine in a balloon, in order to discover whether the Palace Car's passengers might still be down there, living "in a happy republican colony" without means of transportation, means of communication, and palaces.

Another group of Hale's stories might be described as recycled classics. He was perhaps too free in his borrowing. The sources for "The Minister's Black Veil: With Full Particulars," "A New Arabian Night," "A Modern Psyche," and "Crusoe in New York" have been discussed. Defoe's *Robinson Crusoe*, based on the experiences of Alexander Selkirk, meant so much to Hale that he made use of it more than once and in various ways. According to Hale's son Edward Everett Hale, Jr., "My Double and How He Undid Me" borrows its literary form from Defoe's novel. "Nicolette and Aucassin" (*Old and New*, August and September 1874; collected in *Crusoe in New York, and Other Tales*) is a trivial rewrite of the twelfth-century French romance *Aucassin et Nicolette*. "Both Their Houses" (*Harper's*, February 1891; collected in *Susan's Escort, and Others*) is a preposterous travesty of *Romeo and Juliet*, with the two lovers representing the two rival families of expert plumbers.

At least two of Hale's stories in addition to "A New Arabian Night" owe something to the *Arabian Nights*. Of "The Modern Sindbad" (collected in *His Level Best, and Other Stories*) Hale himself wrote that it was about "the adventures of an English merchant from Soho Square who with his wife and children came to this country and did thirty-one states in thirty days. The idea is good, but the execution is crowded and tame, though it requires oceans of work." "Alif-Laila" (*Harper's*, May 1876; collected in *Crusoe in New York, and Other Tales*) is a long-winded and far-out spoof of the *Arabian Nights* in which Scheherazade explains how the genre of the magazine serial was born.

Hale's reputation as an American short-story writer will probably continue to be based on three stories: "The Man Without a Country," "My Double and How He Undid Me," and "The Brick Moon." Popular though he may have been during his lifetime, his contributions as a short-story writer have been largely unexplored in the twentieth century, though Holloway's 1956 biography, Adams's 1977 critical book, and a 1969 doctoral dissertation on his short stories by Nancy Esther James indicate that Hale has maintained at least a modest position among American writers.

Pressures of magazine editing and two never-resolved conflicts–ministerial duties versus the urge to write and Christian witnessing versus artistic judgment–apparently prevented the multifaceted Hale from developing properly as a writer of short fiction. Aside from the great bulk of his religious tales, most of which are simple and contrived moral fables, his short stories reveal his vivacious sense of humor, his love for American history, his fantasy-prone imagination, and his interest in the applications of science and technology. Straddling the Age of Faith and the Machine Age, the witty Hale in a few imaginative leaps compensated for his weakness in writing about commonplace events and ordinary people.

Bibliography:

Jean Holloway, "A Checklist of the Writings of Edward Everett Hale," *Bulletin of Bibliography*, 21 (May-August 1954): 89-92; (September-December 1954): 114-120; (January-April 1955): 140-143.

Biographies:

Edward E. Hale, Jr., *The Life and Letters of Edward Everett Hale*, 2 volumes (Boston: Little, Brown, 1917);

Jean Holloway, *Edward Everett Hale: A Biography* (Austin: University of Texas Press, 1956).

References:

John R. Adams, *Edward Everett Hale* (Boston: Twayne, 1977);

Nancy Esther James, "Realism in Romance: A Critical Study of the Short Stories of Edward Everett Hale," Ph.D. dissertation, Pennsylvania State University, 1969;

William Sloane Kennedy, "Edward Everett Hale," *Century Magazine*, 29, new series 7 (January 1885): 338-343.

Papers:

The official repository for Edward Everett Hale's papers is the New York State Library in Albany, New York. Other important collections of Hale papers are at the Huntington Library, the Massachusetts Historical Society, the Library of Congress, the Houghton Library at Harvard University, the American Antiquarian Society, the John Hay Library at Brown University, the Princeton University Library, the University of Rochester, and the Beinecke Library at Yale University.

James Hall

(29 July 1793-5 July 1868)

Dean G. Hall
Kansas State University

See also the Hall entry in *DLB 73: American Magazine Journalists, 1741-1850.*

BOOKS: *An Oration Delivered in Commemoration of the Festival of St. John the Baptist, 24th. June 1818, Before Lodges Nos. 45, and 113, Ancient York Masons Held in the City of Pittsburgh* (Pittsburgh: Published by request, Ohio Lodge no. 113; printed by Butler & Lambdin, 1818);

Trial and Defence of First Lieutenant James Hall, of the Ordnance Department, United States' Army. Published by Himself (Pittsburgh: Printed by Eichbaum & Johnston, 1820);

Letters from the West; Containing Sketches of Scenery, Manners, and Customs; and Anecdotes Connected with the First Settlements of the Western Sections of the United States. By the Hon. Judge Hall (London: Henry Colburn, 1828);

The Western Souvenir, A Christmas and New Year's Gift for 1829. Edited by James Hall, by Hall and others (Cincinnati: N. & G. Guilford, 1828);

An Address Delivered Before the Antiquarian and Historical Society of Illinois, at Its Second Annual Meeting, in December 1828 (Vandalia: Printed by Robert Blackwell, 1829);

An Oration, Delivered at Vandalia, July 4, 1830 (Vandalia: Printed by Blackwell & Hall, 1830);

Legends of the West (Philadelphia: Harrison Hall, 1832);

The Soldier's Bride and Other Tales (Philadelphia: Key & Biddle, 1833);

The Harpe's Head: A Legend of Kentucky (Philadelphia: Key & Biddle, 1833); republished as *Kentucky,* 2 volumes (London: Newman, 1834);

An Address Delivered Before the Erodelphian Society of Miami University, on the Twenty-Fourth of September, 1833, at Their Eighth Anniversary Celebration (Cincinnati: Corey & Fairbank, 1833);

Sketches of History, Life, and Manners in the West; Containing Accurate Descriptions of the Country and Modes of Life, in the Western States and Territories of North America (1 volume, Cincinnati: Hubbard & Edmands, 1834; extended edition, 2 volumes, Philadelphia: Hall, 1835); republished in part as *The Romance of Western History: or, Sketches of History, Life, and Manners, in the West* (Cincinnati: Applegate, 1857);

Tales of the Border (Philadelphia: Harrison Hall, 1835);

History of the Indian Tribes of North America, With Biographical Sketches and Anecdotes of the Principal Chiefs, by Hall and Thomas L. McKenney, 20 parts (Parts 1-7, Philadelphia: E. C. Biddle, 1836-1837; parts 8-13, Philadelphia: F. W. Greenough, 1837-1838; part 14, Philadelphia: J. T. Bowen, 1841; parts 15-20, Philadelphia: Daniel Rice & James G. Clark, 1842-1844)–bound in three volumes;

A Memoir of the Public Services of William Henry Harrison, of Ohio (Philadelphia: Key & Biddle, 1836);

Statistics of the West, At the Close of the Year 1836 (Cincinnati: J. A. James, 1836); republished as *Notes on the Western States* (Philadelphia: Harrison Hall, 1838); republished as *The West: Its Soil, Surface, and Productions* (Cincinnati: Derby, Bradley, 1848);

The Catholic Question, to Which Are Annexed Critical Notices of A Plea for the West; from the Western Monthly Magazine of 1835 (Cincinnati: Catholic Telegraph Office, 1838);

The Wilderness and the War Path (New York: Wiley & Putnam, 1846);

Address before the Young Men's Mercantile Library Association, of Cincinnati, in Celebration of Its Eleventh Anniversary, April 18, 1846 (Cincinnati: Published by the Association, 1846).

OTHER: "The Soldier's Bride," in *Winter Evenings. A Series of American Tales* (Philadelphia: Ash, 1829); republished as *The Sol-*

dier's Bride and Other Tales (Philadelphia:
J. P. Ayres, 1829), pp. 1-47;

The Western Reader; a Series of Useful Lessons, selected and arranged by Hall (Cincinnati:
Corey & Fairbank/Hubbard & Edmands,
1833);

"Memoir of Thomas Posey," in *The Library of American Biography*, edited by Jared Sparks, second series, volume 9 (Boston: Little &
Brown, 1846), pp. 359-403;

"The Autobiography of James Hall, Western Literary Pioneer," edited by David Donald, *Ohio
State Archaeological and Historical Quarterly*,
56 (July 1947): 295-304.

James Hall was fortunate to be born into a
well-to-do family that encouraged literary creativity. Hall's father, John, was secretary of the Pennsylvania land office and a U.S. marshal, while his
mother, Sarah Ewing Hall, a scholar's daughter ed-

ucated at home, became a formative influence on
James and one of the first women in America to
be recognized for her literary enterprises. In
1816 the Hall family took over Joseph Dennie's
Port Folio, and until its demise in 1827, that magazine was essentially their vehicle: one son, Harrison, published it; another, John Elihu, edited it;
and James and Thomas Mifflin Hall—as well as
their mother—were principal contributors. The
oldest brother, John Elihu, also published the
American Law Journal (1808-1817). Though it was
never his primary occupation, James perceived
writing to be a common part of day-to-day living.
Active as a writer, editor, and publisher for
nearly his entire life, Hall was popular in his
time for his short "western" tales and contributed
greatly to his contemporaries' understanding of
life in the Ohio Valley, which was the western frontier in the early 1800s.

According to the family Bible and the records of the First Presbyterian Church of Philadelphia, James Hall was born in Philadelphia on 29 July 1793. The autobiographical sketch that Hall sent to Evert Duyckinck for use in preparing the *Cyclopaedia of American Literature* and Hall's gravestone, however, give his birth date as 19 August. James was a frail child and kept home, perhaps to his advantage, for the family responsibly educated him and instilled in him a love of books. In 1801 the family moved to Lamberton, New Jersey, a village about thirty miles from Philadelphia. Perhaps dismayed by the roughness of his country playmates and probably spoiled by his nurturing home environment, he had trouble adjusting when he entered a local academy in 1805, and, in what was to be a lasting character trait, pridefully defied authority. As he later wrote in "The Academy" (*Western Monthly Review*, November 1827), he "imbibed a deep-seated disgust against schools, schoolmasters, and school-learning; and against grammars, dictionaries, copybooks" and the school system in general. Hall advocated that teachers should not be allowed to "whip our children," a thesis so startling that the editor, Timothy Flint, included a note that he "did not assent to all the remarks" in the piece. The Hall family suffered a loss of fortune and in 1806 were in residence at the paternal estate on the Susquehanna in Maryland until their permanent return to Philadelphia in 1811. His father then secured James a position in a counting house, which also met with James's disapproval, and by the end of 1811 James was studying law in his uncle Samuel Ewing's law office. Perhaps because of John Elihu Hall's antiwar position published immediately after the declaration of war in 1812, James did not become active in the war effort until March of 1813, when his name appeared at the top of the list of volunteers for the Washington Guards. This group spent three months at Camp Dupont, near Staunton, guarding against British landing parties and were mustered out at the end of July. James reenlisted and spent the following winter at Fort Mifflin under the command of Capt. Thomas Biddle. He was commissioned a third lieutenant in the Second Artillery, promoted to second lieutenant 1 May 1814, fought in the battle of Chippewa in the same year, served in the siege of Fort Erie, undertook several special and dangerous tasks, and for a very short time was a prisoner of war. Hall later wrote "The Soldier's Bride" (first published in *Winter Evenings. A Series of American Tales*, 1829), which uses the battle of Chippewa as its backdrop and includes remarkably vivid and realistic descriptions of military actions.

After the war ended Hall did not want to be mustered out, and under the command of Lawrence Kearney, he sailed on the brig *Enterprise* toward Algiers as part of Stephen Decatur's plan to force restitution from the Dey for disrupting American shipping. Hall's ship arrived too late to be needed, and Hall spent most of his time abroad exploring Spanish sea resorts. In November 1815 he returned to the United States and was assigned duty for the next nine months at Newport, Rhode Island. At the beginning of 1816 he was transferred from the War Department to the Ordnance Department, a move James vehemently protested to no avail, feeling that his acts during the Chippewa and Fort Erie campaigns were being overlooked. His claims were rewarded with a promotion to a first lieutenancy in May and his choice of posts. He opted for the Pittsburgh arsenal, probably because he could continue his law study there with James Ross, a friend of Hall's father, and he arrived there in October 1816. There he encountered Maj. Abraham R. Woolley, a dismally inept officer in Hall's opinion, who challenged Hall's veracity and honor. When Hall delegated to a subordinate the task of bringing back a deserter, a chore Woolley had ordered him to perform himself, and when the subordinate's action resulted in the death of a soldier, Woolley pressed charges and a court-martial was convened on 11 September 1817. Hall was found guilty, stripped of his rank, and cashiered out of the service. Though both men used poor judgment in the situation, Hall was perhaps the wronged party, as evidenced by his eventual restoration to rank and presidential pardon, by the account he renders in his *Trial and Defence of First Lieutenant James Hall, of the Ordnance Department, United States' Army* (1820), and by the fact that Woolley himself was court-martialed and dismissed from the service in 1829. Realizing that his military career was sorely wounded by this episode and that another career was at hand (he had been admitted to the bar 9 April 1818), Hall resigned effective 30 June 1818.

During the four years Hall spent in Pittsburgh, he was an occasional contributor to the *Pittsburgh Gazette*. The newspaper's editor when Hall first arrived in the city was John Irwin Scull, who had also read law under James Ross. Hall's first piece is "Eugenius" (24 December 1816), hardly more than a sketch or fable with the overt moral that people who are good should by necessity therefore be happy and cheerful. Hall signed the piece "Orlando," the pen name he used on and off for more than a decade. Under the encouragement of Morgan Neville, who became Scull's partner and editor in 1817, Hall began a series of essays patterned after the *Spectator* and entitled "The Wanderer, by Edward Ennui." Fourteen pieces appeared in the series between 22 May 1818 and 1 December 1818, and they not only exemplify urbanity and wit worthy of the Addisonian tradition, but they anticipate some of Hall's later work. In the eighth (14 July) he described his captivity during the war and significantly, in the twelfth (3 November), he called for the establishment of a periodical produced in the West and about the West, a venture he brought to fruition himself scarcely more than a decade later. Hall also wrote advocacy journalism for the *Gazette* in which he proposed a turnpike between Philadelphia and Pittsburgh as well as other improvements he felt necessary if these cities were ever to compete commercially with Boston and New York.

In May 1820 Hall rode a keel boat to Shawneetown, Illinois, and within two months had bought half interest in the local newspaper, the *Illinois Emigrant* (later the *Illinois Gazette*), and set up a law practice. He used his newspaper to debate popular issues, published letters impartially though he apparently wrote some of them himself under various pseudonyms, and tried hard to include "literary matters." The most significant pieces he contributed were "Christmas Gambols" (29 December 1821) and "Fiddlers' Green" (5 January 1822); together they form one story (and were so published in the November 1823 *Port Folio* as "The Bachelor's Elysium") which antedates James Fenimore Cooper's creation of the uncouth woodsman as the central character. In a dream of a Mr. Drywit's, Hall's character wears moccasins and buckskin clothes and sports the familiar powderhorn and pouch; the dialect and demeanor of the tall, lanky frontiersman eventually overcomes the prejudices of the fancy ladies present, and one chooses him to be her dancing partner forever. By introducing a character like Cooper's Natty Bumppo into snobbish parlors inhabited by fops, Hall satirizes not the woodsman but the socialites and can be said to have begun the Cooperesque tradition. In addition seven of Hall's well-known "Letters from the

West" first appeared in the *Gazette* (and were republished in the *Port Folio*); most describe the people and places Hall observed when he boated down the Ohio River to Shawneetown and form the nucleus of the later volume which was to gain Hall his reputation as a "western" writer.

Because of political differences with his partner, Hall sold his share in the newspaper and his editorship ended 16 November 1822. In September 1820 Hall had become law partner to John McLean, who by December of that year had been elected speaker of the House of Representatives, becoming a powerful figure in Illinois politics. The rewards were nearly immediate, for on 14 February 1821 Hall was appointed circuit attorney of the Fourth Judicial Circuit. Riding the circuit required that Hall twice a year traverse nearly three thousand square miles of wilderness, stopping at the meagerest villages to represent justice. On 2 February 1823 Hall married Mary Harrison Posey, granddaughter of Gen. Thomas Posey, a Revolutionary-era soldier, governor of the Indiana territory, and later the subject of a biographical account Hall wrote for the *Port Folio* (October 1824) and revised for Jared Sparks's *The Library of American Biography* (second series, volume 9, 1846). On 30 December 1824, after helping McLean gain a U.S. Senate seat, Hall was elected judge of the Fourth Circuit, consisting of Clay, Gallatin, Franklin, Hamilton, Jefferson, and Wayne counties.

After the elections in 1826, the Illinois legislature replaced the circuit judges with justices of the state supreme court, an action which rendered Hall jobless (though the nickname "Judge" Hall followed him until his death) and, when his petitions to overturn the new law were rejected, he was considering at the beginning of 1827 that he might be forced to leave the state. But on 10 February 1827 Hall was elected state treasurer, and by March he had moved his family to Vandalia, the state capital, so that he could better work in his new position. During his stay in Vandalia, Hall became interested in western history (he helped organize the first state historical society) and original literature with the West as its focus. On 17 January 1829 he bought half interest in the *Illinois Intelligencer* and was shortly embroiled in the campaign for governor, taking the side of William Kinney in a fiery contest of newspaper editorializing marked by intense vitriol and personal attacks upon the candidates and their supporters. Kinney was defeated and Hall, though he still had powerful friends, was turned out of office on 14 February 1831. Moreover, he was sued because it was claimed that his books did not balance; eventually Hall turned over real estate to the state for them to sell to settle his debt, but he was never proven to have done wrong during his stint as state treasurer. Because of his growing debts, Hall and his partner offered the *Intelligencer* for sale on Christmas Eve 1831, and Hall wrote his last editorial for that paper on 3 March 1832.

Probably before he left Shawneetown, Hall had written additional material for inclusion in the "Letters of the West" series of the *Port Folio*, but then he decided to rearrange and expand the older letters, combine them with the new work, and seek publication of the collection as a book in London. Hall claims, in his autobiographical sketch, that he had intended that the title page show only "By a Young Gentleman of Illinois" and was greatly embarrassed that it read "By the Hon. Judge Hall" when the volume appeared with the imposing title *Letters from the West; Containing Sketches of Scenery, Manners, and Customs; and Anecdotes Connected with the First Settlements of the Western Sections of the United States* (edited by Henry Colburn, 1828). Hall's embarrassment may be attributed to the unflattering English reviews. One critic, writing in *Quarterly Review* (April 1829), chastised Hall for his democratic (anti-British) prejudices, called him a "judicial blockhead" and the book itself "silly," and Hall later said that he forbade that it be republished. The book is a paean to the democratic experiment moving west and does occasionally fall prey to prolixity or an accountant's eye, but Hall was most often a gifted observer of scenes and people. As Randolph C. Randall notes, "As the early settlement of the Middle West recedes further from our view, the book will grow in value, both as a storehouse for the social historian and as the delight of Americans interested in the West as the early beholders saw it."

In early 1828 Hall decided to fulfill his plan he had announced in the *Pittsburgh Gazette* for a collection of works by western writers and so approached N. and G. Guilford of Cincinnati with a prospectus for a gift book, "its entire devotion to western literature." The result, supposed to be the first of a series of western annuals, was *The Western Souvenir, A Christmas and New Year's Gift for 1829* (1828), which plainly stated its aims in its preface: "It is written and published in the Western country, by Western men, and is chiefly confined to subjects connected with the history

and character of the country which gives it birth." Though it included works by Nathan Guilford and Morgan Neville (it contains Neville's "The Last of the Boatmen" in which the character Mike Fink first appears), Hall had to rely heavily on his own productions, including five tales and nineteen poems amounting to 128 of the volume's 324 pages. Here "The Bachelor's Elysium" is republished, along with "The Billiard Table," "The French Village," "Pete Featherton," and "The Indian Hater." The first two stories are among Hall's best evocations of place and show his versatility in moving from the environs of the city to a Mississippi River village. As examples of verisimilitude, they can hardly be surpassed. "Pete Featherton" portrays the title character, a superstitious backwoodsman prone to drink, as likable but vulnerable to self-delusion. After one notorious drinking bout, Pete imagines that the devil puts a spell on his rifle. Thereafter, Pete misses everything until he consults an Indian conjurer who provides Pete with a charm that allows him to regain his marksmanship. Though the story has a boldness of character delineation of the kind which persuaded Fred Lewis Pattee to call Hall "the real pioneer of Western fiction," Pattee also singled it out to illustrate persuasively the deficiencies of Hall's style. Pattee noticed that Pete does not simply load his rifle but that "he commenced certain preparations fraught with danger to the brute inhabitants of the forest" and that Pete's "keen eye glittered with an ominous lustre as its glance rested on the destructive engine." Nearly all of Hall's works suffer from this same inflated style.

Another story in *The Western Souvenir* deserves mention because it contains the first example of what was to become a stock character in western fiction, the Indian hater, and because it reflects Hall's difficulty in knowing whom to blame for this common racial hatred. In "The Indian Hater" the narrator meets Samuel Monson, a frontiersman apparently normal in every way except that he becomes a bloodthirsty fanatic in the presence of Indians. After Monson murders the narrator's Indian guide in revenge for the Indians' earlier destruction of his family, the narrator is torn in his sympathies for the dead man and the white man, who has obviously been driven insane by brutal memories. Monson is based on a real-life acquaintance of Hall's, Col. John Moredock, whose mother and siblings had been killed by Indians and who devoted most of his remaining energies to vengeance. "Bloody Nathan" in Robert

Montgomery Bird's *Nick of the Woods* (1837) is another early example of such a fanatical character.

In 1829 Hall's "The Soldier's Bride" appeared anonymously in John Elihu Hall's next gift book, *Winter Evenings. A Series of American Tales*, a misleading title for the five stories are not a series and only Hall's tale is set in America. In February 1830 Hall was making plans to publish the next annual edition of the *Western Souvenir* but could not gather enough contributions. Undaunted, in March 1830 he proposed the *Illinois Monthly Magazine* "to develop the character and resources of Illinois" and to include "Tales.– Literary Intelligence" and "Fugitive Poetry"; its first number appeared in October of that year. Though Hall was able to get support from twenty-eight other writers in the two years the *Illinois Monthly* ran, he contributed more than half of the writing published there. Indefatigable, Hall wrote descriptive pieces on Illinois timber, wild animals, soil and productions, land surfaces, public officers, and so on, as well as biographical sketches of Daniel Boone, Thomas Biddle, and others. He wrote a four-part series "On the Intercourse of the American People with the Indians," and as critic he lauded the early productions of Nathaniel Hawthorne. In addition twelve of Hall's short stories appeared in the *Illinois Monthly*, bringing his total output of tales to twenty-five. These he gathered together for *Legends of the West* (1832), published by his brother Harrison Hall, and *The Soldier's Bride and Other Tales* (1833).

Approximately eighty percent of Hall's tales are set in the West and portray western characters. Hall's principal aim, as it appears in the preface to *Legends of the West*, was to render "accurate descriptions of the scenery and population of the country in which the author resides." The goal of verisimilitude is most often achieved in descriptions of scenery, plants, and surface features of the land. When Hall creates characters, even though he nearly always purports to be rendering actual episodes and real-life persons, he embellishes them with dialogue and motivations and in so doing can be said to be one of the earliest writers to move from the simple character sketch to the rudimentary short story. For example, in "The Seventh Son," which humorously satirizes the accommodations easterners must make to western prejudices, Jeremy Geode, a highly trained physician using modern botany and entomology as tools, is forced to present himself as the magical seventh son of an Indian doctor in order to be convincing to his frontier patients.

Hall's only published novel, *The Harpe's Head* (1833), though it contains some believable characters and descriptions of western surroundings, is generally weak because of its sentimentality and overreliance on coincidence to move the plot forward. Essentially a series of poorly integrated episodes, the novel concerns the travails of Virginia Pendleton, who journeys to Kentucky to be with relatives after her uncle dies. En route she is harassed by one of Hall's most memorable characters, Micajah Harpe, an archetype of the menacing backwoods outlaw devoid of "social emotions." Micajah and his brother Wiley, based on real men of the same names, first appeared in an account for the *Port Folio* (April 1824), where Hall's vivid descriptions of their rapine and murder were considered by a writer at the *Cincinnati Literary Gazette* (28 May 1825) to be too gruesome to be historically accurate. At the novel's climax Micajah is hunted like an animal and his head placed in a tree as a gruesome reminder to other miscreants. Another irascible character, Hark Short, is unforgettable as a snake hunter. Perhaps the first literary example of the poor, unbalanced, white swamp dweller, Hark jumps on snakes with his bare feet, wrestles them barehanded, and kills them by swinging them into trees. The episodes which concentrate on Micajah or Hark are lively but unincorporated digressions adversely affecting the unity of the novel. Hall constructs an intrusive happy ending to the main plot by producing Virginia's uncle's hitherto-unmentioned will, which makes her an heiress to a vast estate and a suitable marriage partner for Capt. Lyttleton Fennimore, an entirely wooden hero. Hall's realistic descriptions of frontier landscapes, dwellings, and minor characters are not enough to overcome the novel's shortcomings.

The end of 1832 and beginning of 1833 constituted a period of change for Hall. He had lost his job as state treasurer and was in debt. Not only had he been forced to give up his newspaper but was also forced to sell his press, so some of the issues of the *Illinois Monthly* had to be printed in St. Louis; in June, Corey and Fairbank in Cincinnati took over its printing. By September Hall had made a deal with the printers to move the magazine production entirely to Cincinnati and to publish it as *Western Monthly Magazine*. Hall, however, was stuck in Vandalia, waiting for the state to sell the real-estate holdings he had turned over, and so friends oversaw the first three numbers of the new periodical. His wife

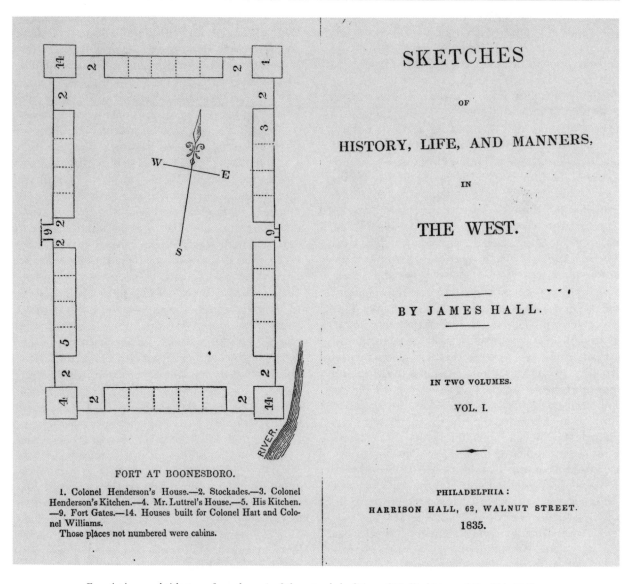

SKETCHES

OF

HISTORY, LIFE, AND MANNERS,

IN

THE WEST.

BY JAMES HALL.

IN TWO VOLUMES.

VOL. I.

PHILADELPHIA:
HARRISON HALL, 62, WALNUT STREET.
1835.

FORT AT BOONESBORO.

1. Colonel Henderson's House.—2. Stockades.—3. Colonel Henderson's Kitchen.—4. Mr. Luttrel's House.—5. His Kitchen. —9. Fort Gates.—14. Houses built for Colonel Hart and Colonel Williams.
Those places not numbered were cabins.

Frontispiece and title page for volume 1 of the extended edition of Hall's history of the Ohio Valley

died 18 August 1832 from a fever contracted at the birth of their fourth child; the baby, James, lived only until 15 October. On 26 February 1833 Illinois finally cleared his account with the state treasurer, and in March Hall went to Henderson, Kentucky, the home of Mary's parents, where he left his three children. He arrived in Cincinnati in late March 1833.

Hall's publishing fortunes improved as editor of the *Western Monthly*, and Hall could legitimately claim that he had three thousand subscribers; the magazine deserved its success. While it included articles from a broad range of eastern or English periodicals, it also published much original factual material about Illinois by Hall himself. Paying high rates for material (a dollar per

page), the magazine attracted and deemed to publish without prejudice works by specialists in science and history as well as poets and short-story writers, including women. Harriet E. Beecher (who married Calvin Stowe in 1836) won the magazine's prize for fiction with "A New England Sketch," which appeared in the April 1834 issue. In 1833 Hall edited *The Western Reader; a Series of Useful Lessons*, a collection of didactic and moralistic works exclusively by American writers such as Benjamin Franklin, Thomas Jefferson, James Fenimore Cooper, John Audubon, and Henry Clay. The book's purposes were "rendering the young reader familiar with the literature of his own land, and of placing before him topics of immediate interest." Hall's point was to make American schoolchildren begin to realize their own heritage and to become less dependent on the European culture for formative examples; the book was adopted by the Cincinnati schools, and more than one hundred thousand copies were sold in the first two years in print.

During this era Hall found time to bring out yet another volume of short stories, his third in three years, *Tales of the Border* (1835). Four of the seven stories had already appeared in the *Illinois Monthly* or *The Western Souvenir* and a fifth, "The Dark Maid of Illinois," had been published in the *Knickerbocker* (July 1833). Perhaps intended as anodynes to the bitter feelings engendered during the Black Hawk War, three of the stories deal with whites' persecution of the Indians. Especially significant is "The Pioneer" because it reworks the material of "The Indian Hater" to provide an enlightened portrait of life in an Indian village as an acceptable alternative to white culture. Hall begins in nearly the same way except that in this story the Indian hater's sister was taken away to live with the Indians after they murdered the rest of his family. With the same singleminded devotion to vengeance evidenced in the earlier version, the Indian hater seeks to exterminate all the savages; but the twist in this tale is that when he does finally find his sister, the Indian hater discovers a woman at peace in her environment and a contented mother and wife–the Indians are not savage at all. He gives up his life of vengeance and leads a religious existence. Likewise in "The New Moon," Menae, daughter of an Omaha chieftain, returns to her tribe after a marriage to a brutal white trader; her idyllic life with the tribe is contrasted effectively with her treatment at the hands of the white man. Hall creates so much sympathy for Menae that her advice to her children to avoid the society and vices of white culture seems sound.

Also in 1835 appeared Hall's *Sketches of History, Life, and Manners in the West*, published by his brother Harrison Hall in two volumes. (Volume one had been printed a year earlier with the longer title *Sketches of History, Life, and Manners in the West; Containing Accurate Descriptions of the Country and Modes of Life, in the Western States and Territories of North America* by the firm of Hubbard and Edmands, but they went broke before the second volume could be produced.) The work consists of six parts, many of which had already appeared in the *Illinois Monthly* or *Western Monthly*: "Intercourse of the American People with the Indians,"

"History of the French Settlements," "Early Settlements on the Ohio," "Events in the Early History of Kentucky," "Military Operations in the Northwestern Territory," and "Civil Institutions of the Territories and New States." Hall's purpose was to write an impressionistic survey of the migrations into the Ohio Valley rather than a meticulous and scholarly history of the area. Unfortunately Hall took from several sources with no acknowledgement, resulting in a negative review by Mann Butler (*Western Messenger*, May 1836), who felt that Hall had made erroneous statements and had taken material from his own *History of the Commonwealth of Kentucky*. A more scathing review in the more prestigious *North American Review* (July 1836) must have hurt Hall deeply, given his commitment to western literature; it concluded that "of the western character he knows little, and of the western spirit he knows nothing." The anonymous review was written by James Freeman Clarke who, as editor of the *Western Messenger*, in which Butler's review had been published, had a conspicuous vested interest in reinforcing Butler's position. The bias in the review was clear; Edgar Allan Poe observed that "personal pique" must be at the root of such an attack. In the preface to *Statistics of the West* (1836), reprinted separately in 1838 as *Reply to Strictures on Sketches of the West*, Hall replied to the critics admitting that a few errors of fact may have crept into his book; he allowed them to impugn his scholarship but took issue with their claim that he lacked a "western spirit."

Hall ran into trouble as editor in May 1835, when he reviewed Lyman Beecher's *A Plea for the West* (1835) revealing it for the thinly veiled attack on Catholics it was. Hall followed with an essay, "The Catholic Question" (June 1835), a reasonable argument that such theological differences had nothing to do with the character or loyalty of Catholics who could practice their religion and yet remain loyal to the democracy. Unfortunately for Hall, Beecher was popular and well connected. Beecher threatened libel and a groundswell of negative public opinion brought subscription cancellations to the magazine. Hall resigned as editor in June 1836, taking up full time another career for which he had been planning several months; he had for some time been in contact with bankers in Philadelphia about the Commercial Bank in Cincinnati. In February 1836 he was elected to the board of directors and on 12 May was elected cashier. From this time, most of Hall's literary output consisted of reworking or gathering previously written pieces and presenting them in different formats. For example, *Statistics of the West*, a collection, with little reworking, of descriptive pieces he had written for magazines was republished with only slight revision as *Notes on the Western States; Containing Descriptive Sketches of Their Soil, Climate, Resources and Scenery* in 1838. It was again republished as *The West: Its Soil, Surface, and Productions* in 1848. And, chapter 12, added to his *Address before the Young Men's Mercantile Library Association* (1846) and two other short, previously published pieces, were published as *The West: Its Commerce and Navigation* (1848). In like manner, *The Romance of Western History: or Sketches, History, Life, and Manners in the West* (1857) consists of a reordering of twenty-two of the original twenty-six chapters of *Sketches of History, Life, and Manners in the West* compiled twenty-two years earlier. He also wrote a campaign biography of William Henry Harrison in 1836 and reworked his biographical sketch of his first wife's grandfather, Gen. Thomas Posey, in 1846.

Hall published one last volume of short stories, *The Wilderness and the War Path* (1846), containing eight tales, five of which had previously appeared in his own earlier volumes and another, "The War Belt," which had been published in the *Knickerbocker* (November 1840). One of the new tales, "The Black Steed of the Prairies," is interesting because Hall retells an Indian legend about a great white horse, swifter and more graceful than all the rest, which assumes dominion over other horses and becomes the object of many hunters. Hall changed the color of the horse to black with the humorous explanation that "we have no ambition to acquire fame as a taker of other men's horses, and we have made ours a horse of a different color." Hall's horse, changed back to the original white of the legend, was perhaps the model for a horse in Herman Melville's *Moby-Dick* (1851), where an extraordinary steed is "elected Xerxes" of the herds of wild horses and is part of Melville's catalogue of animals exhibiting "spiritual whiteness."

The most important product of Hall's late career was *History of the Indian Tribes of North America* (published in twenty parts, 1836-1844, which were later gathered into three volumes), written in collaboration with Col. Thomas Loraine McKenney. Though Hall complained that McKenney was "as lazy a man as ever lived," he chose his partner well, for McKenney had been superintendent of Indian trade for six years, had

been in charge of the Bureau of Indian Affairs (1826-1830), had access to the Indian archives in Washington, had traveled the Great Lakes area visiting Indian tribes, and was sympathetic to Indian rights. He had negotiated various fair treaties and was removed from office by President Jackson when he opposed Jackson's policy of moving Indians across the Mississippi. Hall claimed to have written all of the first two volumes, which were biographical sketches for the Indians appearing in the illustrations, and the last three-fourths of the third, "Essay on the History of the North American Indians," which is a much amplified version of his "On the Intercourse of the American People with the Indians" (*Illinois Monthly*, May-August 1831). Hall devoted his leisure time for more than seven years to perusing official and unofficial sources and transcribing oral accounts. Though the text cannot stand up to more modern criteria of sociology and ethnology, the paintings themselves are valuable historical records, especially so since some of the originals by Charles King and George Catlin were lost in a fire in the Smithsonian (1865). Evidently Hall anticipated that the Indians would retain their territories as sovereign states and argued sympathetically that they be given citizenship and "equality with ourselves." Though the volumes were hardly noticed by reviewers, causing Hall to complain that they are "not known in the literature of the country," the *North American Review* (July 1838), focusing primarily on the illustrations in their praise, said that the work was "second only to Audubon."

For the rest of his life Hall was a leading citizen of Cincinnati, devoting himself and his money to many of the city's cultural events. In approximately 1838 Hall moved the children of his first wife to Cincinnati, and on 3 September 1839 he married Mary Louisa Anderson Alexander, subsequently fathering five additional children. For his last thirty years, Hall concentrated on his financial affairs, achieving a reputation for sound business thinking, caution, and trustworthiness; in 1853 he was elected president of the Commercial Bank and served as such until he retired for health reasons in 1865. He also was renowned locally as a literary figure, as reprints of his works appeared periodically until nearly the end of his life. In 1855 he wrote a brief autobiography for the *Cyclopaedia of American Literature* as well as entries for Dr. Daniel Drake and Benjamin Drake. On 5 July 1868 Hall died and is buried in Spring Grove Cemetery in Cincinnati.

Though many of Hall's tales are not much more than character sketches with added dialogue and weak plotting, it should be remembered that they were written as the short-story form was just emerging. Randall writes that "Hall, by demonstrating that rich narrative veins could be exploited through careful observation and recording of distinctive regional characteristics, was, after Irving . . . the next most significant of the American short story writers who published a large number of tales between 1820 and 1932." His minor place in literary history is preserved because he capitalized on his contemporaries' interest in the newness of the Ohio Valley and because he created early examples of western stereotypes. Hall's strengths as a writer lay in his creation of a sense of place and delineation of characters unknown to easterners and Europeans; thus he may be properly remembered as a chronicler or anecdote teller rather than as a short-story writer in the modern sense. Though much of Hall's work has been superseded by more recent historical treatments of his time and place, his descriptions of land, flora, and customs are valuable for understanding the ambience of the western fringes of American civilization in his era. As a literary ambassador between the East and West, Hall deserves credit for his memorable characters and for his indefatigable efforts to promote his western environment and culture.

References:

Dorothy Dondore, *The Prairie in the Making of Middle America* (Cedar Rapids: Torch Press, 1926);

John T. Flanagan, *James Hall, Literary Pioneer of the Ohio Valley* (Minneapolis: University of Minnesota Press, 1941);

Vernon L. Parrington, *The Romantic Revolution in America, 1800-1860*, volume 2 of *Main Currents in American Thought* (New York: Harcourt, Brace, 1927);

Fred Lewis Pattee, *The Development of the American Short Story* (New York & London: Harper, 1923);

Randolph C. Randall, *James Hall, Spokesman of the New West* (Columbus: Ohio State University Press, 1964);

Ralph Leslie Rusk, *Literature of the Middle Western Frontier*, 2 volumes (New York: Columbia University Press, 1925), pp. 284-295;

William Henry Venable, *Beginnings of Literary Culture in the Ohio Valley: Historical and Biographical Sketches* (New York: Peter Smith, 1949), pp. 361-385.

Papers:

The manuscript for the brief autobiography Hall sent to Evert Duyckinck for his *Cyclopaedia of American Literature*, and seven letters, are among Duyckinck's papers at the New York Public Library. The Historical and Philosophical Society of Ohio, Cincinnati, has a journal for 6 August-16 September 1815, a household account book for 18 February-30 April 1830, and approximately fifteen letters.

Bret Harte

(25 August 1836-5 May 1902)

Henry L. Golemba
Wayne State University

See also the Harte entries in *DLB 12: American Realists and Naturalists* and *DLB 64: American Literary Critics and Scholars, 1850-1880.*

BOOKS: *Condensed Novels, and Other Papers* (New York: Carlton/London: Low, 1867; enlarged edition, Boston: Osgood, 1871);

The Last Galleon and Other Tales (San Francisco: Towne & Bacon, 1867);

The Luck of Roaring Camp, and Other Sketches (Boston: Fields, Osgood, 1870; enlarged, 1870);

Poems (Boston: Fields, Osgood, 1871);

East and West Poems (Boston: Osgood, 1871; London: Hotten, 1871);

Mrs. Skaggs's Husbands, and Other Sketches (London: Hotten, 1872; Boston: Osgood, 1873);

An Episode of Fiddletown and Other Sketches (London: Routledge, 1873);

M'liss. An Idyl of Red Mountain (New York: DeWitt, 1873);

Echoes of the Foot-hills (Boston: Osgood, 1875);

Tales of the Argonauts, and Other Sketches (Boston: Osgood, 1875);

Gabriel Conroy (3 volumes, London: Warne, 1876; 1 volume, Hartford, Conn.: American Publishing Company, 1876);

Two Men of Sandy Bar: A Drama (Boston: Osgood, 1876);

Thankful Blossom, a Romance of the Jerseys, 1779 (Boston: Osgood, 1877; London & New York: Routledge, 1877);

The Story of a Mine (London: Routledge, 1877; Boston: Osgood, 1878);

The Man on the Beach (London: Routledge, 1878);

"Jinny" (London: Routledge, 1878);

Drift from Two Shores (Boston: Houghton, Osgood, 1878);

The Twins of Table Mountain (London: Chatto & Windus, 1879);

The Twins of Table Mountain and Other Stories (Boston: Houghton, Osgood, 1879);

Flip and Other Stories (London: Chatto & Windus, 1882);

Bret Harte

Flip and Found at Blazing Star (Boston: Houghton, Mifflin, 1882);

In the Carquinez Woods (London: Longmans, Green, 1883; Boston: Houghton, Mifflin, 1884);

On the Frontier (London: Longmans, Green, 1884; Boston: Houghton, Mifflin, 1884);

By Shore and Sedge (Boston: Houghton, Mifflin, 1885; London: Longmans, Green, 1885);

Maruja (London: Chatto & Windus, 1885; Boston & New York: Houghton, Mifflin, 1885);

Snow-Bound at Eagle's (Boston & New York: Houghton, Mifflin, 1886; London: Ward & Downey, 1886);

The Queen of the Pirate Isle (London: Chatto & Windus, 1886; Boston & New York: Houghton, Mifflin, 1887);

A Millionaire of Rough-and-Ready and *Devil's Ford* (Boston & New York: Houghton, Mifflin, 1887);

Devil's Ford (London: White, 1887);

A Millionaire of Rough-and-Ready (London: White, 1887);

The Crusade of the Excelsior (Boston & New York: Houghton, Mifflin, 1887; London: White, 1887);

A Phyllis of the Sierras and A Drift from Redwood Camp (Boston & New York: Houghton, Mifflin, 1888; London: Chatto & Windus, 1888);

The Argonauts of North Liberty (Boston & New York: Houghton, Mifflin, 1888; London: Blackett, 1888);

Cressy (2 volumes, London & New York: Macmillan, 1889; 1 volume, Boston & New York: Houghton, Mifflin, 1889; London: Macmillan, 1889);

The Heritage of Dedlow Marsh and Other Tales (1 volume, Boston & New York: Houghton, Mifflin, 1889; 2 volumes, London & New York: Macmillan, 1889);

A Waif of the Plains (London: Chatto & Windus, 1890; Boston & New York: Houghton, Mifflin, 1890);

A Ward of the Golden Gate (London: Chatto & Windus, 1890; Boston & New York: Houghton, Mifflin, 1890);

A Sappho of Green Springs, Lippincott's, 45 (May 1890);

A Sappho of Green Springs and Other Stories (London: Chatto & Windus, 1891; Boston & New York: Houghton, Mifflin, 1891);

A First Family of Tasajara (2 volumes, London & New York: Macmillan, 1891; 1 volume, Boston & New York: Houghton, Mifflin, 1892);

Colonel Starbottle's Client and Some Other People (London: Chatto & Windus, 1892; Boston & New York: Houghton, Mifflin, 1892);

Susy: A Story of the Plains (Boston & New York: Houghton, Mifflin, 1893; London: Chatto & Windus, 1893);

Sally Dows, Etc. (London: Chatto & Windus, 1893); republished as *Sally Dows and Other Stories* (Boston & New York: Houghton, Mifflin, 1893);

A Protégée of Jack Hamlin's and Other Stories (Boston & New York: Houghton, Mifflin, 1894; enlarged edition, London: Chatto & Windus, 1894);

The Bell-Ringer of Angel's and Other Stories (Boston & New York: Houghton, Mifflin, 1894; abridged edition, London: Chatto & Windus, 1894);

Clarence (London: Chatto & Windus, 1895; Boston & New York: Houghton, Mifflin, 1895);

In a Hollow of the Hills (London: Chapman & Hall, 1895; Boston: Houghton, Mifflin, 1895);

Barker's Luck and Other Stories (Boston & New York: Houghton, Mifflin, 1896; London: Chatto & Windus, 1896);

Three Partners or The Big Strike on Heavy Tree Hill (Boston & New York: Houghton, Mifflin, 1897; London: Chatto & Windus, 1897);

Tales of Trail and Town (Boston & New York: Houghton, Mifflin, 1898; London: Chatto & Windus, 1898);

Stories in Light and Shadow (London: Pearson, 1898; Boston & New York: Houghton, Mifflin, 1898);

Mr. Jack Hamlin's Mediation and Other Stories (Boston & New York: Houghton, Mifflin, 1899; London: Pearson, 1899);

From Sand Hill to Pine (Boston & New York: Houghton, Mifflin, 1900; London: Pearson, 1900);

Under the Redwoods (Boston & New York: Houghton, Mifflin, 1901; London: Pearson, 1901);

On the Old Trail (London: Pearson, 1902); republished as *Openings in the Old Trail* (Boston & New York: Houghton, Mifflin, 1902);

Condensed Novels, Second Series: New Burlesques (Boston & New York: Houghton, Mifflin, 1902; London: Chatto & Windus, 1902);

Sue: A Play in Three Acts, by Harte and T. Edgar Pemberton (London: Greening, 1902);

Trent's Trust and Other Stories (London: Nash, 1903; Boston & New York: Houghton, Mifflin, 1903);

The Lectures of Bret Harte, edited by Charles Meeker Kozlay (Brooklyn: Kozlay, 1909);

Stories and Poems and Other Uncollected Writings, compiled by Kozlay (Boston & New York: Houghton Mifflin, 1914);

Sketches of the Sixties, by Harte and Mark Twain (San Francisco: John Howell, 1926).

Collection: *The Writings of Bret Harte*, 20 volumes (Boston: Houghton, Mifflin, 1896-1914).

PLAY PRODUCTIONS: *Two Men of Sandy Bar*, New York, Union Square Theater, 28 August 1876;

Ah Sin, by Harte and Mark Twain, New York, Daly's Theater, 31 July 1877;

Sue, by Harte and T. Edgar Pemberton, New York, Hoyt's Theatre, 15 September 1896.

OTHER: *Outcroppings: Being Selections of California Verse*, edited by Harte (San Francisco: A. Roman/New York: W. J. Widdleton, 1866);

Charles Warren Stoddard, *Poems*, edited by Harte (San Francisco: A. Roman, 1867).

From 1869, the year the final spike was driven into the transcontinental railroad, to 1876, when George Custer died at the Little Big Horn and the United States celebrated its centennial, Bret Harte enjoyed fame as the most popular and original writer in America, largely for his tales of California life. The Union Pacific Railroad had linked East with West, and New Yorkers were eager to know what the country now only five days away by train was like. By the late 1870s American readers were drawn to Ned Buntline's transformation of William F. Cody into Buffalo Bill, Prentiss Ingraham's "shoot-em-ups," and Edward J. Wheeler's western romances featuring outlaws as Robin Hood types. To a great extent Bret Harte earned the obscurity which fell nearly as fast as his fame had soared because to the day he died he did not try much to make any significant developments in the work which had brought him sudden popularity. In fact, his writings before 1872 were more innovative and diverse than any in the rest of the thirty years of his career. As Patrick Morrow has phrased it, the older Bret Harte "was like the highly acclaimed character actor who outgrows the part but is so completely identified with the role that to abandon it in the quest of self-discovery and a new image means courting financial and critical disaster." One could also add "psychological disaster" to Morrow's description, for the fragility of Bret Harte's self-image prevented him from trying new things.

Born in Albany, New York, Bret Harte was christened Francis Brett Hart, and his mother, Elizabeth Rebecca Ostrander Hart, was a low-church Episcopalian; her ancestry was English and Dutch, and she came of solid, cultured, middle-class stock. Harte's paternal lineage is much more complicated. His father, Henry Philip Hart, was the legitimate but unacknowledged son of Bernard Hart, an English Jew who had immigrated to New York and had become rich. In 1799 Bernard had secretly married Henry's mother, Catherine Brett, whose family was proud, prestigious, and owned vast estates along the Hudson River. Bernard publicly married a woman of his own faith in 1806 and apparently took no interest in Henry, who, living with his

Harte, circa 1869, during his tenure as editor of Anton Roman's Overland Monthly *(Brown Brothers)*

mother, was raised in the Dutch Reformed church, went through college but was not granted a diploma because he lacked the ninety-dollar graduation fee, converted to Roman Catholicism, and in 1830 married Elizabeth, whom he met on a visit to the Bretts. Their daughter Eliza was born the next year; their first son, Henry, was born in 1835 and Francis Brett Hart in 1836. Their daughter Margaret, Francis's closest friend, was two years younger. (Though the year of Harte's birth was once disputed, George R. Stewart, Jr., and Richard O'Connor, two of his biographers, agree on 1836.)

As a child, Bret Harte was called Frank or, as a facetious comment on his sickly condition, "Tubbs." He was quiet and moody, and at the age of five, it is said, he already showed his satirical humor by burlesquing the language of his first primer and mimicking school declamations. By the age of thirteen, when his formal schooling ceased, Bret had attended eight different schools because his father had trouble paying tuition. His father, who had changed the family name to Harte in 1844, died in 1845. Elizabeth Harte moved her family to Brooklyn, and while Bret took odd jobs working for a lawyer and a druggist at thirteen and became fully self-supporting at the age of fifteen, brother Henry joined the army and sent home romantic letters full of his adventures first in the Mexican War and then in California. Bret's first poems, written during this period, tended to the satirical and misanthropic. Bret's mother moved to California in 1853; before the year was out, she married Andrew Williams, a college friend of her late husband and soon to be elected Oakland's fourth mayor. On 20 February 1854 Bret and his sister Margaret left New York by steamship to join her, witnessing en route storms at sea, revolution, and shipwreck; these events figure only tangentially in Harte's later fiction.

In late March 1854 Bret began his sixteen-year stay in California, garnering experiences and developing a style that would cause the territory along the Humboldt River to be known as "Bret Harte Country." His first six years were anything but propitious; Harte drifted from job to job and wandered the land. He stayed with his mother and stepfather for a few months, served as tutor to ranchers' children, visited mines, and rode shotgun on a stage in 1857 for "a brief delightful hour," which he had expanded to "several months" by 1894. He wrote poetry that was precious and pretentious. His diaries for this period record that Harte believed himself a failure; he had "suffered considerable" and thought his life was a disappointing blend of "caricature and farce." Seeing no promise in his future, Harte moaned to his diary, "The conclusion forced upon me by observation and not by vain enthusiasm that I am fit for nothing else—must impel me to seek distinction and fortune in literature." One route to literature, he calculated, was to become a printer.

By 1858 Harte was a fair enough hand with the case and stick to be printer for Col. S. G. Whipple and Maj. A. H. Murdock's weekly newspaper, the *Northern Californian* in Union (now called Arcata). Often Harte had the opportunity to fill out pages with his own work, and he had a clear sense of his audience and the booster slant to subject matter they expected. In an uncollected poem, "Why She Didn't Dance" (*Northern Californian*, 30 November 1859), he attempted western dialect for the first time and signed his name "Frank 'Bret.' " The climactic event of this period took place on 26 February 1860 and cost Harte his job. Whipple was away with Harte left in charge of the paper while a tribe of peaceful Indians was holding a three-day religious festival on an island off Eureka, eight miles to the south of Union. Local whites sneaked up on the island at four in the morning and slaughtered every Indian they could find, mostly old men, women, and children. Harte used the 29 February issue of the *Northern Californian* as a forum to denounce the killers, raging against their cowardice and cruelty and intimating that the editor of the *Humboldt Times* and Eureka's sheriff were behind the massacre. Whether driven out of town or brusquely asked to leave, Harte left Union and sailed for San Francisco within the month.

Harte's response to the massacre highlights his true feelings about the West. His works might portray ministers as hypocrites, stockbrokers and bankers as evil with greed, lawmen as corrupt, but his greatest disgust was reserved for those who prospered by the lawlessness and brutality of the frontier. The man who made California famous in literature scorned the West. In his lecture "The Argonauts of '49"–ironically subtitled "California's Golden Age"–which he delivered in the East in 1872-1873 and which was first published as the introduction to volume 2 of *The Writings of Bret Harte* (1896), Harte described the gold-rush days as "a kind of crusade without a cross, an exodus without a prophet. It is not a pretty story; . . . it is a life of which perhaps the best that can be said is that it exists no longer." Harte despised the West, but the West was where he felt he must make his mark and make it by pleasing his local readers. This irony was equaled a decade later when Harte wrote a poem called "Plain Language from Truthful James" (*Overland Monthly*, September 1870; better known as "The Heathen Chinee"), in which whites who try to cheat a Chinese at cards are cheated in turn by their own methods. The poem which Harte called "the worst I ever wrote" was popular from coast to coast, but in California it was used as a weapon to promote racist riots against Orientals. Four years later in "Wan Lee, the Pagan," published in *Scribner's Magazine* (September 1874) and collected in *Tales of the Argonauts, and Other Sketches* (1875), Harte conveyed his anger. Hop-Sing, an urbane, serious, honest, and magical Chinese who is not at all, Harte insists, a pantomime figure, arranges for the Harte persona to become godfather to Wan Lee, who grows up ridiculed, threatened, finally stoned to death in a two-day rampage in 1869 by California's "Christian and highly civilized race." "Chinee" was published the year *after* Wan Lee's fictional death and was used to fuel racist fires while propelling Harte to national fame. This ugly paradox did not escape Harte's awareness.

Another passage from "Wan Lee" may well illustrate Harte's frame of mind when he arrived in San Francisco on 27 March 1860: "He had lived in an atmosphere of trickery and deception; he had learned to look upon mankind as dupes of their senses; in fine, if he had thought at all, he would have been a skeptic; if he had been a little older, he would have been a cynic; if he had been older still, he would have been a philosopher." Like a magician, Harte would cynically (or philosophically) dazzle the world with his art, giving the public whatever it wanted for its entertainment. Thus, in 1860 Harte began to write stories for the *Golden Era* with escape and illusion as their theme: "A Child's Ghost Story" (12 August 1860), "Ran Away" (4 November 1860), and "My Otherself" (originally published as "Our Other Selves," 30 September 1860). But the most psychologically revealing tale was the first one published under Harte's name. Not much good as literature, "My Metamorphosis" (*Golden Era*, 29 April 1860) reveals Harte's psychic intention: a young man, surprised bathing, conceals his naked self by posing among the statuary. (All the stories discussed here were collected for the first time in *Stories and Poems and Other Uncollected Writings*, 1914.)

Harte's life as poseur both socially and literarily begins at this time to be well chronicled. Of medium height and slight build, with an aquiline nose and bright eyes, Bret Harte became noted for his silken Dundreary mustache, his coiffed hair, his manicured nails, his taste for fine clothes and "dude" cravats, his nasal voice, and what one witness described as mincing steps. Samuel Bowles, editor of the *Springfield Republican*, exclaimed over receiving letters from the "Wild West" written by Harte "on thin, dainty, highly finished French note-paper in purple ink, in a delicately, scrupulously finished hand."

Having taken a job as a compositor at the *Golden Era* on his arrival in San Francisco, Harte soon began a regular column called "Town and Table Talk" for that magazine, which paid a dollar a column for prose. In this column he favored drama and opera and touted the actor Dion Boucicault, who specialized in writing plays such as *The Octoroon* (1859; an adaptation of Mayne Reid's novel *The Quadroon*, 1856) and *Rip Van Winkle* (1865; which he and fellow actor Joseph Jefferson adapted from Washington Irving's 1819 story). In both these plays, as in much of Harte's fiction, the protagonists are estranged from their own cultures.

In 1864 Harte helped another *Golden Era* employee, Charles H. Webb, to start a weekly, the *Californian*, which appeared for the first time on 28 May 1864 and continued for two years under their management. Harte started a project well suited to a poseur for the *Californian* in the summer of 1865: *Condensed Novels, and Other Papers*, parodies of authors such as James Fenimore Cooper, Alexandre Dumas, Charlotte Brontë, and Charles Dickens. These *Condensed Novels* (collected, 1867; enlarged edition, 1871) accented the writers' distinctive styles and were a form of fictional criticism. His parody of Cooper, for example, probed far deeper than Mark Twain's essay "Fenimore Cooper's Literary Offences" (*North American Review*, July 1895) and pointed to the killer instinct that D. H. Lawrence later stressed and the fear of miscegenation which Leslie Fiedler explicated a century after Harte. He also cultivated powerful people as patrons, most notably Jessie Frémont, daughter of Sen. Thomas Hart Benton and wife to Gen. John Charles Frémont. His sinecure as clerk in the surveyor-general's office in 1860 provided Harte entry to the elite of San Francisco and introduced him to Thomas Starr King, the diminutive clergyman whose orations helped keep California in the Union during the Civil War. Through King, Harte became clerk and in 1863 superintendent of the new United States Mint, a job he kept until summer 1869. Also through King, he met New Yorker Anna Griswold, an older woman who was a fine contralto, and married her on 11 August 1862.

In his eleven years in San Francisco Harte wrote prolifically, pouring out five poems and more than twenty prose pieces during his first six months. In 1866 he edited *Outcroppings*, an anthology of local poets, and infuriated people because he rejected the efforts of many proud versifiers. He had written twenty-two poems during the Civil War. His most important literary connection was with Anton Roman's new magazine, the *Overland Monthly*, founded in 1868 with Harte as its first editor. At one of the planning sessions Harte perfected its emblem of a snarling grizzly by planting one of its paws firmly on the new transcontinental railroad tracks. As editor, he had the

Caricature of Harte by Spy, published in Vanity Fair, *1879*

distinction of scalping Ralph Waldo Emerson and James Russell Lowell in reviews and of rejecting Walt Whitman's "Passage to India." For this magazine Harte produced the two of his stories which remain most likely to be anthologized: "The Luck of Roaring Camp" (August 1868) and "The Outcasts of Poker Flat" (January 1869). Both stories were collected in *The Luck of Roaring Camp, and Other Sketches* (1870). In addition to satisfying audience demand for local-color sketches and providing formulas for hundreds of western books and movies over the next century, these two stories deployed a cunning narrative strategy which insured their success with genteel readers. The tales argue that society's outcasts—whether gamblers, gold-seekers, prostitutes, or unemployed cowboys—all have hearts of gold. Circumstances can prove them to be nobler than the main-

stream society which rejects them. Yet an elegant, polished, and highly cultivated narrative voice distances the narrator from the subjects, thereby shielding genteel readers from a potentially disturbing theme.

Harte befriended the humorist Charles Henry Webb, Charles Warren Stoddard (whose *Poems* he edited in 1867), Ambrose Bierce, Ida Coolbirth, Ada Clare (known as the "Queen of Bohemia"), and actress Adah Menken. Noted for being tied nearly naked to a horse in the play *Mazeppa*, Menken, whose fourth husband was humor writer Robert H. Newell (Orpheus C. Kerr), ran a literary salon, collected her poems in *Infelicia* (1888), and may have been the model for the sexually free Mrs. Hurlstone in Harte's *The Crusade of the Excelsior* (1887). His most famous friend was Samuel Clemens, who claimed that Harte—whom he met in late 1864—taught him how to write, and who later described Harte as "one of the pleasantest men I have ever known; he was also one of the unpleasantest men I have ever known"—and, when asked by Henry James if he knew Harte, replied tersely: "Yes, I know the son of a bitch." Mercurial in human relationships, Harte wrote steadily. As a critical reviewer, he warned against highly wrought diction, sentimentality, the romanticization of miners and frontiersmen, humor based on mere misspelling or buffoonery; yet as a writer he practiced every sin he preached against, and his reputation soared.

In 1869 the University of California in Berkeley offered him a chair as professor of recent literature, but Harte declined, explaining that his editorial duties already took too much of his time away from writing. In spring 1870 Fields, Osgood and Company of Boston published *The Luck of Roaring Camp, and Other Sketches*, and that company began negotiations with Harte for exclusive rights to publish his stories in their magazines, the *Atlantic Monthly* and *Every Saturday*. At the same time the *Lakeside Monthly* in Chicago offered him editorship and part ownership of that magazine, promising him a substantial increase in income. Harte announced that he was leaving San Francisco on 10 January 1871, and on 2 February he, his wife, and their two sons, Griswold (born 1863) and Francis (born 1865), boarded the Overland Express for Chicago. The Hartes would subsequently have two more children, Jessamy (born 1873) and Ethel (born 1875), but from this time onward husband and wife grew increasingly estranged, and Harte began spending more and more time away from home. Moreover, he would never visit California again, and he avoided western friends when they visited the East.

In Chicago Harte seemed ready to accept the *Lakeside Monthly* offer, but then–after he and his wife failed to attend a dinner in his honor–the Hartes left for the East. Harte never satisfactorily explained his sudden decision. After stops to visit relatives in Syracuse and New York, the Hartes arrived on 25 February 1871 in Boston, where they spent a week with the family of William Dean Howells, who had recently become editor of the *Atlantic Monthly* and who went to great lengths to entertain him and to introduce him to Boston's literati, including Ralph Waldo Emerson, Richard Henry Dana, Jr., Henry Wadsworth Longfellow, Oliver Wendell Holmes, James Russell Lowell, Louis Agassiz, Julia Ward Howe, and Thomas Bailey Aldrich, editor of *Every Saturday*.

The Hartes returned to New York where they spent the next few months and summered in Newport before settling in the Willows, a house in Morristown, New Jersey. By that time Harte had concluded negotiations with publisher James T. Fields and editors Howells and Aldrich for the most lucrative contract given an American author to that date: on 6 March 1871 Harte wrote a letter accepting an "offer of ten thousand dollars for the exclusive publication of my poems and sketches (not to be less than twelve in number) in your periodical for the space of one year...." He continued to be lionized, though his delivery of the Phi Beta Kappa poem at Harvard's 1871 commencement was criticized. He read a nine-year-old imitative poem, speaking in a quiet voice and shocking his audience with his gaudy clothing, especially his bright green gloves.

In the midst of his celebrity he found himself unable to write. He was six months late in honoring his contract with Fields, Osgood, and–also unhappy with the quality of much of the material he sent them–they did not offer him another. In 1873 he wrote only one story; in 1874 he turned out five stories, but the next year only one. Sued for bill payments, he lectured to raise money. From late 1872 until summer 1875 he lectured throughout the East, to Canada and the South, and as far west as Nebraska, often pursued by his creditors and contemptuous of his audience. He wrote candidly to his wife from Kansas, "You can imagine the savage, half-sick, utterly disgusted man who glared at that audience over his desk that night, and d----d them inwardly in his

Harte in 1890 (portrait by J. Pettie, R.A.; Geoffrey Bret Harte, ed., The Letters of Bret Harte, *1926)*

heart.... And yet it was a good audience–thoroughly refined and appreciative, and very glad to see me." He also complained to his wife that he was weary of the stock posturings in his work; yet when he was finally able to stop traveling long enough to finish his only novel, *Gabriel Conroy* (1876), he included these lines in its finale: "Whereat Olly flew into Poinsett's arms, and gave him a fraternal and conciliatory kiss. Tableau." Harte despised the tricks of his craft, but feared moving away from them. Moreover, he apparently was confused about what he should think about life and its hardships. For example, *Gabriel Conroy* contains this sentence: "They were so haggard, so faded, so forlorn, so wan; so piteous in their human aspect, or rather all that was left of a human aspect, that they might have been wept over as they sat there; they were so brutal, so imbecile, unreasoning and grotesque in these newer animal attributes that they might have provoked a smile." The creatures Harte is describing are the people of the Donner party, who are about to be reduced by famine to cannibalism. The man who fairly burst with moral indignation over an Indian massacre in 1860 had by 1876 become so confused about his authorial pose that he was not sure whether he should cry or laugh even with respect to man literally eating man. Though the novel was severely criticized by reviewers, it was financially successful, with *Scribner's Magazine* paying six thousand dollars for serialization rights. Yet once his prepublication advances were charged against royalties Harte was soon in a precarious financial situation again.

Unhappy as a lecturer and faltering as a writer, Harte turned to drama. Although more than a dozen movies would later be made of his stories, including a 1918 film version of *M'liss* starring Mary Pickford and the 1955 movie *Tennessee's Partner* with Ronald Reagan, Harte could not produce a successful play from his fiction. His first effort, *Two Men of Sandy Bar*, opened on Broadway on 28 August 1876 and managed to survive a month despite unfavorable reviews. Later that year he and Mark Twain collaborated on *Ah Sin*, which opened in New York on 31 July 1877 to a similar fate.

Nearly penniless and certainly with a bruised ego, Harte leapt at President Hayes's offer to make him United States commercial agent at Crefeld, Germany. Since 1875 Harte had kept a separate apartment in New York, and he had been spending increasingly less time with his family. He traveled alone to Germany where he took office on 18 July 1878 and arranged for subordinates to perform most of the official work while he took frequent trips to London (for his health, he claimed). He made a holiday visit to Düsseldorf in the company of a "Miss Cooper," whom he presented as his cousin, although records cannot substantiate the kinship. In April 1880 he was appointed as U.S. consul to Glasgow. Taking office in July, Harte held that post five years, fulfilling his duties but spending most of his time in London.

There, he made friends with George Eliot, *Punch* illustrator George Du Maurier, Thomas Hardy, Henry James, James Anthony Froude, and the Duchess of St. Albans, who sponsored Harte much as Jessie Frémont had in California. He became close friends with Arthur Van de Velde and his wife, Marguerite, staying with them and their nine children during his frequent visits to London. In 1882 he began writing again. Although his output was not enormous, a half-dozen stories equaled the merit of those that made him famous a quarter-century earlier. In August 1885 he was relieved of his consulship for "inattention to duty," and from then until his death he made his home with the Van de Veldes, an arrangement many considered scandalous, especially after the death of Arthur Van de Velde in 1892. In 1896 he and T. Edgar Pemberton completed a play, *Sue*, which opened on Broadway on 15 September for a successful run.

His son Frank Harte and his wife settled in England in 1893, and Anna Harte arrived there in late 1898. By that time Harte had moved to a house a few doors away from Marguerite Van de Velde, but he did not invite his wife to join him. He sometimes saw her and their daughter Ethel, who was studying music in Paris, at Frank Harte's house in Caversham; those visits were rare, however, and resulted in quarrels. During his last years he wrote a second series of *Condensed Novels*, published as a book a few months after his death in 1902, but it was a far cry from the quality of the first series of parodies. His last months were spent in weakness and agony from a severe sore throat. On 5 May 1902 he hemorrhaged and died of throat cancer.

In 1857, when Harte had attained the age of twenty-one, he had vowed his dedication to literature. Twenty-one years after that he would complain in a letter, "I grind out the old tunes on the old organ and gather up the coppers. . . ." Twenty-three years after that he spent part of his last day working on another story about the stock character Colonel Starbottle, the pompous southern lawyer whom he had invented in another era six thousand miles away. Bret Harte happened upon a literary method that worked, and he was too insecure to try new forms of self-expression or even to have self-expression as his goal.

The dangers of formulas were known to Harte in his early work. In "Charitable Reminiscences" (first published as "On the Decay of Professional Begging," *Californian*, 17 June 1865; collected in *Mrs. Skaggs's Husbands, and Other Sketches* 1872) Harte is at his desk writing a sketch on poverty while a beggar woman stands outside his window with a sick babe in arms. Her look, Harte says, "plainly said to me, as I bent over my paper, 'Go on with your mock sentimentalities and simulated pathos; portray the imaginary sufferings of your bodiless creations, spread your thin web of philosophy, but look you, sir, here is real misery! Here is genuine suffering!' " After 1868, however, Harte would mention the artifice in his work only in passing. In "The Romance of Madrono Hollow" (*Atlantic Monthly*, September 1871; collected in *Mrs. Skaggs's Husbands, and Other Sketches*), a girl stands at her window with a candle; to her suitor "it was a vestal virgin standing before a hallowed shrine; to the prosaic observer I fear it was only a fair-haired woman" with wicked black eyes. The description shows Harte as a transitional figure who seemed a romanticist and a realist both. Later in the same story another problem with formulas is posed. When Colonel Starbottle curses, Harte records, "I regret that, even in a liberal age, I may not record the exact and even picturesque language."

As the post-Civil War era emphasized the differences within the Union, Harte too depicted the many linguistic variants of his Californians, from Starbottle's pompous diction to a street waif 's stuttering colloquialisms. This language included western humor rife with rough irony, sarcasm, and hyperbole, and it also included elided curses. Harte astutely wrapped these dialectical nuances in a distanced third-person narration of highly polished diction, thereby defusing any offense these vulgarities might cause the gentler reader.

Harte also packed his fiction with figures that have become stock western characters—the likable drunkard, the pretty and spunky young woman who wears pants and laughs like a man, the softhearted gamblers like John Oakhurst and Jack Hamlin, the emotive southern colonel, the prostitute with a heart of gold, the sleazy banker, stockbroker, mine grabber, or landlord, the rough-and-tumble miner who is humanized by the chance appearance of a baby or a prim schoolmistress, the pious Spanish priest—all the types which will continue to inhabit the genre of the western. Scenery too is important to the western, and Harte is extremely deft whether describing the fog rolling in over San Francisco Bay in "The Princess Bob and Her Friends" (*Atlantic Monthly*, December 1871; collected in *Mrs. Skaggs's Husbands, and Other Sketches*) or a miner dying at a bend of the already pollution-clogged Stanislaus River in "Mrs. Skaggs's Husbands" (first published in *Mrs. Skaggs's Husbands and Other Sketches*).

Harte's main, if not his only, theme was the influence of civilization on the West. Although

wary of civilization's artificiality, he generally came down on the side of civilization which he describes as "the tenderness of culture, magic of wealth, and spell of refinement."

Letters:

The Letters of Bret Harte, edited by Geoffrey Bret Harte (Boston: Houghton Mifflin, 1926);

Bradford A. Booth, "Unpublished Letters of Bret Harte," *American Literature*, 16 (May 1944): 131-142;

Booth, "Bret Harte Goes East: Some Unpublished Letters," *American Literature*, 19 (January 1948).

Bibliographies:

George R. Stewart, Jr., *A Bibliography of the Writings of Bret Harte in the Magazines and Newspapers of California, 1857-1871*, University of California Publications in English, volume 3, number 3 (Berkeley: University of California Press, 1933);

Joseph Gaer, ed., *Bret Harte: Bibliography and Biographical Data* (San Francisco: State Emergency Relief Administration, California Library Research, 1935);

Linda D. Barnett, *Bret Harte: A Reference Guide* (Boston: G. K. Hall, 1980).

Biographies:

George R. Stewart, Jr., *Bret Harte: Argonaut and Exile* (Boston: Houghton Mifflin, 1931);

Margaret Duckett, *Mark Twain and Bret Harte* (Norman: University of Oklahoma Press, 1964);

Richard O'Connor, *Bret Harte: A Biography* (Boston & Toronto: Little, Brown, 1966).

References:

Thomas Dykes Beasley, *A Tramp Through Bret Harte Country* (San Francisco: Paul Elder, 1914);

Patrick Morrow, *Bret Harte* (Boise, Idaho: Boise State College Western Writers Series, 1972);

Morrow, *Bret Harte: Literary Critic* (Bowling Green, Ohio: Bowling Green University Popular Press, 1979).

Papers:

The major collections of Harte's papers are at the Beinecke Library, Yale University, and the Huntington Library in San Marino, California.

Nathaniel Hawthorne
(4 July 1804-19 May 1864)

William E. Grant
Bowling Green State University

See also the Hawthorne entry in *DLB 1: The American Renaissance in New England*.

BOOKS: *Fanshawe, A Tale* (Boston: Marsh & Capen, 1828);

Twice-Told Tales (1 volume, Boston: American Stationers' Company, 1837; revised and enlarged edition, 2 volumes, Boston: Munroe, 1842; abridged edition, 1 volume, London: Kent & Richards, 1849);

Peter Parley's Universal History, on the Basis of Geography, ghostwritten by Hawthorne and Elizabeth Hawthorne (Boston: American Stationers' Company, 1837; 1 volume, London: Parker, 1837); republished in 1 volume, slightly abridged and modified, as *Peter Parley's Common School of History* (Boston: American Stationers' Company, 1838);

The Sister Years: Being the Carrier's Address, to the Patrons of the Salem Gazette, for the First of January, 1839 (Salem, 1839);

Grandfather's Chair: A History for Youth (Boston: E. P. Peabody/New York: Wiley & Putnam, 1841; slightly revised and enlarged edition, Boston: Tappan & Dennet, 1842; republished in *Historical Tales for Youth*, 2 volumes (Boston, 1842) and *True Stories from History and Biography* (Boston: Ticknor, Reed & Fields, 1851; London: Low, 1853);

Famous Old People: Being the Second Epoch of Grandfather's Chair (Boston: E. P. Peabody, 1841); republished in *Historical Tales for Youth* (1842) and *True Stories from History and Biography* (1851);

Liberty Tree: With the Last Words of Grandfather's Chair (Boston: E. P. Peabody, 1841); republished in *Historical Tales for Youth* (1842) and *True Stories from History and Biography* (1851);

Biographical Stories for Children (Boston: Tappan & Dennet, 1842; London: Sonnenschein, 1898; republished as *Historical Tales for Youth* (1842) and *True Stories from History and Biography* (1851);

Nathaniel Hawthorne in 1840 (portrait by Charles Osgood; courtesy of the Essex Institute, Salem, Massachusetts)

The Celestial Rail-Road (Boston: Wilder, 1843; London: Houlston & Stoneman, 1844);

Journal of an African Cruiser; Comprising Sketches of the Canaries, the Cape de Verds, Liberia, Madeira, Sierra Leone, and Other Places of Interest on the West Coast of Africa. By an Officer of the U.S. Navy [Horatio Bridge]. *Edited by Nathaniel Hawthorne* (New York & London: Wiley & Putnam, 1845; London: Wiley & Putnam, 1845);

Mosses from an Old Manse, 2 volumes (New York: Wiley & Putnam, 1846; London: Wiley & Putnam, 1846; revised and enlarged edition, Boston: Ticknor & Fields, 1854);

The Scarlet Letter, A Romance (Boston: Ticknor, Reed & Fields, 1850; London: Bogue/Hamilton/Johnston & Hunter/Washbourne;

Edinburgh: Johnston & Hunter/Oliver & Boyd; Dublin: M'Glashan, 1851);

The House of the Seven Gables, A Romance (Boston: Ticknor, Reed & Fields, 1851; London: Bohn, 1851);

A Wonder-Book for Girls and Boys (Boston: Ticknor, Reed & Fields, 1852 [i.e., 1851]; London: Bohn, 1852);

The Snow-Image, and Other Twice-Told Tales (Boston: Ticknor, Reed & Fields, 1852 [i.e., 1851]; London: Bohn, 1851);

The Blithedale Romance (2 volumes, London: Chapman & Hall, 1852; 1 volume, Boston: Ticknor, Reed & Fields, 1852);

Life of Franklin Pierce (Boston: Ticknor, Reed & Fields, 1852; London: Routledge, 1853);

Tanglewood Tales, for Girls and Boys: Being a Second Wonder-Book (London: Chapman & Hall, 1853; Boston: Ticknor, Reed & Fields, 1853);

Transformation; or, The Romance of Monte Beni, 3 volumes (London: Smith, Elder, 1860); republished as *The Marble Faun; or, The Romance of Monte Beni*, 2 volumes (Boston: Ticknor & Fields, 1860);

Our Old Home: A Series of English Sketches (1 volume, Boston: Ticknor & Fields, 1863; 2 volumes, London: Smith, Elder, 1863);

Pansie: A Fragment (London: Hotten, 1864);

Passages from the American Note-Books, 2 volumes, edited by Sophia Hawthorne (Boston: Ticknor & Fields, 1868; London: Smith, Elder, 1868);

Passages from the English Note-Books, 2 volumes, edited by Sophia Hawthorne (Boston: Fields, Osgood, 1870; London: Strahan, 1870);

Passages from the French and Italian Note-Books, 2 volumes, edited by Sophia Hawthorne (London: Strahan, 1871; Boston: Osgood, 1872);

Septimus, A Romance, edited by Una Hawthorne and Robert Browning (London: King, 1872); republished as *Septimus Felton; or The Elixir of Life* (Boston: Osgood, 1872);

Fanshawe and Other Pieces (Boston: Osgood, 1876);

The Dolliver Romance and Other Pieces (Boston: Osgood, 1876);

Doctor Grimshawe's Secret, A Romance, edited by Julian Hawthorne (Boston: Osgood, 1883; London: Longmans, Green, 1883);

Alice Doane's Appeal, Chiefly about War Matters, and Life of Franklin Pierce, volume 24 of the *Wayside Edition* (Boston & New York: Houghton, Mifflin, 1884);

The Ghost of Doctor Harris (N.p., 1900);

Twenty Days with Julian and Little Bunny (New York: Privately printed, 1904);

The American Notebooks, edited by Randall Stewart (New Haven: Yale University Press, 1932);

The English Notebooks, edited by Stewart (New York: Modern Language Association of America, 1941);

Hawthorne as Editor: Selections from the Writings in the American Magazine of Useful and Entertaining Knowledge, edited by Arlin Turner (University: Louisiana State University Press, 1941);

The American Notebooks, edited by Claude M. Simpson, volume 8 of *The Centenary Edition of the Works of Nathaniel Hawthorne* (Columbus: Ohio State University Press, 1973);

The Snow Image and Uncollected Tales, edited by J. Donald Crowley and Fredson Bowers, volume 11 of *The Centenary Edition of the Works of Nathaniel Hawthorne* (Columbus: Ohio State University Press, 1974);

The American Claimant Manuscripts: The Ancestral Footstep, Etherege, Grimshawe, edited by Edward H. Davidson, Claude M. Simpson, and L. Neal Smith, volume 12 of *The Centenary Edition of the Works of Nathaniel Hawthorne* (Columbus: Ohio State University Press, 1977);

The Elixir of Life Manuscripts: Septimus Felton, Septimus Norton, and The Dolliver Romance, edited by Davidson, Simpson, and Smith, volume 13 of *The Centenary Edition of the Works of Nathaniel Hawthorne* (Columbus: Ohio State University Press, 1977);

Hawthorne's Lost Notebook, 1835-1841, edited by Hyatt H. Waggoner and Barbara S. Mouffe (University Park: Pennsylvania State University Press, 1978);

The French and Italian Notebooks, edited by Thomas Woodson, volume 14 of *The Centenary Edition of the Works of Nathaniel Hawthorne* (Columbus: Ohio State University Press, 1980).

Collection: *The Centenary Edition of the Works of Nathaniel Hawthorne*, 20 volumes to date (Columbus: Ohio State University Press, 1963-   ).

When Nathaniel Hawthorne was born in Salem, Massachusetts, on our most patriotic holiday in 1804, his ancestral roots were already deeply planted in New England. Writing in *The Scarlet Letter* (1850) of his sentimental affection for the town of his birth, Hawthorne ascribed his feeling "to the deep and aged roots which my family has struck into the soil." Nearly two centuries after the appearance of his first ancestor "in the wild and forest-bordered settlement," where over time they "mingled their earthly substance with the soil," Hawthorne felt the New England earth itself "must necessarily be akin to the mortal frame wherewith, for a little while, I walk the streets." And, though he acknowledges that this affinity might seem to be merely the "sensuous sympathy of dust for dust," he also perceived a "moral quality" in the feeling engendered by "the figure of that first ancestor," which had been present in his imagination from boyhood and which, he wrote, "still haunts me and induces a sort of home feeling with the past."

It is this rich combination of love of his ancestral soil, a strong sense of the richness of the American past, and that "moral quality" which translates into a concern for the secrets of the human heart that gives Hawthorne's work its unique flavor. William Hathorne (the writer added the *w* as a young man) came to New England with John Winthrop in 1630. Judge John Hathorne, his son, was an unrepentant burner of witches during the notorious Salem witch trials (1692); and Nathaniel's paternal grandfather, Daniel Hathorne, inspired a patriotic ballad during the American Revolution by his valor and courage as a privateer. These ancestors were the writer's strongest links to the past, and his stories and novels turn again and again to the periods their lives touched. Unlike any American writer of short fiction who came before him, Hawthorne was able to link his personal sense of the past with the actual history of his region, as throughout his work he simultaneously plumbed the most private aspects of his own psyche while exploring the shared myths of his community.

Hawthorne's father, Nathaniel Hathorne, followed the family seafaring tradition, handed down, his son wrote, "for above two hundred years"; but with him the tradition of "a gray-headed shipmaster, in each generation, retiring from the quarterdeck to the homestead, while a boy of fourteen took his hereditary place before the mast," ended. Only four when his father died in far off Suriname, Nathaniel grew up in Salem and Maine in the family of his mother, Elizabeth Manning Hathorne, sturdy Maine inlanders who schooled him in other, no less valuable, traditions. He went to school in Salem, and then—rather than going to sea—he entered Bowdoin College in Brunswick, Maine, in 1821. In 1825 he emerged as an apprentice writer. Years of frustra-

tion were ahead of him, but his course was certain.

Returning to his mother's home in Salem after graduation, Hawthorne began his career as what he called "the obscurist man of letters in America." These were the lonely and difficult years when he earned little but learned much. He had begun to write fiction while in college, and soon after graduation he published (at his own expense) *Fanshawe* (1828), his first novel, which was set at a school like Bowdoin. Soon realizing that publication of this apprentice work was a mistake, Hawthorne disposed of as many copies as he could locate and asked his friends and family to do the same. A fire at the Marsh and Capen store in 1831 destroyed all the unsold copies, and Hawthorne continued to deny authorship of the novel for the rest of his life. During this same period he prepared and then destroyed the first of several short-fiction collections that failed to find a publisher. Five of the "Seven Tales of My Native Land" were intentionally consigned to the fire, apparently without "mercy or remorse, (and, moreover without any subsequent regret)," if the preface Hawthorne added to the 1851 edition of *Twice-Told Tales* is to be believed. In the more fictionalized version of this episode, presented in "The Devil in Manuscript" (*New-England Magazine*, November 1835; collected in *The Snow-Image, and Other Twice-Told Tales*, 1852), however, Hawthorne's attitude is quite different as he describes a young writer who in a moment of despair threw his unpublished manuscripts into the flames: "Oberon stood gazing at the conflagration, and shortly began to soliloquize, in the wildest strain, as if Fancy resisted and became riotous, at the moment when he would have compelled her to ascend that funeral pile. His words described objects which he appeared to discern in the fire, fed by his own precious thoughts; perhaps the thousand visions, which the writer's magic had incorporated with those pages, became visible to him in the dissolving heat, brightening forth ere they vanished forever; while the smoke, the vivid sheets of flame, the ruddy and whitening coals, caught the aspect of a varied scenery." While it is probable that neither extreme of these two reactions fully describes Hawthorne's attitude, the appearance of the manuscript-burning episode in his fiction suggests it was a memorable, and perhaps painful, occasion for the young author.

A second group of stories, "Provincial Tales," was apparently sent in 1829 to Samuel Griswold Goodrich, publisher of *The Token*, an annual Christmas gift book in which a number of Hawthorne's early publications appeared. This collection was not published as a book, though Goodrich did include "Sights from the Steeple" in *The Token* for 1831, and "The Wives of the Dead," "Roger Malvin's Burial," "My Kinsman, Major Molineux," and "The Gentle Boy" in *The Token* for 1832. All these stories are believed by scholars to have been among those in "Provincial Tales." A preliminary version of "Alice Doane's Appeal," one of the two surviving stories from the first unpublished collection, was also included. A revised version was published in *The Token* for 1835. A third projected collection was to have been unified through the device of an itinerant young artist who travels through New England telling stories for his livelihood, but, like the other projected collections, "The Story Teller" never saw print as a complete work. Its contents too were published individually in magazines and eventually collected in volumes of short stories.

Though the specific contents of these early collections are not known for certain and though some of the stories, tales, and sketches in them have probably been lost forever, it is still possible, from what is known about them, to characterize the short fiction Hawthorne was writing at this early stage in his career. Though most of the models he encountered in his college reading were British—his favorite author then was Sir Walter Scott—it is clear that from the beginning he had linked his literary fate to his native land, and the titles of these collections suggest the primacy he gave to native American materials. It was these qualities Herman Melville recognized in Hawthorne when he wrote in "Hawthorne and His Mosses," the review of *Mosses from an Old Manse* (1846) that he wrote for the *Literary World* (17 and 24 August 1850): "He is one of the new, and far better generation of your writers. The smell of young beeches and hemlocks is upon him; your own broad prairies are in his soul; and if you travel away inland into his deep and noble nature, you will hear the far roar of his Niagara."

The original, American quality Melville recognized in Hawthorne was there almost from the beginning, though he did need to labor to get out from under the European influences that are so apparent in his earliest work. *Fanshawe* suffers in part because its American setting never emerges from a generalized Gothic vision that

owes more to Scott than to experience, and Hawthorne likely disowned it because he recognized it as imitative. The same realization may lie behind his destruction of other early efforts, as he sought for a new kind of national fiction rooted in the American experience.

For all its artistic faults, *Fanshawe* nevertheless had a positive effect on Hawthorne's career. Among its few readers was Samuel Goodrich. In early 1836 Hawthorne made his entry into the professional literary world of Boston as editor of the *American Magazine of Useful and Entertaining Knowledge*, published by the Bewick Company, of which Goodrich was a director. For the March through September issues Hawthorne and his sister Elizabeth wrote or selected from other publications the entire contents of the journal. Though he complained of a lack of editorial control on his resignation from the magazine in August, it was more probably the publisher's failure to pay his salary that accounts for his early departure. This misunderstanding does not seem to have affected his relationship with Goodrich seriously, however, because he completed in September 1836, again with Elizabeth as his assistant, *Peter Parley's Universal History, on the Basis of Geography* (1837), one of a popular series of children's books published by Goodrich under the pseudonym Peter Parley. More important, however, Goodrich agreed to bring out Hawthorne's first collection of short fiction under the imprint of the American Stationers' Company, which published *The Token* and some of his Peter Parley books.

With Hawthorne's college friend Horatio Bridge, who acted secretly to spare Hawthorne embarrassment, offering $250 as a guaranty against the publisher's losses, an edition of one thousand copies was published on 6 or 7 March 1837. This collection of eighteen stories was enlarged to thirty-nine in 1842, and Hawthorne added a preface to the 1851 edition. Since no other collection of short fiction intervened between the editions of 1837 and 1842 and since many of the stories added to the enlarged edition were written by 1837, the two editions may be treated as a single work.

Some credibility is given to Hawthorne's characterization of himself as "the obscurist man of letters in America" during the period preceding 1837, despite the regular appearance of his work in gift books and magazines for the past half-dozen years, by an anonymous reviewer for the *Boston Courier* (9 March 1837), who announced

TWICE-TOLD TALES.

BY

NATHANIEL HAWTHORNE.

BOSTON:
AMERICAN STATIONERS CO.
JOHN B. RUSSELL.
1837.

Title page for the collection of stories Henry Wadsworth Longfellow described as coming "from the hand of a man of genius"

the work as "the production of 'Nathaniel Hawthorne'–whether a true or fictitious name, we know not–probably the latter." However, that obscurity began to lessen with the appearance of a review by Henry Wadsworth Longfellow in the July 1837 issue of *North American Review* which announced Hawthorne as "a new star . . . in the heaven of poetry." Edgar Allan Poe, in a long two-part review of the 1842 edition for *Graham's Magazine* (April and May 1842), proclaimed, "the style is purity itself. Force abounds. High imagination gleams from every page. Mr. Hawthorne is a man of truest genius." Other critics saw parallels with Germany's Ludwig Tieck and England's Charles Dickens while hailing Hawthorne as a truly American literary voice.

Unlike Hawthorne's earlier, unpublished collections, *Twice-Told Tales* is not organized around a particular theme or idea. To the modern reader, the selections might even seem eccentric, as Hawthorne reserved for later collections some early stories that have come to be regarded as his masterpieces, while including, especially in the 1842 edition, a number of slighter works. Hawthorne himself characterized the selections as "such articles as seemed best worth offering to the public a second time," which might suggest a deliberate effort to attract a popular following by republishing those pieces most attractive to his contemporaries. Unfortunately, however, this effort was not successful, and even though sales of the first edition repaid Bridge's guaranty, Hawthorne realized little profit from it. The 1842 edition fared even worse–and its failure represented a greater problem for the author since he was by then contemplating marriage–as it did not even make the cost of publication. Not until the edition of 1851 was Hawthorne to realize a profit on his early stories. He had, after the critical success of *Twice-Told Tales*, become, in Poe's words, "*the* example, *par excellence*, in this country, of the privately-admired and publicly-unappreciated man of genius."

The stories selected for *Twice-Told Tales* reflect both Hawthorne's interest in New England history and his fascination with daily life in his community. Best among the historical pieces are three stories Hawthorne included in the 1837 edition–"The Gray Champion," "The May-Pole of Merry Mount," and "The Gentle Boy"–as well as two of the four stories grouped as "Legends of the Province House" and "Endicott and the Red Cross"–all added to the 1842 edition. Another story that was first collected in the 1837 edition, "A Rill from the Town Pump," was identified by Hawthorne in his 1851 preface as the most popular piece in the collection, and it is the cornerstone of the second group–which might more accurately be described as personal essays than as short stories in the modern sense. This group also includes "Sunday at Home," "Sights from a Steeple," and "Little Annie's Ramble," all of which were first collected in the 1837 edition. Among other, less easily categorized, notable stories in the collection, "The Minister's Black Veil" and "Wakefield"–both included in the 1837 edition–are excursions into psychological fiction; "Dr. Heidegger's Experiment," also included in the 1837 edition, reveals the fascination with the moral implications of science Hawthorne would develop in other writings. Another story that Hawthorne included in the first edition, "The Prophetic Pictures," concerns itself with the responsibilities of the artist, while "The Ambitious Guest"–added in 1842–introduces the scholar-idealist character type Hawthorne would treat more complexly elsewhere. In the larger context the themes of these stories as well as those of the two major groups reflect lifelong preoccupations in Hawthorne's short stories and novels.

Hawthorne selected a recently published story to open the 1837 edition of *Twice-Told Tales*. "The Gray Champion" first appeared in the *New-England Magazine* for January 1835, and scholars have speculated it may have been written earlier as part of "Provincial Tales." The story is a fictionalized version of an actual event which took place

in Hadley, Massachusetts, in 1675 when King Philip's War set the Indians against the colonists. Surprised by an attack while at Sunday morning worship, the confused and frightened citizens of Hadley were rallied by a dignified elderly man who assumed command to repulse the attackers. Afterward this "Angel of Hadley" disappeared as suddenly as he had come, leaving the delivered townspeople in awe and wonder at their savior's identity. (He was in fact one of the three signers of the death warrant for Charles I who went into hiding in New England after the Restoration of the British monarchy in 1660.)

Hawthorne altered the original event in several respects, but most particularly by changing the crisis from an Indian attack to an April 1689 confrontation between the colonists and the soldiers of Sir Edmund Andros, the royal governor of New England in 1686-1689 and a symbol of British tyranny. As Hawthorne writes, "The whole scene was a picture of the condition of New-England, and its moral, the deformity of any government that does not grow out of the nature of things and the character of the people." With the "religious multitude" on one side, and "the group of despotic rulers" on the other, the "mercenary soldiers" waited for the order "to deluge the street with blood." In answer to a cry from the citizens for God to "provide a Champion for thy people," an aged patriarch appears to confront the attackers. Looking like a resurrected spirit from the first generation of Puritans, the old man speaks with the voice of prophecy as he tells Governor Andros that the rule of James II is over and his own term as royal governor at an end. The people rally behind him, and the British forces retreat. When the episode is over, the old man has disappeared; but, the story ends, "I have heard, that, whenever the descendants of the Puritans are to show the spirit of their sires, the old man appears again," because "he is the type of New-England's hereditary spirit; and his shadowy march, on the eve of danger, must ever be the pledge, that New England's sons will vindicate their ancestry."

An excellent choice for the first story of a first collection, "The Gray Champion" introduces a number of themes and techniques Hawthorne would employ throughout his career. Taking poetic license with the facts, Hawthorne adroitly fashioned a regional, or even national, myth by realizing the symbolic possibilities inherent in his historical source. While the story unfolds plausibly, the uncertainties surrounding the appear-

148

ance, disappearance, and identity of the old warrior provide just the degree of the mysterious that Hawthorne described as the meeting between reality and fantasy. Like his Puritan ancestors, Hawthorne saw the events of history as symbols for deeper truths, but while they sought religious truths he sought to create the "truth of fiction."

The theme of Puritan defiance of royal authority appears again in "Endicott and the Red Cross," which was probably written shortly before it was published in *The Token and Atlantic Souvenir* for 1838. The story again makes use of an actual historical event that Hawthorne turns to his own purposes. When John Endicott, commander of Salem's Puritan militia, tore the red cross of Saint George, the patron saint of England, from a British flag in 1634, it was in all likelihood a religious gesture reflecting his refusal to fight under a flag with a cross upon it because it symbolized the Church of England and, to the Puritans, suggested idolatry. In Hawthorne's story Endicott tells the people that Charles I and the Archbishop of Canterbury "are minded . . . to establish the idolatrous forms of English Episcopacy; so that when [Archbishop] Laud shall kiss the Pope's toe, as cardinal of Rome, he may deliver New England, bound hand and foot, into the power of his master!" In Hawthorne's interpretation the religious element is strongly paralleled by a more political meaning that links Puritan defiance of royal authority to the events of the American Revolution nearly a century and a half later. As Endicott waved the "tattered ensign above his head," the narrator explains, "the people gave their sanction to one of the boldest exploits which our history records. And, for ever honored be the name of Endicott! We look back through the mists of ages and recognize, in the rending of the Red Cross from New England's banner, the first omen of that deliverance which our father consummated, after the bones of the stern Puritan had lain more than a century in the dust."

Interpretations of "Endicott and the Red Cross" center around the extent to which Hawthorne's treatment of the Puritan leader is ironic. Though his passionate stand against Old World tyranny marks him as a legitimate American hero, the scene surrounding the events of the story suggests other possibilities. In an early example of the tableau method he would use so effectively in *The Scarlet Letter*, Hawthorne describes the scene as a reflection in Endicott's

highly polished breastplate, a picture of Puritan intolerance unrivaled in Hawthorne's writings. The whipping post, pillory, and stocks are featured, along with such victims of Puritan authority as a "wanton gospeller" who had "dared give interpretations of Holy Writ, unsanctioned by the infallible judgment of the civil and religious rulers," and a woman who was forced to wear a "cleft stick on her tongue, in appropriate retribution for having wagged that unruly member against the elders of the church." Also among the crowd are men and women marked by cropped ears, branded cheeks, slit nostrils, and other signs of the cruel "justice" of the New England community. Of particular interest is the appearance in this group of "a young woman . . . whose doom was to wear the letter A on the breast of her gown, in the eyes of all the world and her own children. . . . Sporting with her infamy, the lost and desperate creature had embroidered the fatal token in scarlet cloth, with golden thread, and the nicest art of needle-work; so that the capital A might have been thought to mean Admirable, or any thing rather than Adulteress."

In typically ambiguous fashion Hawthorne leaves unresolved the tension between Endicott as symbol of religious intolerance and as emblem of heroic resistance to foreign domination of New England. It has often been argued by Hawthorne's critics that his world is colored in shades of gray, rather than in the extremes of black and white, and such would seem to be the case in this story. Without denying what is admirable in the historic experience of New England, Hawthorne nevertheless recognized that the little commonwealth was, in some respects, compromised from the beginning by evils which mimicked those of the Old World from which the Puritans fled. Given Hawthorne's general sense of human fallibility, it is consistent with his philosophy that he recognize the failures as well as the triumphs in the Puritan past. Just as he found much to deplore as well as much to admire in his own ancestors, Hawthorne finds our common historical past a complex mixture of good and evil.

The Puritan figures who dominate these two stories emerge again as shadowy background characters when Hawthorne treats the period of the American Revolution. In "Howe's Masquerade" (first published in the *United States Magazine and Democratic Review* for May 1838 as one of the four "Legends of the Province-House") a procession of figures from the American past appears to Sir William Howe during the final days of the siege of Boston. It is led by the colony's Puritan governors including "an individual of stern visage" (Endicott) bearing "a rolled-up banner, which seemed to be the banner of England, but strangely rent and torn." They are followed by "a procession of the regicide judges of King Charles," which would include the Gray Champion. Also in the procession is the tyrant Sir Edmund Andros against whom the Gray Champion acted. All the figures in the ghostly parade "form the funeral procession of royal authority in New England," but they also serve to underline the connections Hawthorne clearly sees between the Puritan past and the political history of American independence.

Hawthorne confessed at the end of "Howe's Masquerade" that "it is desperately hard work, when we attempt to throw the spell of hoar antiquity over localities with which the living world, and the day that is passing over us, have aught to do." This lack of a lengthy American past led Hawthorne in the preface to *The Marble Faun* (1860) to complain of "the difficulty of writing a romance about a country where there is no shadow, no antiquity, no mystery, no picturesque and gloomy wrong." It may have been this lack of historical distance that made him less comfortable with the events of the American Revolutionary period than with those of the Puritan years, but whatever the cause, he is only rarely as successful in imaginatively dramatizing this history as that of the seventeenth century. The four tales he called "Legends of the Province House," though they reflect the most momentous change in American history, never achieve the quality of "The Gray Champion" and "Endicott and the Red Cross," and they remain at the periphery of Hawthorne's historical fiction. Only in these two stories and "My Kinsman, Major Molineux" (*The Token* for 1832; collected in *The Snow-Image, and Other Twice-Told Tales*, 1852) did Hawthorne achieve the symbolic power and mythic dimensions characteristic of his best work in a story with a Revolutionary War setting.

Undoubtedly the most successful example of making myth of history in *Twice-Told Tales* is "The May-Pole of Merry Mount," which first saw publication in *The Token and Atlantic Souvenir* for 1836. Some scholarship suggests the story was written early enough to have been included in the projected "Provincial Tales," but the date of composition remains elusive. The story was probably revised or rewritten for publication about 1835, making it one of the more recent tales in the

1837 edition of *Twice-Told Tales*. The confrontation between John Endicott and Thomas Morton is recorded in several Puritan histories to which Hawthorne had access, but the exact source for his story is uncertain.

"The May-Pole of Merry Mount" is Hawthorne's interpretation of the Puritan destruction of a rival colony called Merry Mount at Mount Wollaston (near modern-day Quincy), Massachusetts. In Hawthorne's story, which ignores the complaint by the Puritans that the new colonists were selling guns to the Indians, this episode becomes a classic confrontation between puritanical repression and a prelapsarian spirit of mindless jollity. On one side are John Endicott, "the Puritan of Puritans," and his followers, variously described as "most dismal wretches," "grim," and "dark Puritans." On the other are the followers of Thomas Morton, worshipers at the ancient maypole who, "should their banner be triumphant, were to pour sunshine over New England's rugged hills, and scatter flower-seeds throughout the soil." As Hawthorne describes it, "jollity and gloom were contending for an empire" when the Puritans marched on the Merrymounters.

As the story unfolds, the Merrymounters are dancing around their maypole, celebrating life and fertility. Their costumes evoke pre-Christian rites and even obscure the distinctions between men and beasts: "Had a wanderer, bewildered in the melancholy forest, heard their mirth, and stolen a half-affrighted glance he might have fancied them the crew of some Comus, some already transformed to brutes, some midway between man and beast, and the others rioting in the flow of tipsy jollity that foreran the change." At the center of the festivities are the Lord and Lady of May, an attractive young couple "presently to join in holy matrimony." The Puritans, a band of whom secretly watched this scene of merriment, "compared the masques to those devils and ruined souls, with whom their superstition peopled the forest." As for these enemies of Merry Mount, "their festivals were fast-days, and their chief pastime the singing of psalms. Woe to the youth or maiden, who did but dream of a dance." The whipping post, Hawthorne writes, "might be termed the Puritan May-Pole."

"The May-Pole of Merry Mount" is the most clearly "mythic" story in *Twice-Told Tales*, and as a result it lends itself easily to psychological, philosophical, or theological interpretations. The emphasis in this story on a prelapsarian paradise in

The Old Manse in Concord, Massachusetts, where Hawthorne lived from July 1842 until October 1845 (courtesy of the Concord Free Public Library).

conflict with the postlapsarian world of the Puritan preoccupation with guilt and sin links the story thematically to Hawthorne's novel *The Marble Faun* and suggests the theme of the "fortunate fall" as a likely interpretation. Pointed allusions to the Golden Age as well as descriptions of the Merrymounters suggest that they represent humankind–or the individual–at a level of development prior to knowledge of sin, moral restraint, or guilt. The Puritans, on the other hand, seem so dominated by their sense of sin and guilt as to stand for total repression of those human sexual instincts reflected in the revelry of the Merrymounters. One world is dominated by self-indulgent gaiety and lighthearted sexuality, the other by a self-restraint that seems lifeless and sterile.

The young lord and lady of the maypole emerge as the meeting ground of the two conflicting impulses. Merry Mount is a world existing out of time, lacking a past as well as a future, since no change or evolution occurs there. It is also a world full of superficial pleasure but lacking any real human passion. Thus, Edith, the queen of May, says to her consort, Edgar, "I sigh

amid this festive music. . . . I struggle as with a dream, and fancy that these shapes of our jovial friends are visionary, and their mirth unreal. . . . What is the mystery in my heart?" As the two await their wedding, "a little shower of withering rose leaves" falls from the maypole as a reminder that youth is transitory. Ironically, it is their love, not the appearance of the Puritans, that dooms Edith and Edgar to exile from Merry Mount and life in a postlapsarian world: "from the moment that they truly loved, they had subjected themselves to earth's dooms of care, and sorrow, and troubled joy, and had no more home at Merry Mount."

When the young couple is brought before Endicott, who has felled the maypole with his sword, they are not so much representatives of the world of Merry Mount as young people at a point of transition in their lives. "There they stood, in the first hour of wedlock, while the idle pleasures, of which their companions were the emblems, had given place to the sternest cares of life, personified by the dark Puritans. But never had their youthful beauty seemed so pure and high, as when its glow was chastened by adversity." In an ambiguous ending the young couple are stripped of their festive costumes to be clothed in "garments of a more decent fashion," and Edgar is shorn of his youthful locks, symbolizing their integration into the somber world of Puritanism. As a final gesture, however, Endicott, "the severest Puritan of all," throws the garland from the maypole over their heads. Though they have been forced from the world of Merry Mount to return no more, the wreath suggests that, "in the tie that united them, were intertwined all the purest and best of their early joys." Joining in themselves both the sense of life characteristic of the Merrymounters and the knowledge of suffering and sin taught by the Puritans, we last see them going "heavenward, supporting each other along the difficult path it was their lot to tread." Only by having lost the false paradise of Merry Mount are they free to seek a life that intermingles the joy and sorrow, as well as the love, that is man's true lot in this world.

As "The May-Pole of Merry Mount" deals with questions of sin and guilt in a broadly mythological context, "The Minister's Black Veil," adjacently situated in *Twice-Told Tales*, looks at a similar question on a more individual and personal level. Along with "The May-Pole of Merry Mount" and "The Wedding Knell," it was first published in *The Token and Atlantic Souvenir* for 1836, and, like so many other Hawthorne stories, "The Minister's Black Veil" has a historical basis, though Hawthorne's fiction version varies widely from historical fact. In a footnote to his "parable" Hawthorne refers to a New England clergyman of an earlier period who had "made himself remarkable by the same eccentricity as is here related of the Reverend Mr. Hooper." In that instance, however, the clergyman "had accidentally killed a beloved friend; and from that day till the hour of his own death . . . hid his face from men." Hawthorne's clergyman has far more mysterious motivations for veiling his face.

Secret sin and its effects on the individual were to fascinate Hawthorne throughout his career, and Hawthorne's treatment of the theme in *The Scarlet Letter* is anticipated in this story. The veil that covers Reverend Hooper's face is one of Hawthorne's most effective symbols for "those sad mysteries which we hide from our nearest and dearest, and would fain conceal from our own consciousness, even forgetting that the Omniscient can detect them." Despite tantalizing hints that the minister somehow may have been involved in the death of a young woman parish-

ioner, it is never clear whether the veil conceals "some great crime, too horrible to be entirely concealed," or only Hooper's exaggerated preoccupation with his human, and therefore necessarily sinful, nature. This ambiguity, however, is purposeful. Hawthorne concentrates on the effect of the veil on Hooper's life and ministry, rather than upon the cause for his taking it up. Long before modern psychology described the phenomenon, Hawthorne recognized that guilt can have an existence of its own that bears little relationship to actual causes.

The effect of the veil is twofold: it isolates Hooper from his parishioners and condemns him to the loveless and sterile existence epitomized by the termination of his relationship with his fiancée, Elizabeth; but by the same act he is turned into a powerfully effective preacher: "By the aid of this mysterious emblem . . . he became a man of awful power, over souls that were in agony for sin." Like Dimmesdale in *The Scarlet Letter*, Hooper draws a strange power from the secret he carries in his heart, and while it destroys one aspect of his life it enhances another. Because he is able through his example to lead others to salvation, Hooper's story might be read as another of Hawthorne's variations on the theme of the "fortunate fall," but to limit the reading to that level would ignore other equally important concerns in Hawthorne's fiction.

Hawthorne believed strongly in the natural bond he called the "magnetic chain of humanity." Anything which severs that chain he regarded as inimical to the human spirit and destructive of man's best self. Several of his heroes, both in short stories and novels, have so isolated themselves. Behind his veil, "Mr. Hooper spent a long life, irreproachable in outward act, yet shrouded in dismal suspicions; kind and loving, though unloved and dimly feared; a man apart from men, shunned in their health and joy, but ever summoned to their aid in mortal anguish."

Despite the good he may have accomplished in his ministry, Hooper goes to his grave as a gloomy reminder, not simply of man's fallen nature but of the necessity of coming to terms with one's own human condition. Like his counterparts Goodman Brown and Arthur Dimmesdale, Hooper, who cannot reconcile himself to the reality of his human limitations or accept that good might coexist with evil in a single soul, allows his preoccupation with sin to isolate him from the human community where redemptive love might occur.

During the years immediately following publication of the first edition of *Twice-Told Tales* Hawthorne wrote little adult fiction. His stories scarcely bringing in enough to support his modest bachelor habits, it was impossible for him to contemplate marriage to Sophia Amelia Peabody, with whom he was falling in love, without a steady income. With the help of Sophia's sister Elizabeth Palmer Peabody, Hawthorne was appointed a measurer in the Boston customhouse in January 1839. For the two years he held this post, he apparently wrote little. According to one estimate, between 1838 and 1842 he may have written only two adult sketches, though he did produce the three-volume *Grandfather's Chair* series of stories for children (1841). He also prepared the second edition of *Twice-Told Tales* for publication in 1842, but the twenty-one stories he added had all appeared in magazines and gift books (or in one case–*The Sister Years* [1839]–as a pamphlet) by the end of 1839.

In late 1840 Hawthorne invested in George Ripley's Brook Farm, an experiment in communal living at West Roxbury, Massachusetts, in hope of finding a situation that would enable him both to write and to support a wife. Hawthorne discovered that manual labor left little energy for writing. From April to November of 1841 he labored among the transcendentalist community members before giving up his plan of bringing Sophia to live there after their marriage. Though the Brook Farm experience contributed little to his short fiction, it did provide the basis for his novel *The Blithedale Romance* (1852). Unfortunately for his precarious financial position Hawthorne was never able to recoup his investment in Brook Farm. Soon after leaving he completed another children's book, *Biographical Stories for Children* (1842).

On 9 July 1842 Hawthorne and Sophia Peabody were married and took up residence in the Old Manse at Concord, Massachusetts, where they would live until October 1845. Hawthorne found himself able to write again, and he steadily supplied the magazines with enough somewhat formulaic stories and sketches "to earn . . . so much gold as might suffice" to support his new household, but little beyond that. The approximately twenty stories he published during this short period rarely achieve the high quality of his earlier masterpieces. He said of these years in his introductory essay to *Mosses from an Old Manse*, "all that I had to show, as a man of letters, were these few tales and essays, which had

blossomed out like flowers in the calm summer of my heart and mind." When he came to assemble a new collection of short fiction, he reached into his literary past for "some [stories] that were produced long ago–faded things, reminding me of flowers pressed between the leaves of a book" in order to flesh out the collection. These earlier stories, which he had passed over at least twice in selecting materials for his collections, ironically include "Roger Malvin's Burial" and "Young Goodman Brown," both finished before 1830 and now considered by Hawthorne's critics to be among his authentic masterpieces of short fiction.

A new collection of tales and sketches by Hawthorne was first proposed in late 1845 by Evert Duyckinck, an editor for the firm of Wiley and Putnam who had praised *Twice-Told Tales* in a review. Once again Hawthorne thought in terms of a unified collection and planned an essay which would be "a sort of framework" uniting the stories with each other, and also putting them into the context of the author's life at the Old Manse. By spring 1846 when Hawthorne finished "The Old Manse," he no longer occupied "the most delightful nook of a study" where he wrote during the Manse period. His family augmented by the birth of a daughter, Una (1844-1877), Hawthorne had taken his wife and child in fall 1845 to his mother's house in Salem while he sought a political appointment to supplement his meager income from writing. They were not to find a house in Salem until September 1847, by which time their second child, Julian (1846-1934), had been born. In March 1846 Hawthorne was appointed surveyor of customs in Salem, and it was there–where *The Scarlet Letter* was begun–that he completed his nostalgic sketch. More than just a farewell to the Old Manse, this essay was also meant as his farewell to writing short fiction. *Mosses from an Old Manse* would be, he wrote, "the last collection of this nature, which it is my purpose ever to put forth. Unless I could do better, I have done enough in this kind." Though he would turn his hand occasionally to short works during the next few years, the bulk of his contribution to the short-story genre was behind him. Before him lay the great romances of his maturity as a writer.

Once again Hawthorne's wish for a unified book-length work was frustrated. "The Old Manse" does not do its office. The reflexive voice of the sketch, the ostensible unifying device of the collection, is present in some of the stories and sketches in *Mosses from an Old Manse* but by no means in all of them. The pieces themselves range widely from such authentic masterpieces as "The Birth-mark" (*Pioneer,* March 1843) and "The Artist of the Beautiful" (*United States Magazine,* June 1844) to "Mrs. Bullfrog" (*The Token* for 1838), one of Hawthorne's few efforts to write in a comic mode, and "Buds and Bird Voices" (*United States Magazine,* June 1843), a nostalgic companion piece to "The Old Manse." The result is a work with an even smaller percentage of first-rate pieces than *Twice-Told Tales,* and half of those stories had been written more than fifteen years earlier. One must conclude that the Golden Age of Hawthorne's short-fiction writing was already behind him when he assembled this collection.

The two early masterpieces in *Mosses from an Old Manse,* "Young Goodman Brown" (probably written in 1828 or 1829 and first published in the April 1835 issue of *New-England Magazine*) and "Roger Malvin's Burial" (written in the same period and first published in *The Token* for 1832), return again to the colonial and early republic settings characteristic of much of Hawthorne's best fiction. These stories share with others of the period a symbolic habit of mind combined with an intuitive sense of depth psychology and myth that intrigue the modern reader of Hawthorne. Yet, by the time he included them in *Mosses from an Old Manse,* the author himself had now passed over these tales in making selections for both editions of *Twice-Told Tales,* suggesting that he either saw less in them himself, or expected his readers to see less, than subsequent readers have. It may be that he was not speaking entirely tongue-in-cheek when he wrote of these stories in an 1854 letter to James T. Fields, "Upon my honor, I am not quite sure that I entirely comprehend my own meanings in some of these blasted allegories," though he also complained, "Yet certainly there is more in it than the public generally gave me credit for, at the time it was written."

Regardless of Hawthorne's perception of his allegorical stories, it is largely on them, rather than upon the lighter tales and sketches in which he tried to capture the flavor of contemporary life, that his modern reputation rests. In the allegories Hawthorne explores that "neutral territory, somewhere between the real world and fairyland where the Actual and the Imaginary may meet, and each imbue itself with the nature of the other" he described in the preface to *The Scarlet Letter.* By the time he came to write his major romances, Hawthorne appears to have solved the

conflict between his interest in writing sketches of contemporary life and his attraction to the more imaginative materials of his romances, but that tension seems still clear in *Mosses from an Old Manse.*

"Young Goodman Brown" has been particularly attractive to critics and scholars who read Hawthorne in terms of his anticipation of depth psychology. Hawthorne's repeated intuitive grasp of the effects of guilty knowledge on the unconscious mind assures him a place in the tradition of psychological fiction. Nowhere is this understanding more apparent than in "Young Goodman Brown." Set in the repressive atmosphere of seventeenth-century New England, the story takes the form of a dreamlike journey into the dark, primeval forest, where the protagonist meets at a Black Mass all the familiar figures of his daily life, including his own new wife, Faith.

Salem village provides an image of order, reason, and moral rigidity against which is contrasted the lawless wilderness that Brown enters on his mysterious mission. As he reluctantly makes his way into the forest, Brown seems in the grip of some compulsion over which he lacks control. To his dismay he discovers, when he reaches a clearing where something resembling a Black Mass is about to be held, that all the community leaders–the moral examples and paternal models held up to him in his youth–are among the congregation, including even his own Faith. In this reversal of the orderly world of Salem, Brown learns that "Evil is the nature of mankind. Evil must be your only happiness." Those individuals who seemed so upright and godly in the light of day are revealed in the darkness of the forest to belong equally to the night world of the devil. At the last possible moment Brown cries out to heaven for Faith to join him in resisting this "communion of your race." Ironically, Brown's salvation from the demons in the forest condemns him to a life of misanthropy and isolation, so that when he dies in later years, "they carved no hopeful verse on his tomb-stone; for his dying hour was gloom."

Brown is unable to reconcile himself to the fact that the people he has admired in his youth participate in the sinfulness that for Hawthorne is part of the essential human condition. After his forest visit Brown can see only the darker side of human nature and cannot reconcile himself to the inherent tension in human beings between the forces of light and those of darkness. Through his journey into the wilderness Brown achieves knowledge, but he lacks the wisdom to reconcile the adult experience of sin and guilt as characteristics of human nature with his childishly naive need to view people as unambiguously either good or evil. The result is ignorance of his own complex nature and isolation from the community as well.

Many critics have read this story as a psychological allegory in which the world of the village represents that aspect of the personality Freud characterized as the superego, while the forest scene dramatizes the instinctual qualities characteristic of the id. In this reading, Brown's discovery in the forest frequently is translated as sexual knowledge, an interpretation consistent with both the emphasis on his new marriage and the sexual overtones of the sins described in the communion scene. So read, the story becomes a metaphorical descent into the underworld of the subconscious mind–much as a dream might take one into the depths of his or her emotional being–where Brown discovers his own sexual–that is, sinful–nature. As he revealed in "The May-Pole of Merry Mount," Hawthorne was concerned with the repressive aspects of Puritanism, and the effects on the psyche of rigid denial of natural human qualities. In "Young Goodman Brown" he explores the problems incumbent upon Puritan morality in such a way as to generalize about the universal experience of awakening awareness and the necessity of incorporating one's new knowledge into the adult psyche as a natural aspect of growth.

The effects of guilty knowledge on Goodman Brown are largely internalized, resulting only in his isolation from the community. In "Roger Malvin's Burial" Hawthorne returns to the same topic, but this time he treats much more overt effects of compulsive behavior resulting from a guilty conscience. Probably written in the late 1820s as one of the projected "Provincial Tales," this story, like others of that early group, has a historical event as background, though little use is made of history in the narrative itself. In fact, except for providing a degree of verisimilitude to a somewhat fantastic tale, the historical account of a 1725 raid against the Indians contributes little to Hawthorne's treatment of his material. Once again, history is a point of departure for Hawthorne, not an end in itself. Far more central to "Roger Malvin's Burial" are such themes as the effects of hidden guilt and the psychological conflict between fathers and sons.

Early in the story Hawthorne establishes a father-son bond between Roger Malvin and Reuben Bourne. During the two men's journey home following the raid, Malvin, weak from his wounds, sends the younger man for help, saying, "I have loved you like a father, Reuben, and, at a time like this, I should have something of a father's authority." Reuben replies, "because you have been a father to me, should I therefore leave you to perish, and to die unburied in the wilderness?" He obeys the older man, however, vowing to return "either to save his companion's life, or to lay his body in the grave." Reaching home near death, Reuben is nursed by Roger Malvin's daughter, Dorcas, and later marries her, but he never keeps his promise to her father. The emotion-laden context of Reuben's abandonment of Roger Malvin to die from his wounds achieves even greater significance by the fact that, with Reuben's marriage to Dorcas, he becomes guilty, in his own mind at least, of the crime of parricide.

Hawthorne gives little indication that Reuben could have successfully rescued Roger Malvin, but he should have fulfilled his promise to return to lay the other man's bones in a Christian grave. His failure to do so haunts Reuben and occasions his guilt over "his selfish love of life" that had caused him to leave Roger Malvin before his fate was decided. Trapped in his own lie that he left his wife's father dead and buried, Reuben becomes a victim of "the mental horrors, which punish the perpetrator of an undiscovered crime." His guilt assures the failure of all he puts his hand to, eventually forcing him to relocate with his wife and son, Cyrus–now a young man of fifteen–to the farther settlements. As they set out on this journey, Reuben unconsciously leads them back to the locale of Roger's death. There, in a final guilty sacrifice, Reuben "accidentally" slays his own son at the exact place where he left Roger Malvin years earlier. In an agony of guilt Reuben confesses to Dorcas the fate of her father, telling her, "Your tears will fall at once over your father and your son."

Paralleling Hawthorne's fascination with secret guilt was his interest in the cleansing ritual of confession, but this story offers a complicated variation on the theme that Hawthorne would later employ in *The Scarlet Letter* and *The Marble Faun*. According to the final sentence of "Roger Malvin's Burial," "His sin was expiated, the curse was gone from him; and, in the hour, when he had shed blood dearer to him than his own, a prayer, for the first time in years, went up to Heaven from the lips of Reuben Bourne." This re-

An extract, slightly altered, from "Earth's Holocaust," which Hawthorne prepared for publication in Autograph Leaves of Our Country's Authors *(1864), edited by John P. Kennedy and Alexander Bliss. The story first appeared in the May 1844 issue of* Graham's Lady's and Gentleman's Magazine.

lease of the spirit implies that redemption follows Reuben's fulfilling his vow to return to Roger Malvin and his confession to Dorcas of his earlier failure; but the reader cannot overlook the sacrifice of the innocent Cyrus. Though Hawthorne seems to end the story on an affirmative note, the reader cannot escape the irony that Reuben's salvation has come at the cost of an act that seems more morally compromising than the original cause of his guilt. In all his works Hawthorne never wrote a more morally ambivalent ending.

Obsession, or what his generation called monomania, was an enduring interest of Hawthorne's in both his short fiction and his romances. A group of three stories in *Mosses from an Old Manse* includes some of his best treatments of monomaniacal characters who bring about their own downfalls and frequently those of people closest to them through their pursuits of ideals that lead them to try to improve nature. In "The Birth-mark" and "Rappaccini's Daughter" science is the instrument through which such alterations of nature are undertaken, while in "The Artist of the Beautiful" an artist obsessed with perfection abandons the real substance of life to devote himself to a godlike attempt to make a perfectly realized creation. Both the scientist and the artist are objects of suspicion in Hawthorne's fiction, so it is not surprising that they share some of the same characteristics. In addition to these stories collected in *Mosses from an Old Manse*, "Dr. Heidegger's Experiment" (*Knickerbocker or New York Monthly Magazine*, January 1837; collected in *Twice-Told Tales*, 1837) and "Ethan Brand" (first published as "The Unpardonable Sin" in the *Boston Weekly Museum*, 5 January 1850; collected in *The Snow-Image, and Other Twice-Told Tales*) are other important treatments of the scientist in Hawthorne's short fiction; while "Drowne's Wooden Image" (*Godey's Magazine and Lady's Book*, July 1844; first collected in *Mosses from an Old Manse*) and "The Prophetic Pictures" (*The Token and Atlantic Souvenir* for 1837; first collected in *Twice-Told Tales*, 1837) present similar artist figures. Both these character types reappear in Hawthorne's romances.

In many respects Aylmer of "The Birth-mark" (*Pioneer*, March 1843) is the archetype for all Hawthorne's scientists, since he represents both what is best and what is worst about all of them. His aspirations are truly admirable, his aims ostensibly noble, and his experimental methods essential to human progress. Conversely, however, his obsession with perfection, his drive to achieve some ultimate and transcendental effect through science, and his personal ambition are Faustian qualities that doom him morally. While Aylmer, even at his worst, seems more admirable than his apelike assistant, Aminadab, Hawthorne nevertheless condemns him for his foolish failure to recognize his limitations in a world where Nature "permits us to mar, but seldom to mend, and, like a jealous patentee, never to make."

Married to the beautiful Georgianna, Aylmer is obsessed by the one "visible mark of earthly imperfection" that mars her beauty—a small birthmark shaped like a hand, on one cheek—and he determines to devote all his skill in science to its removal so that "the world might possess one living specimen of ideal loveliness, without the semblance of a flaw." Ironically, Aylmer gives credit to Georgianna for having led him "deeper than ever into the heart of science" until he feels "fully competent to render this dear cheek as faultless as its fellow." Swayed by Aylmer's disgust with her one imperfection, Georgianna willingly enters into the experiment to remove the birthmark, thus persuading some readers to conclude that she is implicated in her own death. Aylmer does succeed in removing the birthmark, but too late they both realize "the fatal Hand had grappled with the mystery of life, and was the bond by which an angelic spirit kept itself in union with a mortal frame." As the mark fades away, Georgianna dies, leaving Aylmer to contemplate the "profounder wisdom" that "ever does the gross Fatality of Earth exult in its invariable triumph over the immortal essence, which, in "this dim sphere of half-development, demands the completeness of a higher state" for its ultimate perfection.

Sometimes classified as early science-fiction fantasies, Hawthorne's stories of science, like his imaginative interpretation of history, have foundations in the actual. With the rise of modern sciences the nineteenth century saw old established principles and authorities for understanding the physical world give way to empirical and experimental methods which sometimes seemed to threaten the bounds of acceptable moral behavior, especially in the minds of essentially conservative thinkers like Hawthorne. The questions raised in the twentieth century over moral and ethical issues related to scientific experiments with genetics and atomic power are scarcely less disturbing than questions raised over science in Hawthorne's day. While his stories of scientists are explorations of the Faustian archetype, they also voice the concerns of a writer who believed that science should exercise great caution before plunging into experiments, the results of which could not be anticipated.

The conflict in values between the experimental attitude represented by Aylmer and a more-conservative tradition in science that relied upon authority is nowhere more succinctly illustrated in Hawthorne's work than by the conflict between Professor Baglioni and Doctor Rappaccini. Baglioni defines Hawthorne's sense of the Faustian quest when he says of his rival, "he cares infinitely more for science than for mankind. . . . He would sacrifice human life, his own among the rest, or whatever else was dearest to him, for the sake of adding so much as a grain of mustard-seed to the great heap of his accumulated knowledge." Later, placing his own views on science in clear juxtaposition to Rappaccini's, Baglioni says, "he is a wonderful man!—a wonderful man indeed! A vile empiric, however, in his practice, and therefore not to be tolerated by those who respect the good old rules of the profession!" Though Hawthorne would seem to remain neutral in this conflict, the tragic results achieved by such empiricists as Aylmer, Rappaccini, and Ethan Brand, whose science proceeds by experiment rather than authority, suggest that he had serious misgivings about the new scientific methods becoming prevalent during his lifetime. Since all three of these stories were composed during his lifetime. Since these stories were composed from the middle to late 1840s, they can fairly be said to reflect his mature attitude toward scientific experimentation.

"Rappaccini's Daughter" (*United States Magazine and Democratic Review*, December 1844) is perhaps the most complex of all Hawthorne's short stories, and the conflict between empirical and traditional science is only a small design in its rich fictional tapestry. Even within a canon characterized by ambiguity and veiled allusions, "Rappaccini's Daughter" stands out for its enigmatic complexity. Rappaccini is an evil genius as well as a loving and protective father; Beatrice is both a model of purity and an emblem of evil; Rappaccini's garden is both "the Eden of the present world" and a poisonous death trap. No reading is ever likely to reconcile all the possibilities of the story into a single coherent pattern, nor is there likely to be even general agreement among scholars upon even the most basic questions of interpretation.

Of all Hawthorne's heroes, Rappaccini most closely resembles Aylmer as the scholar-scientist who uses his science in an attempt to make a world surpassing natural creation. Clearly the old scientist is a Faustian figure in his pursuit of knowledge, a quality which, when combined with his excessive love for and desire to protect his daughter, motivates his attempt to create a new Eden. His garden, however, is the reverse of that in Genesis in almost every respect. The atmosphere of his garden of poisonous plants does not foster life, but death; and, while the created garden is a product of love, it is not a love that integrates its inhabitants into the magnetic chain of humanity Hawthorne talks about elsewhere but one that isolates Beatrice—the daughter Rappaccini has raised to thrive on the garden's toxic atmosphere—and Giovanni, whom the doctor would make Adam to Beatrice's Eve after gradually acclimatizing him to the garden's poisons. The love which fosters the garden is possessive and sterile, not truly creative and productive. It is an ironic Eden at best, at worst a perverted inversion of life-sustaining nature.

Beatrice nevertheless presents the image of a pure and angelic being whose spirit is untouched by the world she inhabits, even though her physical being is so imbued with poison that she has become as "poisonous as she is beautiful." Being unable to separate the scientific laws that govern the world he inhabits from those that govern Beatrice's garden, Giovanni makes the fatal mistake of believing that he can transform her physical nature without harming the spirit within. Somewhat like Aylmer's attempt to transform Georgianna into a perfect being, Giovanni's attempt to "perfect" Beatrice by giving her the antidote to the poison that is her very nature destroys her in the process, but only after they realize that he has become as toxic to beings of the natural world as Beatrice. When Beatrice asks him, "Oh, was there not, from the first, more poison in thy nature than in mine?" it is to his lack of insight into her spiritual nature that she refers. In terms borrowed from "The Birth-mark," Rappaccini sought to make and Giovanni to mend, but in the end they could only mar.

Closely related to the scientist-scholar in Hawthorne's cast of characters is the artist, another figure whose preoccupation with his genius can turn into a monomaniacal obsession. Like the two preceding stories, "The Artist of the Beautiful" (*United States Magazine and Democratic Review*, June 1844) was written while Hawthorne was in residence at the Old Manse. Owen Warland shares with Aylmer and Rappaccini a fascination with the ideal, which he pursues with fanatic zeal. Unlike them, however, no human life is at stake as a result of his creative drive, and the only cost paid is Owen's isolation after he elects to pursue art rather than life.

Somewhat like Aylmer, Owen Warland represents an extreme of intellectual and artistic sensibility, while Robert Danforth, the blacksmith, represents an earthy and sensual man, like Aminadab, who has little use for spiritualized vision. Significantly, Danforth marries Annie, and they have a child, while Owen, who also loves Annie, spends his life bringing forth a perfectly realized mechanical butterfly. Both men are creators, but when the baby, whom Hawthorne calls a "Child of Strength," crushes the fragile little butterfly into oblivion, actual life triumphs over the ethereal product of the artist. For Owen, however, the loss seems to matter little: "he looked placidly at what seemed the ruin of his life's labor, and which was yet no ruin. He had caught a far other butterfly than this." Hawthorne endows the butterfly with significance for Owen beyond its mere physical being.

After he learns of Annie and Robert's engagement, Owen is represented as a man who "had lost his faith in the invisible, and now prided himself, as such unfortunates invariably do, in the wisdom which rejected much that even his eye could see and trusted confidently in nothing but what his hand could touch." By these terms Owen seems to be a materialist who has lost confidence in any reality beyond the physical world and who lacks the spiritual faith necessary to bring out man's best nature; "But, in Owen Warland, the spirit was not dead, nor past away; it only slept." Through his creation of the lifelike butterfly, Owen reawakens his own slumbering spirituality, and, after its destruction, the narrator explains, "when the artist rose high enough to achieve the Beautiful, the symbol by which he made it perceptible to mortal senses became of little value in his eyes, while his spirit possessed itself in the enjoyment of the Reality."

Hawthorne's ambiguous affirmation of the artist's spiritual quest admits no easy conclusions. While Owen achieves a spiritual triumph at the end of the story, he is also an isolated and lonely figure. His creation, unlike Robert and Annie's baby, enhances no life but his own after the few moments of amusement it has provided. Ultimately Hawthorne seems to admire the creative

Hawthorne in 1853 (portrait by G. P. A. Healy; courtesy of the New Hampshire Historical Society)

process for its enhancement of human potential, while at the same time he deplores it for its cutting the artist off from life itself. This profound ambiguity at the heart of "The Artist of the Beautiful" may well represent one of Hawthorne's most personal attempts to resolve his ambivalent feelings about "the comparative value of the Beautiful and the Practical" in his own life.

Reviews of *Mosses from an Old Manse* were generally favorable, most critics preferring it to the two earlier editions of *Twice-Told Tales*. *Mosses from an Old Manse* is well known for having inspired two of the most important reviews in American critical history: Poe's "Tale Writing–Nathaniel Hawthorne" (*Godey's Lady's Book*, November 1847) and Herman Melville's "Hawthorne and His Mosses" (*Literary World*, August 1850). Melville, who would dedicate his *Moby-Dick* to Hawthorne in 1851, said of the older writer, "this great power of blackness in him derives its force from its appeals to that Calvinistic sense of Innate Depravity and Original Sin, from whose visitations, in some shape or other, no deeply thinking mind is always and wholly free." Going on in his review to compare Hawthorne to Shakespeare in the "Art of Telling the Truth," and praising Hawthorne's American originality and freedom from European models, Melville announced, "And now, my countrymen, as an excellent author of your own flesh and blood–an unimitating, and, perhaps, in his way, an inimitable man–whom better can I commend to you, in the first place, than Nathaniel Hawthorne." In many respects Melville's review singles out the qualities in Hawthorne's fiction that modern critics have also found praiseworthy.

Poe, who admired *Twice-Told Tales* more than *Mosses from an Old Manse*, complained that the later collection suffers from "a somewhat too general or prevalent *tone*–a tone of melancholy and mysticism," that "the subjects are insufficiently varied," and that "there is not so much of *versatility*" as he would wish. Nevertheless, he quickly acknowledged that "the style is purity itself. Force abounds. High imagination gleams from every page. Mr. Hawthorne is a man of the truest genius." In the long run, Poe's essay is more important for his definition of the short story than for unique insights into Hawthorne's work.

Despite his assurances in the preface that *Mosses from an Old Manse* would be his last collection of short fiction, Hawthorne produced one more collection of short fiction for adults in 1851. The first two years after he became surveyor in the Salem Custom House in 1846 were not at all productive literary years for him. By the time the election of a Whig, Zachary Taylor, to the presidency in 1848 led to the dismissal of Hawthorne, a Democrat, in June 1849, he seems to have finished only the preface to *Mosses from an Old Manse* and four short stories. After losing his post he turned to work on *The Scarlet Letter*, which he had planned as a long short story, and completed his first major novel on 3 February 1850. That "Ethan Brand," written during his tenure in the customhouse, was first conceived as a novel may suggest that his interest was already turning toward full-length romances, but it is also probably true that he did not find the routine of the customhouse conducive to creativity. Other than "Ethan Brand," the short stories finished at this time are not of the highest quality. "Main Street" (*Aesthetic Papers*, 1849), the best and most popular of them, is more properly classified as a sketch than a short story. Both "The Snow-Image" (*International Miscellany of Literature, Art, and Science*, November 1850) and "The Great Stone Face" (*National Era*, 24 January 1850) were written as children's stories, though they were

later included in *The Snow-Image, and Other Twice-Told Tales*, a collection of stories for adults. At least as far as adult fiction was concerned, Hawthorne was turning his attention to the major novels with which he would complete his literary career.

Encouraged by the success of *The Scarlet Letter* in 1850 and then *The House of the Seven Gables* in 1851, Ticknor, Reed and Fields brought out a new edition of *Twice-Told Tales*–to which Hawthorne added a preface–in 1851, published a collection of his stories for children–*A Wonder-Book for Girls and Boys*–in late 1851 (dated 1852), and began negotiations to buy the copyright to *Mosses from an Old Manse* from Wiley and Putnam. (Ticknor, Reed and Fields brought out a revised and enlarged edition in 1854.) They also published a new collection of his short fiction in late 1851 (dated 1852). Like his other collections, *The Snow-Image, and Other Twice-Told Tales* includes both early and recent stories (including those written while he was in the customhouse). The best of the stories from the customhouse period, "Ethan Brand" (*Boston Weekly Museum*, 5 January 1850), was initially intended as a full-length novel and is subtitled "A Chapter from an Abortive Romance." First published as "The Unpardonable Sin. From an Unpublished Work" in the 5 January 1850 issue of the *Boston Weekly Museum*, it rivals in imaginative power the best of Hawthorne's short fiction, but it lacks the formal distinction that characterizes his best stories. Of the earlier stories published in this volume, only "My Kinsman, Major Molineux" (*The Token* for 1832) can stand beside the early masterpieces. Like others of Hawthorne's best stories, it was written early and probably included among the "Provincial Tales." It is difficult to understand why Hawthorne repeatedly passed over this excellent story in his earlier collections while including clearly inferior work.

The central character in "Ethan Brand," who both looks back to the scholar-idealists of the earlier stories and forward to Chillingworth of *The Scarlet Letter*, explicitly dramatizes Hawthorne's fear that science might subordinate moral values to experimental curiosity. In "Ethan Brand" Hawthorne gives his most elaborate description of the imbalance between the head and the heart that characterizes his scholar-scientists and leads to their downfall: "Then ensued that vast intellectual development, which, in its progress, disturbed the counterpoise between his mind and heart." As a result of Brand's pursuit of the "Unpardonable Sin," "the Idea that possessed his life," he subordinates the heart to the intellect to the extent that his heart withers within him: "He had lost his hold of the magnetic chain of humanity. He was no longer a brother-man, opening the chambers or the dungeons of our common nature by the key of holy sympathy, which gave him a right to share in all its secrets; he was now a cold observer, looking on mankind as the subject of his experiment, and, at length, converting man and woman to be his puppets, and pulling the wires that moved them to such degrees of crime as were demanded for his study."

While Hawthorne's earlier scientists may have erred from misplaced and even monomaniacal worship of the ideal, none of them, including Rappaccini, can be said with certainty to be inherently evil. Not so with the Faustian Ethan Brand. His search for the "Unpardonable Sin" has been undertaken in total disregard of any moral consideration, and he alone of Hawthorne's characters prior to Chillingworth might deserve condemnation as an unpardonable sinner who "had committed the only crime for which heaven could afford no mercy." That sin, which he finds finally within himself, is "the sin of an intellect that triumphed over the sense of brotherhood with man, and reverence for God, and sacrificed everything to its own mighty claims!"

"My Kinsman, Major Molineux" reflects Hawthorne's early fascination with New England history and is his best treatment of the restless period that preceded the American Revolution. Young Robin Molineux leaves his pastoral home in the wilderness to make his way in "the little metropolis of a New England colony," where he hopes to put himself under the protection of a powerful relative, Major Molineux. As the events of the story unfold, Robin meets a succession of figures who not only refuse to help him find his kinsman, but react with increasing hostility to his civil requests for direction. Eventually he is told to wait at a particular corner, where he will see the major pass. He does so, and is eventually rewarded by the sight of a revolutionary mob, led by a diabolically painted figure, carrying Robin's tarred-and-feathered kinsman through the streets. At first appalled, Robin ultimately joins in the mob's laughter at the humiliation of Major Molineux. At the end of the story Robin is planning to depart for home, but then he is persuaded by the gentleman who told him where to find his kinsman that he should remain to make his way in the world without help. Hawthorne's

Hawthorne in London, 19 May 1860 (photograph by Mayall; courtesy of the Essex Institute, Salem, Massachusetts)

best story of the psychological transition from adolescence to young manhood, "My Kinsman, Major Molineux" works also as a political allegory which explores the birth of American democracy—with Robin representing the emerging nation and the major representing England—and reveals its author's somewhat ambivalent attitude toward the events heralding the birth of the United States.

In the last of a series of three sketches called "Old News" (*New-England Magazine*, February, March, and May 1835; collected in *The Snow-Image, and Other Twice-Told Tales*) he writes that the Tory faction in New England mistook "the temporary evils of a change, for permanent diseases of the system which that change was to establish." Hawthorne's portrayal of Major Molineux, whose humiliation is referred to as "the foul disgrace of a head grown grey in honor," suggests that he is not unsympathetic to the Tory position. In a story without any heroic figures with whom Robin might identify, the major is more sympathetically treated than his tormentors. Though it is unlikely that Hawthorne meant to repudiate the achievements of the American Revolution, he seems to have had ambiguous feelings about the violent methods by which independence was achieved.

After *The Snow-Image, and Other Twice-Told Tales* Hawthorne produced no more new collections of short fiction. In July 1852 *The Blithedale Romance*, his third novel in a little over two years, was published in England and the United States. From that time until the appearance of his last completed novel, *The Marble Faun*, he published only two books: a campaign biography of his college friend Franklin Pierce (1852) and a volume of children's stories, *Tanglewood Tales* (1853).

In July 1850 Hawthorne took his family to live in Lenox, Massachusetts, where his third child, Rose (1851-1926), was born the following May. They moved to West Newton, near Boston, in November 1851 but remained there only briefly before buying a house they named the Wayside in Concord and settling there in May 1852.

After Franklin Pierce won the 1852 presidential election, Hawthorne was appointed U.S. consul in Liverpool. The family sailed for England in July 1853, and Hawthorne held office until October 1857. From January 1858 until mid 1859 the family lived in Italy and then spent another year in England before returning home to Concord. On 19 May 1864, while on a tour of New England with Franklin Pierce, Hawthorne died quietly in his sleep in Plymouth, Massachusetts.

Had Hawthorne written no novels, his influence on American literature would have been hardly less than it has been. In his short fiction Hawthorne helped to define the American short-story tradition, giving it its characteristically symbolic and psychological form. Nearly every major American writer in this genre since the Civil War has been influenced by Hawthorne in some way. If the short story is indeed, as some literary scholars have maintained, America's unique contribution to the world's literature, Hawthorne had a major part in securing that place in literary history for his country.

Letters:

Letters of Hawthorne to William D. Ticknor, 1851-1864, 2 volumes (Newark, N.J.: Carteret Book Club, 1910);

The Letters, 1813-1843, edited by Thomas Woodson, L. Neal Smith, and Norman Holmes Pearson, volume 15 of *The Centenary Edition of the Works of Nathaniel Hawthorne* (Columbus: Ohio State University Press, 1984);

The Letters, 1843-1853, edited by Woodson, Smith, and Pearson, volume 16 of *The Cente-*

nary Edition of the Works of Nathaniel Hawthorne (Columbus: Ohio State University Press, 1985).

Bibliographies:

Beatrice Ricks, Joseph D. Adams, and Jack O. Hazlerig, *Nathaniel Hawthorne: A Reference Bibliography, 1900-1971, with Selected Nineteenth-Century Materials* (Boston: G. K. Hall, 1972);

C. E. Frazer Clark, Jr., *Nathaniel Hawthorne: A Descriptive Bibliography* (Pittsburgh: University of Pittsburgh Press, 1978).

Biographies:

Julian Hawthorne, *Nathaniel Hawthorne and His Wife,* 2 volumes (Boston: Osgood, 1884);

Horatio Bridge, *Personal Recollections of Nathaniel Hawthorne* (New York: Harper, 1893);

Rose Hawthorne Lathrop, *Memories of Hawthorne* (Boston: Houghton, Mifflin, 1897);

Julian Hawthorne, *Hawthorne and His Circle* (New York: Harper, 1903);

Randall Stewart, *Nathaniel Hawthorne: A Biography* (New Haven: Yale University Press, 1948);

James R. Mellow, *Nathaniel Hawthorne in His Times* (Boston: Houghton Mifflin, 1980).

References:

Newton Arvin, *Hawthorne* (Boston: Little, Brown, 1929);

Nina Baym, *The Shape of Hawthorne's Career* (Ithaca: Cornell University Press, 1976);

Michael Davitt Bell, *Hawthorne and the Historical Romance of New England* (Princeton: Princeton University Press, 1971);

Millicent Bell, *Hawthorne's View of the Artist* (Albany: State University of New York Press, 1962);

Bernard B. Cohen, ed., *The Recognition of Nathaniel Hawthorne: Selected Criticism Since 1828* (Ann Arbor: University of Michigan Press, 1969);

Michael J. Colacurcio, *The Province of Piety: Moral History in Hawthorne's Early Tales* (Cambridge: Harvard University Press, 1984);

Frederick C. Crews, *The Sins of the Fathers: Hawthorne's Psychological Themes* (New York: Oxford University Press, 1966);

Agnes McNeill Donohue, *Hawthorne: Calvin's Ironic Stepchild* (Kent, Ohio: Kent State University Press, 1985);

Neal F. Doubleday, *Hawthorne's Early Tales: A Critical Study* (Durham: Duke University Press, 1972);

Marjorie J. Elder, *Nathaniel Hawthorne: Transcendental Symbolist* (Athens: Ohio University Press, 1969);

Gloria C. Erlich, *Family Themes and Hawthorne's Fiction: The Tenacious Web* (New Brunswick: Rutgers University Press, 1984);

Bertha Faust, *Hawthorne's Contemporaneous Reputation: A Study in Literary Opinion in America and England, 1828-1864* (Philadelphia, 1939);

James T. Fields, *Yesterdays with Authors* (Boston: Osgood, 1872);

Richard Harter Fogle, *Hawthorne's Fiction: The Light and the Dark* (Norman: University of Oklahoma Press, 1952);

Robert H. Fossom, *Hawthorne's Inviolable Circle: The Problem of Time* (De Land, Fla.: Everett/Edwards, 1972);

Hubert H. Hoeltje, *Inward Sky: The Heart and Mind of Nathaniel Hawthorne* (Durham: Duke University Press, 1962);

Henry James, *Hawthorne* (New York: Harper, 1879);

A. N. Kaul, ed., *Hawthorne: A Collection of Critical Essays* (Englewood Cliffs, N.J.: Prentice-Hall, 1966);

George Parsons Lathrop, *A Study of Hawthorne* (Boston: Osgood, 1876);

Roy R. Male, *Hawthorne's Tragic Vision* (Austin: University of Texas Press, 1957);

Terence Martin, *Nathaniel Hawthorne*, revised edition (Boston: Twayne, 1983);

F. O. Matthiessen, *American Renaissance: Art and Expression in the Age of Emerson and Whitman* (New York: Oxford University Press, 1941);

Hugo McPherson, *Hawthorne as Myth-Maker: A Study in Imagination* (Toronto: University of Toronto Press, 1969);

Lea Bertani Vozar Newman, *A Reader's Guide to the Short Stories of Nathaniel Hawthorne* (Boston: G. K. Hall, 1979);

Jean Normand, *Nathaniel Hawthorne: An Approach to an Analysis of Artistic Creation*, translated by Derek Coltman (Cleveland: Press of Case Western Reserve University, 1970);

Roy Harvey Pearce, ed., *Hawthorne Centenary Essays* (Columbus: Ohio State University Press, 1964);

William Bysshe Stein, *Hawthorne's Faust: A Study of the Devil Archetype* (Gainesville: University of Florida Press, 1953);

Arlin Turner, *Nathaniel Hawthorne: An Introduction and Interpretation* (New York: Barnes & Noble, 1961);

Mark Van Doren, *Nathaniel Hawthorne* (New York: Sloane, 1949);

Edward Charles Wagenknecht, *Nathaniel Hawthorne: Man and Writer* (New York: Oxford University Press, 1961);

Hyatt H. Waggoner, *Hawthorne: A Critical Study*, revised edition (Cambridge: Harvard University Press, 1963).

Papers:

Major collections of Hawthorne papers are at the Berg Collection of the New York Public Library, Boston Public Library, Bowdoin College Library, Essex Institute, Henry E. Huntington Library, and Pierpont Morgan Library.

William Dean Howells

(1 March 1837-11 May 1920)

Paul J. Ferlazzo
Northern Arizona University

See also the Howells entries in *DLB 12: American Realists and Naturalists* and *DLB 64: American Literary Critics and Scholars, 1850-1880.*

BOOKS: *Poems of Two Friends*, by Howells and John J. Piatt (Columbus, Ohio: Follett, Foster, 1860);

Lives and Speeches of Abraham Lincoln and Hannibal Hamlin, life of Lincoln by Howells and life of Hamlin by J. L. Hayes (Columbus, Ohio: Follett, Foster, 1860);

Venetian Life (London: Trübner, 1866; New York: Hurd & Houghton, 1866; expanded, New York: Hurd & Houghton, 1867; London: Trübner, 1867; expanded again, Boston: Osgood, 1872; revised and expanded again, Boston & New York: Houghton, Mifflin, 1907; London: Constable, 1907);

Italian Journeys (New York: Hurd & Houghton, 1867; London: Low, 1868; enlarged, Boston: Osgood, 1872; revised, London: Heinemann, 1901; Boston & New York: Houghton, Mifflin, 1901);

No Love Lost, A Romance of Travel (New York: Putnam's, 1869);

Suburban Sketches (New York: Hurd & Houghton, 1871; London: Low, 1871; enlarged, Boston: Osgood, 1872);

Their Wedding Journey (Boston: Osgood, 1872; Edinburgh: Douglas, 1882);

A Chance Acquaintance (Boston: Osgood, 1873; Edinburgh: Douglas, 1882);

Poems (Boston: Osgood, 1873; enlarged, Boston: Ticknor, 1886);

A Foregone Conclusion (Boston: Osgood, 1875 [i.e., 1874]; London: Low, 1874);

Sketch of the Life and Character of Rutherford B. Hayes . . . also a Biographical Sketch of William A. Wheeler (New York: Hurd & Houghton/ Boston: Houghton, 1876);

The Parlor Car. Farce (Boston: Osgood, 1876);

Out of the Question. A Comedy (Boston: Osgood, 1877; Edinburgh: Douglas, 1882);

A Counterfeit Presentment. Comedy (Boston: Osgood, 1877);

The Lady of the Aroostook (Boston: Houghton, Osgood, 1879; Edinburgh: Douglas, 1882);

The Undiscovered Country (Boston: Houghton, Mifflin, 1880; London: Low, 1880);

A Fearful Responsibility and Other Stories (Boston: Osgood, 1881); republished as *A Fearful Responsibility and "Tonelli's Marriage"* (Edinburgh: Douglas, 1882);

Dr. Breen's Practice, A Novel (Boston: Osgood, 1881; London: Trübner, 1881);

A Day's Pleasure and Other Sketches (Boston: Houghton, Mifflin, 1881);

A Modern Instance, A Novel (1 volume, Boston: Osgood, 1882; 2 volumes, Edinburgh: Douglas, 1882);

The Sleeping Car, A Farce (Boston: Osgood, 1883);

A Woman's Reason, A Novel (Boston: Osgood, 1883; Edinburgh: Douglas, 1883);

A Little Girl Among the Old Masters (Boston: Osgood, 1884);

The Register, Farce (Boston: Osgood, 1884);

Three Villages (Boston: Osgood, 1884);

The Elevator, Farce (Boston: Osgood, 1885);

The Rise of Silas Lapham (1 volume, Boston: Ticknor, 1885; 2 volumes, Edinburgh: Douglas, 1894);

Tuscan Cities (Boston: Ticknor, 1886; Edinburgh: Douglas, 1886);

Poems (Boston: Ticknor, 1886);

The Garroters, Farce (New York: Harper, 1886; Edinburgh: Douglas, 1887);

Indian Summer (Boston: Ticknor, 1886; Edinburgh: Douglas, 1886);

The Minister's Charge, or, The Apprenticeship of Lemuel Barker (Edinburgh: Douglas, 1886; Boston: Ticknor, 1887);

Modern Italian Poets, Essays and Versions (New York: Harper, 1887; Edinburgh: Douglas, 1887);

April Hopes, A Novel (Edinburgh: Douglas, 1887; New York: Harper, 1888);

A Sea-Change, or Love's Stowaway: A Lyricated Farce in Two Acts and an Epilogue (Boston: Ticknor, 1888; London: Trübner, 1888);

Annie Kilburn, A Novel (Edinburgh: Douglas, 1888; New York: Harper, 1889);

The Mouse-Trap and Other Farces (New York: Harper, 1889; Edinburgh: Douglas, 1897);

A Hazard of New Fortunes (1 volume, New York: Harper, 1890 [i.e., 1889]; 2 volumes, Edinburgh: Douglas, 1889);

The Shadow of a Dream, A Novel (Edinburgh: Douglas, 1890; New York: Harper, 1890);

A Boy's Town Described for "Harper's Young People" (New York: Harper, 1890);

Criticism and Fiction (New York: Harper, 1891; London: Osgood, McIlvaine, 1891);

The Albany Depot, Farce (New York: Harper, 1891; Edinburgh: Douglas, 1897);

An Imperative Duty, A Novel (New York: Harper, 1892 [i.e., 1891]; Edinburgh: Douglas, 1891);

Mercy, A Novel (Edinburgh: Douglas, 1892); republished as *The Quality of Mercy* (New York: Harper, 1892);

A Letter of Introduction, Farce (New York: Harper, 1892; Edinburgh: Douglas, 1897);

A Little Swiss Sojourn (New York: Harper, 1892);

Christmas Every Day and Other Stories Told for Children (New York: Harper, 1893);

The World of Chance, A Novel (Edinburgh: Douglas, 1893; New York: Harper, 1893);

The Unexpected Guests, A Farce (New York: Harper, 1893; Edinburgh: Douglas, 1897);

My Year in a Log Cabin (New York: Harper, 1893);

Evening Dress, Farce (New York: Harper, 1893; Edinburgh: Douglas, 1893);

The Coast of Bohemia, A Novel (New York: Harper, 1893);

A Traveler from Altruria, Romance (New York: Harper, 1894; Edinburgh: Douglas, 1894);

My Literary Passions (New York: Harper, 1895);

Stops of Various Quills (New York: Harper, 1895);

The Day of Their Wedding, A Novel (New York: Harper, 1896); republished in *Idyls in Drab* (Edinburgh: Douglas, 1896);

A Parting and a Meeting, Story (New York: Harper, 1896); republished in *Idyls in Drab*;

Impressions and Experiences (New York: Harper, 1896; Edinburgh: Douglas, 1896);

A Previous Engagement, Comedy (New York: Harper, 1897);

The Landlord at Lion's Head (Edinburgh: Douglas, 1897; New York: Harper, 1897);

An Open-Eyed Conspiracy, An Idyl of Saratoga (New York & London: Harper, 1897; Edinburgh: Douglas, 1897);

Stories of Ohio (New York, Cincinnati & Chicago: American Book Company, 1897);

The Story of a Play, A Novel (New York & London: Harper, 1898);

Ragged Lady, A Novel (New York & London: Harper, 1899);

Their Silver Wedding Journey, 2 volumes (New York & London: Harper, 1899);

Bride Roses, A Scene (Boston & New York: Houghton, Mifflin, 1900);

Room Forty-Five, A Farce (Boston & New York: Houghton, Mifflin, 1900);

An Indian Giver, A Comedy (Boston & New York: Houghton, Mifflin, 1900);

The Smoking Car, A Farce (Boston & New York: Houghton, Mifflin, 1900);

Literary Friends and Acquaintance, A Personal Retrospect of American Authorship (New York & London: Harper, 1900);

A Pair of Patient Lovers (New York & London: Harper, 1901);

Heroines of Fiction, 2 volumes (New York & London: Harper, 1901);

The Kentons, A Novel (New York & London: Harper, 1902);

The Flight of Pony Baker, A Boy's Town Story (New York & London: Harper, 1902);

Literature and Life (New York & London: Harper, 1902);

Questionable Shapes (New York & London: Harper, 1903);

Letters Home (New York & London: Harper, 1903);

The Son of Royal Langbrith, A Novel (New York & London: Harper, 1904);

Miss Bellard's Inspiration, A Novel (New York & London: Harper, 1905);

London Films (New York & London: Harper, 1905);

Certain Delightful English Towns With Glimpses of the Pleasant Country Between (New York & London: Harper, 1906);

Through the Eye of the Needle, A Romance (New York & London: Harper, 1907);

Between the Dark and the Daylight, Romances (New York: Harper, 1907; London: Harper, 1912);

Fennel and Rue, A Novel (New York & London: Harper, 1908);

Roman Holidays and Others (New York & London: Harper, 1908);

The Mother and the Father, Dramatic Passages (New York & London: Harper, 1909);

Seven English Cities (New York & London: Harper, 1909);

My Mark Twain, Reminiscences and Criticisms (New York & London: Harper, 1910);

Imaginary Interviews (New York & London: Harper, 1910);

Parting Friends, A Farce (New York & London: Harper, 1911);

New Leaf Mills, A Chronicle (New York & London: Harper, 1913);

Familiar Spanish Travels (New York & London: Harper, 1913);

The Seen and Unseen at Stratford-On-Avon, A Fantasy (New York & London: Harper, 1914);

The Daughter of the Storage and Other Things in Prose and Verse (New York & London: Harper, 1916);

The Leatherwood God (New York: Century, 1916; London: Jenkins, 1917);

Years of My Youth (New York & London: Harper, 1916);

The Vacation of the Kelwyns, An Idyl of the Middle Eighteen-Seventies (New York & London: Harper, 1920);

Mrs. Farrell, A Novel (New York & London: Harper, 1921);

Prefaces to Contemporaries (1882-1920), edited by George Arms, William M. Gibson, and Frederic C. Marston, Jr. (Gainesville, Fla.: Scholars' Facsimiles & Reprints, 1957);

Criticism and Fiction and Other Essays, edited by Clara Marburg Kirk and Rudolf Kirk (New York: New York University Press, 1959);

The Complete Plays of W. D. Howells, edited by Walter J. Meserve (New York: New York University Press, 1960);

W. D. Howells as Critic, edited by Edwin H. Cady (London & Boston: Routledge, 1973);

Editor's Study: A Comprehensive Edition of W. D. Howells' Column (Troy, N.Y.: Whitson Publishing Co., 1983).

Collection: *A Selected Edition of W. D. Howells*, edited by Edwin H. Cady, Ronald Gottesman, Don L. Cook, and David Nordloh, 20 volumes to date (Bloomington: Indiana University Press/Boston: Twayne, 1968-   ).

The son of a Welsh father, William Cooper Howells, and an Irish-German mother, Mary Dean Howells, William Dean Howells was born in Martin's Ferry in Belmont County, Ohio, the second of eight children. Although he had little formal education, the future writer grew up in a home where literature was of great importance. In 1840 his father, a printer, moved his family to Hamilton, Ohio, where he became editor of the *Hamilton Intelligencer*, and in 1849 he bought the *Dayton Transcript*, moving his family once again. The young Howells began working as a printer on his father's newspapers at a very young age. The *Dayton Transcript* folded in 1851, and the next year when his father became editor of the *Ashtabula Sentinel*, the family moved to Ashtabula, Ohio, and six months later to Jefferson, Ohio, where the *Sentinel* became the *Jefferson Gazette*. During these early years Howells wrote extensively for the *Sentinel*. In 1857 he moved to Columbus, Ohio, and worked over the next few years as a correspondent for the *Daily Cincinnati Gazette*, as a reporter and editorial writer for the *Ohio*

State Journal, and as a contributor to other papers.

In 1860 his first book, *Poems of Two Friends,* on which he collaborated with John J. Piatt, was published, and he made his first appearance in the *Atlantic Monthly*–a poem, *Andenken,* in the January 1860 issue. Later that year he traveled to New England, financing his trip with money he earned for writing a campaign biography of Abraham Lincoln. In Boston he established what would prove to be enduring relationships with literati such as James Russell Lowell, James T. Fields, and Oliver Wendell Holmes, and while in New England he met Nathaniel Hawthorne, Ralph Waldo Emerson, and Henry David Thoreau. For his campaign biography he was appointed U.S. consul to Venice, a position he held from late 1861 until summer 1865. He spent his years abroad in literary study. He was married in Paris on 24 December 1862 to Elinor Gertrude Mead of Brattleboro, Vermont, whom he had met in winter 1860, when she had visited a cousin in Columbus. They subsequently had two daughters, Winifred and Mildred, and a son, John.

In 1864 Howells began contributing to the *North American Review,* then under the editorship of James Russell Lowell and Charles Eliot Norton. On his return to the United States in 1865 he worked briefly in New York as a free-lance writer and on the staff of the *Nation,* edited by E. L. Godkin. In spring 1866 he settled in Cambridge, Massachusetts, as assistant to James T. Fields on the *Atlantic Monthly.* He was awarded an honorary M.A. by Harvard in 1867 and was a lecturer on modern literature there in 1869-1871. On 1 July 1871 he was named editor in chief of the *Atlantic* and remained in that position until 1881.

Sketches and travel books appeared before his first novel, *Their Wedding Journey,* was published in 1872. His renown grew through the steady publication of his novels, poetry, and travel books, reaching its height with *A Modern Instance* (1882) and *The Rise of Silas Lapham* (1885).

In January 1886 the first of Howells's regular columns, "The Editor's Study," appeared in *Harper's Monthly,* and he continued to write "The Editor's Study" until March 1892. In February 1886 the first of his social-consciousness novels, *The Minister's Charge* (1887), began to appear serially in *Century* magazine. There followed more novels which revealed his social concerns: *Annie Kilburn* (1888), *A Hazard of New Fortunes* (1890),

The Quality of Mercy (1892), and *The World of Chance* (1893). Thereafter he confined his call for social change to his nonfiction and returned in his fiction to the study of manners and morals with an increased sensitivity to psychology.

Howells had continued to contribute to *Harper's Monthly* after giving up his column in 1892, and the December 1900 issue contained the first of his "Editor's Easy Chair" columns, which he continued to write until his death. He was awarded honorary doctorates by Yale University (1901), Oxford University (1904), Columbia University (1905), and Princeton University (1912). In 1901 he was elected an honorary fellow of the Royal Society of Literature. In 1904 he was elected as one of the first seven members of the American Academy of Arts and Letters and was chosen as president of that group. In 1915 he was awarded the American Academy's Gold Medal for Fiction.

The leading American realist of the later nineteenth century, Howells established the criteria by which realistic fiction was to be judged not only in his own fiction but also through his columns and reviews and by the fiction he chose to publish in the influential *Atlantic Monthly.*

Howells brought his ideas concerning realism together in *Criticism and Fiction* (1891), which comprises articles he wrote for "The Editor's Study" during 1886-1891. "Realism," said Howells, "is nothing more and nothing less than the truthful treatment of material." This dictum required a commonsense fidelity to the characteristics of contemporary life. Howells believed that the fiction writer should provide an accurate though somewhat limited picture of the American scene by choosing familiar settings and plots that concern daily experience, by studying ordinary characters in depth, by maintaining authorial objectivity, and by promoting responsible morality.

There are contradictions, however, between Howells's stated ideals for fiction and his own practice of short-fiction writing. While he maintained that fiction ought to be based upon ordinary observed reality and while most of his short stories might be described as realistic miniatures of familiar scenes and characters, some of his short fiction has as its subject the occult and the supernatural. Furthermore, while Howells professed dislike of romantic fiction, he remained attracted to the possibilities of achieving symbolic truth through romance and gave the subtitle "romance" to some of his short stories. But with regard to the treatment of his subjects, Howells

Howells and his wife Elinor in Venice, where Howells served as U.S. consul from late 1861 until summer 1865 (courtesy of the Ruth-erford B. Hayes Presidential Center, Fremont, Ohio)

maintained an objective approach and a plain style.

Howells's earliest collection of short stories, *Suburban Sketches* (1871), deals with life in and around Cambridge, Massachusetts, during the horse-car era. "Mrs. Johnson" (*Atlantic*, January 1868), the opening story in the collection, is set after the Emancipation Proclamation and provides a detailed portrait of a good-hearted black woman, which reveals racial stereotypes common at the time even among educated and open-minded whites. The brief "Scene" (*Every Saturday*, 7 January 1871) depicts the aftermath of a young woman's suicide, contrasting a romantic version of her death, as seen through the eyes of a member of the "fiction-ridden age," with the pathetic reality of her actual death. Perhaps the most interesting story in the collection is "A Romance of Real Life" (*Atlantic*, March 1870), one of the few short stories by Howells which continue to be anthologized in modern collections. The story develops further the contrast between life as perceived

Howells and Samuel Clemens at Clemens's home in Redding, Connecticut, 1909 (collection of Samuel C. Webster, New York)

by the romantic imagination and life as it is actually lived. A man named Tinker, apparently down on his luck, dupes a naive and well-meaning author into believing a sad story about his difficult life at sea and his consequent separation from his beloved family. The author, believing that he is participating in true-life romance, becomes involved in trying to reunite Tinker with his daughter. He discovers at the end that the ex-sailor is really a bigamous ex-convict who has taken advantage of the author's idealism and sympathy to further his selfish ends.

Several stories in *A Pair of Patient Lovers* (1901) deserve mention. In the title story (*Harper's Monthly*, November 1897) Dr. Anther is surprised when, after many years, Mrs. Langbrith finally decides to refuse his proposal of marriage. The reader must consider whether Dr. Anther is more surprised at her refusal or by the fact that he does not suffer from her rejection as he once thought he might. He wonders whether he had

ever really felt a passion for her. Two playful love stories reflect the limits of the imaginative possibilities for finding a love partner. In "The Pursuit of a Piano" (*Harper's Monthly*, April 1900) a young man's imagination is stimulated to thoughts of a romance with a young woman whose name he has happened to have seen lettered on a piano crate as it is hauled through Boston's Park Square. In "The Magic of a Voice" (*Lippincott's*, December 1899) a man falls in love with a woman after hearing her voice through the wall that separates their rooms. In "A Difficult Case" (*Atlantic Monthly*, July and August 1900) an honest minister fails to convince an old Civil War veteran to believe in immortality of the soul, but in the end the minister seems to receive a divine sign.

Questionable Shapes (1903) is a collection of three tales that deal with the supernatural in a sophisticated rather than a sensational way. "His Apparition" (*Harper's Monthly*, March 1902) is not so much a tale about a ghost as it is a study of the consequences arising from an individual's trying to describe an episode of spiritual visitation to others. "The Angel of the Lord" (first published as "At Third Hand, A Psychological Inquiry," *Century*, February 1901) is a morbid tale of an individual who is haunted by an awareness of mortality. He secludes himself to revel in the English graveyard poets and is finally visited by his obsession in the form of an angel. In "Though One Rose From the Dead" (*Harper's Monthly*, April 1903) a couple whose love during life was unusually strong communicate by mental telepathy after death.

Some of the tales in *Between the Dark and the Daylight* (1907) deal with abnormal phases of consciousness. "The Eidolons of Brooks Alford" (*Harper's Monthly*, August 1906) focuses on that psychophysical phenomenon by which mental images are given physical shape. "A Case of Metaphantasmia" (*Harper's Weekly*, 16 December 1905) treats the subject of dream transference: all the passengers on a sleeping car have the same nightmare. One of Howells's best short stories, "Editha" (*Harper's Monthly*, January 1905), also appears in this collection. It is the story of a young woman, Editha, who out of a romantic notion about the heroism of warriors, drives her unfortunate lover, George, to enlist in the Spanish-American War. She envisions his returning one day in triumphant glory after suffering a slight wound as testament to his courage. Instead, her lover dies ingloriously. In a powerful closing scene between Editha and George's mother, the older woman bluntly and angrily tells Editha that it was her sentimental idealism that killed George.

As the "Dean of American Realism," Howells waged an intense war on its behalf and virtually dominated the literary scene for most of his professional life. His influence was far-reaching, and he affected or directed the careers of more writers than perhaps any other individual in the late nineteenth century; but during the 1920s and 1930s his reputation suffered, with critics such as H. L. Mencken and Sinclair Lewis taking the lead in calling him "the Dean" of an outdated "genteel tradition." During the 1940s a small group of academic scholars who valued his work as both social history and literary art began a quiet revival of Howells. Since the 1950s a steady stream of books, dissertations, articles, and editions of his novels have appeared. Howells is now recognized as a key figure in the creation of the twentieth-century literary sensibility, and he is linked with two other indisputable masters of realistic prose, Mark Twain and Henry James.

Bibliographies:

William M. Gibson and George Arms, *A Bibliography of William Dean Howells* (New York: New York Public Library, 1948);

John K. Reeves, "The Literary Manuscripts of W. D. Howells: A Descriptive Finding List," *Bulletin of the New York Public Library*, 62 (June 1958): 267-278; (July 1958): 350-363; supplement, 65 (September 1961): 465-476;

James L. Woodress and Stanley P. Anderson, *A Bibliography of Writings about William Dean Howells*, *American Literary Realism*, Special Number (1969);

Vito J. Brenni, *William Dean Howells: A Bibliography* (Metuchen, N.J.: Scarecrow Press, 1973).

Biography:

Edwin H. Cady, *The Road to Realism: The Early Years (1837-1885) of William Dean Howells* (Syracuse: Syracuse University Press, 1956); *The Realist at War: The Mature Years (1885-1920) of William Dean Howells* (Syracuse: Syracuse University Press, 1958).

References:

George N. Bennett, *The Realism of William Dean Howells, 1889-1920* (Nashville: Vanderbilt University Press, 1973);

Everett Carter, *Howells and the Age of Realism* (Philadelphia: Lippincott, 1954);

Herbert Edwards, "Howells and the Controversy over Realism in American Fiction," *American Literature*, 3 (November 1931): 237-248;

Henry Gifford, "W. D. Howells: His Moral Conservatism," *Kenyon Review*, 20 (Winter 1958): 124-133;

William McMurray, *The Literary Realism of William Dean Howells* (Carbondale: Southern Illinois University Press, 1967);

Alma J. Payne, "William Dean Howells and the Independent Woman," *Midwest Review*, 5 (Autumn 1963): 44-52;

Lionel Trilling, "William Dean Howells and the Roots of Modern Taste," *Partisan Review*, 18 (September-October 1951): 516-536;

Edward Wagenknecht, *William Dean Howells: The Friendly Eye* (New York: Oxford University Press, 1969).

Papers:

There are significant collections of Howells papers at the Houghton Library, Harvard University; the Huntington Library in San Marino, California; the Library of Congress; the Beinecke Library, Yale University; and the Butler Library, Columbia University.

Washington Irving

(3 April 1783-28 November 1859)

Richard D. Rust
University of North Carolina at Chapel Hill

See also the Irving entries in *DLB 3: Antebellum Writers in New York and the South; DLB 11: American Humorists, 1800-1950; DLB 30: American Historians, 1607-1865; DLB 59: American Literary Critics and Scholars, 1800-1950;* and *DLB 73: American Magazine Journalists, 1741-1850.*

SELECTED BOOKS: *Salmagundi; or, the Whimwhams and Opinions of Launcelot Langstaff, Esq. & Others* by Irving, William Irving, and James Kirke Paulding, 20 parts, republished in 2 volumes (New York: Printed and published by D. Longworth, 1807-1808; London: Printed for J. M. Richardson, 1811; revised edition, New York: D. Longworth, 1814; revised by Irving, Paris: Galignani, 1824; Paris: Baudry, 1824);

A History of New York, from the Beginning of the World to the End of the Dutch Dynasty. Containing Among many Surprising and Curious Matters, the Unutterable Ponderings of Walter the Doubter, the Disastrous Projects of William the Testy, and the Chivalric Achievements of Peter the Headstrong, the three Dutch Governors of New Amsterdam; being the only Authentic History of the Times that ever hath been, or ever will be Published, as Diedrich Knickerbocker, 2 volumes (New York & Philadelphia: Inskeep & Bradford/Boston: M'Ilhenney/Baltimore: Coale & Thomas/Charleston: Morford, Willington, 1809; revised edition, New York & Philadelphia: Inskeep & Bradford, 1812; London: Murray, 1820); republished as volume 1 of *The Works of Washington Irving* (New York & London: Putnam, 1848; revised again, 2 volumes, New York: Printed for the Grolier Club, 1886);

The Sketch Book of Geoffrey Crayon, Gent., as Geoffrey Crayon, 7 parts (New York: Printed by C. S. Van Winkle, 1819-1820); revised edition, 2 volumes (volume 1, London: John Miller, 1820; volume 2, London: Murray, 1820); revised edition (Paris: Baudry & Didot, 1823); republished as volume 2 of

The Works of Washington Irving (New York & London: Putnam, 1848);

Bracebridge Hall, or the Humourists. A Medley, as Geoffrey Crayon, 2 volumes (New York: Printed by C. S. Van Winkle, 1822; London: Murray, 1822); republished as volume 6 of *The Works of Washington Irving* (New York & London: Putnam, 1849);

Letters of Jonathan Oldstyle, Gent., as The Author of *The Sketch Book* (New York: Clayton, 1824; London: Wilson, 1824);

Tales of a Traveller, as Geoffrey Crayon, 2 volumes (London: Murray, 1824; abridged edition, Philadelphia: Carey & Lea, 1824; unabridged edition, New York: Printed by C. S. Van Winkle, 1825); republished as volume 7 of *The Works of Washington Irving* (New York & London: Putnam, 1849);

The Miscellaneous Works of Oliver Goldsmith, with an Account of His Life and Writings, 4 volumes (Paris: Galignani/Didot, 1825); biography revised in *The Life of Oliver Goldsmith, with Selections from His Writings,* 2 volumes (New York: Harper, 1840); biography revised and enlarged as *Oliver Goldsmith: A Biography,* volume 11 of *The Works of Washington Irving* (New York: Putnam/London: John Murray, 1849);

A History of the Life and Voyages of Christopher Columbus (4 volumes, London: Murray, 1828; 3 volumes, New York: G. & C. Carvill, 1828; revised, 2 volumes, 1831); republished in *The Life and Voyages of Christopher Columbus; to Which Are Added Those of His Companions,* volumes 3-5 of *The Works of Washington Irving* (New York & London: Putnam, 1848-1849);

A Chronicle of the Conquest of Granada, as Fray Antonio Agapida, 2 volumes (Philadelphia: Carey, Lea & Carey, 1829; London: Murray, 1829); republished as volume 14 of *The Works of Washington Irving* (New York: Putnam/London: Murray, 1850);

Voyages and Discoveries of the Companions of Columbus (London: Murray, 1831; Philadelphia: Carey & Lea, 1831); republished in *The Life and Voyages of Christopher Columbus; to Which Are Added Those of His Companions,* volumes 3-5 of *The Works of Washington Irving* (New York & London: Putnam, 1848-1849);

The Alhambra, as Geoffrey Crayon, 2 volumes (London: Colburn & Bentley, 1832); as The Author of *The Sketch Book,* 2 volumes (Philadelphia: Carey & Lea, 1832); revised as *The Alhambra: A Series of Sketches of the Moors and Spaniards by the Author of "The Sketch Book"* (Philadelphia: Carey, Lea & Blanchard, 1836); revised as volume 15 of *The Works of Washington Irving* (New York: Putnam, 1851);

A Tour on the Prairies, number 1 of *Miscellanies,* as The Author of *The Sketch Book* (London: Murray, 1835); republished as number 1 of *The Crayon Miscellany* (Philadelphia: Carey, Lea & Blanchard, 1835); republished in *The Crayon Miscellany,* volume 9 of *The Works of Washington Irving* (New York & London: Putnam, 1849);

Abbotsford, and the Newstead Abbey, number 2 of *Miscellanies,* as The Author of *The Sketch Book* (London: Murray, 1835); republished as number 2 of *The Crayon Miscellany* (Philadelphia: Carey, Lea & Blanchard, 1835); republished in *The Crayon Miscellany,* volume 9 of *The Works of Washington Irving* (New York & London: Putnam, 1849);

Legends of the Conquest of Spain, number 3 of *Miscellanies,* as The Author of *The Sketch Book* (London: Murray, 1835); republished as number 3 of *The Crayon Miscellany* (Philadelphia: Carey, Lea & Blanchard, 1835); republished in *The Crayon Miscellany,* volume 9 of *The Works of Washington Irving* (New York & London: Putnam, 1849);

Astoria, or, Enterprise Beyond the Rocky Mountains, 3 volumes (London: Richard Bentley, 1836); published as *Astoria, or Anecdotes of an Enterprise Beyond the Rocky Mountains,* 2 volumes (Philadelphia: Carey, Lea & Blanchard, 1836); revised as volume 8 of *The Works of Washington Irving* (New York: Putnam, 1849);

Adventures of Captain Bonneville, or, Scenes beyond the Rocky Mountains of the Far West, 3 volumes (London: Bentley, 1837); republished as *The Rocky Mountains: Or, Scenes, Incidents, and Adventures in the Far West; Digested from the Journal of Captain B. L. E. Bonneville, of the Army of the United States, and Illustrated from Various Other Sources,* 2 volumes (Philadelphia: Carey, Lea & Blanchard, 1837); republished as *The Adventures of Captain Bonneville, U.S.A., in the Rocky Mountains and the Far West,* volume 10 of *The Works of Washington Irving* (New York & London: Putnam, 1849);

Biography and Poetical Remains of the Late Margaret Miller Davidson (Philadelphia: Lea & Blanchard, 1841; London: Tilt & Bogue, 1843);

Mahomet and His Successors, volumes 12 and 13 of *The Works of Washington Irving* (New York: Putnam, 1850); republished as *Lives of Mahomet and His Successors,* 2 volumes (London: Murray, 1850);

Chronicles of Wolfert's Roost and Other Papers (Edinburgh: Constable, Low/London: Hamilton, Adams/Dublin: M'Glashan, 1855); republished as *Wolfert's Roost and Other Papers,* volume 16 of *The Works of Washington Irving* (New York: Putnam, 1855);

Life of George Washington, 5 volumes (New York: Putnam, 1855-1859; London: Bohn, 1855-1859);

Spanish Papers and Other Miscellanies, Hitherto Unpublished or Uncollected, edited by Pierre M. Irving, 2 volumes (New York: Putnam/Hurd & Houghton, 1866; London: Low, 1866); republished as *Biographies and Miscellaneous Papers by Washington Irving* (London: Bell & Daldy, 1867).

Journals and Notebooks: 5 volumes, edited by Nathalia Wright, Walter A. Reichart, Lillian Schlissel, Wayne R. Kime, and Andrew B. Myers (Madison: University of Wisconsin Press/Boston: Twayne, 1969-1985).

Collection: *The Complete Works of Washington Irving,* edited by Richard Dilworth Rust and others, 30 volumes (Madison: University of Wisconsin Press/Boston: Twayne, 1969-1988).

Washington Irving told an anecdote of his youth which shows both his propensity to delight in stories as well as his skepticism concerning them. A "lively boy, full of curiosity, of easy faith, and prone to relish a story the more it partook of the marvelous," the young Irving met an old "bottle-nosed fellow named Bugbee," who "abused my juvenile ear outrageously with his legendary fables." The boy had a temperament conducive to both these responses. "When I was very young," he wrote in an autobiographical note to Mrs. Amelia Foster, "I had an irrepressible flow of spirits that often went beyond my strength. Everything was fairy land to me." On the other hand this clever youngest son of William and Sarah Sanders Irving indulged in wit and satire dependent on the sort of ironic skepticism found in his first publications, letters in the *New York Morning Chronicle* (1802-1803) published under the signature of "Jonathan Oldstyle, Gent."

Born in New York City at the close of the American Revolution, Washington Irving had eleven years of elementary schooling, after which he studied law in an attorney's office rather than going on to college. His desultory interests included the theater, association with literary-minded young men in New York, and travel (including several trips up the Hudson and a two-year excursion to Europe in 1804 and 1805). A practicing attorney for only a few years, he joined two of his brothers in the hardware business in 1810. In late 1812 he became editor of the *Analectic Magazine,* leaving in late 1814, after

preparation of the January 1815 issue, to become an officer in the militia and to serve in the War of 1812. In 1815 he went to England to help with the failing family business. Remaining abroad until 1832, he went to live in Spain in 1826 but returned to England in 1829 to serve as secretary to the American Legation in London. In 1842 he was appointed U.S. Minister to Spain, where he remained until 1846, when he returned once again to the United States.

Irving's literary career received impetus with the publication of the satirical *Salmagundi* papers, which he had written with other "Knickerbocker wits" in 1807-1808, followed in 1809 by *A History of New York,* published under the pseudonym Diedrich Knickerbocker. When the Irving firm declined into bankruptcy, Washington Irving turned to his pen–with the successful results being *The Sketch Book of Geoffrey Crayon, Gent.* (1819-1820), followed by *Bracebridge Hall* (1822) and *Tales of a Traveller* (1824). With disappointing reviews of the last book Irving turned to history–*A History of the Life and Voyages of Christopher Columbus* (1828), *A Chronicle of the Conquest of Granada* (1829), and *Voyages and Discoveries of the Companions of Columbus* (1831)–before venturing again to write fiction, in *The Alhambra* (1832). Irving's later works include narratives of westward travel such as *A Tour on the Prairies* (1835) and *Astoria* (1836) and biographies such as *Oliver Goldsmith: A Biography* (1849) and *Life of George Washington* (1855-1859).

Recent critical comments by Eugene Current-García reinforce the view of critics such as Fred Lewis Pattee and Arthur Hobson Quinn that Irving was the first American literary artist to intentionally write in the new mode later called the short story. As several letters make clear, Irving was quite aware of what he was trying to accomplish in this "new mode." In an 11 December 1824 letter to Henry Brevoort, Irving said: "I have had the merit of adopting a line for myself instead of following others.... For my part I consider a story merely as a frame on which to stretch my materials. It is the play of thought, and sentiment and language; the weaving in of characters, lightly yet expressively delineated; the familiar and faithful exhibition of scenes in common life; and the half concealed vein of humour that is often playing through the whole–these are among what I aim at, and upon which I felicitate myself in proportion as I think I succeed. I have preferred adopting the mode of sketches & short tales rather than long works, because I chose to

Rip Van Winkle.

a posthumous writing of Diedrich Knickerbocker

By Woden, God of Saxons.
From whence comes Wensday, that is Wodensday,
Truth is a thing that ever I will keep
Unto thylke day in which I creep into
My sepulchre —
                                        Cartwright.

Whoever has made a voyage up the
Hudson must remember the Kaat
Kaalskill mountains. They are a dis-
-membered branch of the great appala-
-chian family, and are seen away to the
west of the river swelling up to a noble
height and lording it over the surroun-
-ding country. Every change of season
every change of weather, indeed every hour
of the day, produces some change in the
magical hues and shapes of these moun-
-tains, and they are regarded by all the

Page from the manuscript for "Rip Van Winkle" (Washington Irving Collection, #4116-a, Clifton Waller Barrett Library, Special Collections Department, University of Virginia Library)

take a line of writing peculiar to myself; rather than fall into the manner or school of any other writer."

From new evidence in volume 2 of *Journals and Notebooks*, edited by Walter Reichart and Lillian Schlissel, and from the *Letters*, edited by Ralph Aderman, Herbert Kleinfield, and Jenifer Banks, the stance of Irving as short-story writer, his artistic intent, and especially the ambivalence with which he approached his materials can be seen more accurately.

Irving's use of multiple and eccentric narrators is a hallmark of his fiction, with a tale such as "The Spectre Bridegroom" deriving "its chief zest from the manner in which it was told, and the peculiar air and appearance of the narrator." Yet it is important not to confuse Irving's personae with Irving himself. The difference between Irving and Geoffrey Crayon, for example, is defined by the variations between Irving's journal entry on his visit to Stratford-on-Avon and the rewriting of that entry as part of his piece on Stratford in *The Sketch Book*. Irving in his journal says:

I am always of easy faith in such matters. I have always an easy belief in these matters and am willing to be deceived, where the deceit produces pleasure and costs nothing–but this was too much even for my credulity. The good lady boasted affinity to Shakespeare and had written several plays and poems; which I came to find had no passing resemblance. I pronounced her of a spurious sort.

Beginning with exactly the same words, Crayon says:

I am always of easy faith in such matters, and am ever willing to be deceived, where the deceit is pleasant, and costs nothing. I am therefore a ready believer in relics, legends, and local anecdotes of goblins and great men; and would advise all travellers who travel for their gratification to be the same. What is it to us whether these stories be true or false, so long as we can persuade ourselves into the belief of them, and enjoy all the charm of the reality. There is nothing like resolute good humored credulity in these matters; and on this occasion I went even so far as willingly to believe the claims of mine hostess to a lineal descent from the poet, when, unluckily for my faith, she put into my hands a play of her own composition, which set all belief in her consanguinity at defiance.

The critical difference is that in spite of his easy belief, Irving quickly found the hostess's claims too much for his credulity. Crayon, on the other hand, is more willing to exhibit "good humored" belief in order to enjoy the charm of a story. The difference is a subtle one, with Irving more clearly aware of what is fancy and what is reality, and with his persona more fascinated with the world of the imagination. It is this same fascination that prompts the poet-painter Crayon to write in *The Sketch Book:* "I delighted to ... gaze upon the piles of golden clouds just peering above the horizon; fancy them some fairy realms and people them with a creation of my own." Again, in the same spirit, Crayon in *Bracebridge Hall* acknowledges, "I feel convinced that the true interests and solid happiness of man are promoted by the advancement of truth; yet I cannot but mourn over the pleasant errors which it has trampled down in its progress.... the delicious realms of fairyland all vanish before the light of true philosophy; but who does not sometimes turn with distaste from the cold realities of morning, and seek to recall the sweet visions of the night?"

An intensification of this attitude is found in Diedrich Knickerbocker's introductory remarks in "The Legend of Sleepy Hollow." A historian who affirms his intention of being "precise and authentic," Knickerbocker treats as his subject the fairy-tale environment of Sleepy Hollow, a neighborhood which abounds with "local tales, haunted spots, and twilight superstitions." He dates his fascination with Sleepy Hollow back to his exploits as a stripling and finds the valley the most promising retreat whither he might, like Rip Van Winkle, "steal from the world and its distractions, and dream quietly away the remnant of a troubled life."

Thus, if Crayon is removed somewhat from Irving, Knickerbocker in turn is distanced even more so. Like one of Mark Twain's deadpan narrators, Knickerbocker seems to believe the fantastic stories he tells, while Crayon indicates ironically that he doubts the veracity of Knickerbocker's tales. In the preface to "Rip Van Winkle" that Crayon is talking tongue-in-cheek can be sensed as he tells the reader that Knickerbocker "found the old burghers, and still more, their wives, rich in that legendary lore so invaluable to true history.... [The chief merit of his work] is its scrupulous accuracy, which indeed was a little questioned on its first appearance, but has since been completely established." Then, in a note to the story, Crayon, with a wink, says the tale is "an absolute fact, narrated with Knickerbocker's usual fidelity." Of course Knickerbocker gives it his "full belief," with historical accuracy ensured by his having talked with Rip Van Winkle himself and by his seeing a certificate on the subject taken before an illiterate country justice.

Subtle treatment of narrators is an essential part of Irving's style, which became a model for later writers with its pictorial power, easy grace, flexibility, subdued humor, symmetry without straining, choice of homely English and American nouns and verbs, elegance without verbosity, abundant metaphors, appeal to sense impressions, and its winning and companionable charm. Irving took great pains with his style because, as he said in a 4 September 1823 letter to his brother Peter, "I wish, in every thing I do, to write in such a manner that my productions may have something more than the mere interest of narrative to recommend them, which is very evanescent; something, if I dare to use the phrase, of classic merit, i.e., depending upon style, etc., which gives a production some chance for duration beyond the mere whim and fashion of the day."

Irving's forty-some short stories (or tales and legends as he would characterize them) can be grouped in various overlapping categories: by locale (set in America, England, France, Germany, Italy, Spain), by types (tales of the supernatural, character sketches, adventures, legends, arabesque tales, and regional and folktales), and by theme (such as mutability, search for wealth or happiness, pursuit of love, folly of imaginative vocations, escape from responsibility, disillusionment born of experience, conflicts between the practical and the imaginative, sanity/insanity, and quest for identity).

A case could be made for calling "The Little Man in Black" (*Salmagundi*, 24 November 1807) Irving's first short story. It moves beyond a simple character sketch to contain plot and revelation of character. Told by Launcelot Langstaff about his grandfather, Lemuel Cockloft, it is a story about "a little black looking man of a foreign aspect" who is ostracized by the suspicious villagers—with the exception of grandfather Cockloft. In his trek one winter night through the village Cockloft follows the howling of a dog to the hovel of the man in black. He arrives in time to show sympathy for the stranger and to hear his sorrowful tale. As a reward for Cockloft's kindness the dying man bequeaths the

treasured volumes of his ancestor, Linkum Fidelius. Irving's story contains the interest of the narrative frame, suspense regarding the character of the man in black, development of the relationship between "my grandfather" and the little man, and the surprise bequeathal of the Fidelius "treasures"–which became a valued part of the Cockloft library.

The tales that are often referred to as making Irving a pioneer of the American short story are "Rip Van Winkle" and "The Legend of Sleepy Hollow," published in 1819 and 1820 in numbers 1 and 6 of *The Sketch Book*. New York printer C. S. Van Winkle put out two thousand copies each of numbers 1 and 2, and presumably there were the same number of copies of the remaining five parts. Irving's friend Henry Brevoort calculated that Irving should have cleared five hundred dollars on each of the first two numbers; it has been estimated that the American profits on *The Sketch Book* were some nine thousand dollars in two years. The first four numbers of *The Sketch Book* were published as one volume in England by John Miller, and John Murray (who initially paid three hundred guineas for the copyright) published numbers 5-7 in another volume. In Irving's lifetime there were some forty-three authorized and unauthorized printings of the book. It was the first literary work by an American author to receive international respect, and it continues to hold a place as an American classic.

While "Rip Van Winkle" owes something to "Peter Klaus" in Othmar's *Volkssagen* (1800) and to Baron Johann Kaspar Riesbeck's *Travels Through Germany* (1783), it centers on Irving's interest in American folklore. As he said some two decades later, "When I first wrote the Legend of Rip Van Winkle, my thought had been for some time turned towards giving a colour of romance and tradition to interesting points of our national scenery which is so deficient generally in our country." The Catskill mountains are the national scenery and the color of romance is given by Rip Van Winkle's encounter with Dutchmen in antique dress. Repeated drafts from their flagon put Rip into a deep, twenty-year sleep. On awaking and returning to his village Rip finds a bustling society of people who do not recognize him. Eventually he is identified by an old woman, his story is corroborated by a local historian, and he returns to his place at the inn where he can repeatedly tell his story in peace.

In "Rip Van Winkle" Irving provides a national fantasy of escape from responsibility, a portrait of an overgrown child who sleeps through the period of adult maturity. Underlying the story are Irving's delight in the magical Catskill region and his partial identification with the storyteller who avoided the cares of business. As Irving said regarding himself, "My whole course of life has been desultory, and I am unfitted for any periodically recurring task, or any stipulated labor of body and mind." The story may also imply Irving's lament that he had "suffered several precious years of youth and lively imagination to pass by unimproved," that in Europe he was a stranger in a strange land, and that he mistrusted the imagination even while exercising it.

On a more general level the story has been seen as a satire on the small-town mind, as an attack on Jeffersonian democracy, as an extension of the political satire of *A History of New York*, and as a portrayal of the tension in early-nineteenth-century America between imaginative endeavor and cultural renunciation of the imagination. On a mythic level, "Rip Van Winkle" has been seen by Philip Young as the American version of the ceremony in the worship of Thor, the God of Thunder. In this version, Rip, like Peter Klaus, is an initiate who is summoned by name to perform a test, communicates with the divinity and his disciples, is given a magic drink, and plunges into a magic sleep—to awaken eventually to a new phase of life.

The story of Rip Van Winkle has become part of the American consciousness. It was dramatized several times in Irving's lifetime and popularized by the actor Joseph Jefferson. Rip figures in American literature as the subject of Herman Melville's sketch and poem, "Rip Van Winkle's Lilac" (published for the first time in 1924), and as the transmuted Van Winkle in Hart Crane's *The Bridge* (1930). It was Crane who said Rip Van Winkle is America's " 'guardian angel' of the journey into the past," and, as Lewis Leary adds, Rip remains its conscience, accusing and amusing at the same time.

"The Legend of Sleepy Hollow" is often seen as a companion piece to "Rip Van Winkle." Both stories are attributed to Diedrich Knickerbocker and thus have an additional degree of narrative distance; both are set in parts of the Hudson River Valley susceptible to "magic hues and shapes" and where the inhabitants "are given to all kinds of marvellous beliefs"; both present supernatural legends of the past; and both present

parables of America developed from European materials. In "The Legend of Sleepy Hollow" Irving adapted parts of G. A. Bürger's "Der wilde Jäger" (1786) and borrowed from the Rübezahl legends.

The story is a familiar one. Into a sequestered Dutch settlement, which has as its chief legend the ghost story of a headless Hessian trooper, comes an itinerant schoolteacher, Ichabod Crane. This Connecticut Yankee has an "appetite for the marvellous" as represented by the story of the headless horseman, but especially he has an appetite for the bounties of Baltus Van Tassel's farm—and his heart yearns for Katrina Van Tassel, who is to inherit it. Ichabod's competition, however, is Brom Bones—a brawling fellow noted for his skill in horsemanship. The conflict comes to a head after a party at the Van Tassels' when Ichabod, on his gaunt horse, Gunpowder, is pursued through the woods by what appears to be a headless horseman. The goblin figure throws his head at Ichabod, and in the morning all that is found of Ichabod is his hat, with a shattered pumpkin close beside it.

While indebted to German sources, Irving drew extensively on native American folklore for "The Legend of Sleepy Hollow." As Daniel Hoffman has shown, Irving tapped Dutch folk superstitions and practical joking in portraying the civilizing Yankee pedagogue in conflict with the shaggy frontiersman. What we have in Brom Bones is a "Catskill Mike Fink, a Ring-Tailed Roarer from Kinderhook" who frightens the tenderfoot out of the district. Hoffman praises Irving's story of a backwoodsman's revenge as the first treatment of this theme and "among the most memorable it has ever received in our literature."

From another angle this story is the first humorous treatment of New England witch lore. It has also been seen by Marjorie W. Bruner as a "rollicking parody of ancient myths and rites of Greek fertility cults, a comic story of death and rebirth, fertility and immortality." In this reading Brom Bones is a rustic Hercules; Katrina is the corn goddess Demeter; and Ichabod is a parody of the river-god Acheloss—with the brook by the churchyard being the river Styx.

In "The Legend of Sleepy Hollow" one can see clearly the kind of polarities found in many of Irving's stories. The burlesque comedy of the Brom Bones-Ichabod Crane conflict is counterpoised by the quiet romantic nostalgia with which the story begins; bold satire of the superstitious schoolmaster and burlesque portrayal of his bor-

An illustration for "The Legend of Sleepy Hollow," drawn by Felix O. C. Darley for an 1848 edition of The Sketch Book

rowed horse accompany gentler humorous descriptions; and the subjective sympathy of Knickerbocker, who sees Sleepy Hollow as an ideal retreat, is counterbalanced by the ironic distance of the postscript with the skeptical storyteller undermining the truth value of his own story.

"The Spectre Bridegroom," in number 4 of *The Sketch Book*, is a story with correspondences to both "Rip Van Winkle" and "The Legend of Sleepy Hollow" in setting, characterizations, sportive Gothicisms, ironic reversals, and creative use of the imagination. Set in "a wild and romantic tract" in the German Odenwald, it tells of Baron Von Landshort–like Ichabod Crane a firm believer in supernatural tales–and of his fair young daughter, who is betrothed to the young Count Von Altenburg. On his way to the Von Landshort castle Von Altenburg is mortally wounded by robbers. His companion, Herman Von Starkenfaust, a stout horseman like Brom Bones, is directed to relay this information to the waiting bride. Old Von Landshort, though, presumes Starkenfaust to be Von Altenburg and keeps the stranger from delivering his true message. Starkenfaust is enamored of the young girl, pretends to be a specter in order to effect his escape, and returns–

posing as a specter to a maiden aunt–to woo and win the girl.

This story is an excellent example of Irving's sportive Gothic, an array of eighteenth-century Gothic devices presented in a playful manner and parodying especially the Gothicisms of Ann Radcliffe. It is also the first of Irving's travelers' tales, anecdotes usually told at inns and related as though they were veracious while at the same time containing many clues that there are reasons for doubt.

Bracebridge Hall (1822), the sequel to *The Sketch Book*, was printed by John Murray, Irving's British publisher, in four thousand copies, for which Irving received one thousand guineas. (The price increased on the next book, *Tales of a Traveller*, to fifteen hundred guineas.) An imperfect edition was published simultaneously in America. American reviewers were annoyed by the bad text and also faulted Irving for not remaining American enough. On the other hand, Edward Everett pronounced the book "quite equal to any thing, which the present age of British literature has produced in this department [the familiar essay]" (*North American Review*, July 1822). In general, British reviews were favorable, although most critics considered the book inferior to *The Sketch Book.*

Bracebridge Hall contains four pieces that can be considered short stories: "The Stout Gentleman," "The Student of Salamanca," "Annette Delarbre," and "Dolph Heyliger." Each is really a story within a story: a thin, nervous man among the company at Bracebridge Hall narrates the first anecdote; the second is read by the captain; the sentimental account of Annette Delarbre, written by an elderly parson, is furnished by Lady Lillicraft; and the story of Dolph Heyliger, set in the province of New York, comes from the papers of Diedrich Knickerbocker and is read by Geoffrey Crayon.

In "The Stout Gentleman" we see Irving's ambivalent attitude toward the imagination; indeed, it might well be considered a parable of his storytelling. On its surface nothing really happens: the narrator tells of staying at an inn in Derby, where he became curious about a traveler spoken of as "the stout gentleman." The nervous gentleman continued to revise his hypotheses about the unknown visitor, striving in vain to see him, and at last getting only a glimpse of the stout gentleman's rear as he climbed into a mail coach.

The story comes alive through the imaginative control of Geoffrey Crayon and the nervous gentleman. Crayon builds up to what he subtitles "A Stage-Coach Romance" by putting the story of the stout gentleman in the context of anecdotes of mysterious personages such as the Wandering Jew and the Man with the Iron Mask, then promises the reader that it has "all the elements of that mysterious and romantic narrative, so greedily sought after at the present day." The only romance turns out to be that created in the mind of the narrator, and the stagecoach of the subtitle is barely referred to in the last two paragraphs.

The marvel of the narrator's story is that it makes something significant out of the dreariest of materials–a rainy Sunday in a country inn, with a view either of tiled roofs or of the stableyard. With the entrance of the stout gentleman the imaginative narrator-artist becomes completely engrossed in his subject. "In such a situation as mine," he says, "every incident is of importance. Here was a subject of speculation presented to my mind, and ample exercise for my imagination." Crayon sets the reader up for a ghost story by closing his introduction to the narrative with an epigraph from *Hamlet:* "I'll cross it, though it blast me!" Then in the story itself many suggestive connections with ghost stories and superstitions are given: reading the almanac, the narrator finds a "direful prediction" of much rain; the stout gentleman becomes "the mysterious stranger"; and, as the church bells chime midnight, the narrator hurries to room number thirteen to investigate "these ghastly great-coats, these gutteral breathings, and the creaking footsteps of this mysterious being." Of course the joke is on the reader; the narrator's eventual view of the stranger is that he is only "the broad disk of a pair of drab breeches," but the pleasure comes from becoming caught up in the narrator's imaginings while at the same time being aware of their triviality.

"The Student of Salamanca," which came primarily from Irving's readings on alchemy, is a story of how Antonio de Castros, the title character, meets an old alchemist, Felix de Vasques, and falls in love with his daughter, Inez. Caring for the old man after a chemical explosion in the philosopher's rundown tower outside Granada, Antonio becomes the alchemist's disciple. He also defends Inez against the amorous advances of an unscrupulous cavalier, Don Ambrosia, then later rescues her again from Ambrosia, helps to prevent the alchemist's execution, and eventually marries Inez.

This story that begins "Once upon a time" thus has a fairy-tale ending as well. It is interesting as Irving's first account of life in Granada (which he had yet to visit) and as an illustration of the imaginative young man (Antonio has a "romantic disposition") who was to be satirized in subsequent stories such as "Adventure of the German Student" and "Mountjoy."

"Annette Delarbre" is presented as a companion piece to "The Student of Salamanca," with Lady Lillicraft furnishing the story for the captain to read in repayment for the story he earlier provided. Both are romantic stories of love frustrated and eventually requited, and both end with satirical undercutting. Much to Lady Lillicraft's consternation, the old general snores through parts of "The Student of Salamanca" and thinks the story a little confused; at the end of "Annette Delarbre" the reader is told that during this sentimental tale Lady Lillicraft, "who knew the story by heart, had led the way in weeping, and indeed had often begun to shed tears before they had come to the right place." The story tells how Annette quarrels with the adoring Eugene La Forgue and, through her temporary disdain, causes him to go to sea. A repentant Annette awaits Eugene's return, only to learn that during a storm he had been washed from the deck of his ship. The news causes Annette to go insane. More than a year later, word comes that Eugene has survived. He returns to the village, blames himself for Annette's condition, and eventually helps bring back her sanity.

Just as the physician tries to cure Annette Delarbre by endeavoring "to engraft, as it were, the reality upon the delusions of her fancy," so too, in the story of Dolph Heyliger does Irving treat the conflict between fancy and reality. "Dolph Heyliger" has the full range of devices and themes that allow for play of the imagination but subtly qualifies them. As with "Rip Van Winkle" and "The Legend of Sleepy Hollow," the story is set in Knickerbocker's Dutch New York– where implausible events seem more likely to happen. Introduced by Knickerbocker's description of a haunted house, the story is that of a ne'er-do-well, Dolph Heyliger, who is apprenticed to a German doctor and who volunteers to stay in the doctor's "haunted house," for Dolph "was fond of adventure, he loved the marvellous, and his imagination had become quite excited by these tales of wonder" concerning the house. With his receptive imagination Dolph sees a ghost at the deserted house, has premonitory dreams of finding money, is led unconsciously to board a sloop going up the Hudson River, is knocked overboard, and eventually ends up in the company of Antony Vander Heyden, who takes Dolph under his wing and with whose daughter Dolph falls in love. Another dream sends Dolph back to an old well near the haunted house from which he extracts a silver porringer filled with gold coins– and forthwith is set up for the rest of his life. In the middle of the story is interspersed a legend of the storm ship and its ghostly crew.

Part of the delight of the story is Irving's playfulness with systems of narration and his ambivalence regarding credibility. While the story originates with Geoffrey Crayon, he actually reads one of Diedrich Knickerbocker's manuscripts; Knickerbocker, in turn, tells a tale told him by John Josse Vandermoere, "a pleasant gossiping" person full of strange anecdotes of the neighborhood. At every stage the truth value of the story is undercut ironically. In the "Haunted House" preface we are assured there is "little doubt the house was haunted, . . . there were so many corroborating stories to prove it–not an old woman in the neighborhood but could furnish at least a

Irving in 1809; portrait by John Wesley Jarvis

score." As for Vandermoere's story Knickerbocker asserts he has endeavored to repeat it as nearly as possible in Vandermoere's words, but then he undercuts his position by saying, "it is now many years since, and I am grown old, and my memory is not overgood. I cannot therefore vouch for the language, but I am always scrupulous as to facts." With similar ironic qualification, Herr Antony, *as far as his memory would serve,* gives us the story of the storm ship in the very words in which it had been written out by Mynheer Selyne, an early poet of the New Netherlands. Then right after that story, Knickerbocker remarks, "Were this a mere tale of fancy, there would be a fine opportunity for weaving in strange adventures. . . ; but as this is absolutely a true story, I must content myself with simple facts, and keep to probabilities." The ironic undercutting here is completed by Knickerbocker's assertion of authority, having the story secondhand from the lips of Dolph Heyliger himself, who never related it till toward the latter part of his life and who was known as the ablest yarn spinner in the whole province.

Irving's next work was his one full short-story collection, *Tales of a Traveller* (1824), a book which disappointed British reviewers (it was derivative, they said, and its style anachronistic) as well as American critics (who thought Irving had abandoned American subjects and condemned his "droll indecencies"), but which Irving considered to contain some of the best things he had ever written. Today, though, it is considered a highly uneven book, what Henry A. Pochmann calls "a patch-work quilt."

Variations on truth-telling provide the main threads of *Tales of a Traveller*. Geoffrey Crayon prefaces his tales with a caveat: "I am an old traveller; I have read somewhat, heard and seen more, and dreamt more than all. My brain is filled, therefore, with all kinds of odds and ends. . . . so that when I attempt to draw forth a fact, I cannot determine whether I have read, heard, or dreamt it; and I am always at a loss to know how much to believe of my own stories." Thus, he can have the pleasure of telling traveler's tales but protects himself from obligations of strict accuracy and truth. He is also apologetic in a playful way, promising that if the tales he has furnished "should prove to be bad, they will at least be found short; so that no one will be wearied long on the same theme."

Crayon's travelers tales are in four cycles. Part 1, "Strange Stories," includes seven "adventures," all owing something to the ghost story and most being primarily sportive Gothic with what Eugene Current-García notes as burlesque, spoofery, hoaxing, and lightly satiric parody. Part 2, "Buckthorne and His Friends," is an interconnected series of stories about the attractions and liabilities of authorship, including sponsoring a dramatic company (akin to authorship in its fostering of the imaginative arts). Part 3, "The Italian Banditti," begins with a frame and two stories that stress the romance of the threat of bandits, but it moves through a real-life story (in the context of the framing situation) to the cruel reality of rape and ritual murder in "The Painter's Adventure" and finally to an emphasis on reality in the last story, "The Adventure of the Englishman." Part 4, "The Money-Diggers," ties in with "Strange Stories" by its sportive Gothic and begins with accounts of buried money, preparation for the comic Faustian story of "The Devil and Tom Walker," and the foolishness of pursuit of pirate treasure in "Wolfert Webber, or Golden Dreams," with an ironic ending in which Webber gains money through subdivisions of his cabbage patch.

The epigraph to "Strange Stories" helps qualify the credibility of the traveler's tales that follow. From John Fletcher's *A Wife for a Month* (1624) this epigraph is an exchange between Tony and Cleanthes in which Tony tells a phenomenal story about a fish with a sword by his side and a gun in his nose. Cleanthes declares, "This is a monstrous lie," to which Tony responds: "I do confess it. Do you think I'd tell you truths?" Tony's story is indeed a tall tale, extreme in its nature and not intended to be believed. His declaration is preparation for the stories that follow; they are "lies"—in other words, fictions—but the pleasure for the reader comes from the way they are told. Each narrator emphasizes the purported authenticity of his tale, but at the same time that believability is undermined repeatedly. At the heart of this deception is a commentary on the nature of fiction, of creations of the imagination, which are not true in the sense of conforming to verifiable external reality, but which have some appearance of authenticity. The auditor or reader wants to believe but expects to be fooled; the main delight is in the way the story is told.

Since he is already known from *Bracebridge Hall* as a person with a highly active imagination, the nervous gentleman is the appropriate narrator of the first set of stories in *Tales of a Traveller*. The credibility of his stories is further thrown into question by dubious responses from a hatchet-faced gentleman and even more so by a Chinese box effect. For example, with "The Adventure of My Uncle," the first of the "Strange Stories," Geoffrey Crayon tells stories related to him by the nervous gentleman, who in turn retells the anecdote he heard from an old gentleman with a "haunted head," who in turn tells a story he once heard his uncle tell. This story of a chamber in a French chateau haunted by a stately woman in ancient dress is set some time before the French Revolution, with each telling being removed in time from the previous one (with the likelihood increasing each time of loss of conformity to actual truth). The innermost box is that the uncle, in turn, learns a story from the marquis who owns the chateau.

The ghost in "The Adventure of My Aunt" turns out to be a former servant, who hides behind a picture in the aunt's chamber with the intent of rifling her strong box. In the rollicking adventure of "The Bold Dragoon," the dragoon's story of dancing furniture in a bewitched room is apparently a cover for drunken antics or a prelude to seductive mischief.

The best-known story of this series, "Adventure of the German Student," is an account of Gottfried Wolfgang, a melancholy young man who arrives in Paris at the outbreak of the French Revolution. There, the visionary recluse encounters a female figure at the foot of the guillotine, protectively takes her home with him, and pledges his love to her—only to discover in the morning a corpse that is subsequently identified as a woman guillotined the previous day. The discovery drives the student mad.

This psychologically complex story ends with a new twist in regard to authenticity. At the beginning of the story the gentleman with the haunted head says he is prepared to vouch for the truth of it. With this in mind the reader sides at the end of the story with the impulsive gentleman who asks, "And is this really a fact?" The other replies that he had it from the best authority, the student himself—whom the narrator met in a madhouse in Paris.

"The Story of the Young Italian," which ends this group of "Strange Stories," develops Irving's themes of mutability and distressed identity. It is a romantic and tragic tale about a young artist, Ottavio, disliked by this father and sent to a convent, where dismal stories of the monks frightened his young imagination. (In this regard, one thinks of the young Washington Irving, who had a hypersensitive imagination which others at times played upon.) This visionary and melancholy Italian becomes a portrait painter and falls in love with Bianca, a young girl in the convent. Later he meets Bianca again, only to leave her temporarily in order to be with his dying father. On his return he finds that his rival has told Bianca that Ottavio is dead and has married her himself. This news throws Ottavio into such a rage that he kills his rival—and then wanders the earth "like another Cain." He tries to diminish his misery by painting the face of his victim. In the closing frame of the tale the baronet who owns the painting pretends to show it to the auditors of the story but instead has them led to see other paintings. Their responses only reveal their superstitions.

The second section of *Tales of a Traveller*, "Buckthorne and his Friends," at first was considered for inclusion in *The Sketch Book* and was later intended to be part of *Bracebridge Hall*, but Irving then was persuaded to develop it into a novel—a plan that did not materialize. However, with its accounts of various travels, particularly those of the poet manqué Jack Buckthorne as he attempts to find his way in the world, the story seems quite appropriate to *Tales of a Traveller*. Further, Buckthorne is connected with other young men, such as Gottfried Wolfgang and Ottavio, who become victims of their own excessive imagination. Paralleling in some ways the young Washington Irving, Buckthorne confesses to have had "the poetical feeling, that is to say, I have always

been an idle fellow, and prone to play the vagabond"; his mother absorbed all his filial affection; he was always "extremely sensible to female beauty"; and he had "a roving, inextinguishable desire to see different kinds of life, and different orders of society." Impatient with school, Buckthorne seizes an opportunity to join an itinerant theater company, playing the part of the lover of Columbine in contest with Pantaloon and the Clown. A fight with Harlequin leads to Buckthorne escaping the ensuing melee with the girl playing Columbine, only to be returned home against his will by agents of his father. Studies at Oxford do not reduce this young buck's poetical inclination, which tempts him "forth into a world of its own creation, which [he] mistook for the world of real life." Eventually Buckthorne receives an inheritance from his "booby" cousin and renounces the "sin of authorship" for life as a country squire at Doubting Castle (a practical action, but hardly one that seems to have Irving's wholehearted endorsement).

Interspersed in Buckthorne's story are accounts of two other failed artists, "the poor-devil author" and "the strolling manager." The first is a village poet who expected to make a name in London society with poems such as "The Pleasures of Melancholy" and "The Pleasures of Memory." As he learns the harsh realities of the publishing world, his expectations are frustrated, and he goes downhill until he eventually finds his niche as an anonymous hack writer who is happy because he is "below the care of reputation." For his part Flimsey, the strolling manager, declines from being the manager of a theater to becoming a bit actor. The moral in each case is the same, one that Irving was phrasing about himself in letters of the time: Fame is fleeting and the public is fickle. As Flimsey says, "I have known enough of notoriety to pity the poor devils who are called favorites of the public."

Irving drew on his own experiences as well for "The Italian Banditti" section. Illustrating this point, Nathalia Wright calls these tales "the earliest appearance of a distinctively American tradition in the treatment of Italian material in fiction." The most gripping traveler's tale in this section is "The Painter's Adventure" with its central story of the young robber. Captured by bandits, the painter is taken along with the robber troop and observes them firsthand. He finds everything "picturesque about these wild beings and their haunts. . . . every thing presented a study for a painter." Yet he learns from a gloomy and

Final page of the manuscript for Bracebridge Hall *(M.A. DeWolfe Howe,* American Bookmen, *1902)*

sardonic young robber the despicable side of the bandit life. This young man has fled to the robber band after killing the bridegroom of a young girl, Rosetta, with whom he was in love. Later he returned to encounter Rosetta, only for her frightened shriek to attract the whole robber band and make her their prisoner. Her abduction was followed by rape, with the young robber seeing his companions as "like so many fiends exulting in the downfall of an angel." Her father refusing ransom, the young robber sought permission to execute Rosetta–which he did as painlessly as possible. By this dismal story the painter is appropriately horror-struck.

The bandit sequence ends with a real-life encounter with robbers after the travelers leave the inn at Terracina. The practical (and previously skeptical) Englishman rescues a fair Venetian bride, and the travelers–and the readers–are disabused of any romantic ideas they may have entertained regarding Italian bandits.

In the fourth part of *Tales of a Traveller,*

"The Money-Diggers," Irving caps the ambivalence toward imagination which he has shown in the previous three sections and again establishes multiple narrative layers to put truth value in serious doubt. Knickerbocker says in a prefatory historical sketch about Captain Kidd, "There is nothing in this world so hard to get at as truth, and there is nothing in this world but truth that I care for." Yet his favorite sources of authentic information are the old Dutch wives of the province, and the story that follows, "The Devil and Tom Walker," is three removes from Knickerbocker (and two more removes from Irving): Knickerbocker has the story from a Cape Cod whaler who recollected a story which was written by a neighbor of his. Then, at the end of the story, the purport of which he told as nearly as he could recollect, Knickerbocker affirms that the truth is not to be doubted since the hole from which Kidd's money came is to be seen to this day.

"The Devil and Tom Walker" is a folktale, which, Henry Pochmann asserts, "in the happy blending of the terrifying and the ludicrous, almost rivals 'The Legend of Sleepy Hollow.' " Integrating German folk motifs with the American story of Captain Kidd's buried treasure, Irving crafted a humorous and engaging story of a man who sells his soul to the devil. Set near Boston around the year 1727, the story tells of Tom Walker's encountering "the wild huntsman," known also as "the black woodsman" and "Old Scratch," and being offered Captain Kidd's money if he would enter into a pact with the devil. His termagant wife tries to enter the pact herself and disappears; Tom finally comes to terms with the devil and then becomes a usurer in Boston until the time when a black man on a black horse whisks Tom away, never to be seen again. His reputed wealth turns out to be reduced to cinders and shavings, and his great house burns to the ground.

Eugene Current-García considers that this narrative "foreshadows the best of Hawthorne's fictional exposure of Yankee shrewdness and Puritan hypocrisy." In "The Devil and Tom Walker" Irving achieved not only the subtle blend of serio-comic pathos seen in "Rip Van Winkle" but also "a species of much starker imagery that transforms such commonplace American activities as money lending, timber cutting, slave trading, treasure hunting, and Bible reading into grotesque emblems of spiritual deprivation, emotional sterility, hypocrisy, and lovelessness." William L. Hedges calls attention to the effective way the narrator's voice brings "studied witticism and wordplay, alliteration, balanced antithesis, hyperbole, literary allusion, and extensive metaphor to bear on the homely subject of Tom Walker's hypocrisy."

The concluding story of *Tales of a Traveller*, "Wolfert Webber, or Golden Dreams," plays on the buried treasure motif. The story is related to Knickerbocker by John Josse Vandermoere, the same person who told him about the adventures of Dolph Heyliger. In both stories the main character fearlessly pursues wild schemes and eventually obtains wealth. "Wolfert Webber" also shares the earlier story's satirical vein, with the superstitious and backward Dutch bearing the brunt of the satire.

Wolfert Webber comes from a long line of cabbage farmers who all have heads resembling cabbages, and his family motto, revealed at the end of the story, is *Alles Kopf*—that is to say, *all head*. Wolfert proves to be a bigger cabbage head than the others: acting on a "golden dream," he digs up his garden looking for buried treasure. Rather than finding wealth, though, "the more he digged, the poorer he grew." Then, acting on a story of Sam, a Negro fisherman, who years earlier had encountered pirates burying what seemed to be treasure, Wolfert seeks out Sam to be his guide to the pirates' landing spot. Accompanied by a German astrologist, they dig for the treasure and find a buried chest—only to be frightened away at that moment by what appears to be the face of a drowned buccaneer. Sickened by the trauma of his escape, Wolfert declines toward what seems to be certain death—only to be revived by his lawyer's information that a new road running through the Webber cabbage patch will bring riches through subdivision developments. Wolfert's fortune is made in spite of himself.

Tales of a Traveller thus comes full circle. The satire on excessive imagination and on the veracity of narrators in "Wolfert Webber" recalls to the spirit of the playful self-deprecation of Geoffrey Crayon in the opening "To the Reader." "I am an old traveller," Crayon says; "I have read somewhat, heard and seen more, and dreamt more than all.... and I am always at a loss to know how much to believe of my own stories.... If the tales I have furnished should prove to be bad, they will at least be found short; so that no one will be wearied long on the same theme."

The Alhambra (1832) contains tales Irving gleaned during his residence in the Alhambra in 1829 and from "various legendary scraps and hints picked up in the course of [his] perambulations." The spirit of these stories, says Henry Pochmann, "is that of *The Arabian Nights*, and their frank supernaturalism rests on magic treasure hidden in the bowels of the earth by the Moors, demon steeds, flying carpets, palaces built by necromancy, enchanted beauties, engulfed convents, and phantom armies that emerge from the heart of a mountain." The initial importance of what William H. Prescott called Irving's "beautiful Spanish Sketch-book" was in its introducing exoticism into American literature. Englishman David Wilkie congratulated Irving on being, with *The Alhambra*, "the founder of a school." Literary historian Mario Mendez Bejarano said that "the soul of Granada is more apparent in the beautiful pages of Irving than in the stories of Chateaubriand, the poems of Zorrilla, or in any of those writers who have celebrated its charms."

Irving sold *The Alhambra* to the London firm of Colburn and Bentley for one thousand guineas; in America the Philadelphia firm of Carey and Lea paid three thousand dollars to publish the two-volume book. Critical reception was largely favorable: the London *Athenaeum* said that *The Alhambra* would not detract from Irving's fame; the *Westminster Review* praised it for its picturesqueness; the *North American Review* said that by the "touch of the enchanter's wand, you are rapt into an enthusiastic reverie of the mystic East, within the crumbling walls of the Alhambra"; the *New-England Magazine* admired "Ahmed al Kamel" for its satire and humor; and the *New-York Mirror* praised "the inimitable freshness and enchanting luxury of the whole description" in *The Alhambra*, calling it a chef d'oeuvre.

"There is nothing I relish more than a marvellous tale," Irving tells Mateo Ximenes as they ramble among the hills above the Alhambra, and Mateo is a perfect person to furnish such stories. This "son of the Alhambra" serves as Irving's guide in and around Granada and as a storehouse of endless legends about the Moors and Christians. As with Diedrich Knickerbocker, Mateo has dubious verification of the truth of his tales. For example, Mateo shows Irving a pit which seems to Irving to have been a Moorish well but which Mateo's father and grandfather firmly believed was an entrance to subterranean caverns of a mountain in which Boabdil and his court lay bound in a magic spell. In another hole there had supposedly been an enchanted pot full of Moorish gold. How did Mateo know? His grandfather was an eyewitness: he saw the hole where the pot had hung.

The first tale in *The Alhambra* is Mateo's anecdote "The Adventure of the Mason." This brief story contains two favorite elements: a ghost (reports about a decaying house being haunted by the priest who had lived there) and the discovery of wealth (by the poor mason who earlier had helped seal up the priest's gold and who later bargained to live in the house rent free while repairing it).

The second tale typifies the context of the legends Irving retells. A visit to a ruin or puzzlement over an unusual carving in a stone elicits an account of the legend associated with the site. With the "Legend of the Arabian Astrologer" a narrative frame is provided by a visit to the ruin of "The House of the Weathercock," which formerly had on one of its turrets a bronze figure of a warrior on horseback. This talismanic figure had been part of a magical warning system created by Ilbrahim Ebn Abu Ayub for the Moorish

king. For his reward the Arabian astrologer has the king furnish him a subterranean cavern–with the last reward being a Gothic princess favored by the king, whom the astrologer wins by requesting the seemingly innocuous favor of obtaining the first beast of burden, with its load, that should pass under a portal. The story ends with the narrator meditating upon the spellbound gateway.

A visit to the Generalife opposite the Alhambra elicits the legend of Prince Ahmed Al Kamel, secluded by his father to prevent him from seeing a female face. Likewise, a beautiful Christian princess living in Toledo was shut up from the world until her seventeenth birthday. Irving's legend employs many elements of fairy tale in bringing these two youths together: a talking owl and a parrot, magic armor and steed, charmed success in a tournament, a sandalwood box with mystic characters, and a flying carpet. The success of his story is in its exotic details; the humorous interchanges among the prince, the owl, and the parrot; and the sensitive portrayal of young love.

Romantic charm is provided to the tower of the Infantas by the "Legend of the Three Beautiful Princesses"–two of whom escape with Christian cavaliers–and by the "Legend of the Rose of the Alhambra," an account of the gentle Jacinta, who receives a silver lute from the third princess, who stayed behind. The garden of Lindaraxa near Irving's room in the Alhambra figures in the "Legend of the Two Discreet Statues," a story of little Sanchica's being directed to treasure and of her father's attempts to outwit a greedy friar.

Irving's most humorous story in *The Alhambra* is "Legend of the Moor's Legacy." The focal character is a comic little strong-backed, bandy-legged water carrier called Peregil, whose aid to a dying Moor brings him enchanted treasure. A grasping alcalde interposes, but his greed leads him and his two assistants to be sealed up in the enchanted cavern. They may be sought after, Irving concludes, "whenever there shall be a lack in Spain of pimping barbers, sharking alguazils, and corrupt alcaldes."

An enchanted cavern also figures in "The Legend of the Enchanted Soldier," about a student led to underground treasure, and in "Governor Manco and the Soldier," a story of a soldier who explains his possession of an Arabian horse by telling of a magical ride to the court and army of Boabdil, shut up in a mountain. In the end the creative soldier escapes with both the horse and the governor's handmaid.

An 1851 drawing of Irving by Felix O. C. Darley (courtesy of Sleepy Hollow Press, Tarrytown, New York)

Wolfert's Roost and Other Papers (1855) contains five pieces that might be called short stories: "Mountjoy," a first-person story that originally was to have been developed into a novel entitled "Rosalie"; "The Widow's Ordeal," a story of judicial combat gleaned from the annals of Spain; "The Grand Prior of Minorca," heard from a Knight of Malta who "loved to let his imagination carry him away"; "Guests from Gibbet Island," a legend of Communipaw found among the Knickerbocker papers at Wolfert's Roost; and "The Adalantado of the Seven Cities: A Legend of St. Brandan." Also of interest are two fanciful pieces which lack sufficient plot development to be called short stories: "Don Juan: A Spectral Research," about an amorous Spanish cavalier's encounter with his own funeral, and "Legend of the Engulphed Convent," about a convent miraculously swallowed up in the earth just as ravaging Moors broke down its gate.

Wolfert's Roost is a hodgepodge of Irving's sketches and tales gathered from the *Knickerbocker Magazine* and elsewhere. It was published

in the United States by George Putnam as volume 16 of *The Works of Washington Irving* (1855). The collection was praised for its mellowness and droll slyness (London *Spectator*), and its "inimitable stories" with a "diversified character" were considered the most valuable recent contribution to the light literature of the day (*United States Magazine and Democratic Review*).

"Mountjoy," subtitled "Some Passages out of the Life of a Castle-builder" (*Knickerbocker*, November and December 1839), can be seen as Irving's tongue-in-cheek deprecation of some of his own earlier excesses. There are some autobiographical echoes in this story of the romantic Mountjoy, who falls in love with a footstep, nearly drowns on the Hudson because of his misguided fancy, and is exposed by the Somervilles, who rescue him, as a shallow thinker and sentimentalist.

Mountjoy, like the young Irving, as a youth read tales of chivalry, adventure, and romance; was captivated by the romantic scenery along the Hudson; and gave full scope to his imagination. A flute player like Irving, Mountjoy–like him–

confesses to a lack of system, saying that "every thing was left to chance and impulse, and native luxuriance." The mature Mountjoy has "grown too wise to be so easily pleased," but the young Mountjoy sentimentally muses on ideal beauties and "mistakes the aberrations of his fancy for the inspirations of divine philosophy."

Looking at "Mountjoy" in relationship to the Common Sense philosophy of Dugald Stewart, James Beattie, and others, Donald Ringe has seen the story as philosophy in the comic mode. Measured against the dicta of the Scottish Common Sense philosophers, Mountjoy's education is the worst possible kind–filling his mind with unrealities at an early age and leading him too early to bewildering metaphysics. The main theme of the story is thus the causes and consequences of, as well as the cure for, a disordered imagination.

"The Widow's Ordeal, or a Judicial Trial by Combat" (*The Magnolia* for 1837) is just the kind of story young Mountjoy would have relished. A beautiful duchess accused of impropriety by her deceased husband's nephew calls for a champion and is vindicated by a young cavalier, who defeats the nephew in the lists and is awarded the hand of the duchess. Mountjoy would also have been thrilled by "The Grand Prior of Minorca" (*Knickerbocker*, February 1840), a ghost story full of Gothic devices: a gloomy and isolated castle, Gothic-looking portraits that come alive at midnight, a mysterious wind, and a swordfight with a ghost.

"Guests from Gibbet Island" (*Knickerbocker*, October 1839) is an adaptation of a Jakob Grimm anecdote about a drunken innkeeper who invites three men hanged on the gallows to sup with him. They do, and soon after he collapses and dies. Walter Reichart notes how Irving has expanded this anecdote of less than a page into an Americanized Knickerbocker story of pirates, hidden booty, and a Dutch innkeeper and his shrewish wife.

Rip Van Winkle is evoked in Irving's last tale, "The Adalantado of the Seven Cities" (*Knickerbocker*, July 1839). The questing Don Fernando de Ulmo is driven by a storm to the phantom island of St. Brandan, is put to sleep by the grand chamberlain, wakes up in a strange cabin bound to Lisbon, and learns on his return that he had been asleep for more than a century. The story is not as smoothly developed as "Rip Van Winkle," nor is Don Fernando developed as fully as the errant Rip. Nevertheless, "The Adalantado" was selected by many contemporary critics for special

mention and continues to exemplify Irving's effective retelling of stories and legends gleaned from old chronicles and oral accounts.

There is no progressive line of development in Irving's short stories. "Rip Van Winkle" is a more memorable tale of charmed sleep than "The Adalantado of the Seven Cities," and "Wolfert Webber" is a better-developed story of pirates and ghosts than "Guests from Gibbet Island." While his stories are uneven in quality, Irving had, as he said, "the merit of adopting a line for myself instead of following others." This pioneer in the short story cleared the path, as Eugene Current-García puts it, "enabling other American writers of short fiction to explore the limitless possibilities of this new literary form." If Irving did not actually invent the short story, he "set the pattern for the artistic re-creation of common experience in short fictional form."

Fred Lewis Pattee notes nine contributions Irving made to the short story. He made short fiction popular; stripped the prose tale of its didactic elements and made it a literary form solely for entertainment; added richness of atmosphere and unity of tone; added definite locality and actual American scenery and people; brought a peculiar nicety of execution and patient workmanship; added humor and lightness of touch; was original; created characters who are always definite individuals; and endowed the short story with a style that is finished and beautiful.

Later in the 1830s and 1840s, Irving was to be surpassed as a short-story writer by Hawthorne and Poe, both of whom he had influenced. Irving was content, though, to "blow a flute in the national concert." While not strong, his musical notes remain clear and audible. He continues to be considered by serious literary critics; his popularity seems assured with a general public appreciative of the picturesqueness, delight, and charm of durable stories such as "Rip Van Winkle" and "The Legend of Sleepy Hollow."

Letters:

Letters, 4 volumes, edited by Ralph M. Aderman, Herbert L. Kleinfield, and Jenifer S. Banks (Boston: Twayne, 1978-1982).

Bibliographies:

William R. Langfeld and Philip C. Blackburn, *Washington Irving: A Bibliography* (New York: New York Public Library, 1933);

Stanley T. Williams and Mary A. Edge, *A Bibliography of the Writings of Washington Irving* (New York: Oxford University Press, 1936);

Haskell Springer, *Washington Irving: A Reference Guide* (Boston: G. K. Hall, 1976);

Springer and Raylene Penner, "Washington Irving: A Reference Guide Updated," *Resources for American Literary Study*, 11 (1981): 257-279;

James W. Tuttleton, "Washington Irving," in *Fifteen American Authors Before 1900*, edited by Earl N. Harbert and Robert A. Rees (Madison: University of Wisconsin Press, 1984), pp. 330-356.

Biographies:

Pierre M. Irving, *The Life and Letters of Washington Irving*, 4 volumes (New York: Putnam, 1862-1864);

Stanley T. Williams, *The Life of Washington Irving*, 2 volumes (New York: Oxford University Press, 1935).

References:

Michael Davitt Bell, "Feelings and Effects: Washington Irving," in his *The Development of American Romance* (Chicago & London: University of Chicago Press, 1980), pp. 63-85;

Marjorie W. Bruner, "The Legend of Sleepy Hollow: A Mythological Parody," *College English*, 25 (January 1964): 274-283;

Eugene Current-García, "Irving Sets the Pattern: Notes on Professionalism and the Art of the Short Story," *Studies in Short Fiction*, 10 (Fall 1973): 327-341;

Richard Ellmann, "Love in the Catskills," *New York Review of Books*, 23 (5 February 1976): 27-28;

Judith G. Haig, "Washington Irving and the Romance of Travel: Is There an Itinerary in *Tales of a Traveller?* in *The Old and New World Romanticism of Washington Irving*, edited by Stanley Brodwin (New York: Greenwood, 1986), 61-68;

William L. Hedges, *Washington Irving: An American Study, 1802-1832* (Baltimore: Johns Hopkins University Press, 1965);

Daniel G. Hoffman, "Irving's Use of American Folklore in 'The Legend of Sleepy Hollow,' " *PMLA*, 68 (June 1953): 425-435;

Lewis Leary, *Washington Irving* (Minneapolis: University of Minnesota Press, 1963);

Terence Martin, "Rip, Ichabod, and the American Imagination," *American Literature*, 31 (May 1959): 137-149;

Robert Allen Papinchak, " 'The Little Man in Black': The Narrative Mode of America's First Short Story," *Studies in Short Fiction*, 22 (Spring 1985): 195-201;

Fred Lewis Pattee, *The Development of the American Short Story: An Historical Survey* (New York & London: Harper, 1923);

Henry A. Pochmann, "Irving's German Tour and Its Influence on His Tales," *PMLA*, 45 (December 1930): 1150-1187;

Arthur Hobson Quinn, *American Fiction: An Historical and Critical Survey* (New York: Appleton-Century, 1936);

Walter A. Reichart, *Washington Irving and Germany* (Ann Arbor: University of Michigan Press, 1957);

Donald A. Ringe, *American Gothic: Imagination and Reason in Nineteenth-Century Fiction* (Lexington: University Press of Kentucky, 1982);

Ringe, *The Pictorial Mode: Space and Time in the Art of Bryant, Irving, and Cooper* (Lexington: University of Kentucky Press, 1971);

Jeffrey Rubin-Dorsky, *"Adrift in the Old World": The Psychological Pilgrimage of Washington Irving* (Chicago & London: University of Chicago Press, 1988);

Edward Charles Wagenknecht, *Washington Irving: Moderation Displayed* (New York: Oxford University Press, 1962);

Nathalia Wright, "Irving's Use of His Italian Experiences in *Tales of a Traveller:* The Beginnings of an American Tradition," *American Literature*, 31 (May 1959): 191-196;

Philip Young, "Fallen from Time: The Mythic Rip Van Winkle," *Kenyon Review*, 22 (Autumn 1960): 547-573;

Charles G. Zug III, "The Construction of 'The Devil and Tom Walker': A Study of Irving's Later Use of Folklore," *New York Folklore Quarterly*, 24 (December 1968): 243-260.

Papers:

Irving's papers are to be found primarily at the New York Public Library, with significant collections also located at Historic Hudson Valley, the Carl H. Pforzheimer Library, the Huntington Library, the University of Virginia Library, and the Columbia, Yale, and Harvard University libraries. See H. L. Kleinfield, "A Census of Washington Irving Manuscripts," *Bulletin of the New York Public Library*, 68 (January 1964): 13-32.

Henry James

(15 April 1843-28 February 1916)

Robert L. Gale
University of Pittsburgh

See also the James entries in *DLB 12: American Realists and Naturalists* and *DLB 71: American Literary Critics and Scholars, 1880-1900.*

BOOKS: *A Passionate Pilgrim, and Other Tales* (Boston: Osgood, 1875);

Transatlantic Sketches (Boston: Osgood, 1875);

Roderick Hudson (Boston: Osgood, 1876; revised edition, 3 volumes, London: Macmillan, 1879; 1 volume, Boston & New York: Houghton, Mifflin, 1882);

The American (Boston: Osgood, 1877; London: Ward, Lock, 1877);

French Poets and Novelists (London: Macmillan, 1878);

Watch and Ward (Boston: Houghton, Osgood, 1878);

The Europeans (2 volumes, London: Macmillan, 1878; 1 volume, Boston: Houghton, Osgood, 1879);

Daisy Miller: A Study (New York: Harper, 1879 [i.e., 1878]);

An International Episode (New York: Harper, 1879);

Daisy Miller: A Study. An International Episode. Four Meetings, 2 volumes (London: Macmillan, 1879);

The Madonna of the Future and Other Tales, 2 volumes (London: Macmillan, 1879);

Hawthorne (London: Macmillan, 1879; New York: Harper, 1880);

Confidence (2 volumes, London: Chatto & Windus, 1880; 1 volume, Boston: Houghton, Osgood, 1880);

A Bundle of Letters (Boston: Loring, 1880);

The Diary of a Man of Fifty and A Bundle of Letters (New York: Harper, 1880);

Washington Square (New York: Harper, 1881);

Washington Square, The Pension Beaurepas, A Bundle of Letters, 2 volumes (London: Macmillan, 1881);

The Portrait of a Lady (3 volumes, London: Macmillan, 1881; 1 volume, Boston & New York: Houghton, Mifflin, 1882);

Henry James, 1905

The Siege of London, The Pension Beaurepas, and The Point of View (Boston: Osgood, 1883);

Daisy Miller: A Comedy in Three Acts (Boston: Osgood, 1883);

Portraits of Places (London: Macmillan, 1883; Boston: Osgood, 1884);

Tales of Three Cities (Boston: Osgood, 1884; London: Macmillan, 1884);

A Little Tour in France (Boston: Osgood, 1885 [i.e., 1884]; revised edition, Boston & New York: Houghton, Mifflin, 1900; London: Heinemann, 1900);

The Author of Beltraffio, Pandora, Georgina's Reasons, The Path of Duty, Four Meetings (Boston: Osgood, 1885);

The Art of Fiction (Boston: Cupples, Upham, 1885);

Stories Revived, 3 volumes (London: Macmillan, 1885);

The Bostonians: A Novel (3 volumes, London: Macmillan, 1886; 1 volume, London & New York: Macmillan, 1886);

The Princess Casamassima: A Novel (3 volumes, London: Macmillan, 1886; 1 volume, New York: Macmillan, 1886);

Partial Portraits (London & New York: Macmillan, 1888);

The Reverberator (2 volumes, London: Macmillan, 1888; 1 volume, New York: Macmillan, 1888);

The Aspern Papers, Louisa Pallant, The Modern Warning (2 volumes, London: Macmillan, 1888; 1 volume, New York: Macmillan, 1888);

A London Life, The Patagonia, The Liar, Mrs. Temperly (2 volumes, London: Macmillan, 1889; 1 volume, New York: Macmillan, 1889);

The Tragic Muse (2 volumes, Boston & New York: Houghton, Mifflin, 1890; 3 volumes, London: Macmillan, 1890);

The American: A Comedy in Four Acts (London: Heinemann, 1891);

The Lesson of the Master, The Marriages, The Pupil, Brooksmith, The Solution, Sir Edmund Orme (New York: Macmillan, 1892; London: Macmillan, 1892);

The Real Thing and Other Tales (New York: Macmillan, 1893; London: Macmillan, 1893);

Picture and Text (New York: Harper, 1893);

The Private Life, The Wheel of Time, Lord Beaupré, The Visits, Collaboration, Owen Wingrave (London: Osgood, McIlvaine, 1893);

Essays in London and Elsewhere (London: Osgood, McIlvaine, 1893; New York: Harper, 1893);

The Private Life, Lord Beaupré, The Visits (New York: Harper, 1893);

The Wheel of Time, Collaboration, Owen Wingrave (New York: Harper, 1893);

Theatricals, Two Comedies: Tenants, Disengaged (London: Osgood, McIlvaine, 1894; New York: Harper, 1894);

Theatricals, Second Series: The Album, The Reprobate (London: Osgood, McIlvaine, 1895; New York: Harper, 1895);

Terminations: The Death of the Lion, The Coxon Fund, The Middle Years, The Altar of the Dead (London: Heinemann, 1895; New York: Harper, 1895);

Embarrassments: The Figure in the Carpet, Glasses, The Next Time, The Way It Came (London: Heinemann, 1896; New York & London: Macmillan, 1896);

The Other House (2 volumes, London: Heinemann, 1896; 1 volume, New York & London: Macmillan, 1896);

The Spoils of Poynton (London: Heinemann, 1897; Boston & New York: Houghton, Mifflin, 1897);

What Maisie Knew (London: Heinemann, 1897; Chicago & New York: Stone, 1897);

In the Cage (London: Duckworth, 1898; Chicago & New York: Stone, 1898);

The Two Magics: The Turn of the Screw, Covering End (London: Heinemann, 1898; New York & London: Macmillan, 1898);

The Awkward Age (London: Heinemann, 1899; New York & London: Harper, 1899);

The Soft Side (London: Methuen, 1900; New York: Macmillan, 1900);

The Sacred Fount (New York: Scribners, 1901; London: Methuen, 1901);

The Wings of the Dove (2 volumes, New York: Scribners, 1902; 1 volume, Westminster: Constable, 1902);

The Better Sort (London: Methuen, 1903; New York: Scribners, 1903);

The Ambassadors (London: Methuen, 1903; New York & London: Harper, 1903);

William Wetmore Story and His Friends, 2 volumes (Edinburgh & London: Blackwood, 1903; Boston: Houghton, Mifflin, 1903);

The Golden Bowl (New York: Scribners, 1904; London: Methuen, 1905);

The Question of Our Speech, The Lesson of Balzac: Two Lectures (Boston & New York: Houghton, Mifflin, 1905);

English Hours (London: Heinemann, 1905; Boston & New York: Houghton, Mifflin, 1905);

The American Scene (London: Chapman & Hall, 1907; New York & London: Harper, 1907);

Views and Reviews (Boston: Ball, 1908);

Italian Hours (London: Heinemann, 1909; Boston & New York: Houghton Mifflin, 1909);

The Finer Grain (New York: Scribners, 1910; London: Methuen, 1910);

The Outcry (London: Methuen, 1911; New York: Scribners, 1911);

A Small Boy and Others (New York: Scribners, 1913; London: Macmillan, 1913);

Notes of a Son and Brother (New York: Scribners, 1914; London: Macmillan, 1914);

Notes on Novelists with Some Other Notes (London: Dent, 1914; New York: Scribners, 1914);

The Ivory Tower, edited by Percy Lubbock (London: Collins, 1917; New York: Scribners, 1917);

The Sense of the Past, edited by Lubbock (London: Collins, 1917; New York: Scribners, 1917);

The Middle Years, edited by Lubbock (London: Collins, 1917; New York: Scribners, 1917);

Gabrielle de Bergerac, edited by Albert Mordell (New York: Boni & Liveright, 1918);

Within the Rim and Other Essays, 1914-15 (London: Collins, 1918);

Travelling Companions, edited by Mordell (New York: Boni & Liveright, 1919);

A Landscape Painter, edited by Mordell (New York: Scott & Seltzer, 1919);

Master Eustace (New York: Seltzer, 1920);

Notes and Reviews (Cambridge, Mass.: Dunster House, 1921);

The Art of the Novel: Critical Prefaces, edited by Richard P. Blackmur (New York: Scribners, 1934);

The American Novels and Stories of Henry James, edited by F. O. Matthiessen (New York: Knopf, 1947; augmented, 1951);

The Notebooks of Henry James, edited by Matthiessen and Kenneth B. Murdock (New York: Oxford University Press, 1947);

The Art of Fiction and Other Essays, edited by Morris Roberts (New York: Oxford University Press, 1948);

The Scenic Art: Notes on Acting & The Drama: 1872-1901, edited by Allan Wade (New Brunswick: Rutgers University Press, 1948; London: Hart-Davis, 1949);

The Ghostly Tales of Henry James, edited by Leon Edel (New Brunswick: Rutgers University Press, 1948 [i.e., 1949]);

The Complete Plays of Henry James, edited by Edel (Philadelphia & New York: Lippincott, 1949; London: Hart-Davis, 1949);

Eight Uncollected Tales, edited by Edna Kenton (New Brunswick: Rutgers University Press, 1950);

The American Essays, edited by Edel (New York: Vintage, 1956);

The Future of the Novel: Essays on the Art of Fiction, edited by Edel (New York: Vintage, 1956);

The Painter's Eye: Notes and Essays on the Pictorial Arts, edited by John L. Sweeney (London: Hart-Davis, 1956; Cambridge, Mass.: Harvard University Press, 1956);

Parisian Sketches: Letters to the New York Tribune, 1875-1876, edited by Edel and Ilse Dusoir Lind (New York: New York University Press, 1957);

The House of Fiction: Essays on the Novel, edited by Edel (London: Hart-Davis, 1957);

Literary Reviews and Essays, edited by Mordell (New York: Twayne, 1957);

French Writers and American Women, edited by Peter Buitenhuis (Branford, Conn.: Compass, 1960);

Henry James: Literary Criticism, edited by Edel and Mark Wilson, 2 volumes (New York: Library of America, 1984);

The Complete Notebooks of Henry James, edited by Edel and Lyall H. Powers (New York: Oxford University Press, 1987).

Collections: *Novels and Tales of Henry James,* 14 volumes (London: Macmillan, 1883);

The Novels and Tales of Henry James, selected and revised by James, New York Edition, 24 volumes (New York: Scribners, 1907-1909); 2 volumes added (New York: Scribners, 1917);

The Novels and Stories of Henry James, edited by Lubbock, 35 volumes (London: Macmillan, 1921-1923);

The Complete Tales of Henry James, edited by Edel, 12 volumes (London: Hart-Davis, 1962-1964; Philadelphia & New York: Lippincott, 1962-1964);

The Bodley Head Henry James, edited by Edel (London: Bodley Head, 1967-   );

The Tales of Henry James, edited by Maqbool Aziz (London: Oxford University Press, 1973-   ).

Henry James was one of the most prolific of major American writers, having written more than four million words of fiction and about the same amount of nonfiction; in addition, about fifteen thousand letters are extant. Since James's fiction, whether long or short, is descriptive, pictorial, and dramatic, it is somewhat arbitrary not only to separate the work into subgenres but even to distinguish it totally from his travel writing, critical pieces, letters, and plays. In prefaces to the New York Edition of his fiction (1907-1909), and elsewhere, James tried to define various types of short fiction. For him the *tale* or *short story* (he employed the terms interchangeably) is most often a "picture" or "anecdote." Though the distinction between the anecdote and the picture is not always clearcut, the picture is the shorter of the two, and, as James noted, it is intended to create "richly summarised and foreshortened effects...." The anecdote, James

Kraft explains, "is an idea that is too complex for this small canvas of the picture, yet is only directed toward a single character and situation."

A representative "picture" is "The Chaperon" (*Atlantic Monthly,* November and December 1891; collected in *The Real Thing and Other Tales,* 1893). Characterized by summary and foreshortening, it depicts a socially ostracized widow who is chaperoned by her spunky daughter back into social acceptance, while Victorian hypocrisy is limned in the background. "The Jolly Corner" (*English Review,* December 1908; collected in volume 17 of the New York Edition) is a typical "anecdote." The American hero of the story so wonders what he would have been like if he had not expatriated himself to Europe that he actually sees his New York alter ego. Despite clear differences between the two stories, the pictorial tale "The Chaperon" is partly anecdotal, while the fictive anecdote "The Jolly Corner" includes intense pictorial moments. As James once wrote, "I rejoice in the anecdote, but I revel in the picture; though having doubtless at times to note that a given attempt may place itself near the dividing-line."

James also applied the French term *nouvelle* to some of his short fiction. As Kraft says, "its flexibility does not necessitate for James the restrictions in length . . . that he feels apply to the English terms 'short story' or 'tale.' "

Of what James calls "on the dimensional ground–for length and breadth–our ideal, our beautiful and blest *nouvelle,*" he named as representative "The Death of the Lion" (*Yellow Book,* April 1894) and "The Coxon Fund" (*Yellow Book,* July 1894), both collected in *Terminations* (1895), and "The Next Time" (*Yellow Book,* July 1895), collected in *Embarrassments* (1896). They are, respectively, 13,400, 21,300, and 15,100 words in length. Other stories by James, both longer and shorter than these three, might be nominated as better *nouvelles.* One of the best, "The Beast in the Jungle" (first published in *The Better Sort,* 1903), succeeds in meeting James's stated challenge for the "blest" genre: "to do the complicated thing with a strong brevity and lucidity–to arrive, on behalf of the multiplicity, at a certain science of control." Dramatizing the numbing fate of the one person in the world to whom nothing happens, the 16,700-word tale displays temporal complication, episodic multiplicity, and pictorial lucidity, and with it controlled compression–given its breadth and range of psychological action. The collection published as *The Better Sort* also includes two other previously unpub-

Henry James, 1862; portrait by John La Farge (courtesy of The Century Association, P1862.3)

lished *nouvelles* of great power: "The Birthplace" (20,200 words) and "The Papers" (35,000).

Despite these distinctions, Kraft notes "that for James the tale could be whatever he created as long as it is not so extended and inclusive as to enter the complexity and breadth of the novel. The important concern for the short fiction is its economy of purpose. The richness of insight possible *within* this economy makes the tale fascinating to James." Indeed, as essential as James's definitions are to the analysis of his writings, it is still valuable to categorize his fiction by length. By this criterion James may be said to have written one hundred short stories (under twenty-five thousand words), twelve long short stories (up to fifty thousand words), eleven short novels (up to seventy-five thousand words), and eleven novels (more than seventy-five thousand words). It is worth noting that James's shortest novel, *The Reverberator* (1888), at fifty-three thousand words, is more than twelve thousand words longer than his longest story, "A London Life" (*Scribner's Magazine*, June-September 1888; collected in *A London Life, The Patagonia, The Liar, Mrs. Temperly*, 1889).

Henry James, Jr., was born at 21 Washington Place (near Waverly Place), in the Greenwich Village section of New York City, on 15 April 1843, the second child of Henry James, Sr., a rich, eccentric philosopher, and Mary Walsh James. The family eventually included four other children: William (1842-1910), Garth Wilkinson (1845-1883), Robertson (1846-1910), and Alice (1848-1892). The future fiction writer's earliest memory was significant: under two years old and in Paris with his parents, he looked out of their carriage and saw the "tall and glorious column" in the Place Vendôme. This moment was the start of his lifelong love affair with Europe. By 1861 he had crossed the Atlantic Ocean six times, his purposely rootless parents having by then taken the family to live in France, England, Switzerland, Germany, and New England. Young James studied literature and languages, including French, which he spoke with enviable fluency.

The most psychic experience of his life occurred during his Parisian residence of 1856-1857, when James first visited the Galerie d'Apollon of the Louvre. The gallery was a blaze of titanic art, and at first James regarded it all as a "bridge over to Style," where he "inhaled . . . a general sense of *glory*." But a few years later this lush memory triggered what he described as "the most appalling yet most admirable nightmare of my life." He dreamed of being trapped in a room, with a "creature or presence" on the other side of the locked door and trying to force its way in. James resisted with his shoulder at first, but then became the aggressor, broke out, and pursued "the awful agent," amid lightning and thunder, down a "glorious hall" resembling the Galerie d'Apollon. As Leon Edel analyzes this dream, "*Sublimity* was indeed the word for it: to resist nightmare, to turn the tables and counterattack, was consonant with the sense of triumph and glory and conquest and power. Henry James had fought back. And he had won."

In September 1860 the James family returned to America, settling in Newport, Rhode Island, so that William could study painting. During this transitional time Henry James sketched a little, turned to more French literature, and made friends with several brilliant young people in the general region. During the Civil War, William abandoned art, turned to science, and enrolled at Harvard University. Wilky and Bob

James joined the Union Army, but Henry stayed out of the war because of an injury. He tried studying at Harvard Law School for the academic year 1862-1863, but he had no intention of pursuing a legal career; instead he attended James Russell Lowell's literature lectures and read in the library. By that time his American friends included John La Farge, Thomas Sergeant Perry, Charles Eliot Norton and his sister Grace Norton, Oliver Wendell Holmes, Jr., William Dean Howells, John Hay, and E. L. Godkin.

At the age of twenty-one he broke into print with an unsigned short story ("A Tragedy of Error," *Continental Monthly*, February 1864; collected in volume one of *The Complete Tales of Henry James*, 1962-1964) and an unsigned book review (*North American Review*, October 1864). He had written more reviews and a dozen more short stories by early 1869, when he began his first adult trip to Europe, going from England to Switzerland to Italy, ultimately his favorite country. This trip helped to form his lifelong pattern of travel, observation, and writing; solitude; friendships with artistic people; and homesickness coupled with an unending puzzlement as to where his true home was. His fourteen months abroad were scarred by the news, received in March 1870, that his beloved cousin Minny Temple had died of tuberculosis. As James remarked in his autobiography, written almost half a century later, his cousin's death marked the end of his youth.

James arrived home in May 1870, went abroad again for two years (May 1872-August 1874), then spent a productive but lonely winter in New York, and finally made the momentous decision to live permanently abroad. By the time he left for Paris in autumn 1875 James had published in periodicals a total of twenty-six short stories and two novels: his first, weak novel, *Watch and Ward* (*Atlantic Monthly*, August-December 1871; published as a book in 1878), and his first mature novel, *Roderick Hudson* (*Atlantic Monthly*, January-December 1875; published as a book in 1876). He had also completed a book of travel essays, *Transatlantic Sketches* (1875), and collected six tales in *A Passionate Pilgrim, and Other Tales* (1875).

In Paris he met Ivan Turgenev (who would be his closest professional friend), Gustave Flaubert, Guy de Maupassant, Emile Zola, Edmund de Goncourt, Ernst Renan, and Alphonse Daudet; but he moved to London in December 1876. In London James met or renewed his acquaintance with Alfred, Lord Tennyson, Robert Browning, George Eliot, William Morris, Anthony Trollope, James Anthony Froude, Leslie Stephen, and other literati. He soon gained notoriety, even fame, with his somewhat shocking short stories "Daisy Miller: A Study" (*Cornhill Magazine*, June and July 1878; published separately in early October of that year, though dated 1879) and "An International Episode" (*Cornhill Magazine*, December 1878 and January 1879; published separately later in 1879). James also wrote the first book-length biographical-critical treatment of Nathaniel Hawthorne (1879) and then began his masterpiece, *The Portrait of a Lady* (1881).

After completing this great novel, James returned to America in October 1881 but soon found himself a stranger there except to his family. In a notebook he wrote, "I needed to see again *les miens*, to revive my relations with them. . . . Apart from this I hold it was not necessary I should come to this country. . . . I have made my choice . . . the old world–my choice, my need, my life." While he was still in America, his mother died, in January 1882. So he stayed on a while, comforting his father, then returned to London in May, only to be summoned across the wintry Atlantic, arriving a few days after the death of his father in December 1882. This time James remained until the following August, helping to settle his parents' estate; but England was now his home; Europe, his professional orientation.

The 1882-1895 period, which James called his "Middle Years," is marked by no fewer than thirty-eight short stories–including many of his finest–as well as "The Art of Fiction" (*Longman's Magazine*, September 1884), his finest critical essay; three long political novels, *The Bostonians* (1886), *The Princess Casamassima* (1886), and *The Tragic Muse* (1890), all of which were unsuccessful with the public; and half a decade of mostly ineffectual play writing, which climaxed with the disastrous staging of his *Guy Domville* in early 1895. James turned again to fiction, writing in his notebook: "I take up my *own* old pen again–the pen of all my old unforgettable efforts and sacred struggles."

From 1896 until the beginning of World War I James was intensely active. In the summer of 1896 he first saw Lamb House while he was vacationing in Rye, a Sussex coastal town southeast of London. Leasing the solid eighteenth-century mansion the following year (he later bought it for two thousand pounds), he made it his home, his retreat, his sacred sanctuary, and his place of

Henry James, circa 1898 (courtesy of Lamb House, Rye)

literary business for virtually the rest of his days. In February 1897, seven months before he signed a twenty-one-year title to Lamb House, he published *The Spoils of Poynton* (serialized in the *Atlantic Monthly*, as *The Old Things*, April-October 1896), and *What Maisie Knew* (serialized in the *Chap Book*, 15 January–1 August 1897) followed in October. Somewhere between these two novels he shifted into the prolix style of the period F. O. Matthiessen labeled his "major phase." Once settled in Lamb House he wrote *William Wetmore Story and His Friends* (1903), a biography of an American sculptor in Rome, and then his best travel book, *The American Scene* (1907), based on his canny observations of his native land during a visit that had lasted from August 1904 to July 1905. Most important, he produced a steady stream of splendid fiction. His short stories from this period include "The Turn of the Screw," "The Beast in the Jungle," "The Birthplace," and "The Jolly Corner." He also wrote two somewhat weak novels, *The Awkward Age* (1899) and *The Sacred Fount* (1901), but the most important works of the period are his three monumental major-phase novels: *The Wings of the Dove* (1902), *The Ambassadors* (1903), and *The Golden Bowl* (1904).

From 1896 through 1900 James published some twenty-two short stories; the years 1901-1910 saw a mere fifteen more, partly because James was also writing novels and a biography, partly also because he had undertaken the Herculean, problematic task of selecting and revising fiction for his twenty-four-volume New York Edition (1907-1909), but mostly because at last the Master was beginning to age.

James suffered a prolonged nervous sickness starting in 1909. William James, though also sick, and his charming wife, Alice James, visited James at Lamb House in 1910, and the three vacationed on the Continent that summer. William James grew worse, and the three returned to America, where William died in New Hampshire, August 1910. Desolated by the loss, James remained in America for a year, then returned to Lamb House, to travel no more. He dictated his autobiographical memoirs: *A Small Boy and Others* (1913), *Notes of a Son and Brother* (1914), and the incomplete third volume *The Middle Years* (posthumously published in 1917).

The start of World War I could not silence James the writer, but it did make him indifferent about bringing his autobiography up to the present or about writing of the contemporary scene. He abandoned a novel, which he had titled *The Ivory Tower* (added in fragmentary form to the New York Edition in 1917). Next, James returned to his long-deferred novel *The Sense of the Past* (added as a fragment in 1917 to the New York Edition), begun about fifteen years earlier, in his excitement following the notoriety surrounding his "The Turn of the Screw," but in December 1915 James sustained a paralytic stroke. His brother's widow, Alice, crossed the Atlantic Ocean to remain with him until the end. In his final delirium, James dictated palace-renovation orders and signed them Napoleon. And The Louvre, that treasure chest of European art, was again on James's mind long after his dream of its Galerie d'Apollon. On 28 February 1916 Henry James died quietly, technically of edema. After a funeral service in Chelsea Old Church, London, his ashes were deposited in the James family plot, in Cambridge, Massachusetts.

Most commentators agree that James went through three stages in his fiction writing: a long period of apprenticeship (1864-1881), the middle years (1882-1895), and his major phase (1896-1916). Critics have also attempted to group his themes into categories, which overlap and tend to blur. In 1948 Osborn Andreas treated each of the novels and stories under one of ten thematic categories: emotional cannibalism, consideration for others, love as a deterrent to the full life, the sense of the past, the artistic homage versus the lure of power, attacks on the sheltered life, the mystery of personal identity, false values, the international theme, and fables for critics. Obviously, a given work of fiction, no matter how short, may dramatize two or more of these themes. For example, "Owen Wingrave" (*Graphic*, Christmas number, 1892, collected in *The Private Life, The Wheel of Time, Lord Beaupré, The Visits, Collaboration, Owen Wingrave*, 1893) features a hero too sensitive to continue his family's tradition of militarism despite pressure from relatives and his fiancée. The themes of this story include emotional cannibalism (Owen's fiancée meddles), love as a deterrent to a richer emotional life, the sense of the past (Owen reviles his imperialistic forebearers' gory history), the false value of blatant patriotism, and even art versus power (Owen prefers a life of the mind to one of courage-carnage). Despite such overlapping, Andreas's thematic categories are immensely helpful. More recently, in 1975, Gordon Pirie divided James's best stories into four groups according to subject: international tales, stories of artists, tales about children and parents, and stories of middle-aged and old people.

The most significant critic to deal with James's short fiction is Leon Edel. In his general introduction to his twelve-volume edition of James's stories, he characterizes the tales of each of James's three main periods. The early stories "contain a good deal of apprentice-work" about "failure in love, renunciation, the reticence of young men, the unfathomableness of young women, the general fickleness of the female sex." They are often melancholy, romantic, lugubrious, painterly, and reflective; are set mostly in America; and concern personal relations more than plot. Edel characterizes the stories of the middle years as typically studies of international manners, which wittily contrast vulgar American egalitarianism with the rudeness and arrogance of British high society. In these stories James concentrates, according to Edel, on studying the American woman "with a mixture of affection, awe, and profound mistrust." Like most other commentators on James's major phase, Edel notes that beginning in the mid 1890s (the start of the so-called major phase) the Master became less concerned with minute descriptions and with discussions of social behavior, and more interested in studying "states of feeling and . . . dilemmas of existence" and in analyzing the unlived life. In these late stories James approaches the existentialist, even the absurdist; he depicts not the visitable, recoverable, and usable past but the empty, useless past, and his realism turns inward, often becoming bleak. At the same time, Edel continues, James delightfully excoriates "the public for its Philistinism."

James published thirty-seven stories between 1864 and 1879. Three of his earliest ones–"The Story of a Year" (*Atlantic Monthly*, March 1865; collected in *The American Novels and Stories of Henry James*, 1947), "Poor Richard" (*Atlantic Monthly*, June 1867; collected in *Stories Revived*, 1885), and "A Most Extraordinary Case" (*Atlantic Monthly*, April 1868; collected in *Stories Revived*)–were inspired by the Civil War. Since James almost never wrote about types of action or specific locales he did not know at first hand, he deals with the Civil War tangentially, reflexively. "The Story of a Year" and "Poor Richard" focus on selfish nonparticipants. The first story concerns a shallow girl whose faithlessness to her soldier-lover vindicates his coldly distrustful mother. The titular hero of the second story is a weak, alcoholic young civilian whose rich young female neighbor prefers uniformed men to him; Richard lies to one of her army suitors and warns her about another. Each story not only hints at James's personal unease during the war years but also prefigures his developing literary powers; furthermore, both stories concern the dangers of love and meddling. "A Most Extraordinary Case" inchoately contrasts the horrible aftereffects of war on men and the poignant charm of women left behind; in it, war is, in a sense, also a metaphor for the inartistic, materialistic jungle in which most people live.

Some of the other early stories are related to these tales of love lost in war. "The Story of a Masterpiece" (*Galaxy*, January and February 1868; collected in *Eight Uncollected Tales*, 1950) is the first of James's works to suggest the vital power of art. Seeming to be following a lead from Hawthorne's "Prophetic Pictures," James's story deals with a jilted lover's painting of his former girlfriend, which reveals her opprobrious inner nature to her present suitor. "The Romance of Certain Old Clothes" (*Atlantic Monthly*, February 1868; collected in *A Passionate Pilgrim, and Other Tales*) is also Hawthornean. As Edel says, James "places the real before us, squarely and objectively, and then skillfully mingles it

James at Lamb House, circa 1900

with the unusual and the eerie, after the fashion of his predecessor [Hawthorne]." In James's tale a man's wife seems to return from the dead to take revenge on the man and her sister, whom he has married in defiance of a vow made to the first wife. A better supernatural tale is "De Grey: A Romance" (*Atlantic Monthly*, 1868; collected in *Travelling Companions*, 1919), which follows the surprising effects of a family curse: all male De Greys are said to vampirize their true loves, but in the story Paul De Grey is drained by Margaret's love for him and dies. This weird story first presents James's sacred-fount theory: that in any sexual relationship one partner ruinously taps the fount of vital energy in the other.

Most of these early pieces, flawed though they are, hint that James was gathering power both stylistic and thematic, but Kraft is correct in noting that their "worst faults . . . are their frequent romantic or melodramatic situations which are often ludicrous, and their unintentionally humorous or mock-sophisticated tone, as if James were not confident enough of what he wanted to say to be serious." Nonetheless, as Edel reports, in 1868 a reviewer for the *Nation* exclaimed after reading "The Story of a Masterpiece" that "within the somewhat narrow limits to which he confines himself, Mr. James is the best writer of short stories in America."

From 1869 through 1872 James published seven more tales. Of these, "A Light Man" (*Galaxy*, July 1869; collected in *Master Eustace*, 1920) is technically the most challenging. As in many of Edgar Allan Poe's tales (including "Ligeia," for example), "A Light Man" contains two stories—one told in the first person by a Europeanized American narrator and the other submerged beneath the lines of his narrative, revealing his contemptible qualities and the dangers of his foreign pseudopolish. Edel notes that in this neglected work James anticipated Joycean stream-of-consciousness by half a century. Better because gentler are "Travelling Companions" (*Atlantic Monthly*, November and December 1870; collected in *Travelling Companions*) and "A Passionate Pilgrim" (*Atlantic Monthly*, 1871; collected in *A Passionate Pilgrim, and Other Tales*), which build on James's first adult trip to Europe. As Cornelia Pulsifer Kelley shows, "Travelling Companions" "is a mixture of travel report and art criticism with the story incidental and not . . . necessary." "A Passionate Pilgrim" may be mainly important because it is the earliest tale which James chose to include in his New York Edition. In "A Passionate Pilgrim" he contrasts two responses to England: one character loves the Old World almost to dementia, while the narrator-observer of this pilgrim's ecstasy avoids such irrationality.

Another pair of stories from this period in James's life reflects his awareness of the dangers of a possessive mother and a competitive brother and thus has interested psychoanalytical critics. The titular hero of "Master Eustace" (*Galaxy*, November 1871; collected in *Stories Revived*) is so spoiled, pampered, and blinded to reality by his widowed mother that he never gains maturity. "Guest's Confession" (*Atlantic Monthly*, October and November 1872; collected in *Travelling Companions*) features an older stepbrother who behaves viciously toward a swindler whose daughter the younger step-brother loves. The story also presents a western millionaire so crude that, if James regarded him as prophetic of future Americans, it is no wonder the young writer opted for Europe.

In none of the stories considered thus far does James give us a traditional, not to say old-fashioned, treatment along the lines of popular

contemporary authors with whom he might be said to have been competing. But in his most unrepresentative short story, "Gabrielle de Bergerac" (*Atlantic Monthly*, July-September 1869; published separately in 1918), he attempted a historical *nouvelle* set in late-eighteenth-century France. Haughty Baron de Bergerac's dowerless maiden sister Gabrielle is courted by a decent though jaded viscount but elopes with her nephew's tutor, Coquelin, to a life of romance, happiness, and ultimate tragedy at the advent of the French Revolution. If it had been written by anyone but James, this story might be better known, for it has romantic charm: Kelley says that it depicts "the anomaly of happy disaster where one suffers for love," while Bruce R. McElderry, Jr., labels it, for that very reason, "probably the least Jamesian of his fiction."

James typically treated love as threatening. For example, "Madame de Mauves" (*Galaxy*, February and March 1874; collected in *A Passionate Pilgrim, and Other Tales*) concerns a beautiful but austerely moral American wife of a philandering French count, who advises that she, too, take a lover. After he repents, fails to win her forgiveness, and commits suicide, her timid American would-be lover thinks of returning to pursue her, but by story's end he has yet to do so.

In other stories written at about this time James dramatized love in unromantic ways. The central painter figure of "The Madonna of the Future" (*Atlantic Monthly*, 1873; collected in *A Passionate Pilgrim, and Other Tales*) adores the model for his projected Madonna, work on which is forever deferred as the model becomes old and faded and the artist sickens and dies. By means of this parable James may be warning all artists, himself included, to stay productive. Parable yields to allegory in "Benvolio" (*Galaxy*, August 1875; collected in *The Madonna of the Future and Other Tales*, 1879), which features a hero vacillating between love of Scholastica (perhaps James's symbol of wise art) and a worldly countess. Only a bit less allegorical is the slightly earlier tale "The Last of the Valerii" (*Atlantic Monthly*, January 1874; collected in *A Passionate Pilgrim, and Other Tales*), which contrasts Martha, the present-day flesh-and-blood American wife of Count Marco Valerio, and an ancient statue of Juno, exhumed on their villa grounds. The count begins worshiping the statue and ignores Martha until she reburies this evidence of the dead, if still potent, Roman past.

Henry James, 1908; portrait by Jacques-Emile Blanche (courtesy of the National Portrait Gallery, Washington, D.C.)

James's apprentice years were climaxed by four tales of great merit and continuing charm: "Four Meetings," "Daisy Miller," "An International Episode," and "A Bundle of Letters." "Four Meetings" (*Scribner's Monthly,* November 1877; collected in *Daisy Miller: A Study. An International Episode. Four Meetings,* 1879) is probably James's best short story to that date. Caroline Spencer, a New England schoolteacher, saves her money and travels to Europe, only to be bilked of her money by a deceitful art-student cousin in France. Some time after she returns to drab America with little of Europe but dreams, her cousin dies, and his shabby "Countess" widow comes to live with her. The condescending narrator, who sees Caroline only four times, is a noncommittal meddler whose supercilious tone carries more irony than he realizes.

"Daisy Miller," whose appearance in the June and July 1878 issues of *Cornhill Magazine* made it the first of James's stories to be published in a British magazine, brought James immediate recognition in England. The story was pirated by magazines in New York and Boston, and

the pamphlet version published by Harper on 1 November 1878 sold twenty thousand copies in just a few weeks. Only "The Turn of the Screw" has matched "Daisy Miller" in popular appeal. James had skillfully depicted women and the contrast between American and European manners before, but those stories are seldom as appealing as his tale of the naive young American Daisy Miller and her encounters with Old World ways in Switzerland and then Italy. Her ignorance of the European code that young ladies must be chaperoned leads to her social ostracism and– after at least one stroll with a young man in Rome's unhealthful night air–her pathetic death. Continuing attention from critics and the general public attests to Daisy's immortal vivacity.

"An International Episode" (*Cornhill Magazine,* December 1878 and January 1879; published separately later in 1879) is James's international "Pride and Prejudice," pitting American pride in hospitality and commercialism, and American prejudice against Britain's social insularism– all this–against British pride in manners, and prejudice against Americans' forwardness and frank talk. In this overly long *nouvelle* (29,300 words) James presents both sides without taking either.

James is said to have written "A Bundle of Letters" in one sitting. Soon after it was published in the French magazine the *Parisian* (December 1879) a pirated edition appeared in Boston (January 1880). The story is in the form of some nine letters, written by six different people–two American girls and one prissy American man, one British girl, a Frenchman, and a chauvinistic German male. Kraft locates the drama of the tale "in the inevitably conflicting points of view and interpretations of reality," adding that the "situation is too clever to be serious, but the story is so well written that it is successful."

In the late 1870s and early 1880s James devoted most of his time to writing novels–*The Europeans* (1878), *Confidence* (1880), *Washington Square* (1881), and *The Portrait of a Lady*–and his *Hawthorne.* It is understandable then that he did not write the first of what Edel classifies as stories of the middle period until 1882. Another epistolary effort, "The Point of View" (*Century,* December 1882; collected in *The Siege of London, The Pension Beaurepas, and The Point of View,* 1883), has been called by S. Gorley Putt not a story but "an animated series of exceedingly witty essays on contemporary America as viewed by different Europeans and Europeanized Americans." A mark of James's general achievement was Macmillan's publication in 1883 of a fourteen-volume edition of his fiction to that date, but this edition includes only thirteen tales, since the first ten slim volumes are taken up with six early novels.

The year 1884 is notable for no fewer than six tales, three of them vintage James: "Lady Barberina" (the spelling was changed to "Barbarina" in the New York Edition), "Pandora," and "The Author of Beltraffio." In "Lady Barberina" (*Country Magazine*, May-July 1884; collected in *Tales of Three Cities*, 1884) a rich American physician virtually purchases the best-limbed wife available in British high society, then lives to rue his bargain. Adeline R. Tintner suggests that James uses "the metaphor of horse trading . . . to analogize the Anglo-American marriage market," and finds parallels between Jonathan Swift's Houyhnhnms and James's bitter version of England's horsy set. James even finds room in this *nouvelle* to satirize western American manhood for being, here at least, ineffective and sycophantic. "Pandora" (*New York Sun*, 1 and 8 June 1884) and "The Author of Beltraffio" (*English Illustrated Magazine*, June and July 1884), both collected in *The Author of Beltraffio, Pandora, Georgina's Reasons, The Path of Duty, Four Meetings* (1885), concern parents and children. The star of "Pandora," one of James's wittiest tales, is Pandora Day, a Daisy Miller bent on surviving. This self-made American girl is so adept that she successfully chaperons her sleepy, wickedly satirized parents, soaring beyond their limited moral horizon and making her way socially in Washington, D.C., to the President himself, from whom she gains a diplomatic post for her fiancé. A brilliant touch is James's introduction of the tone-setting Washington couple the Bonnycastles, based on his friends Henry and Marian Adams. One of James's most morbid pieces, "The Author of Beltraffio," features a Christian wife so rigidly righteous that, rather than see her son grow up and read his pagan father's decadent writings, she withholds the sick boy's medicine and lets him die. Andreas calls this tour de force a tale of art opposed by powerful "worldly vested interests," but in truth it is unclassifiable in its horror.

Exhausted by work on his long novels *The Bostonians* and *The Princess Casamassima*, James grew restless, moved to a different London flat early in 1886, and from December 1886 to July 1887 vacationed in Italy, the setting for one of his finest stories.

One of the most significant *nouvelles* in the English language, "The Aspern Papers" (*Atlantic Monthly*, March-May 1888; collected in *The Aspern Papers, Louisa Pallant, The Modern Warning*, 1888), was popular at once with the public. Edel devotes fourteen pages to it in *Henry James: The Middle Years*, explaining that James's inspiration was a story he had heard in January 1887 about Byron's mistress Claire Clairmont, who until her death in 1879 had lived in Florence with a niece and had certain papers of Byron and of Shelley. An odd American man had tried to obtain them by renting rooms in her house. James converts Shelley into Jeffrey Aspern, American poet, and changes the location to Venice, making his first-person narrator an acquisitive American "publishing scoundrel," whose desire to exploit the papers is greater than his willingness to marry their owner's middle-aged niece, whom he perhaps wrongly describes as "a ridiculous, pathetic, provincial old woman." The reader sees more than James's narrator does, recognizing him as a violator of privacy, who cannot measure the historic value of Venice and fails to appreciate the niece's puzzling last speeches.

"The Liar" (*Century Magazine*, June 1888; collected in *A London Life, The Patagonia, The Liar, Mrs. Temperly*) is another fable about privacy. In "The Liar" James implicitly asks whether it is worse to tell a lie or to trap someone into doing so. Angry because a woman rejected him and much later married a liar named Colonel Capadose, painter Oliver Lyon wonders if she is blinded by love or if she knows the colonel's true nature. Worse, Lyon leads her to second one of the colonel's prevarications. This climax is dwarfed by James's implication that Lyon has done more than his share of spiritual lying. (Often in James's fiction a character's name–such as Lyon–is a subtle clue to his true nature.)

"The Lesson of the Master" (*Universal Review*, 16 July and 15 August 1888; collected in *The Lesson of the Master, The Marriages, The Pupil, Brooksmith, The Solution, Sir Edmund Orme*, 1892) is the earliest of six excellent fables about writers and artists, and their audiences. (The others are "The Real Thing," "The Middle Years," "The Death of the Lion," "The Next Time," and "The Figure in the Carpet.") In "The Lesson of the Master" a long-married master British novelist, Henry St. George, advises an aspiring disciple, Paul Overt, to forego marriage to Marian Fancourt and instead to devote all his energy to writing. Paul does so but later discovers that Henry, whose first wife has recently died, has wed Marian himself. The story leaves this question unan-

LAMB HOUSE.
RYE.
SUSSEX.

Postscript in James's 2 January 1910 letter to Annie Fields, in which James suggests he might write a letter of introduction to Fields's edition of The Letters of Sarah Orne Jewett *(1911). James did not write the introduction (courtesy of the Henry E. Huntington Library and Art Gallery).*

swered: Was Henry sincere? "The Real Thing" (*Black and White*, 16 April 1892; collected in *The Real Thing and Other Tales*), one of James's most frequently anthologized stories, is another fable, the point of which is that impressive-looking people often cannot model as such for an artist. Real life, being rigid and padded, lacks inspiring flexibility; airy hints of beauty best tease the artist into productivity. This story also satirizes stuffy British aristocracy. Incredibly, this splendid fable is one of ten stories James published in 1892. "The Middle Years" (*Scribner's Magazine*, May 1893; collected in *Terminations*) poignantly shows that an ailing novelist in his middle years may die in spite of wanting a second chance to prove himself capable of better work. "A second chance—*that's* the delusion," laments the failing artist.

The simple but devastating point of "The Death of the Lion" (*Yellow Book*, April 1894; collected in *Terminations*) is that high society will lionize a writer or an artist but pay no attention to his work. "The Next Time" (*Yellow Book*, July 1895) contrasts a novelist so superb that he cannot write a sloppy popular book no matter how hard he tries and a lady writer who writes best-sellers but longs to succeed with the discerning few and cannot. The lady writer, possibly patterned in part on the then-popular Francis Marion Crawford, whom James knew and envied to a degree, is named Jane Highmore, whose initials, like her professional traits, are the precise reverse of Henry James's. "The Figure in the Carpet" (*Cosmopolis*, January and February 1896; collected in *Embarrassments*) is James's most complex art anecdote. In recent years, especially since the appearance of Shlomith Rimmon's controversial book *The Concept of Ambiguity—the Example of James* (1977), it has been subjected to critical scrutiny nearly as intense as that applied to "The Turn of the Screw." The "figure in the carpet" is novelist Hugh Vereker's metaphor for the secret pattern underlying and animating his entire life's work. The inept critic-narrator writes a review of Vereker, who calls it routine twaddle but declines to aid the critic, explaining that the artist creates but does not explain, that the audience must respond creatively. That aesthetic dictum is one of James's most central.

Sex, marriage, and parent-offspring relations are also subjects of many short stories written during James's middle period. "The Visits" (published in the 28 May 1892 issue of *Black and White* as "The Visit"; collected in *The Private Life, The Wheel of Time, Lord Beaupré, The Visits, Collabora-*

tion, Owen Wingrave) depicts a young lady so remorseful about having revealed her sexual attraction to a young man that she literally dies of shame. In "Georgina's Reasons" (collected in *The Author of Beltraffio, Pandora, Georgina's Reasons, The Path of Duty, Four Meetings*) the heroine, Georgina Gressie, makes honorable Raymond Benyon promise not to tell anyone that they have secretly married and holds him to it–blithely committing bigamy even as he falls in love hopelessly elsewhere. As Granville H. Jones points out, readers give "neither Georgina nor Benyon . . . much sympathy"; he is too "placid and beaten," while she is a gorgonian horror. The story produced a sensation when it appeared in the *New York Sun* (20 and 27 July, 3 August 1884) and was then republished in the *Cincinnati Enquirer* under a scare headline about bigamy. In "The Modern Warning" (published in the June 1888 issue of *Harper's New Monthly Magazine* as "Two Countries"; collected in *The Aspern Papers, Louisa Pallant, The Modern Warning*) a sensitive woman's marriage is torn apart by cultural and political differences between her British husband and her American brother. "A London Life" (*Scribner's Magazine*, June-September 1888; collected in *A London Life, The Patagonia, The Liar, Mrs. Temperly*) features a single American girl, Laura Wing, shocked by the actions of Selina Berrington, her married sister, who is cavorting with a bearded lover and justifying the affair on the grounds that her husband is a cad. Krishna Baldev Vaid comments on Selina's "moral depravity," but John A. Clair criticizes Laura's "self-righteous moral indignation" and blames her "encompassing naïveté" for her failure to recognize Selina's effort to compromise her so that she cannot testify in Selina's divorce case. In one of James's most unpleasant stories, "The Marriages" (*Atlantic Monthly*, August 1891; collected in *The Lesson of the Master, The Marriages, The Pupil, Brooksmith, The Solution, Sir Edmund Orme*), a daughter wrecks her widowed father's plans for a second marriage and in the process almost ruins the career of her brother, whose marriage to a middle-aged hag their father's fiancée's money could have annulled. The convoluted plot of this rather mediocre story gives the lie to critics who contend that little happens in a typical Jamesian fiction. Submerged in "The Marriages" is queasy evidence supporting Stephen Spender's conclusion that in his novels and stories James alludes to "the sexual act . . . only as the merest formality."

The most powerful "family story" from James's middle phase is unquestionably "The Pupil" (*Longman's Magazine*, March and April 1891; collected in *The Lesson of the Master, The Marriages, The Pupil, Brooksmith, The Solution, Sir Edmund Orme*), one of the finest tales in world literature and often republished. James himself wrote lovingly, in a critical preface, of his inspiration for it: a doctor in Italy gossiped to him about "a wonderful American family, an odd adventurous, extravagant band, of high but rather unauthenticated pretensions, the most interesting member of which was a small boy, acute and precocious, afflicted with a heart of weak action, but beautifully intelligent, who saw their prowling precarious life exactly as it was, and measured and judged it, and measured and judged *them*, all round, ever so quaintly; presenting himself in short as an extraordinary little person." Yale-trained Pemberton accepts employment in the peripatetic Moreen family to tutor their bright son Morgan Moreen, and hangs on in spite of no pay, adversely judging–as does the boy– the parents as, in Putt's words, "dim social frauds and financial failures." But Pemberton may be close to fraudulent himself: he clings to Morgan too intensely for comfort and learns from him more than he teaches him; an Oxford youth whom Pemberton tutors fails; and when the Moreen family offers to let him adopt their little Morgan he hesitates–fatally.

One other type of story James continued to produce during his middle years was the ghostly tale. Some of the eighteen stories, written throughout James's career, included in *The Ghostly Tales of Henry James* (1948 [i.e., 1949]) are not particularly ghostly. The best of these stories from the 1890s are "Sir Edmund Orme," "The Private Life," "Sir Dominick Ferrand," "The Altar of the Dead," and "The Turn of the Screw."

The ghosts in "Sir Edmund Orme" (*Black and White*, Christmas number, 1891; collected in *The Lesson of the Master, The Marriages, The Pupil, Brooksmith, The Solution, Sir Edmund Orme*) and "Sir Dominick Ferrand" (published in the July and August 1892 issues of *Cosmopolitan Magazine* as "Jersey Villas"; collected in *The Real Thing and Other Tales*) are beneficent. In the first tale the ghost of a frustrated man who committed suicide after he was rejected by a woman scares that woman's daughter into accepting her suitor, who thus need not destroy himself. In the second tale the invisible "ghost" is really only an inspiring occult force: when a young writer suddenly elects to respect a dead man's papers, he is as suddenly rewarded by the deceased's illegitimate daughter, an attractive young widow. These two stories have the happiest endings in all of James's fiction. "The Private Life" (*Atlantic Monthly*, April 1892; collected in *The Private Life, The Wheel of Time, Lord Beaupré, The Visits, Collaboration, Owen Wingrave*) is quiet but enormously funny. Symmetrically balanced opposites are the polished statesman Lord Mellifont, so in need of an audience for his windy rhetoric that without it he literally ceases to exist, and playwright Clare Vawdrey, in essence so private that even while he stolidly endures vapid polite socializing his alternate identity is at his desk writing. Vawdrey has a creative private life; Mellifont is nothing but an empty public impression. In their edition of James's notebooks (1947) Matthiessen and Kenneth B. Murdock discuss James's treatment of the artists in public and private: his "treatment of this theme in terms of 'alternate identities' [in *The Private Life*] links the method of his fantasy, as he recognized, with that of his ghost stories." "The Altar of the Dead" (first published in *Terminations*) is one of James's tenderest and most provocative "ghostly tales." Edel sees behind the story James's feelings about the recent suicide of Constance Fenimore Woolson and even memories of dead Minny Temple. Putt praises James's vital description of external details and his "sustained eloquence." The hero, who has the habit of lighting votive candles for dead friends, meets a woman by candlelight in the church and learns that his dead enemy also wronged her; she then inspires him to burn a final candle for that enemy, whom she long ago has forgiven. That last candle eerily serves both men, as the hero, now spiritually whole, soon dies. Putt calls the confluence of the two men's spirits "clockwork coincidence," but the effect is mystically healing.

In James's most splendid tale, "The Turn of the Screw" (*Collier's Weekly*, 27 January-2 April 1898; collected in *The Two Magics: The Turn of the Screw; Covering End*, 1898), an unnamed governess, who narrates the main story, accepts the challenge of tutoring and overseeing the safety of two young children, Miles and Flora, whose parents are dead and whose handsome, wealthy uncle is indifferent to them, frequently leaving them alone with the servants at his estate, Bly. The governess, who is bright but may well be unstable, begins to see ghosts, and in the course of her narration many questions emerge in the reader's mind: Are the children as innocent as they seem? Are the ghosts real or perhaps living people, or are they projections of the governess's sexually inflamed imagination? James called this ambiguous and provocative story "a piece of ingenuity pure and simple, of cold artistic calculation, an *amusette* to catch those not easily caught . . . , the jaded, the disillusioned, the fastidious." Well over a hundred books and articles have offered different and often contradictory explications of "The Turn of the Screw," some electrifying, others ludicrous.

Roger Gard examined sales figures for several of James short-story collections published in the 1890s and concluded that they "only confirm the impression of James's rapid development into the writer of a small minority."

By 1897 James had entered his "major phase," which is marked most memorably by the publication of three of his finest novels–*The Wings of the Dove*, *The Ambassadors*, and *The Golden Bowl*–but which also includes the earlier, stylistically complex novels such as *What Maisie Knew*, *The Awkward Age*, and *The Sacred Fount*.

James also published thirty-five short stories between 1898 and 1910, when the last short story published during his lifetime, "A Round of Visits," appeared in the April and May issues of the *English Review* (collected in *The Finer Grain*, 1910). Edel regards these late tales as radically different from James's earlier short stories, saying that they "might have been written by someone else, so great a change has occurred." He also notes a new trend toward probing the unlived lives of sensitive older men, and concludes that James's vision was becoming more tragic, even existential.

Although no late story by James ever lacks significance, several tales published between 1898 and 1910 are thin. These weaker stories include "John Delavoy" (*Cosmopolis*, January and February 1898; collected in *The Soft Side*, 1900), about a critic whose work is too good to please an editor who wants him to make it more chatty; "The Great Condition" (*Anglo-Saxon Review*, June 1899; collected in *The Soft Side*), in which a widow rejects a suitor when he becomes suspicious of her past, which is blameless; "Maud-Evelyn" (*Atlantic Monthly*, April 1900; collected in *The Soft Side*) featuring an improbable trio–husband and wife, and male traveling companion, whom the couple adopt as their son-in-law, when, in fact, he never met their daughter, who died at age fourteen. Other less important stories include "Miss Gunton of Poughkeepsie" (*Cornhill Magazine*, May

1900; collected in *The Soft Side*), which shows an American girl forcing her Italian fiancé's mother to violate social protocol, and then callously jilting the son; in "Mrs. Medwin" (*Punch*, 28 August-18 September 1901; collected in *The Better Sort*) an American wastrel and his half sister get an out-of-favor woman, Mrs. Medwin, back into British society for a fee; in "Mora Montravers" (*English Review*, August and September 1909; collected in *The Finer Grain*) free-spirit Mora gets revenge on her meddling aunt, who objects to the girl's lodging with an artist in his studio, by accepting an annuity from her aunt as a bribe to marry him, then leaving him and giving him the annuity. In such stories James was occasionally repeating old situations, letting his readers sniff in their background the dry rot of old social conventions.

Perhaps the finest of James's late-phase short works are "The Great Good Place," "The Two Faces," "The Beldonald Holbein," "Flickerbridge," "The Beast in the Jungle," "The Birthplace," "The Papers," "The Jolly Corner," and "The Bench of Desolation." All deal with human failure, and each is rich with verbal embroidery.

"The Two Faces" (published in the 15 December 1900 issue of *Harper's Bazar* as "The Faces"; collected in *The Better Sort*) and "The Beldonald Holbein" (*Harper's New Monthly Magazine*, October 1901; collected in *The Better Sort*) are undervalued little anecdotes concerning jealousy and revenge. The first is filtered decorously through lucidly reflecting points of view; the second is livened by decorous humor. In "The Two Faces" a jilted woman gets even by fatally overdressing her successful female rival for her social debut. The story is critical of high society's penchant for relishing the humiliation of others. In "The Beldonald Holbein" the beautiful Lady Nina Beldonald hires a mousy old woman to be her companion and by her plainness to show off her employer's obvious physical charms; but an artist notices the old woman's resemblance to the subjects of Holbein's paintings and challenges so many painters to want her to sit for them that jealous Nina quickly dumps her and hires a harmlessly drab replacement.

A trio of tales dealing with the dangers of publicity are "Flickerbridge" (*Scribner's Magazine*, February 1902; collected in *The Better Sort*) and "The Birthplace" and "The Papers," both published for the first time in *The Better Sort*. James reviled cheap journalism and sideshows at sacred shrines. In "Flickerbridge" a sensitive American painter visits Flickerbridge, a gracious old estate in northern England, on the recommendation of his pushy journalist fiancée. Charmed by the place and fearing that his fiancée will spoil it with her efforts to publicize it, he breaks their engagement and leaves before she arrives.

"The Birthplace," which F. W. Dupee calls "one of the world's great tales," is a stunning satire. A dreary little librarian who obtains a position as caretaker at the birthplace of a renowned but unnamed English poet is soon grumbling because he is expected to help commercialize the place to increase the tourist trade. He is warned to mend his scholarly ways–and does so with a vengeance: he becomes such a conscienceless barker that he is given a raise. James laments the public's concern with gossip and biographical minutiae, finding it ironic that people would rather visit a famous writer's house than read his writings. "The Papers" focuses on a competent young British reporter and his girlfriend, also a reporter but only mediocre; a publicity-mad nonentity who is a member of Parliament; an equally eager playwright; and a supposedly publicity-shy widow who ultimately hungers to see her name in the tabloids, too. In a notebook entry James identifies the targets of his satire as "different shows of human egotism and the newspaper scramble." In addition, as Putt points out, James cannily included "Edwardian Fleet Street" local-color touches.

James never stopped playing variations on the theme of lost chances. Versions of it appear in a quartet of excellent late-phase stories–"The Great Good Place," "The Beast in the Jungle," "The Jolly Corner," and "The Bench of Desolation." In "The Great Good Place" (*Scribner's Magazine,* January 1900; collected in *The Soft Side*) James invites his readers to sympathize with a probably autobiographical hero who is oppressed one morning by the prospect of unfinished work and a crush of duties in the offing, including breakfast with a young guest who is just arriving. Suddenly he seems to awaken in a new environment, where all is peaceful. Sounds are pleasant, and footsteps are slow all about. When he eventually returns to reality, he finds himself rejuvenated and his affairs simplified by his young guest. McElderry calls the dream locale "a kind of monastic retreat," perhaps symbolizing "some inner resource, some privacy into which the round of daily concerns does not enter." The sense of this Shangri-La within each individual must never be lost, James seems to say, no matter how overwhelming the mundane may become.

"The Beast in the Jungle" (first published in *The Better Sort*), one of James's very best stories, examines psychoneurotic John Marcher, who declines to love May Bartram because he feels that out of the jungle of his life a special beast will spring at him: "a man of feeling didn't cause himself to be accompanied by a lady on a tiger-hunt." He is, however, happy to let her wait with him for the advent of that special something which will make his life extraordinary. As she ages into something resembling an artificial lily under glass, or even an impenetrable sphinx, she comes to understand what that something will be. She dies devotedly hoping that he will never know the truth; but when Marcher visits her grave, he chances to see the face of a nearby mourner seared by grief and realizes too late that his fate is to be the one man in all the world to whom nothing happens. Clifton Fadiman calls "The Beast in the Jungle" a "myth . . . [which] gathers up in its sinuosities a part of the prime and universal experience of mankind. From it even the palest stain of the trivial is absent." Its images of hunting, floating, stabbing, burning, and finally freezing are nightmare elements in a tale of urban loneliness and loss.

"The Jolly Corner" (*English Review,* December 1908; collected in volume 17 of *The Novels and Tales of Henry James,* the New York Edition) presents a long-expatriated American who wonders intensely–as James himself must have wondered, particularly after his 1904-1905 visit to America–what he would have been like if he had stayed in his native land and sought "success" rather than culture. Late at night he visits his boyhood home and suddenly finds himself face to face with his alter ego. Almost as frequently anthologized as "The Beast in the Jungle," this story is enlivened by autobiographical touches, a love interest, and no little ambiguity to challenge its readers.

"The Bench of Desolation" (*Putnam's Magazine,* October-December 1909, January 1910; collected in *The Finer Grain*) is lengthy (18,200 words) and morbid. Long ago warned by his fiancée Kate Cookham that if he did not go through with marriage she would sue him, Herbert Dodd paid her off, married another, became a widower, and staggered for a decade under crushing debt. Then Kate returns with his capital plus interest, explaining that she aimed only to test him and has loved only him. She spurns a suitor to prove that fact and shares a bench with him. In spite of Edmund Wilson's early praise of "The Bench of Desolation" as "beautifully written and wonderfully developed . . . [,] a sort of poem of loneliness and poverty," Putt is surely closer to the truth when he labels the story a "morbidly masturbatory minor achievement. . . ." The work has value as absurdist lyric, but James himself might not have been fully aware of the depth of its implications.

The sales of James's books of short fiction during his major phase were slightly better than those of several earlier collections. Though these books did not sell phenomenally, James became increasingly respected by discerning critics and a loyal coterie of admirers. According to Edel, "the tales he collected in the three volumes of the new century, *The Soft Side* of 1900, *The Better Sort* of 1903 and *The Finer Grain* of 1910, remain among the most important fiction written during America's gilded age and England's Edwardian era." Never popular with the masses, James's works were little read for about a quarter of a century following his death in 1916. But during World War II James began to be appreciated again, and the so-called James boom has shown no letup.

James's writings are psychologically profound and stylistically challenging; yet, as Richard P. Blackmur concludes, not even his two best subjects–social conventions and the artistic vocation–were "ever enough to bring out in James a mastery of substance equal to his mastery of form." Still, he mounted his psychological dramas with taut excitement and painterly charm. In his depictions of the clash of American innocence and Old World sophistication, his naïfs may often fail to achieve personal joy or social success, but they are exemplars of morality. They illustrate the worth of consideration and forgiveness over meddling, coercion, and revenge. They expose false values such as unthinking patriotism, ambition for fame and position, and fatal pride in appearance, pedigree, and social connections. James had faith in art rather than formal religion, established power, and the "things" of this world. Ever antiromantic and individualistic, he espoused professional freedom over personal "love," aesthetic involvement rather than smug Philistinism, aloofness, and the unlived life.

James's complex style attracts only active, ingenious readers. His diction, syntax, descriptions, dialogue, imagery, tone, and indirections are subtly nuanced. His use of the restricted point of view makes his fiction especially difficult to read, and modern; the reader shares the limits and delusions of James's supersubtle fry, as he called his reflectors of fine consciousness. Like Nathaniel Haw-

thorne, Herman Melville, and Eugene O'Neill, among others, James presents more challenging dilemmas than pontifical answers.

Henry James saw ahead of his age, and hence his work wears well. He tentatively explored eroticism, imaginative quests through time and beyond the caged psyche, existential negativism, and even postmodern absurdism. Much refined fiction in English after James, and perhaps a great deal not in English as well, has been at least indirectly influenced by his theory and practice. James perpetually exercised his probing, recording aesthetic consciousness.

Letters:
Henry James: Letters, edited by Leon Edel, 4 volumes (Cambridge & London: Harvard University Press, 1974-1984).

Interviews:
Norman Page, ed., *Henry James: Interviews and Recollections* (New York: Scribners, 1984).

Bibliographies:
Robert L. Gale, "Henry James," in *Eight American Authors: A Review of Research and Criticism*, revised edition, edited by James Woodress (New York: Norton, 1971), pp. 321-375;

Kristin Pruitt McColgan, *Henry James 1917-1959: A Reference Guide* (Boston: G. K. Hall, 1979);

Dorothy McInnis Scura, *Henry James 1960-1974: A Reference Guide* (Boston: G. K. Hall, 1979);

Leon Edel and Dan H. Laurence, *A Bibliography of Henry James*, second revised edition (New York: Oxford University Press, 1982);

Linda J. Taylor, *Henry James 1866-1916: A Reference Guide* (Boston: G. K. Hall, 1982).

Biographies:
Simon Nowell-Smith, *The Legend of the Master: Henry James* (New York: Scribners, 1948);

F. W. Dupee, *Henry James* (New York: Sloane, 1951; revised edition, Garden City, N.Y.: Doubleday, 1956);

Leon Edel, *Henry James: The Untried Years, 1843-1870* (Philadelphia: Lippincott, 1953); *Henry James: The Conquest of London, 1870-1881* (Philadelphia: Lippincott, 1962); *Henry James: The Middle Years, 1882-1895* (Philadelphia: Lippincott, 1962); *Henry James: The Treacherous Years, 1895-1901* (Philadelphia: Lippincott, 1969); *Henry James: The Master, 1901-1916* (Philadelphia: Lippincott, 1972);

these five volumes abridged as *Henry James: A Life* (New York: Harper & Row, 1987);

Robert Charles LeClair, *The Young Henry James, 1843-1870* (New York: Bookman, 1955);

Harry T. Moore, *Henry James* (New York: Viking, 1974).

References:

Elizabeth Allen, *A Woman's Place in the Novels of Henry James* (New York: St. Martin's, 1984);

Osborn Andreas, *Henry James and the Expanding Horizon: A Study of the Meaning and Basic Themes of James's Fiction* (Seattle: University of Washington, 1948);

Paul B. Armstrong, *The Phenomenology of Henry James* (Chapel Hill: University of North Carolina Press, 1983);

Joseph Warren Beach, *The Method of Henry James* (New Haven: Yale University Press, 1918; revised and enlarged edition, Philadelphia: Saifer, 1954);

Richard P. Blackmur, "Henry James," in *Literary History of the United States,* edited by Robert E. Spiller and others, revised edition (New York: Macmillan, 1953), pp. 1039-1064;

Ralph Bogardus, *Pictures and Texts: Henry James, A. L. Colburn, and New Ways of Seeing in Literary Culture* (Ann Arbor: UMI Research, 1985);

Peter Buitenhuis, *The Grasping Imagination: The American Writings of Henry James* (Toronto: University of Toronto Press, 1970);

John A. Clair, *The Ironic Dimension in the Fiction of Henry James* (Pittsburgh: Duquesne University Press, 1965);

Lauren T. Cowdery, *The Nouvelle of Henry James in Theory and Practice* (Ann Arbor: UMI Research, 1986);

Daniel Mark Fogel, *Henry James and the Structure of the Romantic Imagination* (Baton Rouge: Louisiana State University Press, 1981);

Robert L. Gale, *The Caught Image: Figurative Language in the Fiction of Henry James* (Chapel Hill: University of North Carolina Press, 1964);

Gale, *Plots and Characters in the Fiction of Henry James* (Hamden, Conn.: Archon, 1965);

Roger Gard, ed., *Henry James: The Critical Heritage* (London: Routledge & Kegan Paul, 1968);

Granville H. Jones, *Henry James's Psychology of Experience* (The Hague: Mouton, 1975);

Cornelia Pulsifer Kelley, *The Early Development of Henry James* (Urbana: University of Illinois Press, 1930; revised, 1965);

James J. Kirschke, *Henry James and Impressionism* (Troy, N.Y.: Whitston, 1981);

James Kraft, *The Early Tales of Henry James* (Carbondale: Southern Illinois University Press, 1969);

Dorothea Krook, *The Ordeal of Consciousness in Henry James* (Cambridge: Cambridge University Press, 1962);

Glenda Leeming, *Who's Who in Henry James* (New York: Taplinger, 1976);

F. O. Matthiessen, *Henry James: The Major Phase* (New York: Oxford University Press, 1944);

Bruce R. McElderry, Jr., *Henry James* (New York: Twayne, 1965);

Gordon Pirie, *Henry James* (London: Evans, 1975);

Strother B. Purdy, *The Hole in the Fabric: Science, Contemporary Literature, and Henry James* (Pittsburgh: University of Pittsburgh Press, 1977);

S. Gorley Putt, *A Reader's Guide to Henry James* (Ithaca: Cornell University Press, 1966);

Shlomith Rimmon, *The Concept of Ambiguity–the Example of James* (Chicago: University of Chicago Press, 1977);

John Carlos Rowe, *The Theoretical Dimensions of Henry James* (Madison: University of Wisconsin Press, 1984);

Charles Thomas Samuels, *The Ambiguity of Henry James* (Urbana: University of Illinois Press, 1971);

Daniel J. Schneider, *The Crystal Cage: Adventures of the Imagination in the Fiction of Henry James* (Lawrence: Regents Press of Kansas, 1978);

Sister M. Corona Sharp, *The "Confidante" in Henry James: Evolution and Moral Value of a Fictive Character* (Notre Dame: University of Notre Dame Press, 1965);

Muriel G. Shine, *The Fictional Children of Henry James* (Chapel Hill: University of North Carolina Press, 1969);

Stephen Spender, *The Destructive Element: A Study of Modern Writers and Beliefs* (London: Cape, 1935);

Mary Doyle Springer, *A Rhetoric of Literary Character: Some Women of Henry James* (Chicago: University of Chicago Press, 1978);

William T. Stafford, *A Name, Title, and Place. Index to the Critical Writings of Henry James* (Englewood, Colo.: Microcard Editions Books, 1975);

Elizabeth Stevenson, *The Crooked Corridor: A Study of Henry James* (New York: Macmillan, 1949);

Adeline R. Tintner, *The Book World of Henry James: Appropriating the Classics* (Ann Arbor & London: UMI Research, 1987);

Tintner, *The Museum World of Henry James* (Ann Arbor: UMI Research, 1986);

Krishna Baldev Vaid, *Technique in the Tales of Henry James* (Cambridge, Mass.: Harvard University Press, 1964);

William Veeder, *Henry James–The Lessons of the Master: Popular Fiction and Personal Style in the Nineteenth Century* (Chicago: University of Chicago Press, 1975);

Edward Wagenknecht, *Eve and Henry James: Portraits of Women and Girls in His Fiction* (Norman: University of Oklahoma Press, 1978);

Wagenknecht, *The Tales of Henry James* (New York: Unger, 1984);

J. A. Ward, *The Imagination of Disaster: Evil in the Fiction of Henry James* (Lincoln: University of Nebraska Press, 1961);

Katherine Weissbourd, *Growing Up in the James Family: Henry James, Sr. as Son and Father* (Ann Arbor: UMI Research, 1985);

Edmund Wilson, *The Triple Thinkers: Ten Essays on Literature* (New York: Oxford University Press, 1938; revised and enlarged, 1948).

Papers:

Most of James's manuscripts and other papers are in the Houghton Library at Harvard University. Other such materials are in the Collection of American Literature at the Beinecke Library, Yale University, and in the Library of Congress. The libraries of the following institutions also have notable collections: the University of Leeds, Colby College, the University of Rochester, the University of Chicago, the University of California at Los Angeles, the British Museum, the archives of Charles Scribner's Sons at Princeton University, the Huntington Library, the Morgan Library, the New York Public Library, the Buffalo Public Library, and the Century Association in New York City.

Sarah Orne Jewett

(3 September 1849-24 June 1909)

David D. Anderson
Michigan State University

See also the Jewett entry in *DLB 12: American Realists and Naturalists.*

BOOKS: *Deephaven* (Boston: Osgood, 1877; London: Osgood, McIlvaine, 1893);

Play Days: A Book of Stories for Children (Boston: Houghton, Osgood, 1878);

Old Friends and New (Boston: Houghton, Osgood, 1879);

Country By-Ways (Boston: Houghton, Mifflin, 1881; London: Trübner, 1882);

The Mate of the Daylight, and Friends Ashore (Boston: Houghton, Mifflin, 1884);

A Country Doctor (Boston & New York: Houghton, Mifflin, 1884);

A Marsh Island (Boston & New York: Houghton, Mifflin, 1885);

A White Heron and Other Stories (Boston & New York: Houghton, Mifflin, 1886);

The Story of the Normans, Told Chiefly in Relation to Their Conquest of England (New York: Putnam's, 1887; London: Unwin, 1898);

The King of Folly Island and Other People (Boston & New York: Houghton, Mifflin, 1888; London: Duckworth, 1903);

Betty Leicester, A Story for Girls (Boston & New York: Houghton, Mifflin, 1890);

Strangers and Wayfarers (Boston & New York: Houghton, Mifflin, 1890; London: Osgood, McIlvaine, 1891);

A Native of Winby and Other Tales (Boston: Houghton, Mifflin, 1893);

Betty Leicester's English Xmas, A New Chapter of an Old Story (Baltimore: Privately printed, 1894); republished as *Betty Leicester's Christmas* (Boston & New York: Houghton, Mifflin, 1899);

The Life of Nancy (Boston & New York: Houghton, Mifflin, 1895; London: Longman's, 1895);

The Country of the Pointed Firs (Boston & New York: Houghton, Mifflin, 1896; London: Unwin, 1896);

The Queen's Twin and Other Stories (Boston & New York: Houghton, Mifflin, 1899; London: Smith, Elder, 1900);

The Tory Lover (Boston: Houghton, Mifflin, 1901; London: Smith, Elder, 1901);

An Empty Purse: A Christmas Story (Boston: Privately printed, 1905);

Verses, edited by M. A. DeWolfe Howe (Boston: Privately printed, 1916);

The Only Rose and Other Tales (London: Cape, 1937);

*The World of Dunnet Landing: A Sarah Orne Jewett
Collection*, edited by David Bonnell Green
(Lincoln: University of Nebraska Press,
1962);

The Uncollected Short Stories of Sarah Orne Jewett, edited by Richard Cary (Waterville, Maine:
Colby College Press, 1971).

Collections: *Tales of New England* (Boston & New
York: Houghton, Mifflin, 1890; London: Osgood, McIlvaine, 1893);

Stories and Tales, 7 volumes (Boston & New York:
Houghton Mifflin, 1910; London: Constable, 1911);

The Best Stories of Sarah Orne Jewett, 2 volumes, edited by Willa Cather (Boston: Houghton
Mifflin, 1925).

Although not included among major American writers, Sarah Orne Jewett ranks high among
those who have drawn upon the people, places,
and culture of nineteenth-century New England
for the substance of their work, and many of her
"sketches," as she called her short stories, are representative of American regional writing at its
best. She was born in South Berwick, Maine, on
3 September 1849 into an old and wealthy New England family of shipowners and merchants. Her
father, Theodore Herman Jewett, to whom she
was very close, was a respected local physician;
her mother, Caroline Frances Perry Jewett, was a
collateral descendent of Anne Bradstreet. Educated at home with her two sisters and at Miss
Payne's School and Berwick Academy, from
which she graduated in 1866, she later said she
was an indifferent student. She often commented
that her real education came from her father, as
he shared with her his interests in and knowledge of nature and of the English classics. As she
accompanied him on house calls she made many
of the observations and gained many of the insights that later inspired her fiction.

In later years she frequently quoted her father's advice to her in her letters to young writers. Two years before she published the first of
her Maine stories, "The Shore House," in the *Atlantic Monthly* (September 1873), she wrote on the
inside cover of her diary for 1871 the literary principle, gleaned from her father's advice, that was
to control her work:

Father said this one day: "A story should be managed so that it should *suggest* interesting things to
the *reader* instead of the author's doing all the
thinking for him and setting it before him in

black and white. The best compliment is for the
reader to say Why didn't he put in "this" or
"that."

Fond of writing down her ideas and observations, at first in verse and later in prose, from
the time she was quite small, Jewett published
her first story when she was eighteen; her only
melodramatic short story, "Jenny Garrow's Lovers," appeared under the name of A. C. Eliot in
the 18 January 1868 issue of the *Flag of Our
Union*. On the copy of the journal in the Jewett Collection in the Houghton Library at Harvard she
wrote in pencil, "The first story I ever wrote." In
December 1869 she published "Mr. Bruce," also
as A. C. Eliot, in the *Atlantic Monthly*. After these initial successes she began publishing stories and
verse for children in *Our Young Folks*, *St. Nicholas*,
the *Independent*, and other magazines. By 1873,
however, she began to write most frequently for
adults, and her contributions to children's literature declined as she found the vocation that she
had come to regard as her duty. But two of her
last stories were published in the *Youth's Companion*.

In the three decades following her first publications, until she was seriously injured in a carriage accident in 1902, Jewett published nearly
150 stories and sketches in most of the leading
magazines of her time; she also published more
than two dozen children's stories as well as
verses, three episodic novels for adults, two novels for girls, and a children's history. The best of
her stories, in her estimation, were collected in
ten volumes for general readership and one for
children. By 1885 she had become a significant
New England-American writer, and her works between that year and the end of the nineteenth century are her most perceptive and best executed.
This record, a considerable contribution to the literature of her time, was, however, described by
Henry James without irony as "her beautiful little
quantum of achievement."

Such a statement is far from definitive, however, either in James's time or today. Because
James sincerely admired only a few of her stories
he dismissed her substantial chapter in American
and New England writing as essentially subliterary, and, until comparatively recently, when
interest in women writers and regional writing
has increased, most American critics have been
willing to do the same. But whatever her shortcomings as an artist—and they are neither as numerous nor as serious as her detractors insist—

Jewett's role as social observer and recorder is significant, and relatively few of her stories are failures either as art or as commentary.

In her first story, "Jenny Garrow's Lovers," first collected in *The Uncollected Short Stories of Sarah Orne Jewett* (1971), Jewett gave no indication of either the subject matter or the insights that were to mark her best work. Set in the English countryside, the story concerns two brothers, Will and Dick, who compete for Jenny's hand. Will disappears; Dick is accused of his murder and sent to prison; Jenny dies of the plague. After five years Will returns, explaining that after Jenny rejected him he had gone to sea. Dick is released, and the brothers, reunited, live and die unmarried.

The plot, a refurbishing of the most melodramatic stories of her time, is so replete with Victorian clichés–three deaths, false imprisonment, broken hearts, and the plague–that it is beyond belief, but in some ways it foreshadows her later work: its style is sparse–perhaps her father's advice was already being followed–and the story is told in first-person retrospect by an elderly lady, who had known the participants in her youth and who prefaces her tale with the disarming remark that "I'm not much used to writing–I may as well tell you, I'm not used to it at all, for you will find it out soon enough."

The narrator concludes these prefatory remarks, however, with a comment that not only foreshadows Jewett's best work but also perhaps reflects her father's advice: "I've heard people say that sometimes it is the telling, and sometimes the story, and my story is interesting enough, with an old woman to write it, even, instead of one of those young men or women who use such long words, and have the same story over and over again, with different names." Already she was conscious of the art of her craft, although she concludes, naively but in keeping with her persona, with the question, "How do you like my story?"

Her second story, "Mr. Bruce," collected in *Old Friends and New* (1879), combines the narrative technique of her first story with her first use of a New England setting, characters, and tradition. Told by elderly, unmarried Aunt Mary to her twenty-year-old niece, it has an additional narrative complication: it is presumably a story told to Mary by another older woman, Margaret Tarrant, of an incident more than twenty years in the past. With genteel humor reflecting the nature of the double narrative, Jewett sets her story

Ambrotype of Jewett at age eight

firmly into the social pattern of the time: Margaret's tale is told before the fire on a stormy night after a dinner party; the story is that of her older sister, Kitty, and her first meeting with Mr. Bruce, the man who is later to become her husband. Mr. Bruce, an Englishman and a business connection of the girls' father, is invited to dinner, but the Irish maid is ill. As a lark, Kitty, knowing the dinner will bore her, volunteers to take the maid's place and character. The masquerade is carried off perfectly, complete with brogue and mannerisms, and Mr. Bruce responds as he would to a servant, but he is attracted to her. Later Mr. Bruce meets Kitty in her real role; his surprised bewilderment is matched by her amusement, and the two finally marry, to live happily ever after.

The story is framed by Margaret's telling, and the story itself is amusing and light, but its narrative flow is marred by the conventional inclusion of two long letters from Kitty to her sister describing the growing relationship. Nevertheless, the story marks an important advance in Jewett's apprenticeship. Unlike "Jenny Garrow's Lovers," the telling rather than the story has become important; the characters are deftly sketched; the social setting is clearly and sympathetically portrayed;

and the story approaches the realism she was seeking, although it ultimately eludes her at this point.

Following the first of her children's stories, a fantasy, "The Shipwrecked Buttons," written by "Alice Eliot," published in *Riverside Magazine* (January 1870) and collected in *Play Days* (1878), Jewett published the third of her apprenticeship stories, "The Girl with the Cannon Dresses," in the August 1870 issue of *Riverside Magazine*. First collected in *The Uncollected Short Stories of Sarah Orne Jewett*, the story is related to the children's stories with which she was primarily to concern herself during the next several years, but she uses the setting and characters of her own rural New England and her new quiet tone. Unlike the earlier stories, which seem to have been told to Jewett, this one appears to have been drawn from her own experience. The first story published under her own name, it combines the lightness of childhood with the shadow of the darker adult world beyond as it describes the psychological coming-of-age of Alice Channing, an eighteen-year-old girl who is sent to the New Hampshire hills with a former housekeeper to recuperate from an illness. Her illness appears to a kindly country doctor to have a psychological dimension best cured by a closeness to nature and to the former housekeeper, of whom she is fond. The cure works, as Alice not only discovers the natural world of woods and animals but meets Dulcidora Bunt, a younger girl known as Dulcy. The two create a secret world of their own as Alice leads the younger girl toward greater sophistication, in the course of which she discovers her own maturity in the most pleasant summer of her life.

In the story, foreshadowing her own life as well as the substance of future stories, Jewett emphasizes both the closeness of the relationship between the two girls and that between the girls and the natural world of which they are a part. But the idyll of the two girls, momentarily alone in time and in their own natural and created worlds, is, Alice knows, for all its importance, as fleeting as the summer. Alice knows, too, that each must make her own private world alone in the greater and different societies from which each has come. Matured by these realizations, Alice is an adult in her "grown-up clothes."

The story marks an important advance over the earlier two in the indigenous nature of the setting, in the newly discovered psychological dimension, and in the quiet reality of the rural New England world, but these advances were put aside

for two years as Jewett concentrated on her children's stories, most of them to be collected in *Play Days*. Yet, a growing literary relationship with William Dean Howells, assistant editor of the *Atlantic* and, after 1871, editor in chief of that magazine, was to reshape and redirect her literary career. Another professional relationship that became intimate–with James T. Fields, Howells's predecessor as editor of the *Atlantic* and editor at Ticknor and Fields, the leading Boston publishing house, and with Fields's wife, Annie, his unofficial assistant–was to reshape her personal life.

Jewett had first come in touch with Howells when she sent "Mr. Bruce" to the *Atlantic* and Howells, after anonymous comments, agreed to accept it. When in 1873 she submitted "The Shore House" to him, he accepted it also. He was enthusiastic about its realism and its style, encouraging her to continue in that almost plotless but vivid vein and suggesting that she collect "The Shore House" and other sketches and stories in what was to become *Deephaven* (1877), published by Fields's publishing house, which by then had become James R. Osgood and Company.

Fields was also a well-known author and lecturer, one of Boston's most prominent literary figures, and Annie Fields conducted a literary salon at their home, to which Jewett was welcomed after the publication of *Deephaven*. Annie Fields and Jewett became quite close, a relationship that became intense after James T. Fields's death in 1881 and that continued until Jewett's death in 1909. Although ignored or minimized by earlier biographers, the relationship, which may or may not have been lesbian, replaced Jewett's earlier closeness to her father as the central relationship in her life. The Jewett papers at Colby College and at Harvard contain many intimate letters between them, including Jewett's unpublished love letters to Annie Fields. The two traveled to Europe together four times, and Jewett spent half of each year at South Berwick and half with Annie Fields in Boston or at Fields's summer home at Manchester-by-the-Sea. Not only did Annie Fields contribute criticism and encouragement to Jewett during their long relationship, but after Jewett's death she edited and published a volume of Jewett's letters. Unfortunately, however, she deleted the intimacies and consequently misled later scholars and critics about the depth of the relationship, contributing to the enduring mythical portrait of Jewett as passionless in her life as well as in her work. The letters and notes between the two reveal much of Jewett's emotional as well as personal and literary sides.

The publication of *Deephaven*, with the inscription "I dedicate this story of out-of-door life and country people first to my mother and father, my two best friends, and also to all my other friends, whose names I say to myself lovingly, though I do not write them here," marked Jewett's emergence as a writer. John Greenleaf Whittier wrote of it, "I know of nothing better in our literature of the kind," and Howells wrote playfully, "Don't be too proud, now that your book has succeeded so splendidly, to send some sketches and stories to your old friend, the 'Atlantic Monthly.'" *Deephaven* did not, however, receive uniformly glowing reviews. The *New York Times* commented that "It is by some mistake, doubtless, that it got in print at all." Nevertheless, the book appeared at the timely moment when local color was making itself felt in a literature leaving romanticism behind as it moved toward a new realism. It appeared, too, in the decade that Mark Twain, Bret Harte, and George Washington Cable came to national prominence. Jewett, her admirers insisted, had begun to do for New England what the others were doing for the South and the West.

Neither the best nor the most enduring of her work, although it has been frequently republished, *Deephaven* is, however, not entirely the "beginning raw work" that Willa Cather called it. It is, instead, a collection of sketches only loosely and arbitrarily related by the presence of two girls who come to stay for the summer in the town. Consisting of thirteen parts–"Kate Lancaster's Plan" and "The Brandon House and the Lighthouse" from "The Shore House"; "My Lady Brandon and the Widow Jim," previously unpublished; "Deephaven Society," "The Captains," and "Danny" from "Deephaven Cronies," published in the *Atlantic Monthly* (September 1875); "Captain Sands," previously unpublished; "The Circus at Denby," revised from "Deephaven Cronies"; "Mrs. Bonny," "In Shadow," and "Miss Chauncy" from "Deephaven Excursions," published in the *Atlantic Monthly* (September 1876); and "Last Days in Deephaven," revised from "Deephaven Cronies"–the work suffers from attempting to become what it is not, a nearly chronological story of the girls' experiences and observations during the summer. On the threshold of adulthood–although both are twenty-four years old–the girls explore the town and its environs, learning to know the people and their ways.

Front cover for Jewett's first collection of stories, which the author described in her dedication as the "story of out-of-door life and country people"

Through their eyes and especially through Helen's narration, the reader sees the village of Deephaven in decline, its once-strong ties to the sea now little more than a memory, its women dominant, its men, many with the courtesy title of captain, little more than shadows of a once-vigorous past. The young people are largely gone to another life, while the old maintain an archaic caste structure that emphasizes an empty but touching dignity.

The presence of the girls provides a unifying device not unlike that of Sherwood Anderson's use of George Willard in *Winesburg, Ohio* (1919), but unlike George, the girls do not mature, nor do they actively participate in the activities of the town or listen more than superficially to its residents. Many of the residents are grotesques, but because the reader sees them only in relationship to place and time they do not attain the individuality of Anderson's grotesques. Each of them remains unknown to the girls in spite of their propensity to sometimes impertinent questioning, and these grotesques are consequently less than individuals to the reader. Jewett's use of the girls has another unifying dimension: the girls live an intimate life of their own, in but not of the community they observe. Just as the girls are foreign to the town, seen only superficially as strangers, the nature of their relationship is alien to its values as that relationship is suggested, but not defined, by the author.

The book's real merit is the result of its other unifying device: the town that is dying around its people. The first sketch, "Kate Lancaster's Plan," introduces Mrs. Kew, the lighthouse-keeper's wife, memorable for her resigned isolation; "My Lady Brandon" introduces Mrs. Jim Patton, the elderly widowed housekeeper who has found a haven and a refuge in the town and reveals the horror of her marriage; "The Captains" describes the old men who, no longer "seaworthy," endure; "Danny" and "Captain Sands" describe in more detail the once-active lives of the old men and their memories of what once had been; "Mrs. Bonny" is a more detailed portrait of an old woman who leads a solitary but full life in a clearing in the woods; "Miss Chauncy" is the insane but gentle remnant of a once-great family, living in a house full of memories.

Interspersed with the character sketches, each of them placed in a detailed, crystal-clear setting, are sketches of places and traditions: "The Brandon House and the Lighthouse" are seen in Baedecker detail, the Brandon House drawn clearly from the Jewett house in South Berwick; the town's hierarchy is shown in "Deephaven Society"; the dreary, but to the people exciting, performance of a shabby circus and Mrs. Kew's meeting with a tragic old friend, the grossly mislabeled "Kentucky Giantess," is deftly portrayed; the description of the circus is combined with the description of a visit to a lecture on "The Elements of True Manhood"—a dull, inappropriate talk to an audience of children, women, a few old men, and the deaf-as-a-post church sexton. The fishing and sea-story adventure of "Cunner-Fishing" is clear, as are the omnipresence of death and the living tragedies left behind in "In Shadow."

Together, the town and its people are clearly portrayed. The lives of the girls and their eager curiosity are often almost lost in the gloom of the past, and their function as observer-interviewers is extraneous to the town and the story. But in describing the town, the people, and the mores of both, Jewett is at times first-

rate; an atmosphere of serenity at odds with time and decay pervades the work; tragedy is somehow absorbed if not overcome; and life moves inevitably but with dignity to its end.

Two particular characteristics of the work are impressive: Jewett's re-creation of Maine speech, not only in its rhythms but in its vivid idioms; and her portrayal of the sea—the infinite—on the shores and surface of which human life ekes out its brief existence. The town, the people, the times die, but the sea goes on.

Secure in her art, cognizant of what she saw as her duty, Jewett continued to write and to publish in journals, increasingly thinking of her sketches as part of a unified whole; but she would not again use the obvious devices of *Deephaven* to make them so. After publishing *Play Days* in 1878, she put together older and newly published stories in 1879 under the title of *Old Friends and New*. It is composed of seven stories, six of them previously published: "A Lost Lover" (*Atlantic Monthly*, March 1878); "A Sorrowful Guest" (published as "Missing" in *Sunday Afternoon*, July 1879); "A Late Supper" (*Sunday Afternoon*, January 1878); "Mr. Bruce" (*Atlantic Monthly*, December 1869); "Miss Sydney's Flowers" (*Independent*, 16 July 1874); the previously unpublished "Lady Ferry" (when Howells rejected it for the *Atlantic*, Jewett commented "I still think he made a mistake" in a letter to Sara Norton, 12 November 1907); and "A Bit of Shore Life" (*Atlantic Monthly*, August 1879).

Jewett made no attempt to unify the collection through either characters or setting; yet the book, although uneven, presents a clearer definition of the themes and characters that were to dominate Jewett's best work: the elderly woman alone in a society that is passing by her; the worthless husband or lover; contrasts between rich and poor; the omnipresence of a fading past accentuated by vivid natural beauty; the sensitivity of a young woman interested in people; and the recognition of the reality of things neither seen nor understood. Too frequently, however, the stories are marred by the extraneous inclusion of morals that are conventionally Christian and Victorian.

The first story, "A Lost Lover," is improbable in its reliance upon unlikely coincidence and in the sentimentality of the author's comments at the end. The story focuses on the sort of person too frequently found or rumored to exist in nineteenth-century New England seafaring towns: the unmarried woman who waits faithfully for a lover apparently lost at sea. Miss

Horatia Dane, well preserved in her isolation, has waited for nearly thirty years, oblivious to the fading gossip of the town, much of which suggests that she is better off without her apparently lost love. While a romantic twenty-year-old relative, Nellie, is visiting her, a tramp appears at the door. Sensing a sympathetic ear, he tells his fantastic story of his sea journey as a youth, shipwreck and rescue off the China coast, capture by pirates, and establishment of a family somewhere in Australia. While he tells her the story, Miss Dane recognizes him as her lost lover, but, saying nothing as she learns about vice from the man she had loved, she gives him ten dollars and sends him on his way. Confused, she nevertheless keeps the secret, knowing that the romance in her life is gone.

"A Sorrowful Guest," set in Boston, turns on two improbable coincidences that may or may not include the appearance of a ghost. A post-Civil War story based on the chance meeting of former comrades, it records a wartime promise, an apparent death in combat, and the conviction of Whiston, a guest in a fashionable home, that the appearance of a comrade's ghost means that he is going to die. Whiston goes into abrupt decline and dies, whereupon the presumed-dead comrade appears as an injured wastrel who admits that he saw but avoided the weak Whiston. The hosts, a doctor who served in the war and his young sister, keep both secrets, and the young woman ponders on the mysteries of good and evil, courage and cowardice.

"A Late Supper" is an improbable but delightful story set in the country town of Brocton. The story is that of Miss Catherine Spring, a maiden lady living alone, whose income has decreased so that she must leave her home unless she can find paying guests for the summer. No boarders materialize, but relatives from the city stop in, and she goes next door, across the railroad tracks, to borrow milk. On her return a stopped train is blocking her way, and, regretting that her family had sold the land to the railroad, she begins to climb through the cars. The train starts; she is frightened, but a young lady passenger befriends her, and she has an unexpected but delightful journey to the next town. She finally arrives home to give her guests a late supper, and the next day the young lady writes that she and her aunt will become Miss Spring's boarders. Her home is saved; she has pleasant company; and she is able to take in a poor neighborhood child whom she has befriended.

In this story Jewett includes many of her favorite themes and characters: the problems of the elderly unmarried woman living alone, the reality of poverty, the reward of virtue, the intrusion of the new society into the old, the young woman who befriends the old, and the closeness of nature and beauty in the country town. But in this story her touch is light, and the story is marred only by the ubiquitous moral at the end. Miss Spring remains one of Jewett's most memorable ladies.

Following "Mr. Bruce," the fifth of the stories is "Miss Sydney's Flowers," the best in the collection and one of Jewett's most logically and completely developed stories. Set in a country town that is becoming a city, it describes the transition of a proud, selfish, wealthy maiden lady who lives alone, a remnant of the past, into a caring human being. Upset when a new commercial street is cut beside her old house and annoyed by the fascination of idle passersby with the flowers in her greenhouse, she considers screening it but knows the flowers will suffer. Eventually the attention pleases her, and after initial resentment she becomes interested in an old woman who has begun to sell candy on the new street. She invites the woman into her home, and, learning of her dire predicament, she gives help to the old woman and her crippled, lonely sister. Miss Sydney's transition becomes public knowledge as her goodness increases, thus providing a moral involving flowers and goodness, the only jarring note in the story.

"Lady Ferry," like "A Sorrowful Guest," deals with the improbable with overtones of the supernatural. The story is Jewett's first attempt to use Puritan legend—that of the old woman condemned to immortality—in a nineteenth-century setting. Lady Ferry lives mysteriously and presumably immortally with an apparently unrelated family in a house by a ferry. Local lore insists that the old lady has lived forever, and she confuses in her mind the generations she has seen. A young girl visiting the family with which the old lady lives is fascinated by her and befriends her. One night the girl sees—or dreams of—an elegant old-fashioned party in the house, the merry guests finally departing by boat. The next morning the girl finds a silver buckle on the lawn, and the ferry boats are gone, driven away by the wind. The girl keeps her vision—or dream—secret but gives the buckle to the old woman before she returns to her home. Years later she returns to the house; the family is dead, the house is aban-

Dec 22.

A Marsh Island ⓙ III

VIII.

Proof to author
148 Charles St.,
Boston.

That afternoon Mr. Dale made himself delightfully agreeable. Mrs. Owen felt more than equal to the situation, and she had already welcomed back the early strength and reassuring cheerfulness of Temperance Kipp. This excellent person had grown up or been raised as she would have expressed it, on the farm — and remained loyal now to her early friend, in spite of the inducements of well-to-do member of her own family.

Dick rejoiced in his recovered personal belongings, which Temperance herself brought in from the wagon and placed beside him, urged to this service by an insatiable curiosity to see the guest of whom Doris had spoken. Her opinion

Page from the setting copy for Jewett's second novel (Sarah Orne Jewett Collection, #6218, Clifton Waller Barrett Library, Special Collections Department, University of Virginia Library)

doned and haunted. The old woman is almost forgotten, but the girl finds the old woman's grave in a country churchyard.

Jewett leaves much unresolved and unexplained in the story, suggesting but minimizing a rational explanation for the local legend and the child's experience. The story is reminiscent of Nathaniel Hawthorne's "Young Goodman Brown" (1835), and it does work, as adult experience rejects what may or may not have been real and finally no longer believes.

"A Bit of Shore Life" is a sketch reminiscent of those in *Deephaven*, but it is more incisively drawn in its portrayal of the spiritual poverty of the isolated life in the midst of the Maine coast's harsh beauty. The narrator, a summer visitor in a fishing village, befriends Georgie, a boy who fishes as a man, and the boy's taciturn father. With the boy she goes off to visit his aunts, who live alone, on the way stopping at a tragic country auction of the goods of another old woman, who can no longer live alone. Later, while the narrator talks with the aunts, the boy chops wood for them, mindful of his father's injunction that "boys ain't made just to look at."

The narrator enjoys the rural setting, the food, the old women's flowers, and their gossip. Shortly thereafter the summer is over, and the narrator takes home with her the memory of the sturdy boy. She takes with her, too, the memory of the shadow that dominates the village: "I wonder if anyone has not been struck, as I have, by the sadness and hopelessness which seems to overshadow many of the people who live on the lonely farms in the outskirts of small New England villages. It is most noticeable among the women. Their talk is very cheerless, and they have a morbid interest in sickness and deaths; they tell each other long stories about such things; they are very forlorn; they dwell persistently upon any trouble which they have; and their petty disputes with each other have a tragic hold upon their thoughts, sometimes being handed down from one generation to another. . . . their world is so small."

Jewett's narrator, unlike the idle girls of Deephaven, anticipates the forces that led hundreds of young people to leave their late-nineteenth-century village homes and to seek whatever it was that would fill and enrich their lives, the movement that became rejection if not rebellion as it led to *Winesburg, Ohio* and Sinclair Lewis's *Main Street* (1920) two generations later. The story says what *Deephaven* attempted to say,

with touching regret not only because of what had been but because of the shadowy memory of the small boy, a sturdy reminder of the ethic that had once been universal but was gone in the world beyond the village.

The same note of regret permeates *Country By-Ways* (1881), in which Jewett collected sketches and stories written and published since late 1879. Of the eight items in the volume, three are stories, and five are essays in nostalgia, set in the New England countryside—philosophic journeys that try to reconcile the past and present. In these sketches Jewett attempts, too, to reconcile the passage of time and the transience of human activity with the natural setting, the lonely graves, and the empty holes that had once been the basements of homes. In the overgrown pastures of abandoned farms she sees change as inevitable as that of seasons; thus, nature is as permanent as human life, and the societies it creates are not.

The sketches take the narrator along the Piscataqua River as it makes its way to the sea at Berwick. In "River Driftwood," first published in the *Atlantic Monthly*, October 1881, she reflects, "How many men have lived and died on its banks, but the river is always young." The sketches take her through the fall countryside, where she explores an abandoned house and reflects on "the iconoclastic and unpleasant new times" (in "An October Ride," previously unpublished), and through a village where she reflects on the front yards that had given a measure of repose and beauty to "a restricted and narrowly limited life in the old days." But she concludes that, with the passage of parlors and front yards, "a certain element of American society is fast dying out," that "with all our glory and pride in modern progress and success we cling to the old associations regretfully" ("From a Mournful Village," *Atlantic Monthly*, November 1881). "A Winter Drive" (previously unpublished) takes her through the woods and trees near Mount Agamenticus, where she reflects on trees dying and the "wholesale slaughter" of entire forests by the shortsighted men of New England. "An Autumn Holiday" (*Harper's Magazine*, October 1880) takes her through the woods on "a day that loves you" to visit two old ladies who live in the woods and to learn of a strange old man who believed that he was his own dead sister.

With neither the necessity nor the urge to probe human behavior, with the recognition in transcendental fashion of the only permanence, these sketches depict the serenity of nature in all its faces. In them Jewett finds her own Walden Pond, "where I am happiest . . . where I find that which is next of kin to me, in friends, or trees, or hills, or seas, or beside a flower. . . ."

Although the three stories in the collection suffer in comparison with the remarkable unity of the sketches, none is without merit; yet each is marred by improbabilities. In "Andrew's Fortune" (*Atlantic Monthly*, July 1881) a will is lost, depriving a young man of his just inheritance from an uncle, but the will turns up years later, after the nephew has become a success on his own in Boston. The story contains a remarkable sketch of the deathwatch held by the old man's housekeeper and her cronies. "Good Luck: A Girl's Story" (*Good Company*, December 1879) concerns finding a secret room and lost treasure in an old house, as well as a fortunate inheritance; it contains, too, good descriptions of the house itself and of the sense of discovery with which the young people revitalize it.

The best story in the collection is "Miss Becky's Pilgrimage" (*Independent*, 1 September 1881). Miss Rebecca Parsons is delightful; she is another of Jewett's lonely maiden ladies, her life devoted to caring for her bachelor clergyman brother through the drab parsonages that take them farther and farther west, away from their New England village origins. Her pilgrimage, after the brother's sudden death, is her long, reluctant train journey to her old home. Apprehensive of the changes she knows she will find, she meets an old friend on the train; kindly relatives meet her; change is natural and minimal; and she finds romance and purpose with an elderly, respected widower-clergyman of the town.

None of the stories is Jewett at her best. Although she refrains from the arbitrary morals with which she concluded the stories in *Old Friends and New*, the happy endings of these–each of which is a contrived attempt to suggest the rewards of virtue even when the evidence of the story suggests inevitable unhappiness–are neither intellectually adequate nor artistically sound substitutions. In the sketches, however, conventional moralizing is replaced by transcendental awareness, keen observations, vivid sense descriptions, and a sharp insight into the transience of human affairs.

The Mate of the Daylight, and Friends Ashore (1884) is generally less effective than *Country By-Ways* but, nevertheless, introduces a new thematic dimension in her portrayal of strong unmarried women (in "Tom's Husband" [*Atlantic Monthly*, Feb-

ruary 1882]), and it contains two first-rate stories, "Miss Debby's Neighbors" (previously unpublished), which introduces a new technique, and "A New Parishioner" (*Atlantic Monthly*, April 1883), a nearly flawless story.

The first story in the collection, "The Mate of the Daylight" (*Atlantic Monthly*, July 1882), is, however, a weak success story of a handsome but unstable young man. He is not highly regarded by the retired sea captains of the town, but Susan, granddaughter of Captain Ryder, believes in young Daniel Lewis. Lewis goes to sea; in an emergency he proves himself by taking command of the ship, and he wins the approval of the old men, marries Susan, and becomes the ship's master. "The Mate of the Daylight" is one of a very few stories by Jewett in which a young man of the new generation proves himself in accordance with the values of the old.

"A Landless Farmer" (*Atlantic Monthly*, May and June 1883) combines two acknowledged sources, *King Lear* and an inversion of the biblical parable of the Prodigal Son, in another improbable story that, nevertheless, taps universal themes. In the first part–which is redeemed by a fine portrait of Serena, the shrew–an old farmer is cheated and mistreated by his two daughters; in the second part the son returns prosperous from the West to rescue his father from degrading desolation. "Heaven only knows," Jewett concludes, "the story of the lives that the gray old New England farmhouses have sheltered and hidden away from curious eyes as best they might. . . ."

"A New Parishioner" uses the theme of the prodigal's return and the innate skeptical wisdom of an older unmarried woman to produce the best story in the collection, in fact one of Jewett's very best ever. Henry Stroud, the apparently wealthy son of an old family now gone, returns to the village of Walton after many years. Stroud becomes a devout parishioner in the local church and a town benefactor who offers to pay for many town improvements. Among the townspeople, only Miss Lydia Dunn, remembering how Stroud's father had cheated her grandfather, is skeptical, and her position becomes unpopular in the town. Stroud, however, is proved to be a confidence man; his gifts have been paid for by worthless notes; he leaves the town in debt and embittered; and Miss Lydia's reputation for astuteness is enhanced.

Miss Lydia knows that, despite her suspicions, she had come close to accepting his flattery

Annie Fields and Jewett in the library of Fields's home in Boston

and apparent goodness and had even considered him momentarily as a possible husband. The distinction between right and wrong, she knows, so clear in retrospect, is much more difficult to make than she had earlier been willing to admit.

Another story of a returned prodigal son is "An Only Son" (*Atlantic Monthly*, November 1883), in which a young man proves himself, not, however, by going off to return with a fortune, but by becoming one of the taciturn New England tinkerers whose work is successful and profitable. Nevertheless, Jewett comments slyly on the passage of the old crafts and old values, such as those of the town shoemaker, who "didn't do much more than tend shop, nowadays." She goes on to say that "folks would keep on buying cheap shoes and thinking they saved more money on two pairs a year for five dollars than when he used to make 'em one pair for four." Even so, the shoemaker expresses a resigned acceptance: " 'I make better pay than I used to workin' at my trade, and so I ain't going to fret. . . . ' "

"Miss Debby's Neighbors" (previously unpublished) is a dramatic monologue, a delightful tour de force spoken by the shrewd Miss Debby, a "tailoress" and member of "a class of elderly New England women which is fast dying out," those whose wisdom brings a sense of history to their so-

ciety. Miss Debby's craft is, like the shoemaker's, giving way to shoddy factory-made goods, and she regrets the passage of the old ways and her own craft in an age in which "the railroads were making everybody look and act of a piece. . . ," an age of "cheap, ready-made clothes."

The most daring of Jewett's early stories is "Tom's Husband," a story that could perhaps only find acceptance because of the humorous vein in which it is presented. The story of reversed roles within a marriage between Tom Wilson, who has no talent for or interest in his managerial job, and Mary Wilson, who was "too independent and self-reliant" to be a wife, it draws its humor from the completeness with which each exhibits the mannerisms traditionally ascribed to the other sex. Jewett's feminist convictions are clear as she points out that Mary's abilities are the kind that are "often wasted in the more contracted sphere of women." This theme was to provide the substance of her first novel, *A Country Doctor*, published in 1884; but here Jewett mitigates her feminism by suggesting that a woman's "womanliness" is diminished by her participation in men's affairs.

The last two stories in *The Mate of the Daylight, and Friends Ashore*, "The Confession of a House-Breaker" (previously unpublished) and "A

Little Traveler" (*Good Company*, March 1880), are slight but pleasant. The former is a sketch of an early walk in the garden after "breaking out" of the house to watch the coming of a June morning. The latter describes a train journey in which a little girl whose mother has recently died is befriended by the other passengers, whom she charms, on her way to live with an aunt in Boston.

Apparently while writing the stories in this collection, Jewett was at work on *A Country Doctor*, which was followed by another novel, *A Marsh Island* (1885). *A Country Doctor* is an extended metaphor of Jewett's own experience as a female literary artist in a society dominated by male writers and editors. It traces the life of Nan Prince, an orphan adopted by a country doctor modeled on Jewett's own father. The girl determines to be a doctor herself, and the novel traces her life from girlhood ambition through the difficulties of overcoming social disapproval until she succeeds and, convinced that she cannot be both a physician and a conventional wife, returns to her rural home to practice and remains unmarried. Although it was to remain Jewett's favorite among her works, it is marred by sentimentality.

A Marsh Island, a pastoral romance and a tribute to country life aesthetic as experience, is set on Hog Island, on the Massachusetts coast near Annie Fields's summer home. An epic celebration of rural life, it is marred by the plot, a love triangle consisting of Dick Dale, a wealthy young artist from the city; the solid, hardworking Dan Lester, a farmer; and the sensitive Doris Owen, who, true to her origins, chooses Dan.

Both novels are marred by Jewett's most common shortcomings–improbability and sentimentality of plot–while both exhibit her best abilities: a sharp eye for the natural environment; a sense of communion with nature; and a keen ear for the language of New England, whether of the countryside or the city, the north shore or Back Bay. These talents, while enough to save an otherwise mediocre story, are unfortunately not enough to overcome the weaknesses in the novels. While each has fine parts, neither is a great novel.

Nevertheless, Jewett followed the two novels with a consistently high-level collection of short stories, *A White Heron and Other Stories* (1886). Of the nine stories in the volume, five, including the title story, are first-rate, one is good, and two are weaker. Only one of the stories, marred by ambiguous symbolism, is unsuccessful. The others show significant advances in consistent execution, probability, and an increasing willingness to let whatever moral points the stories make emerge from plot, character, and narrative technique rather than from arbitrary omniscient interpretations.

The title story was previously unpublished. After completing it, Jewett wrote Annie Fields, "What shall I do with my 'White Heron' story now she is written? She isn't a very good magazine story, but I love her, and I mean to keep her for the beginning of my next book." The story is her best-known, most widely anthologized, and most frequently analyzed story. Imperfect because of shifts in narrative perspective and time, it is the story of a young girl born and raised in a manufacturing town until she is eight years old. She then goes to live on her grandmother's farm, where she becomes a child of nature, knowing and identifying with the creatures of the woods and swamps. She is offered ten dollars–money badly needed on the farm–to lead a pleasant young ornithologist to the nest of a rare white heron so that he may "collect" it, and she is tempted both by the money and by her attraction to the young man. Early in the morning she climbs a tall pine, reaching the top at dawn, to spot the bird's nest; but when she sees the bird she knows she can never reveal the secret.

Jewett deals successfully with a complex symbolic structure as the girl completes her self-discovery, recognizing, as she spies the heron, the nature of beauty and of nature itself, in the process rejecting the twin lures of money and sexual attraction. The girl's secrets, her self-knowledge, and her recognition of a truth beyond scientific knowledge remain with her as the young man, disappointed, goes off through the woods, never to return.

"The Gray Man," which follows, was also previously unpublished, although it had been submitted to the *Atlantic* and rejected by Thomas Bailey Aldrich, who had replaced Howells as editor in 1881. The weakest story in the collection, it brings a mysterious stranger to a deserted farm on the slope of Mount Agamenticus, where he makes his home. Gray in appearance and grave in demeanor, he is useful and accepted in the neighborhood, but his gloom makes him unwelcome on festive occasions. One day, when war breaks out in the South, he rides off, later to be seen riding his great horse across the battlefields. Neither hostile nor friendly, he is that favorite allegorical figure, Death, the point driven home in a superfluous final paragraph.

Jewett's concern with the usually undeveloped and unrealized talents of a woman appears in "Farmer Finch" (*Harper's Magazine*, January 1885). John Finch, destined by fortune and society to be a farmer, has an intelligent, capable daughter, Polly, who aspires to be a schoolteacher. The family fortunes decline through a bank failure; Finch falls ill; and the job to which Polly aspires is given to the niece of a trustee. Polly, apparently destined to help her mother at home, sees the bright berries growing on the opposite side of an apparently dying barberry bush and decides instead to farm, applying her scholarly talents to studying advanced agricultural techniques. Supported by the kindly family physician, she is marked for success. As the story ends, she has transplanted the bush to the yard, where it flourishes.

"Marsh Rosemary" (*Atlantic Monthly*, May 1886) is a low-key rural tragedy set in the salt marshes of Walpole. Miss Ann Floyd, a self-reliant, strong, unmarried lady and a "tailoress," decides, against her better judgment, to marry a younger, lazy, good-natured, handsome man, Jerry Lane, whom she finds she must support. Her conviction that she can "keep him in better trim" quickly fades as she learns that she is "the better man of the two." Although she has learned to cherish him in spite of his faults, she welcomes his decision to go to sea because she is convinced he will be happy to come home. But he has learned that his comfort has been purchased at the expense of his freedom. When the schooner fails to return and it is learned that it sank with all hands, she settles down to accept her widowhood.

Later, however, she learns that he jumped ship before it sailed and that he is living in another town with another woman. Determined to confront him, she goes there secretly, but she learns from a passerby that he has settled down; at his house she peers through a window at what is apparently a happy home with a baby, and she returns quietly to her home, a lonely supper, and a long old age. Jewett's "Marsh Rosemary," a gray primrose, thereafter stays quietly in her place.

In this story Jewett portrays the poignant loneliness and susceptibility of the older woman with a great deal of insight and skill, and she makes clear the inner strength with which the older woman can accept shame, wrong, and a devastating blow to her self-confidence with dignity and fortitude instead of self-pity. Tautly con-

structed, "Marsh Rosemary" is one of Jewett's best-executed stories.

"The Dulham Ladies" (*Atlantic Monthly*, April 1886), which follows, is another well-executed story in which, however, a quiet humor replaces the pathos of "Marsh Rosemary." The ladies, two older, unmarried sisters of good family, are known in Dulham as "the Dobbin girls," prisoners of their heritage and time past. The two age without knowing it, convinced that they are simultaneously preserving the valuable heritage of the town and their family and keeping up with the times. When baldness approaches for both, they journey to a nearby town to purchase, secretly, stylish artificial frisettes. But in their self-delusion they buy ridiculous wigs with long bangs, sold to them by an unscrupulous fake-French salesman. Their appearance is, unknown to them, funny, but the town keeps their illusions intact, and they continue to the end, denying change and preserving their vanished past, in spite of their vague dissatisfaction with the wigs. They remain those "innocent Christian babes," "the Dobbin girls," until they die.

"A Business Man" (previously unpublished) marks the passing of time and the increasing redundancy of John Craven, a widower who had devoted his life single-mindedly to business. Changing business practices as his sons take over the business make him idle and obsolete, but in wandering about the town he meets a struggling young businessman, provides capital, and works for the young man as a clerk. As the small business prospers and the young man marries, the old man finds a new fulfillment that lasts to his death. Although Jewett insists upon the folly of such dedication at the expense of a richer life, Craven is sympathetically portrayed, and it is clear that his skills, expended in a good cause, have given him the fulfillment that had earlier eluded him.

"Martha and Mary," the story of "the old Miss Deans" (*Christian Union*, 26 November 1885), is one of the weaker stories in the collection, a brief tale in which two aging "tailoresses," patterned after their biblical namesakes, invite an old, well-fixed widower cousin to Thanksgiving dinner. Their mixed motives are fulfilled as a family feud is vanquished, and the old man gives them his late wife's modern sewing machine. Jewett carefully draws the contrasting characters of the old women but does not exploit the situation, and the story drifts off.

Jewett in an 1892 photograph by Frederick Hollyer

"The News from Petersham" (*Youth's Companion*, 3 April 1884) is a brief, well-executed piece in which the news of an old man's slight illness in Petersham becomes, a short time later and a few miles away, the news of his death. This unobtrusively moral tale is followed by "The Two Browns" (*Atlantic Monthly*, 6 August 1886), a light but well-executed story, set in New York, of a young lawyer who has two identities: J. Benedict Brown at home and in his profession, and John B. Brown, secretly a manufacturer. Narrowly escaping a situation in which he may be forced to sue himself, he and a partner sell the business at a profit. The two Browns become one, and he confesses all to his wife, one of Jewett's few obtuse, tradition-bound younger women.

A White Heron and Other Stories is a clear advance over previous collections, not only marking a clearer understanding of the changing nature of the New England economy and social structure and a growing acceptance of those changes, but showing increasing sureness and consistency in execution, a defter touch in the light stories, and a confidence in her work that minimizes, when it does not eliminate, moral didacticism.

Following this collection, Jewett published *The Story of the Normans, Told Chiefly in Relation to Their Conquest of England* (1887), a children's history combining fact, myth, and impressions. This book was the first of three children's works that were to include *Betty Leicester, A Story for Girls* (1890) and *Betty Leicester's English Xmas* (1894), both considered classics and both dealing with the growing maturity of a strong young woman. Her next collection of stories was *The King of Folly Island and Other People*, published in 1888.

All but the last, weakest story in this collection reflect the bleak New England underside of what Jewett calls "this lavish America," where people live in quiet desperation marked by calm dignity. In the title story (*Harper's Magazine*, December 1886) both setting and predicament are clear, and Jewett suggests that, metaphorically if not literally, neither is unique to the lonely island off the Maine coast. There George Quint, known to mainlanders as "King George," holds lonely dominion over his ailing daughter, Phebe, the rugged landscape, a few sheep, and the sea in which he fishes for a living. Having vowed that he will never set foot on another man's land, he does whatever business he transacts from his boat at the town dock. A stranger, a lonely man who has devoted his life to a successful business (in effect, a king of his own island), comes to the village, and, as a rustic joke, he is sent to board with Quint. He comes to know Quint and his daughter, who is apparently seriously ill, and ultimately to know himself. A friendship grows between the stranger and Phebe, and then he goes back to his lonely business kingdom while she awaits the winter that will kill her.

This story is Jewett's bleakest and the closest to an incipient naturalism. The girl, like her mother before her, accepts her bondage and her fate, dreaming of a world she can never know; and the businessman, having known a dim beauty so briefly, accepts his own bondage without illusions in a world he thought he had chosen. Only Quint, defiant but sometimes oddly tender, is spared the knowledge, not of his kingdom, but of his thralldom.

"The Courting of Sister Wisby" (*Atlantic Monthly*, May 1887) is a humorous, earthy story told to the narrator on a late summer day by old Mrs. Goodsoe, a lonely widow and practitioner of the art of natural healing. As the old woman and her avid listener gather mullein against the chills of the coming winter, the old lady tells, in a story redolent of a primitive revivalistic religious fervor, of the strange, stormy courtship of Deacon Brimblecorn, alias Brimful the evangelistic dowser, and the spirited, spiteful Sister Lizy Wisby, and finally of the old man's lonely widowerhood, bent twig in hand, searching out water in the fields. The story, ludicrous rather than grim, mitigates the gloom of its predecessor.

"The Landscape Chamber" (*Atlantic Monthly*, November 1887) is a brief interlude in a summer trip by horseback. When the horse becomes lame, the narrator seeks a place to stay, to let the horse heal, in a once-magnificent, now-decayed house isolated in grown-over pasture. The house is occupied by an old man, admittedly a hereditary "monomaniac," a doomed, hopeless tyrant, and his pathetic, lonely daughter, living out their isolated existence in Calvinistic, near-naturalistic poverty. The horse recovers through the old man's ministrations, while the narrator tries to befriend the daughter, who alternately reaches out and withdraws. The narrator departs, remembering the woman's words that "we shall all disappear some night in a winter storm, and the world will be rid of us–father and the house and I, all

three" and her father's assertion that "we are of those who have no hope in a world of fate."

Paired with "The Landscape Chamber" is a lighter story, establishing the pattern of the collection. "Law Lane" (*Scribner's Magazine*, December 1887) is a story of continued, ruinous rural litigation, a feud over a two-foot-wide strip of land along a lane shared by the Crosby and Barnet families; of two delightful old ladies who gossip while picking blackberries; and of a mischievous boy who overhears them and repeats their secret– that the Crosby girl and the Barnet boy are secretly in love. After family conflicts, illness, and the temporary self-exile of the Barnet boy, the feud ends happily, appropriately on Christmas day.

"Miss Peck's Promotion" (*Scribner's Magazine*, June 1887) is a bleak story of the frustrated near-romance of a trustworthy older woman whose loneliness is briefly interrupted when she is called to care for the young child of the local minister, who has been recently widowed. The town links their names, and Miss Peck overcomes her initial repugnance to allow herself to think more of him; but the minister marries a "townish, empty-faced, tiresomely pretty girl." Miss Peck refuses to keep house for them, and she returns to her windy hilltop home, free and secure in the knowledge that the minister rather than she will "reap the whirlwind."

"Miss Tempy's Watchers" (*Atlantic Monthly*, March 1888) is a remarkable reconstruction of the life of Miss Temperance Dent through the gossip and reminiscences of her two old friends, Mrs. Crowe and Miss Binson, while they are watching Miss Dent's corpse. Eventually the old ladies doze off, knowing that "Tempy" would like them to rest. Miss Tempy emerges as one of Jewett's selfless maiden ladies, generous and lonely, while the world of the two old ladies is both diminished by her death and enhanced by the remembering, as Mrs. Crowe gains a measure of humility and Miss Binson a sense of compassion while they talk through the long night.

"A Village Shop" (previously unpublished) is the story of Miss Esther Jaffrey and her unmarried brother Leonard, the last of a long, distinguished line in the town of Grafton. Fortune fails, and Miss Jaffrey opens a ladies' shop in what had been her father's study, her grandfather's law office, and even a remote colonial ancestor's counting room. Leonard, upon graduation from Harvard College, announces himself to be a scholar and spends his days taking obscure notes in a fine copperplate hand. Their fortunes fade further as the town grows away from its heritage and Miss Jaffrey's shop, until a wealthy farmer, who remembers and respects them, asks them to take in his bright, pretty daughter so that she can attend the academy in town while learning to emulate Miss Jaffrey and being tutored by Leonard. Leonard and the girl fall in love, and Miss Jaffrey is both horrified by the difference in their ages and terrified and humiliated by the prospect of the loss of the girl's board and the consequent dependence of all three on the farmer's charity. Unexpectedly, Leonard is offered the job of librarian in the town's new library, and, suddenly confident, he offers to support Miss Jaffrey from his new largess if she will close the shop: " 'Never!' said the pale old woman . . . and she went in, stately as a princess, to wait upon an early customer." In spite of the undertone of fear and uncertainty in the face of change, Jewett maintains a light tone, and Miss Jaffrey remains proud, indestructible, and independent to the end.

The last, weakest story, "Mére Pochette" (*Harper's Magazine*, March 1888), is Jewett's first attempt to portray French Canadians, a people maintaining their culture and religion in isolation in an alien country. Grandmother and granddaughter (the orphaned daughter of a mother who had run off with the American she loved) clash until the granddaughter repents and, with an unexpected legacy from her father, is free to marry and to go to the United States with her husband. Weak in concept and execution, the story's only redeeming feature is the sharp portrait of the strong, tightfisted old matriarch, a portrait ruined by her unlikely conversion to accepting the granddaughter's plans.

With the exception of this last story the collection is sound and uniformly well executed; the characters and incidents are both believable and acceptable; and Jewett's New England, in transition as well as in stagnation, is real. Its people, imprisoned by the old way or new, are helpless to understand or mitigate forces that, whether economic, hereditary, or material, keep them poised on the edge of destruction. But her capable old women maintain the control and dignity with which they live in spite of the odds against them.

Published two years later, Jewett's next collection of stories, *Strangers and Wayfarers* (1890), is less satisfactory than *The King of Folly Island* because in several of the stories she attempts to make improbable plots probable, and in others she attempts unsuccessfully to reproduce black American dialect and Irish brogue. Nevertheless, her portrayals of New England character and her reproduction of New England idioms are sure, and her insights into what remains behind the gray exteriors of New England houses and faces is clear. It is equally clear, however, that Jewett has attempted to broaden her perspective and to mitigate the harsh determinism that permeated the previous collection.

The first story, "A Winter Courtship" (*Atlantic Monthly*, February 1889), is a light, pleasant tale of a seven-mile journey between North Kilby and Sanscrit Pond, during which the widowed Mrs. Fanny Tobin captures the heart of Mr. Briley, the old bachelor who carries mail and passengers between the two points in his two-seated covered wagon. It is followed by "The Mistress of Sydenham Plantation" (*Atlantic Monthly*, August 1888), in which Jewett attempts unsuccessfully to transplant her insight into New England change and individual tragedy to the lush, rural South. Mrs. Sydenham, absorbed in the tragedies of her losses during the Civil War, remains a shadowy figure imprisoned in her memory, and her faithful servant Peter is a caricature, rather than a portrait, of a black former slave.

"The Town Poor" (*Atlantic Monthly*, July 1890) is, however, Jewett at her compassionate best as she explores the plight of two old, unmarried sisters who, infirm and unskilled, are forced to "go on the town," to be put out to board in a ramshackle house where they desperately maintain some semblance of dignity. But two ladies who visit them discover compassion for them, and as the tale ends, they are determined to take the selectmen to task and restore the sisters to their old home.

Like "A Winter Courtship," "The Quest of Mr. Teaby" (*Atlantic Monthly*, January 1890) is the story of a brief rural courtship. Old Mr. Teaby, a bachelor peddler rapidly losing customers to the new stores, and his old friend Sister Pinkham meet by chance at a country railroad station. Their gossip, memories, and loneliness drive them together. They part, but Sister Pinkham knows that the old man needs someone to look after him, and it appears that she has selected herself for the role, as she pursues him with his forgotten umbrella.

"The Luck of the Bogans" (*Scribner's Magazine*, January 1889) is Jewett's first attempt to write about the Irish who had come to New England, and, as in her earlier attempt to use the

French Canadians, she is largely unsuccessful. An ambitious story, it traces the life of Mike Bogan, a hardworking, ambitious young man, from his Kerry home to Boston, where he rises through hard work and thrift to prosperity as a saloon owner. But Bogan's luck turns bad. His son Dan, whom he was determined would become an American gentleman, turns to drink and carousing with toughs. When Dan is brought home dead, Mike goes into decline and dies of a broken heart, dreaming of his Irish home. Unfortunately, the tragedy of change and misguided ambition is not quite real; the Irishmen are too stagy and their brogue too artificial, leaving the reader with the impression of peering through a window at strangers.

Conversely, "Fair Day" (*Scribner's Magazine*, August 1888) is superb, a story in which the hopes, dreams, tragedies, and misfortune of an old widow's life are defined in one day while her son, his inept wife, and their children are at the fair. Mrs. Mercy Bascom has raised four children alone and well, married off the three daughters successfully, and then, with the son, upon whom she depends, married, has gone reluctantly to live with him. On the day of the story, the family, carelessly neglecting to ask her along, leaves her alone with the housework and her memories. She walks through the fields to the old place. Recalling an old feud with her sister-in-law, also a widow, she determines to make up with her so that she will have someone to talk to of the old days. When the son returns from the fair to a well-prepared supper, she announces that her sister-in-law has been there, has asked about her, and has suggested they visit. The portrayal of old Mrs. Bascom, of her memories and her habits of a lifetime, her loneliness, sense of rejection, and useful uselessness, is effectively drawn.

In "Going to Shrewsbury" (*Atlantic Monthly*, July 1889) the narrator hears of the uprooting of an old farm woman from her home by an unscrupulous heir when she chances to meet the lady, who shares fears, apprehensions, and memories with her, on the train. Particularly delightful are the old woman's perceptions of the new world of the "cars" and her fellow travelers. The narrator is pleased when later she learns that the old woman enjoys the concerts, plays, and lectures of the city so much that she does not want to return home.

"The Taking of Captain Bull" (*Harper's Magazine*, December 1889) is a well-executed, amusing story with memorable characters: Captain Bull, a retired, crusty bachelor sea captain left alone with mixed regret and relief after his religious sister's death; and Mrs. French, the capable housekeeper, a stranger in the community, who comes to work for him and maintains the house as a captain maintains his ship. Much town gossip ensues until Mrs. French reveals that she is his niece, having kept her identity secret because she was uncertain whether or not she wanted to live with him. The captain is pleased, but he secretly regrets that she is not the "jiggeting" girl he had expected her to be, to liven up the old house.

"By the Morning Boat" (*Atlantic Monthly*, October 1890) is a slight but archetypal story in which fifteen-year-old Elisha leaves his bleak Maine-coast home for Boston and his future, carrying with him for luck an old neighbor's watch and mixed good wishes and warnings. "In Dark New England Days" (*Century Magazine*, October 1890) is an archetypal story of another sort, drawing on the old New England fear of the power of curses spoken and things not seen. Accused but acquitted of stealing the gold hoarded by the dead father of two miserable old sisters, Enoch Holt swears by his right hand that he is innocent. One of the old ladies curses his right hand and that of all his descendants, thus beginning a strange, unnatural series of circumstances. While the old women sink into destitution and Enoch prospers, especially after an apparently successful voyage, the old women of the town count the effects of the curse: Enoch's wife is thrown out of a wagon and her right hand crippled; his son has his right hand shot off in a fight; Enoch falls while building a fine new house and suffers the amputation of his mangled right hand. When new babies are born in Holt's family, the women inspect their hands first of all.

The gloom of this New England tale is mitigated by the last sketch in the book, "The White Rose Road" (*Atlantic Monthly*, September 1889), a quiet account of a drive along a quiet road, encounters with the past in the form of old houses and a passing funeral, and reflections on a time when the streams were unpolluted and rich with salmon. Caught up in the pleasantness of the day and the road, the narrator concludes, "I believed that with a little more time we should grow wiser about our fish and other things besides."

The defects of the collection lie in Jewett's attempt to transpose New England characters and incidents to alien settings, constructing stories about strangers, particularly as those stories contrast with the reality and sureness with which she

Jewett was awarded an honorary D.Litt. degree from Bowdoin College in 1901 (photograph by Elise Tyson)

treats her fellow New England wayfarers. Perhaps an innate dissatisfaction with the collection led Jewett to publish later in 1890 *Tales of New England*, a retrospective collection of the stories she liked best from the four collections preceding *Strangers and Wayfarers*. Not until three years later, in 1893, did she publish her next book, *A Native of Winby and Other Tales*, another uneven collection containing only a few first-rate stories, the others marred by improbability and sentimentality.

The title story, "A Native of Winby" (*Atlantic Monthly*, May 1891), is slight and sentimental, the story of a distinguished westerner–a war hero, a wealthy man, and a U.S. Senator–who returns to Winby to visit his old school and to spend an evening with the old woman who had

been his first love half a century before.

"Decoration Day" (*Harper's Magazine*, June 1892) is somewhat sentimental but a fine story in which three middle-aged men, veterans of the Civil War, decide to hold a Decoration Day observance in the tiny village of Barlow Plains. Their conversations, plans, and relationships with the community reveal what has been–the fortunes and misfortunes of their comrades and themselves–as they hold their nostalgic but proud parade through the village to the burying ground beyond.

In "Jim's Little Woman" (*Harper's Magazine*, December 1890) Jewett moves her characters and the plot between St. Augustine, Florida, and the

Maine coast, along the old timber-shipping route, but the story is not successful. Jim, southern-born descendent of New England and Spanish ancestry, marries Marty, a Maine coastal girl, and leaves her stranded and impoverished in St. Augustine while he, presumed dead of a fever in Jamaica, is actually adventuring in the Caribbean. But he comes back and reforms, and all of them return north. The unlikely plot is clearly secondary to Jewett's detailed descriptions of St. Augustine.

Conversely, "The Failure of David Berry" (*Harper's Magazine*, June 1891) is a near-perfect story of the decline and ruination of a village shoemaker-craftsman in competition with factories and a newer, more complex economic system that has no place for the old intimate human ways. David Berry, a wise man as well as a skilled craftsman, has his own shop in his yard, where people come to him to have shoes made or repaired or simply to loaf and to talk. But the village grows and fewer customers come, so he moves his shop to rented quarters on the main street. There expenses are greater, and the new local shoe factory, where "second-choice" shoes can be had for "next to nothing," reduces his trade. Pressure from his wife and others leads him to put in a line of ready-made shoes which Berry can neither recommend nor " 'palm off . . . on folks that respect either me or themselves.' " His wife's illness, together with increasing costs, leads him to borrow and to delay paying the rent, the wood and coal man, and the factory shoe agent. Suddenly Berry is rumored to be insolvent, and creditors foreclose. His tools are auctioned to pay his debts, and the old man, rejected for employment at the shoe factory because he is too old, goes into decline and dies.

The theme of this story, the decline of hand craftsmanship in an increasingly industrial America, is, with the exodus of young people from the farms and villages to the cities, another of Jewett's strongest themes, one of the classic themes of American writing in the late nineteenth and early twentieth centuries. Both were to become particularly significant in the writing that came out of the Midwest in the early years of the twentieth century, works by Theodore Dreiser, Sherwood Anderson, F. Scott Fitzgerald, and others. "The Failure of David Berry" anticipates Anderson's *Poor White* (1920), his best and profoundest novel, by nearly thirty years.

In contrast, "The Passing of Sister Barsett" (*Cosmopolitan*, May 1892) is a light, well-executed story in which an elderly woman hypochondriac is believed dead. Two delightful old ladies, Mrs. Mercy Crane, who never leaves her house but depends on others for the news, and Miss Sarah Ellen Dow, who had taken care of Sister Barsett until sent away by the lady's relatives, discuss over tea the nature of Sister Barsett's illness, the range of remedies and physicians she used over the years, the character of her relatives, and Miss Dow's unemployment. But the word "gone," overheard by Miss Dow, has been misinterpreted, and the old woman is alive, calling for Miss Dow and her tea.

"Miss Esther's Guest" (previously unpublished) is another light, delightful story, in which Miss Esther Porley, alone after the death of her mother, agrees doubtfully to participate in the "Country Week," a program to give poor people from Boston a week in the country. Because she has cared for her mother and is afraid of young children, she asks specifically for an elderly woman. But the committee, to her horror, sends a quiet, retired old man. They adjust, however, and as he returns to Boston at the end of the week, it is clear that they have an understanding and he will return.

The strongest and best story in the collection is "The Flight of Betsey Lane" (*Scribner's Magazine*, August 1893). Set in Byfleet Poor-house, it is the story of three old, infirm women–Mrs. Dow, Miss Bond, and Miss Betsey Lane–who not only live in the past but dominate the poor farm, its residents, and the selectmen who are in charge of it. The poor farm is a lively, busy place, and the residents are not unhappy, having accepted the fact that they are "on the town." Miss Betsey, however, has a not-too-well-kept secret dream: to go to the centennial celebration at Philadelphia. An unexpected gift of a hundred dollars from the daughter of an old employer provides the means, and off she goes, early in the morning before the others are awake, riding to Boston in a freight train with a friendly brakeman whose clothes she mends on the way.

While bewilderment, consternation, searches, and finally mourning reign in the poorhouse, Miss Betsey has a magnificent time, pampered and enjoyed by fairgoers and employers alike. On the ninth day, as Mrs. Dow and Miss Bond go to a nearby pond to await the rising of her body–they are convinced she had drowned herself because an ancestor had–Miss Betsey comes down the path, laden with memories and presents for all.

"Between Mass and Vespers" (*Scribner's Magazine*, May 1893) and "A Little Captive Maid" (*Scribner's Magazine*, December 1891), the last two stories in the collection, are further evidence that, when Jewett uses subject matter and characters alien to her native New England, the stories are inferior. In the first story a wise old Irish priest, transplanted with his flock to a New England town, one Sunday between mass and vespers saves a young parishioner, Dan Nolen, from going further down the path of crime and drink. "A Little Captive Maid" focuses on the relationship between a young Irish servant girl, sent to America by an avaricious aunt to break up her romance, and the aged, wealthy Captain Balfour, her employer. The two become close, and when the old man dies he leaves her a hundred dollars and passage to Ireland so that she can go back to marry her young love.

In these, as in almost all the similar stories, Jewett substitutes for the clear exposition and insight into her characters improbable, sentimental plots and artificial, almost unreadable, caricatured dialect. Her stories of the French-Canadian and Irish immigrants to New England are always sympathetic but also condescending, as adjectives replace insights. As a whole, *The Native of Winby and Other Tales* is clear indication of Jewett's strengths in the short-story form, but unfortunately it demonstrates her weaknesses as well.

The Life of Nancy (1895) is a more consistent collection than its immediate predecessor although, too, is marred by weak, improbable, or sentimental stories. Nevertheless, it contains one of Jewett's best stories and three that are almost as good. The title story, however (*Atlantic Monthly*, February 1895), is the weakest, most improbable, most sentimental story in the collection. Inconsistent in setting and character, disjointed in structure, it recounts an attraction between a country girl from the Maine coast and a young man from Boston that results in what the reader is told is a lifelong friendship, although there is almost no correspondence and they meet only three times: in Maine, by chance in Boston, and again a generation later in Maine. The last occurs when Nancy, crippled and bedridden after teaching school, has become from her bed the town's teacher of dancing and deportment. In spite of an initial section that is both believable and well presented, the story deteriorates into maudlin pathos. Nancy, a believable and capable young woman, becomes too good to be true as she overcomes her physical handicap through an undefined spiritual strength. Unfortunately, Jewett excuses the improbabilities by taking refuge in "the curious inconsistency of fate."

"Fame's Little Day" (*Harper's Magazine*, March 1895) is a slight but pleasant tale of the New York visit of Mr. and Mrs. Abel Pinkham of Wetherford, Vermont. An idle newspaper reporter writes a brief notice of their visit as a joke; other papers embellish it, and Mr. Pinkham becomes a fictional entrepreneur instead of a maple-sugar farmer. The notices give them a sense of importance that belies their fear of the city and overcomes Mr. Pinkham's earlier unpleasant experiences. Having conquered the city–and sent home clippings–they are eager to return home with their new dignity, a dignity that exists nowhere in New York except in their own minds.

"A War Debt" (*Harper's Magazine*, January 1895) attempts to bridge the gulf between North and South as it stresses old ties between families and a new sense of relationship. The story is, however, too ambitious for its substance: a young man from Beacon Street is sent by his grandmother to return a silver cup, rescued from the debris of war by her dead son and the boy's father, to its rightful owners. The boy does so, and he is well received by the old patriarch of the southern family, a former Harvard roommate of the boy's grandfather. On the journey the boy catches a glimpse of a young woman, suggesting that new ties between North and South will emerge in the future.

"The Hilton's Holiday" (*Century Magazine*, September 1893) is a slight but sound story that takes a father and his two small daughters from their remote farm on a day's excursion to town, where the father, caught up in the girls' excitement, forgets the errands that served as an excuse for the trip. In the same vein, light and amusing but well done, is "The Only Rose" (*Atlantic Monthly*, January 1894). Old Mrs. Bickford, who has buried three husbands and remembers each fondly for his good but different points, has a problem. Given a magnificent bouquet by Miss Poindexter, she divides it into three for the three graves; but she has only one rose. Mr. Fraley, the first and the love of her youth, seems to be the sentimental favorite, but the possibility of neglecting the others makes her feel guilty. Deciding to leave the problem to chance, she lets her nephew distribute the bouquets. The rose falls out, and the boy announces that he'll give it to his Lizzie. " 'My first husband, was just such a tall, straight young man as you be,'" she tells him. "'The flower he first give me was a rose.'"

"A Second Spring" (*Harper's Magazine*, December 1893) is another story that combines late love and a practical arrangement, as Israel Haydon, devastated at sixty-seven by the loss of his wife, leads a solitary life, his pride and independence threatened by entreaties that he live with his son. Struck by the old man's declaration that he will never live "in the chimbly-corner of another man's house," the son and his wife find him a housekeeper, the remarkably efficient Maria Durrant. While Haydon settles into his renewed routine, gossip fired by jealousy among other unmarried women threatens what has become a growing relationship, and Israel and Maria marry. The story is serious and sound in spite of the tendency of Maria to be too even, too mild, and too efficient to be true.

In "Little French Mary" (*Pocket Magazine*, November 1895) Jewett addresses the French-Canadian influx into New England. When the town of Dulham receives its first French-Canadian family, the town is curious at first, finding Alexis, the father (they do not attempt to pronounce his last name) valuable and efficient as a handyman. His daughter Mary charms the old men at the store. When they depart at the end of summer to return to Canada, Dulham seems somehow diminished.

The three best stories in the collection, each a fine story in its way, are the last: "The Guests of Mrs. Timms" (*Century Magazine*, February 1894); "A Neighbor's Landmark" (*Century Magazine*, December 1894); and "All My Sad Captains" (*Century Magazine*, September 1895). The first is social comedy based on the New England ritual of invitations and visits among ladies, involving the scrupulously polite confrontation of two memorable, if unlikable, ladies. The second story turns on a man's confused pride and the threatened "harvesting" of two landmark pines. The third pits three old sea captains in competition for the hand of a coquettish widow.

"The Guests of Mrs. Timms" hinges upon four visits, all of them the results of invitations extended and perhaps misunderstood. In the first visit Miss Cynthia Pickett calls upon Mrs. Persis Flagg after an invitation extended at a church county conference. Mrs. Flagg emerges as snobbish, domineering, condescending, and nearly rude as she makes it clear that her toleration of the timid Miss Pickett's visit is a favor to one socially beneath her, and she dismisses Miss Pickett

just before tea. Nevertheless, Mrs. Flagg persuades Miss Pickett to accompany her on a visit to Mrs. Captain Timms of Baxter, seven miles away, who had, at the county conference, invited both of them to call. Mrs. Flagg is particularly curious about Mrs. Timms's house, especially the living-room carpet, which is said to be unusual. The next day the two set off, Miss Pickett restrained in her second-best dress, while Mrs. Flagg wears her best, carrying a huge, bulky purse, which, she tells Miss Pickett, contains two jars of her best jam for Mrs. Timms.

The two are witnesses to the second visit. On the stage they strike up an acquaintance with a woman from a nearby town who is on her way to an extended visit with Mrs. Beckett, at Beckett's Corners, halfway to Baxter. She has been invited by Mrs. Beckett at her church's county convention. When the stage stops at Mrs. Beckett's house, the woman and her trunk are put down, and as the stage pulls out the ladies overhear Mrs. Beckett insisting that she does not remember either meeting the woman or having invited her.

Mrs. Flagg and Miss Pickett become increasingly excited as they near Mrs. Timms's house, Mrs. Flagg especially anticipating a stay overnight. Miss Pickett timidly suggests they also visit a mutual old friend who lives in the town in genteel poverty, a suggestion that Mrs. Flagg deprecates but does not reject.

Mrs. Timms is coolly polite, inviting them in but not even asking them to take off their bonnets. Conversation flags, and in a short time the two are out on the street, upset and unfed. At Mrs. Flagg's suggestion they go to visit the old friend, Miss Nancy Fell.

That visit, they recount on the stage returning home, was a delight: a warm welcome, a good if simple dinner, and much good conversation. As they near Beckett's Corners they anticipate another passenger and her trunk, but they see the woman sitting in a window fanning herself, while Mrs. Beckett cheerfully instructs the driver to bring the woman's other trunk on his next trip. Mrs. Flagg suggests a future call on Mrs. Beckett, who seems friendly and with whom she has a vague connection, but Miss Pickett does not reply.

The story is perfectly executed, and Jewett's ironic portrayal of the irrepressible Mrs. Flagg is superb, clear evidence of her ability to satirize effectively, if seldomly. "The Guests of Mrs. Timms" is among the best of her stories.

"A Neighbor's Landmark" is nearly as effective. It contrasts the grim individualism of farmer-fisherman John Packer and the greed of Mr. Ferris, one of those lumbermen who "stripped land to the bare skin . . . left nothing to grow; no sapling-oak or pine stood where his hand had been," with whom Packer has made a deal in order to assert Ferris's ownership of the trees that were used as landmarks by fishermen at sea as well as travelers by land. Neither the pleas of Packer's wife and daughter nor the concerns of the neighborhood change his mind, but Packer goes out in his boat to fish and to think. While he remembers the role the trees have played in his family, they take on symbolic dimensions representing his own marriage, and he rows rapidly to shore, runs the three-quarters of a mile up the hill, and saves the trees from the axe, as well as from Ferris's greed and his own misguided stubbornness.

"All My Sad Captains" combines humor and pathos as Captain Witherspoon, the poorest and smallest captain, known emphatically as *The* Captain," Captain Shaw, the wealthiest of the three, and Captain Crowe, who owns the finest house, compete for the hand of Mrs. Maria Lunn, the widow of Capt. Peter Lunn. The town itself, like the tradition that the captains represent, is in decline–pleasure boats have replaced the old brigs that the captains remember, and the once-busy wharves and warehouses decay slowly, emitting the odors of the riches they once held. Mrs. Lunn plays her role coquettishly but carefully; while saving face for the others, she selects the most caring, *The* Captain.

The collection contains some of Jewett's best stories as well as some of her weakest, and the contrasts are clear. In the last three stories, dealing with elderly ladies, delightful or not, in her portrayal of the decline of New England tradition as well as its economy, in her plot structures that grow out of the combination of both, and in her clear definition of the setting out of which character seems to emerge, her talents are clear. Conversely, when she ventures into the improbable and the unknown, her work invariably suffers.

In 1896 Jewett published *The Country of the Pointed Firs*, her best-known novel and the work that is often considered her masterpiece. Called by Carlos Baker "the best piece of regional fiction to have come out of nineteenth century America," it includes everything Jewett had learned about her craft, her people, and her region in nearly thirty years of writing fiction. Like *Deephaven* and many of her stories, it is narrated by a woman. Partially serialized in the *Atlantic Monthly* (January, March, July, and September 1896) in segments that stand well as individual stories and sketches, its unifying features are setting, time, and the unobtrusive narrator, who–as a summer visitor to the decaying port of Dunnet Landing–is in but not of the town, "a hermit crab in a new shell." The setting–the village, the country, and seaside of which it is intrinsically a part–embraces the people, the sad captains, the elderly ladies alone, the eccentrics. Each becomes not merely a focal point of the narrator's observation but part of Jewett's epic of place, with past and present fused through ceremony, ritual, and symbolism of artifact and idea into a remarkably unified whole that is real yet epic in tone.

Later editions of the novel have not remained as Jewett organized it in the first edition, thus contributing to some confusion among scholars and students. The first edition contains twenty-one chapters, ending with "Along Shore" and "The Backward View." In 1910 the publishers added "A Dunnet Shepherdess" (*Atlantic Monthly*, December 1899; collected in *The Queen's Twin and Other Stories*, 1899) and "William's Wedding" (*Atlantic Monthly*, July 1910). In 1919 "The Queen's Twin" (*Atlantic Monthly*, February 1899; collected in *The Queen's Twin and Other Stories*) was added, before "The Backward View," used as the last chapter. In 1925, in the Willa Cather edition, the last four chapters, including the three additions, were again rearranged.

The inclusion of the stories from *The Queen's Twin and Other Stories*, the last collection of Jewett's stories published in her lifetime, suggests some of the strong points of that collection. The title story defines the reality of illusion as it recounts a visit to an old widow who lives alone, surrounded by pictures of Queen Victoria, to whom she feels a mystic coincidental kinship. Regally alone, her self-delusion, which she knows realistically is just that, has given her life focus and meaning.

"A Dunnet Shepherdess" recounts another visit to the hills beyond Dunnet Landing, to an old woman who lives with her unmarried daughter, who has given up teaching to live out her remarkable rapport with sheep. In the background is a touching, unfulfilled romance between William, the aging bachelor who uses trout fishing as an excuse to visit the farm, and the lonely shepherdess. They eventually marry in "William's Wedding." The three stories together, as Jewett intended, complement *The Country of the Pointed Firs.*

"Where's Nora?" (*Scribner's Magazine*, December 1898) and "Bold Words at the Bridge" (*McClure's Magazine*, April 1899) are weak Irish-American stories, in the first of which Nora makes a success in America by selling her little "cakeens" to railroaders. In the second, two Irish women, after "bold words at the bridge" over their respective gardens and the affinity of pumpkins for melons, become friends again.

"Martha's Lady" (*Atlantic Monthly*, October 1897) is a slight, improbable story of the lifetime affection, in spite of long separation, between Martha, a servant from a bleak farm, and a Boston lady. Only Miss Harriet Pyne, mistress and aunt respectively to the two women, emerges as one of Jewett's strong, individual women.

The last three stories in *The Queen's Twin and Other Stories*—"The Coon Dog" (*Scribner's Magazine*, August 1898), "Aunt Cynthy Dallet" (previously unpublished), and "The Night Before Thanksgiving" (*Boston Evening Transcript*, 16 November 1895)—are slight stories, the second and third of which are holiday tales. The first is a story of coon hunting, in which old faithful Rover, rather than the allegedly valuable hound, trees the coon. The story has a fine portrait of a female rural confidence person reminiscent of those in Mark Twain's *The Adventures of Huckleberry Finn* (1884). "Aunt Cynthy Dallet" brings together on New Year's Day an old woman who lives alone on a hilltop and her impoverished niece; and "The Night Before Thanksgiving" brings a prodigal home from the West to care for the poor old woman who had befriended him as a boy, thus saving her from a lonely, hungry Thanksgiving. The collection is unfortunately a weak way in which to conclude Jewett's long career as a writer of short fiction.

Jewett published only one more full-length book before the accident that ended her active career, and a handful of stories and poems after the accident. The book is *The Tory Lover* (1901), a historical romance set in New England. The principal characters are Mary Hamilton, an aristocratic young patriot, and her lover, Roger Wallingford, whom Mary persuades to abandon his family's loyalties to the English crown and become a patriot. The story includes all the trappings of popular romance: secret trysts, unsympathetic parents, exciting chases at sea, historical characters, imprisonment, reunions, and a happy ending. The characters, with the exception of a few minor

ones, are thinly portrayed, and the plot is contrived. Nevertheless, in spite of the clichés that abound, Jewett's real talent occasionally breaks through in the scenes and settings in eighteenth-century New England and in the portraits of the traditions of its people.

One of the most prolific contributors to American literature of her time and to the canon of the literature of her region, Jewett has a small but secure place in literary history. The bulk of her work consists of clear, careful expositions of some of the great themes of American and New England history: America's decline as a seafaring nation, the transition from a rural and village economy to urban industrialism, the cross-cultural impact of immigration, the decline of individualism and craftsmanship, and the great migrations to the towns and the cities. These themes are not developed in national or regional terms; they are developed through portraits of the people and places that give them meaning: the old women left alone by chance or circumstances, the sad captains who stare out to sea, the taciturn individualists who wrest a hard living from the thin earth and the bleak ocean, and the young people who seek fortune in the city. Important, too, are the old houses, the vivid natural settings, and the tentative feminism that is etched in her work. The time, place, and people of late-nineteenth-century New England have had no more faithful chronicler, and they endure in her work.

Letters:

Letters of Sarah Orne Jewett, edited by Annie Fields (Boston & New York: Houghton Mifflin, 1911);

Letters of Sarah Orne Jewett now in the Colby College Library (Waterville, Maine: Colby College Press, 1947);

Sarah Orne Jewett Letters, edited by Richard Cary (Waterville, Maine: Colby College Press, 1956; revised and enlarged, 1967);

"Two Letters of Sarah Orne Jewett," edited by David B. Greene, *Notes & Queries*, new series 5 (August 1958): 361-362;

"Letters of Sarah Orne Jewett to Anna Laurens Davies," edited by C. Carroll Hollis, *Colby Library Quarterly*, 8 (September 1968): 97-138.

Bibliographies:

Clara C. Weber and Carl J. Weber, *A Bibliography of the Published Writings of Sarah Orne Jewett* (Waterville, Maine: Colby College Press, 1949);

Clayton L. Eichelberger, "Sarah Orne Jewett (1849-1909): A Critical Bibliography of Secondary Comment," *American Literary Realism*, 2 (Fall 1969): 189-262;

Gwen L. Nagel and James Nagel, *Sarah Orne Jewett: A Reference Guide* (Boston: G. K. Hall, 1978).

Biographies:

F. O. Matthiessen, *Sarah Orne Jewett* (Boston: Houghton Mifflin, 1929);

John T. Frost, *Sarah Orne Jewett* (Kittery Point, Maine: Gundalow Club, 1960).

References:

Louis Auchincloss, *Pioneers and Caretakers: A Study of Nine American Women Novelists* (Minneapolis: University of Minnesota Press, 1965);

Richard Cary, Introduction to *Deephaven and Other Stories* (New Haven: College & University Press, 1966), pp. 7-23;

Cary, Introduction to *The Uncollected Short Stories of Sarah Orne Jewett*, edited by Cary (Waterville, Maine: Colby College Press, 1971), pp. iii-xviii;

Cary, "Jewett on Writing Short Stories," *Colby Library Quarterly*, 6 (June 1964): 425-440;

Cary, "Jewett's Literary Canons," *Colby Library Quarterly*, 7 (June 1965): 82-87;

Cary, "Miss Jewett and Madame Blanc," *Colby Library Quarterly*, 7 (September 1967): 467-488;

Cary, *Sarah Orne Jewett* (New York: Twayne, 1962);

Cary, "Sarah Orne Jewett (1849-1909)," *American Literary Realism*, 1 (Fall 1967): 61-66;

Cary, "Some Bibliographic Ghosts of Sarah Orne Jewett," *Colby Library Quarterly*, 8 (September 1968): 139-145;

Cary, "Violet Paget to Sarah Orne Jewett," *Colby Library Quarterly*, 9 (December 1970): 235-243;

Cary, ed., *Appreciation of Sarah Orne Jewett: Twenty-nine Interpretative Essays* (Waterville, Maine: Colby College Press, 1973);

Willa Cather, Preface to *The Best Stories of Sarah Orne Jewett*, 2 volumes, edited by Cather (Boston: Houghton Mifflin, 1925), I: ix-xix;

Josephine Donovan, *Sarah Orne Jewett* (New York: Ungar, 1980);

Donovan, "The Unpublished Love Poetry of Sarah Orne Jewett," *Frontiers*, 4 (January 1980): 26-31;

Donovan, "A Woman's Vision of Transcendence: A New Interpretation of the Works of Sarah Orne Jewett," *Massachusetts Review*, 21 (Summer 1980): 365-381;

Carolyn Forrey, "The New Woman Revisited," *Women's Studies*, 2 (1974): 37-56;

Katherine T. Jobes, "From Stowe's Eagle Island to Jewett's 'A White Heron,'" *Colby Library Quarterly*, 10 (December 1974): 515-521;

Robin Magowan, "Fromentin and Jewett: Pastoral Narrative in the Nineteenth Century," *Comparative Literature*, 16 (Fall 1964): 331-337;

Jean Sougnac, *Sarah Orne Jewett* (Paris: Jouve et Cie, 1937);

Catherine B. Stevenson, "The Double Consciousness of the Narrator in Sarah Orne Jewett's Fiction," *Colby Library Quarterly*, 11 (March 1975): 1-12;

Margaret F. Toth, *Sarah Orne Jewett* (Minneapolis: University of Minnesota Press, 1966);

Susan A. Toth, "Sarah Orne Jewett and Friends: A Community of Interest," *Studies in Short Fiction*, 9 (Summer 1972): 233-241;

Rebecca West, Introduction to *The Only Rose and Other Tales* (London: Cape, 1937), pp. 7-14;

Percy D. Westbrook, *Acres of Flint: Writers of Rural New England, 1870-1900* (Washington, D.C.: Scarecrow Press, 1951).

Papers:

The most important collections of Jewett's letters and manuscripts are in the Houghton Library at Harvard University, in the Boston Public Library, and at Colby College. Other collections include those at the Folger Shakespeare Library and the Library of Congress.

Richard Malcolm Johnston

(8 March 1822-23 September 1898)

Bert Hitchcock
Auburn University

BOOKS: *The English Classics: A Historical Sketch of the Literature of England from the Earliest Times to the Accession of King George III* (Philadelphia: Lippincott, 1860); revised and enlarged by Johnston and William Hand Browne as *English Literature: A Historical Sketch of English Literature From the Earliest Times* (New York: University Publishing Company, 1873);

Georgia Sketches, as Philemon Perch (Augusta, Ga.: Stockton, 1864); revised and enlarged as *Dukesborough Tales* (Baltimore: Turnbull Brothers, 1871; enlarged again, 1874; revised and enlarged again, New York: Harper, 1883); revised and abridged as *Dukesborough Tales: The Chronicles of Mr. Bill Williams* (New York: Appleton, 1892);

Address, Spoken at the Georgia Academy of the Blind, June 27th, 1867 (Baltimore: Sun Book & Job Printing Establishment, 1867);

Address Spoken Before the Phi Kappa and Demosthenian Societies of the University of Georgia, on Commencement Day, August 2d 1869, On the Dead of Georgia (Athens, Ga., 1869);

School and College Discipline: An Address Delivered before the Philomathean Society of St. John's College, Annapolis, Maryland, on December 11th, 1873 (Baltimore: Printed by Charles Harvey & Company, 1874);

Life of Alexander H. Stephens, by Johnston and Browne (Philadelphia: Lippincott, 1878);

Old Mark Langston: A Tale of Duke's Creek (New York: Harper, 1884);

Two Gray Tourists: From Papers of Mr. Philemon Perch (Baltimore: Baltimore Publishing Company, 1885);

Mr. Absalom Billingslea and Other Georgia Folk (New York: Harper, 1888);

Ogeechee Cross-Firings: A Novel (New York: Harper, 1889);

Widow Guthrie: A Novel (New York: Appleton, 1890);

The Primes and Their Neighbors: Ten Tales of Middle Georgia (New York: Appleton, 1891);

Richard Malcolm Johnston

Studies, Literary and Social, first series (Indianapolis: Bowen-Merrill, 1891);

Mr. Fortner's Marital Claims and Other Stories (New York: Appleton, 1892);

Mr. Billy Downs and His Likes (New York: Webster, 1892);

Studies, Literary and Social, second series (Indianapolis: Bowen-Merrill, 1892);

Little Ike Templin and Other Stories (Boston: Lothrop, 1894);

Lectures on Literature: English, French and Spanish (Akron, Ohio: D. H. McBride, 1897);

Old Times in Middle Georgia (New York: Macmillan, 1897; London: Macmillan, 1897);

Pearce Amerson's Will (Chicago: Way & Williams, 1898);

Autobiography of Colonel Richard Malcolm Johnston (Washington: Neale, 1900).

OTHER: "Early Educational Life in Middle Georgia," part 1, published as chapter 42 in volume 2 of *Report of the Commissioner of Education for the Year 1894-95* (Washington, D.C.: U.S. Government Printing Office, 1896), pp. 1699-1733;

"Early Educational Life in Middle Georgia," part 2, published as chapter 16 in volume 1 of *Report of the Commissioner of Education for the Year 1895-96* (Washington, D.C.: U.S. Government Printing Office, 1897), pp. 839-886.

PERIODICAL PUBLICATIONS: "Reading Bores," *Lippincott's*, 47 (March 1891): 401-403;

"Middle Georgia Rural Life," *Century*, 43 (March 1892): 737-742;

"The Planter of the Old South," *Southern History Association Publications*, 1 (January 1897): 35-44;

"Dogs and Railroad Conductors," *Lippincott's*, 61 (June 1898): 862-864.

Richard Malcolm Johnston holds an important place in that improbable line of nineteenth- and twentieth-century writers of short fiction who emerged from central Georgia to win national acclaim. From Augustus Baldwin Longstreet, this unusual literary succession moves to William Tappan Thompson and Charles Henry Smith (Bill Arp), through Johnston to Joel Chandler Harris and Harry Stillwell Edwards, and to Flannery O'Connor and Alice Walker, women who reveal their middle-Georgia roots as strikingly as any of their male predecessors. Johnston, at the height of his popularity, from the early 1880s through the mid 1890s, had as big a name as any. He was a maker as well as a major beneficiary of the vogue of local-color fiction, that curious, phenomenal blend of romanticism and realism that so enthralled America's reading public. Beginning a professional writing career at the age of fifty-seven and bursting into national prominence when he was sixty-one, Johnston is the key figure linking the robust realism of Old Southwest humor and the quaint romanticism of southern local-color literature. No other individual illustrates so well the postbellum adaptations of the southern short-story writer in order to continue to entertain the nation. The southern literary renascence of the twentieth century would react to those genteel conventions, to the nostalgia and the apologetics, but it would also fruitfully draw upon the regional self-consciousness and portrayal of the "common folk" of this earlier renascence. In doing so, it could not fail to have a debt to Richard Malcolm Johnston, the man who, according to Edmund Clarence Stedman in 1898, was "the founder of a school of fiction and the dean of Southern men of letters."

Johnston, the next to youngest of the six children of Catherine and Malcolm Johnston, was born on a plantation near the village of Powelton in Hancock County, Georgia. Educated at Powelton Academy and Mercer University, from which he graduated in 1841, he taught school briefly before being admitted to the bar in 1843. For fifteen years he alternated between the professions of education and law until in 1857 he was forced to choose between three offers of prestigious positions. He made the decision for teaching: the professorship of belles lettres and oratory at Franklin College (now the University of Georgia) instead of a circuit judgeship or the presidency of his alma mater, Mercer. After serving as a faculty member in Athens for four years, he returned to Hancock County in 1862 to open a private boarding school, Rockby, near Sparta. Johnston, who had married Mary Frances Mansfield on 26 November 1844 and who would become the father of ten children, found life difficult in Reconstruction Georgia. By 1867 he had made the decision to move north to Maryland–specifically, to the village of Waverly, several miles north of Baltimore. Here he relocated his family and opened another school, which he called Pen Lucy. His new school stayed open until 1883, although enrollment began to drop after its first six years, a decline contributed to by Johnston's conversion to Roman Catholicism in 1875.

In Maryland, Johnston was, as he desired, close to centers of literary publishing. His textbook on English literature, one of the first in the country, was published by J. B. Lippincott and Company of Philadelphia in 1860, but except for a humorous sketch that had appeared in *Porter's Spirit of the Times* in 1857 he had been able to secure only local publication for the short fiction he began to write in the late 1850s. During the Civil War, Stockton and Company of Augusta printed four Johnston stories in periodical or pamphlet form and then put them together into a book entitled *Georgia Sketches* (1864). This basic publication pattern Johnston was able to repeat, with enlargement and improvement, when the *New Eclectic* of Baltimore ran five of his previously published tales plus three new ones and Turnbull Brothers then collected the eight as *Dukesborough Tales* (1871). A second edition of *Dukesborough Tales*, which added one story, was published by the Turnbulls in 1874. Still Johnston gained no national audience, nor, in fact, did he receive any financial remuneration for his fiction until five years later when, with the help of Sidney Lanier, he placed a story with *Scribner's Monthly*. *Scribner's* carried one other, and *Harper's* printed five more of his tales in 1881 and 1882. In 1883 Harper and Brothers published a new *Dukesborough Tales* that collected all of his published pieces, a total now of sixteen. Almost overnight Richard Malcolm Johnston found himself a national literary figure.

Although some of its stories (after successive revisions) were now being "collected" for the fourth time and although it would have yet another, a reduced and refined, edition in 1892, the 1883 *Dukesborough Tales* is the definitive version of Johnston's best-known book. The title itself reveals a typicality of form as well as substance: the tale or sketch as opposed to either longer fiction or the classic short story of Nathaniel Hawthorne or Edgar Allan Poe, and the fictional setting of Dukesborough, based on the Powelton, Georgia, of the author's early years and drawing upon his intimate knowledge of the white middle-class inhabitants of that region. At this time Johnston was still in a relatively early stage of moving from the mode of Old Southwest humor to the molds of genteel local-color writing. His stories would become increasingly polished, but at the expense of original vitality and engaging freshness.

Characterization, not plot, was Johnston's strength, and his most memorable characters people his earlier stories. In quick, deft strokes he created such humorous originals as the schoolmasters Israel Meadows (who was not "restrained from taking office by the consciousness of attainments inadequate to the discharge of its duties") in "The Goosepond School" and Josiah Lorriby ("his body was good enough, but his other parts were defective") in "How Mr. Bill Williams Took the Responsibility." Used engagingly as narrators, the characters of Philemon Perch and Bill Williams are the means for revealing far more interesting personages: the wig-wearing title character of "Investigations Concerning Mr. Jonas Lively" and the pompous title character of "The Expen-

sive Treat of Colonel Moses Grice," for example. While his most vivid characters emerge from the Old Southwest humor tradition (individuals such as the deaf and dumb Billy Moon who beats Oglethorpe Josh Green in a militia muster-day fight), Johnston was also capable of striking characterization when he worked at almost the other extreme. The foolish puppy love for a teacher in "The Early Majority of Mr. Thomas Watts" is deeply and directly autobiographical, for example. In between, in *Dukesborough Tales*, in a stratum and from a perspective that would become standard for local-color writing, many other characters from middle Georgia are given fictional life. Such names as Williamson Slippey, Adiel Slack, and Neelus Peeler reveal Johnston's bias for raw humor, a predilection that would never be lost but that increasingly gave way to the demand for placid quaintness.

Launched by the success of *Dukesborough Tales*, Johnston worked to place his stories in leading national magazines (*Harper's*, *Century*, *Cosmopolitan*, for example) and then to have them collected in a book by a major publisher (Harper, or Appleton, for example). Predictably, this larger scheme had a formulaic counterpart in the fiction itself. As, in a total of sixty-six more stories, the rural Georgia world he created became more and more populous, individuality of characters diminished, and plots became repetitious. This trend evolved over six collections, however—from *Mr. Absalom Billingslea and Other Georgia Folk* (1888) to *Old Times in Middle Georgia* (1897), and includes also *The Primes and Their Neighbors* (1891), *Mr. Billy Downs and His Likes* (1892), *Mr. Fortner's Marital Claims* (1892), and *Little Ike Templin* (1894). Excluding six tales that remain in manuscript, only four of Johnston's stories were never collected.

In the collected stories several societal or institutional subjects establish themselves as favorite authorial interests: schools and education, the judiciary, denominational church activities, courtship, and marriage. Translated repeatedly into plot, these subjects lose some of their interest for readers. Still, in many of the tales there remains a certain distinctive appealing whimsy and charm proceeding from Johnston's own personality. Reflected fairly consistently in style or tone, this distinctiveness also continued sometimes to be manifested in eccentric character creations. Moving a reader beyond simple amusement are moments with the Reverend Rainford Gunn, hotel-keeper Pink Fluker, domestically entangled Ephrodtus

Johnston as Southern man of letters, caricatured by J. H. Garnsey for the Atlanta magazine Alkahest *in 1897*

Twilley, the speedy Peeky Grizzle, the self-congratulating Littleberry Roach, the grotesque Poly Cobble, or big, mean Jim Rakestraw. Employed recurrently as a narrator, old Mr. Pate endearingly reveals himself as he relates the antics and activities of his Georgia friends and neighbors. Central Georgia was obviously central to Johnston the writer. To make up "a story of imagination," he said, he had to begin with an actual place he knew well. Possessed of a keen ear and sharp eye, quickly then he focused on the human inhabitants of this place. The rural society in which he spent his youth and early manhood provided "striking rustic individualities" and "oddities of deportment and dialect" that clearly provided the stimuli if not the actual models for his most impressive literary creations.

For a dozen years after closing his school

and moving into Baltimore in 1883, Johnston attempted to be a professional man of letters, earning a living from writing and giving public readings and lectures. Although he worked best and was most popularly successful in shorter fiction form, he also tried his hand at long fiction. Four works published as separate volumes are perhaps more properly called romances rather than novels. Two of them, *Old Mark Langston* (1884) and *Widow Guthrie* (1890), appeared first as books, while *Ogeechee Cross-Firings* (1889) and *Pearce Amerson's Will* (1898), shorter works, initially appeared in periodicals. Similar to his short fiction in their local color, Johnston's novels are quite unlike his short stories in their more serious intents and somber outlook. Exhibiting neither technical skill nor much of the author's natural geniality, none is a very distinguished production. While Johnston had "no equal in his short stories, in humor and character," wrote Charles Dudley Warner in a letter in 1890, "I doubt him on a long novel."

His literary mine playing out and his popularity and income waning, Johnston successfully sought civil service employment in Washington, D.C., first with the U.S. Department of Labor in 1895 and then the U.S. Bureau of Education in 1896. In this second capacity he wrote "Early Educational Life in Middle Georgia" for two annual commissioner's reports. Containing some of his best prose, the study has been seen by some as both the epitome and the most valuable of all of his writings. Nonfiction was a mode he had long worked in, from biography (*Life of Alexander H. Stephens*, 1878) to European-travel account (*Two Gray Tourists*, 1885), to general historical essay or formal literary study (*Studies, Literary and Social*, 1891 and 1892; *Lectures on Literature: English, French and Spanish*, 1897). But, as was true for his fiction, Johnston's best nonfiction came deep from his own personal experience. Representatively noteworthy both for its subject matter and fond, commanding treatment, "Middle Georgia Rural Life" appeared in the March 1892 issue of *Century*. "Reading Bores" and "Dogs and Railroad Conductors," published in *Lippincott's* in 1891 and 1898 respectively, are appealing familiar essays not so much rooted in place as in personality. They particularly make a reader regretful that Johnston did not work much more in the genre of the personal essay.

Very likely a model for Francis Hopkinson Smith's character Colonel Carter of Cartersville, "Colonel" Richard Malcolm Johnston had an extremely attractive personality and an unusually impressive personal presence. By the end of his life, on 23 September 1898 in Baltimore, he was far removed both in time and place from the antebellum rural Georgia that had created and sustained him. The fragmentary, posthumous *Autobiography of Colonel Richard Malcolm Johnston* (1900) is disappointing for its relative lifelessness as well as for its incompleteness and attention to persons other than its author.

Her father's personality, said one of Johnston's daughters, was greater than any of his writings. The literary achievement that Johnston can boast came directly out of his personality, however, and there is irony that the sportive fiction in which he excelled ranked very low on his own classical scale of literary value. He spoke disparagingly of "mere story-telling," claimed that he became a writer of fiction "partly by accident" and only out of financial necessity, and worried about being remembered "only as an aged clown." These opinions notwithstanding, Johnston's skill in sketching memorable humorous characters is undeniable, and his short fiction has considerable value for both American literary and social history. Johnston was to the southern local-color movement what Edward Eggleston was to the western, and he is the preeminent transition figure between late-nineteenth-century southern local-color writing and the earlier Old Southwest humor, now increasingly recognized as the fecund forerunner of much of the best twentieth-century literature of the South. In his creation of the fictional Dukesborough and in collections of short stories with a common geographical setting, Johnston set a precedent for Sherwood Anderson and his *Winesburg, Ohio* (1919), for William March and his Reedyville and Pearl County, Alabama, stories, for Eudora Welty and her Morgana, Mississippi, in *The Golden Apples* (1949), and for William Faulkner and his famed creation of Jefferson and Yoknapatawpha County, Mississippi. If less artistic in form and more superficial in effect than these later works, Johnston's tales and sketches deserve to be remembered. Ten or twelve of his stories will amply reward readers of future generations. "Within their slight translated world," as Edd Winfield Parks has written, they vividly re-create "a few humorous, pathetic, simple, vital characters, a little town in middle Georgia, and a culture which grew out of a way of living."

References:

Robert Bush, "Richard Malcolm Johnston's Marriage Group," *Georgia Review*, 18 (Winter 1964): 429-436;

Corliss Hines Edwards, Jr., "Richard Malcolm Johnston's View of the Old Field School," *Georgia Historical Quarterly*, 50 (December 1966): 382-390;

Sophia Bledsoe Herrick, "Richard Malcolm Johnston," *Century*, 36 (June 1888): 276-280;

Bert Hitchcock, *Richard Malcolm Johnston* (Boston: Twayne, 1978);

Jay B. Hubbell, *The South in American Literature* (Durham, N.C.: Duke University Press, 1954), pp. 777-782, 940-941;

Francis Taylor Long, "Part I of The Life of Richard Malcolm Johnston in Maryland, 1867-1898: Country Gentleman, Teacher, and

Writer, 1867-1881," *Maryland Historical Magazine*, 34 (December 1939): 305-324;

Long, "Part II of The Life of Richard Malcolm Johnston in Maryland, 1867-1898: Some Literary Friendships–The Lecture Platform, 1882-1889," *Maryland Historical Magazine*, 35 (September 1940): 270-286;

Long, "Part III of The Life of Richard Malcolm Johnston in Maryland, 1867-1898: The Closing Years, 1889-1898," *Maryland Historical Magazine*, 36 (March 1941): 54-69;

Edd Winfield Parks, "Professor Richard Malcolm Johnston," *Georgia Historical Quarterly*, 25 (March 1941): 1-15;

Parks, "Richard Malcolm Johnston," in his *Segments of Southern Thought* (Athens: University of Georgia Press, 1938), pp. 223-244;

Charles Forster Smith, *Reminiscences and Sketches* (Nashville, Tennessee: Publishing House of the Methodist Episcopal Church South, 1908), pp. 164-188;

Edmund Clarence Stedman and Stephen B. Weeks, "Literary Estimate and Bibliography of Richard Malcolm Johnston," *Southern History Association Publications*, 2 (October 1898): 315-327;

Jimmy Ponder Voyles, "Richard Malcolm Johnston's Literary Career: An Estimate," *Markham Review*, 4 (February 1974): 29-34;

William A. Webb, "Richard Malcolm Johnston," in *Southern Writers: Biographical and Critical Studies, Volume II* (Nashville & Dallas: M. E. Church, South, 1903; New York: Gordian Press, 1970), pp. 46-81.

Papers:
The R. M. Johnston collections at the Enoch Pratt Free Library in Baltimore and the Georgia Historical Society in Savannah and the Alexander H. Stephens Papers in the Library of Congress are the three largest, most important manuscript collections for Johnston materials. Other papers, primarily letters, may be found in manuscript collections at Duke University, Emory University, Trinity College, Columbia University, Indiana University, and the New York Public Library.

Caroline M. Kirkland
(11 January 1801-6 April 1864)

William V. DeTora
Temple University

See also the Kirkland entries in *DLB 3: Antebellum Writers in New York and the South* and *DLB 73: American Magazine Journalists, 1741-1850.*

BOOKS: *A New Home–Who'll Follow? Or, Glimpses of Western Life, By Mrs. Mary Clavers* (New York: C. S. Francis/Boston: J. H. Francis, 1839); republished as *Montacute* (London: E. Churton, 1840); republished as *Our New Home in the West; or, Glimpses of Life among Early Settlers* (New York: James Miller, 1872);

Forest Life, 2 volumes (New York: C. S. Francis/Boston: J. H. Francis, 1842);

Western Clearings (New York: Wiley & Putnam, 1845; London: Wiley & Putnam, 1846);

Holidays Abroad; or, Europe from the West, 2 volumes (New York: Baker & Scribner, 1849);

The Evening Book; or, Fireside Talk on Morals and Manners, with Sketches of Western Life (New York: Scribner, 1852);

The Book of Home Beauty (New York: Putnam, 1852);

A Book for the Home Circle; or, Familiar Thoughts on Various Topics, Literary, Moral and Social (New York: Scribner, 1853);

The Helping Hand, Comprising an Account of the Home for Discharged Female Convicts and an Appeal in Behalf of That Institution (New York: Scribner, 1853);

Autumn Hours, and Fireside Reading (New York: Scribner, 1854);

Personal Memoirs of George Washington (New York & London: Appleton, 1857).

OTHER: *Spenser and the Faëry Queen*, edited, with an introduction, by Kirkland (New York & London: Wiley & Putnam; 1847; London: Wiley & Putnam, 1847);

Garden Walks with the Poets, edited by Kirkland (New York: Putnam, 1852);

The School-Girl's Garland, first and second series, edited by Kirkland (New York: Scribner, 1864).

Caroline M. Kirkland

PERIODICAL PUBLICATIONS:
FICTION

"The Blighted Heart," *Graham's Lady's and Gentleman's Magazine*, 23 (July 1843): 1-7;

"Courting by Proxy: A Tale of New York," *Graham's Lady's and Gentleman's Magazine*, 24 (May 1844): 215-218;

"Vincent Hervey, or the Man of Impulse," *Columbian Lady's and Gentleman's Magazine*, 2 (August 1844): 49-55;

"The Hard Winter," *Union Magazine of Literature and Art*, 2 (January 1848): 43;

"The Log-House," *Union Magazine of Literature and Art*, 2 (June 1848): 274-275;

"Bush-Life," *Sartain's Union Magazine of Literature and Art*, 6 (January 1850): 70-74.

NONFICTION

"Literary Women," *Sartain's Union Magazine of Literature and Art*, 6 (February 1850): 150-154.

The appearance of *A New Home—Who'll Follow?* in 1839 caused, in the words of Edgar Allan Poe, "an undoubted sensation." Written by an actual western settler, this collection of wilderness sketches by Caroline M. Kirkland was as bold and uncompromising as the frontier it described. The book was a popular and a critical success, and reviewers praised Kirkland's realistic depictions, which, they noted, were rare during a time when sentimental fluff was all too common in popular fiction. Even in its own day, *A New Home* seemed to be something out of the ordinary. Yet it is only in retrospect that Kirkland's real contribution to American letters can be fully appreciated, for this eastern migrant to the West was a literary as well as a literal pioneer. In an age which condoned the imaginative excesses of popular romancers and adventure-tale hacks, Kirkland insisted on the presentation of "actual reality" in fiction. When she succeeded in applying this principle to her own writing, she produced works which signal the early beginnings of realism in American fiction.

Caroline Matilda Stansbury was born 11 January 1801 in New York City. Her father and mother, Samuel and Elizabeth Alexander Stansbury, were a highly literate middle-class couple who passed on to their daughter their own love for literature and reading. A precocious child, Caroline gained the attention of her aunt, Lydia P. Mott, who as headmistress of several academically distinguished seminaries, undertook the task of educating her talented niece. Under her aunt's direction, Kirkland excelled as a scholar, and in her late teens she began teaching in one of Mrs. Mott's schools in New Hartford, New York. There, in 1819, she met William Kirkland, a tutor in the classics at Hamilton College. Soon thereafter the couple became engaged, and on 10 January 1828, following William's return from a two-year study program abroad, they married.

After their marriage the Kirklands moved to Geneva, New York, where their four children— three daughters and a son, Joseph, who would himself become a well-known realist writer—were

born. In Geneva the Kirklands started a girls' school. Despite their best efforts, the venture was financially unsuccessful, and William Kirkland sought employment elsewhere. In 1835 he became principal of the Detroit Female Seminary, and he and his family moved West. During his tenure as principal, William Kirkland began buying land in the Michigan backcountry, and within two years he had amassed, counting his father's holdings, more than thirteen hundred acres of Michigan woodland. In the fall of 1837 the family left Detroit to settle on their land near the frontier village of Pickney.

The move to the frontier proved to be the impetus which Caroline Kirkland's innate literary talents needed. Like so many recently arrived pioneers, Kirkland was appalled at the disparity between the idealized literary portrayals of the West and the much harsher actual conditions of frontier life. In the opening sketch of *A New Home* she confesses that "all I knew of the wilds was from [Charles Fenno] Hoffman's Tour, or Captain [James] Hall's 'graphic' delineations. I had some floating idea of 'driving a barouche-and-four any where through the oak-openings'–and seeing 'the murdered Banquos of the forest' haunting the scenes of their departed strength and beauty. But I confess these pictures, touched by the glowing pencil of fancy, gave me but incorrect notions of a real journey through Michigan." Determined to produce "an unimpeachable transcript of [the] reality" of frontier life, Kirkland spent the next five years in Pickney writing *A New Home* and *Forest Life* (1842), two collections of sketches which chronicle the actual experiences of "Mrs. Mary Clavers" on the Michigan frontier.

To understand just how innovative these chronicles were, one must first understand the nature of the popular western fiction of the time. In *The Rediscovery of the Frontier* (1931) Percy H. Boynton identified "two main kinds" of "conscious literature of frontier days": "what was written from frontier communities–almost invariably affected, unrevealing of anything except the desire of the writers to compose the kind of thing approved by tradition; and what was written about the frontier by more or less careless and more or less unscrupulous observers and sojourners who put in writing a sentimentalized and rapidly conventionalized account to be marketed in the older country."

In many ways, *A New Home* and *Forest Life* are reactions against such idealized portrayals of the West. Eschewing tales of conventional heroism and adventure, Kirkland ignores "romantic incidents" in her work, focusing instead on the daily routine and mundane occurrences of frontier life. *A New Home* opens, for instance, with a graphic and comically delightful description of crossing a Michigan mud hole in a carriage. In the same volume Kirkland evokes the unpleasantness of living in a leaky, drafty, often unbearably hot log cabin, the circumstances of which were never "alluded to in any of the elegant sketches of western life which had fallen under my notice." *Forest Life* reveals a similar concern for accurate presentation. An entire sketch discusses the various kinds of insects that plagued the Michigan pioneer, the frontier being "a rare region for the study of entomology." Clearly Kirkland's frontier is not the pastoral Eden of popular legend, and its inhabitants are equally unidealized. The typical homesteader in *Forest Life* is hardly the self-reliant and robust yeoman of western romance; on the contrary, he is an overworked, often sickly individual suffering from perennial bouts with "ague" and a host of other frontier ailments. Similarly, the woodsman, a wildly idealized figure in so many frontier tales, becomes in Kirkland's hands an opportunistic vagabond whose wondrous adventures in the forest usually involve being "continually subject to accidents of the most appalling kind." Such debunking of frontier stereotypes is a major part of the strategy in *A New Home* and *Forest Life*.

Yet if Kirkland's characters are not the traditional heroes of frontier fiction, they are, nevertheless, peculiarly western. Attempting to depict "some of the very ordinary scenes, manners, and customs of Western Life," Kirkland approaches a kind of regionalist writing which would not become generally popular until after the Civil War. Like the later local-color writers, for instance, Kirkland carefully records dialect because "even language," like everything else in the West, has its own "peculiarities." Mrs. Danforth and Mrs. Titmouse in *A New Home* and Mr. Butts in *Forest Life* speak an "indescribable twang," which is at once indigenous to their particular region and extremely comical to the eastern narrator for whom it is sometimes "scarce intelligible." Kirkland frequently uses regional touches as a source of humor. In *Forest Life* Mrs. Ainsworth practices the annoying habit of using her apron for a handkerchief, and Aunty Parshalls unthinkingly relies on the same pot for cooking, washing, and carrying pig food. Similarly, the distinctively western

custom of borrowing anything a neighbor happens to have is as frustrating to the narrator as it is funny. To have "money or mere household conveniences," writes Kirkland in *A New Home*, and "not be willing to share them in some sort with the whole community, is an unpardonable crime." This kind of detail, which records the individual peculiarities of a particular region, combines the kind of realism and humor usually found only in the historically accurate but comically exaggerated western tall tale.

In her choice of fictional materials, then, Kirkland departed from most conventional frontier writing of her time. The distinctively feminine point of view which is everywhere evident in *A New Home* and *Forest Life* is equally outside the mainstream of traditional western adventure fiction and that of the tall tale as well. Focusing on her actual experiences in the wilderness, Kirkland, not surprisingly, portrays life on the frontier as seen from the female perspective. As a result, many of the best portions of *A New Home* and *Forest Life* deal with the daily routine of the frontier woman's life. In *A New Home* Kirkland observes that "the ironing and the baking were imperious," that "the circumstances of living all summer, in the same apartment with a cooking fire" are intolerable, and that "the inexorable dinner hour, which is passed *sub silentio* in imaginary forests, always recurs, in real woods, with distressing iteration." Such tedium, as is evident in the group quilting scene in *Forest Life*, is only occasionally relieved by moments of leisure. These sketches, which depict a life stripped to its essentials, evoke aspects of the frontier that had been portrayed by authors before her. What is significant in Kirkland's writing is the choice of detail that she uses to paint her picture of wilderness life. Indeed, the fact that such domestic activities as baking and ironing are discussed at all is remarkable given the normal fare of frontier fiction, which almost inevitably focuses on heroic adventure. In this respect, Kirkland's fiction signals, as Judith Fetterley observes, "a realism in American fiction designed not simply to counter previous romanticism" but "designed equally to counter that masculine 'realism' that believes the whole story has been told when the man's story has been told." On various levels, then, Kirkland's work initiates a break with most portrayals of western life, especially in her contribution to our understanding of the hardships of frontier women.

Aesthetically, Kirkland's experience on the frontier was most rewarding, yet the frontier experiment had serious monetary repercussions which the Kirklands had hardly anticipated. By 1843 William had become the victim of a swindling land agent, and the Kirkland family, their financial resources exhausted, was forced to return to New York City. Like so many disappointed frontier settlers, the Kirklands returned to the East in desperate need of money, and both Kirkland and her husband, in addition to teaching, began contributing essays and tales to various popular periodicals. The economic motivation that prompted this writing perhaps best explains the disappointing fiction that Kirkland produced during her first few years in New York. Abandoning the realistic style of her earlier work, Kirkland began writing the kind of economically safe romances that were the staples of the popular magazines of her day. "The Blighted Heart," published in *Graham's* in July 1843, is a sentimental tale narrated by a once proud man who after losing his wife becomes a recluse waiting for death to bring "an union with the loved and lost." "Courting by Proxy: A Tale of New York," appearing in the May 1844 issue of *Graham's*, recounts the story of Alonzo Romeo Rush who, after trying to "love a rich girl," finally discovers that he really loves a poor "little tailoress." "Vincent Hervey, or the Man of Impulse," published in the August 1844 issue of the *Columbian Lady's and Gentleman's Magazine*, focuses on a man who, after many obstacles, finally achieves "the crowning grace of a supremely happy marriage." Even the western tales of this period, originally published in the *Knickerbocker Magazine* and *Graham's* and later collected in *Western Clearings* (1845), reveal a similar preoccupation with sentimental romance. In "Love vs Aristocracy" Persis Allen rejects a haughty village aristocrat and marries a poor but sincere schoolmaster. "Chances and Changes" presents the story of twins who, after a series of comic mix-ups, marry the respective husbands for whom each is best suited. In "The Schoolmaster's Progress" Mr. Horner wins the heart of his beloved Ellen despite the schemes of the jealous Harriet Bangle to prevent the match. There are, of course, a few sketches in *Western Clearings*, such as "The Bee-Tree," that are as good as any in *A New Home* or *Forest Life*. Overall, however, the fiction of this period is inferior to Kirkland's earlier work, although it did, in conjunction with William's publications, provide the Kirklands with financial security.

Such security, however, was short-lived. In 1846 William Kirkland drowned. His death placed a severe financial burden on his wife, who now had to educate and provide for her children "on my own and their earnings principally." Relying on native resiliency and her New York connections, Kirkland eventually found steady employment in 1847 as the sole editor of a new monthly, the *Union Magazine of Literature and Art*, a position she held by herself until 1849, when the sale of the *Union* brought in John S. Hart as coeditor, and the magazine became *Sartain's Union Magazine of Literature and Art*. As an editor, Kirkland objected to the "vapid and valueless" love stories so common in her time; yet sentimental romance frequently appeared in the *Union*, most likely in deference to popular tastes. Kirkland's own contributions to the *Union*, however, marked a return to the realistic style and western settings of her earlier work. "The Hard Winter" (January 1848), for example, is a realistic and bitterly sarcastic portrayal of the effects of a drought on a western community. "The Log-House" (June 1848) presents a "description of the real primitive log house," the one "in which it was our fate first to look western life in the face." "Bush-Life" (January 1850) cautions readers "who have only heard or read of life in the wilderness" not to expect adventures such as "wolf-hunts" and "deer shooting," "following Indian trails, or wading streams in search of fish" because "this view of things is a poor preparation for the reality of life in the wilderness." The success of these tales helped make Kirkland's association with the *Union* a happy and productive one, and by mid century Kirkland's was a well-known name in the most important literary circles of New York City.

Although Kirkland's name as editor continued to appear in the *Union* until 1851, she contributed only a few articles to the periodical after 1849. Indeed, the 1850s initiated yet another change in Kirkland's literary career as she began, over the next decade and a half, to market her own publications, which included three gift books– *The Evening Book* (1852), *A Book for the Home Circle* (1853), *Autumn Hours* (1854)–two verse miscellanies–*Garden Walks with the Poets* (1852), *The School-Girl's Garland* (1864)–and a biography– *Personal Memoirs of George Washington* (1857). Her interests, however, were not solely literary. In 1853 she published *The Helping Hand*, a plea for the rehabilitation of discharged female convicts, and after 1860 she wrote various magazine pieces on the Civil War. Her busy life came to an abrupt end, however, when on 6 April 1864 she died of a stroke in New York City.

Caroline M. Kirkland received favorable reviews from important contemporaries such as William Cullen Bryant and Edgar Allan Poe, yet her work, like that of many women writers of her day, was largely ignored during the century after her death. Revisionist criticism is now rectifying this situation. William S. Osborne's *Caroline M. Kirkland* (1972), an insightful treatment of the entire canon, discusses Kirkland as an early realist, and similar discussions are appearing more frequently in anthologies and book-length critical studies of women writers. The renewed interest in nineteenth-century female authors seems to guarantee that Kirkland will continue to be the subject of further critical evaluation and that this attention, in turn, will allow future readers to see the true significance of this early American realist and feminist.

References:
Percy H. Boynton, *The Rediscovery of the Frontier* (Chicago: University of Chicago Press, 1931), p. 24;
Judith Fetterley, ed., *Provisions: A Reader from 19th-Century American Women* (Bloomington: Indiana University Press, 1985), pp. 117-124;
Langley C. Keyes, "Caroline M. Kirkland: A Pioneer in Realism," Ph.D. dissertation, Harvard University, 1935;
William S. Osborne, *Caroline M. Kirkland* (New York: Twayne, 1972);
Edgar Allan Poe, "The Literati of New York City," *Godey's Lady's Book,* 4 (August 1846): 75-76.

Papers:
There are small collections of Kirkland's letters in the Alderman Library, University of Virginia; in the John M. Olin Library, Cornell University; in the Bentley Historical Library, University of Michigan; at the Historical Society of Pennsylvania; at the Massachusetts Historical Society; in the Houghton Library, Harvard University; and in the Milton S. Eisenhower Library, Johns Hopkins University. A few manuscripts are scattered among the Cincinnati Historical Society; the Harry Ransom Humanities Research Center, University of Texas, Austin; and the Newberry Library in Chicago (which also has letters).

Augustus Baldwin Longstreet

(22 September 1790-9 July 1870)

Doty Hale

California State University, Los Angeles

See also the Longstreet entries in *DLB 3: Antebellum Writers in New York and the South* and *DLB 11: American Humorists, 1800-1950.*

BOOKS: *An Oration, Delivered Before the Demosthenian & Phi Kappa Societies, of the University of Georgia, at the Commencement of August, 1831* (Augusta, Ga.: Printed by W. Lawson, 1831);

An Oration Delivered in the City of Augusta, on the Centennial Birth-Day of George Washington (Augusta, Ga.: Printed by W. Lawson, 1832);

Georgia Scenes, Characters, Incidents, &c. in the First Half Century of the Republic. By A Native Georgian (Augusta, Ga.: Printed at the State Rights Sentinel Office, 1835);

Address Delivered Before the Faculty and Students of Emory College, Oxford, Ga. (Augusta, Ga.: Printed by W. T. Thompson, 1840);

Eulogy on the Life and Public Services of the Late Rev. Moses Waddel, D.D. (Augusta, Ga.: Chronicle & Sentinel, 1841);

Letters on the Epistle of Paul to Philemon, or the Connection of Apostolical Christianity with Slavery (Charleston, S.C.: Printed by B. Jenkins, 1845);

A Voice from the South: Comprising Letters from Georgia to Massachusetts, and to the Southern States (Baltimore: Western Continent Press, 1847);

The Letters of President Longstreet . . . The Alien and Sedition Laws and Virginia and Kentucky Resolutions of 1798 and 1799 . . . The Democratic Platform of 1852 (New Orleans: Printed at the Office of the Louisiana Courier, 1852?);

Know Nothingism Unveiled. Letter of Judge A. B. Longstreet, of Mississippi, Addressed to Rev. William Winans (Washington, D.C.: Printed at the Office of the Congressional Globe, 1855?);

Fast-Day Sermon: Delivered in the Washington Street Methodist Episcopal Church, Columbia, S.C., June 13, 1861 (Columbia, S.C.: Townsend & North, 1861);

Shall South Carolina Begin the War? (Charleston, S.C., 1861);

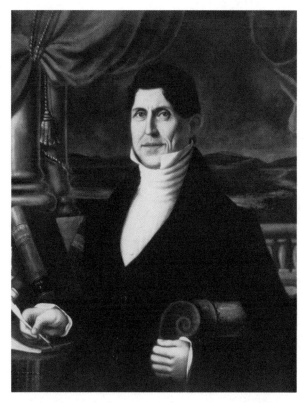

Augustus Baldwin Longstreet (courtesy of Special Collections, Robert W. Woodruff Library, Emory University)

Master William Mitten (Macon, Ga.: Burke, Boykin, 1864);

Valuable Suggestions Addressed to the Soldiers of the Confederate States (Macon, Ga.: Soldiers' Tract Association of the M. E. Church, South, 1864?);

Stories with a Moral Humorous and Descriptive of Southern Life a Century Ago, edited by Fitz R. Longstreet (Philadelphia: Winston, 1912).

Augustus Baldwin Longstreet held four college or university presidencies and was a lawyer, a judge, a captain in the Georgia militia, a state assemblyman, a farmer, a teacher, a polemicist, a newspaper owner, and a Methodist minister. Yet today he is best remembered for his *Georgia*

Scenes (1835), a series of short stories that is generally regarded as setting the pattern for the realistic local-color humor of the American South.

Longstreet's father, William, like his son a man of many careers, at various times tried inventing, mechanics, farming, business, real estate, and politics, prospering in most but losing money in others. His tombstone summed up his general attitude to life: "All the days of the afflicted are evil, but he that is of a merry heart hath a continual feast."

William Longstreet's elder sons followed him into business, but Augustus, born in Augusta, Georgia, on 22 September 1790, showed early signs of intellectual promise. When he was eight his mother, Hannah Randolph Longstreet, wrote her aunt that he "reads and writes, and often makes observations that would surprise you for a child of his age." They sent him to the local academy, where instead of fulfilling his family's hopes he became the class clown, making the other students laugh at his funny faces even while he sat on the dunce stool. A despairing teacher sent him home, suggesting that he belonged in a lunatic asylum.

Augusta was then a bustling frontier city, full of cotton and tobacco warehouses, stage-coaches, theaters, and race courses. Young Longstreet found the atmosphere in its streets and in the countryside near Edgefield, South Carolina (where his family lived from the time he was eleven or twelve until 1805), more congenial than school. His chief ambition in his early teens was to "outrun, outjump, outshoot, throw down any man in the district." He was later to enliven his short stories with descriptions of such activities, but the schooling he needed to translate real life into literature did not interest him until he met young George McDuffie, who roomed in Mrs. Longstreet's boardinghouse. Greedy for education, McDuffie read everything from newspapers to classics aloud to his young roommate. Longstreet found it "first irksome, then tolerable, then delightful. Thus I acquired my first taste for reading. . . ."

After attending Dr. Moses Waddel's well-known boarding school in Willington, South Carolina, Longstreet went to Yale, graduating in 1813. He then entered the law school of Judges Tapping Reeve and James Gould in Litchfield, Connecticut. In New England he applied himself to his studies (Emory University Library has one of his notebooks from that time); his classmates also remembered him as a raconteur and jokester.

He returned to Augusta in late 1814 when his father died and was admitted to the Georgia bar the next year. In March 1817 the young lawyer married Frances Eliza Parke of Greensboro, Georgia, and moved his practice there. Their union lasted fifty-one years and produced eight children, only two of whom survived to adulthood. After several years as a lawyer, he served as a Georgia assemblyman in 1821, and the next year he was appointed to a three-year term as a Georgia Superior Court judge. In 1827 the Longstreets moved to Augusta.

Politically Longstreet found himself caught up in the controversy between the Federalists, who wanted a strong central government, and those who called for broader powers for state governments. Longstreet gradually became a states' rights advocate, and in 1833, when a Federalist newspaper, the *North American Gazette*, came up for sale in Augusta, Georgia, he bought it and changed its name to the *State Rights Sentinel*.

The first issue of the *Sentinel* (9 January 1834) advised old subscribers that the new paper would not follow the Federalist political sentiments of "the late Editor, but apart from politics, we hope to lay before them . . . useful and interesting matter enough to repay them amply for the support they may give us." The best–and most popular–features Longstreet offered his readers were his nonpolitical, local-color stories. Some of them had already been published in the *Milledgeville* (Georgia) *Southern Recorder:* "The Dance" (30 October 1833), "The Song" (6 November 1833), "The Horse-Swap" (13 November 1833), "The Turf" (20 November 1833), "The Fight" (27 November 1833), "The Turn Out" (11 December 1833), "The Character of a Native Georgian" (1 and 8 January 1834), and "The Gander Pulling" (15 January 1834). Though the issues containing them are no longer in existence, three other stories, which later appeared in the *State Rights Sentinel*, are reported to have been published first in the *Recorder:* "The Ball" (*Recorder*, 1832; *Sentinel*, 6 March 1834), "Georgia Theatrics" (*Recorder*, 1833; *Sentinel*, 10 March 1834), and "An Interesting Interview" (*Recorder*, 1834; *Sentinel*, 17 March 1834).

Once he had his own newspaper, Longstreet republished these stories and then some new ones: "The 'Charming Creature' as a Wife" (14 April 1834), "The Mother and Her Child" (2 June 1834), "The Fox Hunt" (12 February 1835), "The Wax Works" (19 February 1835), "Dropping to Sleep" (26 February 1835), "The Debating Society" (5 March 1935), and "A Sage Conversation" (17 March 1835).

Later in 1835 the *State Rights Sentinel* published the first book edition of *Georgia Scenes*, containing all these stories except the short sketch "Dropping to Sleep," as well as "The Shooting Match," whose original periodical appearance has not been located, and "The Militia Drill" (*State Rights Sentinel*, 15 May 1834), by a friend later identified as Oliver H. Prince. Longstreet says in his preface that some of the stories are "literally true" and others are combinations of events, some imagined, but "usually *real* . . . happening at different times and under different circumstances."

The author of *Georgia Scenes* was listed as "A Native Georgian," and even though Longstreet was known to have written the book, he claimed to be "extremely desirous of concealing the author, and, the more effectually to do so, I wrote under two signatures"–Hall and Baldwin. Hall is the narrator of the twelve stories with male protagonists and Baldwin of the six with female protagonists. Longstreet subsequently explained that the stories were written not just for entertainment but to fill "a chasm in history which has always been overlooked–the manners, customs, amusements, wit, dialect, as they appear in all grades of society" and especially of those in the "common walks of life. . . . their remarks upon the dresses of their characters, the horses, their mode of driving, and their blunders; upon the pugilistic combatants, their appearance, their muscle, their remarks; . . . their own private games, quarrels, and fights." While Longstreet wished to provide a broad social history, the details he lists were, especially in his time, chiefly of interest to males. It is not surprising, therefore, that Hall's stories are not only more numerous than Baldwin's, but also more lively. In fact, they are so lively that Longstreet felt constrained in his preface to remind "those who have taken exceptions to the coarse, inelegant, and sometimes ungrammatical language . . . *that it is language accommodated to the capacity of the person to whom he represents himself as speaking.*" Certainly by today's standards, the language is mild enough.

Today's readers are likely to find Longstreet's attempt to render southern dialect more interesting than shocking. Like many writers, Longstreet used dialect as an indication of class; educated southerners are accorded standard spelling and grammar unless they are (like Ned Brace) deliberately imitating their lessers. Black

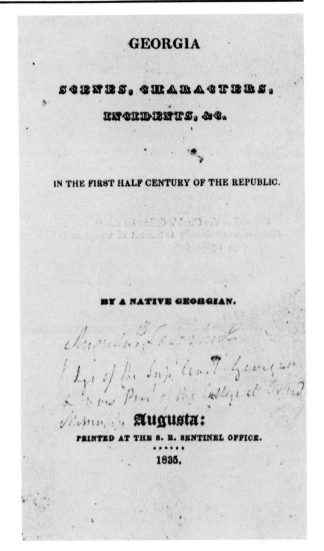

Title page for Longstreet's first book, an early example of southern local-color humor (courtesy of the South Caroliniana Library, University of South Carolina)

speech is consistently dialectical in spelling and syntax; the speech of rural and lower-class whites is between the two, with only occasional dialectical spellings ("sarment" for sermon) and grammatical errors to indicate departure from the standard.

Today some of the gory descriptions of the events themselves may seem more "coarse" than the language. In "The Fight" one combatant loses his left ear, his middle finger, and "a large piece from his left cheek"; the other loses a third of his nose. In "The Gander Pulling" a gander's feet are bound, his neck is greased, and he is suspended from a rope. Men on horseback gallop by, pulling on the neck until the head is wrenched from the body. In such stories narrator Hall usually disassociates himself from these activities at some point, calling them "cruel" or "abhorrent" and sure to give way before the spread of democracy or Christian doctrine. Once having issued these caveats, however, Hall resumes the stories with further vivid, lively, and realistic details.

Not all of narrator Hall's stories are as bloody, but they generally reflect Longstreet's early ambition to "outrun, outjump, outshoot, throw down any man in the district." One exception is "The Debating Society," drawn from Longstreet's later experiences: he and George McDuffie played a prank on their forensic club by creating a nonsensical subject and arguing it with pretentious language. In the story the subject is "whether, at public elections, should the votes of faction predominate by internal suggestions or the bias of jurisprudence?"

Only three of Baldwin's stories are as lively as most of Hall's, largely because Baldwin most often deals with upper-class women. Longstreet, like most of his contemporaries, presented women as either paragons of virtue or silly, selfish manipulators. Most of Baldwin's paragons, such as the mother in "A 'Charming Creature' as a Wife," are described secondhand rather than shown in action. Their lesser sisters are either made ridiculous (Miss Aurelia Emma Theodosia Augusta Crump of "The Song" and the Misses Feedle, Deedle, Rino, and Gilt of "The Ball") or cruel and stupid (the slapping, shouting, baby-talking mother in "The Mother and Her Child"). In the longest and worst story narrated by Baldwin, "A 'Charming Creature' as a Wife," the title character bedazzles Baldwin's nephew into marriage and then insults his family and friends, sleeps late, and mismanages his household. She promises to reform and tries; but it is a "struggle against nature," and after three months she returns to her old habits. At the end the young husband abruptly dies "the drunkard's death."

Baldwin is a far more believable narrator, however, when he enters what Longstreet called "the common walks of life." In "The Dance" the unaffected, merry, but plainly dressed young women from "one of the frontier counties" are openly contrasted with "some weakly, sickly, delicate, useless, affected, 'charming creature' of the city." Similarly, in "A Sage Conversation" Baldwin claims that he loves, respects, and is amused by the "aged matrons of our land." Some critics insist that he is more amused than respectful and implicitly jeers at the gossipy old women by calling their conversation "sage." The women do, however, have their own homespun wisdom and understanding of people. Moreover, Longstreet's own sense of fun and his mastery of dialogue come through as their conversation shows the wandering, tangential turns that casual talk usually takes.

Nineteenth-century critical reception of the book was generally enthusiastic and adulatory. Edgar Allan Poe said, "Seldom–perhaps never in our lives–have we laughed so immoderately over any book as over the one now before us." Harper and Brothers reprinted *Georgia Scenes* in 1840 and from then until 1884 put out nine printings, all called the "second edition." Other editions followed, and various stories have been anthologized, usually in collections of southern or "frontier" humor.

In 1836 Longstreet sold the *Sentinel*, but in spring 1838, when William Tappan Thompson, who had worked with Longstreet on the *Sentinel*, began to publish his own newspaper, the *Augusta Mirror*, Longstreet gave him three stories–"Little Ben," "A Family Picture," and "Darby Anvil"– which appeared in the *Mirror* in 1838 and 1839. In autumn 1838, embittered by the machinations of politics, Longstreet decided to become a Methodist minister and was admitted to the ministry "on trial." He received full ordination in January 1843. In August 1839 he was appointed president of Emory College and held that post until 1848. After serving for five months in early 1849 as president of Centenary College in Louisiana, Longstreet became president of the University of Mississippi and remained there until 1856. In 1858 he accepted the presidency of the University of South Carolina and served until late 1861, when the student body resigned en masse to join the Confederate Army. After the war Longstreet went to live with his granddaughter in Oxford, Mississippi, where he died in 1870.

For a short time between 1838 and the early 1840s Longstreet discontinued short-story writing, but he resumed his efforts when it was pointed out to him that his stories were really "*moral*," if only through their "delicate satire." It was, as John Donald Wade notes, "an argument which an already half-hearted opponent could not well resist." Consequently, when William Gilmore Simms sought contributions for the Savannah, Georgia, *Magnolia, or Southern Monthly*, Longstreet sent three more stories: "The Old Soldiers" (March 1843), "The Gnatville Gem" (June 1843), and "Julia and Clarissa" (September-October 1843). Two others, "John Bull's Trip to

Illustration from the second edition of Georgia Scenes *(1840)*

the Gold Mines" and "The India Rubber Story," were apparently never published; Wade thinks they have been lost, along with five others reputed to have been written by Longstreet: "The Corn Shucking," "Climbing the Greasy Pole," "A Night at College," "The Coquettes," and "The Snake Bite." Five of the six stories from the *Augusta Mirror* and the *Magnolia* were posthumously published in Oscar P. Fitzgerald's biography (1891) and in *Stories with a Moral* (1912). In the sixth, "Little Ben," a man with a speech defect narrates two stories, which, according to Wade, "make very hard reading." The other five later stories differ from those in *Georgia Scenes* because they deal more with the urban middle class; yet—again—the stories with male protagonists are better than those with females. "Darby Anvil" is an entertaining story about a hypocritical politician. "The Gnatville Gem" shows the problems of editing a newspaper, especially when one caters to the desires of the subscribers instead of writing from one's own knowledge and convictions. "The Old Soldiers" is a melodramatic tale in which two old men discover that they served in the Revolutionary War together. "Julia and Clarissa" is an interminable tale of female backbiting and marriage-jockeying. "A Family Picture," also long and quite

loosely structured, is nevertheless enlivened by the scenes of normal children playing pranks and quarreling among themselves.

As far as has been determined, these stories marked the end of Longstreet's short-story writing. Rev. J. T. Wightman told Fitzgerald that Longstreet "said to me on one occasion that he intended to redeem the humor of this book [*Georgia Scenes*] by writing another 'Georgia Scenes' of a religious character, but the war kept his pen at rest." (Longstreet was against a civil war, but once the South had seceded, he used his pen to promote its cause.) Fitzgerald wonders if a strictly religious *Georgia Scenes* would have succeeded. If *Master William Mitten* (1864)—a novel begun in 1849, set aside after five chapters, and then completed in 1859—is any indication, Fitzgerald is right to wonder. Unlike *Georgia Scenes*, where the depiction of manners, customs, and wit was his aim, *Master William Mitten* was written to improve the morals of overindulgent mothers and their indolent children. After its publication Longstreet said that some few readers appreciated this aim, "but by a large majority of readers, who expected at the opening of it a rehash of the 'Georgia Scenes,' it was considered a dead failure." Most subsequent critics agree with the "large majority," for the book alternates between William Mitten's repeated sinning (stealing, cigar smoking, cheating, drinking, consorting with bad company) and his mother's weakness in allowing it. The best parts of the book come when Mitten, like Longstreet, attends Dr. Waddel's school and engages in nothing more than lively schoolboy pranks. After Mitten leaves Waddel's school, he resumes his repetitious bouts with most of the known sins. He actually makes some money gambling until "he was arrested in his career by that disease so common to gamblers, and so fatal to all, consumption." Following an unlikely conversion, he "preached powerfully" for a month, and then died.

After the publication of *Master William Mitten* Longstreet continued to enjoy stories, and told them privately, but his later publications are religious, political (mainly supporting the Southern cause), or academic (inaugural and commencement addresses). Thus his literary reputation largely rests on some twenty-five short stories. They were enough. Twentieth-century critics such as Walter Blair and Bernard DeVoto agree that, in DeVoto's words, "So far as any man may be credited with the discovery that this realistic humor of the backwoods was the material of literature, the distinction is Longstreet's."

Letters:
J. R. Scafidel, ed., "Letters of Augustus Baldwin Longstreet," 2 volumes, Ph.D. dissertation, University of South Carolina, 1976.

Biographies:
Oscar P. Fitzgerald, *Judge Longstreet, A Life Sketch* (Nashville, 1891);

John Donald Wade, *Augustus Baldwin Longstreet: A Study of the Development of Culture in the South* (New York: Macmillan, 1924); new edition, edited by M. Thomas Inge (Athens: University of Georgia Press, 1969).

References:
Jesse Bier, *The Rise and Fall of American Humor*

(New York: Holt, Rinehart & Winston, 1968), pp. 61-65;

Walter Blair, *Native American Humor, 1800-1900* (New York: American Book Co., 1937), pp. 287-298;

Bernard DeVoto, *Mark Twain's America* (Boston: Little, Brown, 1932), pp. 96-97;

Emory Phoenix, special Longstreet number, 18 (November 1903);

Kenneth Lynn, *Mark Twain and Southwestern Humor* (Boston: Little, Brown, 1959), pp. 61-72;

B. R. McElderry, Jr., Introduction to *Georgia Scenes* (New York: Sagamore Press, 1957), pp. v-x;

Vernon Louis Parrington, "Augustus Baldwin Longstreet," in his *The Romantic Revolution in America, 1800-1860*, volume 2 of *Main Currents in American Thought* (New York: Harcourt, Brace, 1927), pp. 166-172;

Edgar Allan Poe, Review of *Georgia Scenes, Southern Literary Messenger*, 2 (March 1836): 287-292.

Papers:
A fire at Longstreet's Oxford, Mississippi, home destroyed most of his papers. The South Caroliniana Library at the University of South Carolina and the Robert W. Woodruff Library at Emory University have small collections of manuscripts and letters. Other letters are scattered among the William R. Perkins Library, Duke University; the University of Georgia; the Beinecke Library, Yale University; the Library of Congress; the Georgia Historical Society, Savannah; the Lilly Library, Indiana University; the Boston Public Library; the Houghton Library, Harvard University; the University of Mississippi; the University of North Carolina at Chapel Hill; Morristown National Historic Park, Morristown, New Jersey; the Ohio Historical Society, Columbus; Dickinson College; the Historical Society of Pennsylvania; and the Robert Muldrow Cooper Library, Clemson University.

Herman Melville

(1 August 1819-28 September 1891)

A. Robert Lee
University of Kent at Canterbury

See also the Melville entry in *DLB 3: Antebellum Writers in New York and the South.*

BOOKS: *Narrative of a Four Months' Residence among the Natives of a Valley of the Marquesas Islands; Or, A Peep at Polynesian Life* (London: Murray, 1846); republished as *Typee: A Peep at Polynesian Life. During a Four Months' Residence in a Valley of the Marquesas, With Notices of the French Occupation of Tahiti and the Provisional Cession of the Sandwich Islands to Lord Paulet*, 2 volumes (New York: Wiley & Putnam/London: Murray, 1846); revised edition, with "The Story of Toby," 2 volumes (New York: Wiley & Putnam/London: Murray, 1846);

The Story of Toby, A Sequel to "Typee" (London: Murray, 1846);

Omoo: A Narrative of Adventures in the South Seas, 2 volumes (London: Murray, 1847; New York: Harper/London: Murray, 1847);

Mardi: And a Voyage Thither (3 volumes, London: Bentley, 1849; 2 volumes, New York: Harper, 1849);

Redburn: His Voyage. Being the Sailor-Boy Confessions and Reminiscences of the Son-of-a-Gentleman, in the Merchant Service (2 volumes, London: Bentley, 1849; 1 volume, New York: Harper, 1849);

White Jacket; Or, The World in a Man-of-War, 2 volumes (London: Bentley, 1850); republished as *White-Jacket; Or The World in a Man-of-War*, 1 volume (New York: Harper/London: Bentley, 1850);

The Whale, 3 volumes (London: Bentley, 1851); republished as *Moby-Dick; Or, The Whale*, 1 volume (New York: Harper/London: Bentley, 1851);

Pierre; Or, The Ambiguities (New York: Harper, 1852; London: Sampson Low, 1852);

Israel Potter: His Fifty Years of Exile (New York: Putnam, 1855; London: Routledge, 1855);

The Piazza Tales (New York: Dix & Edwards/London: Sampson Low, 1856);

Herman Melville, 1870 (portrait by J. O. Fenton; courtesy of the Ganesvoort-Lansing Collection, Manuscripts and Archives Division, the New York Public Library, Astor, Lenox and Tilden Foundations)

The Confidence-Man: His Masquerade (New York: Dix, Edwards, 1857; London: Longman, Brown, Green, Longmans & Roberts, 1857);

Battle-Pieces and Aspects of the War (New York: Harper, 1866);

Clarel: A Poem and Pilgrimage in the Holy Land, 2 volumes (New York: Putnam's, 1876);

John Marr and Other Sailors, With Some Sea-Pieces (New York: De Vinne, 1888);

Timoleon Etc. (New York: Caxton, 1891);

The Apple-Tree Table and Other Sketches, edited by
Henry Chapin (Princeton: Princeton University Press, 1922);

Billy Budd and Other Prose Pieces, edited by Raymond Weaver, volume 13 of *The Works of Herman Melville*, Standard Edition (London, Bombay & Sydney: Constable, 1924); "Billy Budd, Foretopman," republished in *Shorter Novels of Herman Melville*, edited by Weaver (New York: Liveright, 1928);

Poems . . . Battle-Pieces, John Marr and Other Sailors, Timoleon and Miscellaneous Poems, edited by Michael Sadleir and Weaver, volume 16 of *The Works of Herman Melville*, Standard Edition (London, Bombay & Sydney: Constable, 1924);

Journal Up the Straits, October 11, 1856-May 5, 1857, edited by Weaver (New York: The Colophon, 1935); republished as *Journal of a Visit to Europe and the Levant, October 11 1856-May 6, 1857*, edited by Howard C. Horsford (Princeton: Princeton University Press, 1955);

Journal of a Visit to London and the Continent by Herman Melville, 1849-1850, edited by Eleanor Melville Metcalf (Cambridge, Mass.: Harvard University Press, 1948; London: Cohen & West, 1949).

Editions and Collections: *The Works of Herman Melville*, Standard Edition, 16 volumes (London, Bombay & Sydney: Constable, 1922-1924);

Billy Budd Sailor (An Inside Narrative) . . . Reading Text and Genetic Text, edited by Harrison Hayford and Merton Sealts, Jr. (Chicago: University of Chicago Press, 1962);

The Writings of Herman Melville, Northwestern-Newberry Edition, edited by Hayford, Hershel Parker, and G. Thomas Tanselle, 9 volumes to date (Evanston: Northwestern University Press, 1968-   ).

OTHER: Merton M. Sealts, *Melville as Lecturer*, includes the texts of three lectures by Melville, "based on contemporary newspaper accounts" (Cambridge, Mass.: Harvard University Press, 1957), pp. 127-185.

"You must have plenty of sea-room to tell the truth in," wrote Herman Melville in "Hawthorne and His Mosses," the pseudonymous, two-part review of Nathaniel Hawthorne's *Mosses from an Old Manse* (1846) that he published in the *Literary World* for 17 and 24 August 1850. Melville

had made his bow as an author with an outpouring of sea and adventure fiction whose centerpiece would shortly be *Moby-Dick* (1851), as capacious a narrative as nearly any in Western fiction. He had been obliged in his early twenties to escape the genteel poverty of his New York family by signing on as a seaman aboard a whaling ship, which sailed from New Bedford on 3 January 1841. He was not to return to the United States until October 1844, after having seen the great Atlantic and Pacific whale fisheries, and having been, at different times, a common sailor before the mast, a harpooner, a deserter from the crew of a whaling ship, a freebooter in the Marquesas, Tahiti, and Honolulu, and eventually an enlistee aboard a returning man-of-war. If any one hallmark has come to be associated with his work, it has to be its oceanlike scale, nothing less than the restless "diving" for "vital truth" as well as the "real originality" he also invokes in the course of "Hawthorne and His Mosses."

The tendency to see Melville as a writer who required "sea-room" and to view *Moby-Dick* as its most dramatic apotheosis has been understandable, but over time readers have discerned in Melville's life and work a greater variety, other quite unexpected facets and claims. "Mighty" as *Moby-Dick* may be ("To produce a mighty book, you must have a mighty theme," says Ishmael), it takes its place within the yet larger body of his writing, his nonfiction and poetry as well as his other fiction, an output which began with *Typee* (1846) and concluded with the posthumously published novella *Billy Budd* (1924). This output, of necessity, embraces his short stories, the best of them–"Bartleby, The Scrivener," "The Encantadas," and "Benito Cereno"–included with two others–"The Lightning-Rod Man" and "The Bell-Tower"– and the story-sketch "The Piazza" in *The Piazza Tales* (1856), the only collection of his short stories published during his lifetime.

Set in the context of both his writing and life, the stories occupy a strikingly compact and convenient niche, three busy years at mid career, 1853-1856, during which he wrote sixteen stories and published fourteen of them in *Harper's New Monthly Magazine* or *Putnam's Monthly Magazine*. His other short fiction comprises only early and late miscellaneous pieces and "The Town Ho's Story," published in *Harper's New Monthly* in October 1851 and included in *Moby-Dick* as chapter 54. But, despite the acclaim that "Bartleby" and the best of Melville's other stories have come to enjoy, none was well regarded in his lifetime.

Rather, they gave their few readers the impression of minor *exercises de style*. They seemed odd, knotty stories, full of offbeat disgruntlement and jokery, and to some they appeared to be evidence of a career in decline, or one which had dissolved into obscurity and too private a manner. Melville's stories, particular and distinct as they may be, are recognizably the products of the same vital imagination that created *Moby-Dick*.

"Until I was twenty-five, I had no development at all. From my twenty-fifth year I date my life," Melville wrote to Nathaniel Hawthorne in June 1851. His twenty-fifth year was the year he began writing *Typee*, his first work of fiction. A key "development" the book may have been, but it was not entirely out of keeping with a life already marked by a whole run of changes and reversals. Born on 1 August 1819, the third of eight children, he spent his boyhood in New York City, where his father Allan Melvill (Melville himself added the final *e*) did business as an "importer of French Goods and Commission Merchant." His mother, Maria Gansevoort Melvill, descended from a leading New York Dutch-American, or Knickerbocker, family. Much to their mutual satisfaction both sides could lay claim to kin prominent in the Revolutionary War: Maj. Thomas Melvill, who took a leading part in the Boston Tea Party, and Gen. Peter Gansevoort, who held his commission under George Washington. This stock was also to be of considerable pride to Melville, the basis of high personal expectations. "Somewhat slow in comprehension" as his father called him at seven, he entered the New York Male High School in 1827, took occasional family holidays in Boston and Albany, ingested a fair dose of Calvinism from one of his grandmothers, and appears to have grown up a pliant, convivial, if at times somber, youngster.

The first shock to this cushioned environment came with the bankruptcy–closely followed by the delirium and death–of his revered father in the trade recession of 1832. (Allan Melvill had moved the family to Albany in 1830.) Melville was to reconfront these events in *Pierre* (1852), and the effect on the family at large was also profound. Money became tighter than ever, and Maria Melvill found herself and the children edging toward genteel poverty if not outright indigence. For Melville it began a series of false starts. In 1833 and 1834 he worked at an uncle's farm in Pittsfield, Massachusetts (where he would buy his own farm, Arrowhead, in 1850). During

1834-1836 he clerked in his brother Gansevoort's store in Albany. In 1837 he tried teaching in a Pittsfield country school, an experience which no doubt lies behind Ishmael's allusion to schoolmastering in *Moby-Dick*. In 1838 he made his authorial debut, writing in a debating club controversy for the *Albany Microscope*, and studied surveying and engineering at the Lansingburgh Academy, most probably in the hope of working on the Lake Erie Canal system. No permanent job presented itself. In June 1839 he sailed down the Hudson to New York and secured a place to Liverpool and back as a deckhand aboard the packet ship *St. Lawrence*. He portrayed his encounters with the brute equations of Victorian sailor and city life, with some irony, in *Redburn* (1849). Once back in New York and again jobless he tried another spell of teaching, and in 1840 he took off to Illinois, where he traveled the Mississippi, an experience reworked in his canny "metaphysical" satire, *The Confidence-Man* (1857).

In near desperation, in January 1841 he sailed out of Fairhaven, Massachusetts, as a whaleman and harpooner aboard the *Acushnet*, the beginning of four years of Polynesian and whaling adventure. His outward journey took him to Rio de Janeiro, round Cape Horn, through the Galápagos Islands, and eventually to the Marquesas, where, with his friend Toby Greene, he jumped ship at Nukuhiva in July 1842. His escape into an inland valley would become the basis of *Typee*. By signing on with two further whalers, the *Lucy Ann* out of Australia and the *Charles & Henry* out of Nantucket, he island-hopped through Tahiti and the Hawaiian islands before disembarking at Honolulu in May 1843. These travels would provide him with the material for *Typee*'s sequel, *Omoo* (1847). In August 1843 he signed on as an enlisted seaman aboard the frigate *United States*, returning to Boston in October 1844 after stopovers once again in the Marquesas and Tahiti, then Valparaiso, Callao, and Rio. From this journey he had the basis for *White Jacket* (1850). Back one more time in Lansingburgh and as much as anything to amuse his mother and sister, he started to write up his Marquesan experiences. The upshot was *Typee*.

Ostensibly a "narrative" of a young sailor's desertion and escape into a tropical Marquesan valley, this first full-length venture was neither quite fiction nor fact. Its adventure-filled story blends suspense with romance, a daring mix of sailors' high jinks, amateur anthropology, and reportings of cannibalism and other hidden tribal rituals and rites. To his more staid contemporaries Melville was shocking, a sailor-turned-teller whose book bordered on the lewd and called into question "civilized" standards. To admirers, however, he became the find of the season, full of derring-do in his unveiling of an alternative, primitive other world. His tongue-in-cheek reportage and general mischief merely added to the flavor. In retrospect *Typee* has come to be seen as even subtler, unexpectedly well designed, a tale whose different skeins play into an unfolding whole. Certainly the book points forward to the stories with its use of paradox and ambiguity in the confusion over which tribe—the Typees or the Happars—is cannibalistic or friendly, over the contrast of Polynesian totem and taboo with their equivalents in Western life: Pacific, tropical ways of being against Yankee uptightness, and over the stain of cannibalism in the one domain against the stain of colonialism and disease in the other. Anything but a book of "unvarnished truth," as the narrator Tommo alleges, *Typee* shows Melville's instinctual adeptness at the essential elements of storytelling.

In 1847 not only was *Omoo* published, but a number of new turns in his domestic life took place. In February Evert Duyckinck, editor of the newly created *Literary World,* asked him to contribute book reviews—a sign that he amounted to something more than a mariner home from the seas with a passing literary flair. In July 1847 he produced a run of satirical sketches on "Old Zack," President Zachary Taylor, for the journal *Yankee Doodle.* On 4 August 1847 he married Elizabeth Shaw, daughter of the Chief Justice of Massachusetts, a widely applauded match. Their first son, Malcolm, was born in February 1849, their second, Stanwix, in October 1851; two daughters followed, Elizabeth in 1853 and Frances in 1855.

Omoo, however much it may be regarded as an appendix to *Typee,* shows the same flair. Again one encounters episodes and short dramatic events made over into a single line of narrative, each glossed and given life by the energy of Melville's storytelling voice. This energy emerges in accounts of island-hopping; the portrait of the gargoyled Dr. Long Ghost; attacks on the baleful influence of the colonizers, missionaries, and sailors who have brought malaria (and worse) to the islanders; and in the evidence of declining self-esteem among the different peoples, especially those of Honolulu. Melville's play never eclipses his underlying seriousness; his narrative is at once an entertainment and an act of witness, even instruction.

With *Mardi* (1849) the ability to weave each episode and digression into a convincing whole failed him. Subtitled *And a Voyage Thither,* this "Book of Dreams"–as Melville chose to call it–takes its narrator and companions across an archipelago of island kingdoms, most of them mythicized and fantastical, others versions of Europe and America. The book is an endeavor to create nothing less than a world allegory, but its tooevident symbolism and literariness fail to come off; it is a "romance" which simply runs afoul of its own contrivance. For all its flaws, however, one cannot fail to sense an inveterate storyteller at work, Melville always and everywhere willing himself to more and more fabulation.

Not surprisingly, *Mardi* brought stinging dismissals down upon Melville's head. Reviewers asked why had he not stuck to the sunshine, the apparent simplicity, of his first two ventures. He saw himself, as a consequence, obliged to return to journeyman writing, a fiction of *facts,* as he observed with regret. The results, "two *jobs,* which I have done for money," were *Redburn* and *White Jacket.* Neither, in truth, deserve Melville's low estimate. Both are lively, dramatic shipboard stories, which in all of their documentation and "fact" reveal deeply inward rites of passage. Melville cast *Redburn* as a journey to Liverpool and back, aboard a merchant ship. For the wellborn, ingenuous, awkward Wellingborough Redburn, it is a passage out of innocence into experience as the boy faces the shock of loneliness, of depravity aboard ship and in the city, and of the different sights and sounds of death. Again one senses Melville experimenting in the tactics of first-person narration, the way a storyteller "creates" his audience, playing to its expectations and needs, pacing each element in the narration.

White Jacket is another chronicle, this time narrated by a more mature, more seasoned sailor, an older and less put-upon witness who tells of life aboard a U.S. frigate returning from Peru to Boston. Depicting a "man-of-war" world with its fixed hierarchies of command and behavior, *White Jacket* is notable for Melville's ability to create an organizing symbol, in this case a caullike badge of innocence–the white jacket worn by the narrator. In ripping himself free of it, the narrator rips free of past illusion and vulnerability. In this work, too, Melville shows that he knows how to people a narrative, creating the noble captain Jack Chase, or the poet-companion Lemsford, and a company of officers and men. However best read, as "novels," or "confession," or "fictions of fact," both *Redburn* and *White Jacket* confirm Melville's growing powers as a maker of fiction, at once instinctual yet equally canny and inventive at every turn.

On completion of *Redburn*, and with the American proofs of *White Jacket* in hand to persuade the London publisher Richard Bentley of the need for a British edition (which he did successfully), Melville made a two-month trip to Europe, visiting London, Paris, Brussels, Cologne, and the Rhineland. Back in New York in February 1850, he borrowed money from his father-in-law to buy a farm in Pittsfield, Massachusetts, where he worked furiously to complete his "hell-fired" whale book, published in England as *The Whale* and in America as *Moby-Dick.* Meanwhile he had taken to reading Shakespeare like a man possessed, and the impact is clear to all who read *Moby-Dick.* He also published "Hawthorne and His Mosses," his profoundly admiring account of Hawthorne's *Mosses From An Old Manse.* By the time the article was published he had discovered that Hawthorne was living in nearby Lenox. There began a friendship, a short-lived but momentous encounter between two of America's major authors, albeit stronger on the part of Melville who dedicated *Moby-Dick* to Hawthorne, "In token of my admiration for his genius."

Distinctive as all five of his first books are, they all point forward to *Moby-Dick.* A "story," or "drama done," stunning in its own right, the book also functions as a compound of other stories—the nine "gams" for instance, or the different "lowerings" after the whale, or the apocalyptic final confrontation with Moby-Dick. Other kinds of "story" also play into the whole. One has only to think of Ishmael as a would-be embarkee, whether suffering fits of depression in Manhattan, or seeking a room at the Spouter Inn, or in a marriage bed with Queequeg, or—even more tellingly—as the "teller" of his own thoughts and speculations. There is also "story" in the book's omnipresent "ballast," the bedrock of authenticating fact which secures its every flight into metaphysics and myth. This double play of meaning can take the form of a pastiche classification of whales; or the mat woven by Queequeg and Ishmael, which Melville artfully turns into a metaphor for the interaction of Free Will, Chance, and Necessity in the shaping of human affairs; or the gold doubloon from Equador nailed to the masthead by Ahab and used to expose human-

kind's competing solipsisms in defining the world; or the "voyage" of the *Pequod* itself, which despite the destruction of its captain and crew never actually ends but continues always as mankind's "devious cruising" after "truth." In all of these aspects and others *Moby-Dick* serves as Melville's landmark fable of Man against Other, a historic tale of the New England oil industry transformed magnificently into a quest for metaphysical "light." A would-be Book of Revelation, a narrative of First and Last meanings, *Moby-Dick* represents Melville's storytelling brought to epic pitch.

Pierre, Melville's "kraken" book according to his letters, shows his thematic interest turning inland—as in "Bartleby" and some of his other city stories—a weblike, convoluted story of its titular hero's pursuit of absolutes only to come up against relativity and so to be led on to stasis and ultimately self-destruction. So stylized, and, as is now acknowledged, so self-reflexive, a fiction could hardly have done less to court approval, and it received a drubbing from the reviewers.

In part it was this disaster and the need to secure a dependable income to support his wife and family that caused Melville to turn to writing short stories for publication in magazines. *The Piazza Tales* and other stories were the result, a new kind of storytelling for him. In the same period he also wrote the novella *Israel Potter*, first serialized in nine installments in *Putnam's Monthly* from July 1854 to March 1855 and then published in book form later in March 1855. A half-factual, cryptic story of the life, decline, and final prairie exile of a onetime American mariner, it offers at the same time an unflattering perspective on both the national credo of optimism and all unduly self-persuading and patriotic versions of history.

The same temper, or distemper, runs through *The Confidence-Man*, the last of Melville's prose fiction to be published in his lifetime. Generally ignored, the novel, when reviewed at all, prompted the same dismaying response as *Mardi* and *Pierre.* Structured around a twenty-four-hour All Fools' Day journey down the Mississippi from St. Louis to New Orleans, it depicts a frontier citizenry as deluded by its own foibles and naive wishes to believe the best of the "metaphysical scamp" whom Melville puts through successive incarnations aboard the riverboat *Fidèle.* Melville's fast-moving fades and dissolves, his agile, equivocal prose, and his ringing of the changes on words such as "confidence," "trust," "charity,"

Melville, circa 1847 (portrait by Asa W. Twitchell; courtesy of the Berkshire Athenaeum)

and "charm," show him to be a consummate master of satiric skills. The central story of a river journey in which a standard of "confidence" is set against that of "No Trust" also includes five key interfoliated subplots, involving the supposedly abused wife Goneril, the alms-seeking cripple, the Indian-hater John Moredock, the Prodigal Son Charlemont, and the candle maker and light bringer China Aster—all in their separate ways commentaries upon the larger narrative. Including—in chapters 14, 39, and 44—story-essays on the ways narrative relates to reality and takes on its characteristic shape, *The Confidence-Man* has now rightly been assigned a higher place in the Melville canon than at any time previously. The book has also, perhaps understandably, been seen as something of a defiant last act of storytelling on Melville's part, his final Swiftian vision of the human "masquerade."

The fiction written after *Pierre*—the stories, *Israel Potter*, and *The Confidence-Man*—would be the last published in his lifetime. Sales continued to be poor. *Moby-Dick*, like *Mardi* before it, was considered too much taken up with metaphysics and skepticism ever to be popular. The stories neither sold nor won admirers, and *The Confidence-Man* was judged simply impenetrable. In 1853 the family tried unsuccessfully to secure a consular post for Melville. Domestic strains began to show between him and his wife, and by 1856 Melville was close to nervous collapse. In October 1856, with money borrowed from his father-in-law, he left for an extensive tour of Europe and the Levant in hopes of restoring his health. He had a brief reunion with Hawthorne in Liverpool, after which Hawthorne, the American consul there, wrote of Melville in his diary, "He can neither believe, nor be comfortable in his unbelief; and he is too honest and courageous not to try to do one or the other." Melville's journey took him on to the Holy Land–which in time would yield the material for his epic poem of doubt and faith, *Clarel* (1876)–and to Italy, Switzerland, Germany, and the Netherlands. He shipped back to New York from Liverpool in May 1857, seemingly much recuperated.

But for a one-time best-selling author he had become a commercial failure. In 1858, 1859, and 1860 he gave lectures on the lyceum circuit on topics such as the South Seas and Italian statuary; in 1860 he took a trip aboard his brother Tom's ship *The Meteor* to San Francisco, returning to New York by himself; in 1861 at the outbreak of the Civil War he tried for a naval appointment without success; and in 1863 he reluctantly sold his Pittsfield farm to return with the family to New York City, where he would have his residence until his death in 1891. In December 1866, all other avenues appearing closed to him, he took an oath as a minor customs inspector for the New York harbor authority, a post he discharged with resigned diligence until 1885, when a slightly earlier bequest to his wife eased his way into retirement. Despite the publication of his poetry (principally *Battle-Pieces and Aspects of the War* in 1866 and *Clarel* a decade later), his times saw little improvement. His work continued largely unread. In 1867 he came upon his son Malcolm dead at home of a self-inflicted gunshot wound. Malcolm's brother Stanwix was to die of fever in San Francisco in 1886. Despite occasional expressions of interest–from Julian Hawthorne, Nathaniel Hawthorne's son, and various British admirers and correspondents–Melville's later years were marked by anonymity and eclipse. The papers found at his death, however, did yield one last triumph.

Though *Billy Budd*, written during 1888-1891, did not appear in print until 1924 and then in an erroneous text, it would show itself as honed and concentrated an effort as anything Melville wrote. An "inside narrative," as Melville called it, this valedictory work once again confronts the puzzle of iniquity and is a parabolic drama of sacrificial innocence and murderous legality. Set against the immediate background of British naval insurrection at the Nore and Spithead, it discloses the fateful encounter of three "phenomenal" men, Captain Edward Vere of the *Bellipotent*, the master-at-arms John Claggart, and the impressed foretopman Billy Budd. A truly Orphic "welkin-eyed," "Handsome Sailor," Billy also suffers the blight of being a stutterer. When wrongfully accused of mutiny by Claggart, he cannot speak his innocence. He kills his accuser with a blow of the fist, finds himself sentenced to hang by Vere's drumhead court, and to his fellow shipmates becomes a messiah, their foundling Christ who has suffered a new crucifixion. Even without "plenty of sea-room," Melville could "tell the truth," keeping his canvasses small and his writing precise. As in Melville's short stories, *Billy Budd* relies upon a voice held discreetly at a distance, unwilling to spell out meanings or instruct the reader in how to reach any one mastering interpretation of the narrative's events.

Melville has been recognized as more than a writer of fiction. His poetry, for instance, has increasingly won higher regard, whether the "strife as memory" and "moods variable" of his Civil War verse in *Battle-Pieces*, or *Clarel*, the daunting verse-epic (longer than *Paradise Lost*) that he wrote as a modern "pilgrimage" of the loss of and search for faith, or the retrospective sailor and travel pieces which make up *John Marr and Other Sailors* (1888) and *Timoleon Etc.* (1891). He has also won recognition as a letter writer of unexpected versatility. His letters in general show his playful side, even when they speak of business and publishing. But it is his correspondence with Hawthorne during 1852, in the wake of "Hawthorne and His Mosses" and his first meeting with the older writer, which amounts to the high point, at once companionable yet serious and singular in its insights into the creative process. Melville as diarist also invites attention, especially for his logs of his visits to London and Europe in 1849-1850 and to the Holy Land in 1856-1857. Both again emphasize Melville's talent for the telling observation, his sensitivity to human difference and variety, and the contrasting textures of place and culture. Nor–as not only "Hawthorne and His Mosses" but his several early book reviews and the reports of the lectures he gave in 1860 on the South Seas and other travel topics bear witness–can Melville as essayist be passed over lightly. As much as his longer fiction, these compositions belong in the general context of his writing, and in a number of cases they have direct implications for the short stories.

Given the general rebirth of interest in Melville that began in the 1920s, the neglect of Melville's short fiction in particular can be seen as a radical disservice. For quite as much as *Moby-Dick* and the other longer fiction, his stories show his imagination at full strength. Each is a unique further communication of truth, told in a small and often oblique way. In this respect, two of the departure points for Melville's short-story writing take on added relevance, first "The Town-Ho's Story" and then the "Agatha" letters, as they have come to be known, which Melville wrote to Hawthorne in 1852. "The Town-Ho's Story" can be read as one of *Moby-Dick*'s nine "gams," a story-within-a-story and an augury of the whale's later role in meeting and punishing Ahab's monomania. But despite its integral part in that larger whole, "The Town-Ho's Story" is as freestanding as any of the stories in *The Piazza Tales*. In large measure this has to do with its appeal as a single, unfolding dramatic event aboard the *Town Ho*, where the Mate Radney's insult to the Lakeman Steelkilt results in a skirmish in which the Mate's jaw is broken and an abortive mutiny is led by Steelkilt, who is flogged by Radney and plans to kill him. Before Steelkilt can carry out this deed, however, Radney goes after Moby-Dick, and the whale bears off the hate-consumed Mate, a fate which haunts Radney's widow as if in a nightmare. Steelkilt escapes to Tahiti.

Much of the story's appeal has to do with the virtuosity of Melville's storytelling, his meticulous, lively staging of the narrative. Ishmael, his narrator, pretends first of all to reassume "the style in which I once narrated it at Lima," in the Golden Inn. His storytelling is interrupted by questions about American terms and usages from his highborn Peruvian drinking cronies, and finally, mock solemnly "sworn to" on "a copy of the Holy Evangelists." This Golden Inn retelling, in fact, makes its very artifice an integral part of the drama, from the story's alleged genesis as a statement made under oath to the harpooner Tashtego, his then equally alleged mumbling aloud of it while asleep on the *Pequod*, and on to the ensuing insistence of Ahab's crew that the whole account be put before them. As Ishmael tells it one more time, it becomes a bar story, a fable to hold the attention of recently met drinking companions. The locale of a South American port, the hot sun, the pauses and clarifications, all form elements in Ishmael's "styling" of the story, his wish to entertain but also astound his listeners. His is the perfect simulation of spontaneous and oral storytelling, the live voice. So exemplary a match of tale and telling, furthermore, lays down the pattern for a near perfect match of the stories to follow.

The "Agatha" correspondence, in essence one extended letter of 13 August 1852 and two short notes of 25 October and 25 November, might be construed as a story left in embryonic and untransposed note form. In offering Hawthorne the outline of an episode originally told to him by a New Bedford lawyer, Melville clearly intended an act of homage and friendship in the same vein as he had shown in "Hawthorne and His Mosses." But he intended, too, a professional gift of story material for Hawthorne to act on "with your great power in these things." Melville made his offer at a turning point in their respective careers. Hawthorne, as *The Scarlet Letter* had given notice in 1850, was moving away from the short story to the longer "romance." Melville, on the other hand, was turning precisely the opposite way, into short-story writing. As Melville's letter of 25 November indicates, Hawthorne had tactfully "urged" Melville to work up the material himself. That the evidence suggests he did not—or at least did not in the manner he proposed to Hawthorne—can truly be thought a loss.

The "Agatha" material concerns the sad, enduring loyalty of a Nantucket woman abandoned by her weak and bigamist sailor-husband. Her life becomes a monument to stoicism, and in his letters, as if thinking of how he himself might have written the story, Melville counsels Hawthorne to build each "tributary" item into a whole—Agatha's patience and resignation, the rotting of her wooden post box as she waits across the years for word from her husband, her cliff-side habitat, the husband's subsequent duplicities and betrayals, the ancillary family skeins of the story, and the general contextual New England bleakness of the sea and weather. He speaks of "a skeleton of actual reality" to be "built about with fulness & veins & beauty" as to produce a transcending and quite other imaginative reality. In effect he was indicating his own compositional procedures, storytelling thoroughly grounded in "fact" but remade or "built about" into art. As a type Agatha anticipates the gallery of figures in Melville's short fiction, characters whose human spirit has undergone ravage, most notably the eviscerated Bartleby and the lost Hunilla in "The Encantadas."

"Bartleby," first published in the November and December 1853 issues of *Putnam's Monthly* as "Bartleby, The Scrivener" and the first story proper in *The Piazza Tales*, is a haunting, prophetically modern tale of exile and self-loss. Its story of a "forlorn," anorexic law copyist who comes to work in a Wall Street domain of "rich men's bonds, and mortgages, and title-deeds" at once unsettles and compels. In part it offers a mystery. Who is Bartleby? What is the significance of his repeated statement "I would prefer not to," his sheer aloneness, his odd, unexplained withdrawal of labor, his eventual removal to The Tombs, his "pallor" and "emaciation" and eventual death "huddled at the base of the wall" with his "dim eyes" nonetheless still open? The role of the lawyer-narrator similarly poses problems. It can by no means be taken for granted that his self-estimate as "unambitious" and "eminently safe" applies. Readers might be tempted to think him, for instance, ironic at his own expense, aware of his own past shortcomings and complacencies in confronting the copyist. Nor can we be certain of his own attitude to the revelation that Bartleby previously held a position in the "Dead Letter Office at Washington," the custodian of "errands of life" put bureaucratically to "death." Most especially can we not be sure of how the lawyer himself understands his concluding equation, "Ah, Bartleby! Ah, humanity!"

"Bartleby" has been seen first as a "parable of walls," a depiction of "self" as irrecoverably immured and unfree, and thereby a companion piece to Franz Kafka's *The Trial* (1925), Albert Camus's *The Plague* (1947), or Samuel Beckett's *Waiting For Godot* (1952). Other interpreters look at "Bartleby" more as a quasi-religious fable, Bartleby himself as the spurned Christ or Buddha, and his eventual muteness as the token of God's inscrutable withdrawal from, or irrelevance to, the world. Less cosmically, it has been argued that "Bartleby" offers a classic portrait of catatonia or schizophrenia, in which copyist and lawyer constitute divided facets of a single personality, a doppelgänger story in the manner of Edgar Allan Poe's "William Wilson" (1839) or Henry James's "The Jolly Corner" (1908). Or, "Bartleby" is a story of Wall Street, in which this business epicenter of nineteenth-century America is seen as murderous to the human creative spirit, a site only of commodification and of the fetish of property and profit. A much favored recent interpretation sees the story as deeply autobiographical. Bartleby functions as a surrogate for Melville himself, that is, Melville as a scrivener who "would prefer not" to "check his copy" and write to the required norm. His books, too, at least *Mardi* and *Pierre*, had quickly enough become "dead letters," left to dust and obscurity in out-of-the-way libraries.

As always in Melville's storytelling, the organizing tactics of the tale need close examination.

Not only does the narrator play an equivocal part in the tale, shifting in register from apparent self-satisfaction, to irritation, to panic, to would-be divestment of all responsibility for Bartleby, and to a final, uncertain glimpse of the total significance of his copyist's life and death; but around Bartleby gather other kinds of witness, other guesses at his strange purposes. There is the testimony of Turkey and Nippers, his fellow clerks, one of whom can work properly only in the morning and the other only in the afternoon. Half-men, robotic, having lost full humanity, they each give a half-version of Bartleby, full of hostility or accommodation, according to their mood swings. Then there is the testimony of Ginger Nut, the dollar-a-week office boy, anxious always to emulate and placate his elders. The story also puts before the reader a body of other testimony, that of the lawyer who rents the offices after the narrator has vacated the premises in the vain hope of freeing himself of his clerk and of the narrator's former landlord, both of whom complain that he has left behind his office stock in the person of Bartleby who refuses to leave. The landlord speaks of clients leaving and a possible mob, to be brought on by Bartleby's "stationary" and unspeaking sentinelship. Once Bartleby is imprisoned in the Tombs and visited there by the lawyer, still other testimony makes itself heard. One of the turnkeys calls him "the silent man." The grubman, anxious to make a quick dollar, thinks Bartleby "odd" and "a gentleman forger," a term which gives support to the interpretation of the story as indicative of Melville's own experience in the literary trade. The story also makes reference to the lawyer's baffled resort to yet another pair of voices, those of "philosophic" authority, "Edwards on the Will" and "Priestly on Necessity."

But against all these voices, the lawyer's above all, we are confronted with Bartleby's, minimalist in speech, stating his preference not to copy, not to check, not to do anything which will affirm or validate the Wall Street domain in which he finds himself. In this negation he has been seen by many as a figure of almost absurd Thoreauvian resistance, a true anarch and dissenter. When visited by the lawyer at the Tombs he says accusingly: "I know you . . . and I want nothing to say to you." Having receded into wordlessness, silence, an accusing absence of all speech, he incarnates the dead letters which once he destroyed, a figure of absence, nonbeing, otherness. However we react to the lawyer's self-

Last page of the manuscript for what Melville called an "inside narrative," the novella Billy Budd *(courtesy of the Houghton Library, Harvard University)*

posturings ("unambitious," unprone to "dangerous indignation at wrongs and outrages," the self-vaunting friend of John Jacob Astor), there can be little doubt that Melville intends the reader to be drawn into his difficulties and confusion. "Eminently safe" he may believe himself, but in reality his "safeness" counts for little. The encounter with Bartleby has turned his world—its values, idiom, assurance, ethics—upside down; it is neither eminent nor safe. Such are the subversive implications of "Bartleby," as sure and consequential a story as any Melville wrote.

Melville's second triumph in *The Piazza Tales* is "The Encantadas"—first published in *Putnam's Monthly* (March-May 1854)—his ten allegorized sketches of the Galápagos Islands. He makes over this South Pacific island chain, which he had visited in the 1840s, into a portrait of Hell, a barren, alien, seemingly arrested, or misevolved world. Paradoxically, Charles Darwin's *The Origin of Species*, the canonical text of evolution published a mere five years later in 1859, takes its data from the same Galápagos Islands. Melville heads each of his sketches with an extract from

Edmund Spenser's *The Faerie Queen*, as if to give notice that his is not the role of simple geographer or explorer. Rather, "The Encantadas" sketches are indeed to be regarded as "built about," seamed and layered with fantasy, speculation, a whole overlay of commentary, and yet other storytelling.

Initially, the islands are set forth as a domain of "cinders," "extinct volcanoes," "a vacant lot," which Melville also glosses as "uninhabitable and woe-begone" and in all a "plutonian sight." What life is to be encountered exists at ground level, whether the "mosses" and "wiry shrubs" which cling at the volcanic soil, or the crawling insect and reptile life, which Melville lists cryptically as "tortoises, lizards, immense spiders, snakes, and that strangest anomaly of outlandish nature, the *iguana*." Calling on long-stored memories, he transforms the actual Galápagos into an imagined nether place, infernal, elemental islands forged out of the earth's larval upheavals, and the perfect backdrops for human calamity.

Yet Melville does not give way to solemnity in "The Encantadas." His antic Yankee wit and sardonicism put in frequent appearances. "Sketch Second," for instance, invokes "wondrous tortoises," stately, time-burdened "mystic creatures" with shells "grim as blacksmiths." But affecting as they are, bearers of history as they seem, they can also be put to other purposes, such as supper for the crews of visiting whalers.

"Sketch Third" turns to Rock Rodondo, a natural promontory which has long served as a lookout post and bird sanctuary. Standing high above a chain of "fish-caves," it seems to Melville to resemble in turn "a tall light-house" and "the lofty sails of a cruiser." Unlike other parts of the islands, Rodondo is not bathed in silence. Around it wheel birds of every variety, their piercing and cacophonous cries creating a "demonic din." "Sketch Fourth" is "A Pisgah View from the Rock," a wry, mock-panoramic sweep of "yonder Burnt District of the Enchanted Isles." Melville even includes a splendid mock census, a set of "the most reliable estimates made upon the spot." In the fifth, sixth, and seventh sketches, Melville plays the chronicler of the whale ship *Essex* (whose story is a source for *Moby-Dick*), nearly wrecked at Rodondo, of the past sojourns of Elizabethan buccaneers, and of a Creole adventurer made ruler of Charles Island by the Peruvians for his part in their war of liberation against Spain. This adventurer runs afoul of his own motley subjects and leaves behind only a "permanent Riotocracy."

"Sketch Eighth" tells the tragic, painful story of Hunilla, "the dark-damasked Chola widow" who has been abandoned at Norfolk Isle by a treacherous captain. Witness to the deaths of her husband and brother and implied to have been the victim of rape, she has also had to suffer the affliction of having been seen but ignored by passing vessels. Melville attributes to her "nameless misery" and calls her a "lone shipwrecked soul." In almost every respect Hunilla resembles Agatha in Melville's letters to Hawthorne, a figure whose grief, endurance, and last return to her native town of Payta in Peru, mark her as one of Melville's true sacrificial beings. Her life has indeed made her into a "silent passenger," a lone survivor.

"Sketch Ninth" gives the history of "the hermit Oberlus," another Creole outlander and isolato who rules Hood's Island. A Caliban in appearance–"beast-like," "heavy," "earthy," and "unshorn"–he, too, eventually makes his way to Payta. But there, as the leader of "a mongrel and assassin band," he finds himself in a Peruvian

jail, his island exile exchanged for another sort of isolation on the mainland. "Sketch Tenth," "Runaways, Castaways, Solitaries, Grave-Stones, Etc.," gives a summary of the Galápagos as "cindery solitude," Nature's own hellish topography. Melville thinks of the castaways, the escapees, the hermits, and the outcasts who have ended up on the islands, either by chance or choice, as life's refugees. He also recalls "a stake and a bottle" found near the shore and imagines it to be a type of South Seas "post-office." Over time, the stake rots, and the bottle falls, "no very exhilarating object," one more emblem of isolation and broken communication in line with the details he had enumerated for Hawthorne in the "Agatha" letters. But in typical spirit Melville refuses to close on a note of simple bleakness. He cites an "epithet" allegedly found on a grave marker "in a bleak gorge of Chatham Isle," a piece of "gimcrack" doggerel about being buried under Galápagos "cinders," evidence that none of Melville's antic turn of wit had left him. But despite the wit, the close observation of nature, and the historical recall of "The Encantadas," the dominant impression of these sketches is somber. If they point to any encompassing view of life, it is that failure and isolation yield the most revealing measure of the human condition.

Just as *Pierre* shifts imaginative location to inland after the ocean space of *Moby-Dick*, so in several of his lesser stories after "The Encantadas" Melville turns to domestic and family scenarios. Behind each of them one discerns an unease, a chafing at being housebound and hemmed in, or so at least their touchy, easily rattled narrators seem to imply. In "The Lightning-Rod Man" (first published in the August 1854 issue of *Putnam's Monthly* and collected in *The Piazza Tales*) Melville mocks the idea of buying protection against the "grand irregular thunder" of things. The story no doubt reflects his experience of being huckstered at his Arrowhead farmhouse by actual lightning-rod salesmen, but he makes it into a smack at all "transcendental" salesmen of false religions, bromides, panaceas, and salvations. Narrated in the first-person, crusty voice of a country householder, it portrays the salesman as a modern devil, a doorstep Mephistopheles, whose true identity breaks through when he throws his "tri-forked thing" at the narrator's heart.

A similar disposition can be discerned in "I and My Chimney"–first published in the March 1856 issue of *Putnam's Monthly* and posthumously collected in *The Apple-Tree Table and Other Sketches* (1922)–the story of an edgy, defensive attachment to a "corpulent old Harry VIII of a chimney," an image of the narrator's own besieged selfhood. Pressed by his wife and daughters to change, or even dismantle, both his house and its chimney centerpiece, the narrator dodges and weaves, retreats into convenient absences, sidesteps the architect, and at all times makes clear his unshakable affinity with the chimney ("I and my chimney, two gray-headed old smokers"). The story's play of effects might be that of virtual domestic black comedy, the writer-self under duress to the point of suspected breakdown and madness–but, in reality, sure of his own values and style.

In "The Apple-Tree Table" (first published in the May 1856 issue of *Putnam's Monthly* and collected in *The Apple-Tree Table and Other Sketches*) Melville again affects the voice of the put-upon paterfamilias narrator. Ostensibly the tale is the history of a bug which has long lain dormant inside a piece of domestic furniture, but which "ticks" and eventually achieves its release. To the narrator's womenfolk the event arouses fright and superstition, creating a great deal of bother, before the truth gains ground. A slight piece, it again shows Melville in the persona of the husband or father as victim of the domestic round.

A second grouping of his stories might be thought of as parables, narrative as a form of warning against the hold of illusion and misplaced confidence. First published in *Harper's New Monthly* (December 1853) and collected in *The Apple-Tree Table and Other Sketches*, "Cock-A-Doodle-Do!" is the account of a "noble," "lusty," "glorious" cockerel, "Signor Beneventano," whose crowing thrills and exhilarates the narrator. Compelled to search it out, he finds it, after most diligent inquiry, to be the property of the Merrymusk family, whose pauperism, emaciation, and eventual deaths lie at quite the opposite end of the spectrum from the bird's "exultant" acts of crowing. The crowing has been parodic, false, a spurious call to self-resolution and sexual and existential well-being. Its work done, the cockerel after sounding "one supernatural note," falls dead, ever to go on crowing in the mind and senses of the narrator. Also a cautionary tale, "The Happy Failure"–first published in *Harper's New Monthly* (July 1854) and collected in *The Apple-Tree Table and Other Sketches*–extols the virtue of abandoning the incapacitating "invention," the dream of the perfectly created thing. The nar-

Melville in 1885 (photograph by Rockwood)

rator's uncle, a cranky "inventor" of the "Great Hydraulic-Hydrostatic Apparatus for draining swamps and marshes" in an upper stretch of the Hudson River, finally comes to see the futility of his efforts, and his invention's anacondalike grip on his life and energies. In front of his nephew and his black manservant Yorpy, he finally abandons his "huge, shabby, oblong box, hermetically sealed." Unburdened, he advises only the "invention" of happiness. Melville doubtless intended a satire of rampant Franklinism, his age's obsession with get-rich-quick gadgetry and machines, but, as in "Bartleby," he could well have been thinking of his own past literary "inventions" and the imagined relief at giving up his similarly unwanted and unappreciated creative labor.

"The Fiddler" (*Harper's New Monthly*, September 1854; collected in *The Apple-Tree Table and Other Sketches*) also addresses itself to the nature of "failure" and "success." The poet Helmstone has just suffered a disaster from the critics for his latest literary effort. Through his friend Standard he meets Hautboy, once a musical prodigy and the darling of the concert circuit, who has settled for playing entertainer and "fiddler" to his friends. In him Helmstone at last sees the very figure of contentment, the instance of the man–the artist–who has settled for less, a man "happier than a king" because he acknowledges only "facts" and eschews all dream, fantasy, or false and debilitating ambition. In consequence Helmstone tears up his manuscripts, buys himself a fiddle, and goes "to take regular lessons of Hautboy." Yet, despite the poet's conversion to Hautboy's perspective, Melville leaves a sting in the story's ending, suggesting that Hautboy's approach may not be the only or the best way forward for the "failed" creative temperament and that Hautboy and Helmstone's "happiness," despite its celebrated levelheadedness, signifies a betraying loss of desire. Melville leaves no doubt that "fiddling" carries its pejorative as well as benign implication.

The "failure" in "Jimmy Rose"–first published in *Harper's New Monthly* (November 1855) and collected in *The Apple-Tree Table and Other Sketches*–is that of a one-time New York merchant, whose ships have sunk just outside port and brought him to bankruptcy and ruin. At first abandoned by the friends he once so lavishly entertained, he gradually works his way back into their good graces. He settles for a lesser role– that of avoiding being a "man-hater" and of offering himself as a model of good taste, informedness, and general goodness of heart, which the narrator asssociates with the continuing "rosiness" of his cheeks. Despite penury and adversity, he has managed to keep faith of a sort, a moral redemption transcending his material ruin. Like "Cock-A-Doodle-Do!" and "The Fiddler," however, "Jimmy Rose" offers a paradoxical conclusion. Its narrator, William Ford, may well acknowledge that Jimmy Rose has made his failure into success, a life of good-natured stoicism and manners. But his "roses" bloom on a "ruined" cheek, suggesting that he has attained his equilibrium at a high price. And at his death, though he is nursed by the "only daughter of an opulent alderman" and still proud of his genteel beggardom, the esteem in which he is held by his fellow citizenry and humankind seems in question.

The last story in *The Piazza Tales*, "The Bell-Tower" (first published in the August 1855 issue of *Putnam's Monthly*), involves a shift in time and place, from Melville's nineteenth-century America to Renaissance Italy. Written in a suitably baroque style, at times almost deliberately stilted, the story warns against monstrous technology and the rule of the head over the heart. Bannadonna, a "great mechanician" but an "unblest

foundling," constructs for his Italian patrons an exquisite, "titanic" bell and clock tower, a supreme feat of engineering. Its cogs, pulleys, springs, and allegorical figures personifying time seem harmonized into the perfect contrivance, the ultimate machine. But during the preparation, the inspired, exhilarated Bannadonna, in his furious impatience to get his project completed, strikes a workman. A "splinter" of the workman's bone gets into the main molten "domino," imperceptibly altering the necessary fine balance and tuning of the bell tower's workings. As the machinery is put through its paces in preparation for its presentation to the republic, an "absorbed" Bannadonna fails to observe his own creation, the "domino," and is struck fatally upon his "intervening brain" by a falling figure. Another Frankenstein thus falls afoul of his creation, the master destroyed by the servant. At his state funeral in the very cathedral for which the bell tower was initially designed, the "groined belfry" crashes down like some "lone Alpine landslide." Unlike Hawthorne's "Ethan Brand" (1851), however, to whose treatment of the theme of the "unpardonable sin" it bears considerable resemblance, "The Bell-Tower" rather overinsists upon its moral: "So the creator was killed by the creature . . . and so pride went before the fall." More telling and more subtle is Melville's preface to the story. Taken, as he pretends, *"from a private MS,"* its essential two lines read: *"Seeking to conquer a larger liberty, man but extends the empire of necessity."*

Equally gnomic in purpose but more adroit in style are Melville's three diptychs or paired tales, each told through a single narrative voice and exploring two counter or alternative versions of life. In "The Two Temples," which was written in 1854 but remained unpublished until it appeared in *Billy Budd and Other Prose Pieces*, Melville addresses himself to "charity," in the first charity unexpectedly denied and in the second charity unexpectedly given. In "Temple First"– controversial in its time when Charles F. Briggs rejected the story for publication in *Putnam's Monthly* because he believed that it mocked the monied fashionability of New York's Grace Church–the narrator is denied entry to worship. He sneaks in undetected, however, by an unwatched door, hears the service from high within a vertiginous, stained-glass gallery, and finally brings attention to himself by touching a bell rope and causing an "astounding reverberation." The same "beadle-faced" church warden who refused him a place in the church takes him to court for trespassing, and there he receives a reprimand, a fine, and, to his added chagrin, a "pardon" for having "humbly indulged myself in the luxury of public worship." By contrast, in "Temple Second," as a "stranger in London," the narrator is given by "some sort of a working-man," a free ticket to hear the actor Macready perform, an act of "sterling charity" that contrasts with his expulsion from a snobbish church in his own New York City. Melville casts both parts of the story as "drama," the one a tale of arbitrary exclusion and the other–set literally in a theater–of arbitrary inclusion.

First published in the June 1854 issue of *Harper's New Monthly* and collected in *The Apple-Tree Table and Other Sketches,* "Poor Man's Pudding and Rich Man's Crumbs" also juxtaposes two versions of "charity," though in both cases it is spurious. In "Picture First," set in rural America, the narrator is taken by the "Poet Blandmour" to observe Nature as some imagined "blessed almoner," a tirelessly beneficent and ingenious provisioner. Under Blandmour's dispensation "soft March snow" becomes "Poor Man's Manure," melted snow "Poor Man's Eye-Water," a "cup of cold rain-water" "Poor Man's Egg." Set against this "poetry," however, are the poverty and starvation of the Coulter family, whom the narrator recognizes as victims of an actual, inhospitable Nature that contrasts with the falsifying, literary version given out by Blandmour and his fellow nature writers. The "damp," demeaning life of the Coulters causes the narrator to eschew all future temptations to "poeticize" the lives of the poor, especially as he nearly chokes on "Poor Man's Pudding," an indigestible, dried-out dessert served up by Dame Coulter in the wake of equally indigestible plates of old salt pork. "Picture Second" moves from the American countryside to London, to describe another foray into just as unreal and upside-down a case of "charity." The narrator meets "a very friendly man" in Cheapside and allows himself to be taken to the scene of a "grand Guildhall Banquet." There, on the day after the banquet, he sees "charity" dispensed: leftovers are given to London's beggars and starving. This demeaning ritual, for which the "mass of lean, famished, ferocious creatures" have had to acquire tickets, points up the lavishness of the surroundings and the huge cost of the original banquet. Melville lists the "remnants" of this sumptuous, stately banquet in Dickensian fashion: "disembowelled pasties, plundered pheas-

Melville's gravestone, Woodlawn Cemetery, Bronx, New York

ants, and half-sacked jellies." The upshot is a fray from which the narrator and his guide barely escape. "Bruised and battered," the narrator pleads to be "saved equally" from the mockery of both kinds of "charity."

A single narrator also speaks through the two parts of "The Paradise of Bachelors and the Tartarus of Maids," first published in the April 1855 issue of *Harper's New Monthly* and collected in *The Apple-Tree Table and Other Sketches.* In "The Paradise of Bachelors" Melville's narrator describes a "bachelor" London evening at the Temple, formerly a cloister for the Knights Templars and later the site of two Inns of Court where "benchers" studied law, but now a men's club for lawyers given to "good living, good drinking, good feeling, and good talk." Claiming descent from the original Knights Templars and benchers, these are men without women who have put work, family, and Eros in abeyance. To the admiring narrator, the evening in a well-appointed dining room, with mutton, turkey, chicken pie, claret, and port, becomes the very instance of sociality, male fraternity. "The Tartarus of Maids," however, tells a quite opposite story, one of grim impregnation and the human reproductive system, disguised as the account of a traumatizing visit to a paper mill in "Woedolor Mountains in New England." A "bachelor" story, also, it gives a bachelor's view of women and sex, with a sense of the terrors of sexual life. It is a story of some daring on Melville's part, one of his many oblique narratives. The landscape itself reads two ways: it is literally a "bleak" Massachusetts, Maine, or Vermont, but its crevices, gorges, place names, points of entry and exit also patently symbolize a sexual or bodily terrain. The paper mill, overseen by a diabolized, "dark-complexioned, well-wrapped personage" and his boy assistant Cupid, and worked by blank, pale, compliant "virgins," produces the paper in "nine minutes to the second." A "bachelor" story which subverts "bachelor" innocence and evasion, it equally offers a sympathetic picture of women as the victims of men's sexual needs and domination. One can also discern Melville's critique of New England factory and work practices and the general exploitation of female labor. That its extraordinary treatment of sex, covert and explicit, escaped general notice, not to say disapprobation and censorship, pays tribute to Melville's storytelling adeptness. Among other features, it anticipates a later current of debate about sexual role and gender.

First published in the October and November 1855 issues of *Putnam's Monthly* and collected in *The Piazza Tales*, "Benito Cereno" represents Melville again at his greatest strength. A chill, tense, and exhilarating novella-length story of slave insurrection off the Chilean coast, it probes brilliantly and disconcertingly the whole complex "knot" of race and the historic ascendancy of white over black. Told through another bachelor viewpoint, that of Amasa Delano, sealer-captain of Duxbury, Massachusetts, a "person of a singularly undistrustful good nature," it involves the reader in deciphering what has occurred aboard the *San Dominick*, a slave ship under the ostensible command of Benito Cereno, his few white crewmen, and a company of Africans whose spokesman is Babo, Cereno's Senegalese body servant. In fact, the *San Dominick* masquerades as a slave ship, and Delano accepts that appearance as reality. Yet, the ship is actually a world turned inside out and made to emulate itself. For Babo and his fellow slaves have revolted, killed all but a token number of the crew as well as Cereno's kinsman and the co-owner of the ship, replacing the ship's figurehead with his skeleton, which is kept covered. Through a whole ritual of visits and would-be "gamming," Delano and his *Bache-*

lor's Delight shipmates are made witness to a stunning charade: black slave insurrectionists "acting out" the intolerable historic role into which they have been cast by slavery. Only after the charade has been played through, the skeleton-figurehead uncovered, and Cereno and his remaining crew dramatically rescued, does Delano experience a "flash of revelation," a full understanding of the spectacle in which he has been implicated.

The story puts before the reader a complex weaving of language and metaphor, the interplay of references to black, white, and gray. Then, too, the story relies upon two seeming "versions" of the events under narration: the story as reported from Delano's viewpoint and the story as "sworn to" in a lengthy legal deposition and taken down by Doctor Rozas from the depleted Cereno, who dies from the shock of his experience not long after Babo's execution in Lima. In Delano's version Melville might again be said to have written a "fiction of fact," and in Cereno's deposition, a "non-fiction of fact." Neither version, actually, gives the entire, elusive truth of the matter. For if any one truth can be said to make itself available, it has to do with the very dynamics of the situation, the charade aboard the *San Dominick*, the signals which pass among Cereno, Babo, and Delano, and the past circles of history which have locked Africa, Europe, and the Americas into a disastrous slave equation.

In turn Melville develops a collocation of keys and clues to the story, as in the story's opening, where half-colors, shadow, and the intermediary play of mist and vapor set the tone for the drama to follow: "The morning was one peculiar to the coast. Everything was mute and calm; everything gray. The sea, though undulated into long roods of swells, seemed fixed, and was sleeked at the surface like waved lead that has cooled and set in the smelter's mold. The sky seemed a gray surtout. Flights of troubled gray fowl, kith and kin with flights of troubled gray vapors among which they were mixed, skimmed low and fitfully over the waters, as swallows over meadows before storms. Shadows present, foreshadowing deeper shadows to come." Shadow operates everywhere in "Benito Cereno," a story of compound half-perceptions and misperceptions. "Truths" become warped and distorted according to the vision of those to whom history has given the power of definition.

The story first of all likens the *San Dominick* to a Pyrenean "white-washed monastery after a thunder-storm" patrolled by inquisitional "Black

Friars"–as if a reenactment of the abdication of Charles IV and the vengeful upsurge of "purification" he caused to be visited upon Spain will be seen here, amid Chilean coastal waters. In turn Melville releases his other "keys": the "shield-like stern-piece" depicting "a dark satyr in a mask, holding his foot on the prostrate neck of a writhing figure likewise masked"; Aranda's body serving as the ship's figurehead; the striking of the white boy by the black; the parodic imperial dumbshow of padlock and key as the giant, former ruler Atufal makes his ritual appearances and bows before Cereno; the "hubbub of voices" of the Ashanti women and the sound of the elders clashing knives echoing through the ship at the slightest hint of danger; and Babo's supreme, obsequious, parodic double role through which he at once fawns over and rules the helpless Cereno, the "master" to whom he gives his "devoted service." The *San Dominick* thus becomes Melville's version of a "Heart of Darkness" in which darkness inside as well as outside in the form of skin color becomes the modus vivendi. Whatever Cereno embodies as a fading scion of ancient "Castile and Leon," whatever Babo's rights or wrongs in seizing the ship, even the "white noddy" Delano is drawn into the ritual of enslavement when he offers to buy Cereno's manservant. Melville centers these masquerades, rites, powers, and confusions in the metaphor of a Gordian knot, described as "a combination of double-bowline-knot, treble-crown-knot, back-handed-well-knot, knot-in-and-out-knot, and jamming-knot." Enjoined to "Undo it, cut it, quick," Delano might himself be a surrogate for the reader put upon to decipher the "knotted" text before him.

Cereno may think that "the negro" has "cast such a shadow" upon him. But for Babo and his fellow mutineers, slavery has cast its shadow equally upon them. When, after Cereno's rescue, the blacks have been tried and executed, Babo's decapitated head is left on view, "fixed on a pole in the Plaza." Gazing "unabashed" at the whites who come to see this "hive of subtlety," Babo is imagined by Melville's narrator to be saying: "since I cannot do deeds, I will not speak words." Cereno dies, ghostly, white, the "dead" presence of an imperial dynasty. But Babo's is the "live" enduring silence, the unwillingness to say anything in or to a world which has stolen from him and his fellow slaves the right to speak and act in their own names. Of all Melville's stories "Benito Cereno" contains his most challenging drama; it is narrative as an inquiry into freedom and revolt, blackness and whiteness, and the denial and liberation of self.

There remain a few other contenders for inclusion in Melville's story canon. His two-part "Fragments from a Writing Desk" (published in the *Democratic Press & Lansingburgh Advertiser* for 4 and 18 May 1839 and collected in *Billy Budd and Other Prose Pieces*), a piece of juvenilia, is a near-parodic Gothic fantasy of a beautiful deaf-and-dumb woman. His "Authentic Anecdotes of 'Old Zack,'" seven minor satiric pieces on President Zachary Taylor, were published in *Yankee Doodle* (24 July-11 September 1847). "The 'Gees" is "a general sketchy view" of tough Cape Verde "Portuguese" sailors, a "singular people" even by the standards of the oceangoing community, which appeared in *Harper's* in March 1856 (collected in *The Apple-Tree Table and Other Sketches*). "Daniel Orme" (published in *Billy Budd and Other Prose Pieces*) and "John Marr" (published in *John Marr and Other Sailors*), two sailor sketches written to accompany Melville's later sea poetry, depict "solitary" veterans of shipboard life. "The Marquis of Grandvin" and "Three 'Jack Gentian' Sketches," both posthumously published in *Billy Budd and Other Prose Pieces*, present visions of the cavalier good life and character. Two other efforts have an even stronger claim to be classified as short fiction.

In "The Piazza" Melville ostensibly wrote no more than a frontispiece for *The Piazza Tales*, a piece of scene-setting to create a context for other stories. In fact "The Piazza" amounts to infinitely more. Narrated as if in the voice of yet another landlocked former sailor who has taken to "poesie," it plays off the oppositions of "fact" and "fantasy," or as Hawthorne's analogous "The Custom-House" in *The Scarlet Letter* expresses it, "the Actual and the Imaginary." The story of the narrator's construction of his north-facing piazza, his withstanding of his neighbors' derision, and his "inland voyage to fairy-land" in search of a mountainside cottage whose glowing window he sees from his piazza, it also tells of disillusionment, his discovery that the cottage is inhabited not by fairies but by Marianna, a lonely orphan who daydreams about the inhabitants of his house below. His discovery suggests that to confuse life with art is to run the risk of shock and pain. So rebuked, the narrator–a devotee of *The Faerie Queen* and *A Midsummer Night's Dream*–gives up "romance" as a standard in life. Rather, he will create his Mariannas and fairylands in his art, thereby avoiding the disillusion of discovering mere country poverty, and a put-upon, sad, country girl. He vows to "stick to the piazza," to take joy and inspiration from the "ampitheatre" about him, and to seek truth at night, in darkness, and "when the curtain falls." There, in the wellsprings of the creative imagination, darkly and in private, can he best think of a Marianna or "many as real a story." In each of these respects "The Piazza" offers a gloss on his storytelling in the rest of the book, but it remains a story of itself, typically subtle in theme and execution.

"Hawthorne and His Mosses," too, might be read as fiction. As a review of Hawthorne's *Mosses From An Old Manse*, it is a most telling estimate of the "cadence," "magic," "wondrous effects," and philosophic "NO! in thunder!" of his New England contemporary. But "Hawthorne and His Mosses" assumes fictional dress as well. Narrated pseudonymously by a "Virginian Spending July in Vermont," it offers a setting ("A papered chamber in a fine old farm-house.... surrounded by mountains, old woods, and Indian ponds"), a plot dealing with the narrator's "ravishment" by Hawthorne's stories, a discernible storylike rhythm (an overnight pause, the rising excitement as one revelation follows another), and a pervasive imagery of "shock," "diving," "seduction," and "implementation." For all that "Hawthorne and His Mosses" has rightly been lauded as a clarion cry for a national literature, as well as an analysis of both Hawthorne and Shakespeare, it displays throughout Melville's best resources as a short-storyteller. It at once belongs to, and gives further luster to, his overall story repertoire.

Melville's place in the history of American literature is no longer in doubt. Nor, central though it is, can *Moby-Dick* be called the sole reason for assigning him that place. For just as his other novels, his poetry, his logs and correspondence contribute to the achievement, so, too, do his short stories. Inevitably they differ in weight, some of them taken up with profoundest human tragedy, others with domestic life or literary setbacks and disgruntlements. But the best of them dazzle and challenge, at once serious yet able to call upon both Melville's longstanding Yankee wit and his unmistakable virtuosity as a storyteller.

Letters:
The Letters of Herman Melville, edited by Merrell R. Davis and William H. Gilman (New Haven: Yale University Press, 1960).

Bibliographies:
Meade Minnigerode, *Some Personal Letters of Herman Melville and a Bibliography* (New York: E. B. Hackett, 1922);
Herbert Cahoon, *Herman Melville: A Check List of Books and Manuscripts in the Collections of the New York Public Library* (New York: New York Public Library, 1951);
Theodore L. Gross and Stanley Wertheim, eds., *Hawthorne, Melville, Stephen Crane: A Critical Bibliography* (New York: Free Press, 1971);
Brian Higgins, *Herman Melville: An Annotated Bibliography,* volume 1: 1846-1930 (Boston: G. K. Hall, 1979);
Jeanetta Boswell, *Herman Melville and the Critics: A Checklist of Criticism, 1900-1978* (Metuchen, N.J. & London: Scarecrow, 1981).

Biographies:
Raymond Weaver, *Herman Melville, Mariner and Mystic* (New York: Doran, 1921);
John Freeman, *Herman Melville,* English Men of Letters Series (New York & London: Macmillan, 1926);
Lewis Mumford, *Herman Melville: A Study of His Life and Vision* (New York: Harcourt, Brace, 1929);
Newton Arvin, *Herman Melville* (New York: Sloane, 1950);
Leon Howard, *Herman Melville: A Biography,* (Berkeley: University of California Press, 1951);
Jay Leyda, *The Melville Log: A Documentary Life of Herman Melville, 1819-1891,* 2 volumes (New York: Harcourt, Brace, 1951); republished, with a supplementary chapter (New York: Gordian, 1969);
Eleanor Melville Metcalf, *Herman Melville: Cycle and Epicycle* (Cambridge, Mass.: Harvard University Press, 1953);
Edwin Haviland Miller, *Melville* (New York: Braziller, 1975).

References:
Charles Roberts Anderson, *Melville in the South Seas* (New York: Columbia University Press, 1939);
James Baird, *Ishmael: A Study of the Symbolic Mode of Primitivism* (Baltimore: Johns Hopkins Press, 1956);
John Bernstein, *Pacifism and Rebellion in the Writings of Herman Melville* (The Hague: Mouton, 1964);

Warner Berthoff, *The Example of Melville* (Princeton: Princeton University Press, 1962);

Marius Bewley, *The Eccentric Design* (New York: Columbia University Press, 1959);

R. Bruce Bickley, *The Method of Melville's Short Fiction* (Durham: Duke University Press, 1975);

Merlin Bowen, *The Long Encounter: Self and Experience in the Writings of Herman Melville* (Chicago: University of Chicago Press, 1960);

Watson G. Branch, ed., *Melville, The Critical Heritage* (London & Boston: Routledge & Kegan Paul, 1974);

William Braswell, *Melville's Religious Thought* (Durham: Duke University Press, 1943);

Richard Brodhead, *Hawthorne, Melville, and the Novel* (Chicago: University of Chicago Press, 1976);

John Bryant, ed., *A Companion to Melville Studies* (New York & Westport, Conn.: Greenwood Press, 1986);

Richard Chase, *The American Novel and Its Tradition* (Garden City, N.Y.: Doubleday, 1957);

Chase, *Herman Melville: A Critical Study* (New York: Macmillan, 1949);

Chase, ed., *Melville: A Collection of Critical Essays* (Englewood Cliffs, N.J.: Prentice-Hall, 1962);

William B. Dillingham, *Melville's Short Fiction 1853-1856* (Athens: University of Georgia Press, 1977);

Edgar Dryden, *Melville's Thematics of Form: The Great Art of Telling the Truth* (Baltimore: Johns Hopkins Press, 1968);

Régis Durand, *Melville, signes et metaphores* (Lausanne: Editions de l'age d'homme, 1980);

Charles Feidelson, Jr., *Symbolism and American Literature* (Chicago: University of Chicago Press, 1953);

Leslie Fiedler, *Love and Death in the American Novel*, revised edition (New York: Stein & Day, 1966);

Marvin Fisher, *Going Under: Melville's Short Fiction and the American 1850s* (Baton Rouge: Louisiana State University Press, 1977);

Richard Harter Fogle, *Melville's Shorter Tales* (Norman: University of Oklahoma Press, 1960);

H. Bruce Franklin, *The Wake of the Gods: Melville's Mythology* (Stanford: Stanford University Press, 1963);

Robert L. Gale, *Plots and Characters in the Fiction and Narrative Poetry of Herman Melville* (Hamden, Conn.: Archon Books, 1969);

Tyrus Hillway, *Herman Melville* (New York: Twayne, 1963);

Daniel Hoffman, *Form and Fable in American Fiction* (New York: Oxford University Press, 1961);

A. R. Humphreys, *Melville* (Edinburgh & London: Oliver & Boyd, 1962);

M. Thomas Inge, ed., *Bartleby the Inscrutable: A Collection of Commentary on Herman Melville's Tale "Bartleby the Scrivener"* (Hamden, Conn.: Archon Books, 1979);

C. L. R. James, *Mariners, Renegades, and Castaways, The Story of Herman Melville and the World We Live In* (New York: C. L. R. James, 1953);

A. N. Kaul, *The American Vision: Actual and Ideal Society in Nineteenth-Century Fiction* (New Haven: Yale University Press, 1963);

D. H. Lawrence, *Studies In Classic American Literature* (New York: Seltzer, 1923);

Alan Lebowitz, *Progress Into Silence, A Study of Melville's Heroes* (Bloomington: Indiana University Press, 1970);

A. Robert Lee, ed., *Herman Melville: Reassessments* (London: Vision Press, 1984);

Lee, ed., *The Nineteenth-Century American Short Story* (London: Vision Press, 1986);

Harry Levin, *The Power of Blackness: Hawthorne, Poe, Melville* (New York: Knopf, 1958);

R. W. B. Lewis, *The American Adam: Innocence, Tragedy, and Tradition in the Nineteenth-Century* (Chicago: University of Chicago Press, 1955);

Leo Marx, *The Machine in the Garden, Technology and the Pastoral Ideal in America* (New York: Oxford University Press, 1964);

Ronald Mason, *The Spirit Above The Dust* (London: John Lehmann, 1951);

F. O. Matthiessen, *American Renaissance: Art and Expression in the Age of Emerson and Whitman* (New York: Oxford University Press, 1941);

Jean-Jacques Mayoux, *Melville par lui-même* (Paris: Editions de Seuil, 1958); translated by John Ashbery as *Melville* (New York: Grove, 1960);

James E. Miller, Jr., *A Reader's Guide To Herman Melville* (New York: Farrar, Straus & Cudahy, 1962);

Perry Miller, *The Raven and the Whale: The War of Words and Wit in the Era of Poe and Melville* (New York: Harcourt, Brace, 1956);

Lea B. Newman, *A Reader's Guide to the Short Stories of Herman Melville* (Boston: G. K. Hall, 1986);

Charles Olson, *Call Me Ishmael: A Study of Melville* (New York: Reynal & Hitchcock, 1947);

Faith Pullin, ed., *Melville: New Perspectives* (Edinburgh: Edinburgh University Press, 1978); republished as *New Perspectives on Melville* (Kent: Kent State University Press, 1978);

Michael Paul Rogin, *Subversive Genealogy: The Politics and Art of Herman Melville* (New York: Knopf, 1983);

Edward H. Rosenberry, *Melville* (London, Henley & Boston: Routledge & Kegan Paul, 1979);

Rosenberry, *Melville and the Comic Spirit* (Cambridge, Mass.: Harvard University Press, 1955);

Constance Rourke, *American Humor: A Study of the National Character* (New York: Harcourt, Brace, 1931);

Viola Sachs, *The Game of Creation* (Paris: Editions de la Maison des sciences de l'homme, 1982);

William Ellery Sedgwick, *Herman Melville: The Tragedy of Mind* (Cambridge, Mass.: Harvard University Press, 1944);

John Seelye, *Melville: The Ironic Diagram* (Evanston: Northwestern University Press, 1970);

Milton R. Stern, *The Fine Hammered Steel of Herman Melville* (Urbana: University of Illinois Press, 1957);

Geoffrey Stone, *Melville* (New York: Sheed and Ward, 1949);

K. H. Sundermann, *Herman Melville's Gedankegut: Eine Kritische Untersuchung Seiner Weltanschaulicher Grundieen* (Berlin: Verlag Arthur Collignon, 1937);

Lawrance Thompson, *Melville's Quarrel With God* (Princeton: Princeton University Press, 1952);

Kingsley Widmer, *The Ways of Nihilism: Herman Melville's Short Novels* (Los Angeles: California State Colleges, 1970);

Edmund Wilson, *The Shock of Recognition, The Development of Literature in the United States by the Men Who Made It* (New York: Farrar, Straus & Cudahy, 1943);

Nathalia Wright, *Melville's Use of the Bible* (Durham: Duke University Press, 1949).

Papers:

The Houghton Library at Harvard University has letters, travel journals, and manuscripts for *Billy Budd*, short stories–including notes and a partial rough draft for "The Confidence Man," poems, and other shorter writings. The Duyckinck Collection and the Berg Collection at the New York Public Library include letters from Melville and his family. The University of Virginia Library also has letters and manuscripts.

Mary N. Murfree
(Charles Egbert Craddock)

(24 January 1850-31 July 1922)

Wade Hall
Bellarmine College

See also the Murfree entry in *DLB 12: American Realists and Naturalists*.

BOOKS: *In the Tennessee Mountains* (Boston & New York: Houghton, Mifflin, 1884; London: Longmans, Green, 1884);

Where the Battle Was Fought (Boston: Osgood, 1884; London: Trübner, 1885);

Down the Ravine (Boston & New York: Houghton, Mifflin, 1885; London: Ward, Lock, 1886);

The Prophet of the Great Smoky Mountains (Boston & New York: Houghton, Mifflin, 1885; London: Chatto & Windus, 1885);

In the Clouds (Boston & New York: Houghton, Mifflin, 1886; London: Ward, Lock, 1886);

The Story of Keedon Bluffs (Boston & New York: Houghton, Mifflin, 1887; London: Ward, Lock, 1887);

The Despot of Broomsedge Cove (Boston & New York: Houghton, Mifflin, 1888; London: Low, 1889);

In the "Stranger People's" Country (New York: Harper, 1891; London: Osgood, 1891);

His Vanished Star (Boston & New York: Houghton, Mifflin, 1894; London: Chatto & Windus, 1894);

The Phantoms of the Foot-Bridge, and Other Stories (New York: Harper, 1895);

The Mystery of Witch-Face Mountain and Other Stories (Boston & New York: Houghton, Mifflin, 1895);

The Young Mountaineers (Boston & New York: Houghton, Mifflin, 1897);

The Juggler (Boston & New York: Houghton, Mifflin, 1897; London: Gay & Bird, 1898);

The Story of Old Fort Loudon (New York & London: Macmillan, 1899);

The Bushwackers & Other Stories (Chicago & New York: Stone, 1899);

The Champion (Boston & New York: Houghton, Mifflin, 1902);

A Spectre of Power (Boston & New York: Houghton, Mifflin, 1903);

The Frontiersmen (Boston & New York: Houghton, Mifflin, 1904);

The Storm Centre (New York & London: Macmillan, 1905);

The Amulet (New York & London: Macmillan, 1906);

The Windfall (New York: Duffield, 1907; London: Chatto & Windus, 1907);

The Fair Mississippian (Boston & New York: Houghton Mifflin, 1908);

The Raid of the Guerilla, and Other Stories (Philadelphia & London: Lippincott, 1912);

The Ordeal; A Mountain Romance of Tennessee (Philadelphia & London: Lippincott, 1912);

The Story of Duciehurst: A Tale of the Mississippi (New York: Macmillan, 1914).

Most of the fifty short stories that Mary Noailles Murfree wrote in a career of almost fifty years were about the mountaineers of East Tennessee; but the dominant theme of all her fiction is, as she stated in her first published story, "The Dancin' Party at Harrison's Cove," that "Human nature is the same everywhere. . . ." It was not, however, the universal human qualities of Murfree's stories that made them popular and made her a master of local-color fiction. Instead, the particular details of backwoods life in the isolated Tennessee mountains accounted for their appeal to readers, particularly in the North and the East.

The daughter of William Law Murfree and Fanny Priscilla Dickinson Murfree, Mary Noailles Murfree was born 24 January 1850, near Murfreesboro, a town in middle Tennessee named for her great-grandfather. For fifteen years–from 1855 to 1870–her family spent summers at Beersheba Springs, a popular resort for affluent southern families in the Cumberland Mountains. It was here that she gained firsthand knowledge of the character and customs of the mountain people. In a letter dated 30 September 1884 she reported to Thomas Bailey Aldrich, editor of the *Atlantic*, "I struck upon the mountaineers as a topic at hap-hazard, perhaps because I was myself greatly interested by them; but I did not then appreciate how very little was known of them elsewhere. I was early familiar with their primitive customs, dialect, and peculiar ways of life, for I used to spend much time in the mountains long before I knew of the existence of such a thing as 'literary material.' " She and her sister Fanny also spent time in the Smoky Mountains, some one hundred miles to the east of Beersheba Springs, where the mountains were higher and the scenery more spectacular. In her fiction she combines the topography and people of the Cumberlands with those of the Smokies.

Murfree spent the first six years of her life at Grantland, the Murfreesboro estate on which she was born. In 1856 the family moved to Nashville, where they lived for most of the next seventeen years. The young writer in the making was fortunate to have been born into a wealthy, refined, and intellectually inclined family. Although southern women of her day were not expected to pursue intellectual vocations, Murfree's parents took great pains to educate her, first at home and later in schools in Nashville and Philadelphia, where she attended Chegary Institute from 1867 to 1869. Her family also encouraged her developing literary ambitions. Thus her temperament, her education, and her family environment were ideal for the aspiring writer. In addition, a fever contracted when she was four had caused a partial paralysis and a light lameness, which made it impossible for her to participate actively in sports and turned her to reading as her principal pastime.

In 1872, when the Murfrees moved into New Grantland (their old home had been destroyed during the nearby Battle of Stone's River in 1862), twenty-two-year-old Mary began making plans to write professionally. Two years later her first work, "Flirts and Their Ways," a light satirical essay, appeared in the May 1874 issue of *Lippincott's Magazine* under the pen name of R. Emmet Dembry.

In 1876 she sold her first two mountain stories to *Appleton's Weekly*, but the magazine ceased publication before they appeared. In May 1878 the *Atlantic Monthly* published "The Dancin' Party at Harrison's Cove" and, therefore, had the honor of introducing "Charles Egbert Craddock" to the public. The upheavals of the Civil War and its aftermath had made educated people curious about the cultural backwaters. Because little had been written about the mountain people of the southern Appalachians, the time was right for Craddock, a male pseudonym Murfree had borrowed from the hero of a story she had just begun. "He" became one of the most important of the local-color pioneers, who exploited the unique characteristics of the "odd corners" of America in the last third of the nineteenth century. Craddock's stories were immediately popular, particularly with genteel readers, because they were, in the words of a contemporary critic, "wholesome and pure, without a hint of the erotic, or of prurient suggestion." In addition, although her Civil War sympathies were Southern, her stories avoid controversy and seldom mention racial matters.

From 1878 until the late 1890s, when the local-color lode was almost exhausted, Charles Egbert Craddock's name was familiar to readers of such popular magazines as the *Atlantic, Harper's Monthly, Harper's Weekly, Century, Lippincott's, Youth's Companion,* and the *Christian Union.* In 1881 the Murfree family moved to St. Louis, where her brother practiced law, but nine years later they returned to Murfreesboro, which the writer called home for the rest of her life.

The identity of "that man Craddock" was kept secret until 1885, when Murfree traveled to Boston and revealed her true identity to Thomas Bailey Aldrich. In 1884 Aldrich had urged Houghton, Mifflin to publish a collection of the eight Craddock stories that had appeared in the *Atlantic* since 1878. *In the Tennessee Mountains* (1884) was an instant best-seller, going into more than a dozen editions within two years. Little wonder, then, that the unveiling of Craddock as Mary Noailles Murfree was one of the literary exposés of the era.

Easily the best of Murfree's books, *In the Tennessee Mountains* was praised by contemporary critics as a milestone in American regional writing. Singled out for special compliments were Craddock's accurate details, close observations, gift for recording mountain dialect, and the unpretentiousness of the stories. Murfree would write a total of twenty-five books, including seven collections of short stories, but she would seldom improve upon the stories in her first collection. Indeed, *In the Tennessee Mountains* contains the characters, the incidents, and the settings that she would return to throughout her career. These stories are the first and strongest chapters in the loosely constructed epic of the Tennessee mountains she was to spend her life writing. Her first published story, "The Dancin' Party at Harrison's Cove," is a good introduction to Murfree's fictional world and method. Little more than an incident of mountain life, the story focuses on a dancing party a backwoods father decides to give so that his four marriageable daughters can meet some eligible young men. A killing at the party is narrowly avoided when a guest at the New Helvetia Springs Hotel, "old Mr. Kenyon," a "fightin' preacher," interrupts the two combatants, tells them a properly conducted dance is not sinful, and leaves them with the newfound appreciation "that a Christian may be a man of spirit also, and that bravado does not constitute bravery."

The story introduces not only Murfree's mountaineer types and the mountain setting but also two themes that run through her fiction, the universality of human nature and—at the same time—the contrasts of the folk life in the mountains and the more refined life of wealthy visitors. In providing a rationale for the party, Murfree reminds her readers that "strange as it may seem, the prudent father exists even among the 'mounting folk.' Men there realize the importance of providing suitable homes for their daughters as men do elsewhere, and the eligible youth is as highly esteemed in those wilds as is the much scarcer animal at a fashionable watering-place." Nevertheless, the mountain people believe that dancing is a sin, and even the girls' father, Mr. Harrison, "stood in bodily fear of the judgment day and the circuit-rider." His wife is terrified of such wickedness: "Such trifles as killing a man in a quarrel, or on suspicion of stealing a horse, or wash-tub, or anything that came handy, of course, does not count; but a dancing party! Mrs. Harrison could only hold her idle hands, and dread the heavy penalty that must surely follow so terrible a crime." The young people do not seem to consider dancing a serious crime, and they turn out in large numbers at the Harrisons' log cabin for the party. While "the sinful votaries of Terpsichore" celebrate, their elders sit on rush-bottomed chairs along the walls, and the men make frequent trips to an adjoining shed for cider and moonshine whiskey. The story illustrates the often-jarring clash of Murfree's elevated literary style, used for description and narration, and her folk style, used for recording backwoods speech. The first two paragraphs of the story also demonstrate the gulf between the writer and her subject:

> "Fur ye see, Mis' Darley, them Harrison folks over yander ter the Cove hev determined on a dancin' party."

> The drawling tones fell unheeded on old Mr. Kenyon's ear, as he sat on the broad hotel piazza of the New Helvetia Springs, and gazed with meditative eyes at the fair August sky. An early moon was riding, clear and full, over this wild spur of the Alleghanies; the stars were few and very faint; even the great Scorpio lurked, vaguely outlined, above the wooded ranges; and the white mist, that filled the long, deep, narrow valley between the parallel lines of mountains, shimmered with opalescent gleams.

One of the most unsettling juxtapositions of high and low language occurs in "The Romance of Sunrise Rose" (*Atlantic Monthly*, December 1880; collected in *In the Tennessee Mountains*). These lines describing a "paint-rock" occur in the first two paragraphs: "What momentous morning arose with so resplendent a glory that it should have imprinted its indelible reflection on the face

Murfree during the visit to Boston when her identity was revealed: (left to right) Edwin Booth, Murfree, Thomas Bailey Aldrich, Lilian Woodman Aldrich, Fanny Murfree, Miss Houghton, and James M. Bugbee, 1885

of this great Cumberland cliff; what eloquence of dawn so splendid that the dumb, insensate stone should catch its spirit and retain its expression forever and forever?" This euphuistic description is followed by a mountaineer's explanation of the painted rock's origins: " 'Twar painted by the Injuns,–that's what I hev always hearn tell. Them folks war mos'ly leagued with the Evil One."

The mountain people in Murfree's stories speak variations of a single dialect, a debased English supposedly handed down from their Elizabethan ancestors. Attempts by local colorists to represent such provincial speech patterns frequently resulted in almost unreadable phonetic misspellings. Yet Murfree's rendering of dialect is usually accurate and readily decipherable.

Murfree implies also that all mountain people are cut from the same cloth. Her men are usually shiftless, though they can develop considerable enthusiasm over hunting, fishing, or fighting. Her most industrious males are the miller, the blacksmith, the preacher, and the moonshiner. They are fiercely independent and are generally contemptuous of the law, especially those restricting the making of whiskey. Her women are frequently pretty when they are young, but they marry early and soon fade under the burdens of childbearing, child rearing, and house and field work. Murfree describes one such mountain woman in "The Dancin' Party at Harrison's Cove": "she was tall and lank, and with such a face as one never sees except in these

mountains,–elongated, sallow, thin, with pathetic, deeply sunken eyes, and high cheek-bones, and so settled an expression of hopeless melancholy that it must be that naught but care and suffering had been her lot; holding out wasted hands to the years as they pass,–holding them out always, and always empty."

Although the cultural barrier between writer and subject never came down, Murfree was consistently sympathetic with her mountain people and their lives. In the final paragraph of "The 'Harnt That Walks Chilhowee" (*Atlantic Monthly*, May 1883; collected in *In the Tennessee Mountains*) she boldly asserts their potential superiority: "The grace of culture is, in its way, a fine thing, but the best that art can do–the polish of a gentleman–is hardly equal to the best that Nature can do in her higher moods."

Following the success of *In the Tennessee Mountains*, Murfree wrote fifteen more mountain stories. Literary taste, however, began to change in the 1890s, and by the end of the century historical fiction had replaced local color in popularity. In an attempt to accommodate the changing times, she did extensive research on the pioneer period of Tennessee history and wrote three historical novels and seven short stories about the state's colonial past. Five of the stories deal with the conflict between the British and the French for the Indian trade between 1734 and 1762. Two stories are based on Indian legends. One of her colonial stories, "The Exploit of Choolah, the

Chickasaw," was first published in *The Bushwackers & Other Stories* (1899), and the remaining six make up the content of *The Frontiersmen* (1904).

In several of her mountain stories there are references to the Civil War, and Murfree wrote two novels and three short stories that directly relate to the war. The stories—"The Bushwackers" (first published in *The Bushwackers & Other Stories*), "The Raid of the Guerillas" (*Harper's Magazine*, July 1909; collected in *The Raid of the Guerilla, and Other Stories*, 1912), and "The Lost Guidon" (*Lippincott's Magazine*, August 1911; collected in *The Raid of the Guerilla, and Other Stories*)—are all set in the mountains. "The Bushwackers" is a rambling narrative about a series of incidents involving Hilary Knox, a country boy with romantic notions of war like those of Henry Fleming in Stephen Crane's *The Red Badge of Courage* (1895): "He longed to be in the midst of action, to take a man's part in the great struggle, to live the life and do the faithful devoir of a soldier." Soon, however, he is disabused of such ideals, when he is confronted by a man in his army unit, "a big, brutal cavalryman" named Jack Bixby, who delights in poking fun at the raw recruit. Later, after he is captured and paroled by Federal soldiers, Knox is maliciously attacked by Bixby with a bowie knife and loses his right arm. The pathetic young man is discharged and returns home "maimed and helpless" to find that a gang of bushwackers, including Jack Bixby, are hanging out at an abandoned resort hotel nearby. When the bushwackers, one of the many "vagrant bands of stragglers and marauders" who prey upon victims for their own gain, are surrounded by a posse of local loyalists, Knox forgets the wrong done him by the wicked Bixby and helps him escape. The story is filled to the brim with a then-popular mixture of pathos and religious sentiment. It is, nonetheless, an exciting narrative that holds the reader's attention to the last paragraph.

During the last phase of her literary career, Murfree turned to Mississippi, where her family had owned a plantation before the Civil War. Between 1908 and 1914 she wrote two novels and two short stories set in Mississippi. The stories—"The Phantom of Bogue Holauba" (*Lippincott's Magazine*, March 1912), a ghost story, and "The Crucial Moment" (*Lippincott's Magazine*, April

1912), a melodrama of murder and justice—were collected in *The Raid of the Guerilla, and Other Stories*.

Mary Noailles Murfree's last published piece was an article, "Muscle Shoals in Colonial Days," which appeared in the December 1921 issue of *Youth's Companion*. Near the end of her life her lameness became chronic, and she spent her last years blind and restricted to a wheelchair. When she died, on 31 July 1922, her reputation had declined to the point that her obituary in the *New York Times* (2 August 1922) was a mere four lines at the bottom of page seventeen. For her lifetime of literary labor in the Tennessee mountains, she deserved better. Although no serious critic today would call her a major writer, she is an important figure in the American local-color movement. Despite stylistic and structural weaknesses, her intrusive editorializing, and her stereotyping of mountain people, her stories present a world that comes alive in sight, sound, color, and action—and many of them continue to be enjoyable to read.

References:

G. H. Baskette, "Mary Noailles Murfree," in *Library of Southern Literature*, 16 volumes, edited by Edwin A. Alderman and Joel Chandler Harris (New Orleans, Atlanta & Dallas: Martin & Hoyt, 1909-1913), VIII: 3721-3745;

Richard Cary, *Mary N. Murfree* (New York: Twayne, 1967);

Wade Hall, *The Smiling Phoenix: Southern Humor from 1865 to 1914* (Gainesville: University of Florida Press, 1965);

Edd Winfield Parks, *Charles Egbert Craddock (Mary Noailles Murfree)* (Chapel Hill: University of North Carolina Press, 1941);

Merrill Maguire Skaggs, *The Folk of Southern Fiction* (Athens: University of Georgia Press, 1972);

Thomas Daniel Young, *Tennessee Writers* (Knoxville: University of Tennessee Press, 1981).

Papers:

The most significant holdings of Murfree manuscripts are at the Tennessee State Library and Archives and the Robert W. Woodruff Library, Emory University.

Fitz-James O'Brien

(1828-6 April 1862)

Gary Hoppenstand
Michigan State University

BOOKS: *A Gentleman from Ireland. A Comedy in Two Acts* (New York: Samuel French, 1858);
The Poems and Stories of Fitz-James O'Brien. Collected and Edited, with a Sketch of the Author, by William Winter (Boston: Osgood, 1881).
Collections: *The Diamond Lens with Other Stories*, edited by Winter (New York: Scribners, 1885; London: Ward & Downey, 1887);
Collected Stories by Fitz-James O'Brien, edited by Edward J. O'Brien (New York: A. & C. Boni, 1925);
The Supernatural Tales of Fitz-James O'Brien, edited, with notes and an introduction, by Jessica Amanda Salmonson (New York: Doubleday, 1988).

In his *Supernatural Horror in Literature* (1945) Howard Phillips Lovecraft called Fitz-James O'Brien one of Edgar Allan Poe's earliest disciples, and from the time of Poe's death to the turn of the century, O'Brien was the foremost American writer of supernatural and science-fiction short stories. Though he established his literary reputation as a poet and essayist, O'Brien's handful of collected short stories established him as a master of the macabre.

Michael Fitz-James O'Brien was born in Cork, Ireland, between April and 31 December 1828. His father, James O'Brien, Esquire, was a county coroner. His mother, Eliza O'Driscoll O'Brien, described as a beautiful woman, was some twenty years younger than her husband, and not long after his death in 1839 or 1840 she married DeCourcy O'Grady, a man of wealth and distinguished ancestry. Though Fitz-James survived the first of the great Irish famines in 1845, which resulted in large-scale immigration of Irish peasants to America, his voyage to New York was not motivated by famine but was induced by financial impoverishment and a sense of reckless adventure.

Upon arriving in New York in early 1852, O'Brien is said to have lodged himself in an expensive hotel, run up a high bill, and departed with-

Fitz-James O'Brien

out paying. Rumors also persist that O'Brien had squandered his patrimony before leaving Ireland. Though none of these rumors can be substantiated, it is certain that O'Brien possessed an aristocrat's taste for luxury. To maintain his standard of living, O'Brien turned to a form of labor that he had found quite profitable and untaxing back in Ireland: writing for newspapers and magazines. By the time he died in 1862 O'Brien had contributed to nearly all the major American magazines, most frequently to *Harper's New Monthly Magazine,* for which he wrote thirty-three poems, thirty-five short stories, and five articles, and *Harper's Weekly,* to which he contributed thirty-two

"Man about Town" columns (31 January-26 September 1857), eight poems, and one short story. He also wrote plays, two of which–*A Gentleman from Ireland* and *The Sisters*–opened in December 1854 for successful runs in New York.

O'Brien's major contribution to American supernatural literature was the contemporary urban setting. Most practitioners of the Gothic horror story, including Poe, set their fiction in socially decadent European environments. O'Brien was one of the first authors to describe, as realistically as possible, the everyday city milieu. Such settings, when used as the backdrop for O'Brien's rather conventional supernatural themes, led to a mix of realism and fantasy that was to be copied later by major horror writers.

O'Brien has also been recognized as one of the originators of the American short story. After his death O'Brien was represented in most major short-story collections of the nineteenth century. His masterful treatment of suspense guaranteed him a popular audience among his contemporaries. After the turn of the century O'Brien's tendency toward the melodramatic and highly artificial character development caused his reputation to decline. Only his two most popular short stories, "The Diamond Lens" and "What Was It? A Mystery," have continued to be anthologized.

The first of O'Brien's significant short stories, "The Bohemian" (*Harper's New Monthly Magazine*, July 1855; collected in *The Poems and Stories of Fitz-James O'Brien*, 1881), satirizes artistic bohemianism, through a title character who seems much like O'Brien himself. The Bohemian of the story–a man named Philip Brann who describes himself as "clever, learned, witty, and tolerably good looking," with "a contempt for labor"–joins forces with the narrator, Henry Cranstoun a man driven by dreams of wealth. Greed unites these two men in a conspiracy that ultimately destroys the beautiful and sensitive Annie Deane, the narrator's fiancée. "The Bohemian" is an allegory of vision, employing a metaphor that is used elsewhere in O'Brien's fiction. The Bohemian, recognizing the narrator's greed, proposes a scheme in which Annie Deane–a "clairvoyante" who has fantastic visions–would be used to discover the location of hidden treasure left and forgotten by the inhabitants of New York on Coney Island. After the discovery of the treasure leads to Annie's destruction, the Bohemian, a self-proclaimed mesmerist, blinds the narrator to the greater treasure of love. By the conclusion of the

story, the narrator has discovered how much "wealth" he has forfeited.

"Duke Humphrey's Dinner" (*Harper's New Monthly Magazine,* August 1855; collected in *The Poems and Stories of Fitz-James O'Brien*) is one of O'Brien's most melodramatic story. Though spoiled, love-stricken children at the beginning of the story, Dick and Agnes are saved by their commitment to each other after they squander their inheritances and are financially abandoned by their families. Dick's final act of selflessness, selling a treasured book, comes to the attention of a friend whom Dick once saved from drowning. The friend offers Dick and Agnes a new start. By honest labor, Dick raises himself to be a "great merchant," and their happiness is guaranteed. "Duke Humphrey's Dinner" predates both Horatio Alger, Jr.'s myth of material success and O. Henry's myth of noble poverty.

"The Pot of Tulips" (*Harper's New Monthly Magazine,* November 1855; collected in *The Poems and Stories of Fitz-James O'Brien*) appears at first glance to be a traditional ghost story. A wealthy, jealous husband, Van Koeren misjudges his beautiful younger wife, condemning her and their young son to a life of poverty and misery, but after his death, he desires to undo his mistake. The narrator of the story is thus "haunted" by the ghost of Van Koeren until he can unlock the secret of Van Koeren's hidden wealth by following the clues given him by Van Koeren's ghost. The motif of unrequited justice, though common in ghost stories, is secondary to the process of mystery and detection, making "The Pot of Tulips" one of the earliest syntheses of the ghost story and the detective story: the ghost-hunter tale.

"The Dragon Fang Possessed by the Conjuror Piou-Lu" (*Harper's New Monthly Magazine,* March 1856; collected in *The Poems and Stories of Fitz-James O'Brien*) differs considerably from most of O'Brien's other short stories. Departing from the contemporary setting, the story takes place in a mythical Chinese fairyland. Magic is commonplace, and the fantastic is mundane. The protagonist, Piou-Lu, undergoes a series of adventures with a moral being delivered at the conclusion of each. As in O'Brien's less fantastic work, however, there is great emphasis placed upon the acquisition and management of money. In one of the short adventures, Piou-Lu informs an unfortunate fruit vendor: "Gather your plums, Liho . . . and think this one of your fortunate days; for he who runs after his losses with open mouth does not always overtake them." For O'Brien, the loss

O'Brien as a Union army recruiter, caricatured by Mullen for Vanity Fair, *1861*

of money was bad, but lamenting such losses was worse.

The narrator of "The Lost Room" (*Harper's New Monthly Magazine*, September 1858; collected in *The Poems and Stories of Fitz-James O'Brien*), who lives in a large boardinghouse, unwillingly enters another dimension in his own room. The house is described as a conglomeration of crannies, windings, cul de sacs and corridors that, "like mathematical lines, seemed capable of indefinite extension." One night, after a frightening stranger tells him that the house's other inhabitants are cannibals, the narrator seems to discover six "decadently" dressed men and women feasting in his room. During the evening's encounter with these phantom libertines the narrator doubts his sanity, and as the night wears on the narrator does in fact descend deeper into madness. Finally he runs out of the house and is never again able to find his room. The loss of home, the fear of the unknown, the evil of opulence, and the dread that one is not in control of his fate—such things combine in this story to create a dark and "surrealistic nightmare that later influenced new generations" of horror writers. Lovecraft employed the "eerie geometric building" motif in some of his stories, and both hard-boiled detective writers and existentialists have employed the "man's lack of control" motif.

"The Diamond Lens" (*Atlantic Monthly*, January 1858; collected in *The Poems and Stories of Fitz-*

James O'Brien) is O'Brien's best-known and most frequently anthologized story. The narrator's interest in lenses and microscopes is another example of O'Brien's concern with vision and knowledge. The narrator's drive to perfect the microscope is an extension of his desire for divine knowledge. An odd transcendentalist, the narrator has a vision of a microworld in which there exists a celestial realm inhabited by a female who is a "divine revelation of perfect beauty." The narrator falls madly in love, but for a glimpse of perfection he must pay a price, and that price is witnessing the destruction of his miniature sylph. Man is flawed, and the sylph's world, a tiny cosmos located in a drop of water, evaporates because the narrator fails to care properly for the microscope slide.

"What Was It? A Mystery" (*Harper's New Monthly Magazine*, March 1859; collected in *The Poems and Stories of Fitz-James O'Brien*) offers an enigma in which the lack of vision confounds the narrator, in a story that incorporates the theme employed in "The Lost Room," the notion that man is at the mercy of unknown hostile powers. In this story the narrator encounters an invisible creature that has attacked him in bed. The narrator and a friend subdue the creature and tie ropes around it. They make a plaster of Paris mold of the creature but discover little about the creature's origins or eating habits, and eventually the creature starves to death. The narrator draws an analogy between the invisible creature and a glass, implying that both are products of the natural world. By providing a scientific explanation for a seemingly preternatural event, the story locates itself in the relatively new genre of science fiction. The literary impact of "What Was It?" in the middle and late 1800s was staggering. The French master of the short story Guy de Maupassant borrowed from it for his tale "The Horla."

"The Wondersmith" (*Atlantic Monthly*, October 1859; collected in *The Poems and Stories of Fitz-James O'Brien*) is O'Brien's last significant short story, though he continued publishing fiction until his death. For the first time in O'Brien's work, the setting is fully realized. Golosh Street and its bizarre inhabitants are described in careful detail, aiding the reader's willing suspension of disbelief, so that Herr Hippe's devilish plans for his miniature, toylike automatons seem less outlandish. The notion of the robot was one of O'Brien's major contributions to science fiction. O'Brien, at his best, blended fact and fancy, myth and reality, so that the enchanted reader failed to notice where the one ended and the other began.

At the beginning of the Civil War O'Brien enlisted in the Union army, zealously aiding in attempts to enlist recruits and writing songs and poems filled with patriotic fervor. He was cited for bravery in action at Bloomery Gap, West Virginia, on 14 February 1862. On 16 February while on a scouting expedition, O'Brien was wounded in the breast by a Confederate bullet, but he shot and killed his attacker and was able to ride the twenty-four miles back to camp. Less than two months later he died of tetanus caused by improper treatment of his wound. Some of his fiction and his poetry continued to be published several months after his death.

Although Fitz-James O'Brien is largely forgotten, he was one of America's earliest popular short-story writers. His supernatural fiction influenced generations of horror writers. His work, unlike the invisible creature in "What Was It?," should not remain hidden.

Biographies:

William Winter, "Sketch of O'Brien," in *The Poems and Stories of Fitz-James O'Brien*, edited by Winter (Boston: Osgood, 1881), pp. xv-xxviii;

Francis Wolle, *Fitz-James O'Brien: A Literary Bohemian of the Eighteen-Fifties*, University of Colorado Studies, series B, volume 2, number 2 (Boulder, May 1944).

Reference:

Howard Phillips Lovecraft, *Supernatural Horror in Literature* (New York: Abramson, 1945).

Papers:

O'Brien manuscripts are scattered among the following libraries: the Beinecke Library, Yale University; the Folger Shakespeare Library; the Milton S. Eisenhower Library, Johns Hopkins University; the New York Public Library; the William R. Perkins Library, Duke University; the Cincinnati Historical Society, and the Alderman Library, University of Virginia.

Sara Payson Willis Parton
(Fanny Fern)
(9 July 1811-10 October 1872)

Miriam S. Gogol
Fashion Institute of Technology, State University of New York

See also the Parton entry in *DLB 43: American Newspaper Journalists, 1690-1872.*

BOOKS: *Fern Leaves From Fanny's Port-Folio* (Auburn: Derby & Miller/Buffalo: Derby, Orton & Mulligan, 1853; London: Cooke, 1853);

Little Ferns for Fanny's Little Friends (Auburn: Derby & Miller, 1853);

Fern Leaves From Fanny's Port-Folio, second series (Auburn & Buffalo: Miller, Orton & Mulligan/London: Low, 1854); republished as *Shadows and Sunbeams: Being a Second Series of Fern Leaves From Fanny's Port-Folio* (London: Orr, 1854);

Ruth Hall (New York: Mason Brothers, 1855);

Rose Clark (New York: Mason Brothers, 1856);

The Play-Day Book (New York: Mason Brothers, 1857);

Fresh Leaves (New York: Mason Brothers, 1857);

A New Story Book for Children (New York: Mason Brothers, 1864);

Folly As It Flies (New York: Carleton/London: Low, 1868);

Ginger-Snaps (New York: Carleton/London: Low, 1870);

Caper-Sauce: A Volume of Chit-Chat about Men, Women, and Things (New York: Carleton/London: Low, 1872).

"The woman writes as if the devil was in her," said Nathaniel Hawthorne (letter to William D. Ticknor, 2 February 1855) of Sara Payson Willis Parton, who was known to the world as Fanny Fern, the first American woman newspaper columnist and the highest-paid one of her day. In her nine volumes of newspaper columns and two novels, *Ruth Hall* (1855) and *Rose Clark* (1856), she wrote fervently about the rights of women, the protection of children, and the need to improve social conditions.

Sara Payson Willis Parton (courtesy of the New-York Historical Society)

Until recently, however, twentieth-century critics have characterized Fern as nothing more than an extreme sentimentalist. Overlooking most of her writing, they usually point to her short stories as the objects of their derision. Consequently, they do a disservice both to her other works and also to the short stories, which deserve far greater recognition than they have yet received. Some are sentimental indeed, written to meet the demands of her newspaper audience, but they also give insight into everyday life in the 1850s. Moreover, they express a depth of feeling that she considered an essential part of human life.

The daughter of Nathaniel and Hannah Parker Willis, Fern was born into a family of strong journalistic and literary traditions. Her grandfather Nathaniel Willis published a Whig newspaper in Boston during the Revolutionary War. Not long after her birth in Portland, Maine, her father moved the family to Boston, where he started a printing business; in 1827 he founded another newspaper, the *Youth's Companion.* Her elder brother was the literary lion Nathaniel Parker Willis.

Described as a rosy-cheeked beauty with a torrent of yellow curls in her early years, Fern had a propensity for mirth and impudence. Her third husband, eminent biographer James Parton, believed she decidedly "was not formed for a saint. . . . And, I presume, she gave her father some troublesome hours with her wild ways. At least, I heard him tell her so, when he was past eighty-eight, with a chuckle and a grin. 'How do you manage her?' Said he: 'I never could.' "

Her beauty and mirth did not spare her a life fraught with struggle as melodramatic and even as heroic as that of any of her characters. Married to Charles Harrington Eldredge, a cashier at the Merchant's Bank in Boston, in May 1837, Fern spent seven happy years with him until her life was transformed in 1844 with the first of a series of tragedies. In February of that year her youngest sister died, followed by her mother six weeks later. In 1845 Fern's oldest daughter died after a brief illness. The following year her husband died. A widow with two small daughters, she married S. P. Farrington in 1849. The marriage was unhappy. After she separated from her husband in 1851, she was so poor that she temporarily had to send her eldest daughter away. Her early stories repeatedly recount the pain and struggle of these times.

Scorned by relatives outraged by her divorce (1852), she struck out on her own to support her family. She worked as a seamstress, applied to be a schoolteacher, and finally became a newspaper writer. The first of her pieces to be published was accepted by the editor of a small Boston newspaper, the *Mother's Assistant.* He reluctantly agreed to pay her the small sum of a half dollar, for which she had to call several times. This experience was so discouraging that she

might not have continued except that she saw her piece copied in the *Boston Transcript.* Before the end of the week, almost every paper in Boston had pirated it. She had no difficulty placing her writings after that, but she still received little remuneration.

By September 1852 Fern was writing articles exclusively for the *New York Musical World and Times,* where they appeared under the heading "Fanny Fern's Column." Thus, she became the first woman columnist in the United States. Other women–such as Lydia Maria Child and Margaret Fuller–had been correspondents or editors, but Fern was the first columnist in the modern sense of the word: a professional journalist paid a salary for a regular column stating her personal views on social and political issues.

Just one year later, in 1853, her first collection, *Fern Leaves From Fanny's Port-Folio,* was published. Most of the pieces were culled from the Boston papers *Olive Branch* and *True Flag,* as well as *Musical World and Times.* As are all of her later volumes, except her novels, *Fern Leaves* is a miscellany of short stories, vignettes, and brief essays. Her short stories should rightly be published as a separate volume.

Many of Fern's pieces appearing in the guise of fiction (thus palatable to her reading public) are actually based on fact and satirize conventions of the day. *Fern Leaves From Fanny's Port-Folio* contains more short stories than subsequent collections. The stories cover a multitude of topics, from autobiographical accounts of Fern's troubles, to realistic portrayals of the struggles of women and the plight of unprotected children. These stories are compelling reading, in spite of their sentimentality, because they are told from the perspective of a woman who knew and felt what she was describing.

Every aspect of women's lives is examined, with special attention given to how they live and what they value. Fern takes them to task for being frivolous in their concerns with dress, warning that their lives may be impoverished by their vanity. Through gentle parody, she also mocks those men who prevent women from leading fulfilling lives. Much of the feminism revealed at this early stage of her fiction writing is confined within the accepted parameters of the day. Fern repeatedly counsels that women have as much power as they are willing to conceal: " 'Tis better policy to play possum, and wear the mark of submission. No use in raising any unnecessary antagonism."

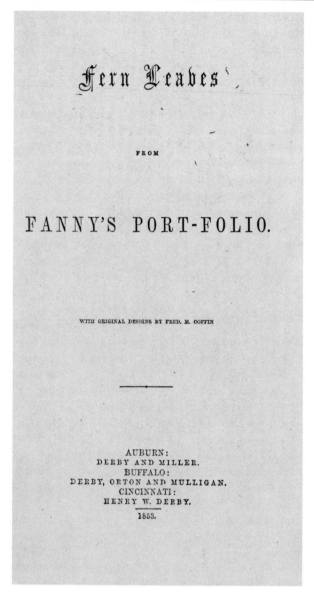

Fern Leaves

FROM

FANNY'S PORT-FOLIO.

WITH ORIGINAL DESIGNS BY FRED. M. COFFIN

AUBURN:
DERBY AND MILLER.
BUFFALO:
DERBY, ORTON AND MULLIGAN.
CINCINNATI:
HENRY W. DERBY.
1853.

Title page for Parton's critically acclaimed first collection of stories, which examined women's issues

From the start of her writing career, Fern was preoccupied with the issue of children's rights. Her strong portrayals call for the protection of children from the abuse and neglect of parents and from the devastation of poverty. Some of the best short stories in this volume describe her love of children and the love they need if they are not only to survive but also to flourish.

Many of the clearly autobiographical stories reflect her spontaneous reaction to issues she has observed or experienced. "The Widow's Trials," for example, mirrors the devastating emptiness Fern felt after her first husband's funeral: "All the usual phrases of stereotyped condolence had fallen upon her ear; and now they had all gone, and the world would move on just the same that there was one more broken heart in it." Other stories reflect her effort to hide her grief from her children, her need temporarily to give up one of her daughters, her children's reminiscences about their dead father, and, when destitute, her efforts to find employment. A major theme throughout her work is the world's callousness and indifference to those in need: "Alas! poor human nature," she exclaims. "Everybody looking out for number one, and caring little who jostled past, if their rights were not infringed." But she also notes the exceptions, those who are kind: "God's image is only marred, not destroyed."

Their ornate and flowery language and their mid-Victorian conventionality aside, these stories are powerful evocations of real events. They manifest her commitment to telling the truth about tragic social conditions, and they show the obvious pain she felt for the victim of society. It should be recognized that her capacity to express this compassion makes her a precursor of such humanistic, twentieth-century writers as Theodore Dreiser and Sherwood Anderson.

Fern Leaves was a runaway best-seller with its extraordinary sale of close to eighty thousand copies in America in less than one year's time. Much of the popular press applauded its sentimental pieces. The *Canadian Christian Advocate* commented typically: "We do not believe the author exists who can equal her sketches." But this same volume was criticized by mid-twentieth-century critics. Most dismissed it as sentimental drivel. Fred Lewis Pattee, in *The Feminine Fifties* (1940), did much to promulgate this distorted view of Fern's work, calling her the "most tearful and convulsingly 'female' moralizer" of the period. Some more recent critics, such as Nina Baym, consider this judgment absurd. Baym describes Fern's pieces as jaunty and irreverent, written in a style responsive to the rhythms and vocabulary of ordinary speech. She sees in Fern an accomplished practitioner of a vernacular prose style.

After the enormous success of *Fern Leaves*, a second series bearing the same title was published in 1854. Again, these pieces are a miscellany of stories, essays, and discourses culled from her newspaper columns and framed as parables, soliloquies, and meditations. Many elaborate on themes developed in the first series, this time with a vengeance. Here a new side of Fern is appearing. More confident in her own voice and in the public's acceptance of it, she takes strong stands against the inequities of marriage, child abuse, and other social ills. Her style has changed markedly. No longer so sentimental, she is humorous, satirical, and even crude in her language.

Her stories dared to challenge the sanctity of marriage in an era when women were made to feel it was "unfeminine" to criticize men, much less to do so in such an unsuitable and masculine vehicle as a newspaper. Several of these stories focus on wrong marriages: on marrying too quickly ("Love and Duty"), on forced marriages ("The Fatal Marriage"), and on wife battering and psychological abuse ("Our Nelly"). Again and again wives die after a year or two because their husbands have broken their spirit. Fern affirms her stance in "Our Nelly": "Ah! there is no law to protect woman from negative abuse!–No mention made in the statute book (which *men frame for themselves*) . . . No! if she can show no mark of brutal fingers on her delicate flesh, he has fulfilled his legal promise to the letter. . . . *Out* on such a mockery of justice!"

Perhaps Fern's most rhythmic and moving writing in this collection is found in the stories about children and the mothering of them (which she later describes as "all that is left us of paradise"). She is able to capture the way children feel and how they suffer, especially by being deprived of a mother. In "Willy Grey" a young boy loses his mother and is left with a stern, unsympathetic father. Fern conveys his need of "tears of sympathy" and "unconditional" love, unconditional because of the newness of feelings in him with which adults have long been familiar.

The second series was also a success with the public and sold at least twenty thousand copies. Some recent commentators, such as Ann Douglas Wood, see an improvement in her second volume; as Wood puts it, there is more "Fanny" and less "Fern." No longer flowery in her prose, Fern has turned from the praise of suffering to the advocacy of fighting.

During this period of remarkable productivity, another of her volumes was published, *Little Ferns for Fanny's Little Friends* (1853). This book was the first of three devoted exclusively to juvenile stories–which also include *The Play-Day Book* (1857) and *A New Story Book for Children* (1864). Another best-seller, *Little Ferns* immediately sold thirty-two thousand copies in the United States and forty-five thousand more in Great Britain,

where Fern was always popular. Unlike the adult collections, *Little Ferns* is almost exclusively devoted to fiction. Many of the stories are told from the viewpoints of children themselves, perceptively revealing what they think, feel, and desire.

Although some of these stories are maudlin (especially those about dying children), what is most striking about this volume is its overall maturity. The language is relatively sophisticated, the images complex, and the messages didactic. The stories become increasingly indistinguishable in tone and tenor from Fern's "adult" pieces, with the introduction of such topics as prostitution, suicide, and imprisonment. They are not so much *for* children as *about* them and, as such, deserve further study as part of the canon of adult fiction.

The next years were lively and remunerative ones for Fern. In 1855 she contracted with Robert Bonner to write a column for the *New York Ledger* at the unprecedented salary of one hundred dollars a week. She maintained that association for the rest of her life and is said never to have missed an issue. At this time she moved to New York City, where on 5 January 1856 she married James Parton. By now she was known as Fanny Fern, publicly and privately. Her husband addressed her as Fanny, friends wrote to Fanny Fern Parton, and she herself signed her correspondence Fanny Fern. She successfully litigated to stop publication of a book using that name and thus also won the legal right to her popular pseudonym.

Between 1857 and 1872 she published four more adult collections from her columns. These later volumes include few short stories. *Fresh Leaves* (1857) contains a novella and a handful of short stories and soliloquies. The volume opens with one of the best stories, "A Business Man's Home," in which Fern shows both sides of a marriage: a husband inextricably trapped within a temperament formed from his bitter childhood experience and a wife who must defy him if she is to maintain her selfhood. The novella, "Fanny Ford," is a parable of vengeance wreaked on a father who hoards his money and exploits his workers. Maudlin and melodramatic, this story is a throwback to the weakest of Fern's earliest works.

The three remaining volumes, *Folly As It Flies* (1868), *Ginger-Snaps* (1870), and *Caper-Sauce* (1872), contain few stories. Those that do appear in the guise of fiction dissolve into Fern's editorializing within the opening paragraphs. For instance, in *Folly As It Flies* a story entitled "Bridget As She Was, And Bridget As She Is" opens with a simple country girl wooed into the sophisticated but frivolous ways of city people. It is not long before Fern's persona appears to proffer opinions on what constitutes a good or a bad servant.

Fern's last book, *Caper-Sauce*, has a subtitle that reveals its emphasis: *A Volume of Chit-Chat about Men, Women, and Things*. Yet much of what she guilefully calls "chit-chat" is her strongest and most polemical work and, as such, deserves close examination.

Fern continued writing right up to her death from cancer in 1872. When she lost the use of her right hand, she wrote laboriously and painfully with the left. "Write she would," James Parton wrote in his memorial volume. In the last weeks of her life, unable to write with either hand, she dictated her column.

The resurgence of interest in Fanny Fern with the republication of *Ruth Hall* in 1986 and with fresh recognition from such distinguished critics as Ann Douglas Wood and Nina Baym points to the necessity of republishing her short stories, along with her nonfiction and vignettes. Her essays contain some of her best and most vitriolic statements about society and the status of women; as such, they deserve the attention of a new generation of readers.

References:

Florence Bannard Adams, *Fanny Fern, or a Pair of Flaming Shoes* (West Trenton, N.J.: Hermitage, 1966);

Nina Baym, "Melodramas of Beset Manhood: How Theories of American Fiction Exclude Women Authors," in *The New Feminist Criticism*, edited by Elaine Showalter (New York: Pantheon, 1985), pp. 63-80;

Baym, *Woman's Fiction: A Guide to Novels by and about Women in America, 1820-1870* (Ithaca: Cornell University Press, 1978), pp. 251-252;

James C. Derby, *Fifty Years Among Authors, Books and Publishers* (New York: Carleton, 1884), pp. 208-220;

Robert P. Eckert, Jr., "Friendly, Fragrant Fanny Ferns," *Colophon*, 18 (September 1934): n. pag.;

Grace Greenwood, "Fanny Fern–Mrs. Parton," in *Eminent Women of the Age*, edited by James Parton (Hartford: S. M. Betts, 1868), pp. 66-84;

James D. Hart, *The Popular Book* (New York: Oxford University Press, 1950);

John S. Hart, *The Female Prose Writers of America* (Philadelphia: E. H. Butler, 1857);

Linda Huf, *A Portrait of the Artist as a Young Woman: The Writer as Heroine in American Literature* (New York: Ungar, 1983);

Mary Kelley, *Private Woman, Public Stage: Literary Domesticity in Nineteenth-Century America* (New York: Oxford University Press, 1984);

The Life and Beauties of Fanny Fern (New York: Long, 1855);

Patricia McGinnis, "Fanny Fern, American Novelist," *Biblion*, 2 (1969): 2-37;

Ethel Parton, "Fanny Fern at the Hartford Female Seminary," *New England Magazine*, 24 (March 1901): 94-98;

Parton, "A Little Girl and Two Authors," *Horn Book Magazine*, 17 (March-April 1941): 81-86;

Parton, "A New York Childhood: The Seventies in Stuyvesant Square," *New Yorker* (13 June 1936): 32-39;

James Parton, *Fanny Fern, A Memorial Volume* (New York: Carleton, 1873);

Ishbel Ross, *Ladies of the Press* (New York: Harper, 1936);

Elizabeth Bancroft Schlesinger, "Fanny Fern: Our Grandmother's Mentor," *New-York Historical Society Quarterly*, 38 (October 1954): 501-519;

Schlesinger, "Proper Bostonians as Seen by Fanny Fern," *New England Quarterly*, 27 (March 1954): 97-102;

Jane Tompkins, *Sensational Designs: The Cultural Work of American Fiction, 1790-1860* (New York: Oxford University Press, 1985);

Ann Douglas Wood, "Scribbling Women and Fanny Fern: Why Women Wrote," *American Quarterly*, 23 (September 1971): 3-14.

Papers:

Some of Parton's letters are in the Sophia Smith Collection at Smith College.

James Kirke Paulding

(22 August 1778-6 April 1860)

Dean G. Hall
Kansas State University

See also the Paulding entries in *DLB 3: Antebellum Writers in New York and the South* and *DLB 59: American Literary Critics and Scholars, 1800-1850.*

BOOKS: *Salmagundi; or, the Whim-whams and Opinions of Launcelot Langstaff, Esq. & Others*, by Paulding, Washington Irving, and William Irving, 20 parts, republished in 2 volumes (New York: Printed and published by D. Longworth, 1807-1808; London: Printed for J. M. Richardson, 1811; revised edition, New York: D. Longworth, 1814; revised by Irving, Paris: Galignani, 1824; Paris: Baudry, 1824); revised by Paulding as volumes 1 and 2 of *The Works of James K. Paulding* (New York: Harper, 1835);

The Diverting History of John Bull and Brother Jonathan. By Hector Bull-Us (New York: Inskeep & Bradford/Philadelphia: Bradford & Inskeep, 1812; London: Sherwood, Neely & Jones, 1813); republished as *A Brief and Humorous History of the Political Peculiarities of England and America* (London: Sherwood, Neely & Jones, 1814); revised as *The Diverting History of John Bull and Brother Jonathan*, volume 9 of *The Works of James K. Paulding* (New York: Harper, 1835);

The Lay of the Scottish Fiddle; A Tale of Havre de Grace, Supposed to Be Written by Walter Scott, Esq. (New York: Inskeep & Bradford/Philadelphia: Bradford & Inskeep, 1813; London: Cawthorn, 1814);

The United States and England: Being a Reply to the Criticism on Inchiquin's Letters (Philadelphia: Bradford & Inskeep/New York: Inskeep & Bradford, 1815);

Letters from the South, Written during an Excursion in the Summer of 1816, 2 volumes (New York: James Eastburn, 1817); revised and enlarged as *Letters from the South. By a Northern Man*, volumes 5 and 6 of *The Works of James K. Paulding* (New York: Harper, 1835);

The Backwoodsman. A Poem (Philadelphia: M. Thomas, 1818);

James Kirke Paulding (courtesy of the Frick Art Reference Library)

Salmagundi, Second Series, 10 parts, republished as volumes 1 and 2, with volume 3 (parts 11-15, probably not separately published) (Philadelphia: M. Thomas/New York: Haly & Thomas, 1819-1820); revised as volumes 3 and 4 of *The Works of James K. Paulding* (New York: Harper, 1835);

A Sketch of Old England by a New-England Man, 2 volumes (New York: Charles Wiley, 1822);

Koningsmarke, The Long Finne, A Story of the New World, 2 volumes (New York: Charles Wiley, 1823; London: Whittaker, 1823); revised as *Koningsmarke, or, Old Times in the New World,* volumes 7 and 8 of *The Works of James K. Paulding* (New York: Harper, 1834, 1835);

John Bull in America: or, The New Munchausen (New York: Charles Wiley, 1825: London: Miller, 1825; enlarged edition, New York: Charles Wiley, 1825);

The Merry Tales of the Three Wise Men of Gotham (New York: G. & C. Carvill, 1826);

The New Mirror for Travellers, and Guide to the Springs, by an Amateur (New York: G. & C. Carvill, 1828); enlarged as *A Book of Vagaries; Comprising the New Mirror for Travellers And Other Whim-Whams*, edited by William Irving Paulding (New York: Scribner, 1868);

Tales of the Good Woman, by a Doubtful Gentleman (New York: G. & C. & H. Carvill, 1829);

Chronicles of the City of Gotham from the papers of A Retired Common Councilman (New York: G. & C. & H. Carvill, 1830);

The Dutchman's Fireside, 2 volumes (New York: Harper, 1831);

Westward Ho!, 2 volumes (New York: Harper, 1832);

Sketch of the Early Life of Joseph Wood, Artist (Washington, D.C.: Temperance Union, 1834);

A Life of Washington, 2 volumes (New York: Harper, 1835);

Slavery in the United States (New York: Harper, 1836);

The Book of Saint Nicholas, volume 14 of *The Works of James K. Paulding* (New York: Harper, 1836);

A Christmas Gift from Fairy Land (New York: Appleton, 1838);

The Old Continental: or, The Price of Liberty, 2 volumes (New York: Paine & Burgess, 1846; London: Routledge, 1849);

The Puritan and His Daughter, 2 volumes (New York: Baker & Scribner, 1849);

The Literary Life of James K. Paulding, compiled by William Irving Paulding (New York: Scribner, 1867).

The Lion of the West Retitled the Kentuckian, or a trip to New York A Farce in Two Acts, written by Paulding in 1830, revised by John Augustus Stone and William Bayle Bernard, edited by James N. Tidwell (Stanford: Stanford University Press/London: Oxford University Press, 1954).

Collection: *The Works of James K. Paulding*, 15 volumes (New York: Harper, 1834-1839).

OTHER: *The Bucktails; or, Americans in England*, in *American Comedies* (Philadelphia: Cary & Hart, 1847), pp. 17-100.

James Kirke Paulding, born in Great Nine Partners, New York, to William and Catherine Ogden Paulding, took great pride in his Dutch ancestry; and the English subjection of the Dutch was partial cause for the anti-British feelings which dominate much of the work of his middle period. James's father, a colonel and commissary in the New York militia during the American Revolution, ruined himself financially by extending credit to the army, eventually lost his home, and was imprisoned for debt. Paulding's schooling in rural Tarrytown, New York, was erratic. He claimed, however, to have read Oliver Goldsmith's *The Citizen of the World* (1762) twenty times and stated that it was his model for English prose. In one of his autobiographical tales, "Dyspepsy" (first published in *Tales of the Good Woman*, 1829), he wrote of nature hikes and characterized his youth thus: "I was eternally thinking and doing nothing."

In 1797 Paulding moved to New York City and was drawn toward becoming a man of letters chiefly through his association with the Irving family. (His sister was married to William Irving, Washington Irvings's older brother.) During this time Paulding supported himself as a clerk in the United States Loan Office and used the setting of a "commercial emporium" for many of his tales. The most important consequence of mingling with the Irvings was his friendship with Washington Irving, who started a group to discuss mostly literary matters. Other members of these "Lads of Kilkenny" were Henry Brevoort, Gouverneur Kemble, David Porter, and Richard McCall. Though the group met most of the year at Dyde's public house, during the weekends and summers they met at the Kemble family mansion on the banks of the Passaic above Newark. The mansion became the Cockloft Hall of the *Salmagundi* papers. These meetings had additional importance for Paulding because he married Kemble's sister, Gertrude, on 15 November 1818.

On 24 January 1807 the first of the twenty parts of *Salmagundi; or, the Whim-whams and Opinions of Launcelot Langstaff, Esq. & Others* was published as a thirty-page pamphlet in New York and very shortly became a success. Stating that its purpose was to "instruct the young, reform the old, correct the town, and castigate the age," *Salmagundi* masterfully exercised wit and satire through all twenty parts, the last of which appeared on 25 January 1808. Paulding's role in the authorship was at least equal to Washington Irving's. *Salmagundi* consists chiefly of humorous accounts of theater and dance performances, English travelers in America, the continuing literary views and products of Pindar Cockloft, and the adventures of other members of the Cockloft family. The authors, who also included William Irving, were surprised that *Salmagundi* was so successful (eight hundred copies of one part at a shilling each were sold in one day) and that sales amounted to between ten thousand and fifteen thousand dollars. Because, however, Paulding and Irving received only one hundred dollars each from the publisher, they refused to continue. Critical reception was as warm as the popular reception. Sir Walter Scott thought the work could easily become popular in England; the *Monthly Review* in London thought the writers did "certainly excel in an adroit species of irony," and the *North American Review* said it was "the ablest work of wit and humor which we had produced."

Little is known of Paulding's life between 1808 and 1812, but in 1812 he published his first independent work, *The Diverting History of John Bull and Brother Jonathan*. The subject is the settlement and growth of the colonies in America and political developments before and after the American Revolution. The participating countries are portrayed as a family having problems with its neighbors–the ocean is a millpond and the colonies are farms–and the satire exhibits Paulding's sharp ear and eye for national idiosyncracies.

Between 1813 and 1819 Paulding was a steady contributor to the *Analectic Magazine*, which was under the editorship of Washington Irving until 1815. Fifteen of Paulding's thirty contributions deal with the War of 1812. Though generally popular features in the magazine, the sketches eventually came to rely less on researched fact than on excessive patriotic sentiment and rhetoric. As a result Irving came to wish that Paulding would dissociate himself from the magazine. Paulding's other contributions span a broad range from a review of Charles Phillips's "The Emerald Isle" (July 1813) to "The Idea of a True Patriot" (February 1814), which satirizes false patriotism, to "Americanisms" (May 1814), which defends the development of a native American language, to fairy stories such as "May-Day (August 1814) and "Cupid and Hymen–An Allegory" (September 1813).

During this same period Paulding also wrote a five-canto poem, *The Lay of the Scottish Fiddle,* parodying Scott's verse tales. Paulding's poem, published in Philadelphia in 1813 and a year later in London, was damned in the British periodical *Quarterly Review,* which also took the opportunity to censure American writers and America in general. Paulding took offense and the offensive: in the heat of his anger he wrote a defense of America that was published in 1815 as *The United States and England.* Paulding closely examined several charges against Americans that were then current in English review-articles, maintaining that their real motivation was to vitiate the anti-English feelings in America engendered by Congressional investigations into atrocities committed by British soldiers during their invasion of Washington and the burning of the Capitol and the White House in 1814. The work is a thorough, systematic, and reasonable rebuttal of most of the English accusations, and it made Paulding a national hero in many people's eyes. Most important among these was President James Madison, who in 1815 appointed Paulding secretary of the Board of Navy Commissioners which resulted in Paulding's removal to Washington for the next eight years.

Paulding's piece was only one early shot in a fusillade of literary bombardments in the ensuing written war with England. In fault-finding travel books, English travelers to America had deprecated the American people and mores as crude, unsophisticated, and undeveloped. Paulding wrote several works all in one way or another focusing on the same themes. His *Letters from the South* (1817) are observations and essays on people and natural scenery of the South told with patriotic enthusiasm. Though less focused than Timothy Dwight's *Travels in New-England and New-York* (1821-1822) and less scientific and scholarly than Thomas Jefferson's *Notes on the State of Virginia* (1785), Paulding's work compares favorably with them for its realistic descriptions and reasonable opinions. Though the main thrust is to show the humane nature of southern living, Paulding took note of the lack of cultural activities, attributing them to the burdensome responsibilities of making a living from the physical activity of farming.

In May 1819 Washington Irving and Paulding, probably unaware of each other's intentions, each attempted new serial publications. Irving's product was *The Sketch Book of Geoffrey Crayon, Gent.* (1819-1820) while Paulding's was a revival of *Salmagundi*. Irving's work was richly conceived and wrought, carefully revised and edited, while Paulding's was hastily written and poorly reworked. Paulding satirizes fashions and foibles of society (including his favorite topic, English travelers), and, though the revivified *Salmagundi* ran for only fifteen numbers, some of the material is quite good. In two later numbers the Oneida Indian culture is examined and cleverly shown to be superior to European culture in many ways, and Paulding also champions literary realism ("rational fictions") and makes his own claims of literary independence.

Paulding again entered the ongoing Anglo-American literary war with *A Sketch of Old England by a New-England Man* (1822). Though he vilified other writers for writing travel books about places they had never visited, Paulding's claim to firsthand knowledge was only a pretense. The work purports to be a volume of letters written from London to the author's brother in New England and compares America and England to America's benefit on nearly every aspect of English life. Paulding's first novel, *Koningsmarke, The Long Finne, A Story of the New World* (1823), while an obvious imitation of Henry Fielding's *Tom Jones* (1749), is American in its setting: a Swedish settlement in seventeenth-century Delaware.

In 1824 Paulding became a naval agent in New York, and shortly thereafter he returned to his favorite subject in *John Bull in America: or, The New Munchausen* (1825), reportedly written in just three weeks. The volume served as the last volley in Paulding's personal literary war with England. He was recognized by his contemporaries as the most effective agent in those wars, and most critics felt if he had not won, certainly he had given as much as he had taken.

Paulding's next, and generally considered his best, novel was *The Dutchman's Fireside* (1831) set in New York, near Albany, and again using Dutch characters. It was followed in 1832 by *Westward Ho!*, a novel about a family's move from Virginia to Kentucky. His reputation more than firmly established, Paulding received fifteen hundred dollars for it, and J. & J. Harper confidently ran five thousand copies for the first edition.

During the 1830s Paulding was at the height of his creative powers, moving freely from novels to sketches to tales to biography to drama. Contemporary critics included his name with Irving's and James Fenimore Cooper's. His play *The Lion of the West*–now apparently lost–won a

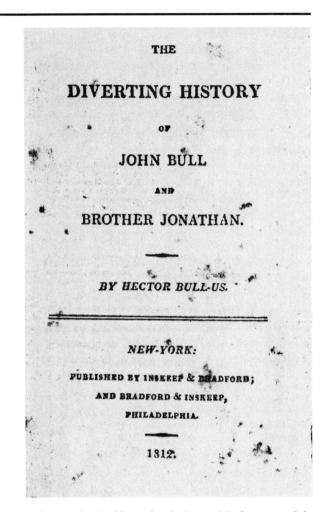

THE

DIVERTING HISTORY

OF

JOHN BULL

AND

BROTHER JONATHAN.

BY HECTOR BULL-US.

NEW-YORK:

PUBLISHED BY INSKEEP & BRADFORD;
AND BRADFORD & INSKEEP,
PHILADELPHIA.

1812.

Title page for Paulding's first book, a satirical account of the settlement and political development of the British colonies in America

prize of three hundred dollars for the best original comedy with an American as the leading character. Exhibiting Paulding's facility at dialogue and comedy, the play was presented by James H. Hackett on and off for nearly twenty years. In 1835 Paulding published *A Life of Washington*, in two volumes that went through ten American editions before it was replaced by Irving's popular treatment of the same figure. Poe gave Paulding's biography an extremely positive review in the *Southern Literary Messenger*. The next year Harper and Brothers brought out Paulding's apology for slavery, *Slavery in the United States*. Though realizing "the atrocity of slavery" and that it directly opposed "fundamental principles of our government," Paulding maintained that the evil of slavery was secondary to the breakup of the Union, a consequence he considered inevitable if the South were not allowed to continue the practice.

In May 1838 President Martin Van Buren, after offering the position to two others (one of whom was Irving), asked Paulding to become Secretary of the Navy. Paulding accepted and held the post until March 1841, during which time he lived in Washington, D.C. With the inauguration of William Henry Harrison, Paulding returned to New York, where his wife died in May 1841. Though in temporary ill health, Paulding later accompanied Van Buren on a seven-thousand-mile speaking tour through the South and West. For the next ten years Paulding continued to contribute to periodicals, mainly *Graham's Magazine, Godey's Lady's Book,* and the *Literary World.* He also revised *The Bucktails; or, Americans in England,* a play probably written circa 1812, for inclusion with three plays by his son, William Irving Paulding, in *American Comedies* (1847).

In 1846 Paulding wrote an ambitious novelistic treatment of the American Revolution, *The Old Continental: or, the Price of Liberty,* whose hero is based upon John Paulding, the author's first cousin. His final novel, *The Puritan and His Daughter* (1849), is generally considered his weakest and perhaps an indication of diminished mental powers.

Though Paulding's mental powers dimmed and his literary production ceased, he lived until the age of eighty-one. In 1846 he had retired to an estate near Hyde Park, New York, where he died on 6 April 1860. He was buried in the Greenwood Cemetery in Brooklyn. He had bequeathed his manuscripts and copyrights to his son, William, whose *Literary Life of James K. Paulding* (1867) is a rather impressionistic biography, which in typical nineteenth-century fashion includes sizable extracts from Paulding's works.

The significance of Paulding's career as a short-story writer is often overlooked by modern scholars. Yet in the 1830s, when Hawthorne and Poe were beginning to think about and perfect the genre, Paulding had already experimented with the short-story form and published many tales in the most popular magazines. He was a respected literary figure, who contributed to the early development of the American short story. He was one of the earliest writers to claim that America was not a wasteland with insufficient materials for a fine homegrown national literature. He also felt that real experience could and should be the basis for good fiction; he wrote in 1820, "The best and most perfect works of imagination appear to me to be those which are founded upon a combination of such characters

as every generation of men exhibits, and such events as have taken place in the world, and will again." Thus, before Cooper wrote any of his American novels, Paulding had already indicated that the American pioneers' experiences should be the subjects of our national literature.

Paulding's "frontiersmen" were the New York Dutch, and, though the stories many times revolve around Dutch superstitions and beliefs, they are essentially realistic. The best example of this type is "Cobus Yerks"(*The Atlantic Souvenir* for 1828; collected in *Tales of The Good Woman*) in which Cobus, under the influence of too much liquor and too many ghostly yarns, wrecks his wagon on the way home from the tavern. In another more Poelike ghost story, "The Ghost" (*The Atlantic Souvenir* for 1830; collected in *The Book of Saint Nicholas,* 1836), Paulding reveals the human origin of apparently spirit-initiated happenings at the end of the tale: a sailor who has fallen overboard and is thought drowned, has, in fact, safely reboarded the frigate and plays pranks which are unexplained until many years after. Many of the tales examine, in the manner of Hawthorne, the effects on the mind of foolish living or psychological pressures. He traces creeping degeneration in "The Drunkard" (first published in *Tales of the Good Woman*), fanatic religious mania in "The Mother's Tragedy" (*Graham's Magazine,* February-March 1846), and the consequences of overvaluating passion in "The Mother's Choice" (*New-York Mirror,* 25 September 1831) and "The Dumb Girl" (first published in *Chronicles of the City of Gotham,* 1830). In "The Poet's Tale" (*The Atlantic Souvenir* for 1828) he writes, "A story with a moral is always worth telling," and many of his tales are overtly didactic. The most obvious example in this category is "The Magic Spinning Wheel" (*The Token and Atlantic Souvenir* for 1836) which dramatizes the then-popular philosophy of work.

Paulding was a good stylist. In his review of Paulding's *Life of Washington,* Poe wrote, "There is no better literary manner than the manner of Mr. Paulding. Certainly no American, and possibly no living writer of England, has more of those numerous peculiarities, which go to the formation of a happy style." Paulding was also productive. Between 1807 and 1848 he produced more than seventy stories, and he was the most prolific American short-story writer of the 1830s, a decade usually thought of as dominated by other writers.

His stories and letters call for a national literature. In a letter to the editor of the *Southern Literary Messenger* (July 1834) he wrote, "Give us something new—something of your native feelings.... I want to see something, wholesome, natural, and national." He recognized Poe's abilities and is credited with spurring Poe to write *The Narrative of Arthur Gordon Pym*, after Harper had refused to publish a volume of Poe's tales. Moreover, Paulding is thought to have had a direct influence on Hawthorne's ideas for *The Scarlet Letter* (1850). Hawthorne carefully recorded the plot of Paulding's "The Dumb Girl" in his *American Notebooks* for 7 September 1835. Living up to his own call, Paulding combined the defense of America and his own fiction. In "The Yankee Roué" (first published in *Tales of the Good Woman)* the main character, Sopus, gives up America to travel and eventually to live in Europe. After losing his money and failing to find employment, Sopus returns home to "refine, enlighten, and civilize" his "semi-barbaric countrymen." Sopus's ridicule is entirely self-reflexive, and Paulding demonstrates his dissatisfaction with Americans who criticize other Americans as if they themselves were exempt.

Had Paulding written less and with more care, he might well be remembered as a key progenitor of both the American short story and the novel. His best work is, however, surrounded by masses of inferior journalistic prose, and no authoritative edition of his work exists. Though Fred Lewis Pattee is correct in observing that Paulding's best fiction contains "often really brilliant narrative and description," Paulding is most remembered as a "defender of America" in a long-past literary war and as Irving's contemporary without Irving's constant ability.

Letters:
The Letters of James Kirke Paulding, edited by Ralph M. Aderman (Madison: University of Wisconsin Press, 1962).

References:
Ralph M. Aderman, "James Kirke Paulding as Social Critic," *Papers on English Language and Literature*, 1 (Summer 1965): 217-229;

Aderman, "James Kirke Paulding's Contributions to American Magazines," *Studies in Bibliography*, 17 (1964): 141-151;

Aderman, "James Kirke Paulding's Literary Income," *Bulletin of the New York Public Library*, 64 (1960): 117-129;

Amos L. Herold, *James Kirke Paulding, Versatile American* (New York: Columbia University Press, 1926);

Herold, "Paulding's Literary Theories," *Bulletin of the New York Public Library*, 66 (1962): 236-243;

Louis D. Owens, "James K. Paulding and the Foundations of American Literature," *Bulletin of the New York Public Library*, 79 (1975): 40-50;

Owens, "Paulding's 'The Dumb Girl,' A Source of *The Scarlet Letter*," *Nathaniel Hawthorne Journal* (1974): 240-249;

Fred Lewis Pattee, *The Development of the American Short Story* (New York: Harper, 1923);

William Irving Paulding, *Literary Life of James K. Paulding* (New York: Scribner, 1867);

Larry J. Reynolds, *James Kirke Paulding* (Boston: Twayne, 1984);

Papers:
Paulding's papers are widely scattered. Some may be found at the Boston Public Library, Brown University Library, Clemson University Library, Columbia University Library, Duke University Library, Harvard University Library, Henry E. Huntington Library and Art Gallery, New York Public Library, New York State Library, University of Virginia Library, and Yale University Library.

Elizabeth Stuart Phelps

(31 August 1844-28 January 1911)

Jean Ferguson Carr
University of Pittsburgh

BOOKS: *Ellen's Idol* (Boston: Massachusetts Sabbath School Society, 1864; London: Ward, Lock, 1864);

Up Hill; or, Life in the Factory (Boston: Hoyt, 1865);

Mercy Gliddon's Work (Boston: Hoyt, 1866; London: Ward, Lock, 1873);

Gypsy Breynton (Boston: Graves & Young, 1866; London: Ward, Lock, 1872);

Gypsy's Cousin Joy (Boston: Graves & Young, 1866; London: Strahan, 1873);

Gypsy's Sowing and Reaping (Boston: Graves & Young, 1866; London: Strahan, 1873);

Tiny (Boston: Massachusetts Sabbath School Society, 1866; London: Ward, Lock, 1875);

Tiny's Sunday Nights (Boston: Massachusetts Sabbath School Society, 1867; London: Ward, Lock, 1875);

Gypsy's Year at the Golden Crescent (Boston: Graves & Young, 1868; London: Strahan, 1873);

I Don't Know How (Boston: Massachusetts Sabbath School Society, 1868; London: Ward, Lock, 1873);

The Gates Ajar (Boston: Fields, Osgood, 1869 [i.e., 1868]; London: Low & Marston, 1869);

Men, Women, and Ghosts (Boston: Fields, Osgood, 1869; London: Low & Marston, 1869);

Hedged In (Boston: Fields, Osgood, 1870; London: Low & Marston, 1870);

The Trotty Book (Boston: Fields, Osgood, 1870); republished as *That Dreadful Boy Trotty: What He Did and What He Said* (London: Ward, Lock, 1877);

The Silent Partner (Boston: Osgood, 1871; London: Low, 1871);

What to Wear? (Boston: Osgood, 1873; London: Low, 1873);

Trotty's Wedding Tour, and Story-Book (Boston: Osgood, 1874 [i.e., 1873]; London: Low, Marston, Low & Searle, 1873);

Poetic Studies (Boston: Osgood, 1875);

The Story of Avis (Boston: Osgood, 1877; London: Routledge, 1877);

My Cousin and I (London: Sunday School Union, 1879);

An Old Maid's Paradise (Boston: Houghton, Osgood, 1879; London: Clarke, 1879);

Sealed Orders (Boston: Houghton, Osgood, 1879);

Friends: A Duet (Boston: Houghton, Mifflin, 1881; London: Low, 1881);

Doctor Zay (Boston: Houghton, Mifflin, 1882);

Beyond the Gates (Boston & New York: Houghton, Mifflin, 1883; London: Chatto & Windus, 1883);

Songs of the Silent World, and Other Poems (Boston & New York: Houghton, Mifflin, 1885 [i.e., 1884]);

Burglars in Paradise (Boston & New York: Houghton, Mifflin, 1886; London: Chatto & Windus, 1886);

The Gates Between (Boston & New York: Houghton, Mifflin, 1887; London: Ward, Lock, 1887);

Jack the Fisherman (Boston & New York: Houghton, Mifflin, 1887; London: Chatto & Windus, 1887);

The Madonna of the Tubs (Boston & New York: Houghton, Mifflin, 1887; London: Low, 1887);

A Gracious Life: A Eulogy on Mrs. Charlotte A. Johnson (Boston: Privately printed, 1888);

A Lost Winter (Boston: Lothrop, 1889);

The Struggle for Immortality (Boston & New York: Houghton, Mifflin, 1889; London: Low, 1889);

Come Forth!, by Phelps and Herbert D. Ward (London: Heinemann, 1890; Boston & New York: Houghton, Mifflin, 1891 [i.e., 1890]);

The Master of the Magicians, by Phelps and Ward (Boston & New York: Houghton, Mifflin, 1890; London: Heinemann, 1890);

Austin Phelps; A Memoir (New York: Scribner, 1891; London: Nisbet, 1891);

Fourteen to One (Boston & New York: Houghton, Mifflin, 1891; London: Cassell, 1891);

A Lost Hero, by Phelps and Ward (Boston: Roberts, 1891);

The Lady of Shalott (Boston & New York: Houghton, Mifflin, 1892);

Donald Marcy (Boston & New York: Houghton, Mifflin, 1893; London: Heinemann, 1893);

A Singular Life (Boston & New York: Houghton, Mifflin, 1895; London: Clark, 1895);

Chapters from a Life (Boston & New York: Houghton, Mifflin, 1896; London: Clark, 1897);

The Supply at St. Agatha's (Boston & New York: Houghton, Mifflin, 1896);

The Story of Jesus Christ: An Interpretation (Boston & New York: Houghton, Mifflin, 1897; London: Low, 1897);

Loveliness; A Story (Boston & New York: Houghton, Mifflin, 1899; London: Clarke, 1899);

A Plea for the Helpless (New York: American Humane Association, 1901);

The Successors of Mary the First (Boston & New York: Houghton, Mifflin, 1901);

Within the Gates (Boston & New York: Houghton, Mifflin, 1901);

Vivisection and Legislation in Massachusetts (Philadelphia: American Anti-vivisection Society, 1902);

Avery (Boston & New York: Houghton, Mifflin, 1902; London: Richards, 1903);

Confessions of a Wife, as Mary Adams (New York: Century, 1902);

Trixy (Boston & New York: Houghton, Mifflin, 1904; London: Hodder & Stoughton, 1905);

The Man in the Case (Boston & New York: Houghton, Mifflin, 1906; London: Constable, 1906);

Walled In; A Novel (New York & London: Harper, 1907);

Though Life Us Do Part (Boston & New York: Houghton Mifflin, 1908);

Jonathan and David (New York & London: Harper, 1909);

The Oath of Allegiance, and Other Stories (Boston & New York: Houghton Mifflin, 1909; London: Constable, 1909);

A Chariot of Fire (New York & London: Harper, 1910);

The Empty House, and Other Stories (Boston & New York: Houghton Mifflin, 1910); republished as *A Deserted House, and Other Stories* (London: Constable, 1911);

Comrades (New York & London: Harper, 1911).

OTHER: Chapter 7, in *Sex and Education, A Reply to Dr. E. H. Clarke's "Sex in Education,"* edited by Julia Ward Howe (Boston: Roberts, 1874), pp. 126-138;

"The Boys of Brimstone Court," in *The Boys of Brimstone Court, and Other Stories*, by Phelps and others (Boston: Lothrop, 1879);

"Mary A. Livermore," in *Our Famous Women. An Authorized Record of the Lives and Deeds of American Women* (Hartford: A. D. Worthington/ Chicago: A. G. Nettleton, 1883), pp. 386-414;

"The Married Daughter," chapter 8 of *The Whole Family: a novel by twelve authors: William Dean Howells, Mary E. Wilkins Freeman, Mary Heaton Vorse, Mary Stewart Cutting, Elizabeth Jordan, John Kendrick Bangs, Henry James, Elizabeth Stuart Phelps, Edith Wyatt, Mary R. Shipman Andrews, Alice Brown, Henry Van Dyke* (New York & London: Harper, 1908), pp. 185-218;

In After Days: Thoughts on the Future Life, essays by Phelps, W. D. Howells, and others (New York & London: Harper, 1910).

PERIODICAL PUBLICATIONS:
FICTION

" 'Tenty Scran'," sometimes attributed to Rose Terry Cooke, *Atlantic Monthly*, 6 (November 1860): 587-601;

"A Sacrifice Consumed," *Harper's New Monthly*, 28 (January 1864): 235-240;

"Mrs. Braddon's Home," *Harper's New Monthly*, 28 (March 1864): 519-527;

"Andrew Kent's Temptation," *Harper's New Monthly*, 31 (June 1865): 42-56;

"Margaret Bronson," *Harper's New Monthly*, 31 (September 1865): 498-504;

Jane Gurley's Story, Hours at Home, 2 (March 1866): 406-412; (April 1866): 494-502; 3 (May 1866): 19-30; (June 1866): 168-174; (July 1866): 250-259; (August 1866): 339-347; (September 1866): 421-426; (October 1866): 538-545;

"Miss Stuyvesant," *Harper's New Monthly*, 33 (August 1866): 336-345;

"Both Sides," *Harper's New Monthly*, 38 (May 1869): 778-787;

"Not a Pleasant Story," *Scribner's Monthly*, 3 (November 1871): 98-105;

"An Hour with Gwendolyn," *Sunday Afternoon*, 3 (March 1879): 230-234;

"Zerviah Hope," *Scribner's Monthly*, 21 (November 1880): 78-88;

A Brave Girl, Wide Awake, 18 (December 1883): 27-31; (January 1884): 105-111; (February 1884): 169-174; (March 1884): 237-241; (April 1884): 297-303; (May 1884): 361-365; 19 (June 1884): 27-31; (July 1884): 92-96; (August 1884): 156-162;

"A Lovely Girl," *Ladies' Home Journal*, 5 (August 1888): 1-2; (September 1888): 1-2;

"The Secretary's Murder," by Phelps and Ward, *Harper's Bazar*, 24 (31 January 1891): 83;

"His Creed and His Deed," *Two Tales*, 2 (27 August 1892): 263-281;

"The Story of a Grudge," *Independent*, 44 (29 December 1892): 1881-1883; 45 (5 January 1893): 30-31;

"A Point of Order," *Chautauquan*, 18 (October 1893): 35-43;

"The Veteran," *Pocket Magazine*, 1 (November 1895): 59-84.

NONFICTION

"Chaucer: How He Lived, How He Looked, and

What He Was," *Watchman and Reflector*, 51 (27 January 1870): 5;

"The 'Female Education' of Women," *Independent*, 25 (13 November 1873): 1409-1410;

"Confession of St. Augustine," *Atlantic Monthly*, 37 (February 1876): 129-140;

"George Eliot," *Independent*, 33 (3 February 1881): 1;

"Last Words from George Eliot," *Harper's New Monthly*, 64 (March 1882): 568-571;

"George Eliot," *Harper's Weekly*, 29 (14 February 1885): 102-103;

"George Eliot's Short Stories," *Independent*, 37 (30 April 1885): 545-546;

"In Memoriam, Edward Rowland Sill," *Independent*, 39 (28 April 1887): 517-518;

"Edward Rowland Sill," *Century*, 14 (September 1888): 704-708;

"The Short Story," *Independent*, 44 (3 November 1892): 1541-1542;

"Heaven: The Gates Ajar—25 Years After," *North American Review*, 156 (May 1893): 567-576;

" 'Afterwards': A Study of a Story by Ian Maclaren," *McClure's*, 5 (September 1895): 329-332;

"The World Invisible," *Harper's Bazar*, 42 (April 1908): 354-356; (May 1908): 419-422; (July 1908): 619-623;

"How to Endure Invalidism," *Harper's Bazar*, 43 (June 1909): 544-547;

"Stories that Stay," *Century*, 59 (November 1910): 118-123;

"The Windsor Club Stories," *Independent*, 72 (1 February 1912): 231-238.

Elizabeth Stuart Phelps's career exemplifies the range of interests and achievements of nineteenth-century women writers. An acknowledged voice for woman's rights, antivivisection, and temperance causes, she wrote more than a hundred and fifty stories, twenty novels for adults, children's books, poetry, plays, an autobiography, biographies of her father and of Jesus Christ, and essays on every imaginable subject, from the afterlife and homeopathy to women's names and dress. Phelps was both popular and acclaimed in her day; yet since then she was virtually unread until the recent revival of work by women writers. Her novel *The Gates Ajar* (1869 [i.e., 1868]) made her internationally famous and controversial at the age of twenty-four. "The Tenth of January" (*Atlantic Monthly*, March 1868), her story of the collapse of the Pemberton Mills, brought her recognition from such luminaries as John Greenleaf Whittier and Thomas Wentworth Higginson, who later praised her as having "more genius" than Louisa May Alcott or Harriet Beecher Stowe. She is gradually being rediscovered for such novels as *The Story of Avis* (1877) and *The Silent Partner* (1871), valued for her ardent investigations, in fiction and prose, of the unarticulated lives of the industrial poor, of the elderly, and of women.

Phelps was part, as James T. Fields joked, "of a family of large circulations." Born Mary Gray Phelps, she was the child of two successful writers: clergyman and later Andover professor of theology Austin Phelps, author of books on rhetoric and religion, and popular writer Elizabeth Stuart Phelps, author of *The Sunny Side* (1851) and "Angel over the Right Shoulder" (1852). In *Chapters from a Life* (1896) Phelps wrote that it was "impossible to be *their* daughter and not to have something to say, and a pen to say it." After her mother died from childbirth and "cerebral disease" when Phelps was eight, Phelps took, or was given, her mother's name and described herself as "proud to wear" it. She also shared her mother's belief that "it was as natural for her daughter to write as to breathe." She grew up in the intensely intellectual atmosphere of Andover, Massachusetts, which she described as "a heavily masculine place. . . . used to eminent men," under the influence of her father and yet driven by the memory of her "unusual" mother's "difficult reconciliation between genius and domestic life." She made a virtue of such a polarized inheritance, developing what she described in one of her characters as a "strong dual nature which gave her something of brilliance and eminence among her less composite neighbors–the people of monochrome or monologue." Phelps saw her childhood as setting her apart from dominant cultural practices of her day. Urged to inquire into the "questions of life" and to be "serious," to avoid confusing "sounds or appearances with values," she refused to accept without question the world's definitions of things. She valued her own opinions even when they countered those of her friends and of authorities, as her account of Ralph Waldo Emerson's visit to Andover illuminates. Phelps announced herself "too much of a modern" to share her schoolmates' idolatry of Chaucer as "the Father of English Poetry," a remark that earned her Emerson's "rebuke." Although she somewhat mockingly described herself as "demolished" by

Emerson in this debate, she persisted in her opinion, defending it as only "common honesty." She appreciated the modern poets her father read to her (Thomas De Quincey and William Wordsworth), but she preferred her own discovery, Elizabeth Barrett Browning. As she later wrote, "what Shakespeare or the Latin Fathers might have done for some other impressionable girl, Mrs. Browning . . . did for me. . . . I owe to her, distinctly, the first visible aspiration (ambition is too low a word) to do some honest, hard work of my own."

In her autobiography, *Chapters from a Life*, as well as in many essays, Phelps articulated the literary importance of story writing and of its practitioners, defending from charges of triviality the form she called "the lion of our intellectual day." Insisting that its days as an "apologetic form" were over, she predicted that the story "of the future will not be a bit of bric-à-brac. It will be a work of faultless construction and of exquisite finish." Phelps admired Nathaniel Hawthorne as "colossal," but her extended discussions focused on two women writers, Harriet Beecher Stowe and George Eliot. In an 1876 lecture series at Boston University, she discussed Eliot as the "representative" of "modern fiction," and in an 1885 essay she proclaimed, "the short story is to literature what the opal is to jewels: simply the most delightful or the dreariest of things." As Emerson and Walt Whitman had done for poetry, she announced an ambitious program for the American story: "Our huge extent of territory, . . . our extremes of wealth and poverty, our assorted races, our feverish restlessness of temper, our sudden changes of fortune, our popular education, our enormous seaboard life, give us unique chances for swift and splendid effects."

Phelps published two collections of stories for children, five collections for adults, and was planning a sixth ("The Windsor Club Stories") when she died. Her stories experiment with narrative strategies of both written and oral tales, exploring the constraints on narrators unused to literary language and storytelling traditions. Although primarily set in her native New England, Phelps's stories also venture away to South Carolina's fever islands, Maine's lumbering camps, the Civil War's front lines, Colorado's silver mines, and the eastern seaboard's fishing vessels. They tell of the Ku Klux Klan, stowaways, unemployment, wicked vivisectors, rich men's guilt, poor men's powerlessness, lovers long lost to war or drink, forgotten veterans, modern inventions,

Phelps with her mother and infant brother, circa 1850

adorable and demanding dogs. They chart the difficult course between husband and wife, writing of things that "thousands of women know" but few had expressed.

Phelps published her first story at thirteen, when she received $2.50 for a contribution to the *Youth's Companion*. She kept her work to herself, choosing not to "submit" it to her father's scrutiny and carrying on "the writer's profession for many years as if it had been a burglar's." But she also celebrated the "sense of dignity which marks the hour when one becomes a wage-earner . . . I felt that I had suddenly acquired value–to myself, to my family, and to the world" (she received $100 for each volume in the "Tiny" series of children's books and $150 for each "Gypsy" book). Although she later dismissed these early books as "hack work" ("very proper, and very pious, and very much like what well-brought-up little girls were taught to do, to be, to suffer, or to write in those days") and praised only their "va-

riety" and "considerable dash of fun," her ten children's novels and many stories far exceed conventional expectations. The stories, regular contributions to *St. Nicholas, Youth's Companion,* and *Our Young Folks,* and collected in two volumes of "Trotty" stories, *The Trotty Book* (1870) and *Trotty's Wedding Tour, and Story-Book* (1874), depict slave children, street urchins, and factory workers, as well as tomboyish middle-class girls running the family business or hiring a replacement to tend the baby brother. Even the most sentimental of topics is handled with skeptical wit, as, for example, in "Baby-Birds: A Story for Baby-Women" (*Youth's Companion,* 25 November 1869; collected in *Trotty's Wedding Tour*), in which a toddler dresses herself as a boy in "naughty clothes" and recounts the scolding she receives from the birds outside for such "sinful" behavior. Although smaller in scale and development, the children's fiction works through issues and narrative strategies to which Phelps returns in her work for adults, and she shows an early confidence and independence.

The event that shaped Phelps's life and impelled her to expand the scope of her writing was the Civil War, whose effects she described as a national "disease," a "material miasma" which "the most superficial cannot escape." At seventeen she had watched the graduating class of Andover march off to Bull Run and Antietam and had suffered from the death of Samuel Hopkins Thompson, a close friend whom, biographers speculate, Phelps may well have loved and planned to marry. Phelps saw an unpassable gulf between those who had "lived the war" and the following generations, who "looked upon Memorial Day as a questionable popular festival." The heroine of her uncollected story "Margaret Bronson" (*Harper's New Monthly*, September 1865), who disguises herself as a soldier to fight beside her lover, finds herself "so surrounded and hemmed in by . . . scenes of peril and blood and death, that they must necessarily interweave themselves with the controlling events of her life." Phelps was particularly concerned about how "in those fiery days, personal tragedy was but the little tongue of flame in the great conflagration," and she saw literary responses to the war ignoring the humbler suffering away from the battle lines. Most of her war stories explore the pain and the silence of those left at home, especially those in the constrained position of the "widowed girl," who was forbidden by custom and propriety to articulate her feelings. In "The Oath of Allegiance" (*Atlantic Monthly*, April 1894; collected in *The Oath of Allegiance, and Other Stories*, 1909) Phelps compares such "unnamed, unauthorized, unmaidenly anguish" to the feeling of a "creature under vivisection, who understands what the men of science are saying around the torture-table." The experience presents "one of the challenges that God himself must find hard to answer": "How do women bear their lives?" In such stories as "A Sacrifice Consumed" (*Harper's New Monthly*, January 1864; uncollected) and "Annie Laurie" (*Harper's New Monthly*, December 1887; collected in *Fourteen to One*, 1891) Phelps tries to develop this hidden story of the "unconsulted women," the "martyrs at humble firesides," who gave not their lives but "their happiness instead."

In her autobiography Phelps located her ambition as a writer with this sympathetic understanding of a nation "dark with sorrowing women," to whom "even the best and kindest forms of our prevailing beliefs" had little to offer. "Creeds and

Phelps, circa 1880 (photograph by Notman Photographic Co.; courtesy of the Treasure Room, Haverford College Library, Haverford, Pennsylvania)

commentaries and sermons were made by men," Phelps wrote. "What tenderest of men knows how to comfort his own daughter when her heart is broken?" Rejecting the traditional forms of men, of the preacher whose prayer "sounded like the language of an unknown race to a despairing girl," Phelps decided she ought to write about "the peculiar needs of woman as a class." In an unpublished essay on Abigail Adams (written in 1876) she explained: "Sex, like other prejudices, has an incalculable influence upon the interpretation of facts. History is written by men; therefore, capricious in its treatment of women. . . . We read of the Pilgrim Fathers. Who tells us of the Pilgrim Mothers?" Phelps thus mined personal and cultural experience as authority for her career as a woman writer, justifying her feminist critique as a highly moral, social, and patriotic cause. The specific historical problem of women, who understand but are mute, who experience something that cannot be told in proscribed forms, becomes a rationale for Phelps's larger project of writing about women's secret lives outside the war context, and by extension, about the lives of the poor and the unrecorded, what she called "histories of denied capacity" ("The World Invisible," *Harper's Bazar*, April-May-July 1908).

Phelp's first collection for adults, *Men, Women, and Ghosts* (1869) contains ten stories, including her well-received story "The Tenth of January" (*Atlantic Monthly*, March 1868), a powerful imagining of the inner life of a crippled factory girl who is trapped in the collapse of a mill. The volume's title, provided by her editor, James T. Fields, and praised by Phelps as "one of the best ever given to any book of mine," refers to most of the stories' concern about the difficult worldly relations between men and women, between fathers and their fallen daughters, husbands and wives, girls and suitors. It refers to the stories' interest in the imaginary realm of the spiritual, necessary perhaps to jolt men and women into some form of understanding. Many of the stories use the device of spiritualism or second sight to question humanity's understanding of how the world operates, as in "The Day of my Death" (*Harper's New Monthly*, October 1868), in which a man is forced to examine his life and relationships under the pressure of believing he knows his death date, or as in "No News" (*Atlantic Monthly*, September 1868), in which a betrayed wife's near drowning forces her husband to imagine the reality of her domestic life. What is otherwise dismissed as "women's imagination," becomes through the pressure of ghosts and spiritual vision a powerful way of reimagining the world, of seeing what is normally blocked by more ordinary ways of making sense ("philosophic" speculation, "fact," reason, and "common" sense).

Her second and most-ambitious collection, *Sealed Orders* (1879), contains seventeen stories. Oliver Wendell Holmes praised the volume, and Whittier compared it to Hawthorne's *Twice-Told Tales*. The stories, especially the title piece (*Independent*, 14 August 1873) and "The Lady of Shalott" (*Independent*, 6 July 1871), which Elizabeth T. Spring cited as "the best American short story" in her 1883 essay, are consistently accomplished, rigorously questioning established authority and imagining what it is to live at odds with one's culture. The deprived narrator of "Sealed Orders" jingles the few coins in his pocket during his sweetheart's wedding to a richer man, creating a bitter rhythm for the thoughts that remain unarticulated, blocked by his lack of education. In "Since I Died" (*Scribner's Monthly*, February 1873) a daring reverie reminiscent of Emily Dickinson's poetry in its precise account of life after death, the

dead narrator wonders how to communicate with her mourning friend, asking "is there an alphabet between us?" Phelps tells the "factual" story that "Mr. Tennyson has omitted to mention" in his version of Shalott and offers the "true" story of Guenevere. She imagines the song of a drunken old woman and the hidden romance of a Puritan couple, the difficulty of understanding the life of a black servant who is "without even the crude conditions of heroism, of romance, of poetry."

On 20 October 1888 she surprised her friends by marrying Herbert Dickinson Ward, seventeen years her junior and the son of William Hayes Ward, her longtime friend and editor at the *Independent*. A graduate of theology school at Andover, Herbert Ward wanted to be a writer. They collaborated on several stories and books, and Phelps tried to help his career, but their marriage was an unhappy one. Ward left for long stretches of time to go sailing or traveling and was away when she died. They had no children. In her autobiography Phelps insisted, "a literary woman's best critic is her husband," but she curiously thanked Ward only for never having "hindered" her. Other local writers supported her more productively. She corresponded with such eminent women as Julia Ward Howe, Lucy Larcom, and Mary Claflin, with the Boston literati (James and Annie Fields, Longfellow, Phillips Brooks, James Osgood, Oliver Wendell Holmes), and with her New York editors (Edward Rowland Sill and Richard Gilder). In the 1870s and 1880s her close friend was Mary Briggs Harris, a doctor in Andover and the inspiration for her portrayals of strong women doctors in *Doctor Zay* (1882) and "Zerviah Hope" (*Scribner's Monthly*, November 1880; uncollected).

Having suffered a physical breakdown in 1877 after writing *The Story of Avis*, Phelps was a semi-invalid much of her life. Despite her severe illnesses, she continued to be productive, publishing her third collection *Fourteen to One* in 1891. The volume contains fourteen stories, including several of her most popular, such as "Jack the Fisherman" (first published as "Jack," *Century*, June 1887; separately published later that year) and "The Madonna of the Tubs" (first published in *Harper's New Monthly*, December 1885; separately published in 1887) that drew on her experiences with working-class people in Gloucester, Massachusetts, where she had summered since 1876. She mined her painful knowledge of illness for "Shut In" (previously unpublished), the story of an invalid who rebels against the authority of her powerful doctor. Several stories return to the subject of the Civil War, including one of her own favorites, "The Bell of St. Basil's" (*Atlantic Monthly*, May 1889), set in the postwar South.

Toward the end of her life she became absorbed by the antivivisection cause, writing many pamphlets and too many stories about cruel scientists and grieving children. But in the last two years before her death of heart disease in 1911, she produced two further collections–one of eleven stories, *The Oath of Allegiance, and Other Stories*, and one of eight stories and a play, *The Empty House, and Other Stories* (1910). Although several stories in these volumes fall below the usual standards of her work, there are also important and powerful stories, many of which have a striking modernity, skillfully using modern inventions such as the automobile or the telephone, the telegraph or the electric fan, as controlling images. The title story of the 1910 volume, "The Empty House" (*Woman's Home Companion*, April-May 1910) presents the bleak abandoned life of businessmen and their complicated dependence on their secretaries; "Unemployed" (*Harper's New Monthly*, November 1906; collected in *The Oath of Allegiance and Other Stories*) explores the terrifying self-destruction of being outmoded in a society wanting only material goods and labor. The stories worry through divorce, separation, affairs; they assess the pain of "The Rejected Manuscript" (*Harper's New Monthly*, January 1893; collected in *The Empty House, and Other Stories*) of a woman writer, and the heroism of "The Chief Operator" (*Harper's New Monthly*, July 1909; collected in *The Oath of Allegiance and Other Stories*) during the Johnstown flood.

Most of the collected stories and almost sixty uncollected stories appeared initially in the leading periodicals of the day: *Harper's New Monthly*, the *Atlantic Monthly*, *Scribner's Monthly*, the *Century*, and the *Independent*. Phelps also published in religious papers (*Watchman and Reflector*) and women's magazines (*Hours at Home, Ladies' Home Journal*). She was well paid for her efforts, receiving $75 to $100 for each story in *The Independent* and $200 to $300 for stories in the monthly journals. When, in 1908, William Dean Howells and the editor of *Harper's Bazar* invited twelve eminent American writers to collaborate on a serial novel, *The Whole Family*, Phelps asked for a payment of $750, far more than that received by coauthors Henry James or Mary Wilkins Freeman. A thorough professional, Phelps wrote letters to

her editors that are full of stipulations about royalties and insistence on accurate proofreading. She offered as advice to young writers: "Respect the market laws. Lean on nobody."

Although Phelps identified herself as a woman's writer, she also received recognition from many male critics, such as Holmes (who ranked her in his autobiography with the best short-story writers of the century) and Whittier, but her professional confidence antagonized some of her male peers. Howells, who was generally supportive of her work, publishing much of it in the *Atlantic* and, writing to her that one of her novels was "wonderfully delicate and . . . fine" (11 July 1881), wrote to James on 6 March 1870 about "her most gasping and shuddering style." In a gesture reminiscent of Hawthorne's earlier worry about the power of "scribbling women" to write books that outsold his, Howells confided that Phelps's writing "discomforts me . . . and it is pretty sure to sell twenty thousand." Many of her contemporaries shared the judgment of her 1939 biographer Mary Angela Bennett, who found Phelps too "combative." Others, like Fred Lewis Pattee, domesticate her achievements by seeing her as not "consciously" a realist and not "intentionally" an innovator. But there were surprising appreciations. Phelps was moved by Henry Wadsworth Longfellow's "kind" response to *The Story of Avis*, for which, as a "woman's book," she had expected "small hospitality at the hands of men," and she praised his "marvelous intuition in the comprehension of an unusual woman." She has received renewed attention as a successful woman writer, although critics focus more on the shape of her career and biography than on detailed examination of specific works, often treating the stories only as they illuminate the longer fiction. Bennett's biography contains the most complete bibliography, and Kessler's 1982 study is the most thorough analysis of Phelps's career and work.

Phelps often referred to her views as those of a "dissenter," of a "modern" who is made stronger from having been raised by "orthodoxy" or the "Old school." She regularly portrayed her position as modern or commonsensical, in touch with "the world's people" as opposed to overly rigid, outmoded, and authoritative. At the same time, she saw her historical circumstances as providing her with an insight and depth lost by the "modern world." She rejected William Makepeace Thackeray's view that the "public is a jackass," responding with warmth and diligence to the many personal letters from readers, but, like Anthony Trollope and George Eliot before her, she defensively claimed to ignore professional reviews. She was, however, willing to assert her literary credo, as when she challenged Howells's critique of Harriet Beecher Stowe (and by extension, of Phelps) as overly moralistic and argued instead for a realism of moral vision: "Life is moral struggle," she insisted. "Portray the struggle, and you need write no tract." She often framed her stories with a proud admission that her subject or mode of storytelling was out of style; such "apologies" serve to warn the readers that they must adapt their expectations or ways of reading to her fictional world. Like the narrator of Rebecca Harding Davis's "Life in the Iron Mills" (1861)—a story Phelps cited as seminal and which prefigured her attitude toward industrial subjects—she proposed a reconstructed way of "reading" both her fiction and the world. Like many women of her day, she presented her social and literary position as an advantage, enabling her to serve as a valuable cultural go-between or translator who can understand the "strange" languages of past and present and can articulate the worlds of women and the poor for male or middle-class readers.

Biographies:

Elizabeth T. Spring, "Elizabeth Stuart Phelps," in *Our Famous Women* (Hartford: A. D. Worthington/Chicago: A. G. Nettleton, 1883), pp. 560-579;

E. F. Harkins, *Famous Authors (Women)* (Boston: Page, 1901), pp. 11-26;

Mary Angela Bennett, *Elizabeth Stuart Phelps* (Philadelphia: University of Pennsylvania Press/London: Oxford University Press, 1939);

Lori D. Kelly, *The Life and Works of Elizabeth Stuart Phelps, Victorian Feminist Writer* (Troy, N.Y.: Whitston, 1983).

References:

Mari Jo Buhle and Florence Howe, Afterword to *The Silent Partner*, by Phelps (Old Westbury, N.Y.: Feminist Press, 1983), pp. 353-386;

Susan M. Coultrap-McQuin, *Elizabeth Stuart Phelps: The Cultural Context of a Nineteenth-Century Professional Writer*, Ph.D. dissertation, University of Iowa, 1979;

Ann Douglas, *The Feminization of American Culture* (New York: Knopf, 1977);

Carol F. Kessler, *Elizabeth Stuart Phelps* (Boston: G. K. Hall, 1982);

Kessler, Introduction to *The Story of Avis*, by Phelps (New Brunswick: Rutgers University Press, 1985), pp. xiii-xxxiii;

Fred Lewis Pattee, *The Development of the American Short Story* (New York & London: Harper, 1923), pp. 178-182;

Barton Levi St. Armand, "Paradise Deferred: The Image of Heaven in the Work of Emily Dickinson and Elizabeth Stuart Phelps," *American Quarterly*, 29 (Spring 1977): 55-78;

Michael Sartisky, Afterword to *Doctor Zay*, by Phelps (New York: Feminist Press, 1987), pp. 259-321;

Helen Sootin Smith, Introduction to *The Gates Ajar*, by Phelps (Cambridge, Mass.: Harvard University Press, 1964), pp. v-xxxiv;

Christine Stansell, "Elizabeth Stuart Phelps: A Study in Female Rebellion," *Massachusetts Review*, 13 (1972): 239-256;

Susan Ward, "The Career Woman Fiction of Elizabeth Stuart Phelps," in *Nineteenth-Century Women Writers of the English-Speaking World*, edited by Rhoda B. Mason (New York: Greenwood, 1986), pp. 210-219;

Barbara Welter, *Dimity Convictions: The American Woman in the Nineteenth Century* (Athens: Ohio University Press, 1976), pp. 111-120.

Papers:

Phelps destroyed much of her private correspondence. Manuscripts and correspondence with authors and publishers can be found at the Houghton Library, Harvard University; the New York Public Library; the Beinecke Library, Yale University; the Huntington Library, San Marino, California; the Schlesinger Library, Radcliffe College; the James Duncan Phillips Library, The Essex Institute; the Rutherford B. Hayes Library; the Boston Public Library; the Clifton Waller Barrett Library, Alderman Library, University of Virginia.

Albert Pike

(29 December 1809-2 April 1891)

Joseph M. Flora
University of North Carolina at Chapel Hill

SELECTED BOOKS: *Prose Sketches and Poems, Written in the Western Country* (Boston: Light & Horton, 1834); extended edition, edited by David J. Weber (Albuquerque: Calvin Horn, 1967);

Lays of the Humbuggers, &c. By Sam. Barnacle, Poet Laureate (Little Rock: Pike, 1836);

An Address Delivered by Albert Pike, Esq., to the Young Ladies of the Tulip Female Seminary, and Cadets of the Arkansas Military Institute: At Tulip, on 4th June, 1852 (Little Rock: Printed by William W. Woodruff, 1852);

Nugæ (Philadelphia: Printed by C. Sherman, 1854);

Morals and Dogma of Ancient and Accepted Scottish Rite of Freemasonry (Charleston, S.C.: Privately printed, 1870);

Hymns to the Gods and Other Poems (Washington, D.C.: Privately printed, 1872; revised, 1873 [i.e. 1872]);

The Silver Wedding. A Masque (Washington, D.C., 1878);

Gen. Albert Pike's Poems. With Introductory Biographical Sketch by Mrs. Lilian Pike Roome (Little Rock: Fred. W. Allsopp, 1900);

Lyrics and Love Songs, edited by Roome (Little Rock: Fred. W. Allsopp, 1916);

Irano-Aryan Faith and Doctrine as Contained in the Zend-Avesta (Louisville: Standard Printing, 1924);

Lectures of the Arya (Louisville: Standard Printing, 1930);

Indo-Aryan Deities and Worship as Contained in the Rig-Veda (Louisville: Standard Printing, 1930).

Although there is some uncertainty about the origins of the song "Dixie," the most popular version, also probably the first, is that of Daniel Decatur Emmett (1859). Of the many variations, one of the most interesting is by Albert Pike, who made it a war hymn in 1861, beginning his version with the lines:

> Southrons, hear your country call you!
> Up lest worse than death befall you!

Courtesy of the Mathew Brady Collection, National Archives

> To arms! to arms! to arms! in Dixie!
> Lo! all the beacon fires are lighted,
> Let all your hearts be now united!
> To arms! to arms! to arms! in Dixie!
>
> Advance the flag of Dixie!
> Hurrah! Hurrah!
> For Dixie's land we'll take our stand,
> To live or die for Dixie!

Pike's battle cry continues through several stanzas. It is indicative of his literary reputation that his hymn is now hardly known at all.

Had Pike's contemporaries envisioned a literary assessment of his work in the late twentieth century, they would doubtless have predicted that scholars would commemorate him above all as a poet. Indeed, Pike turned his hand readily to verse on many occasions. He marked, for example, his 1831 departure for the western frontier in "Ballad. Written on leaving New England," which begins:

> Farewell to thee, New England,
>   Farewell to thee and thine;
> Farewell to leafy Newbury,
>   And Rowley's woods of pine.
>
> Farewell to thee, old Merrimack,
>   Thou deep, deep heart of blue;
> Oh! could I say, while looking back,
>   That all, like thee, are true!

Readers encountered Pike's poetry in magazines such as *Blackwood's*, *Knickerbocker*, and *Spirit of the Times*, as well as in his own newspaper, the *Arkansas Advocate*. Pike's assessment of his verse is suggested by his privately publishing his poetry collections *Nugæ* (1854) and *Hymns to the Gods and Other Poems* (1872). Pike's only formally published book was *Prose Sketches and Poems, Written in the Western Country* (1834), but his poetry appeared in several nineteenth-century anthologies. Edgar Allan Poe liked Pike's verse, claiming, "there are few of our native writers to whom we consider him inferior," and some readers have claimed that Pike's "To Isadore" influenced Poe's "The Raven." Yet Pike's poetry—too imitative of the British Romantics—is now of little interest.

Twentieth-century readers find greater value in his sketches and tales, for he sensed the value of economy in narrative prose. He was not only literate and a lover of books, but he discovered in the far Southwest a history and culture that had yet to receive expression in English. Although he spent less than a year in New Mexico, he can be called its first Anglo-American poet as well as its first Anglo-American short-story writer, and certainly a pioneer of the literature of the Southwest.

Albert Pike was born to Benjamin and Sarah Andrews Pike on 29 December 1809, in Boston, Massachusetts. Soon after his birth the Pikes returned to the family home in Byfield, later moving to Newburyport, where Albert received his early education. Pike also studied at an academy in Framingham, Massachusetts. He taught school from 1824 to 1831, always saving time to read widely and to write poetry. He had Harvard as a goal and was admitted as a junior on the strength of tests, but Harvard wanted him to pay tuition for the first two years as well, and Pike was too poor and too proud to accede to the requirement. Harvard gave him an honorary A.M. in 1859, a tribute to Pike's extraordinary abilities to teach himself.

The schoolteacher's life could not long content Pike. So in March 1831 he turned, as other adventurous Americans had done, to the West. From St. Louis he proceeded to Independence, Missouri, and joined a party of hunters and traders going to Santa Fe, New Mexico. Adept at languages, he listened and observed to the eventual ends of literature already noted. After some time in Santa Fe, Pike accompanied another expedition that eventually took him in March 1833 to Arkansas, where briefly he again taught school at Fort Gibson. He settled in Little Rock that October and began writing political articles for the *Little Rock Arkansas Advocate*, supporting Robert Crittenden, a Whig, for Congress. On the strength of these articles he was invited to join the *Advocate* staff. He also became assistant clerk in the territorial legislature.

A romantic in several senses, Pike fell in love with Mary Ann Hamilton. She was ill-suited to him, but on 18 November 1834 they married—to the lasting happiness of neither. Mary Ann brought some property to the marriage, however, enabling Pike to purchase an interest in the *Advocate*. In 1835 he became sole owner and editor and had a ready-made vehicle for his literary efforts.

In need of a steady flow of cash to support a rapidly growing family, Pike sold the *Advocate* in 1837 and turned to practicing law. Self-taught in that as in much else, he had been licensed as a lawyer in August 1834 and made an impressive career of it. In late 1836 he was appointed the first reporter of the Arkansas State Supreme Court, and by 1842 he was admitted to practice before the U.S. Supreme Court.

Pike set aside legal and political debate in Arkansas when the United States and Mexico went to war in 1846, but his role as captain of the cavalry troop he had recruited brought its own turmoil. He sent a letter criticizing his regimental colonel, Archibald Yell, and lieutenant colonel, John Selden Roane, to the *Arkansas Gazette*, where it appeared in the 24 April 1847 issue. Roane and his friends had also written letters in which they criticized Pike. On 2 July Roane and Pike dueled.

After each combatant fired two shots and neither was hit, the attending surgeons interceded to argue successfully that honor had been served. After the war Pike continued to be active in Whig politics and later was a vigorous advocate of the Know-Nothing party. In 1853 he moved his law practice to New Orleans, but he returned to Little Rock in 1857.

Pike's attitudes toward slavery were curious. He had supported the slavery provision in the Arkansas constitution of 1836 on the grounds that Arkansas was a border state settled largely by slaveholders, but he was not friendly to slavery. It was uncertain where he would cast his support when the Civil War broke out, but he finally decided for the Confederacy. Because of his experience in the West, the new government sent him to negotiate treaties with Indian tribes west of Arkansas. On 22 November 1861 the Indian country west of Arkansas and north of Texas was constituted the Indian Territory and Pike was named its commissioner. Although Pike understood that the Indians were to fight only in defense of their own territory, in March 1862 they took part in the Battle of Pea Ridge (Arkansas), committing atrocities for which Pike was criticized. He resented what he considered the intrusion of Gen. Thomas C. Hindman into his affairs, and on 3 July 1862 he prepared a circular, *Letter to the President of the Confederate States*. President Davis considered the publication a grave military offense and so informed Pike. Never one to take criticism easily, Pike stated his case in letters to various officials; on 31 July 1862 he wrote an address to the Indian tribes that caused Col. Douglas H. Cooper to declare that Pike was "either insane or untrue to the South." When Pike continued to press his case, General Hindman ordered his arrest. Pike was sent home to Arkansas and never tried. During the course of the war he was vilified in both North and South, and he spent the last months of that national agony in retirement in Arkansas and, probably, Texas.

Having lost much of both his reputation and his property, Pike found the years after the war to be hard. For a time, fearing arrest because of his wartime activities, he was constantly on the move to secure his own safety. Responding to appeals from Pike's friends, President Andrew Johnson issued an order permitting Pike to return to his home on condition that he take the oath of allegiance and promise to conduct himself as a loyal citizen. But life in Arkansas was again difficult, and in 1867 Pike moved to Memphis, Tennessee, where he practiced law. In 1868 he moved to Washington, D.C., where, in addition to practicing law, he was associate editor of the *Patriot* (1868-1870). Pike again found solace in books and turned his energies to Freemasonry, whose philosophy helped sustain him in his last years.

A Mason since 1850, Pike had been elected sovereign grand commander of the Supreme Grand Council, Southern Jurisdiction of the United States, in 1859 and held that office for thirty-two years. His reputation for Masonry became international, and he worked many years rewriting the rituals of the order.

After Pike died at age eighty-one in the house of the Scottish Rite Temple in Washington, his written request that his body be cremated and his ashes put around the roots of two acacias in front of the home of the Supreme Council was disregarded. He was buried in Oak Hill Cemetery, Washington, but the Supreme Council erected a statue in his honor. In Freemasonry he found the fame that he had once hoped to find through his poetry. The political turmoil of the South and Southwest as the nation grappled with the question of slavery took too much of his energy (first in the war with Mexico and then in the Civil War) for Pike to give to literature what he might have. Yet, even as the record of Pike's political and legal skirmishes provide interesting commentary on his time, he also deserves to be remembered for his prose sketches and tales of the early West.

When Pike began writing the sketches in *Prose Sketches and Poems*, there was only the slimmest tradition of short fiction in America. Washington Irving's *The Sketch Book of Geoffrey Crayon, Gent.* (1819-1820) had appeared, and Pike knew Irving's work. Publication of Pike's "Narrative of a Journey in the Prairie" and "Narrative of a Second Journey" antedates Irving's *A Tour on the Prairies* (1835) by a year, and Pike later lamented that he had not met Irving's party, for he could have given Irving much description of the Far West, about which many in the East were immensely curious. Pike captured much of the spell of the prairie in descriptions such as this passage:

> I have seen the prairie, and stood long and weary guard in it, by moonlight and starlight and storm. It strikes me as the most magnificent, stern, and terribly grand scene on earth—a storm in the prairie. It is like a storm at sea, except in one respect—and in that it seems to me to be superior. The stillness of the desert and illimitable plain, while the snow is raging over its surface, is

Pike in the library of his home at Little Rock, Arkansas

always more fearful to me than the wild roll of the waves; and it seems unnatural–this dead quiet, while the upper elements are so fiercely disturbed; it seems as if there ought to be the roll and the roar of the waves. The sea, the woods, the mountains, all suffer in comparison with the prairie–that is, on the whole–although in particular circumstances either of them is superior. We may speak of the incessant motion and tumult of the waves, the unbounded greenness and dimness, and the lonely music of the forests, and the high magnificence, the precipitous grandeur, and the summer snow of the glittering cones of the mountains: but still, the prairie has a stronger hold upon the soul, and a more powerful, if not as vivid an impression upon the feelings. Its sublimity arises from its unbounded extent, its barren monotony and desolation, its still, unmoved, calm, stern, almost self-confident grandeur, its strange power of deception, its want of echo, and, in fine, its power of throwing a man back upon himself and giving him a feeling of lone helplessness, strangely mingled at the same time with a feeling of liberty and freedom from restraint. It is particularly sublime, as you draw nigh to the Rocky Mountains, and see them shot up in the west, with their lofty tops looking like white clouds resting upon their summits. Nothing ever equalled the intense feeling of delight

with which I first saw the eternal mountains marking the western edge of the desert.

Pike had an eye for people as well as landscape, and one of his sketches, "Trappers on the Prairie," gives a pointed description of the mountain man: "There are probably as many brave men among the mountain trappers, as among the same number of men in any part of the world. Inured to danger, they soon learned to disregard it–and hearing the Indian yell frequently sounding around them, they soon learned to yell in their turn, and frequently to imitate the Indians in some of their barbarities. There is also a great fund of originality among them, and many men may be found there, who could at once convince the world that the characters of Hawk Eye and Mike Finn are by no means exaggerated." Pike proceeds with brief sketches of several trappers before giving a more extensive portrait of one he found especially remarkable, Bill Williams. Using dialogue, Pike presents a couple of informative anecdotes, instructing the reader in the course of one of these on buffalo hunting. He ends the sketch with a more extended account of battle with some Utah warriors. Pike's aim is clearly to inform his readers about the rugged life of the West in an entertaining way. In the manner of Irving's *The Sketch Book of Geoffrey Crayon, Gent.*, there is the flavor of the familiar essay in "Trappers of the West" as well as in many of Pike's other pieces, especially the "Letters" he wrote for the *Boston Pearl and Literary Gazette*.

Some of Pike's prose sketches are quite clearly tales with dominant plot lines. "A Mexican Tale" recounts the woes of two young lovers, Rafael and Inacia, whose hopes for a life together are doomed because Inacia's foolish parents see advantage in their daughter's marrying sixty-year-old Lopez, who has a powerful ally in the corrupt village priest. The story ends in a dramatic scene: Rafael buries his knife in the bosom of Inacia, who has been stolen from him after living with him in brief bliss in the mountains near Taos; then he manages to kill Lopez before himself falling victim to the spears of Lopez's party. Lopez dislikes Rafael, in part, for his favorable disposition toward Americans, including the narrator, Pike himself. Pike found that most Mexicans liked and respected Americans–but he was overlooking some realities by holding this view.

The narrator of "A Mexican Tale" hears the account of Rafael and Inacia when he is a guest in a home in the valley of Taos; the technique of the "twice-told tale" was Pike's natural method for his stories, and his own views sometimes color the story in ways that original source for the story would not have colored them. For example, Pike, after telling the reader that Inacia was "pretty, almost a beautiful girl," observes: "There is no taste in the dress of a New Mexican female–not a spark–and they never develop any thing of that grace of bust and outline, which enchants us in our own delightful girls." Later, he is at pains to assure the reader that the corrupt priest of this tale was not exceptional: "The priests of Santa Fe, of Taos, of San Miguel, and other places which I could mention–were name of avail–are all notorious gamblers, and scruple not to cheat in this branch of their sacred profession. The priest of Serollata [Pike's spelling for Sebolleta or Cebolleta?] is rarely seen except disguised with liquor, and the priest of Taos scruples not to intoxicate himself at a fandango. As to their deism, several of them have Volney in their libraries, and as to their chastity, they make no profession of it, and speak of their mistresses and their amours as a matter of course." Although "A Mexican Tale" presents a dramatic story, Pike tells it to inform American audiences of life in the western country.

"Refugio" also has a dramatic story line. The title character, an American of Santa Fe, is wrongly accused of murder by a couple of treacherous no-accounts. The last words of the tale assure the reader that the memory of Refugio "will long live in the country which witnessed his sufferings, his disgrace, his undaunted boldness, and his final triumph." Once Pike has begun telling Refugio's story, he keeps steadily on course. He begins, however, by describing his own hard journey to Santa Fe. He discovers the city to have more splendor than does Taos and describes it along with something of its history. He reports that he met several of the "great men" of the province and then presents several brief unflattering portraits. Hardly with a view to reaching a New Mexican audience, he summarizes the general population: "As to the common herd, they are rather better; they have some generosity and hospitality. They will all lie and steal, to be sure, and have no idea of gratitude. There is neither honor among the men nor virtue among the women. In fact, honor in New Mexico would be apt to lie on the owner's hands. Character is a mere drug, a valueless article; and he who has little of it is as well off, and as rich, as he who has much." Finally, against such a backdrop, Pike is ready to tell the story vindicating the American Refugio.

Pike did not always call attention to his views in his tales. "San Juan of the Del Norte" moves quickly to its primary business, a sketch of a Spaniard whose peace is destroyed after he leaves his village with a trader and succumbs to a desire for great riches, which he never achieves. In "The Gauchupin" Pike claims to be relating a story in the words of a "very excellent and worthy friend," thus dismissing himself in the first paragraph so that his friend can recount his humorous role in bringing about the marriage of a fellow American and a beautiful Spanish girl.

The narrator plays a sustained part in "Manuel The Wolf Killer." He shares some of his impressions of the New Mexico people and country, but he then focuses on the history of the strange Manuel, who has been crazed by a desire to kill wolves ever since his young brother was killed by one while in Manuel's charge on a bear hunt. Because his horse was injured, the narrator has to stay several days in Manuel's village; thus he is present when an accident in the mountains triggers Manuel's recovery to sanity, and three months afterward he dances at Manuel's wedding.

"The Inroad of the Nabajo" is a much more diffuse tale. Describing early Taos and the life in that village, Pike also recounts warfare between the Navajo and the Indians of Taos. The reader also learns that the Indians "have very little of that sententious gravity and unbending sobriety of appearance generally ascribed to Indians. . . . Not that I mean to say that they are never grave—sometimes they are; but generally, an Indian is the most merry and apparently lighthearted thing in the world. Do you think that they are like Chingachgook, who would not embrace Uncas till they were alone by their campfire? No." The central episode is the story of competition between two suitors, one Spanish and one American, for the hand of a lovely young woman, a widow whose beauty Pike notices at a fandango in Taos. Ana Maria's story is interrupted frequently; it is also a twice-told tale, repeated, in the words of one of Pike's American friends, "as nearly as I can."

Pike knew that he had an important subject in the western experience: "I love a western man. There is so much open, brief, off-hand kindness—so much genuine honesty—excellence of heart, and steadiness of purpose in them, that they always claim, from him who knows them well, the utmost affection and respect. You, who have never left the shores of the Atlantic, cannot appreciate, you know nothing about their character." Pike's sketches of these men helped to inform his readers about their character, and those efforts are still of interest. He might have done more to present western man had his own life not become so hectic. And he needed an example other than Irving's. Nathaniel Hawthorne's tales did not begin appearing until after Pike's book was in print, and by the time Edgar Allan Poe had written a critical theory for the short story, Pike was caught in other activities. He might have benefited, too, from the example of a Stephen Crane or an Ernest Hemingway, who recognized the possibilities of using one's own dramatic life for fictional ends. For in Pike's life, both during and after his New Mexican journeys, there was ample material.

Bibliography:

William Boyden, *Bibliography of the Writings of Albert Pike* (Washington, D.C., 1921).

Biographies:

Fred W. Allsopp, *Albert Pike: A Biography* (Little Rock: Parke-Harper, 1928);

W. L. Brown, "Albert Pike," Ph.D. Dissertation, University of Texas, 1955;

Robert Lipscomb Duncan, *Reluctant General: The Life and Times of Albert Pike* (New York: Dutton, 1961).

Papers:

Pike's unpublished manuscripts are in the library of the Supreme Council, Scottish Rite of Freemasonry, Southern Jurisdiction, Washington, D.C.

Edgar Allan Poe
(19 January 1809-7 October 1849)

Eric W. Carlson
University of Connecticut

See also the Poe entries in *DLB 3: Antebellum Writers in New York and the South; DLB 59: American Literary Critics and Scholars, 1800-1850;* and *DLB 73: American Magazine Journalists, 1741-1850.*

BOOKS: *Tamerlane and Other Poems. By a Bostonian* (Boston: Printed by Calvin F. S. Thomas, 1827);

Al Aaraaf, Tamerlane, and Minor Poems (Baltimore: Hatch & Dunning, 1829);

Poems by Edgar A. Poe. Second Edition (New York: Elam Bliss, 1831);

The Narrative of Arthur Gordon Pym. Of Nantucket, anonymous (New York: Harper, 1838; London: Wiley & Putnam, 1838);

Tales of the Grotesque and Arabesque, 2 volumes (Philadelphia: Lea & Blanchard, 1840);

The Prose Romances of Edgar A. Poe, No. I. Containing the Murders in the Rue Morgue, and The Man That Was Used Up (Philadelphia: William H. Graham, 1843);

Tales by Edgar A. Poe (New York: Wiley & Putnam, 1845; London: Wiley & Putnam, 1845);

The Raven and Other Poems (New York: Wiley & Putnam, 1845; London: Wiley & Putnam, 1846);

Eureka: A Prose Poem by Edgar A. Poe (New York: Putnam, 1848; London: Chapman, 1848).

Editions and Collections: *The Works of the Late Edgar Allan Poe, with A Memoir by Rufus Wilmot Griswold and Notices of his Life and Genius by N. P. Willis and J. R. Lowell,* 4 volumes, edited by Griswold (New York: J. S. Redfield, 1850-1856);

The Works of Edgar Allan Poe, 10 volumes, edited by Edmund Clarence Stedman and George Edward Woodberry (Chicago: Stone & Kimball, 1894-1895);

The Complete Works of Edgar Allan Poe, 17 volumes, edited by James A. Harrison (New York: Thomas Y. Crowell, 1902);

Selections from the Critical Writings of Edgar Allan Poe, edited by F. C. Prescott (New York:

Edgar Allan Poe, September 1849

Holt, 1909); republished, with new preface by J. Lasley Dameron and new introduction by Eric W. Carlson (New York: Gordian Press, 1981);

Collected Works of Edgar Allan Poe, 3 volumes, edited by Thomas Ollive Mabbott (Cambridge, Mass.: Belknap Press of Harvard University Press, 1969-1978);

Collected Writings of Edgar Allan Poe, edited by Burton R. Pollin, volume 1, *The Imaginary Voyages: The Narrative of Arthur Gordon Pym, The Unparalleled Adventure of one Hans Pfaall, The Journal of Julius Rodman* (Boston: G. K. Hall,

1981); volume 2, *The Brevities of Edgar Allan Poe* (New York: Gordian Press, 1985);

Edgar Allan Poe: Poetry and Tales, edited by Patrick F. Quinn (New York: Library of America, 1984);

Edgar Allan Poe: Essays and Reviews, edited by G. R. Thompson (New York: Library of America, 1984).

OTHER: *Poe's Contributions to the Columbia Spy: Doings of Gotham, as described in a series of letters to the editors of the Columbia Spy, together with various editorial comments and criticisms by Poe now first collected*, compiled by Jacob E. Spannuth, with an introduction by Thomas Ollive Mabbott (Pottsville, Pa.: Jacob E. Spannuth, 1929).

Edgar Allan Poe's importance as a short-story writer may be seen in his pioneering contributions to the genre, in his theory of the tale, in the rich variety, meaning, and significance of his stories, and in their influence on writers the world over. Poe was a pivotal figure in converting the traditional Gothic tale of mystery and terror into variations of the romantic tale and the modern short story by shifting the emphasis from surface sensationalism, suspense, and plausibility of plot pattern to the "under current of meaning" suggested by the symbolic play of language, the subtle use of style, tone, and point of view, the subconscious motivation of character, and serious interpretive themes. The diversity of his seventy works of short fiction (including some sketches) represents not only a response to the demands of the literary marketplace but also an expression of his own deeper evolving outlook on life and his theory of the short story, especially "the tale of effect."

Ever since Poe's short stories first began to appear in the 1830s readers have been intrigued by the nature of the man or the mind that produced them. Was he as demonic or demented as the protagonists of his horror tales, and as analytical or psychic as the heroes of his detective and mystery stories? Contrary to popular legend, Poe was neither an alcoholic nor a drug addict, though he did struggle during much of his adult life against a predisposition to drink during periods of stress and despair. A highly complex character, Poe was capable of the strictest artistic control and intellectual acumen, at other times suffering from emotional instability and dependence.

Born in Boston on 19 January 1809, he was not yet three when his mother died on 8 December 1811 in Richmond. A talented leading lady in the American theater of the day, Elizabeth Arnold Poe, of English birth, had married David Poe, Jr., a mediocre actor who later abandoned his family. After his mother's death Poe was taken in by the childless John and Frances Allan; brother William Henry was taken in by his paternal grandparents; and sister Rosalie was cared for by foster parents. Allan, a Scottish-born tobacco merchant, was as strict and unemotional as his wife was overindulgent. When Allan's business interests took him to Scotland and London in 1815, Mrs. Allan and Poe accompanied him, returning to Richmond in 1820. Poe was educated in private academies, excelling in Latin, in writing verse, and declamation. He enjoyed swimming, skating, and shooting. In 1825 Allan inherited the sizable fortune of his uncle, William Gault; even so, being the child of former actors, Poe was regarded as an outsider by the Richmond elite. At sixteen, young Poe fell in love with Sarah Elmira Royster, to whom he became "engaged" without parental consent.

In February 1826 Poe entered the University of Virginia, where he excelled in Greek, Latin, French, Spanish, and Italian. When his allowance from Allan did not cover the cost of books and clothes, Poe resorted to playing cards for money, incurring debts of two thousand dollars. Refusing to pay these "debts of honor" at the end of the term in December, Allan withdrew Poe from the university. When all attempts at reconciliation with Allan failed, Poe went to Baltimore in March 1827, then sailed to Boston, where in May he enlisted in the United States Army as "Edgar A. Perry" and was assigned to duty with the coast artillery at Fort Independence, Boston Harbor and later at Fort Moultrie on Sullivan's Island in Charleston Harbor. It was in Boston that a young printer was persuaded to publish Poe's anonymous first book, *Tamerlane and Other Poems. By a Bostonian* (1827). After Mrs. Allan died in February 1829, Poe quit the army and sought help in getting an appointment to West Point. A second volume, with six new poems, was published under Poe's own name in Baltimore in December 1829. On 1 July 1830 he entered West Point, but by October, learning that Allan had remarried and despairing of reconciliation or inheritance (he had never been legally adopted), Poe ignored orders, thus obtaining his dismissal from the academy on 31 January 1831.

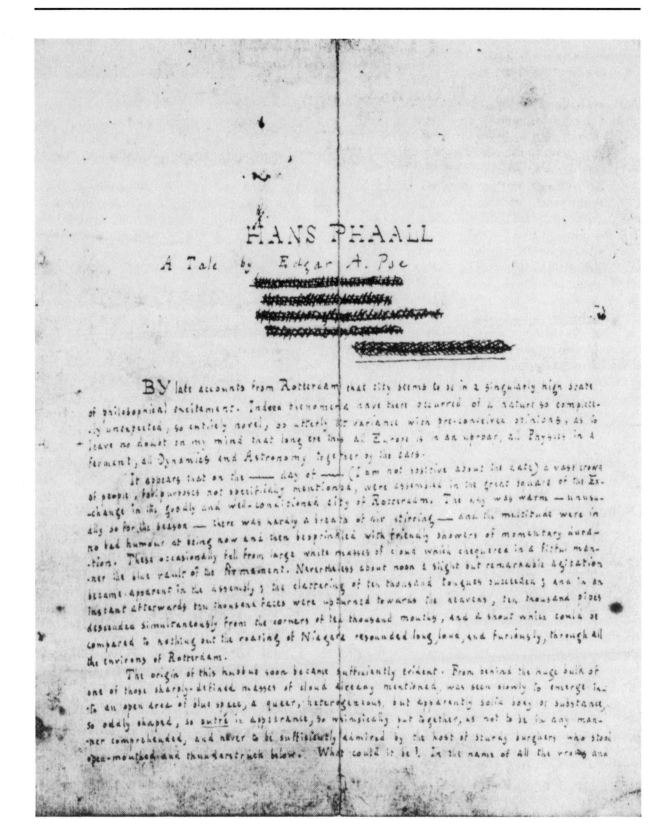

First page of the manuscript for Poe's 1835 story of a balloon journey to the moon (courtesy of the Pierpont Morgan Library)

Poe's writing career falls into three major periods, each marked by a shift in perspective. During the first period, 1827 to 1831, his three slim volumes of poetry expressed a strong attachment to the romantic myth of a pastoral and poetic ideal, made up of "dreams" and "memories" of a pristine paradise or Eden. These early poems celebrated Beauty and Innocence, Love and Joy as dynamic life values in the poet's feeling for the potential of harmony of mind with nature, of the "soul" with "God" or the universal "Ens." In 1831, a transition year, three of Poe's poems ("Romance," "Israfel," and "To Helen") expressed a new commitment to a poetry of heartfelt conviction in the face of life's burdens and sorrows. During the decade that followed, 1831 to 1841, a radical change was reflected in poems and tales on the theme of death as a finality in a cosmic void of darkness and silence. His third and final period, 1841 to 1849, was marked by a return to poetry and by essays and fiction on the theme of psychic transcendentalism. Through all three of these stages Poe continued to publish comic and satiric tales, mainly parodies, burlesques, grotesques, and hoaxes.

When Poe's three volumes of poetry from 1827 to 1831 went largely unnoticed and when he failed in his applications for editorial work and teaching, he turned to humorous and satiric fiction, then in demand. In June 1831 he submitted five stories to a contest sponsored by the *Philadelphia Saturday Courier* with one hundred dollars offered as a prize for the best work of fiction. Although Poe did not win the prize, his five tales were published by the *Courier* from January to December 1832. "Metzengerstein," the first of these stories, has been appreciated for its unity of tone and effective suspense. It is better read as a powerful allegory than a parody, burlesque, or hoax. Its Gothic devices and plot support a serious moral theme: the evil of pride and arrogant power brings about self-destruction by retributive forces from within. In "The Duc de L'Omelette" and "The Bargain Lost" (republished as "Bon-Bon," *Southern Literary Messenger*, August 1835) the Devil appears as the antagonist in the form of a mysterious stranger. The first story neatly satirizes French aristocratic vanity, hauteur, and cunning so clever as to outface and outwit the Devil himself. In part it satirizes the French affectations of Nathaniel Parker Willis, editor of the *American Monthly Magazine*. "The Bargain Lost" is the colorful account of Pedro Garcia, a Venetian chef and metaphysician of sorts. The satiric treatment

of the character types widens into a tour de force of wit and erudition at the expense of classical philosophers, tyrants, authors, and the conventional figure of the Devil himself. "A Tale of Jerusalem," based on an old theme and episode found in Horace Smith's long novel, *Zilla, a Tale of the Holy City* (1828), is largely a play on words. "A Decided Loss" (revised as "Loss of Breath," *Messenger*, September 1835) satirizes "the extravagances of Blackwood," that is, the tales of "sensation" published in *Blackwood's Magazine*. When the protagonist expresses a "wild delight" in analyzing his sensations, Poe adds a note linking this analysis with "much of the absurd *metaphysicianism* of the redoubted Schelling." The reliance on grossly implausible events, comic details, historical allusions, humorous word play, and caricature in the story of a man who loses his "breath" (his voice), who is hanged but does not die, gives humorous support to the playful subtitle, "A Tale Neither In Nor Out of 'Blackwood,'" appended to the piece upon its revision.

Although little is known of Poe's activities throughout 1832, in May 1833 he proposed for publication "Eleven Tales of the Arabesque," consisting of the five *Saturday Courier* tales plus six new stories which were submitted to a contest sponsored by the *Baltimore Saturday Visiter*. The first prize of fifty dollars went to Poe's "MS. Found in a Bottle," which was published on 19 October, and an honorary second prize to his poem "The Coliseum." The eleven tales "are supposed to be read at table," Poe explained to Joseph T. and Edwin Buckingham, editors of the *New-England Magazine*, "by the eleven members of a literary club, and are followed by the remarks of the company upon each. These remarks are intended as a burlesque upon criticism. In the whole, originality more than anything else has been attempted. . . ." As representative of the collection, Poe enclosed "Epimanes" (*Messenger*, March 1836; republished as "Four Beasts in One—The Homo-Cameleopard," *Broadway Journal*, 6 December 1845), a story for which he drew upon both ancient and modern history, only the main incident being an invention. Although Jacksonianism may have been an intended target, the satire is less applicable to American democracy than to monarchical regimes. An overlooked aspect of the story is the point of view, the use of a witness-reporter who, like a modern-day "eyewitness" newscaster, describes the unfolding event in the dramatic tones of one who is baffled, amazed, and finally (and ironically) caught

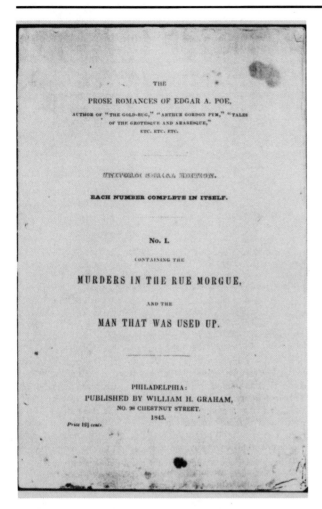

Front cover for the first in an intended series of pamphlet reprintings of Poe stories. No others were published (courtesy of the Pierpont Morgan Library).

up in the crowd's hysterical celebration.

These eleven tales, literary rather than autobiographical in origin, became the basis for Poe's "The Tales of the Folio Club," a scheme introduced in an 1833 manuscript. In the introduction the narrator, a disaffected member of the club, unflatteringly describes the members as "quite as ill-looking as they are stupid." In principle, members are forbidden "to be otherwise than erudite and witty; and the avowed objects of the confederation were 'the instruction of society, and the amusement of themselves.' " It should be noted that Poe's original title, "Eleven Tales of the Arabesque," implied something more than satires and grotesques. Poe referred to "most" of these early stories as "*intended* for half-banter, half-satire—although I might not have fully acknowledged this to be their aim even to myself "; he identified only "Lionizing" (*Messenger*, May 1835) and "Loss of Breath" as "satires properly speak-

ing." Reference to a larger purpose—to illustrate a range of creative "Imaginative Faculties"—accompanied Poe's proposed seventeen-tale version of the Folio Club collection in September 1836. Among the nonsatiric Folio Club tales that are neither burlesques nor parodies, several fantasies of the human condition exemplify the impressionistic use of the "Imaginative Faculties." The companion pieces "Siope—A Fable" (*Baltimore Book* for 1838; republished as "Silence," *Broadway Journal*, 6 September 1845) and "Shadow—A Fable" (*Messenger*, September 1835; revised as "Shadow—A Parable," *Broadway Journal*, 31 May 1845) belong in this category, being distinguished by an arabesque design and "existentialist" themes. In "Siope" the Roman figure of a man on the rock of *Desolation* "trembled in solitude" at the sight of a restless and hostile universe, but when confronted by SILENCE as the ultimate nature of existence, he shudders and flees in terror. At this, the Demon narrator laughs. But the human "I" "could not laugh with the Demon" (life is no laughing matter); only the lynx "looked at him [the Demon] steadily in the face" (only the philosophical lynx-eye, as Poe noted elsewhere, can see the deeper Dignity of Man). In "Shadow," when questioned, the shadow replies in the frightening tones of "a multitude of beings," in the varying cadences, "the well remembered and familiar accents of many thousand departed friends." This ending is reminiscent of the early poem "The Spirits of the Dead" (1827), where the voices of the dead revive the speaker's will to live in the face of loss and grief. But here that idea is not implied, as if the loss of his mother, Frances Allan, brother William Henry (who died in 1831) and Mrs. Jane Stanard—the "well remembered" mother of a schoolmate—had left him inconsolable.

Poe's tales and poems during this period (1831-1841) made him one of the foremost nineteenth-century "literary conquerors of the Void." But if the Poe hero confronted by Nothingness stands alone in "fear and trembling," God is not therefore "dead" nor life-in-the-large Absurd. In his sea tales Poe's protagonist encounters a boundary situation with "no exit," but in the process his terror is transformed from physical fear to something more. In "MS. Found in a Bottle" the narrator, a rationalist and skeptic, quickly finds himself one of two survivors stranded on a ship in a simoom. Despite the "pitchy darkness" and raging tempest and in contrast to the "superstitious terror" felt by his companion, an old Swed-

The System of Doctor Tarr and Professor Fether.

By Edgar A. Poe.

During the autumn of 18—, while on a tour through the extreme Southern provinces of France, my route led me within a few miles of a certain Maison de Santé, or private Mad-House, about which I had heard much, in Paris, from my medical friends. As I had never visited a place of the kind, I thought the opportunity too good to be lost; and so proposed to my travelling companion (a gentleman with whom I had made casual acquaintance, a few days before) that we should turn aside, for an hour or so, and look through the establishment. To this he objected; pleading haste, in the first place, and, in the second, a very usual horror at the sight of a lunatic.

Fair copy of the manuscript for Poe's 1845 study of patients and caretakers in a French insane asylum (Donald G. Mitchell, American Lands and Letters, *volume 2, 1899)* ish sailor, he is "wrapped up in a silent wonder." When he is hurled onto a gigantic, strange ship that is very old and porous, he finds himself surrounded by an equally strange crew of aged men with "decayed charts of navigation" and "scattered mathematical instruments of the most quaint and obsolete construction." At this point the narrator is overcome by "a new sense–a new entity," presumably a new, intuitive mode of realization, suggested also by his "thoughtless touches of the brush" on a folded sail which when "spread out" spell "the word DISCOVERY." These and other similar details turn the ship and its captain into a symbol of ancient wisdom; the ship's plummet into a whirlpool at the story's conclusion signals a passive, mystical resignation to the tragic destiny of life. But the narrator's own "eagerness of hope" and curiosity is transformed into a glimpsed vision of the sublime, however terrifying and fatal.

In April 1841 Poe's "A Descent into the Maelström," a reworking of material used in "MS. Found in a Bottle," appeared in *Graham's Magazine*. Here, an old mariner, in contrast to his brother, whose sheer fright turns him into a raving maniac, takes note of the full moon streaming down into the black funnel in which their ship is trapped, in "a flood of golden glory." A magnificent and symbolic rainbow appears, and an agonizing "yell" up to heaven rises out of the mist. Then he is overcome with curiosity, fear, and "a more exciting *hope*" as he realizes that his only escape is to leave the ship and cling to a water cask. But the real denouement consists of the final four sentences on how the white-haired mariner's story met with disbelief from "the merry fishermen of Lofoden," who thus denied their primal, higher consciousness of the nature of existence.

"The Visionary" (*Godey's Lady's Book*, January 1834; revised as "The Assignation," *Broadway Journal*, 7 June 1845) was Poe's first story to appear in a national monthly with a wide circulation. As one of the Folio Club tales it had been assigned to "Mr. Convolvulus Gondola, a young gentleman who had travelled a good deal." Due, in part, to its inflated bathos, it has been regarded as a lampoon of Byronic passion or as a parody of Thomas More. Neither of those views reckons with Poe's preference for the visionary hero, the classical, Hellenic heroine, the conventional villain, the symbolic rescue, the arabesque apartment, the love poem written in London, the painting of the Marchesa Aphrodite, or the final

suicide pact. W. H. Auden's comment on Poe's style as "operatic" suggests that these stock elements, coupled with the overwrought diction, may, within the narrator's maturing perception, comprise a psychodrama of the self's quest for origins, for identity, and for unity. So considered, it has been read as a paradigm of Poe's own search for a lost unity of the primal self.

Although the tales of the Folio Club were never published as a group, Poe's friendship with John Pendleton Kennedy helped open the pages of the *Southern Literary Messenger*, where "Berenice" appeared in March 1835. With the aid of Kennedy, one of the judges in the *Visiter* contest, Poe became an editor on the *Messenger*, to which he contributed poems, tales, and reviews (over eighty), helping to increase the circulation from five hundred to over thirty-five hundred.

Meanwhile, Poe had married his cousin Virginia Clemm on 16 May 1836; she was not quite fourteen. Poe had been living in the Clemm household, consisting of Virginia, her mother, Maria Clemm, and Poe's grandmother, Elizabeth Poe, since 1831. After the grandmother's death in 1835 Poe and the Clemms moved from Baltimore to Richmond. In February 1837, with Mrs. Clemm, Poe and Virginia moved to New York, where they stayed for about a year and a half before relocating in Philadelphia.

"Berenice" was the first of five symbolic dramas of the self, published between 1835 and 1839, that are best appreciated as tales of psychic conflict and tales of vision. "In them," Richard Wilbur once wrote, "Poe broke wholly new ground, and they remain the best things of their kind in our literature. . . . I think he will have something to say to us as long as there is civil war in the palaces of men's minds" ("The House of Poe"). This group includes also "Morella" (*Messenger*, April 1835), "Ligeia" (*American Museum*, September 1838), "The Fall of the House of Usher" (*Burton's Gentleman's Magazine*, September 1839), and "William Wilson" (*Gift* for 1840). Despite its rich language, "Berenice" has posed a problem for the general reader: the ending (the pulling of Berenice's teeth) is often seen as too gruesome, too repulsive. Poe admitted that "The subject is far too horrible. . . . I allow that it approaches the very verge of bad-taste–but I will not sin quite so egregiously again," adding the observation that famous magazines are indebted to stories "*similar in nature to Berenice.* . . . You asked me in what does this nature consist? In the ludicrous heightened into the grotesque: the fearful coloured into the

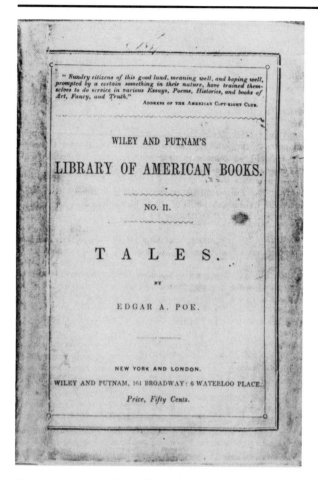

Front cover for the 1845 collection of twelve Poe stories (courtesy of the Richard Gimbel Collection, Philadelphia Free Library)

horrible: the witty exaggerated into the burlesque: the singular wrought out into the strange and mystical.... To be appreciated you must be *read*, and these things are invariably sought after with avidity."

"Berenice" is best read as not only a study in monomania but also an allegory of the bipart self suffering a radical split. The tale is narrated by Egaeus, whose abstracted, dreaming imagination is his only world of reality. Berenice, in all her natural loveliness, embodies the memory of his original, true identity. However, due to frequent epileptic seizures, her beauty has begun to fade, and Egaeus becomes fixated on her teeth as a sign of her attenuation. In extracting her teeth during Berenice's most severe cataleptic fit (it appears that she has died), Egaeus (the heartless intellect) violates the very unity of mind and heart that his fragmented self so desperately seeks to recover. "Morella" is a variation on the same theme: the tragedy of a cold, unloving rationality that is unable to respond to the "mystical"

studies of "the imaginative Morella." Morella's readings in Johann Gottlieb Fichte, Friedrich Wilhelm Joseph von Schelling, and the Pythagoreans left her husband, the narrator, whose guide is Locke's definition of identity as "the sameness of rational being," confused and afraid. Morella's decline parallels Berenice's in symbolic meaning, but her return through her daughter, born immediately after her death, adds another dimension, the idea of psychic continuity or indestructible will, along with the secondary theme of retribution from within.

At least twice Poe singled out "Ligeia" as his "best" tale, probably because of its intricate symbolic design and its theme: life has no meaning or purpose unless spiritual integrity can be recovered from the repressed "will." When Poe remarked that "I should have intimated that the *will* did not perfect its intention–there should have been a relapse . . . and Ligeia . . . should be at length entombed as Rowena," he hinted that either the act of willing requires repeated renewal, or human purpose is at the mercy of the fates, forces beyond human control. The epigraph ascribed to Joseph Glanvill, however, still holds true: "Man doth not yield himself to the angels, nor unto death utterly, save only through the weakness of his feeble will."

Published the year after "Ligeia," "The Fall of the House of Usher" is Poe's most popular tale and perhaps his best. It has been a favorite of anthologists since Rufus Griswold. In its group it is the only tale with three instead of two characters, suggesting the three faculties in Poe's "world of mind"–Pure Intellect, Taste (or "poetic intellect"), and Moral Sense–which Poe elsewhere terms "mental power," "sensibility," and "intense vitality" or "Energy." The narrator functions as an observer-interpreter, as a voice for the meaning of it all, the only "central intelligence" in the story. Roderick Usher is the creative mind ("poetic intellect") in the hypnagogic or visionary state, now suffering from a psychic conflict caused by the repression of his Moral Sense or will (entombment of his sister, Madeline). Though his eye was "large, liquid, and luminous beyond comparison"–a sign of his sensibility–he lacks the "moral energy" or "vitality" necessary to true genius as defined by Poe. As with the "lofty" and "ethereal" Lady Ligeia, so here on the "threshhold" (of consciousness) "there *did* stand the lofty and enshrouded figure of the lady Madeline of Usher," whose fatal embrace of Roderick becomes (in the words of one noted critic) a "foreview of the soul's reconstitution and purification in death."

As a classic of its genre, "William Wilson" is Poe's clearest embodiment of the Double. In it the protagonist's counterpart dramatizes not only conscience but a Jungian "anima" or Primal Self in deep discord with the willful ego. Here, as elsewhere in Poe, this shadow self comes to momentary consciousness in "dim visions of my earliest infancy ... the belief of my having been acquainted with the being who stood before me, at some epoch very long ago." Suppressed in his self-willed boyhood, this deeper Moral Sense remains undeveloped as Wilson pursues a life of increasing folly, dissipation, and crime, heedless of the repeated visitations and warnings of his alter ego. Although a transparent allegory in its general outline, here, too, Poe blends the supernatural and the psychological through the symbolic use of architectural details and neo-Gothic elements, thus adding nuance and depth of meaning.

By now Poe had entered upon his greatest period as a writer of prose fiction (1837-1845), which coincided more or less with his years in Philadelphia (1838-1844). He remained busy from May 1839 as coeditor of *Burton's Gentleman's Magazine*, doing most of the reviews and one feature per month. The twenty-five tales published to date were collected in *Tales of the Grotesque and Arabesque* (1840), specially arranged and prefaced by Poe, thus providing new clues to Poe's artistic purpose and form. Applying to the table of contents his remark that he "desired to preserve, as far as a certain point, a certain unity of design," one sees immediately that the arabesques are alternated with the grotesques: "Morella," "Lionizing," "William Wilson," "The Man That Was Used Up," "The Fall of the House of Usher," "The Duc de L'Omelette," and so on through the first twelve tales, after which the sequence becomes less regular, with four arabesques among the last five. It would seem that Poe carefully distinguished these two modes of fiction, although elsewhere he may have used the terms loosely; even here he refrains from any attempt at definition. In speaking of "this prevalence of the 'Arabesque' in my serious tales" Poe furnishes another clue to his use of the term, especially as he then distinguishes his 'phantasy-pieces' from the vogue of " 'Germanism' and gloom." In his own tales of terror, he claims "that terror is not of Germany, but of the soul,—that I have deduced this terror only from its legitimate sources, and urged it only to its legitimate results." The placement of

"MS. Found in a Bottle," "Shadow," and "The Visionary" among the arabesques suggests that the Folio Club plan was more complex than supposed or that it had undergone revision in Poe's mind. In short, it becomes absurd to erect a theory of Poe's fiction based on the notion that Poe did not distinguish arabesque from grotesque.

Beyond the sixteen tales already discussed, there are seven satires and two serious stories included in the collection; one of the latter, "Hans Phaall" (*Messenger*, June 1835; later "Hans Pfaall"), has by some been considered a long narrative rather than a short story. Except for "King Pest the First. A Tale Containing an Allegory" (*Messenger*, September 1835), most of these satires appeared in the late 1830s. "The Man That Was Used Up: A Tale of the Late Bugaboo and Kickapoo Campaign" (*Burton's*, August 1839) relates not only to problems with the Kickapoo tribe of Indians in Florida in 1839 but also to the heroic action of Col. Richard M. Johnson (later vice-president under Martin Van Buren) at the Battle of the Thames in October 1813, leaving his body shattered. More significant is the satire of the specious social lion and his empty-headed admirers. In the next tale, "The Devil in the Belfry" (*Saturday Chronicle*, 18 May 1839), written in the manner of Washington Irving's Knickerbocker history, Poe amused himself by caricaturing the inhabitants of the Dutch borough of Vondervotteimittiss in all their complacency and clock-ridden existence. When a devilish stranger arrives and causes the town clock to strike thirteen, pandemonium sets in. This story is very likely one of Poe's jabs at smug bourgeois America; but more particularly it satirizes President Van Buren, who was preparing for a visit in June 1839 to Kinderhook and New York.

In "King Pest" Poe's black humor is so extreme that it ceases to be funny. Many readers reacted with loathing and horror to the description of the company drinking out of skulls. Robert Louis Stevenson, for instance, was overcome with disgust: "He who could write 'King Pest' had ceased to be a human being." Others have noted the angry, cruel, grim humor in some of these tales, as if Poe were unburdening his resentments against the world and against God's indifference to man—further evidence of Poe's bitterness and skepticism during the 1830s. On the other hand, Constance Rourke, in *American Humor* (1931), appreciates "King Pest" as "one of the most brilliant pure burlesques in the language, transmuting ter-

Poe's burial site in Baltimore, Maryland

ror into gross comedy, as it had often been transmuted in the western tall tales."

Next came two satires of how to concoct a *Blackwood's Magazine* story according to Poe's tongue-in-cheek version of the formula. Given Poe's predilection for exaggeration, implausible incidents, caricature, sophomoric puns, farfetched coinages, and other wordplay, it is not surprising to find him lampooning his own use of these outrageous devices in "The Signora Zenobia" and its companion piece, "The Scythe of Time" (*American Museum*, November 1838; revised as "How to Write a Blackwood Article" and "A Predicament," *Broadway Journal*, 12 July 1845). These two offer the reader an essay definition and an illustration of Poe's precise, as well as broad use of, the "grotesque" as burlesque. Psyche Zenobia, the first-person narrator of both parts, is a snobbish literary bluestocking from Philadelphia come to Edinburgh to seek out Mr. Blackwood, editor of the famous journal that bears his name. Besides recommending several examples of preposterous fiction, he advises her to strive for the sensational incident, and "Should you ever be drowned or hung, be sure and make a note of your sensations–they will be worth to you ten guineas a sheet." Then there is the tone or manner of narration–ranging from "the tone didactic" to "the tone transcendental . . . a little reading of the *Dial* will carry you a great way." Finally, "an air of erudition" is essential and can be achieved by including "little scraps of either learning or *belespritism*," especially phrases and snatches of poetry in French, Spanish, Italian, Latin, and Greek.

"Von Jung, the Mystic" (*American Monthly Magazine*, June 1837; revised as "Mystification," *Broadway Journal*, 27 December 1845) is situated at Göttingen, one of the German universities where dueling was in favor when the Baron Ritzner Von Jung arrived. Poe not only undercuts the whole dueling mystique but also exposes the pretentious reputations and presumed special knowledge of the participants. The next selection, "Why the Little Frenchman Wears His Hand in a Sling" (previously unpublished), is an amusing anecdote told by a first-person narrator, the self-styled "Sir Patrick O'Grandison, Baronitt, 39 Southampton Row, Russell Square, Parrish o'Bloomsbury." Very popular, it became one of the first Poe stories to be pirated in London.

Despite the originality, subtlety, and variety of these stories, reviews of the collection were few, sales poor. In the so-called "interlude" year of 1840 "The Journal of Julius Rodman" was serialized in six installments (January-June) in *Burton's Gentleman's Magazine*, and Poe made plans for his own critical journal, to be called the "Penn Magazine," but his prospectus failed to attract financial support. "Peter Pendulum (The

Business Man)" (*Burton's*, February 1840), a little-known parody of Joseph C. Neal's *Charcoal Sketches* (1838), ironically describes the narrator's pride in being a "methodical" businessman, but whose actual "business" consists of petty schemes of a ridiculous, marginal nature for extorting a pittance here and there by such "methods" as "Mud-Dabbling," "Cur-Spattering," and "Organ-Grinding."

"The Man of the Crowd" (*Graham's*, 1840) has increasingly become a favorite of the general reader and the Poe scholar. As a study in compulsive behavior, it is the first of five dramatizations of pathological states. Readers have variously seen "the old man" of the story, who is pursued and observed by the narrator, as a lost soul, an outcast, a lonely drunkard, the narrator's own future self, or Everyman burdened by "the mystery hidden in every human soul." But the overt statement of theme, repeated in the final paragraph, refers to him as "the type and the genius of deep crime. He refuses to be alone. *He is the man of the crowd.* The worst heart of the world is a grosser book than the 'Hortulus Animae,' and perhaps it is but one of the great mercies of God that '*es lässt sich nicht lesen* [it does not allow itself to be read].' " The old man is not Everyman, then, but rather the perpetrator of a crime so heinous that it cannot be expiated, nor identified by others.

From 1841 to 1849 Poe's transcendentalism, cosmic and psychic, was chiefly developed in the final two parts of a trilogy of "angelic colloquies" and in the closely related "The Island of the Fay" (*Graham's*, June 1841) and "Mesmeric Revelation" (*Columbian Magazine*, August 1844). The first colloquy, "The Conversation of Eiros and Charmion" (*Burton's*, December 1839), reprinted in *Tales of the Grotesque and Arabesque*, contains several of Poe's psycho-transcendental themes: death-as-metamorphosis and the revelation of a supernal existence in which the senses have "the keenness of their perception of *the new.*"

By far the most important of these philosophical fantasies is "The Colloquy of Monos and Una" (*Graham's*, August 1841), detailing the process by which Monos was "born again" as he passed through Death into "the Life Eternal." In what is a major statement of Poe's social and philosophical perspective, Monos proceeds to diagnose "man's general condition," as marked by the "evil days" of "general misrule," ugly industrialization, sorry attempts at "omniprevalent Democracy" (equalitarianism), and, worst of all, the tyranny of the mechanical arts and the "harsh mathematical reason" over the poetic intellect–alas for the "majestic intuition of Plato!" The dominant rationalism (the "leading evil, Knowledge," infected with system and abstraction) led to the exploitation of nature and the corruption of cultural values. In this sick society "the world of mind" suffered from fragmentation and psychic conflict (as reflected in Poe's murder tales). Only by a recovery of poetic sensibility and the "sentiment of the natural" can the individual be redeemed and regenerated into the reintegrated Self.

The third of these angelic dialogues, "The Power of Words" (*Democratic Review*, June 1845), is the briefest and by some considered the best. One of Poe's chief philosophical concerns in the piece is the idea that happiness is not to be found in knowledge, but in the acquisition of knowledge–"the thirst *to know* which is for ever unquenchable within it [the soul]–since to quench it would be to extinguish the soul's self." This theme of spiritual individualism echoes "MS. Found in a Bottle," where the narrator feels "a curiosity to penetrate the mysteries of these awful regions ... hurrying onwards to some exciting knowledge...."

Somewhat earlier Poe composed one of his finest symbolic fantasies, "The Island of the Fay," a prose poem that first expounds on the dependence of perception on solitude and perspective. Then comes this key passage: "As we find cycle within cycle without end–yet all revolving around one far-distant centre which is the Godhead, may we not analogically suppose, in the same manner, life within life, the less within the greater, and all within the Spirit Divine?"–words restated at the end of *Eureka* (1848), Poe's long essay on the cosmogony of "the material and the spiritual universe." The dream vision that follows, of the fay in a fragile canoe, adds the polarity of light and dark, of life and death, as symbolic of the cyclical life process.

"Mesmeric Revelation" is both a sequel to "The Island of the Fay" and a prelude to *Eureka*. It is basic to an understanding of Poe's framework of language and ideas on matter, spirit, God, and the universe, ideas that he was to set forth in much greater detail in *Eureka*. Vankirk, a hypnotized "sleep-waker," reports from a vision of "the ultimate life" beyond the gulf. In so doing he repeats, almost verbatim, ideas Poe stated in his letters of 2 July 1844 to James Russell Lowell and of 10 July 1844 to Dr. Thomas Holley Chivers, a Georgia poet who much admired Poe's work. While under hypnosis, Vankirk states that God is the original "unparticled matter [that] not only permeates all things, but impels all things; and thus *is* all things within itself." What is called "death" is but "the painful metamorphosis" of the "rudimental" organic life into the "ultimate" inorganic, angelic life of "the nearly unlimited perception." For this essay tale, Poe drew on Chauncey Hare Townshend's *Facts in Mesmerism* (1840), which he called "one of the most truly profound and philosophical works of the day–a work to be valued properly only in a day to come."

Closely related to these works is the earlier "Eleonora" (*Gift* for 1842), the most striking example of what Poe called "the singular wrought out into the strange and mystical," as expressed in its rich imagery, subtle tonalism, structural development, and symbolism. Interpretations have ranged from the autobiographical, the ethical (the matured Eleonora absolves the narrator of his broken vow), and the idea of paradise lost and regained, to the gnostic or neo-Platonic pattern of the soul's experience.

Another arabesque called "Life in Death" (*Graham's,* April 1842) is best known by the title "The Oval Portrait," the shortened and improved version which appeared in the 26 April *Broadway Journal.* It is a brief but complex story of a painter who spends many weeks portraying his wife, young and beautiful at the outset, until he finds, to his shock, that the final touches of his brush coincide with her dying breath. The painter is "confounded, subdued, and appalled" by the "absolute *life-likeness* of expression" in the painting. What appalls him about this expression he does not say. But the omniscient narrator lets fall the clue at the very end: when the work was finished, "for one moment, the painter stood entranced . . . but in the next, while yet he gazed, he grew tremulous and very pallid, and aghast, and crying with a loud voice, 'This is indeed *Life* itself!' turned suddenly to regard his beloved:–*She was dead*!" At that moment, just before his wife's death, there was something in the painting itself that appalled him, and that something could only be her look as the dying victim of his artistic monomania (the "passionate" absorption of the "wild and moody man" in his art), for which she had come to hate him and his work. It is that realization that caused him to cry out in despair, not in triumph, even before seeing that his wife had died, for she had died less from physical causes than from being denied the right to recognition and love as a human being. The vague and shadowy setting, the painter's self-described "dreamy stupor," and the candles with which he lights his studio are suggestive of another psychic experience.

In January 1842 Virginia Poe suffered her first attack of tuberculosis, placing her health in jeopardy for years, during which Poe agonized with every relapse. In May Poe resigned the editorship at *Graham's Magazine* that he had held since April 1841. In his third essay on Nathaniel Hawthorne, for the November 1847 issue of *Godey's Lady's Book,* Poe composed a discriminating and revealing definition of originality as something more than novelty: "true originality . . . is that which, in bringing out the half-formed, the reluctant, or the unexpressed fancies of mankind, or in exciting the more delicate pulses of the heart's passion, or in giving birth to some universal sentiment or instinct in embryo, thus combines with the pleasurable effect of *apparent* novelty, a real egoistic delight," leaving the reader to feel that he and the author "have, together, created this thing." Even allegory–which is usually to be avoided–if "properly handled, judiciously subdued, seen only as a shadow or by suggestive glimpses" may fulfill the function of the tale, namely to stimulate the reader to intense, psychic excitement. Most famous of all is this definition:

> A skilful artist has constructed a tale. He has not fashioned the thoughts to accommodate his incidents, but having deliberately conceived a certain *single effect* to be wrought, he then invents such incidents, he then combines such events, and discusses them in such tone as may best serve him in establishing this preconceived effect. If his very first sentence tend not to the out-bringing of this effect, then in his very first step has he committed a blunder. In the whole composition there should be no word written of which the tendency, direct or indirect, is not to the one preestablished design. And by such means, with such care and skill, a picture is at length painted which leaves in the mind of him who contemplates it with a kindred art, a sense of the fullest satisfaction.

Taken alone, this definition may seem to relate only to rational art, in which everything is preconceived, but if taken with the definition of "true originality" above, it describes the organic nature of subconsciously determined creative art–as in the symbolic and impressionistic "tales of effect."

Of Poe's richly varied output in 1841-1842, two were comedies. In "Never Bet Your Head: A Moral Tale" (*Graham's,* September 1841; republished as "Never Bet the Devil Your Head," *Broadway Journal,* 16 August 1845) Poe created a witty burlesque of the transcendentalists. Toby Dammit, affected by a disease called "the transcendentals," insists on leaping the stile at a covered bridge. At Toby's offer "to bet the Devil his head," the Devil himself appears, to insist on a trial and "to see whether you go over it handsomely and transcendentally, and don't omit any flourishes of the pigeon-wing." In the end the "transcendentalists" refuse to pay the narrator for Toby's funeral expenses. The other humorous tale, "A Succession of Sundays" (*Saturday Evening Post,* 27 November 1841), is a situation comedy spiced with a bit of wordplay and caricature in the description of the granduncle Rumgudgeon, the "rusty, crusty, musty, fusty" curmudgeon. The story was republished as "Three Sundays in a Week" in the 10 May 1845 *Broadway Journal.*

By midsummer of 1842 two other tales of major rank had been finished. "The Masque of the Red Death" (*Graham's,* 30 April 1842) transformed what Poe knew of the bubonic plague and the Philadelphia cholera epidemics into a highly artistic Gothic fantasy symbolizing the irresponsibility of attempting to escape the realities of Life, of Time, and of Death. This work deserves the high place it holds among Poe's impressionistic tales of effect, both for its dramatic irony and its rich color symbolism. In "The Pit and the Pendulum" (*Gift* for 1843) Poe utilized the dramatic monologue for emotional intensity and psychological and "spiritual effect," improving upon his *Blackwood's* model. The popularity of this tale in Poe's time is attributed to the fact that many of his readers were familiar with its source stories, which were widely printed. Despite the rational calculations of the protagonist, this story goes beyond the tale of ratiocination in its emphasis on the hero's will to live in the face of inexorable fate (the pendulum), rewarded by a last-moment rescue. Several critics have seen the hero as existential man undergoing fear and dread, with the pit as the Void and the wall as the boundary situation of No Exit.

In late 1842 Poe finished two more tales of terror, "The Tell-Tale Heart" (*Pioneer,* January 1843) and "The Black Cat" (*Saturday Evening Post,* 19 August 1843). Along with "The Imp of the Perverse" (*Graham's,* July 1845) and "The Cask of Amontillado" (*Godey's Lady's Book,* November 1846) they comprise a group of murder tales or studies in the pathology of crime. To some ex-

tent Poe attributed such self-destructive behavior to "the imp of the perverse," but in his diagnosis of the sick society in "The Colloquy of Monos and Una," Poe noted that with the loss of Taste (sensibility) and Moral Sense consequent upon the "diseased commotion, moral and physical," disruption of the tripartite self led to acute psychic conflict. In his murder stories of the years immediately following, such conflict is dramatized as violence, sadism, and self-deception. "William Wilson" is often included in this group, being the first and clearest example of the psyche at war with itself. "The Tell-Tale Heart," a dramatic monologue, is marked by intensity of tone, "totality of impression," and psychorealism. These aspects of the story are especially noticeable in the hallucinative "tell-tale" heartbeats which drive the speaker, who has murdered an elderly man, to confess his crime. Also effective are Gothic elements such as the old man's deformed "evil eye" and the "death watch" sound the narrator hears coming from the wall: "I knew the sound well. Many a night, just at midnight, when all the world slept, it has welled up from my own bosom, deepening, with its dreadful echo, the terrors that distracted me." The "dread" of death as destiny in a universe of Nothingness or Nada adds a philosophical dimension to this tale of terror.

In "The Black Cat" a confessional narrator relives the drama of his perverse conflicts with his cats, his wife, and himself. His persistent rationalizing, masochism, and final compulsion to confess underscore the dramatic irony of his stated purpose as that of simply recounting "a series of mere household events." As the cats become the agents of retribution, so the narrator becomes his own victim: the cats project his own demonic nature and ultimate fate. Two years later Poe published "The Imp of the Perverse," in which he attributes much of human conduct to the irrational compulsion to do oneself harm. Not diabolic, this "imp" also is "occasionally known to operate in furtherance of good," as in the subconscious urge to confess in order to lighten the heavy burden of guilt. It is the telltale beating of the "heart" (the Moral Sense) that becomes louder and louder until it can no longer be ignored. Although there is no such explicit confession in "The Cask of Amontillado," which rounds out this group of tales, Montresor's narrative some fifty years after the event (he has entombed his rival, Fortunato, alive in a catacomb) suggests a desire to unburden the soul of its secret guilt. And when, after Fortunato's cries have ceased, Montresor says,

"My heart grew sick on account of the dampness of the catacombs. I hastened to make an end of my labour," the reader knows it was not only dampness that "sickened his heart." The dramatic irony in this tale so coldly told lies in the unawareness of Fortunato that he is being lured, through his own vanity and boasting, to his doom–Fortunato, whose name means both fortunate and fated, and who is described by Montresor as "rich, respected, admired, beloved; you are happy, as I once was." "The Cask of Amontillado" is "unsurpassed for subtly ironic touches . . . on its surface completely amoral, [it] is perhaps the most moral of his [Poe's] tales," Thomas Ollive Mabbott noted.

Still suffering from economic hardship, in March 1843 Poe went to Washington in search of a government job, but the search came to naught because of a drinking spree. Friends put the penniless Poe on the train for Philadelphia. In June, however, he became instantly famous when his story "The Gold Bug" won a one-hundred-dollar prize offered by the *Dollar Newspaper*. It appeared on 21 and 28 July in two installments and was often reprinted and even dramatized. In July *The Prose Romances of Edgar A. Poe*, the first of a pamphlet series, reprinted "The Murders in the Rue Morgue" (which first appeared in the April 1841 issue of *Graham's Magazine*) and "The Man That Was Used Up." During the winter months Poe lectured in several cities on poetry in America.

From 1844 to 1846 a dozen comic and satiric pieces in what Poe called "the plausible or verisimilar style" were published. Like his earlier humorous tales of the 1830s, these were popular and sold well, being either amusing or suspenseful, or both. "Raising the Wind; or Diddling Considered as One of the Exact Sciences" (*Saturday Courier*, 14 October 1843; revised as "Diddling Considered as One of the Exact Sciences," *Broadway Journal*, 13 September 1845) was so called after a London farce about a Jeremy Diddler, who made a living by petty swindles. After describing nine of the admirable qualities of the diddler, including perseverance, ingenuity, and audacity, Poe presented eleven examples of diddles, classified as simple, bold, neat, and so on, each wittily told in a lively, colloquial, concise style. "The Spectacles" (*Dollar Newspaper*, 27 March 1844), Poe's next effort, is an overlong bit of implausible comedy about a young man of weak eyesight who, refusing to wear glasses, falls "in love at first sight," not realizing until too late that he has married his great-great-grandmother, aged eighty-two. When it is revealed that he has been the object of a plot to get him to wear glasses and that he is not really married, he is free to wed the lovely Stephanie, heir to his grandmother's fortune. This happy ending, rare in Poe's fiction, does not occur in "The Oblong Box" (*Godey's Lady's Book*, September 1844), in which the artist Wyatt brings aboard ship a mysterious box, an object of great curiosity to his friend, the narrator. In an epilogue, the captain explains that the box contained not a famous painting, as had been supposed, but the corpse of Wyatt's wife, whose loss Wyatt so mourned that during a storm he lashed himself to the box and plunged to his death in the ocean. However, the Wyatt who could not go on living was the grief-stricken husband, not–as some critics would have it–Wyatt the artist overcome by "the death of a beautiful woman." In "Thou Art the Man" (*Godey's Lady's Book*, November 1844) another oblong box containing a corpse plays a key role in the surprise ending, a happy one in that justice is done. As the first comic detective story, it has been described by Howard Haycraft as "a trail-blazing tour de force" in using "the scattering of false clues by the real criminal" and "the psychological third degree."

Poe's knowledge of the mountains southwest of Charlottesville, Virginia, gave him the title and the setting for "A Tale of the Ragged Mountains" (*Godey's Lady's Book*, March 1844). In his first use of mesmerism Poe presents Augustus Bedloe's first-person account, while in a hypnotic trance, of his seeming reincarnation as a British officer named Oldeb fighting and dying in a Middle-Eastern city during an insurrection in 1780. Rather than conclude that the narrator is unreliable or that the story is a clever ratiocinative hoax, the reader would do better to invoke a "suspension of disbelief." In "The Angel of the Odd– An Extravaganza" (*Columbian Magazine*, October 1844), the most absurdly comic of all Poe's tales, the author seems to be describing himself as one of "these fellows, knowing the extravagant gullibility of the age, [who] set their wits to work in the imagination of improbable possibilities–of odd accidents." The incredibilities that follow turn out to be the Angel of the Odd's revenge on the skeptical narrator, if only in a dream after imbibing too much brandy. Another overdone satire, "The Literary Life of Thingum Bob, Esq." (*Messenger*, December 1844), showed up the pretentiousness and hypocrisy of the literary establishment of magazine editors of his day–their lack of standards and integrity, their reliance on puffery and on the jargon of praise and condemnation of fellow editors and authors.

The Poes returned to New York City in April 1844, and during the next five years Poe wrote such famous poems as "The Raven," "Ulalume," "For Annie," and "Annabel Lee." The popularity of "The Raven," which was often reprinted, parodied, and anthologized, made Poe more famous. *Graham's Magazine* for February 1845 carried James Russell Lowell's long essay-appreciation of Poe, praising him as "the most discriminating, philosophical and fearless critic upon imaginative works who has written in America." Aided by Lowell, Poe became editor of the *Broadway Journal*, for which he wrote over sixty reviews and essays, a few new stories, and in which he reprinted revised versions of his tales and poems. By fall he had, with borrowed money, bought the journal, but when it lost money, Poe, ill and depressed, stopped publication early in January 1846. In 1845, also, two volumes of his work were published: *Tales by Edgar A. Poe*, containing twelve stories selected by Evert A. Duyckinck, and, in November, *The Raven and Other Poems*.

At this time Poe wrote two tales concerned with historical perspective. In "The Thousand-and-Second Tale of Scheherazade" (*Godey's Lady's Book*, January 1845) Poe made effective use of factual wonders from various sources in continuing the adventures of Sinbad, up to the invention of the telegraph, the daguerreotype, the bustle skirt, and other marvels of the nineteenth century. In "Some Words with a Mummy" (*American Review*, April 1845) it is the Egyptian mummy, brought back to life by a galvanic battery, who not only astonishes a company of doctors and scholars by his quick comprehension but also reports the superiority of ancient science and arts, at the expense of modern technology and spurious claims for progress and democracy (which Poe equated with "mobocracy"). Here Poe also made fun of the vogue of Egyptology.

That perspective determines perception became the theme of two stories, one serious, the other comic-satiric. In "The Premature Burial" (*Dollar Newspaper*, 31 July 1844), after establishing the degree of "appalling and intolerable horror," the narrator describes his sensations while undergoing an attack of catalepsy, when "all was void, and black, and silent, and Nothing became the universe." As a result his whole outlook on life changed for the better when he ceased to

dwell on sepulchral terrors: "they must sleep, or they will devour us–they must be suffered to slumber, or we perish"–the same conclusion reached by the narrator of "The Man of the Crowd." In one of his most radical experiments with perspective, "The System of Doctor Tarr and Professor Fether" (*Graham's Magazine*, November 1845), Poe both playfully and seriously reverses the roles of patients and caretakers in a French asylum for the insane. As a result, the narrator, a visitor to the institution, is taken in by the "soothing system" then in use in England, Italy, and the United States. Critics disagree as to whether Dickens is satirized in Poe's narrator, Dickens having described visits to asylums in Boston and Hartford, one in particular: "I very much questioned within myself as I walked through the Insane Asylum, whether I should have known the attendants from the patients." More interesting is the general question of who is "sane" or "insane" and whether Poe was speaking for himself when Monsieur Maillard, the asylum's superintendent, comments that "the dexterity with which he [the lunatic] counterfeits sanity, presents, to the metaphysician, one of the most singular problems in the study of mind."

When "The Facts in the Case of M. Valdemar" (*American Review*, December 1845) appeared, mesmerism was being used, in the United States and abroad, by physicians as well as spiritualists. After his shocker became a subject of special interest, Poe responded coyly and cleverly to inquiries: "*Why* cannot a man's death be postponed indefinitely by Mesmerism? *Why* cannot a man talk after he is dead? *Why? Why?*" But a year later, he replied differently: " 'Hoax' is precisely the word suited to M. Valdemar's case." In London it was published as a pamphlet, with a preface describing it as "only a plain recital of facts, of so extraordinary a nature as almost to surpass belief." A rather implausible piece, "The Sphinx" (*Arthur's Ladies' Magazine*, January 1846) is noteworthy as an experiment in visual perspective as a source of fear and confusion.

Of Poe's famous detective stories, "The Murders in the Rue Morgue" is, if not the first of its kind, the first in which a crime is solved by analysis. The popularity of these tales Poe attributed to their being "something in a new key. . . . people think they are more ingenious than they are–on account of their method and *air* of method. In the 'Murders in the Rue Morgue,' for instance, where is the ingenuity of unraveling a web which you yourself (the author) have woven for the express purpose of unraveling?" "The Murders in the Rue Morgue" quickly became popular in the United States and by 1846 had been published in France. Although some critics have found fault with the inaccurate references to the setting in Paris, Poe was not troubled by them, nor was his translator Charles Baudelaire: "Do I need to point out that Edgar Poe never came to Paris?" The description of Dupin's domicile, his daytime dream state, his nocturnal activities, and his "abstract" trancelike quality of eyes and voice identify him as a "Bi-Part Soul," both creative and resolvent–in short, a psychotranscendental hero. In contrast to the story's narrator and the Parisian police, who are "cunning but no more," relying on measurement and direct, diligent investigation, Poe's detective, C. Auguste Dupin, trusts the half-closed eye, the sidelong glance ("by undue profundity we perplex and enfeeble thought"). All told, however, Dupin's success results from close inquiry and keen observation as well as profound intuitions.

Historically, "The Mystery of Marie Rogêt" (*Ladies' Companion*, November 1842, December 1842, February 1843) is significant as the first detective story to attempt the solution of a real crime. Otherwise, it has been regarded as too long, too involved, too discursive, and lacking in plot suspense–more of an essay analyzing a crime than a work of fiction. Poe had completed two thirds of his fictional version when new facts became known in the real murder case. At that point he felt obliged to add new matter suggesting death by abortion. In his fictional parallel about the fate of Marie, a Parisian grisette, Poe said that his purpose was to analyze "the true principles which should direct inquiry in similar cases." To Dupin "this is a far more intricate case than that of the Rue Morgue," testing his intuitive insight into "the seemingly irrelevant," the "collateral, or incidental, or accidental events," "the unlooked for and the unimagined," even the "Calculus of Probabilities"–or so he claimed. Dupin's psychological insight is shown in his speculative analysis of the murderer's state of mind.

"The Purloined Letter" (*Gift* for 1845) is, in Poe's words, "perhaps the best of my tales of ratiocination" and is the favorite of most readers as well. Immediately popular, it was among his first translated into French. Here again Dupin is presented as the seer relying on trancelike reflection, intuitive identification, sharp observation, and the clever ruse–in contrast to the "persevering, ingenious, cunning" police. Dupin is able to fathom the thoughts of the culprit, Minister D＿＿＿, because, like D＿＿＿, he is both poet and mathematician. As so-called hero-god he operates within society but outside its conventions and limits.

Though published before "The Purloined Letter," "The Gold Bug," Poe's most successful tale, also embodies a combination of deductive reasoning (the solving of the famous cryptogram), hunches, emotional intensity, and accidental circumstances. Although Poe knew Sullivan's Island and vicinity from his tenure in the army, he modified his setting for the story with romantic details, being more intent on writing a romantic mystery, a blend of fantasy and realism. Usually overlooked by critics is the fact that the story's protagonist, William Le Grand, like Dupin, is not only a rationalist but a man of "vision," "absorbed in reverie," with "deep-set eyes," at times excited to the point of apparent "madness."

In his three balloon hoaxes spanning the years 1835 to 1849, Poe put his long-standing interest in astronomy and mechanics to work. His first hoax, "Hans Phaall–A Tale" (*Messenger*, June 1835), is an account of an allegedly triumphant pioneer trip to the moon, full of human horror, terror, and suffering, and documented with plausible scientific detail. Whereas this hoax features a sustained narrative and conventional satire, the much later "The Balloon Hoax" (published by the *New York Sun* on 13 April 1844 as a one-page broadside entitled "The Extra Sun") seems to have been written mainly to appeal to the desire of the popular press to feed the public's hunger for news of actual, not just imaginary, flights. Poe relied mainly on Monck Mason's account of a real trip by balloon from London to Weilburg. And, to stir up excitement over his own story, Poe played a major role in announcing and advertising the famous first crossing of the Atlantic in Mason's Flying Machine, claiming that the air will now become "a common and convenient highway for mankind." In contrast to the incredibly sensational crises of Hans Phaall, this tale achieved credibility from its calmly objective tone and style as much as from its supposed verisimilitude.

Poe's late and last balloon story, "Mellonta Tauta" (*Godey's Lady's Book*, February 1849), is a more ambitious mixture of science fiction and social criticism. In fact, the voyage beginning on 1 April 2848 is little more than a device for futuristic criticism of blind American faith in technology, mass man (mobocracy), the "Humanity" doctrine (humanitarianism), transcendentalism, progress, bigness (which caused New York City to be destroyed in the disastrous earthquake of 2050), and "churches" for the worship of the idols Wealth and Fashion. As Republicanism degenerates into the rule of the Mob, so "democracy is a very admirable form of government–for dogs" (by analogy with the social system of prairie dogs). The story is critical of the deductive logic of Aristotle, the inductive method of Francis Bacon, the former's absurd faith in immutable axioms, and the latter's dogmatic trust in details and "facts." In contrast to these *creeping* and *crawling* modes of thought, Poe advocates the intuitive leap, as in the way Johannes Kepler *guessed*, that is, *imagined* certain laws. Except for some joking metaphors, here Poe is serious in restating his epistemological credo.

His final piece of science fiction, "Von Kempelen and His Discovery," opportunistically exploited the Gold Rush mania by means of what Poe called an "exercise" or experiment in "the plausible or verisimilar style." However, upon its publication on 14 April 1849 in the *Boston Flag of Our Union*, there was no excitement among readers. Shortly before, on 17 March 1849, "Hop-Frog: Or, the Eight Chained Orang-Outangs" appeared in the same Boston paper. Despite its being "one of Poe's great tales of horror," the reader may feel, according to Mabbott, that "the vengeance is too much for poetic justice," and that it is "notable mainly as a terrible exposition of the darkness of a human soul." But, of course, here, as elsewhere, the sensational Gothic plot must be read for its neo-Gothic "undercurrent of meaning."

In 1846, with Poe only irregularly employed, the family suffered from economic hardship, illness, and depression. At the Fordham Cottage, now their residence, Virginia died of consumption on 30 January 1847. During her final illness, Poe, with "the horrible never-ending oscillation between hope and despair," tried to drown his grief in alcohol. Despite his continuing illness, Poe produced tales, essays, reviews, and poems.

In 1848 Poe lectured on "The Poetic Principle" and *Eureka*. Now more in need of emotional security than ever, he developed romantic friendships with several women, notably Sarah Helen Whitman, Mrs. Annie Richmond, and Mrs. Elmira Shelton (formerly Sarah Elmira Royster, his former fiancée); these platonic friendships are echoed in some of the poems and letters, but not in the fiction. Poe's conditional engagement to the forty-five-year-old Mrs. Whitman was ended when he ("wisely," Mabbott thought)

called on her after drinking. Years later she published *Edgar Poe and His Critics* (1860), a sympathetic defense of Poe as person and writer. Poe's final year, 1849, was divided among lecturing, writing poetry and narrative, and visiting friends, old and new, in Philadelphia, Richmond, and Baltimore. Two months in Richmond were his happiest; there he visited Mrs. Shelton, now a widow, who apparently accepted his marriage proposal. Seemingly in fair health when leaving Richmond for New York to fetch Maria Clemm, he stopped in Baltimore and several days later, on election day, 3 October, was found "extremely ill," half conscious and delirious, outside a polling place. On 7 October he died.

Part of Poe's influence on world literature consists of his theory of the short story: in his definitions of the "tale of effect," "the tale proper," and the tale of "*single effect*," Poe laid the theoretical base for his organic concept of the story, both dramatic (as in the "The Tell-Tale Heart") and symbolic (as in "Ligeia" and "Eleonora"). Poe distinguished "the tale proper" from the novel by the former's "far more imperatively" demanding a tight *construction* of plot. This criterion was applied in Poe's tales of ratiocination in a concentrated, economical plot, climax, and denouement. Though sometimes marked by "Defoe-like detail," the Poe story is carried along psychologically by the momentum of suspense and the narrator's stream of consciousness, reflected in the mood and atmosphere of the setting. But no single definition, not even Poe's own, does justice to the variety of his short stories. When asked about "Berenice" he briefly characterized four types of tales–the grotesque, the tale of horror, the burlesque, and the arabesque, not including the detective story. As "romances," the arabesques create a unity or "totality of impression," a design comparable to musical form in the interweaving of motifs and "accompanying tones" and rhythms suited to the sense (Poe here borrowing from his theory of poetry). As a poem must be brief–not over one hundred lines–so the tale of effect must be limited to the reader's capacity for a sustained, heightened response. In these impressionistic tales Poe made the most "imperative" demands on the reader through a style powerful in feeling and mood, in hypnotic tonalities and rhythms, and in symbolic suggestiveness. Rather than "explaining away his incredibilities," Poe insisted, the author should give them "the character and the luminousness of truth," thus bringing about, "unwittingly, some of the most vivid creations of human intellect," creations which, in their dramatizing of "the agonizing consciousness of consciousness," have become the indispensable keystone to much modern psychological fiction, as Allen Tate, D. H. Lawrence, Lewis Simpson, and others have maintained.

Poe's influence may also be measured by his many admirers among creative writers, from Thomas Holley Chivers, Margaret Fuller, Hawthorne, Henry Wadsworth Longfellow, and Lowell, among Poe's American contemporaries, to his followers in France–Charles Baudelaire, Jules Verne, the Goncourts, Stéphane Mallarmé, Paul Valéry, André Gide, and many others; to Fyodor Dostoyevski, Charles Algernon Swinburne, August Strindberg, Walt Whitman (the poems), Henry James (the fiction), Robert Louis Stevenson, William Butler Yeats (the poems), Edmund Gosse, George Saintsbury, Thomas Hardy, Hamlin Garland, Ambrose Bierce, Edwin Markham, Conrad Aiken, Walter de la Mare, Edwin Arlington Robinson, George Bernard Shaw, Vachel Lindsay, D. H. Lawrence, Ezra Pound (the poems), Lafcadio Hearn, Ruben Dario, Willa Cather, W. H. Auden, Allen Tate, Richard Wilbur, Joseph Conrad, Theodore Dreiser, Vladimir Nabokov, Konstantin Balmont, James Branch Cabell, Arthur Conan Doyle, Wilkie Collins, Dorothy Sayers, Ellery Queen, and many others, in Spanish America, Germany, Italy, Spain, Hungary, Romania, Russia, Scandinavia, Japan, and China. Poe has also influenced Claude Debussy, Maurice Ravel, Sergey Rachmaninoff, Sergey Prokofiev, Jean Sibelius, and the painter René Magritte, among others. In his Nobel Prize acceptance speech Isaac Bashevis Singer said, "I found comfort in such pessimists and decadents as Baudelaire, Verlaine, Edgar Allan Poe, and Strindberg. . . . The pessimism of the creative person is not decadence but a mighty passion for redemption of man. While the poet entertains he continues to search for eternal truths, for the essence of being. In his own fashion he tries to solve the riddle of time and change, to find an answer to suffering, to reveal love in the very abyss of cruelty and injustice." This statement is especially true of Poe, who wrote, "It is only the philosophical lynxeye that, through the indignity-mist of Man's life, can still discern the dignity of Man" (*Marginalia*, June 1849).

Letters:
The Letters of Edgar Allan Poe, edited by John Ward Ostrom (Cambridge, Mass.: Harvard University Press, 1948); republished with three supplements (New York: Gordian Press, 1966); fourth supplement, *American Literature*, 45 (January 1974): 513-536.

Bibliographies:
J. Lasley Dameron and Irby B. Cauthen, Jr., *Edgar Allan Poe: A Bibliography of Criticism 1827-1967* (Charlottesville: University Press of Virginia, 1974);
Esther K. Hyneman, *Edgar Allan Poe: An Annotated Bibliography of Books and Articles in English, 1827-1973* (Boston: G. K. Hall, 1974).

Biographies:
Rufus Wilmot Griswold, "Memoir of the Author," in *The Works of the Late Edgar Allan Poe*, 4 volumes (New York: J. S. Redfield, 1850-1856), III: vii-xxxix;
Sarah Helen Whitman, *Edgar Poe and His Critics* (New York: Rudd & Carleton, 1860);
John H. Ingram, *Edgar Allan Poe: His Life, Letters and Opinions*, 2 volumes (London: John Hogg, 1880);
George Edward Woodberry, *The Life of Edgar Allan Poe, Personal and Literary*, 2 volumes (Boston: Houghton Mifflin, 1909);
Hervey Allen, *Israfel: The Life and Times of Edgar Allan Poe*, 2 volumes (New York: Doran, 1926);
Joseph Wood Krutch, *Edgar Allan Poe: A Study in Genius* (New York: Knopf, 1926);
Mary E. Phillips, *Edgar Allan Poe, the Man*, 2 volumes (Chicago: John C. Winston, 1926);
Arthur Hobson Quinn, *Edgar Allan Poe: A Critical Biography* (New York: D. Appleton-Century, 1941);
Marie Bonaparte, *The Life and Works of Edgar Allan Poe: A Psycho-analytic Interpretation*, translated by John Rodker (London: Imago, 1949);
William Bittner, *Poe: A Biography* (Boston: Little, Brown, 1962);
Sidney P. Moss, *Poe's Literary Battles: The Critic in the Context of His Literary Milieu* (Durham: Duke University Press, 1963);
Edward Wagenknecht, *Edgar Allan Poe: The Man Behind the Legend* (New York: Oxford University Press, 1963);
Thomas Ollive Mabbott, "Annals of Poe's Life," in *Collected Works of Edgar Allan Poe*, 3 volumes (Cambridge, Mass.: Belknap Press of Harvard University Press, 1969-1978), I: 527-572;

Moss, *Poe's Major Crisis: His Libel Suit and New York's Literary World* (Durham: Duke University Press, 1970);

John Carl Miller, ed., *Building Poe Biography* (Baton Rouge: Louisiana State University Press, 1977);

Wolf Mankowitz, *The Extraordinary Mr. Poe* (New York: Simon & Schuster, 1978);

Julian Symons, *The Tell-Tale Heart: The Life and Works of Edgar Allan Poe* (New York: Harper & Row, 1978);

Dwight R. Thomas, "Poe in Philadelphia, 1838-1844: A Documentary Record," Ph.D. Dissertation, University of Pennsylvania, 1978;

John Carl Miller, ed., *Poe's Helen Remembers* (Charlottesville: University Press of Virginia, 1979);

David K. Jackson and Dwight Thomas, *The Poe Log: A Documentary Life of Edgar Allan Poe, 1809-1849* (Boston: G. K. Hall, 1987).

References:

W. H. Auden, Introduction to *Edgar Allan Poe: Selected Prose and Poetry* (New York: Rinehart, 1950);

Harold Beaver, Introduction to *The Science Fiction of Edgar Allan Poe* (New York: Penguin, 1976), pp. vii-xxi;

Martin Bickman, "Animatopoeia: Morella as a Siren of the Self," *Poe Studies*, 8 (December 1975): 29-32;

Eric Carlson, "Poe's Vision of Man," in *Papers on Poe: Essays in Honor of John Ward Ostrom*, edited by Richard P. Veler (Springfield, Ohio: Chantry Music Press, 1972), pp. 7-20;

Carlson, ed., *Critical Essays on Edgar Allan Poe* (Boston: G. K. Hall, 1987);

Carlson, ed., *The Recognition of Edgar Allan Poe: Selected Criticism Since 1829* (Ann Arbor: University of Michigan Press, 1966);

Ottavio Casale, "Poe's Transcendentalism," *ESQ*, 50 (first quarter 1968): 85-97;

J. Lasley Dameron and Louis Charles Stagg, *An Index to Poe's Critical Vocabulary* (Hartford, Conn.: Transcendental Books, 1966);

Edward H. Davidson, *Poe: A Critical Study* (Cambridge, Mass.: Harvard University Press, 1957);

Joan Dayan, *Fables of Mind: An Inquiry into Poe's Fiction* (New York: Oxford University Press, 1987);

Dennis W. Eddings, *The Naiad Voice: Essays on Poe's Satiric Hoaxing* (Port Washington, N.Y.: Associated Faculty Press, 1983);

T. S. Eliot, "From Poe to Valéry," *Hudson Review*, 2 (Autumn 1949): 327-342;

Richard Finholt, "The Vision at the Brink of the Abyss," *Georgia Review*, 27 (Fall 1973): 356-366;

Roger Forclaz, *Le Monde d'Edgar Allan Poe* (Bern: Herbert Lang / Frankfurt: Peter Lang, 1974);

Forclaz, "Psychoanalysis and Edgar Allan Poe," in *Critical Essays on Edgar Allan Poe*, edited by Carlson (Boston: G. K. Hall, 1987);

David Galloway, ed., *The Other Poe: Comedies and Satires* (New York: Penguin, 1983);

James Gargano, "The Question of Poe's Narrators," *College English*, 25 (February 1963): 177-181;

Clark Griffith, "Poe and the Gothic," in *Papers on Poe*, edited by Veler (Springfield, Ohio: Chantry Music Press, 1972);

Griffith, "Poe's 'Ligeia' and the English Romantics," *University of Toronto Quarterly*, 14 (October 1954): 8-25;

David Halliburton, *Edgar Allan Poe: A Phenomenological View* (Princeton: Princeton University Press, 1973);

Howard Haycraft, *Murder for Pleasure* (New York & London: D. Appleton-Century, 1941);

Daniel Hoffman, *Poe Poe Poe Poe Poe Poe Poe* (Garden City, N.Y.: Doubleday, 1972);

Robert D. Jacobs, *Poe: Journalist & Critic* (Baton Rouge: Louisiana State University Press, 1969);

Barbara Johnson, "The Frame of Reference: Poe, Lacan, Derrida," in *Psychology and the Question of the Text: Selected Papers from the English Institute 1976-1977*, new series no. 2, edited by Geoffrey Hartman (Baltimore: Johns Hopkins University Press, 1978), pp. 149-171;

David B. Kesterson, ed., *Critics of Poe* (Coral Gables: University of Miami Press, 1973);

David Ketterer, *The Rationale of Deception in Poe* (Baton Rouge: Louisiana State University Press, 1979);

D. H. Lawrence, "Edgar Allan Poe," in *Studies in Classic American Literature* (New York: Seltzer, 1923; London: Secker, 1924);

Stuart C. Levine, *Edgar Poe: Seer and Craftsman* (De Land, Fla.: Everett/Edwards, 1972);

Kent Ljungquist, "The Short Fiction of Poe," in *Survey of Modern Fantasy Literature* (Englewood Cliffs, N.J.: Salem Press, 1983), IV: 1665-1678;

John F. Lynen, "The Death of the Present: Edgar Allan Poe," in *The Design of the Present: Essays on Time and Form in American Literature* (New Haven: Yale University Press, 1969), pp. 205-271;

Joseph J. Moldenhauer, "Murder as a Fine Art: Basic Connections between Poe's Aesthetics, Psychology, and Moral Vision," *PMLA*, 83 (May 1968): 284-297;

Stephen L. Mooney, "The Comic in Poe's Fiction," *American Literature*, 33 (January 1962): 433-441;

Mooney, "Comic Intent in Poe's Tales: Five Criteria," *Modern Language Notes*, 76 (May 1961): 432-434;

Mooney, "Poe's Gothic Waste Land," *Sewanee Review*, 70 (January-March 1962): 261-283;

John P. Muller and William J. Richardson, eds., *The Purloined Poe: Lacan, Derrida, and Psychoanalytic Reading* (Baltimore: Johns Hopkins University Press, 1988);

Burton R. Pollin, *Dictionary of Names and Titles in Poe's Collected Works* (New York: Da Capo Books, 1968);

Pollin, *Word Index to Poe's Fiction* (New York: Gordian Press, 1982);

Patrick F. Quinn, *The French Face of Edgar Allan Poe* (Carbondale: Southern Illinois University Press, 1957);

Quinn, "A Misreading of Poe's 'The Fall of the House of Usher,' " in *Critical Essays on Edgar Allan Poe*, edited by Carlson (Boston: G. K. Hall, 1987);

Claude Richard, ed., *Edgar Allan Poe: Journaliste et Critique* (Paris: Klincksieck Press, 1978);

Barton Levi St. Armand, "Usher Unveiled: Poe and the Metaphysic of Gnosticism," *Poe Studies*, 5 (June 1972): 1-8;

Donald Barlow Stauffer, "Poe as Phrenologist: The Example of Monsieur Dupin," in *Papers on Poe*, edited by Veler (Springfield, Ohio: Chantry Music Press, 1972);

Stauffer, "Style and Meaning in 'Ligeia' and 'William Wilson,' " *Style*, 1 (1967): 107-120;

Allen Tate, "The Angelic Imagination," *Kenyon Review*, 14 (Summer 1952): 455-475;

Tate, "Our Cousin, Mr. Poe," *Partisan Review*, 16 (December 1949): 1207-1219;

G. R. Thompson, *Poe's Fiction: Romantic Irony in the Gothic Tales* (Madison: University of Wisconsin Press, 1973);

Richard P. Veler, ed., *Papers on Poe: Essays in Honor of John Ward Ostrom* (Springfield, Ohio: Chantry Music Press, 1972);

John Walsh, *Poe the Detective: The Curious Circumstances Behind "The Mystery of Marie Roget"* (New Brunswick, N.J.: Rutgers University Press, 1968);

Richard Wilbur, "Eleonora," in *Critical Essays on Edgar Allan Poe*, edited by Carlson (Boston: G. K. Hall, 1987);

Wilbur, "The House of Poe," in *Anniversary Lectures 1959* (Washington, D.C.: Library of Congress, 1959);

Wilbur, Introduction and notes to *Poe: Complete Poems*, edited by Wilbur (New York: Dell, 1959);

Michael J. S. Williams, *A World of Words: Language and Displacement in the Fiction of Edgar Allan Poe* (Durham: Duke University Press, 1988).

Papers:

Significant collections of Poe's papers are located at the University of Texas (M. L. Stark Library and Humanities Research Center–the Koerster Collection); Pierpont Morgan Library, New York; Free Library of Philadelphia (the Richard Gimbel Collection); Henry E. Huntington Library and Art Gallery, San Marino, California; Indiana University (Lilly Collection); New York Public Library (Manuscript Division and the Berg Collection); University of Virginia (Ingram Collection); Enoch Pratt Free Library, Baltimore; Poe Foundation, Richmond (State Library of Virginia); Boston Public Library (Griswold Papers); Library of Congress (Ellis and Allan Papers); Columbia University Libraries; Duke University Library (Whitty Collection); Yale University, Beinecke Rare Book and Manuscript Library; also the private collection of H. Bradley Martin, New York City, which can be viewed in the Pierpont Morgan Library.

Catharine Maria Sedgwick

(28 December 1789-31 July 1867)

Laura M. Zaidman
University of South Carolina, Sumter

See also the Sedgwick entry in *DLB 1: The American Renaissance in New England.*

BOOKS: *A New-England Tale; or, Sketches of New-England Character and Manners*, anonymous (New York: Bliss & White, 1822; London: Miller, 1822); extended as *A New England Tale and Miscellanies* (New York: Putnam, 1852);

Mary Hollis. An Original Tale (New York: New York Unitarian Book Society, 1822);

Redwood; A Tale, 2 volumes (New York: Bliss & White, 1824);

The Travellers: A Tale. Designed for Young People (New York: Bliss & White, 1825);

The Deformed Boy (Brookfield: E. & G. Merriam, 1826);

Hope Leslie; or, Early Times in Massachusetts, 2 volumes (New York: White, Gallaher & White, 1827);

A Short Essay to Do Good (Stockbridge: Printed by Webster & Stanley, 1828);

Clarence; or, A Tale of Our Own Times, 2 volumes (Philadelphia: Carey & Lea, 1830; London: Colburn & Bentley, 1830; revised edition, New York: Putnam, 1849);

Home (Boston: Munroe, 1835; London: Simpkin Marshall, 1836);

The Linwoods: or, "Sixty Years Since" in America, 2 volumes (New York: Harper, 1835; London: Churton, 1835);

Tales and Sketches (Philadelphia: Carey, Lea & Blanchard, 1835);

The Poor Rich Man, and The Rich Poor Man (New York. Harper, 1836; London: Tegg, 1837);

Live and Let Live; or, Domestic Service Illustrated (New York: Harper, 1837; London: Green, 1837);

A Love Token for Children (New York: Harper, 1838);

Means and Ends; or, Self-Training (Boston: March, Capen, Lyon & Webb, 1839);

Stories for Young Persons (New York: Harper, 1841; London: Tilt & Bogue, 1841);

Catharine Maria Sedgwick (engraving of a portrait by Charles C. Ingham)

Letters from Abroad to Kindred at Home, 2 volumes (London: Moxon, 1841; New York: Harper, 1841);

Tales and Sketches. Second Series (New York: Harper, 1844);

Morals of Manners; or, Hints For Our Young People (New York: Wiley & Putnam, 1846; London: Wiley, 1846);

Facts and Fancies for School-Day Reading (New York & London: Wiley & Putnam, 1848);

The Boy of Mount Rhigi (Boston: C. H. Pierce, 1848);

Tales of City Life. I. The City Clerk. II. "Life Is Sweet" (Philadelphia: Hazard & Mitchell, 1850);

Married or Single? (1 volume, London: Knight, 1857; 2 volumes, New York: Harper, 1857);

Memoir of Joseph Curtis, a Model Man (New York: Harper, 1858).

OTHER: "Le Bossu," in *Tales of Glauber-Spa*, 2 volumes, edited by William Cullen Bryant (New York: Harper, 1832), I: 25-108;

"A Memoir of Lucretia Maria Davidson," in *Lives of Sir William Phips, Israel Putnam, Lucretia Maria Davidson, and David Rittenhouse*, in volume 7 of *The Library of American Biography*, edited by Jared Sparks (Boston: Hilliard, Gray/London: Kennett, 1837), pp. 219-294.

PERIODICAL PUBLICATIONS: "The Irish Girl," *United States Magazine and Democratic Review*, 10 (February 1842): 129-140;

"A Huguenot Family," *Godey's Lady's Book*, 25 (September 1842): 144-148, 189-193;

"Imelda of Bologna," *Columbia Lady's and Gentleman's Magazine*, 5 (1846): 253-261;

"Owasonook," *Sartain's Union Magazine*, 6 (June 1850): 399-407.

None of Catharine Maria Sedgwick's short-story collections is in print today, but from the 1820s to the 1850s she was extremely popular. In fact, she has been called the best-known American female writer before Harriet Beecher Stowe. Although in recent years feminist scholars in particular are rediscovering Sedgwick's short stories, it would be a fair assessment to say that Sedgwick's stories have not stood the test of time. Her failure to survive as a popular writer may be explained by changes in literary tastes; nevertheless, her stories are notable for their strong moral values, believable women characters, and interesting subjects. She not only wrote historical romances but also created realistic pictures of early-nineteenth-century New England society—fifty years before the rise of regionalism in America. Her best-known novel, *Hope Leslie* (1827), which depicts home life in colonial New England, helped to establish the domestic-novel subgenre.

Born in Stockbridge, Massachusetts, on 28 December 1789, Sedgwick closely identified with this region of the Berkshires throughout her life. Her descriptions of the area's natural beauty and local traditions are among the earliest attempts to set American fiction in native surroundings. Her family had lived in that area for generations. Theodore Sedgwick and Pamela Dwight Sedgwick, his second wife, raised a family of seven children, of which Catharine Maria was the sixth. Speaker of the United States House of Representatives during Washington's administration and a judge on the Massachusetts Supreme Court, her father achieved prominence and modest wealth. The family was surrounded by cultivated people. Sedgwick learned much from their intellectual discussions of literature and theology and attended boarding schools in Boston and Albany. Because her mother was often ill, she was also well trained to perform household duties. Sedgwick's fiction promotes the virtues of domesticity as well as the values of a strong family—both reflections of her personal life.

Yet Sedgwick also believed that unmarried women should be strong and independent. In a eulogy delivered on the Sunday after Sedgwick's funeral the Reverend Dr. Dewey of Stockbridge recalled that even Sedgwick's gait demonstrated a sense of independence "not often seen in a New England woman"; people noticed that she walked with "an unconventional freedom, a bearing independent of all constraint, and yet so generous and kind-hearted to all around her." Dewey also recalled that her central position in her family—as well as in literary, philanthropic, and social groups—placed many demands upon her, for she once wrote him, "My normal condition is one of fatigue."

Active in the Unitarian church, which she joined in 1821 for greater religious freedom, Sedgwick became known as a fervent religious writer. Her first novel, *A New-England Tale* (1822), began as a tract on the joys of Unitarianism compared to the spiritual restrictions of Calvinism. Greatly influenced by the Reverend William Ellery Channing, Sedgwick extolls the virtues of kindness, courtesy, honesty, and self-improvement—moral values instilled in her by her early religious training. Her stories emphasize the domestic rather than the ecclesiastical side of Sabbath worship. Sunday is a sacred day not merely because of church sermons, but mainly because of devout prayer and conversation between parents and children.

Her voluminous diaries, journals, and letters reveal the earnestness of her religious and social interests, continually sparked by the intellectual discussions of her Unitarian circle, which included the cream of Boston's intelligentsia: the Channings, the Peabodys, the Wares, and the Follens. Ann Douglas has compared this group to "an extension of a Harvard Divinity School seminar," and it provided support and literary advice. Although many of her friends were reformers, Sedgwick refused to join the Abolitionists and woman's rights supporters because she considered them too extreme.

From 1848 until her death, she was the first president of the Women's Prison Association in New York, a position indicative of her desire to improve society in a less radical way. She wrote two stories calling for improved property rights for married women, but she generally believed that in time women would gain social and political equality if they demonstrated their moral and intellectual qualities. Thus, although her fiction does not champion feminism, she remains an important spokesperson for women. While Unitarian pastors Channing and Ware inspired her writing about moral causes, the most important influences on her literary career were her brothers and sisters and their families. They inspired her many popular works, most of which can be characterized as pious stories with housewives as heroines.

In 1807 her mother died; and a year later, after her father remarried, she went to live with older siblings. After her father's death in 1813, she returned to her Stockbridge home. For most of her life she lived with her brother Charles in Lenox, Massachusetts, during the summer and with brother Robert in New York City in the winter. While extolling the roles of wife and mother in her fiction, Sedgwick rejected several marriage proposals, choosing spinsterhood (along with only about ten percent of nineteenth-century women). She deplored the stereotype of the pitiable, even laughable spinster. In her last novel, *Married or Single?* (1857), she praises a single life if it be the alternative to an unhappy marriage. In an 1854 journal entry she wrote, "I certainly think a happy marriage the happiest condition of human life"; yet "it is the high opinion of its capabilities which has perhaps kept me from adventuring in it." Her fiction stresses her belief that woman's greatest achievement is within the family, that through selfless devotion to husband and children she contributes to both her family and her community. She had extremely close relationships with her brothers and their families. Their homes were always open to her for support, guidance, and affection, and her nieces and nephews were like surrogate children. In fact, she referred to herself as the "virgin mother" of her namesake, niece Kate. In return for this closeness, her niece cared for her during several years of invalidism, and Sedgwick died of "paralysis" at seventy-seven at her niece's home in West Roxbury, Massachusetts, on 31 July 1867.

Sister Mary Michael Welsh has classified Sedgwick's longer fiction as novels–*A New-England Tale* (1822), *Redwood* (1824), *Hope Leslie* (1827), *Clarence* (1830), *The Linwoods* (1835), and *Married or Single?* (1857)–and didactic tales–*Home* (1835), *The Poor Rich Man, and The Rich Poor Man* (1836), *Live and Let Live* (1837), *Means and Ends* (1839), *Morals of Manners* (1846), and *Facts and Fancies for School-Day Reading* (1848). Some of Sedgwick's shorter tales were collected in volumes for children–*A Love Token for Children* (1838) and *Stories for Young Persons* (1841)–and for young adults–*Tales and Sketches*, first and second series (1835 and 1844). Many other stories appeared in magazines, anthologies, and annual gift books, and a few were published separately as pamphlets.

Many of Sedgwick's stories for children were intended for Sunday-school reading. The eight stories in *A Love Token for Children* all present moral lessons. Sedgwick uses allegory to impress upon children the virtues of hard work ("The Widow Ellis and her Son Willie"), religious belief ("The Magic Lamp"), and choosing right over wrong ("The Bantem" [*sic*]). "Mill-Hill" is a narrative about a young man–"reared in squalor and neglect, without any intellectual or moral training whatever"–who succumbs to the temptation of crime and dies, blaming his dreadful misfortune on his failure to be "faithful to Miss Emma's Sunday school and the lessons imparted there."

A sequel to *A Love Token, Stories for Young Persons* is a collection of a dozen short stories to teach children moral lessons such as the virtues of charity to the poor ("The Deformed Boy"), the obligation of being kind to animals ("Fanny and Her Dog Neptune"), and the importance of forgiving wrongdoing ("Jacot: An Adventure on Board the St. George"). Their didacticism and sentimentality made the book popular with adults as a gift for children. Some of these brief stories were previously published in *Juvenile Miscellany* and *Godey's Lady's Book*.

Sedgwick's historical fiction, inspired by the novels of Sir Walter Scott, led Fred Lewis Pattee to describe her as "a weaver of her native New England history and tradition into long sentimental fictions or of wild romances laid in the Pyrenees and the Apennines with heroes and villains, mad monks, revengeful queens, rescuing knights and fainting maidens superlative in beauty." Two typical sentimental fictions are "The Irish Girl" (*United States Magazine and Democratic Review*, February 1842), a plea for greater compassion toward immigrants, and "Fanny McDermott" (*Godey's Lady's Book*, January 1845; added to the 1852 edition of *A New-England Tale*), a seduction story advocating reticence. "The White Scarf" (*The Token and Atlantic Souvenir* for 1839; added to the 1852 edition of *A New-England Tale*), set in the days of Charles VI of France, typifies her "wild romances" in foreign lands.

Another story with a European setting, "Le Bossu," which at eighty-three pages might be called a novella, appeared in *Tales of Glauber-Spa* (1832), edited by William Cullen Bryant. The introduction claims that the tales were found in a deserted inn at Glauber-Spa, having been left by visitors who departed hurriedly when a case of cholera was discovered there. Actually the tales were contributed by well-known authors: Sedgwick, Robert C. Sands, James K. Paulding, William Leggett, and Bryant. Bryant later commented that Sedgwick skillfully used picturesque elements in her story to depict "the semibarbarous magnificence" of Charlemagne's court.

"Le Bossu" demonstrates how Sedgwick molded history to her didactic purposes. The title character, Charlemagne's eldest and illegitimate son Pepin, called Le Bossu because of a slight spinal deformity from an accident in his infancy, is forced to lead his soldiers in battle against his father, but refuses to kill his father when he has the chance. Le Bossu is taken prisoner but later escapes with the aid of a monk who reveals himself to be the long-lost father of Blanche of Aquitaine, Le Bossu's true love. Blanche has been raised as an orphan in the court because her nurse concealed her identity when her family was persecuted by Fastrade, Charlemagne's "crafty, cruel, and still beautiful" queen. The diabolical wiles of the queen are no match for the goodness of Blanche, described as the "ideal beauty" with "rich brown tresses" and "eyes of the deepest violet hue." The author recognizes her profuse descriptions of characters, for she begs the readers to "forgive the prolixity of our ceremony of introduction, remembering, in our behalf, that court presentations cannot be brief. . . ." Indeed, "Le Bossu" is not brief; in the end, justice finally prevails: the hero and heroine are reunited on a "celestial" little island. They become priest and priestess of a chapel that brings prosperity to the long reign of Charlemagne. The moral of this tale, briefly stated, seems to be that despite adversity the righteous will be victorious.

Among other historical tales set in Europe is "Imelda of Bologna" (*Columbian Lady's and Gentleman's Magazine*, 1846), a story with many similarities to *Romeo and Juliet*. "St. Catharine's Eve" (*The Token* and *Atlantic Souvenir* for 1835; collected in *Tales and Sketches*, 1835), which takes place at the thirteenth-century court of Philip Augustus, deals with religious persecution. This theme recurs in several other Sedgwick stories, including "A Huguenot Family" (*Godey's Lady's Book*, September 1842), set in seventeenth-century France during the Catholic church's persecution of the Protestant Huguenots.

Sedgwick also wrote many American historical tales about the Puritans, dealing with both their goodness and their religious fanaticism. "Mary Dyre" (*The Token* for 1831; collected in *Tales and Sketches*), which deals with the Puritans' expulsion of Quakers from Massachusetts, points out that " the persecuted had become the persecutors." In contrast, "A Berkshire Tradition" (added to the extended edition of *A New-England Tale*, 1852) presents a sympathetic portrait of Miss Sylvy, "a kind, warm-hearted, Puritan spinster [who] strengthens one's faith in human nature." In Sedgwick's severest indictment of the Puritans, "Owasonook" (*Sartain's Union Magazine*, June 1850), Deacon Nathan Bay is portrayed as a rigid, crafty Puritan who tries unsuccessfully to take advantage of his young ward, Jessie Blair. Sedgwick described this period in colonial history as a time when "there were no dissenters from the established doctrine and independent government of the Puritan church," and although she admitted in a letter to Swiss historian J. C. L. Simonde de Sismondi that she "unintentionally committed [a fault] in delineating the Puritans as to degrade them," she concluded that "their bigotry, their superstition, and above all their intolerance, were too apparent on the pages of history to be forgotten."

Other historical stories focus on Native Americans. "The Catholic Iroquois" (*The Atlantic Souvenir* for 1826; collected in *Tales and Sketches*) tells of the massacre of an entire settlement, pointing out that Indians felt justified in their cruelty because they were avenging the deaths of family members.

"Old Maids," first published in *The Offering. A Christmas and New Year's Present* for 1834 and collected in *Tales and Sketches*, has recently been republished in *Old Maids: Short Stories by Nineteenth Century U.S. Women Writers* (1984), edited by Susan Koppelman, who calls Sedgwick's story a

The Homestead

Certain it is these walls of our old home give out to the attentive ear of memory the harmonies of family love — the soft glad whisper of the birth-day — the merry music of the marriage-bell — the shout of joyous meeting — the sighs of parting, the noisy, idle, & yet most wise joys of childhood — the ringing gaieties of youth — the free, fearless discussions of manhood — the loving admonition of age — the funeral wail; laments! — And there we hold communion with spirits unseen "Both when we wake & when we sleep"

CM Sedgwick

Sedgwick's fair-copy contribution to Autograph Leaves of Our Country's Authors, *edited by Alexander Bliss and J. P. Kennedy (1864)*

"truly germinal work," particularly in its defense of unmarried women. Yet Koppelman's assertion that Sedgwick's stories, including "Old Maids," "claimed no purpose other than to entertain," is inaccurate. Sedgwick's didactic purpose is as obvious today as it was to her contemporaries. In an instructional dialogue between Mrs. Seton, who is happily married, and Anne, an unmarried young woman, Anne questions the wisdom of twenty-three-year-old Emily Dayton's engagement to "the most testy, frumpish, stupid man you can imagine." Emily is "perfectly independent" financially, and Anne speculates that she is marrying only to avoid becoming an old maid–that hideous stereotype of a "faded, bony, wrinkled, skinny, jaundiced" woman "whose mind has dwindled." To repudiate this myth Mrs. Seton tells about several single women. For example, Violet Flint devotedly took over household responsibilities (including nine or ten children) for her invalid sister-in-law; Sarah Lee generously shared whatever she had with her neighbors as well as taking care of young and old alike; Agnes gives up her fiancé because her younger sister and he have fallen in love. Ironically, the man becomes "unfaithful," "inconstant in his pursuits–self-indulgent, and idle, and finally intemperate, in his habits" even though Lizzy "loved him to the end." In contrast, Agnes, the old maid, has a profitable teaching career and remains devoted to her sister's happiness.

Despite Mrs. Seton's stories of admirable unmarried women who "dwell in light, the emanation of their own goodness," there is never any question that marriage is the choice recommended by Sedgwick. Mrs. Seton reaffirms society's traditional belief that marriage is "the *happiest* destiny of women." When Anne says she is half persuaded to remain single, Mrs. Seton quickly admonishes her: "No, Anne, I would by no means persuade you or any woman to *prefer* single life. It is not the primrose path . . . married life is the destiny Heaven has allotted to us." Moreover, the epigraph to the story states, "To be the mistress of some honest man's house . . . is the most creditable lot a young woman can look to. . . ." Modern readers misconstrue Sedgwick's message if they see in this story a plea for the equal status of single and married life; however, here and in her 1857 novel, *Married or Single?*, she disproves the assumptions that marriage is absolutely essential for a useful life or that women must remain adjuncts of men. In the preface to that novel she states that she seeks to elevate the single woman to a more honorable level than the vulgar, ridiculed stereotype of "old maid"; yet she refers to women as "the feebler sex."

Sedgwick's success as a novelist during the first half of the nineteenth century led to a demand for her short stories by editors of magazines and the annual gift books that were then extremely popular. In the very first volume of the first American gift book, *The Atlantic Souvenir and New Year's Offering* for 1826, Sedgwick is included with William Cullen Bryant and James Kirke Paulding in a list of contributors who are "highly distinguished in this and foreign countries by their writings."

Sedgwick's stories were featured as lead articles and were highlighted in prefaces to the annuals. Judith Fetterley has noted that popular and critical praise for Sedgwick's writing established "the right of women to the territory of American fiction." She was a trailblazer for the women who, by the 1850s, dominated the popular-fiction market. Fetterley calls Sedgwick's authorial voice "strong, clear, confident, unconflicted"; nevertheless, her short story "Cacoëthes Scribendi" suggests that she was ambivalent about her own career and about women writers in general.

First published in *The Atlantic Souvenir* for 1830 and collected in *Tales and Sketches*, "Cacoëthes Scribendi" (translated as "writer's itch," the phrase appears in the seventh *Satire* of Juvenal) has been republished in Fetterley's anthology *Provisions: A Reader from 19th Century American Women* (1985) with an excellent introduction. Twenty-five years before Hawthorne complained about the competition from the "d----d mob of scribbling women" who dominated American literature in the 1850s, Sedgwick questioned the quality of the vast outpouring of feminine prose. "Cacoëthes Scribendi" portrays a young woman and man who choose not to be writers and sev-

eral older women who delight in their newfound occupation.

Perhaps inspired by Juvenal's satire, Sedgwick's authorial persona pokes fun at the annuals, telling how Ralph Hepburn (a young man "full of good humor, kindheartedness, spirit, and intelligence") buys two of the pretty annuals for his cousin Alice Courland (a lovely seventeen-year-old, "unassuming, unostentatious, and unspoiled") when he is in Boston during "the season of the periodical inundation of annuals." Tongue in cheek, Sedgwick implies that Alice's gift books are only for show: "Ah! little did she think they were to prove Pandora's box to her. Poor simple girl! she sat down to read them, as if an annual were meant to be read, and she was honestly interested and charmed." Alice tells her mother that she delights in love stories that end in the happy marriages of faithful lovers. In fact, though they are first cousins, Ralph and Alice eventually marry. Alice becomes "the happiest of wives" and dashes her mother's and aunts' hope that she become an author.

The widowed Mrs. Courland and her sisters have the "itch to scribble." Inspired by seeing stories by childhood friends in Alice's gift books, Mrs. Courland heeds the call to become an author. She writes a story the same day she reads the annuals, presents it to her family and friends the next morning (with all applauding except Alice), sends it off to a publisher, and soon sees it gracing the pages of an annual. She writes about anything: "a sudden calamity, a death, a funeral, were fortunate events to her. . . . She wept as a woman, and exulted as an author." The "poor heroine," Alice, is "destined to be the victim of this *cacoëthes scribendi*." Everything Alice says appears in her mother's stories. A "literary fever" attacks the Courland family as Mrs. Courland convinces her unmarried sisters to write stories, too.

Alice has more sense, for she refuses to attempt the "easy writing" her mother encourages her to try. As Ralph says, "Easy writing, but hard reading." When her mother proudly shows off Alice's school composition, which has been published in an annual without Alice's permission, Alice angrily throws it into the blazing fire. Mrs. Courland also fails to persuade Ralph to become a writer; when he is forced to write, he composes a letter asking for Mrs. Courland's permission to marry Alice.

Sedgwick is critical of Mrs. Courland's lack of talent and of her allowing writing to infringe on her family life. She favors the good sense of Alice, who "fulfilled the destiny of women" by putting home and family first. Nevertheless, Sedgwick clearly states that these women without men are happy in their pursuits.

In her own life writing was not her first priority: "My *author* existence has always seemed something accidental, extraneous, and independent of my inner self. My books have been a pleasant occupation and excitement in my life. The notice, and friends, or acquaintance they have procured me, have relieved me from the danger of ennui and blue devils, that are most apt to infest a single person. But they constitute no portion of my happiness. . . ." This attitude is reflected in the satire of "Cacoëthes Scribendi."

Another writer who found fault with the annual gift books was William Cullen Bryant, who attributed their popularity to the rich, "who do not read" yet are "not generally insensible to the pleasures of show." Writing in his *United States Review*, Bryant stated that the annuals' "splendid binding, beautiful type, fine paper, and elegant engravings," as well as their "tales and poems furnished by the most popular writers," make them "a pretty object for a parlor window or a dressing table." Nevertheless, he praised Sedgwick's "well-devised adventures of imaginary persons." Poe stated in "The Literati of New York City" (*Godey's Lady's Book*, May-October 1846) that Sedgwick "has marked talent but no genius," yet he acknowledged her excellent, simple style and considerable reputation.

Sedgwick also received "very tempered praise" in Margaret Fuller's *Woman in the Nineteenth Century and Kindred Papers* (1845). In fact, Sedgwick was the only American woman writer to whom Fuller paid tribute. Although she condemned contemporary women's fiction ("flimsy," a mere "opiate"), she liked Sedgwick's freedom from sentimentality, her common sense, and her interest in history. Sedgwick's moralistic tales were praised by William Ellery Channing and Ralph Waldo Emerson, whose reviews applauded her strong Unitarian beliefs that people are inherently good and that those who use their God-given talents will lead happy lives.

Teaching good manners (the only major difference between social classes, she thought) became the central objective of Sedgwick's writing, for she believed that the similar behavior of all classes would result in a true democracy. Edward Halsey Foster believes that the great popularity of her stories with her contemporaries may be explained by "her pietistic philosophy . . . her moralized endings, her prim avoidance of everything not in most proper form and repute"; thus, her works were allowed in even "the most Puritanic parlors." Foster has called her short stories "literary exercises" that are "not especially interesting," for they are "obvious reworkings, at a minor level, of ideas she had treated in her novels and didactic tales." Several feminist scholars have attached great importance to stories such as "Old Maids" and "Cacoëthes Scribendi."

Sedgwick's roles are both as a leader in forging native subjects into a new national literature and as a transitional figure between the Gothic romance and realistic fiction. Her stories warrant attention for their believable women and realistic settings. Bridging romanticism and realism, Catharine Maria Sedgwick successfully portrayed the literary and social traditions of her society.

Biography:
Mary E. Dewey, ed., *Life and Letters of Catharine M. Sedgwick* (New York: Harper, 1871).

References:
Gladys Brooks, *Three Wise Virgins* (New York: Dutton, 1957);

Ann Douglas, *The Feminization of American Culture* (New York: Knopf, 1977);

Edward Halsey Foster, *Catharine Maria Sedgwick* (New York: Twayne, 1974);

Mary Kelley, "A Woman Alone: Catharine Maria Sedgwick's Spinsterhood in Nineteenth-Century America," *New England Quarterly*, 51 (June 1978): 209-225;

Fred Lewis Pattee, *The First Century of American Literature, 1770-1870* (New York & London: Appleton, 1935);

Sister Mary Michael Welsh, *Catharine Maria Sedgwick: Her Position in the Literature and Thought of Her Time up to 1860* (Washington, D.C.: Catholic University of America, 1937).

Papers:
Sedgwick's letters, diaries, and journals are deposited at the library of the Massachusetts Historical Society in Boston.

Harriet Prescott Spofford

(3 April 1835-14 August 1921)

Thelma J. Shinn
Arizona State University

BOOKS: *Sir Rohan's Ghost. A Romance* (Boston: Tilton, 1860);

The Amber Gods and Other Stories (Boston: Ticknor & Fields, 1863);

Azarian: An Episode (Boston: Ticknor & Fields, 1864);

New-England Legends (Boston: Osgood, 1871);

The Thief in the Night (Boston: Roberts, 1872; London: Low, 1872);

Art Decoration Applied to Furniture (New York: Harper, 1878);

The Servant Girl Question (Boston: Houghton, Mifflin, 1881);

Poems (Boston: Houghton, Mifflin, 1882);

The Marquis of Carabas (Boston: Roberts, 1882);

Hester Stanley at St. Marks (Boston: Roberts, 1882);

Ballads about Authors (Boston: Lothrop, 1887);

A Lost Jewel (Boston: Lee & Shepard, 1891);

House and Hearth (New York: Dodd, Mead, 1891);

A Scarlet Poppy and Other Stories (New York: Harper, 1894);

A Master Spirit (New York: Scribners, 1896);

An Inheritance (New York: Scribners, 1897);

In Titian's Garden and Other Poems (Boston: Copeland & Day, 1897);

Stepping-Stones to Happiness (New York: Christian Herald, 1897);

Priscilla's Love-Story (Chicago & New York: Stone, 1898);

Hester Stanley's Friends (Boston: Little, Brown, 1898);

The Maid He Married (Chicago & New York: Stone, 1899);

Old Madame & Other Tragedies (Boston: Badger, 1900);

The Children of the Valley (New York: Crowell, 1901);

The Great Procession and other Verses for and about Children (Boston: Badger, 1902);

That Betty (New York, Chicago, Toronto, London & Edinburgh: Revell, 1903);

Four Days of God (Boston: Badger, 1905);

Old Washington (Boston: Little, Brown, 1906);

Harriet Prescott Spofford

The Fairy Changeling. A Flower and Fairy Play (Boston: Badger, 1911);

The Making of a Fortune. A Romance (New York & London: Harper, 1911);

The King's Easter (Boston: World Peace Foundation, 1912);

A Little Book of Friends (Boston: Little, Brown, 1916);

The Elder's People (Boston & New York: Houghton Mifflin, 1920).

OTHER: "Priscilla," in *Three Heroines of New England Romance* (Boston: Little, Brown, 1894), pp. 15-60.

PERIODICAL PUBLICATIONS: "Six by Seven," *Knickerbocker*, 55 (January 1860): 17-36;

"Yet's Christmas Box," *Harper's New Monthly Magazine*, 20 (April 1860): 644-659;

"Fauntleroy Verrian's Fate," *Knickerbocker*, 57 (January 1861): 57-70; (February 1861): 186-194; (March 1861): 278-285; (April 1861): 388-398; (May 1861): 465-474;

"How Charlie Came Home," *Harper's New Monthly Magazine*, 22 (January 1861): 186-198;

"The Tale of the Trefetheness," *Harper's New Monthly Magazine*, 22 (March 1861): 489-512;

"Vallandigham," *Harper's New Monthly Magazine*, 23 (September 1861): 468-485;

"Madeleine Schaeffer," *Harper's New Monthly Magazine*, 25 (June 1862): 37-52; (October 1862): 651-660; (November 1862): 753-764;

"The Strathsays," *Atlantic Monthly*, 11 (January 1863): 99-118;

"The Dark Ways," *Atlantic Monthly*, 11 (May 1863): 545-565;

"Rosemary," *Harper's New Monthly Magazine*, 26 (May 1863): 803-809; 27 (June 1863): 41-52; (July 1863): 195-200;

"Fiery Colliery of Fiennes," *Harper's New Monthly Magazine*, 27 (October 1863): 613-627;

"Ray," *Atlantic Monthly*, 13 (January 1864): 19-39;

"Our Bridget," *Harper's New Monthly Magazine*, 28 (February 1864): 388-395;

"The Rim," *Atlantic Monthly*, 13 (May 1864): 605-615; (June 1864): 701-713; 14 (July 1864): 63-73;

"Sold for a Song," *Harper's New Monthly Magazine*, 28 (May 1864): 745-752;

"Mrs. Gisborne's Way," *Harper's New Monthly Magazine*, 29 (October 1864): 585-594;

"The True Story of Luigi," *Atlantic Monthly*, 14 (October 1864): 411-423;

"On the Way to the Diamond Mines," *Harper's New Monthly Magazine*, 29 (November 1864): 724-734;

"Mrs. Buswell's Christmas," *Harper's Weekly*, 8 (31 December 1864): 842-843;

"The Portrait," *Our Young Folks*, 1 (February 1865): 85-93;

"Poor Isabel," *Harper's New Monthly Magazine*, 30 (March 1865): 469-475;

"Mr. Furbush," *Harper's New Monthly Magazine*, 30 (April 1865): 623-626;

"Out of Prison," *Harper's New Monthly Magazine*, 31 (July 1865): 215-222;

"Down the River," *Atlantic Monthly*, 16 (October 1865): 468-490;

"A Mad Night," *Beadle's Monthly*, 1 (February 1866): 160-167; (March 1866): 235-242;

"An Hour at Sea," *Harper's New Monthly Magazine*, 33 (July 1866): 250-254;

"D'Outre Mort," *Galaxy*, 2 (15 November 1866): 516-529;

"The Marshes," *Harper's New Monthly Magazine*, 35 (June 1867): 94-107;

"A Pleasant Morning," *Harper's New Monthly Magazine*, 35 (September 1867): 450-453;

"The Hungry Heart," *Harper's New Monthly Magazine*, 35 (November 1867): 740-748;

"Elisabetta's Christmas," *Galaxy*, 5 (January 1868): 60-77;

"Flotsam and Jetsam," *Atlantic Monthly*, 21 (January 1868): 7-16; (February 1868): 186-198; (March 1868): 313-325;

"The Black Bess," *Galaxy*, 5 (May 1868): 517-528;

"The Spanish Lace," *Harper's Bazar*, 1 (9 May 1868): 442-443;

"The Strange Passengers," *Lippincott's Magazine*, 1 (June 1868): 647-657;

"Arabella and Her Bonnet," *Harper's Bazar*, 1 (1 August 1868): 630-631;

"In the Maguerriwock," *Harper's New Monthly Magazine*, 37 (August 1868): 348-355;

"Lost and Found," *Atlantic Monthly*, 22 (August 1868): 243-251;

"A Ride in the Dark," *Harper's Bazar*, 1 (15 August 1868): 662-663;

"The Hazel-Nut Pearls," *Harper's Bazar*, 1 (19 September 1868): 742-743;

"The Moonstone Mass," *Harper's New Monthly Magazine*, 37 (October 1868): 655-661;

Aunt Lenore's Burglar," *Harper's Bazar*, 1 (17 October 1868): 810-811;

"One of the Thanksgivings," *Harper's Bazar*, 1 (12 December 1868): 934-935;

"Ben's Turkey," *Harper's Bazar*, 2 (2 January 1869): 6-7;

"The Insurance on the 'Highflyer,' " *Harper's New Monthly Magazine*, 38 (February 1869): 397-405;

"The Magnetic Patient," *Harper's Bazar*, 2 (20 February 1869): 118-119;

"The Unknown Guest," *Lady's Friend*, 6 (February 1869): 116-121;

"The Miracle of the Dice: A True Story," *Lady's Friend*, 6 (April 1869): 266-272;

"Rougegorge," *Lippincott's Magazine*, 3 (May 1869): 501-516;

"An Arrest," *Lady's Friend,* 7 (July 1870): 433-437;

"Our House Warming," *Harper's Bazar,* 3 (30 July 1870): 486-487;

"Two Hearts," *Harper's New Monthly Magazine,* 41 (August 1870): 374-383;

"Little Ben," *Atlantic Monthly,* 26 (September 1870): 309-321;

"A Pilot's Wife," *Harper's New Monthly Magazine,* 41 (November 1870): 860-868;

"Louie," *Lippincott's Magazine,* 6 (December 1870): 589-604;

"A Beautiful Idiot," *Harper's Bazar,* 4 (21 January 1871): 38-39;

"Miss Moggaridge's Provider," *Atlantic Monthly,* 27 (January 1871): 17-27;

"Footpads," *Atlantic Monthly,* 27 (April 1871): 401-413;

"Giulia," *Aldine,* 4 (April 1871): 65-67;

"The Brocade," *Harper's Bazar,* 4 (10 June 1871): 362-363;

"The Old Plum-Tree," *Harper's Bazar,* 4 (1 July 1871): 406-407;

"Miss Phippeny's Heir," *Harper's Bazar,* 4 (16 September 1871): 582-583;

"Maud's Mishaps," *Harper's Bazar,* 4 (4 November 1871): 694;

"Bella's Beginnings," *Harper's New Monthly Magazine,* 44 (December 1871): 113-118;

"Royal's Raffle," *Harper's Bazar,* 5 (20 January 1872): 50-51;

"Wedding Presents," *Harper's New Monthly Magazine,* 44 (February 1872): 441-447;

"Mrs. Grey's Two Dreams," *Harper's Bazar,* 5 (9 March 1872): 174-175;

"A Rose," *Harper's Bazar,* 5 (27 April 1872): 286-287;

"Mr. Sutherland's Sickness," *Harper's Bazar,* 5 (11 May 1872): 322-323;

"Aunt Pen's Funeral," *Harper's New Monthly Magazine,* 45 (June 1872): 60-64;

"At Rye," *Harper's Bazar,* 5 (21 September 1872): 626-627;

"Thanksgiving at the Big Rock," *Harper's Bazar,* 5 (7 December 1872): 802-803;

"Rapall's New-Year," *Harper's Bazar,* 6 (11 January 1873): 26-27;

"Lilian's Life," *Harper's Bazar,* 6 (22 March 1873): 186-187; .

"Adelaide," *Harper's Bazar,* 6 (17 May 1873): 314-315;

"The Beautiful Miss Vavasour," *Harper's New Monthly Magazine,* 46 (May 1873): 852-858;

"Rosy's Wedding Portion," *Harper's Bazar,* 6 (31 May 1873): 346-347;

"Ebb and Flow," *Harper's New Monthly Magazine,* 47 (June 1873): 121-126;

"Honora," *Harper's Weekly,* 17 (19 July 1873): 626-627;

"Old Margaret's Boy," *Harper's Bazar,* 6 (19 July 1873): 454-455;

"By-and-By," *Harper's Bazar,* 6 (27 September 1873): 618-619;

"Anstice's Thanksgiving," *Harper's Bazar,* 6 (6 December 1873): 778;

"Delgrado," *Harper's New Monthly Magazine,* 48 (December 1873): 98-104;

"Mrs. Eccleby's Economy," *Harper's Bazar,* 7 (24 January 1874): 66-67;

"Jo and I," *Harper's New Monthly Magazine,* 48 (March 1874): 562-572;

"Rosamund and Her Lovers," *Harper's Weekly,* 18 (7 March 1874): 214;

"A Stroke of Luck," *Harper's Bazar,* 6 (28 March 1874): 206-207;

"Our Ball Dresses," *Harper's Bazar,* 6 (11 April 1874): 238;

"At Last," *Scribner's Monthly,* 8 (May 1874): 90-99;

"Mrs. Rothely's Emeralds," *Harper's Bazar,* 7 (4 July 1874): 434-435;

"Aunt Magruder's Management," *Harper's Bazar,* 7 (1 August 1874): 494-495;

"The New Carpet," *Harper's Bazar,* 7 (29 August 1874): 562-563;

"A Sequestered Letter," *Harper's Bazar,* 7 (26 September 1874): 626-627;

"Sunshine," *Harper's Bazar,* 7 (24 October 1874): 690-691;

"The Wedding Morning," *Harper's Bazar,* 7 (19 December 1874): 834-835;

"The Campaign of the Calico," *Harper's Bazar,* 8 (23 January 1875): 62;

"Playing with Fire," *Lippincott's Magazine,* 15 (March 1875): 357-370;

"Striking Silver," *Harper's Bazar,* 8 (6 March 1875): 162-163;

"Miss Desmond," *Harper's Bazar,* 8 (20 March 1875): 194-195;

"A Lion in the Way," *Harper's New Monthly Magazine,* 50 (April 1875): 722-727;

"Mrs. Penrhyn's Trip," *Harper's Bazar,* 8 (12 June 1875): 382-383;

"A Last Card," *Harper's Weekly,* 19 (26 June 1875): 518-519;

"Two Sides to a Bureau," *Harper's Bazar,* 8 (24 July 1875): 478-479;

"An Apple of Sodom," *Harper's New Monthly Magazine*, 51 (August 1875): 384-391;

"The Little Black Fiddle," *Harper's Bazar*, 8 (7 August 1875): 514;

"One of Them," *Harper's Bazar*, 8 (28 August 1875): 562-563;

"Arneld and His Violin," *St. Nicholas*, 3 (November 1875): 17-20;

"A Christmas Gift," *Harper's Bazar*, 8 (25 December 1875): 834-835;

"One New Year in a Thousand," *Harper's Bazar*, 9 (8 January 1876): 26-27;

"A Little Brimstone," *Harper's Bazar*, 9 (29 January 1876): 70-71;

"Rats," *Harper's New Monthly Magazine*, 52 (May 1876): 888-892;

"Miss Susan's Love Affair," *Harper's New Monthly Magazine*, 53 (June 1876): 26-32;

"The Little People's New Year," *Harper's New Monthly Magazine*, 54 (January 1877): 284-290;

"Romance of a Barn-Yard," *Harper's New Monthly Magazine*, 54 (February 1877): 446-448;

"In A Storm," *Harper's New Monthly Magazine*, 57 (June 1878): 108-113;

"The Boy Astronomer," *St. Nicholas*, 6 (April 1879): 378-383; (May 1879): 441-444;

"The Drift-Wood Fire," *Harper's New Monthly Magazine*, 61 (November 1880): 888-893;

"Halcyon Days," *Harper's Bazar*, 15 (21 January 1882): 42-43;

"By the Winter's Moon," *Harper's New Monthly Magazine*, 64 (February 1882): 392-398;

"A Little Aesthete," *Harper's Bazar*, 15 (4 March 1882): 135;

"Miss Wildrose," *Our Continent*, 1 (8 March 1882): 52;

"Miss Mary Dunlap," *Harper's Bazar*, 15 (29 April 1882): 263;

"Rose in Bloom," *Our Continent*, 2 (19 July 1882): 45-48;

"Rock Creek Church," *Harper's Bazar*, 15 (29 July 1882): 470-471;

"Two Missionaries," *Harper's Bazar*, 15 (16 September 1882): 582-583;

"Fire and Snow," *Our Continent*, 2 (20 September 1882): 332-333;

"An All-Hallowe'en," *Harper's Bazar*, 15 (11 November 1882): 710-711;

"The Colonel," *Continent*, 3 (11 April 1883): 459-461;

"A Dead Man's Shoes," *Harper's Bazar*, 16 (2 June 1883): 342-343;

"The Mount of Sorrow," *Harper's New Monthly Magazine*, 67 (June 1883): 623-626;

"A Coincidence," *Harper's Bazar*, 16 (11 August 1883): 502-503;

"The Little Pulsifer," *Harper's Bazar*, 16 (6 October 1883): 630-631;

"Olivia," *Swinton's Story-Teller*, 10 October 1883;

"Something to be Thankful For," *Swinton's Story-Teller*, 28 November 1883;

"Mrs. Severance's Trip Over," *Harper's Bazar*, 17 (26 January 1884): 58-59;

"Transformation," *Manhattan*, 3 (February 1884): 115-122; (March 1884): 206-212;

"The Day of the Month," *Harper's Bazar*, 17 (15 March 1884): 167;

"At The Princess Ida's," *Lippincott's Magazine*, 34 (July 1884): 50-58;

"Aunt Magillop's Tea-Cups," *Harper's Bazar*, 17 (16 August 1884): 522-523;

"Three Quiet Ladies of the Name of Luce," *Harper's New Monthly Magazine*, 69 (November 1884): 887-892;

"Malgre Lui," *Harper's Bazar*, 17 (15 November 1884): 730-731;

"The 'Countess Nina,'" *Harper's Young People*, 6 (9 December 1884): 88-91;

"Under the Mistletoe," *Harper's Weekly*, 28 (13 December 1884): 828-829;

"An Angel in Disguise," *Harper's Bazar*, 18 (31 January 1885): 83-84;

"Mrs. Wybert's Daughter," *Harper's Bazar*, 18 (9 May 1885): 302-303;

"A Breakfast Dish," *Harper's Bazar*, 18 (8 August 1885): 510-511;

"Louise and Her Lover," *Harper's Bazar*, 18 (5 December 1885): 786-787;

"Mrs. Hetty's Husband," *Cosmopolitan*, 1 (May 1886): 135-142;

"Under the Mistletoe," *Cosmopolitan*, 2 (December 1886): 201-208;

"One Whole Day," *Harper's Bazar*, 20 (1 January 1887): 6-7;

"The Freshet," *Harper's Bazar*, 20 (23 April 1887): 299;

"Mr. Poindexter," *Harper's Bazar*, 20 (30 July 1887): 538-539;

"Uncle Mason's Money," *Cosmopolitan*, 4 (September 1887): 15-27;

"A Royal Cat's Eye," *Harper's Bazar*, 20 (1 October 1887): 682-683;

"The Pretty Spendthrifts," *Cosmopolitan*, 4 (November 1887): 244-253;

"Two Gentlemen from Spain," *Harper's Bazar*, 20 (10 December 1887): 858;

"Elizabeth," *Boston Transcript*, 24 December 1887;

"The Old Year Out and the New Year In," *Harper's Bazar*, 21 (7 January 1888): 10-11;

"A Little Brown Witch," *Boston Transcript*, 25 February 1888;

"Little Rosalie," *St. Nicholas*, 15 (May 1888): 494-501;

"The Brathwaite Ghost," *Harper's Bazar*, 21 (25 August 1888): 562-563;

"My Jo," *Harper's Bazar*, 22 (19 January 1889): 46-47;

"A Saint's Halo," *Harper's Bazar*, 22 (20 April 1889): 290-291, 297;

"The Willoughby Baby," *Harper's Bazar*, 22 (13 July 1889): 514-515;

"The Doctor's Thanksgiving," *Harper's Bazar*, 22 (7 December 1889): 887-888;

"A New-Year's Banquet," *Harper's Bazar*, 23 (4 January 1890): 10-11;

"An Easter Bridal," *Harper's Bazar*, 23 (19 April 1890): 289, 293-294;

"Hester's Love Story," *Housewife*, 6 (May 1890): 1-2, 14; (June 1890): 1-2, 5 (July 1890): 16;

"Wise Pietro," *Harper's Bazar*, 23 (7 June 1890): 450-451;

"Christmas That Was Christmas," *Harper's Young People*, 12 (2 December 1890): 74-79;

"At the Symphony," *Harper's Bazar*, 24 (10 January 1891): 26-27;

"Grandma'am," *Harper's Bazar*, 24 (11 April 1891): 286-287;

"A Jar of Pot Pourri," *Harper's Young People*, 12 (7 July 1891): 599-601;

"The Stars and Stripes," *Harper's Bazar*, 24 (18 July 1891): 554-555;

"A Quarrel," *Harper's Bazar*, 24 (24 October 1891): 814-815;

"The People of the Water House," *Harper's Young People*, 13 (23 February 1892): 290;

"The Twenty-Ninth of February," *Harper's Bazar*, 25 (27 February 1892): 165-167;

"Beyond the Horizon," *Harper's Bazar*, 25 (9 April 1892): 290-291;

"A Taste of the World," *Harper's Bazar*, 25 (23 July 1892): 597-599;

"Tom's Way of Getting There," *Harper's Young People*, 13 (9 August 1892): 689-690;

"Christmas-Tide at Old Benbow," *Harper's Young People*, 14 (6 December 1892): 100-105;

"A Merry Christmas," *Harper's Bazar*, 25 (24 December 1892): 1049-1051;

"Priscilla's Love-Story," *Harper's Bazar*, 26 (18 Feb-

Engraving of Spofford as a young woman

ruary 1893): 126-127; (25 February 1893): 150-151; (4 March 1893): 166-167;

"Angela," *Harper's Bazar*, 26 (26 August 1893): 698-699;

"A Watch in the Night," *Harper's New Monthly Magazine*, 88 (December 1893): 147-152;

"Jesse," *Harper's Bazar*, 27 (26 May 1894): 422-423;

"Elizabeth's Charities," *Harper's Bazar*, 28 (5 January 1895): 6-7;

"Serena's Mourning," *Independent*, 47 (17 January 1895): 94-95;

"Jule's Garden," *Harper's Young People*, 16 (12 March 1895): 333-335;

"At the Menagerie," *Independent*, 47 (28 March 1895): 424;

"An Easter Gift," *Harper's Bazar*, 28 (6 April 1895): 269-270;

"A Career," *Harper's Bazar*, 28 (3 August 1895): 622-623;

"A Christmas Revel," *Harper's Bazar*, 28 (21 December 1895): 1049-1050;

"A Suffering Saint," *New Orleans Times Democrat*, 9 February 1896, p. 14;

"The Godmothers," *Cosmopolitan*, 20 (March 1896): 461-471;

"A Piece of Pasture," *Independent*, 48 (7 May 1896): 638-639;

"A Tea-Rose," *Harper's Bazar*, 29 (22 August 1896): 707, 718-719;

"In the Time of the Sweetbriar," *McClure's Magazine*, 7 (September 1896): 305-311;

"Book-Larnin'," *Harper's Bazar*, 29 (7 November 1896): 930-931;

"Up in Maine," *Harper's Bazar*, 29 (21 November 1896): 983-984;

"A Perpetual Thanksgiving," *Independent*, 48 (26 November 1896): 1621-1623;

"The Match-Makers," *Harper's Bazar*, 30 (20 March 1897): 237-239;

"Before a Fall," *Harper's Bazar*, 31 (19 February 1898): 157-159;

"Talking it Over," *Harper's Bazar*, 31 (17 September 1898): 798-799;

"Mrs. Derlar's Reasons for Thanksgiving," *Independent*, 50 (24 November 1898): 1473-1478;

"Mr. Mountjoy's Christmas Gift," *Harper's Bazar*, 31 (17 December 1898): 1088-1090;

"The Nemesis of Motherhood," *Cosmopolitan*, 26 (April 1899): 692-696;

"Thanksgiving Indeed," *Independent*, 51 (30 November 1899): 3223-3226;

"Christmas Bells," *Independent*, 51 (21 December 1899): 3420-3425;

"Paquito," *Harper's Bazar*, 33 (30 June 1900): 535-540;

"Mrs. Varney's Freedom," *Harper's Bazar*, 33 (11 August 1900): 918-924;

"The Conquering Will," *Smart Set*, 4 (June 1901): 109-115;

"Betty and Thanksgiving," *Independent*, 53 (28 November 1901): 2825-2829;

"A Case of Nerves," *Harper's New Monthly Magazine*, 104 (December 1901): 61-65;

"Clarice," *Harper's Bazar*, 36 (January 1902): 15-19;

"The Birthday," *Outlook*, 70 (1 March 1902): 581-585;

"Sereny," *Frank Leslie's Popular Monthly*, 54 (August 1902): 344-351;

"An Idyll of a Summer Night," *Independent*, 54 (21 August 1902): 2006-2010;

"His Mother's New Year," *Independent*, 55 (8 January 1903): 84-87;

"A Sacrifice," *Atlantic Monthly*, 91 (May 1903): 616-626;

"An Angel in the House," *Harper's New Monthly Magazine*, 107 (June 1903): 78-82;

"The Ray of Displacement," *Metropolitan*, 19 (October 1903): 37-47;

"The Story of the Queen," *Atlantic Monthly*, 92 (November 1903): 586-594; (December 1903): 775-786;

"Dr. Lloyd's Christmas Gift," *Delineator*, 62 (December 1903): 881-885;

"Mrs. Bassett and the Wedding," *Woman's Home Companion*, 31 (August 1904): 3-4, 27;

"Miss Virginia's Christmas," *Harper's Weekly*, 49 (16 December 1905): 34-38;

"The Sparrow-Hawk," *Delineator*, 68 (November 1906): 790-793;

"Jolly's Father," *Harper's Monthly Magazine*, 115 (October 1907): 761-770;

"Two in a Garden: An Interlude," *Harper's Bazar*, 42 (June 1908): 552-556;

"Zoe's Masterpiece," *Harper's Bazar*, 43 (August 1909): 795-800;

"Miss Melissa's Miracle," *Outlook*, 94 (26 March 1910): 720-725;

"The Emperor and the Baby," *Strand Magazine* (London), 40 (October 1910): 406-410;

"Cap'n Tom's Christmas Supper," *Outlook*, 96 (26 November 1910): 675-681;

"An Easter Blessing," *Outlook*, 97 (15 April 1911): 822-826;

"The Weaver of Spells," *Century Magazine*, 60 (September 1911): 635-642;

"A Question," *Bellman*, 11 (28 October 1911): 553-556;

"The Rose," *Harper's Monthly Magazine*, 105 (October 1912): 739-744;

"Billy's Christmas Angel," *Bellman*, 13 (14 December 1912): 765-766;

"A Christmas Blessing," *Lippincott's Monthly Magazine*, 90 (December 1912): 710-717;

"A Christmas Eve Happening," *Harper's Weekly*, 56 (14 December 1912): 24;

"Nancy's Southern Christmas," *St. Nicholas*, 40 (December 1912): 161-164;

"Miss Clementine's Christmas Present," *Harper's Bazar*, 47 (January 1913): 11-12;

"A Fortune in a Flower," *St. Nicholas*, 40 (May 1913): 592-596;

"Mr. Castle's Fortunate Christmas Eve," *Bellman*, 15 (6 December 1913): 728-729;

"A Homely Sacrifice," *Harper's Monthly Magazine*, 129 (November 1914): 853-860;

"The Mad Lady," *Scribner's Magazine*, 59 (February 1916): 238-245;

"Miss Diantha's Divorce Case," *Ladies' Home Journal*, 33 (September 1916): 14, 68.

Beginning her long writing career toward the end of Nathaniel Hawthorne's and producing her last book in the same year that saw the publication of F. Scott Fitzgerald's first, Harriet Prescott Spofford was inevitably buffeted by the winds of literary change. Initially admired for her romantic color, she was soon condemned for such "fatal fluency" and finally praised for her stark portraits of New England natives in *The Elder's People* (1920). Yet Spofford's style did not evolve as much as the attitudes of her critics and publishers; both realistic stories and romantic tales can already be found in her first collection, *The Amber Gods and Other Stories* (1863). Seldom do her stories lack the texture of careful research and observed reality whether she is imagining the streets and cataloguing the wines of a Paris she had never seen or recalling the villages and people of her native New England. The real evolution in Spofford's fiction lies instead in her observations of daily life for turn-of-the-century women, and her stylistic importance lies in her revelation of those lives through domestic imagery. Yet the young Henry James criticized both. In his critique of *The Amber Gods and Other Stories* for the *North American Review* (October 1863) James labeled her frequent attention to "illicit love" as "a grave artistic fault," while his review of her novel *Azarian: An Episode* (1864) for the same magazine in January 1865 criticized her possession of "the fatal gift of fluency," which he saw her sharing with "the majority of female writers–Mrs. Browning, George Sand, Gail Hamilton, Mrs. Stowe."

The eldest of the five children of Joseph Newmarch Prescott and Sarah Jane Bridges Prescott, Harriet Elizabeth Prescott was born in Calais, Maine. In 1849, when her father left for Oregon hoping to make a fortune, her mother took the children to live in Newburyport, Massachusetts. She studied for four years at the Putnam Free School in Newburyport and then attended Pinkerton Academy in Derry, New Hampshire (1853-1855). Spofford's literary interests in both puritan realities and romantic possibilities arise naturally from her New England heritage. William Dean Howells in his *Literary Friends and Acquaintance* (1900) attributes her romanticism to "the pathos of revolt from the colorless rigidities which are the long result of puritanism in the physiognomy of New England life." Her insights into the lives of women must have been enhanced by

an extended family circle which often included under one roof her grandmother and four aunts as well as her mother, three younger sisters and a brother.

Her father had never been successful financially, and his hopes of earning wealth in Oregon while the women supported each other through teaching and running a boarding house resulted only in his returning to Newburyport an invalid by 1856. Barely in her twenties, Harriet Prescott began writing to support her parents and younger siblings.

These early money-making ventures were published anonymously in Boston family story papers and were never collected or acknowledged later. Her literary career officially began with the appearance of "In A Cellar" (collected in *The Amber Gods and Other Stories*) in the February 1859 issue of the *Atlantic Monthly*. Vividly tracking a stolen diamond and uncovering European intrigues, the romantic tale provides such realistic pictures of Paris that *Atlantic* editor James Russell Lowell called in Thomas Wentworth Higginson to convince the *Atlantic* staff that "a demure little Yankee girl could have written it," as Higginson records in his *Letters and Journals of Thomas Wentworth Higginson* (1921). *Atlantic* publication earned Harriet Prescott acquaintance with the New England literary elite of her time, including Lowell, John Greenleaf Whittier, Oliver Wendell Holmes, Henry Wadsworth Longfellow, and Harriet Beecher Stowe, among others. In the next few years she would also meet Howells and Hawthorne, and her future husband, Richard S. Spofford, Jr.

Having published *The Amber Gods and Other Stories* and two book-length romances before she married Spofford on 19 December 1865, Prescott had already gained recognition and criticism for her literary individuality. In her first short-story collection "Circumstance" (*Atlantic Monthly*, May 1860), "Knitting Sale-Socks" (*Atlantic Monthly*, February 1861), and "The South Breaker" (*Atlantic Monthly*, May and June 1862) offer realistic depictions of New England life. "Circumstance" is in fact based on a true incident in Prescott family history; yet Emily Dickinson is reported by Martha Dickinson Bianchi in *Emily Dickinson Face to Face* (1932) to have told Austin Dickinson's wife, Sue, that "it is the only thing I ever read in my life that I didn't think I could have imagined myself!"

Already in "Circumstance" can be seen Spofford's attention to the lives of women and her portrayal of those lives through domestic imagery. Here musical images provide structure, as a young woman postpones an animal's attack by singing, tracing her own life in the songs she chooses. Equally rooted in female experience are the metaphors which define the contrasting characters of Yone and Lu in the collection's title story. A romantic tale offered from the point of view of the passionate–but dead–Yone, "The Amber Gods" (*Atlantic Monthly*, January and February 1860) employs jewelry and fabric as clues to character. Yone can wear "regal Venice point. Fling it around you. No, you would look like a ghost in one,–Lu like a corpse." Yone identifies with amber jewelry shaped from once-living matter into images of pagan gods, while Lu is "light" and "limpid" like aquamarine and is characterized by "mechlin, with its whiter, closer, chaster web." Perhaps because the spheres of men and women had moved so far apart and because the traditional images of the romantics were giving way to more personal images as realism gained ground, James mistook similar images in *Azarian* for mere costuming effects: "Imagine Thackeray forever pulling Rebecca's curls and settling the folds of her dress." Yet such domestic images convey individual characteristics and universal realities in Spofford's fiction.

Yone and Lu are Spofford's first contrasting pair of women, a common device not only in Spofford's fiction but all nineteenth-century literature, which tended to stereotype women. The passionate but dangerous Yone loses to the proper but colorless Lu in this first story, but tradition does not always win over passion in Spofford's fiction. In fact, Spofford's later pairs of women are less contrastive as Spofford concerned herself more with sisterhood than symbolic stereotyping. Yone and Lu may be patterned on the colorful Prescott herself and her religious girlhood friend Louisa Stone. Hal and Lole, as they called each other, maintained a lifelong friendship, as evidenced by the poem "Translation–To L.P.H.," which Harriet wrote when Lole (since 1859 Mrs. John Hopkins) died in 1895.

Also included in this initial collection are "Desert Sands" (previously unpublished) and "Midsummer and May" (*Atlantic Monthly*, November and December 1860), each of which presents a pair of women. In "Desert Sands" the "good" woman of the pair, Eos, sacrifices her talent and ultimately her life for her husband. Confinement and self-sacrifice, often leading to insanity or death, also occur in later stories by Spofford

Front cover for one of Spofford's story collections

(and in the works of many of her female contemporaries). In Eos they produce what her cousin calls "a spiritual asphyxia," and her death leaves her husband spiritually and physically blind. The talent that Eos sacrifices is easily recognized and appreciated by the "bad" woman, the seductive Vespasia. Less effective is the rambling romantic concoction that contrasts "Midsummer," the dark and queenly Mrs. Laudersdale, with "May," her blonde daughter Marguerite, whom she calls Rite. Mrs. Laudersdale narrowly escapes breaking her marriage vows for young Roger Raleigh, who is destined after a decent interval of thirteen years to fall in love with and marry Rite. Unnecessary plot complications and unclear contrasts mar the story.

According to Elizabeth K. Halbeisen, the thirty-one-year gap between Spofford's first collection of short stories and her second, *A Scarlet Poppy and Other Stories* (1894), was filled with the publication of eight books and "374 periodical appearances, including short stories, novels, poems, and articles, . . . a count in all probability far from complete. Of the periodical group, 141 are short stories for adult America." Those chosen for inclusion in *A Scarlet Poppy and Other Stories* are light satire, while–as the title suggests–her next adult collection, *Old Madame & Other Tragedies* (1900), contains tragedies.

The Spofford marriage was long and successful, marred only by the death of their only child in infancy in 1867. Alternating their home between Massachusetts and Washington, D.C., where Richard Spofford was involved in political and legal work, they were particularly happy in 1874 with the purchase of the five-acre Deer Island, in the Merrimack River, which became their permanent home and a haven for them both. Harriet's parents shared Deer Island with the younger couple until her father's death in 1881 and her mother's in 1883. Both relatives and friends were frequently entertained there, among them Harriet's literary friends Sarah Orne Jewett, Elizabeth Stuart Phelps Ward, Julia Ward Howe, and Whittier, the last of whom wrote in "June on the Merrimac" of how "Deer Island's mistress sings." Richard's mother died at Deer Island in September 1887; in less than a year he too was dead. Harriet Spofford turned to her Boston friends and her writing to sustain her for the remaining thirty-three years of her life. Besides those already mentioned, only two other collections of adult short stories, *Old Washington* (1906) and *The Elder's People*, would appear; many fine stories still remain uncollected.

In a few stories in *A Scarlet Poppy and Other Stories* humor offers new insights into the pairs of women characters. In "An Ideal" (*Continent*, 24 October 1883), for instance, the "gay, tormenting sprite" Rosalie triumphs over the "pensive saint" Alicia when Rosalie's husband discovers during a visit that the woman he has enshrined in memory during his fifty-year marriage is now unrecognizably ugly, old, and querulous. Yet Spofford has sympathy for both women in most tales, as is apparent in her presentation of Priscilla Mullins in her contribution to *Three Heroines of New England Romance* (1894). While Priscilla is described as "gentle," Spofford suggests that there might be "a spice of feminine coquetry in her famous speech to John Alden. . . . Or was it that she understood the dignity and worth of womanhood, and was the first in this new land to take her stand upon it?"

Spofford's spirited women gain some victories within marriage, as does Rosalie, but Spofford is aware of just how tenuous these victories are. Also in *A Scarlet Poppy*, for instance, the reader meets Mrs. Claxton, whose husband "would have been as much surprised to find his wife differing from him as he would have been to hear his wooden dining table speak up and complain of the dinner." In "Mrs. Claxton's Skeleton" (*Harper's New Monthly*, March 1883) she gains her husband's approbation and apology when she saves him and their neighbors from a flood, but she realizes as well that "that despotic principle was bred in his bones, and Noah's flood itself could not have washed it out." Another domestic quarrel is resolved in the title story (*Harper's Bazar*, 31 March 1888), while her observation that husbands fail to realize the individuality of their wives informs Spofford's "The Composite Wife" (previously unpublished): when Mr. Chipperley plans to take a fourth wife, he sees her as a composite of and interchangeable with his previous wives. Satirical attacks on vegetarianism in "Best-Laid Schemes" (*Harper's New Monthly*, August 1883) and on snobbishness in "Mr. Van Nore's Daughter-in-Law" (*Our Continent*, 18 October 1882) complete the collection.

What is recognized with humor and grace in these tales written by a happy wife is seen as more ominous in some of the stories collected in *Old Madame & Other Tragedies*. The domestic imagery conveys the somber realities of the confinement of women. Insanity traps the woman of "Her Story" (*Lippincott's Magazine*, December 1872) in a sanatorium she describes as "this prison, this grave" while she shares with her friend Elizabeth her hopes of recovering and rejoining her husband and children. Ten years in a French insane asylum is only the beginning for Helen Vance in "A Lost Identity" (originally published as "Metamorphosis" in the May 1883 issue of the *Manhattan*). She comes home to find that her husband, believing she has died in a shipwreck, has remarried. Rather than destroy his happiness, Helen returns to the asylum.

But home and a husband themselves imprison Emilia in "Ordronnaux" (*Scribner's Monthly*, September and October 1874). Treating both sides of the female stereotype with empathy, Spofford shows that all women are prisoners of that stereotype and its social reflections, even in marriage. Married to a man she does not love, Emilia conveys her sense of entrapment in even her clothing: as she "put on the royal silk, the web-like lace, bound the golden bands around her wrists, . . . the clink of her heavy bracelets was like the clank of chains; and her face burned with disgrace." The house offers "not a single room whose atmosphere Emilia could assimilate with that of her own interior life, and the whole place was only a beautiful prison, a prison that she loathed from the first day she crossed its threshold."

The strength of woman emerges in two stories in *Old Madame & Other Tragedies*. The title story (*Century Magazine*, January 1882) offers historical romance–a sketch of Elizabeth Champernoune, last matriarch of a powerful New England family–which would be republished in 1889 in *The Woman's Story as Told by Twenty American Women*. In "The Wages of Sin," first published after her husband's death, Spofford admires the "fallen woman," despite Judith Dauntry's betrayal of the institution of marriage. "The Wages of Sin" first appeared in the October 1898 issue of *Cosmopolitan* as "Judith Dauntry." This tale of illicit love and social ostracism presents an uncompromising woman who survives community punishment and personal tragedy in her commitment to nature and to love. She is finally recognized by the minister as being "like some great angel of succor to the suffering," and she has "ceased to think of herself as an abandoned woman; so far as she thought of it at all she had a dim sense of being virtuous." Clearly delineating the ragged edges of the New England villages Spofford knew so well, "The Wages of Sin" combines Spofford's "romantic concern" with madness and the atypical life with her "realistic depiction" of New England; as such, it leads naturally to the subtle realism that dominates her twentieth-century fiction.

Memories of her Washington days with her husband provide setting and characters for the stories collected in *Old Washington*. All five of these interconnected tales involve the landlady Mrs. McQueen, modeled on Mrs. Roach who ran the boarding house at 520 Thirteenth Street, N.W., in which the Spoffords lived. The stories are "A Thanksgiving Breakfast" (*Harper's New Monthly*, November 1895), "A Guardian Angel" (*Harper's New Monthly*, May 1897), "In a Conspiracy" (previously unpublished), "A Little Old Woman" (previously unpublished), and "The Colonel's Christmas" (*Harper's New Monthly*, December 1894). These sentimental tales are not the best of Spofford's late romantic works, which remain uncollected and include two treatments of madness, "The Rose" in the October 1912 issue of *Harper's Monthly* and "The Mad Lady" in the February 1916 issue of *Scribner's Magazine*. Even a science-

fiction story appears among her twentieth-century periodical publications: "The Ray of Displacement" (*Metropolitan*, October 1903) examines a scientific theory of a "Y ray" which would allow humans to become invisible and to pass through solids.

A single story, "Her Eyes are Doves," which appeared originally in the *Harper's Monthly Magazine* of January 1910, was republished by the World Peace Foundation of Boston as a pamphlet, *The King's Easter* (1912), and edited by Edwin D. Mead. This story, which debates the issues that would lead to World War I, is an implicit plea for peace. Spofford's stature in the early twentieth century is suggested by Howells's inclusion of "Circumstance" in *The Great Modern American Stories* (1920) and Alexander Jessup's choice of her first story, "In A Cellar," for *Representative American Short Stories* (1923).

By the standards of realism, however, Spofford's final collection, *The Elder's People*, is her best. The dry humor, the day-to-day realities of life in a New England village, the believable dialect, and the restraint with which she individualizes each character earned her praise in reviews, including those in the *Literary Digest* (23 October 1920) and the *New York Times Review of Books* (18 April 1920). The fourteen stories share locale and characters, particularly the title character, Elder Perry. The stories include "The Deacon's Whistle" (*Harper's Monthly*, July 1907), "A Change of Heart" (*Harper's Monthly*, April 1908), "A Rural Telephone" (*Harper's Monthly*, May 1909), "The Step-Father" (first published in *Woman's Home Companion*, August 1911, as "An Act of Grace"), "John-a-Dreams" (*Harper's Monthly*, February 1910), "Miss Mahala's Miracle," "An Old Fiddler" (*Harper's Monthly*, December 1905), "The Blessing Called Peace," "Father James" (*Harper's Monthly*, June 1904), "The Impossible Choice," "A Village Dressmaker" (*Atlantic Monthly*, January 1906), "Miss Mahala's Will," "A Life in a Night," and "Miss Mahala and Johnny" (*Harper's Monthly*, October 1913). Each is written in dialect; each captures the voices and idiosyncrasies of its New England villagers. Although Spofford's domestic imagery is not as lush as in earlier stories, the same domestic realities convey her universal themes. Clothes still serve as metaphors, especially in "A Village Dressmaker." In this tale of self-sacrifice Susanne gives the wedding gown she had made for herself to Rowena Mayhew, who is marrying the man they both loved. Each woman has been defined by clothes and colors, including Susanne's two maiden aunts, who live for the joy she gives them. Sisterhood emerges triumphant in this story, sustaining even the rejected Susanne, who has gained happiness through her decision. By the very choice she has made, Susanne has won, as her aunts observe:

> "Wal! I think a woman'd orter be translated
>   thet's happy givin' another woman her weddin'
>   gownd!"
> "Susanne *is* translated."
> "Ann, a cross is a cross your life long."
> "Cely," said her sister, "you've heern Elder Perry
>   say thet there ain't no cross w'en there ain't
>   no self to suffer under it!"

Although she was known best throughout her life for her poetry, it is in her short stories that Spofford excels. Whether romantic or realistic, their insights into the lives of and attitudes toward women are clearly conveyed through domestic imagery. Through their characters and images emerge human and universal truths clothed in the colors of her imagination. So subdued are those colors in her later work that she once confided a fear to Mary Gray Morrison that "something had escaped into the air. I never could get it back" (quoted in *Bookman*, November 1925).

Yet the colors are there, and the very texture of the lives she captured can still be felt. When Prescott died quietly at Deer Island on Sunday, 14 August 1921, she was eighty-six years old. To her readers, mostly women, of sixty years of her contributions to their favorite periodicals, her message of sisterhood clearly survived her.

References:

Edwin M. Bacon, *Literary Pilgrimages in New England* (New York & Boston: Silver, Burdett, 1902), pp. 65-70;

Albert L. Bartlett, "Some Annals of Old Haverhill," *New England Magazine*, new series 2 (July 1890): 505-507;

Helen Coffin Beedy, *Mothers of Maine* (Portland: Thurston, 1895), pp. 354-355;

William I. Cole, "Maine in Literature," *New England Magazine*, new series 22 (August 1900): 741;

Rose Terry Cooke, "Harriet Prescott Spofford," in *Our Famous Women* (Hartford: A. D. Worthington/Chicago: A. D. Nettleton, 1884), pp. 521-538;

Etta R. Goodwin, "The Literary Women of Washington," *Chautauquan*, 27 (September 1898): 585-586;

Elizabeth K. Halbeisen, *Harriet Prescott Spofford: A Romantic Survival* (Philadelphia: University of Pennsylvania Press, 1935);

John L. Haney, *The Story of Our Literature* (New York: Scribners, 1903), p. 252;

A. A. Hopkins, *Waifs, and Their Authors* (Boston: Lothrop, 1880), pp. 303-316;

F. M. Hopkins, "American Poets of Today: Harriet P. Spofford," *Current Literature*, 25 (February 1899): 122-123;

William C. King, *Woman. Her Position, Influence and Achievement throughout the Civilized World . . . From the Garden of Eden to the Twentieth Century* (Springfield: King Richardson, 1902), p. 422;

Mary Gray Morrison, "Memories of Harriet Prescott Spofford," *Bookman*, 62 (November 1925): 315-318;

Fred Lewis Pattee, *The Development of the American Short Story* (New York & London: Harper, 1923), pp. 159-163;

Elizabeth Stuart Phelps, "Stories That Stay," *Century Magazine*, new series 59 (November 1910): 119;

Wilder D. Quint, "Harriet Prescott Spofford at Deer Island," *New York Times Saturday Review of Books and Art*, 26 November 1898, p. 793;

Charles F. Richardson, *American Literature (1607-1885)*, 2 volumes (New York: Putnam's, 1902), II: 443-445;

Thelma J. Shinn, "Harriet Prescott Spofford: A Reconsideration," *Turn-of-the-Century Women*, 1 (Summer 1984): 36-45;

Edmund C. Stedman, *Poets of America* (Boston & New York: Houghton, Mifflin, 1886), p. 445;

R. H. Stoddard and others, *Poets' Homes*, 2 volumes (Boston: Lothrop, 1877), I: 196-229;

E. P. Whipple, *American Literature and Other Papers* (Boston: Ticknor, 1899), p. 125;

Helen M. Winslow, *Literary Boston of To-day* (Boston: Page, 1903), pp. 114-117;

J. B. M. Wright, "Some Authors and their Homes, Mrs. Harriet Prescott Spofford," *Literary World*, 30 (16 September 1899): 300.

Papers:

Most of the Prescott family letters are held by the Essex Institute in Salem, Massachusetts. At least one other letter by Spofford is preserved in the Simon Gratz Autograph Collection at the Historical Society of Pennsylvania.

Frank R. Stockton

(5 April 1834-20 April 1902)

Henry L. Golemba
Wayne State University

See also the Stockton entry in *DLB 42: American Writers for Children Before 1900.*

BOOKS: *A Northern Voice Calling for the Dissolution of the Union of the United States of America* (N.p., 1860);

Ting-a-ling (New York: Hurd & Houghton, 1870; London: Ward & Downey, 1889);

Round-about Rambles in Lands of Fact and Fancy (New York: Scribner, Armstrong, 1872);

The Home: Where It Should Be and What To Put In It, by Stockton and Marian Stockton (New York: Putnam, 1873);

What Might Have Been Expected (New York: Dodd, Mead, 1874; London: Routledge, 1874);

Tales Out of School (New York: Scribner, Armstrong, 1876);

Rudder Grange (New York: Scribners, 1879; London: Hamilton, 1883; extended edition, New York: Scribners, 1879);

A Jolly Fellowship (New York: Scribners, 1880; London: Kegan Paul, 1880);

The Floating Prince and Other Fairy Tales (New York: Scribners, 1881; London: Ward & Downey, 1889);

The Lady, or the Tiger? and Other Stories (New York: Scribners, 1884; London: Hamilton, 1884);

The Story of Viteau (New York: Scribners, 1884; London: Low, 1884);

The Late Mrs. Null (New York: Scribners, 1886; London: Low, 1886);

The Christmas Wreck and Other Stories (New York: Scribners, 1886);

The Casting Away of Mrs. Lecks and Mrs. Aleshine (New York: Century, 1886; London: Low, 1886);

The Bee-Man of Orn and Other Fanciful Tales (New York: Scribners, 1887; London: Low, 1888);

The Hundredth Man (New York: Century, 1887; London: Low, 1887);

The Dusantes. A Sequel to "The Casting Away of Mrs. Lecks and Mrs. Aleshine" (New York: Century, 1888; London: Low, 1888);

Frank R. Stockton

Amos Kilbright: His Adscititious Experiences, with Other Stories (New York: Scribners, 1888; London: Unwin, 1888);

The Great War Syndicate (London: Longmans, Green, 1889; New York: Collier, 1889);

Personally Conducted (New York: Scribners, 1889; London: Low, 1889);

The Stories of the Three Burglars (New York: Dodd, Mead, 1889; London: Low, 1890);

Ardis Claverden (New York: Dodd, Mead, 1890; London: Low, 1890);

The Cosmic Bean; or, The Great Show in Kobol-Land (London: Black & White Publishing, 1891);

The Rudder Grangers Abroad and Other Stories (New York: Scribners, 1891; London: Low, 1891);

The Squirrel Inn (New York: Century, 1891; London: Low, 1891);

The House of Martha (Boston & New York: Houghton, Mifflin, 1891; London: Osgood, McIlvaine, 1891);

The Clocks of Rondaine and Other Stories (New York: Scribners, 1892; London: Low, 1892);

The Watchmaker's Wife and Other Stories (New York: Scribners, 1893);

Pomona's Travels (New York: Scribners, 1894; London: Cassell, 1894);

The Adventures of Captain Horn (New York: Scribners, 1895; London: Cassell, 1895);

Stories of New Jersey (New York, Cincinnati & Chicago: American Book Co., 1896);

Mrs. Cliff's Yacht (New York: Scribners, 1896; London: Cassell, 1896);

Captain Chap or The Rolling Stones (London: Nummo, 1896; Philadelphia: Lippincott, 1897);

A Story-Teller's Pack (New York: Scribners, 1897; London: Cassell, 1897);

The Great Stone of Sardis. A Novel (New York & London: Harper, 1898);

The Girl at Cobhurst (New York: Scribners, 1898; London: Cassell, 1898);

The Buccaneers and Pirates of Our Coasts (New York & London: Cassell, 1898);

The Associate Hermits (New York & London: Harper, 1899);

The Vizier of the Two-Horned Alexander (New York: Century, 1899);

The Young Master of Hyson Hall (Philadelphia: Lippincott, 1900; London: Chatto, 1900);

Afield and Afloat (New York: Scribners, 1900; London: Cassell, 1900);

A Bicycle of Cathay. A Novel (New York & London: Harper, 1900; London: Harper, 1900);

Kate Bonnet. The Romance of a Pirate's Daughter (New York: Appleton, 1902; London: Cassell, 1902);

John Gayther's Garden and the Stories Told Therein (New York: Scribners, 1902; London: Cassell, 1902);

The Captain's Toll-Gate (New York: Appleton, 1903; London: Cassell, 1903);

The Lost Dryad (Riverside, Conn.: Printed at Hillacre for the United Workers of Greenwich, 1912);

The Poor Count's Christmas (New York: Stokes, 1927).

Collection: *The Novels and Stories of Frank R. Stockton*, Shenandoah Edition, 23 volumes (New York: Scribners, 1899-1904).

PERIODICAL PUBLICATIONS: "The Pilgrim's Packets," *Scribner's Monthly*, 5 (January 1873): 333-336;

"Mark Twain and His Recent Works," *Forum*, 15 (August 1893): 673-679;

"How I Served My Apprenticeship as a Man of Letters," *Youth's Companion*, 70 (5 March 1896): 119;

"My Favorite Novelist and His Best Book," *Munsey's Magazine*, 17 (June 1897): 351-366;

"A Philippine Embarrassment," *New York Sunday World*, 12 November 1899, p. 3.

An author whose best-sellers were discussed from California to India in his time, Frank Stockton is known today mainly for "The Lady, or the Tiger?" (*Century*, November 1882; collected in *The Lady, or the Tiger? and Other Stories*, 1884), fairy tales such as "The Bee-Man of Orn" (originally published as "The Bee-Man and His Original Form" in the November 1883 issue of *St. Nicholas*) and "The Griffin and the Minor Canon" (*St. Nicholas*, October 1885)–both collected in *The Bee-Man of Orn and Other Fanciful Tales* (1887) and republished with illustrations by Maurice Sendak in the 1960s–and for his science fiction novels such as *The Great War Syndicate* (1889) and *The Great Stone of Sardis* (1898), which were widely imitated. The writings of this genteel humorist will probably never regain the popularity and critical respect accorded them during Stockton's lifetime. Even in his own time his refusal to belong to any literary movement puzzled–as Stockton records in "The Pilgrim's Packets" (*Scribner's Monthly*, January 1873) and "Plain Fishing" (first published in *Amos Kilbright*, 1888)–the various realists, rationalists, materialists, and naturalists of his era. Yet, after his death in 1902, an anonymous obituary writer called him "as distinct an embodiment of the American spirit in one sort as Mark Twain was in another."

Francis Richard Stockton was born in Philadelphia on 5 April 1834 to an elderly father, William Smith Stockton, and his young second wife, Emily Hepsibeth Drean Stockton. William Stockton was a strict Methodist leader and pamphleteer who descended collaterally from Richard Stockton, a signer of the Declaration of Independence. William Stockton was actively involved in the creation of a schism within the Methodist church in America and vied for leadership of the offshoot, the Methodist Protestant church, with his oldest son, Frank Stockton's half brother Thomas Hewlings Stockton, who shared the podium with Abraham Lincoln at Gettysburg and whom Henry Clay called the best pulpit orator of the day. Emily Hepsibeth Drean was from Leesburg, Virginia, and her influence is apparent in Stockton's sympathy for the South before the

Civil War, his choice of wife, and the whimsical, fanciful tone of his stories as well as the subject matter for many of his southern stories.

Although one of the slightly built youth's legs was shorter than the other, he had an active childhood, organizing a gang of boys who indulged in madcap pranks that would have made Tom Sawyer proud. He had to restrain his youthful exuberance after 1844 after his father was dismissed as superintendent of the Philadelphia Alms House for mismanagement of funds and spent more time at home writing religious tracts. Frank Stockton was closest to his brother John, two years his junior, who reinforced Frank's interest in literature. Together they would make up stories and continue to develop them well into the night. Upon graduation from Philadelphia's Central High School in February 1852, Frank joined a Forensic and Literary Circle and wanted to be a writer, but his father demanded he do something more practical, so he became a wood engraver. (Samples of his work survive in the volume of brother Thomas's poems he illustrated in 1862.) He did not abandon his literary ambitions, however; his first published story, "The Slight Mistake," appeared in the 1 September 1855 issue of the *Philadelphia American Courier*.

In 1860 Stockton moved his engraving office to New York after marrying on 30 April Mary Ann Edwards Tuttle (who was called Marian) from Georgetown, South Carolina, who had been a literature teacher in the school for women which his mother had founded in Philadelphia. Later in 1860, objecting to war and sympathetic to the Southern cause, he had privately printed *A Northern Voice Calling for the Dissolution of the Union*. His father died on 20 November 1860, and by the end of the decade he had entirely abandoned wood engraving, an increasingly supererogatory craft due to technological advances, and followed his brother John into journalism. He wrote for the *Philadelphia Press* and *Post*, supported Jay Cooke's banking plan and Horace Greeley's presidential campaign, and wrote a "how to" book with his wife: *The Home: Where It Should Be and What To Put In It* (1873), which Stockton later discovered to be utterly useless when he tried to buy and furnish a house.

Also during the 1860s he contributed more imaginative pieces to J. G. Holland's *Punchinello*, Edward Eggleston's *Hearth and Home*, *Puck*, and other humor magazines. Most important, he published *Ting-a-ling* (1870), which is considered a milestone in children's literature. Eschewing the saccharine form made popular by Sarah Josepha Hale's "Mary Had a Little Lamb" and C. C. Moore's "A Visit from St. Nicholas," the stories in *Ting-a-ling* are closer in kind to Grimm's fairy tales and Lewis Carroll's Alice stories. Problems are not patly resolved; the happy ending is ambiguous; maxims collapse into irony; and, after the heroine is beheaded inadvertently by the hero, her head is magically reattached to her body–but backwards.

These efforts caught the attention of Mary Mapes Dodge, who asked Stockton in 1873 to become her assistant editor at the new *St. Nicholas Magazine*. Stockton accepted the post in 1873 and worked at it so diligently that he was forced to take a recuperative vacation to Virginia, Florida, and Nassau in 1876 because he had become temporarily blind. His anxiety was aggravated by the premature death of his brother John in 1877, and he finally quit *St. Nicholas* in 1878 after his vision had become permanently impaired.

By that time Stockton had produced two more successful novels, *What Might Have Been Expected* (1874), which had been serialized in *St. Nicholas* (November 1873-October 1874), and *Rudder Grange* (1879), which began as a story published in the November 1874 issue of *Scribner's Monthly*. Popular as *Rudder Grange* and its sequels *The Rudder Grangers Abroad* (1891) and *Pomona's Travels* (1894) were, Stockton's name did not become a household word until after the publication of "The Lady, or the Tiger?" in the November 1882 issue of *Century Magazine*. Stockton had called the story "The King's Arena" but William Carey, an editor at *Century*, requested and received Stockton's permission to change the name to "The Lady, or the Tiger?" In this frequently republished story a middle-class male falls in love with a princess whose father is so enraged that he commands the man to appear in the king's arena and open one of two doors. Behind one is a beautiful middle-class woman whom the man must marry; behind the other is a voracious tiger. The princess has discovered what lurks behind each door, and she signals her lover to open the door on the right. What comes out–the lady, or the tiger?–Stockton leaves his readers to decide. Robert Browning offered a solution; American high-school students debated it; Hindu sages exchanged opinions. Deluged by requests for the correct answer, Stockton refused to take sides, saying to one letter writer that the answer she proposed revealed more about her own personality than it did about the story. Stockton responded to popular demand by writing two sequels. In the first, "His Wife's Deceased Sister" (*Century*, January 1884; collected in *The Lady, or the Tiger? and Other Stories*), he complains about the restrictive demands of the audience who threatened to stifle him with love, and he vows never again to publish a story that runs the risk of becoming vastly popular. (Stockton sometimes failed in this resolve; for example, in 1895, the first year for which accurate book-publishing statistics exist, his novel *The Adventures of Captain Horn* was a best-seller, and after "The Buller-Podington Compact" was published in the August 1897 issue of *Scribner's Magazine*, it led to a chain of "Pass-It-On" societies whose members exchanged entertaining stories.) The second sequel to "The Lady, or the Tiger?" is "The Discourager of Hesitancy" (*Century*, July 1885), another open-ended story for which a reader's solution reveals more about himself than about the story.

Stockton's later years were literarily prolific but socially inactive. He granted interviews but declined many invitations to banquets and receptions. He took a trip to Chicago and to the West in 1894, but he spent most of his time at his large homes with extensive grounds: in 1890 he bought The Holt near Morristown, New Jersey, not far from Thomas Alva Edison's Menlo Park (Stockton's hero in *The Great Stone of Sardis* is loosely based on the popular image of Edison); and in 1899 he moved to Claymont in the Shenandoah Valley not far from his mother's country and on land once owned by George Washington near Charles Town, West Virginia. Ill and suffering impaired vision, he dictated most of his later stories to his wife or to an amanuensis. He spoke out publicly on only two issues: the international copyright law, in which he had a vested interest; and his old abhorrence, war.

He contributed an essay to the *Critic* symposium (February 1897) on the Venezuelan dispute between the United States and Great Britain, thus joining an array of American writers who presented a solid front against imperialism; but he preferred fiction as a means of waging war on war. In stories such as "The Skipper and El Capitan" (*Cosmopolitan*, November 1898) and "The Governor-General" (*Cosmopolitan*, October 1898)—both collected in *Afield and Afloat*, 1900—he pointed out war's absurdities in a manner used by Leonard Wibberly a half century later in his *The Mouse that Roared*. In *The Great War Syndicate* (1889) he followed Edward Bellamy's lead in *Looking Backward* (1888) by suggesting that business consortia could end war, but, unlike Bellamy, Stockton is mainly interested in using business to strip war of all glamour and romance. His war is made to be as dull, mechanical, and unheroic as the filling out of insurance forms. He also mistakenly expressed the hope that development of ultimate weapons would serve as a martial deterrent.

Although he was a well-known writer, Stockton feared that so much of his money went to his taxes that his wife might not be provided for after his death. Moreover, he feared his style of writing was rapidly becoming old-fashioned. In a 5 November 1900 letter to his friend Robert Underwood Johnson, editor for *Century Magazine*, Stockton described a dream in which his beloved home was burned down, leaving him with nothing but the clothes he wore. Homeless with nowhere else to go, he dreamt he traveled to New York and informed the *Century* editors that he intended to quit writing. When the editors in his dream insisted that he could write as well as ever, Stockton answered, "Oh, it is not that! I can write humorous stories if I want to, but the readers of to-day do not care for them; the public taste has altered; humor is no longer fashionable."

In 1902 Stockton made a business trip to New York. On the way home he stopped in Washington, D.C., to attend a National Academy of Sciences banquet. He became ill and died of a cerebral hemorrhage in his room at the Willard Hotel on 20 April.

As his dream had foreshadowed, Stockton's fiction quickly became unfashionable. Considered the equal of Mark Twain in 1885, voted to fifth place among the best living American writers by readers of *Literature Magazine* in 1899, he was soon forgotten by most readers. His fan clubs remained loyal; special editions of his stories were still published. In 1913 Etta De Camp published a volume of stories which she claimed Stockton had dictated to her from the spirit world. Movie directors sought permission to make film versions of Stockton's stories. Some scholars wonder why Stockton is not more esteemed. While certainly not a Mark Twain, a Henry James, or a Stephen Crane, he is clearly a more skillful and more versatile writer than Richard Harding Davis, Horatio Alger, or Thomas Bailey Aldrich. Sporadically, champions of this "civilized humorist" have attempted to rekindle the old fervor over Stockton. The strongest attempt came between World War I and World War II.

Stockton at his desk, 1896

The main reason for Stockton's decline may be that he seems too amused by life for twentieth-century tastes. Where Twain decided that "Man is the cruellest of animals and life a tragic mistake," Stockton's version might have read, "Man is the quirkiest of animals and life an amusing absurdity." An exchange from *The Squirrel Inn* (1891) illustrates the point. A woman character complains that Stockton's plot is becoming as bewilderingly complicated as the queer architectural design of the Squirrel Inn, but her lover, speaking on Stockton's behalf, replies:

> It strikes me, Susan, that our lives are very seldom built with a hall through the middle and the rooms alike on both sides. I don't think we'd like it if they were. They would be stupid and humdrum. The right sort of a life should have its ups and downs, its ins and outs, its different levels, its outside stairs and its inside stairs, its balconies, windows, and roofs of different periods and different styles. This is education. These things are the advantages that our lives get from the lives of others.
>
> Now, for myself, I like the place I live in to resemble my life and that of the people around

me. And I am sure that nothing could be better suited to all that than the Squirrel Inn.

This passage is more remarkable for what it leaves out than for what it includes. There are no Melvillean highs and lows. The universe may be chaotic, life absurd, humanity driven by biological forces and destructive drives, but flowers still bloom near the deep ravine of Stockton's literary garden. In *The Captain's Toll-Gate* (1903) Stockton has a romantic poet, as unlucky in love as he is in his poetic craft, walk off a pier in frustration. But Stockton handles the suicide lightly. Before killing himself, the poet cries out to his beloved, "Am I not to know whether I am to rise into paradise, or to sink into the infernal regions?" and the heroine answers calmly, "Don't do either, Mr. Locker. This earth is a very pleasant place. Stay where you are." Yet, what greatness Stockton may have achieved may ultimately rest on the disjunction between what he said and what he believed. He might say with the heroine of *The Captain's Toll-Gate* that this earth is a pleasant place, but what he in truth believed is that pleasantry can be a vastly inhibiting and irritating phenomenon. Many of his stories virtually cry out in stifled screams against the cozy suffocation of civilized conduct.

A brief look at four stories can clarify this point while also providing a sense of Stockton's range. In "Mr. Tolman" (*Harper's Monthly*, August 1880; collected in *The Lady, or the Tiger? and Other Stories*), the story William Dean Howells liked best because of its realistic technique, the title character is bored stiff with the business corporation he has built and takes a vacation to ponder whether he should retire. He is charmed by an old woman's bookshop, buys it, brings together two lovers to whom he later sells the shop, and returns refreshed to his corporation, dashing his manager's hopes of becoming president. Tolman will apparently persist at the grind, feeding on the memory of once having done worthwhile work. In "Derelict–a Tale of the Wayward Sea" (first published in *The Rudder Grangers Abroad and Other Stories*) there is a literal derelict ship, but the main characters are also derelicts motivated by extreme selfishness while mawkishly pretending to themselves that they are in love. Only their deep ignorance preserves their bliss. In "Our Archery Club" (*Scribner's Monthly*, August 1879; collected in *The Lady, or the Tiger? and Other Stories*) one of the club's two best archers is a mechanic with less personality than a robot; the other is snubbed if not despised because his manner is unorthodox. Indeed, his method of shooting his arrows from below his belt is a bit too suggestive even to be noted by more than glances between the genteel club members. The mechanic is a stylish fool who keeps his equipment in a coffinlike box, who dreams of shooting eagles but settles for straw-filled targets, and who wins the club medal–and his sweetheart–only because the other contestants shoot badly on his behalf.

Stockton wrote "The Knife That Killed Po Hancy" (first published in *The Great War Syndicate*) deliberately to do Robert Louis Stevenson's Jekyll and Hyde one better. Stockton's hero, a flabby lawyer so out of condition that he sweats playing billiards, accidentally nicks himself with a knife that has killed Po Hancy, a pantherlike Burmese Dacoit bandit, thereby intermixing their two bloods. The golden mean of the vigorous, high-spirited but civilized male is not achieved. The hero swings schizophrenically from one extreme to the other, from destructive violence to dull domesticity. He has courted two women–one a modest, reliable maiden, the other a lively vixen–and has made himself fit for neither.

A novel published the year of Stockton's death treats this theme in more extended length. The main character of *Kate Bonnet* (1902) is Stede Bonnet, an eighteenth-century plantation owner in the Caribbean who throws off the stultifying cloak of domestic life to become what he truly desires–a pirate who kills men, rapes women, pillages towns, and sinks ships, much to the dismay of his family and friends. He is a marked contrast to those males in "The Transferred Ghost" (*Century*, May 1882) and "The Spectral Mortgage" (*Century*, February 1883)–both stories collected in *The Lady, or the Tiger? and Other Stories*–who have as little force in the world as do ghosts. Bonnet ends up as Blackbeard's bookkeeper, but when the Bible-quoting Ben Greenway observes him toiling away at Blackbeard's ledgers and expresses his pleasure that Bonnet to all appearances has accepted the mild yoke of civil behavior, Bonnet replies in a groan, "I tell you, Ben Greenway, you are mistaken; I am just as wicked as I ever was." If given the chance, Bonnet would return to his bloody, destructive ways at once, but Bonnet's quest for adventure is frustrated at every turn, and his fate is appropriate to his strangulated impulses: he is hanged. *Kate Bonnet* may be Stockton's response to his early sketch "Kate" (*Southern Literary Messen-*

ger, December 1859). In "Kate" the male's very ineptitude makes him a desirable mate; in *Kate Bonnet* Stede's destructive drives have no outlet, no place in civilized society. He is a willing outcast.

Feelings of frustration or entrapment are not restricted to Stockton's males, and many of his women also fight for their freedom. In Stockton's personal favorite among his works, *Ardis Claverden* (1890), the heroine is smarter, more handsome, richer, more competent, and more mature than anyone male or female in her community, and because of her virtues she is misunderstood and mistreated. In "The Great Staircase at Landover Hall" (*Harper's Weekly*, 17 December 1898) a woman trips over a child's toy and falls down a staircase to her death, and her unfulfilled spirit haunts the house thereafter. In *The Late Mrs. Null* (1886) a woman finds she can be most active and independent when she merely pretends to be married; her nonexistent husband, Null, is the best husband a woman could have, she says. In "The Magic Egg" (*Century*, June 1894; collected in *A Story-Teller's Pack*, 1897) Edith Starr breaks her engagement to Herbert Loring because she concludes that the principal intention of her husband-to-be is "to cloud my perceptions, to subject my intellect to his own, to make me believe a lie."

Loring amiably admits that her accusation is correct, and "The Magic Egg" thereby becomes one of Stockton's most complex and probably most revealing stories. What Loring in his magic show and Stockton in his fiction seek to achieve is to distill the essence of a magical reality for the enjoyment of their audiences; yet they soon discover that their audiences are entertained but for a day and refuse to accept their art on its own terms.

One important effect of Stockton's inversion of conventions and his stylistic experimentation was to force frustration upon his reader aesthetically as well as thematically. In addition to the shattered orthodoxies of his children's stories and the inconclusion of "The Lady, or the Tiger?" he has a lawyer in "Struck by a Boomerang" (first published in *Afield and Afloat*) attempt to unravel a murder mystery only to discover that he himself is the accidental perpetrator of the crime. In Stevenson's favorite Stockton story, "The Remarkable Wreck of the *Thomas Hyke*" (*Century*, August 1884; collected in *The Christmas Wreck and Other Stories*, 1886), the characters cannot decide if a ship has sunk even though they have all the facts. In "Our Story" (*Century*, September 1883; collected in *The Lady, or the Tiger? and Other Stories*) the reader presumes that the first-person narrator is telling his own story, but in the last paragraph the reader learns that the story was written by another writer–a deception which Gertrude Stein later used in *The Autobiography of Alice B. Toklas. John Gayther's Garden* (1902), which Stockton left not quite finished at his death, was planned as a group of short stories told and responded to by various members of a household and their guests, the internal narratives complicated by the diverse responses of an audience ranging from the liberated next-door neighbor to the romantic daughter of the house, her matronly mother and rather blunt father, and the gardener, John Gayther (a persona for Stockton). Had Stockton completed this work, it might have been his best.

As it is, although one could list thirty or more first-rate Stockton stories, Stockton will continue to be remembered for only those few children's stories and "The Lady, or the Tiger?," which he considered to be among the least important works in his canon.

Interviews:

Clarence C. Buel, "The Author of The Lady, or the Tiger?," *Century Magazine*, 10 (July 1886): 404-408;

Edith M. Thomas, "A Dialogue between Frank R. Stockton and Edith M. Thomas," *McClure's Magazine*, 1 (November 1893): 466-477;

James Herbert Morse, "Authors at Home," *Critic*, 32 (16 April 1898): 259-261.

Biography:

Martin I. J. Griffin, *Frank Stockton; A Critical Biography* (Philadelphia: University of Pennsylvania Press, 1939).

References:

Henry Golemba, *Frank Stockton* (Boston: Twayne, 1981);

William Dean Howells, "Stockton's Novels and Stories," *Atlantic Monthly*, 87 (January 1901): 136-138;

Howells, "Stockton's Stories," *Atlantic Monthly*, 59 (January 1887): 130-132.

Papers:

There are collections of Stockton's papers at the Pierpont Morgan Library, Princeton University Library, and the Clifton Waller Barrett Library, University of Virginia.

Harriet Beecher Stowe

(14 June 1811-1 July 1896)

Theodore R. Hovet
University of Northern Iowa

See also the Stowe entries in *DLB 1: The American Renaissance in New England,* *DLB 12: American Realists and Naturalists,* and *DLB 42: American Writers for Children Before 1900.*

*SELECTED BOOKS: *Primary Geography for Children on an Improved Plan,* by Stowe and Catharine Beecher (Cincinnati: Corey, Webster & Fairbank, 1833);

Prize Tale: A New England Sketch (Lowell, Mass.: Gilman, 1834);

The Mayflower; or, Sketches of Scenes and Characters among the Descendants of the Pilgrims (New York: Harper, 1843); expanded as *The Mayflower and Miscellaneous Writings* (Boston: Phillips, Sampson, 1855);

Uncle Tom's Cabin; or, Life Among the Lowly, 2 volumes (Boston: Jewett/Cleveland: Jewett, Proctor & Worthington, 1852);

Uncle Sam's Emancipation; Earthly Care, a Heavenly Discipline; and Other Sketches (Philadelphia: Hazard, 1853);

Sunny Memories of Foreign Lands, 2 volumes (Boston: Phillips, Sampson/New York: Derby, 1854);

The Christian Slave. A Drama Founded on a Portion of Uncle Tom's Cabin (Boston: Phillips, Sampson, 1855);

Dred; A Tale of the Great Dismal Swamp, 2 volumes (Boston: Phillips, Sampson, 1856); republished as *Nina Gordon: A Tale of the Great Dismal Swamp,* 2 volumes (Boston: Ticknor & Fields, 1866);

Our Charley, and What to Do With Him (Boston: Phillips, Sampson, 1858);

The Minister's Wooing (New York: Derby & Jackson, 1859);

The Pearl of Orr's Island: A Story of the Coast of Maine (Boston: Ticknor & Fields, 1862);

Agnes of Sorrento (Boston: Ticknor & Fields, 1862);

---

*This list omits British editions for books first published in the United States.

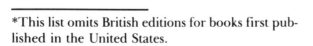

A Reply to "The Affectionate and Christian Address of Many Thousands of Women of Great Britain and Ireland to Their Sisters, the Women of the United States of America" (London: Low, 1863);

House and Home Papers, as Christopher Crowfield (Boston: Ticknor & Fields, 1865);

Little Foxes, as Crowfield (Boston: Ticknor & Fields, 1866);

Religious Poems (Boston: Ticknor & Fields, 1867);

Stories About Our Dogs (Edinburgh: Nimmo, 1867);

The Daisy's First Winter, and Other Stories (Boston: Fields, Osgood, 1867); republished with differing contents as *Queer Little Folks* (London: Nelson, 1886);

Queer Little People (Boston: Ticknor & Fields, 1867);

The Chimney-Corner, as Crowfield (Boston: Ticknor & Fields, 1868);

Men of Our Times; or, Leading Patriots of the Day (Hartford, Conn.: Hartford Publishing Company/New York: Denison, 1868); republished as *The Lives and Deeds of Our Self-Made Men* (Hartford, Conn.: Worthington, Dustin, 1872);

Oldtown Folks (Boston: Fields, Osgood, 1869);

The American Woman's Home, by Stowe and Catharine Beecher (New York & Boston: Ford, 1869); revised and enlarged as *The New Housekeeper's Manual* (New York: Ford, 1874);

Lady Byron Vindicated. A History of the Byron Controversy, from Its Beginning in 1816 to the Present Time (Boston: Fields, Osgood, 1870);

Little Pussy Willow (Boston: Fields, Osgood, 1870);

My Wife and I; or, Harry Henderson's History (New York: Ford, 1871);

Pink and White Tyranny. A Society Novel (Boston: Roberts, 1871);

Six of One by Half a Dozen of the Other. An Every Day Novel, by Stowe, Edward Everett Hale, Lucretia Peabody Hale, and others (Boston: Roberts Brothers, 1872);

Oldtown Fireside Stories (Boston: Osgood, 1872); expanded as *Sam Lawson's Oldtown Fireside Stories* (Boston: Houghton, Mifflin, 1881);

Palmetto-Leaves (Boston: Osgood, 1873);

Woman in Sacred History (New York: Fords, Howard & Hulbert, 1873); republished as *Bible Heroines* (New York: Fords, Howard & Hulbert, 1878);

Betty's Bright Idea. Also Deacon Pitkin's Farm, and The First Christmas of New England (New York: National Temperance Society & Publishing House, 1875);

We and Our Neighbors; or, The Records of an Unfashionable Street (New York: Ford, 1875);

Footsteps of the Master (New York: Ford, 1877);

Poganuc People: Their Loves and Lives (New York: Fords, Howard & Hulbert, 1878);

A Dog's Mission; or, The Story of the Old Avery House and Other Stories (New York: Fords, Howard & Hulbert, 1880).

Collections: *The Writings of Harriet Beecher Stowe*, 16 volumes (Boston & New York: Houghton, Mifflin, 1896);

Harriet Beecher Stowe (New York: Library of America, 1982)–includes *Uncle Tom's Cabin, The Minister's Wooing*, and *Oldtown Folks*, with notes and chronology by Kathryn Kish Sklar.

OTHER: *A Key to Uncle Tom's Cabin; Presenting the Original Facts and Documents upon which the Story is Founded*, compiled by Stowe (Boston: Jewett/Cleveland: Jewett, Proctor & Worthington, 1853).

Until fairly recently Harriet Beecher Stowe has been remembered almost exclusively for *Uncle Tom's Cabin* (1852). For almost a half century, however, she not only wrote some of the finest regional novels in American literature but was also a steady contributor of short stories to widely circulated family publications, annual gift books, and influential magazines such as the *Atlantic Monthly*. For the past three decades, a steady stream of scholarship and criticism has provided a much more balanced view of her literary accomplishments, and today her fiction has assumed a significant place in nineteenth-century American literature.

Born in Litchfield, Connecticut, Harriet Elizabeth Beecher was the daughter of the well-known Congregational minister Lyman Beecher and his first wife, Roxana Foote Beecher. Among her seven brothers and sisters were Catharine Beecher, an older sister who is notable for her theories of women's education and health (theories which receive prominent treatment in some of Stowe's short stories), and Henry Ward Beecher, pastor of Plymouth Church in Brooklyn, New York, and a prominent participant in American religious life during the middle decades of the nineteenth century.

Between 1824 and 1832 Harriet attended Catharine Beecher's Hartford Female Seminary, eventually assisting her sister with teaching duties. Lyman Beecher moved his family to Cincinnati in 1832 when he assumed the presidency of Lane Theological Seminary. Harriet Beecher taught at Western Female Seminary, founded by Catharine Beecher, and in 1834 began her long writing career with "Isabelle and Her Sister Kate" (*Western Monthly Magazine*, February 1834) and–the first story to which she signed her name–"A New England Sketch," which won first prize in a contest sponsored by *Western Monthly Magazine* and was published in that magazine's April 1834 issue. Republished as a pamphlet (1834), as "Uncle Tim" in *The Mayflower* (1843) and as "Uncle Lot" in the 1855 enlarged edition of *The Mayflower*, this story–vividly contrasting handsome young James Benton and his Yankee "cuteness" (that is, "acuteness") with Uncle Lot, the "chesnutt burr"–is a noteworthy presage of Stowe's later contributions to regional literature.

In January 1836 she married widower Calvin Stowe, a respected biblical scholar and theologian whose sophisticated religious speculations, stories of the New England past, and personal experiences with the supernatural were an important source for some of his wife's best fiction. They had seven children.

Amid a steady stream of children, onerous household duties, and the uncongenial environment of a frontier town, Stowe continued writing. By the end of the 1840s her stories and sketches had appeared in the popular magazine *Godey's Lady's Book*, in annual gift books such as *The Religious Souvenir* and *The Temperance Offering*, and in E. D. Mansfield's Cincinnati *Chronicle*. She had also published *The Mayflower*, a collection of stories and sketches. Her name consistently appeared alongside those of such literary luminaries of the period as Lydia Maria Child, T. S. Arthur, Catharine Maria Sedgwick, Caroline Lee Hentz, and Lydia Sigourney. As the *North American Review* pointed out in 1855, the "world-famous tale" *Uncle Tom's Cabin* "was not the miraculous outblooming of a genius that had previously given no sign, but that in the 'Miscellaneous Writings' of earlier years there had been the distinct presage of high and enduring reputation."

Much to Harriet Stowe's delight, the Stowes returned to New England in 1850, after Calvin Stowe accepted a position at Bowdoin College. In June 1851 the first episode of *Uncle Tom's Cabin* appeared in the *National Era*, and the book was published in March 1852. During that same year, Calvin Stowe moved the family to Andover, Massachusetts, where he assumed a professorship at Andover Theological Seminary.

Uncle Tom's Cabin not only made Stowe famous, but the royalties freed her from the most oppressive effects of family responsibilities. Between 1853 and 1860 she made three trips to Europe and became an influential spokesperson on national affairs, religious developments, and domestic practices. These years were also productive ones for the author of *Uncle Tom's Cabin*. After the publication of *Dred* (1856), her second antislavery novel, she published *The Minister's Wooing* (1859), a perceptive fictional treatment of eighteenth-century New England Calvinism; *The Pearl of Orr's Island* (1862), a flawed but interesting regional novel; and *Agnes of Sorrento* (1862), a romantically sentimental tale of Renaissance Italy. The death of her son Henry Ellis Stowe in

Theologian and biblical scholar Calvin Stowe, who married Beecher in 1836

1857 and the Civil War cast a shadow over these otherwise rich and productive years.

After Calvin Stowe's retirement from Andover in 1864 the Stowes moved to Hartford, Connecticut, where they remained for the rest of their lives except for winter stays in Florida. During this time she became a regular contributor to the *Atlantic Monthly*. She also wrote what critics consider her most artistically enduring works: *Oldtown Folks* (1869), *Oldtown Fireside Stories* (1872), and *Poganuc People* (1878). During this period she also produced the controversial *Lady Byron Vindicated* (1870), several religious works, collections of essays and stories, and three society novels–*My Wife and I* (1871), *Pink and White Tyranny* (1871), *We and Our Neighbors* (1875)–which, while careless artistically and hopelessly sentimental, are of interest to social and intellectual historians for Stowe's response to the modern city and her portrayal of feminine and masculine "spheres" in middle-class life. From the early 1880s until her death in 1896, Stowe lived in material comfort and senility.

Stowe's reputation as an American short-story writer rests on *Oldtown Fireside Stories*. Her other stories, however, are not without interest. *The Mayflower; or, Sketches of Scenes and Characters among the Descendants of the Pilgrims* contains sketches and a few stories which are early contributions to regional literature. Like the aged clergyman in "Old Father Morris," Stowe learned how to "create a gallery of New England paintings" in "Yankee form." This art is most evident in "Love versus Law" (first published as "Deacon Enos" in *The Gift* for 1840). The narrator has returned to his native village in New England and is musing in the graveyard, the most "picturesque and peculiar . . . feature of the landscape." The gravestone of Deacon Enos Dudley reminds him of the story of a romance between Susan "Sukey" Jones and Joseph Adams, which had almost been undone by a feud between Sukey's sister, the misnamed Silence, and Joseph's litigious father, Uncle Jaw, who always looks like "a northeast rainstorm." The dispute was ended by the deacon, who is "a very proverb for peacefullness of demeanor and unbounded charitableness." As is characteristic of Stowe's later New England novels and stories, "Love versus Law" succeeds in its poetic evocation of the New England past, its vivid portrayal of village characters, and its inspired use of Yankee dialect. "Cousin William" (*The Gift* for 1839) is less successful at "New England painting" but is noteworthy for the early appearance of Stowe's New England heroine, that tough-minded, physically vigorous, free young woman who stands in delightful contrast to the birdlike, feminine, cloistered, domestic idols who populate the popular fiction of the nineteenth century, including that of Stowe. "Aunt Mary" (*Western Monthly Magazine*, July 1834)—a sketch rather than a story—throws light on Stowe's inner life. The narrator confesses to "an unreasonable heart which is not conformed unto the nature of things" and a "longing for something which should touch it right."

Unfortunately, *The Mayflower* also demonstrates Stowe's most serious artistic weaknesses: moralistic intrusions on the narrative and the undercutting of realistic portrayal with Christian sentimentality. These flaws are most fully exemplified in "The Tea Rose" (*Godey's Lady's Book*, March 1842), in which the beautiful and sorrowful Florence gives her tea rose plant to a poor family before leaving for New York. This act of charity results in her long lost love's seeing the rose and thus finding her again. As the narrator points out to the reader, "he had traced her, even as a hidden streamlet may be traced, by the freshness, the verdure of heart, which her deeds of kindness had left wherever she had passed. This much said, our readers need no help in finishing my story for themselves."

The Mayflower was later expanded. The additions, most of which had appeared in periodicals, are sketches such as "The Canal Boat" (*Godey's Lady's Book*, October 1841), the most interesting to the modern reader, and embarrassing moralistic exempla such as "The Seamstress" (*The Gem Annual* for 1840), or tales of Christian uplift in the manner of "The Mourning Veil" (*Atlantic Monthly*, November 1857).

Stowe published one other collection of stories before the Civil War, *Uncle Sam's Emancipation; Earthly Care, a Heavenly Discipline; and Other Sketches* (1853). The most substantial of the stories, "The Yankee Girl" (*The Token and Atlantic Souvenir* for 1842), portrays a New England woman who rejects a Canadian aristocrat because she does not want to be "a sort of ornamental appendage to his station." The title story, which is supposed to be "literal matters of fact . . . clothed in dramatic form," recounts a young southern slaveowner's discovery of why slaves want their freedom and his decision to emancipate Sam and his family. The other pieces in this collection are sketches and moral essays dealing with such favorite topics of the popular magazines as the drunkard who commits suicide rather than shame his mother, the death of a beautiful young child, the comfort that Christianity and the Bible bring to the poor, and a philanthropist's vision of heaven. One of these, "The Two Altars" (*Autographs for Freedom*, edited by Julia Griffins, 1853), stands out because of Stowe's bitter contrast between the ideals of the American Revolution and the realities of the America of the Fugitive Slave Law.

The artistry that Stowe could achieve in the short story is illustrated in *Oldtown Fireside Stories*, an "amount of curious old Natick tradition" which, as she told James T. Fields, she had not been able to fit into her novel *Oldtown Folks*. These stories were collected as *Oldtown Fireside Stories*, later expanded as *Sam Lawson's Oldtown Fireside Stories* (1881).

These stories, which might have been mere exercises in dialect writing, Yankee humor, and sketching of village characters, achieve emotional texture and thematic depth through the skillful exploitation of the frame structure. Horace Holyoke, who made his appearance as the narrator of *Oldtown Folks*, is the voice of the outer frame as he looks back from the midst of the machine age to the lost world of Oldtown when "two-thirds of New England was . . . dark, unbroken forests" and "the stormful Atlantic" deadened and deafened "any voice that might tell of the settled life of the old civilized world. . . ." Sam Lawson, the voice of the inner frame, is not only the oral historian of the era but an embodiment of values that fly in the face of the New England work ethic that created Horace's world. He is the village "do-nothing," who refuses to be controlled by "the incessant steam-power in Yankee life" of "work, thrift, and industry." To complete the effect of these contrasting sensibilities, Horace's memories of the settings for Sam's stories are capable of wrenching the heart of the reader. Before beginning Sam's story "The Bullfight," Horace comments, "It all comes back to me again,–the image of that huckleberry pasture, interwoven with fragrance of sweetfern, and the ground under our feet embroidered with starmoss and wintergreen, or foamy patches of mossy frost-work, that crushed and crackled delightfully beneath our feet. Every now and then a tall, straight fire-lily–black, spotted in its centre–rose like a little jet of flame; and we gathered it eagerly, though the fierce August sun wilted it in our hands."

Sam's stories, masterpieces of the kind of oral art one associates with Mark Twain, are in themselves a pillar of fire slowly leading Horace and the reader into the promised land of the New England past. Like "some modern novel-writers," Horace explains, Sam employs a narrative art which is "like the course of a dreamy, slow-moving river through a tangled meadow-flat,–not a rush nor a bush but was reflected in it." But the slow-moving flow of the narrative is enlivened by ripples of linguistic surprise. Similar to Huck's ruminations on the raft or on the island, Sam's stories in New England pastures or next to the winter fire take flights into poetic fancy. "When a feller is Indianin' round," Sam observes, "a feller's thoughts gits like a flock o' young partridges: they's up and down and everywhere. . . ." Thus the reader learns to wait for those moments when from the leisurely flow of the story there bursts forth such comments as "So ye see it goes, boys, gettin' yer bread by the sweat o' your brow; and sometimes sweatin' and not gettin' yer bread. That 'ere's what I call the *cuss*, the 'riginal cuss, that come on man for hearkenin' to the voice o' his wife. . . ."

The "rushes and bushes" reflected in the slow-flowing narrative encompass an astonishing variety of human nature. The characters range from the Indian woman Ketury, a "rael wild sort" who comes to a meeting to rattle her necklace "o' rattlesnakes' tails and wildcat teeth" at the parson, to Aunt Lois, who is "the very impersonation of that obstinate rationalism that grew up at the New England fireside"; from the beautiful Huldy, a "factualized" New England woman who can master anything, to the jolly black Caesar, who is incapable of learning from his Puritan betters that "this life's a dream, an empty show."

Sam's stories, like those Calvin Stowe was fond of relating to his wife, fall into two kinds: ghost stories and tales about the people of Oldtown or their ancestors. In the best of the ghost stories, what may or may not be the supernatural appears in the midst of the prosaic New England setting: no ancient haunted houses; no windswept heaths; no mysterious forests; only Oldtown with its "elm-trees, its great square white houses, its meetinghouse and tavern and blacksmith's shop and mill." At certain times, however, such as during a howling snowstorm or at sunset, the "real" and "commonplace" begin to grow "vague and supernatural" as the objects of Oldtown "loom through the gloom." The stories also, like Henry James's *The Turn of the Screw* (1898), skillfully raise questions about the reliability of the observer of unusual events. What might be ghosts, real people, or nothing at all are seen through an alcoholic haze, in the shadow world between sleep and waking, or in the uncertain light of a brilliant moon. Finally, these stories draw forth revelations about the inner life of Oldtown as they reopen old wounds, set the gossip mill turning, and test the rationality, or lack of it, of its leading citizens.

Two stories exemplify Stowe's skillful use of these elements. In "The Ghost in the Cap'n Brown House" (*Atlantic Monthly*, December 1870) Horace sets up Sam's story by noting how Oldtown at sunset becomes "vague and supernatural." Sam then tells the story of a sea captain who lives in a house built like a ship with Quassia, a black serving woman who looks like an "ugly Indian idol" and who wears "gold hoops in her ears, made right in the middle o' Africa among the heathen there." The town seamstress, respectable and level-headed Cinthy Pendleton, is spending a few days at the house mending Brown's clothes. She keeps sensing "somebody or somethin' round the house." One night, during a

Stowe after she achieved her literary reputation

terrific snowstorm and after she has drunk some of the captain's flip, Cinthy suddenly wakes from her sleep to find a woman with long black hair and mournful eyes staring at her. She is convinced the woman is a ghost, but the town gossips insist it was a hidden mistress of the captain's. Sometime later, another woman, Sally Robinson, claims that she saw a carriage drive up to the captain's house at three in the morning and that Brown put a woman into it. Which is more mysterious to Oldtown, Cinthy's ghost or Sally's mistress? As Sam concludes, "which on 'em was awake, or which on 'em was asleep, is what ain't settled in Oldtown yet."

Similarly, in "The Ghost in the Mill" (*Atlantic Monthly*, December 1870) Captain Eb Sawin gets caught in a snowstorm and is forced to take refuge in a mill belonging to the heavy-drinking Cack Sparrock. They start drinking. Suddenly the Indian witch Ketury shows up (Eb swears later that she has left no tracks in the snow). After sitting on the floor for a while, she looks up at the chimney and calls, "Come down, come down! Let's see who ye be!" A pair of feet appears in the hearth. She calls again, and the legs join the feet. This process continues until the whole body of a murdered peddler stands in the hearth. During a sudden burst of the storm, the

body and Ketury disappear. Terrified, Cack confesses that his father had killed the peddler years ago and that he had helped him put the body in the chimney. After Cack's death, the men of the town pull down the mill, and they find a skeleton in the chimney. After Sam finishes the story, one of his auditors, the rationalistic Aunt Lois, insists that Captain Eb was drunk and dreamed the whole thing. Horace's grandmother, however, asks, if all people were like Aunt Lois, what would happen to Cotton Mather's "Magnilly"? Sam ends the dispute with his version of the golden mean, a code that undoubtedly shapes his stories: "if ye want to lead a pleasant and prosperous life, ye must continue allers to keep jest the *happy medium* between truth and falsehood."

The other ghost stories have less texture and, to their detriment, rely less on the context of Oldtown culture. "The Sullivan Looking-Glass" is a romantic tale of how a young woman who has "the gift of seein'" regains her rightful inheritance after looking in an old mirror from Venice and seeing herself finding the lost will. "Capt. Kidd's Money" (*Atlantic Monthly*, November 1870) tells how a group of shiftless villagers find Captain Kidd's buried treasure and then lose it because they cannot keep quiet, thereby invoking a charm which spirits the treasure into the ground.

Sam, who was along, admits that he fell asleep during the most critical events. "Tom Toothacre's Ghost Story" (*Christian Union*, 1872) and "A Student's Sea Story" (*Atlantic Monthly*, January 1879)—both added to the 1881 edition—simply recount stories of men who have seen ghosts.

Sam's stories about the people of Oldtown rest upon sharply etched character studies and incongruous situations. "The Minister's Housekeeper" (*A Library of American Literature*, 1852) describes how the dignified and learned Parson Carryl is driven by the town gossips, who wish to unseat his beautiful housekeeper, Huldy, to take over his own domestic chores. His first project is to force a tom turkey to hatch eggs. After an extended battle with the turkey, he sets it onto the nest with a corn basket and a stone. The turkey soon smashes the eggs and appears "struttin' and gobblin' as if he'd come through the Red Sea, and got the victory." Not only does the parson give up on the turkey, but he decides to marry Huldy. As he puts it, "I thought as folks wanted to talk about Huldy and me I'd give 'em somethin' worth talkin' about."

In a similar vein Parson Williams in "The Parson's Horse-Race" (*Atlantic Monthly*, October 1878; added to the 1881 edition) takes great pride in his horse, a horse which his black servant secretly races. Unaware of his own horse's "sins," the parson hears about the secret races and decides to put a stop to them. When he and the deacons appear at the track, the town cutup yells "Go it boys!" to start the race. The parson's horse, of course, joins the race and carries his rider to victory. The parishioners are scandalized that their minister's horse was racing and bring charges against him. "The sins of the horse" were "imputed to the Doctor," Sam explains. The parson, however, takes it all in good fun and tells the story so delightfully that he is forgiven for his one experience with racy living.

Other stories also deal with how the incongruous event suddenly breaks the rigid pattern of New England village life. "Laughin' in Meetin'" (*Christian Union*, 1872; added to the 1881 edition) recounts how Parson Morrel bursts out laughing in front of his congregation when a sheep attacks the severe Deacon Titkins in the doorway of the church and takes his wig. Some of the congregation want to discipline the parson, but the movement fails. As Sam points out, to punish the parson for laughing would be like chastising the ice for "breakin' up in the Charles River." In "The Bull-fight" Sam tells how the

greedy Bill Moss has his bull fight that of Ike Sanders, his popular foster brother and rival for the pretty Delily Sawain. When Bill's bull is killed, Bill attacks the victor with a board. Ike's bull chases Bill into the house, where he has to shoot it. After this disaster, Bill has to go west, leaving the field clear for the likeable Ike. "How to Fight the Devil" describes how the nasty Black Hoss tries to frighten a converted Indian, Sarah Bunganuck, by wearing a bull's hide and horns and telling her he is the devil. Sarah completely routs Black Hoss—thereby upsetting the villager's negative stereotype of converted Indians—by replying with simple dignity, "Poor old critter, how I pity ye!" "Miss Elderkin's Pitcher" (*Atlantic Monthly*, August 1870) is about the beautiful but "briery, scratchy" Miry Brown, whose father, the devilish Black Hoss, opposes her romance with the academy teacher because of his poverty. Black Hoss dies unconverted and leaves Miry only an old cracked pitcher which she has always hated. In a rage, she throws it across the room, and it breaks to pieces. Out roll hundreds of gold pieces "as thick as dandelions in the meadow." "Allers see what there is in a providence afore you quarrel with it," is Sam's moral, " 'cause there's a good many things in this world turns out like Mis' Elderkin's pitcher."

The stories of Oldtown's past are much less colorful than these tales of village folk. "The Widow's Bandbox" (*Atlantic Monthly*, July 1870) is a tale of the American Revolution. A British officer disguises himself as a woman and talks an American ship captain, to whom "every woman's an angel," into carrying what is said to be the body of "her husband." The coffin contains another British officer, who is supposed to help capture the ship. Tom Toothacre sees through the disguise and breaks up the plot. "Colonel Eph's Shoe-Buckles" (*Atlantic Monthly*, October 1870) deals with the Indian uprisings of the early days of the colony. The story describes how the colonel escapes torture by the Indians when his guard becomes so attracted to his shoe buckles that he gets too close. The colonel subdues him and manages to outrun his captors. "Oldtown Fireside Talks of the Revolution" (added to the 1881 edition) is a simple patriotic recounting of how Horace's grandfather and neighbors participated in the battle of Concord and other skirmishes of the Revolution.

Stowe's other contributions to short fiction after the Civil War are children's stories far less noteworthy than those in *Sam Lawson's Oldtown Fireside Stories*. Stowe's short stories display both the best and the worst aspects of periodical literature during the second and third quarters of the nineteenth century. In her stories for religious publications, family magazines, and gift books she provided the moral uplift and Christian sentiment which her editors and her readers wanted, and she became a major voice in the popular literature of the period, much to the detriment of her literary reputation during the decades following her death. For the *Atlantic Monthly* or a sophisticated religious publication such as the *Christian Union*, she provided some of the better short fiction of the nineteenth century. With their sensitive evocation of the New England past, vivid portraits of village people, and the unforgettable presentation of Sam Lawson, a Yankee poet unassimilable by either the Puritan power structure or the forces of machine culture, the best of *Sam Lawson's Oldtown Fireside Stories* provided a lasting contribution to regional literature and introduced an American voice as unforgettable as Twain's master of the raft.

Letters:

Life of Harriet Beecher Stowe Compiled from Her Letters and Journals, edited by Charles Edward Stowe (Boston: Houghton, Mifflin, 1889);

Life and Letters of Harriet Beecher Stowe, edited by Annie A. Fields (Boston: Houghton, Mifflin, 1897).

Bibliographies:

Margaret Holbrook Hildreth, *Harriet Beecher Stowe: A Bibliography* (Hamden, Conn.: Archon, 1976);

Jean Ashton, *Harriet Beecher Stowe: A Reference Guide* (Boston: G. K. Hall, 1977).

Biographies:

Charles Edward Stowe and L. B. Stowe, *Harriet Beecher Stowe, The Story of Her Life* (Boston: Houghton Mifflin, 1911);

Forest Wilson, *Crusader in Crinoline: The Life of Harriet Beecher Stowe* (Philadelphia: Lippincott, 1941);

References:

John R. Adams, *Harriet Beecher Stowe* (Boston: Twayne, 1963);

Elizabeth Ammons, ed., *Critical Essays on Harriet Beecher Stowe* (Boston: G. K. Hall, 1980);

Charles Foster, *The Rungless Ladder: Harriet Beecher Stowe and New England Puritanism* (Durham: Duke University Press, 1954);

Edward Charles Wagenknecht, *Harriet Beecher Stowe: The Known and the Unknown* (New York: Oxford University Press, 1965).

Papers:

Harriet Beecher Stowe's papers are in the Beecher-Stowe Collection at Schlesinger Library, Radcliffe College, Harvard University.

Maurice Thompson
(9 September 1844-15 February 1901)

Bernard F. Engel
Michigan State University

See also the Thompson entry in *DLB 71: American Literary Critics and Scholars, 1880-1900.*

BOOKS: *Hoosier Mosaics* (New York: Hale, 1875);
The Witchery of Archery: A Complete Manual of Archery (New York: Scribners, 1878);
How to Train in Archery, by Thompson and Will H. Thompson (New York: Horsman, 1880);
A Tallahassee Girl (Boston: Osgood, 1882);
Songs of Fair Weather (Boston: Osgood, 1883);
His Second Campaign (Boston: Osgood, 1883);
By-Ways and Bird Notes (New York: Alden, 1885);
At Love's Extremes (New York: Cassell, 1885); republished as *Milly: At Love's Extremes* (New York: New Amsterdam Book Company, 1901);
A Banker of Bankersville (New York: Cassell, 1886);
Sylvan Secrets, in Bird-songs and Books (New York: Alden, 1887);
The Story of Louisiana (Boston: Lothrop, 1888);
A Fortnight of Folly (New York: Alden, 1888);
Poems (Boston & New York: Houghton, Mifflin, 1892);
The King of Honey Island (New York: Bonner, 1893);
The Ethics of Literary Art: The Carew Lectures for 1893, Hartford Theological Seminary (Hartford: Hartford Seminary Press, 1893);
Lincoln's Grave (Cambridge, Mass. & Chicago: Stone & Kimball, 1894);
The Ocala Boy, A Story of Florida Town and Forest (Boston: Lothrop, 1895);
How To Study History, Literature, The Fine Arts, by Thompson, Albert Bushnell Hart, and Charles Mason Fairbanks (Meadville, Pa.: Flood & Vincent, 1895);
Stories of Indiana (New York & Cincinnati: American Book Company, 1898);
Stories of the Cherokee Hills (Boston & New York: Houghton, Mifflin, 1898);
Alice of Old Vincennes (Indianapolis: Bowen-Merrill, 1900);
My Winter Garden (New York: Century, 1900);

Maurice Thompson

Rosalynde's Lovers (Indianapolis: Bowen-Merrill, 1901);
Sweetheart Manette (Philadelphia & London: Lippincott, 1901).

PERIODICAL PUBLICATIONS: "A Prairie Home," *St. Nicholas,* 18 (September 1891): 859-862;
"Smithers," *Lippincott's Monthly Magazine,* 49 (June 1892): 723-734.

While modern critics regard some of Maurice Thompson's work as a step toward realism, Thompson rightly perceived himself as writing in the older romantic mode. His "local color" aimed to set down "those incidents of human life that flicker along the vanishing line" that marks "the close of every period of civilization." His intention was not to portray dominant social circumstances, but to summon nostalgia for a world whose colors were fading. Yet, Thompson's dream world is one where outcomes are determined by luck and shrewdness. Achievement in the arts or professions is remote, the highest accomplishment is outdoing the other fellow by means that often amount to the use of force or to cheating, and people are pathetically dependent on the approval of their peers.

Thompson was born on 9 September 1844 in Fairfield, Indiana, to the Reverend Matthew Grigg and Diantha Jaeger Thompson. He got a few years of backwoods schooling in Indiana; in north Georgia, where he passed his late boyhood and early manhood on his parents' plantation, he learned, with the help of his mother, something of literature and mathematics. Thompson served in the Confederate army from 1861 to 1864, then returned to Georgia, where he studied engineering and law. Finding little opportunity in the defeated South, he moved to Crawfordsville, Indiana, in 1868 and made a living briefly as a civil engineer and then as a lawyer, in partnership with his brother, Will Henry Thompson, until the 1880s, when he was able to live on the earnings of his pen.

Thompson had begun writing while in the South and eventually published numerous poems, reviews, literary articles, and nature sketches, as well as a handful of short stories. His first success came with tales of his experiences as an archer, sometimes written in collaboration with his brother, an even more noted bowman. These tales stimulated national interest in the sport and remained a source of income throughout his career.

Thompson selected the poems for his two collections, *Songs of Fair Weather* (1883) and *Poems* (1892), from several hundred published verses. These poems are conventional in form and betray an attenuated romanticism that represents itself as a search for ideal truth. His novels also are in the mode of the middlebrow writer. Except for his nature writing, his work sold only indifferently well until *Alice of Old Vincennes* (1900), a historical novel, became a best-seller.

In his writing Thompson demonstrates an attachment to the past and the rural. He finds low-life characters amusing or pathetic and regards city life and industrialization as inimical to the imagination and the humane. He draws on his own observations to depict cabin and farm, clothing, behavior, and speech habits, but such detail is only an anchor to keep his fiction from escaping reality entirely.

Thompson published only two collections of short stories: *Hoosier Mosaics* (1875), set in Indiana, and *Stories of the Cherokee Hills* (1898), drawing on his experiences in the South. The people and places in both books are remote from the world of immigrants, industry, and urban life. The stories–or "sketches," as Thompson called them–make use of regional dialects, often indicated by quirky spelling and rural locutions. The habit of inserting before a decisive development or action a static description of trees, grasses, and birds suggests that Thompson supposed there to be a connection between nature and events in the human world; he does not, however, indicate what that relationship between man and nature might be. In several stories characters are defeated, usually in love affairs. While these people may be considered forerunners of the grotesques who, a generation later, would populate Sherwood Anderson's *Winesburg, Ohio* (1919), Thompson–unlike Anderson–does not perceive his losers to be trapped in situations that allow no fulfillment: they may be rueful, or baffled, but they do not become grotesque.

In *Hoosier Mosaics*, by far the better of Thompson's two collections, the common theme is pride, exposed by a shrewdness that for Thompson represented folk wisdom. In many of these stories a man believes himself in love–from a distance–with a woman who does not share his feelings and shrewdly puts him down. In "Was She a Boy?" a young person–first in the guise of a man, then appearing to be female–dallies with a gullible townsman while working a confidence racket. In "Big Medicine" and "Hoiden" unsuccessful male lovers leave town. Big Medicine moons over a young woman but finds that she has a lover. Thompson recognizes the admiration that lies behind the small-town dwellers' humorously disparaging descriptions of the well-dressed businessman. The villagers are indirectly confessing their own limitations, as they do in heeding the insulting, though humorous, advertisements that Big Medicine paints on fences, gates, pig-pens, and wagon beds. The pathos of Big Medicine's lot is paralleled in "Hoiden," an account of how Luke, a prosperous farmer, is attracted by the tomboy daughter of a civil engineer. When the girl is abruptly taken away by another, Luke is left "morose and petulant." Pathos is also evoked in "Trout's Luck," a sketch presenting a young man who, losing his money to a county fair pitchman, must endure the rest of the evening in torment, as his rival entertains the girl on whom both have set their hearts. In one way or another, the victims in these stories have failed to meet the challenges of the shrewd competitors they have faced.

In the best of the tales, "The Pedagogue," the central character is similarly outwitted. The teller of the story recalls the severe teachers that once were accepted by the community as intellectual and moral authorities. His example is Blodgett, a teacher who was shown to have translated a Latin work in error and was so humiliated as a result that he left his job, his lady love, and the town. Thompson's aim is to arouse feelings of nostalgia, but the reader will see in the tale an unflattering depiction of the pride that is the dominant civic attitude.

Failure in love is comedic in "The Venus of Balhinch." The narrator and his friend Ben become rivals for the local belle, Susie. At one point the narrator takes revenge on Ben by setting fire to his haystacks, an action suggesting meanness, but Thompson does not develop this aspect of the narrator's character. When the narrator finally gets up the nerve to propose, Susie dumps a churnful of milk on him. Rather like the rural comedy of Oliver Goldsmith, the tale is meant to appeal through its portrayal of the swain's comeuppance. Thompson's description of the young woman's house, with its bare-board floors and its picture of George Washington, is convincingly realistic.

Coincidence creates a doleful sort of humor in "Legend of Potato Creek." A city girl on the farm for the summer heals a horse that was to be shot as incurable and also nurses Zach, a young farmer, back to health. But neither horse nor man can hold onto life; as Zach lies on his deathbed, news comes that the horse, too, is dying. Thompson seems to be attempting to give the Indiana countryside some of the association with the mysterious that Washington Irving sought for New York. His immediate purposes, however, are only to wring out a tear and to amuse by paralleling the experiences of horse and man.

The two stories in *Hoosier Mosaics* not centering on a love relationship both celebrate cleverness. The boy in "The Idyl of the Rod" is to be admired for insulating himself from the effects of a

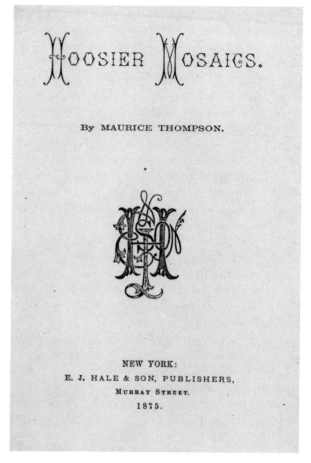

Title page for Thompson's first volume of stories, about life in small-town Indiana

beating by his father. Thompson does not wonder why the father wants to give the boy such a terrible drubbing just because of a childish oversight. In "Stealing a Conductor," the liveliest of the stories in the book, the penniless central character gets out of difficulty by using his wits to steal a ride on a train and, in a final display of cleverness, to escape from the train crew arriving at the station.

Hoosier Mosaics celebrates winners and finds pathos or humor in the fates of losers. The larger aim is to suggest that people from the small towns and farms of the Midwest have wits that make them the equals of the better educated and more sophisticated. As a local colorist, Thompson feared that the growing domination of the city was eliminating the native common sense that he saw in people of the backcountry.

Though it has since gained moderate esteem from literary historians for its use of observed details, *Hoosier Mosaics* had no sale outside the state of Indiana and little within it. *Stories of the Cherokee Hills* had somewhat more acceptance. Its stories also often illustrate what Thompson took to be native wit. Its aim, however, is to give sentimental views of relations between blacks and whites in the South. Though in *Lincoln's Grave* (1894), an ode, Thompson wrote that abolition of slavery was necessary, and that he had fought as a Confederate only to stem northern aggression, he argues in these tales that, in the Georgia hill regions where he grew up, slave life was idyllic. The opening piece, "Color-line Jocundities," is a rambling, half-autobiographical preface giving an idealized view of the situation of blacks, whose inferior status, Thompson's narrator says, is God's will and Nature's way. The sort of black the narrator prefers is Tuck, a former slave who is proud that, after he once dared to vote, a white man hit him so hard that he has never again gone near the ballot box. Tuck, the story implies, knows his "place." The book ends with the exemplary anecdote "Ben and Judas," which illustrates what the speaker sees as the ideal harmonious pairing of white (Ben) and black (Judas). Judas has a chance to vote but gracefully steps aside, saying that it is right that only Ben's vote should count.

Pretension of blacks to equality is punished in "Rudgis and Grim" and shown to be disastrous to whites in "A Race Romance." Such stories are somewhat balanced by two tales showing that certain blacks may have unusual capabilities. "A Dusky Genius" portrays sympathetically, if patronizingly, the achievement of the black man Rack, who makes an excellent banjo from a juice-soaked board and an opossum skin. Rack is approved because he kowtows humbly to his master and claims neither fortune nor social recognition.

Similarly, in "The Balance of Power" the freedman Barnaby maneuvers local politics so that his former master is nominated for the legislature. Barnaby represents the black who works to bring happiness to his white superior and makes no uppity demand for acknowledgment.

The only story not dealing directly with race relations, "Hodson's Hide-out," works for the effect of pathos, not by recording the mistreatment of a black man, a matter seen as incidental in the 1870s, but by showing a father's inability to comprehend that his son, reported missing in action in the Civil War, must be considered dead. The narrator speaks of using Hodson as representative "of that region"; such value as the story has is, indeed, in its description of hills, cabins, and isolated people.

Thompson's short fiction achieved the local colorist's aim of recording the ways of a time and place. His underlying motive was to defend values that he located in the past and the rural. It seems clear, finally, that the views of Thompson's narrators are shared by the author.

References:

R. E. Banta, comp., *Indiana Authors and Their Books 1816-1916* (Crawfordsville, Ind.: Wabash College, 1949);

Dorothy R. Russo and Thelma Sullivan, *Seven Authors of Crawfordsville, Indiana* (Indianapolis: Indiana Historical Society, 1952), pp. 173-283;

George A. Schumacher, *Maurice Thompson, Archer and Author* (New York: Vantage Press, 1968);

Otis B. Wheeler, *The Literary Career of Maurice Thompson* (Baton Rouge: Louisiana State University Press, 1965).

Nathaniel Parker Willis

(20 January 1806-20 January 1867)

William V. DeTora
Temple University

See also the Willis entries in *DLB 3: Antebellum Writers in New York and the South; DLB 59: American Literary Critics and Scholars, 1800-1850;* and *DLB 73: American Magazine Journalists, 1741-1850.*

BOOKS: *Sketches* (Boston: S. G. Goodrich, 1827);
Fugitive Poetry (Boston: Pierce & Williams, 1829);
Poem, Delivered Before the Society of United Brothers, at Brown University on the day Preceding Commencement, September 6, 1831, with other poems (New York: Harper, 1831);
Melanie and Other Poems (London: Saunders & Otley, 1835; enlarged edition, New York: Saunders & Otley, 1837);
Pencillings by the Way (3 volumes, London: Macrone, 1835; 2 volumes, Philadelphia: Carey, Lea & Blanchard, 1836);
Inklings of Adventure (3 volumes, London: Saunders & Otley, 1836; 2 volumes, New York: Saunders & Otley, 1836);
A l'Abri; or, the Tent Pitch'd (New York: Colman, 1839); republished as *Letters from under a Bridge* (London: G. Virtue, 1840; New York: Morris, Willis, 1844);
Bianca Visconti; or, the Heart Overtasked (New York: Colman, 1839);
Tortesa; or, the Usurer Matched (New York: Colman, 1839);
American Scenery, 2 volumes (London: G. Virtue, 1840);
The Romance of Travel (New York: Colman, 1840); republished as *Loiterings of Travel* (London: Longman, Orme, Brown, Green & Longmans, 1840);
The Sacred Poems of N. P. Willis (New York: Morris, Willis, 1843);
The Lady Jane, and Other Humorous Poems (New York: Morris, Willis, 1844);
The Poems, Sacred, Passionate, and Humorous (New York: Clark & Austin, 1844);
Dashes at Life with a Free Pencil (1 volume, New York: Burgess, Stringer, 1845; 3 volumes, London: Longman, Brown, Green & Longmans, 1845);

Nathaniel Parker Willis, 1856

Rural Letters and Other Records of Thought at Leisure (New York: Baker & Scribner, 1849);
People I Have Met; or, Pictures of Society and People of Mark, Drawn under a Thin Veil of Fiction (Auburn: Alden, Beardsley / Rochester, N.Y.: Wanzer, Beardsley, 1849; London: Bohn, 1850);
Life Here and There (New York: Baker & Scribner, 1850);
Hurry-graphs; or, Sketches of Scenery, Celebrities & Society, Taken from Life (Auburn & Rochester: Alden & Beardsley, 1851);

Summer Cruise in the Mediterranean (Auburn: Alden & Beardsley, 1853; London: Nelson, 1853);

Fun-Jottings; or, Laughs I Have Taken a Pen To (New York: Scribner, 1853);

Health Trip to the Tropics (New York: Scribner, 1853; London: Sampson, Low, 1854);

Famous Persons and Places (New York: Scribner, 1854; London: Ward & Lock, 1854);

Out-doors at Idlewild; or, The Shaping of a Home on the Banks of the Hudson (New York: Scribner, 1855);

The Rag Bag, A Collection of Ephemera (New York: Scribner, 1855);

Paul Fane; or, Parts of a Life Else Untold (New York: Scribner/Boston: Williams, 1857; London: Clarke, 1857);

The Convalescent (New York: Scribner, 1859).

Collections: *The Complete Works of N. P. Willis* (New York: J. S. Redfield, 1846);

The Prose Works of N. P. Willis (Philadelphia: Carey & Hart, 1849);

Poems of Nathaniel Parker Willis, edited, with a memoir, by H. L. Williams (New York: Hurst, 1882);

The Poetical Works of N. P. Willis (London: Routledge, 1888).

OTHER: *The Legendary, Consisting of Original Pieces, Principally Illustrative of American History, Scenery, and Manners*, 2 volumes, edited by Willis (Boston: S. G. Goodrich, 1828);

The Token: A Christmas and New Year's Present, edited by Willis (Boston: S. G. Goodrich, 1829);

The Opal: A Pure Gift for the Holy Days, edited by Willis (New York: J. C. Riker, 1844);

The Prose and Poetry of Europe and America, compiled by Willis and George Pope Morris (New York: Leavitt & Allen, 1845);

The Gem of the Season, for 1850, edited by Willis (New York: Leavitt, Trow, 1850);

Memoranda of the Life of Jenny Lind, edited by Willis (Philadelphia: Peterson, 1851);

Trenton Falls, Picturesque and Descriptive, edited by Willis (New York: Putman, 1851).

PERIODICAL PUBLICATION: "Death of Edgar A. Poe," *Home Journal* (30 October 1849).

The decline of the critical reputation of Nathaniel Parker Willis, wrote Arthur Hobson Quinn, provides "a shining example of the price a gifted man pays in terms of lasting fame for con-

temporary popularity." This kind of assessment of Willis's work has become a critical cliché, accurate enough in general, but insufficient because it discounts Willis's pervasive influence on short fiction as an editor and arbiter of taste during the 1830s and 1840s. Indicative of popular tastes and the demands of the magazine market, Willis's work informs the literary historian who seeks to know something of the state of the art of popular short fiction during the first half of the nineteenth century. Willis, whatever his shortcomings, had an uncanny ability to anticipate what the literary market would bear.

Nathaniel Parker Willis was born 20 January 1806 in Portland, Maine, the son and grandson of journalists. His grandfather, Nathaniel, founded the *Independent Chronicle* in Boston, Massachusetts. His father, Nathaniel, who married Hannah Parker on 21 July 1803 (Nathaniel Parker was the second of nine children), was a Boston clergyman and founder of the religious newspaper the *Boston Recorder*. Willis received all the advantages of a first-class education, attending Boston Latin School, preparing for college at Andover, and eventually attending Yale. His years at Yale set the pattern for his later public career. As an undergraduate Willis became a well-known figure for both his literary productions and his flamboyant life-style. While at Yale he gained a national reputation as a poet, first by publishing verse in his father's newspaper and later with a thin volume of poems entitled *Sketches* (1827). Even as a student-author, Willis knew his audience well. His early poetry, mostly verse interpretations of biblical themes, exploited the contemporary rage for religious revivalism. His college years, however, were only partially devoted to literary endeavors. Possessing social graces equal to his literary talents, Willis quickly developed a taste for fashionable society and earned the reputation of dandy, which would follow him the rest of his life.

Upon graduation from Yale, Willis set out for Boston to pursue a career in journalism. In 1828 he edited *The Legendary* for Samuel G. Goodrich; a year later he edited Goodrich's popular gift annual, *The Token*. Always brash and confident, Willis released, in April 1829, a publication of his own—the *American Monthly Magazine*. The extravagant editorial pose which he created for himself enhanced his reputation as a dandy. His column, "The Editor's Table," introduced in the fourth issue, quickly became the magazine's centerpiece, presenting Willis's usually appreciative book reviews in an urbane, conversational style. Within two and a half years, however, dwindling subscriptions and mounting debt forced Willis to discontinue the magazine. He also dashed out a few tales for popular magazines during his time in Boston, but in later years he republished only fragments of these stories, which were the efforts of an apprentice.

After the folding of the *American Monthly* Willis left Boston for New York and quickly formed a relationship with George Pope Morris and the *New York Mirror*. He became an associate editor for the *Mirror* and was asked to submit a series of weekly travel letters from Europe. On 10 October 1831 he sailed for Europe on a trip that would have a major effect on his short-fiction writing.

In the fashionable circles of Old World society Willis found his natural element, and his flamboyance as well as his creativity blossomed. Traveling in England and on the Continent, Willis became a darling of European high society. He recounted his experiences with European nobility in *Pencillings by the Way* (1835), a collection based on the letters he sent to the *Mirror*. The book was a success in America, but Willis's candor enraged some of his European acquaintances, who accused him of abusing their hospitality and turning it into "copy." For a while he was lambasted in the British press, but only one incident connected with *Pencillings by the Way* came close to having serious consequences. Capt. Frederick Marryat, editor of the *London Metropolitan Magazine* and author of books that Willis called "gross trash," attacked Willis in print and challenged him to a duel. The intercession of seconds prevented the meeting, but the incident caused an exciting stir in England and America and added to Willis's reputation as a rake.

The European sojourn, however, was also the beginning of a decade-long period of prolific short-fiction writing. While still in England, Willis issued *Inklings of Adventure* (1836), a collection of thirteen tales which had appeared in English magazines under the pseudonym "Philip Slingsby." Four years later and back in America, his second book of short fiction appeared. *The Romance of Travel* (1840), a collection of stories previously published in the *Mirror*, the *New Monthly*, and the *Corsair*, (which Willis edited from 1839 to 1840) was immediately successful. Willis's popularity as a magazinist was now at its height. Biographer Henry A. Beers reports that by 1842 Willis was writing four monthly articles for four

Willis in later life (photograph by Rockwood)

magazines (the *Mirror, Graham's, Godey's,* and *Ladies' Companion*) at an annual income of forty-eight hundred dollars per year. Most of these stories would eventually appear in *Dashes at Life with a Free Pencil* (1845), Willis's third and final collection of previously uncollected short fiction.

Willis's sense of the business of literature helps explain the nature of his short-fiction writing. Always aware of popular tastes, Willis tailored both the form and the content of his work to conform to the demands of the marketplace for imaginatively extravagant, though technically conservative romances. Fred Lewis Pattee correctly asserts that the "short story as an independent literary form did not exist for Willis." Indeed, Willis wrote short fiction only because longer American works simply would not sell. In the preface to *Dashes at Life with a Free Pencil* Willis complains that "the author, in the following collection of brief tales, gives material, that, but for a single objection, would have been molded into works of larger design. That objection is the unmarketableness of American books in America." While Willis trimmed the length of his stories, he never bothered to develop a new form for them. As a result, most of his stories are simply safe, condensed forms of the romance novel. Often, for example, he relies on "chapters" that function in ways similar to those of their counterparts in longer narratives. Chapter divisions set up cliff-hangers in "Lady Ravelgold," present digressive descriptive passages in "F. Smith," initiate scene changes or shifts in action in "The Gypsy of Sardis," and provide background information necessary to the plot in "The Bandit of Austria." Such devices were necessary because the emphasis throughout all of Willis's fiction is on the story. There is little attempt at character development and often no connection between behavior and motivation.

Most often the action in a Willis story unfolds through the traditional narrative method of exposition, complication, and easy, usually optimistic, resolution. "Tom Fane and I," one of Willis's most characteristic stories, provides a good example of his narrative method. The situation is quickly introduced–Tom Fane, a young ne'er-do-well, becomes involved in a scheme to help his fortuneless friend, Philip Slingsby, marry the ward of a rich trader in rice and molasses. The comic complication involves Philip hearing Tom's apparent proposal to Katherine, the girl Tom is supposed to help Philip marry. A quick and decidedly unbelievable resolution ensues. Philip was simply mistaken. As the tale concludes, Philip gets his Katherine and her fortune, Tom marries Philip's sister, and everybody is happy. The story is easily comprehended and narratively unchallenging. Yet its economy of design and simplistic narrative formula would have appealed to even the indiscriminate reader of popular fiction, described by Herman Melville in "Hawthorne and His Mosses" (1847) as the "superficial skimmer of pages." More innovative short-story forms, as conceived by Edgar Allan Poe and Nathaniel Hawthorne, were simply alien to, or more likely ignored by, Willis throughout his career.

Just as the form of Willis's stories catered to popular tastes, so, too, was the content of his short fiction completely controlled by the demands of the marketplace. Pandering to the popular thirst for the exotic, Willis frequently set his stories in remote or picturesque parts of the world. In "Pasquali, The Tailor of Venice" the setting is contemporary Italy. "The Gypsy of Sardis" is a prose travelogue of Asia Minor. "The Belle of the Belfry, or the Daring Lover" is set in France, while "The Bandit of Austria" takes

place in Vienna and its environs. Occasionally, Willis resorts to the remote in both time and place. "The Inlet of Peach-Blossoms," for example, recounts a legend from ancient China. When Willis does deal with the American scene, his settings still seem exotic to his middle-class readers because he confines himself almost exclusively to the favorite haunts of the rich. "Tom Fane and I," "Larks in Vacation," and "The Ghost-Ball at Congress Hall" all take place in Saratoga, New York. In "F. Smith" the fashionable seaside resort of Nahant, Massachusetts, is described in loving and sometimes gratuitous detail.

Exotic settings require exotic characters, and Willis's stories are full of an assortment of counts, dukes, princesses, gypsies, and American belles. These characters tend to be stock romantic representations. There is little attempt to individualize any character. Willis's heroines, for example, are completely idealized. Iminild in "The Bandit of Austria," the countess in "The Countess Nyschriem, and the Handsome Artist," Princess Leichstenfels in "Love and Diplomacy," and Maimuna in "The Gypsy of Sardis" all share common characteristics. They are exquisitely beautiful, and they all fall in love. Willis's heroes are equally romantic figures. Tyrell in "The Bandit of Austria," Robertin in "The Belle of the Belfry," and even Philip Slingsby in "The Gypsy of Sardis" are devil-may-care adventurers whose spirited intrigues rival those of any of the popular heroes of early-nineteenth-century romance. Willis's stories are also filled with stock romantic plot machinery. "The Gypsy of Sardis" revolves around disguises and rescues. In "The Bandit of Austria" duels, abductions, and extraordinary chase scenes proliferate. "Lady Ravelgold" presents the themes of star-crossed love and the recovery of a title and fortune, while "The Belle of the Belfry" focuses on the dramatic revelation of a lost heiress. However, by far, Willis's favorite romantic theme is the gaining of unexpected fortune. Tremlet, the banker in "Lady Ravelgold," turns out to be a Russian nobleman and inherits land and money. Thénais in "The Belle of the Belfry" is transformed from a poor working girl to an estate owner when she discovers her noble parentage. Percie, a servant, marries nobility in "The Bandit of Austria," and Graeme McDonald, a poor artist, marries a rich and powerful countess at the conclusion of "The Countess Nyschriem, and the Handsome Artist."

Willis's experiments in other genres reveal a similar romantic impulse. Both *Bianca Visconti; or,* the Heart Overtasked (1839) and Tortesa; or, the Usurer Matched (1839), his two attempts at drama, are sentimentalized romances that were only partially successful even in his own day. Willis's one novel, *Paul Fane; or, Parts of a Life Else Untold* (1857), continues on the romantic preoccupations of his short fiction in longer form. It was for his short fiction that Willis was best known; during the years between the publication of *Inklings of Adventure* and *Dashes at Life with a Free Pencil*, Willis was perhaps the most popular magazinist in America.

After 1846, however, Willis's major period of short fiction writing was over, and during the succeeding seven years he began remarketing already collected material, in *People I Have Met* (1849), *Life Here and There* (1850), and *Fun-Jottings* (1853). Although he continued to contribute tales to magazines, he was too busy with fulltime editorial duties with Morris's *Home Journal* to maintain his earlier pace.

Willis's previous experiences as an editor prepared him well for the job with Morris, which he began in 1846. In addition to editing his own *American Monthly* and serving as nominal editor on Morris's original *New York Mirror*, he had also edited the short-lived *Corsair*, through which he introduced William Makepeace Thackeray to the American public. After the *Corsair* Willis worked with Morris again on the weekly *New Mirror* (1843-1844) and on its later manifestation, the daily *Evening Mirror*. As editor of the *Evening Mirror* in 1844-1845 Willis engaged Poe as critic and subeditor and lent Poe the support of the paper. In 1846 Willis joined the *Home Journal*, where his position as editor forced him to make what was undoubtedly an uncomfortable decision to reject contributions by his sister Sara Payson Willis Parton (Fanny Fern). For exercising his editorial right, Willis was ruthlessly caricatured in Fanny Fern's *Ruth Hall, a Domestic Tale of the Present Time*

(1854). Despite this unpleasant experience, Willis continued as editor of the *Home Journal* until his death on 20 January 1867.

Despite the praise of contemporaries like Poe, Willis's literary reputation has continuously declined since his death. Although Pattee credits him with adding touches of humor and unexpectedness to the short story, he is dismissed, even by Pattee, as an author who devoted real talent to insignificant purposes. Nowhere is this opinion more apparent than in the scholarly community's near neglect of Willis, especially in the last two decades. But Willis's brand of marketable fiction was precisely the kind of writing against which authors like Hawthorne and Melville were reacting. Thus, to know Willis is to know something of the milieu out of which greater writing emerged.

Biographies:

Henry A. Beers, *Nathaniel Parker Willis* (Boston & New York: Houghton, Mifflin, 1885);

Harry Thurston Peck, "N. P. Willis and His Contemporaries," *Bookman*, 24 (September 1906): 33-43.

References:

Robert F. Marler, "From Tale to Short Story: The Emergence of a New Genre in the 1850's," *American Literature*, 46 (May 1974): 153-169;

Fred Lewis Pattee, *The Development of the American Short Story* (New York: Harper, 1923), pp. 78-88;

Arthur Hobson Quinn, *History of the American Drama* (New York: Harper, 1923), p. 255.

Papers:

Willis's letters are housed at the Yale University Library. A fragmentary diary is in the public library at Morristown, New Jersey.

Constance Fenimore Woolson

(5 March 1840-24 January 1894)

Mary P. Edwards
Randolph-Macon College

See also the Woolson entry in *DLB 12: American Realists and Naturalists.*

BOOKS: *The Old Stone House,* as Anne March (Boston: Lothrop, 1872);

Castle Nowhere: Lake-Country Sketches (Boston: Osgood, 1875);

Two Women: 1862. A Poem (New York: Appleton, 1877);

Rodman the Keeper: Southern Sketches (New York: Appleton, 1880);

Anne: A Novel (New York: Harper, 1882; London: Low, 1883);

For the Major: A Novelette (New York: Harper, 1883; London: Low, 1883);

East Angels (New York & London: Harper, 1886; London: Low, 1886);

Jupiter Lights: A Novel (New York: Harper, 1889; London: Low, 1889);

Horace Chase: A Novel (New York: Harper, 1894; London: Osgood, 1894);

The Front Yard and Other Italian Stories (New York: Harper, 1895);

Dorothy and Other Italian Stories (New York: Harper, 1896);

Mentone, Cairo, and Corfu (New York: Harper, 1896);

Constance Fenimore Woolson, volume 2 of *Five Generations (1785-1923), Being Scattered Chapters from the History of the Cooper, Pomeroy, Woolson and Benedict Families, with Extracts from Their Letters and Journals, as Well as Articles and Poems by Constance Fenimore Woolson,* edited by Clare Benedict (London: Ellis, 1930).

According to Fred Lewis Pattee, during the 1870s Constance Fenimore Woolson "was the most 'unconventional' feminine writer that had yet appeared in America." Woolson's fiction of the 1870s and 1880s places her among the female local colorists, whose stories were replacing the sentimental and effusive fiction of the first generation of American women writers. As Ann Douglas Wood has noted, "Constance Fenimore

Constance Fenimore Woolson

Woolson, a descendant of James Fenimore Cooper and a friend of Henry James, began her own career in declared hostility to her rhapsodical sisters." Woolson's early stories appeared in major periodicals, including *Atlantic Monthly, Scribner's Monthly, Harper's New Monthly,* the *Galaxy,* and *Appletons' Journal.* These stories were so successful that after the publication of "Rodman the Keeper" in 1877 Harper and Brothers asked "whether or not it would be possible" for her to send all the stories she wrote to them. "The Native Element in Fiction," an anonymous article in the July 1883 issue of *Century,* listed Woolson among those American writers "who hold the front rank today in general estimation. . . ." The others named in the same article were William Dean Howells, Henry James, George Washington Cable, and Frances Hodgson Burnett. By the end of the nineteenth century, four collections of Woolson's short stories had been published: *Castle Nowhere: Lake-Country Sketches* (1875), *Rodman the Keeper: Southern Sketches* (1880), *The Front Yard and Other Italian Stories* (1895), and *Dorothy and Other Italian Stories* (1896). The first two volumes, set in northern Michigan and the South (the Carolinas, the mountain regions of Tennessee, and northern Florida), respectively, have been of special interest to recent critics, such as Anne Rowe, who have emphasized Woolson's role as a local colorist who "attempted to capture in her work the uniqueness of the places about which she wrote— to value their differences rather than to urge their conformity with the rest of the nation." Some contemporary scholarship has focused on those stories in *Rodman the Keeper*, in which Woolson pictures Northerners who went to live south of the Mason-Dixon line following the Civil War. These stories, such as "King David," illustrate Woolson's interest in the psychology of such "transplanted" persons. As Evelyn Helmick notes, "Miss Woolson's major theme in all her southern work is the contrast between the northern and southern temperaments." The stories in the posthumously published volumes *The Front Yard* and *Dorothy* are tales of American characters in European settings which analyze the effect of European culture upon Americans and examine their responses to the Old World. Woolson also wrote travel sketches, critical essays, and reviews for "The Contributors' Club" in the *Atlantic Monthly;* and five novels: *Anne* (1882), *For the Major* (1883), *East Angels* (1886), *Jupiter Lights* (1889), and *Horace Chase* (1894). At the end of the nineteenth century the *Boston Globe* called her the "novelist laureate" of America.

The sixth and youngest daughter of Charles Jarvis and Hannah Cooper Pomeroy Woolson, Constance Fenimore Woolson was born on 5 March 1840, in Claremont, New Hampshire. Not long after her birth the family moved to Cleveland, Ohio, where she attended Miss Hayden's School during the 1840s and the Cleveland Female Seminary in the 1850s. Woolson continued her education at Madame Chegaray's School in New York City, where in 1858 she graduated at the head of her class. Her early experiences in northern Ohio and the Great Lakes region, including many summer journeys to Mackinac Island, form the background for her first stories. As her name suggests, her literary antecedents include her mother's uncle, James Fenimore Cooper. This relationship seemed of particular signifi-

cance to her English publishers, who advertised her first novel, *Anne,* in the London *Times* and *Daily News* as "the New American Novel by a Niece of Fenimore Cooper."

Woolson began writing in earnest in 1870-1871, following her father's death in 1869. She lived with her mother, traveling with her to New York City and throughout the South. They were often accompanied by Woolson's sister Clara Benedict as they visited Philadelphia, Washington, Richmond, Charleston, and Jacksonville, en route to Florida, usually St. Augustine. John Dwight Kern notes that "just as Mackinac Island was the focal point of Miss Woolson's writings about the lake region, so St. Augustine was to become her literary capital in the South." Woolson and her mother also spent time in the Carolinas, Tennessee, and Georgia, and the experiences of these years furnished the materials for Woolson's southern stories. Devastated by her mother's death in 1879, Woolson left America and traveled abroad. Although she occasionally contemplated returning to live in her mother's birthplace, Cooperstown, New York, Woolson's professional and personal interests, as well as her preference for the Italian climate during the winter months, kept her abroad. From 1880 until her death in 1894, she lived for varying periods of time in Florence, Venice, Rome, Switzerland, the Black Forest, London, Warwickshire, Cheltenham, and Oxford, and made trips to Greece and Egypt. Her friendship with Henry James began in the spring of 1880 and continued until the time of her death. The stories in her third and fourth volumes of tales reflect their shared interest in the international theme, while some of those same stories also illuminate her struggle to comprehend the nature and role of the woman artist. In 1894, suffering from a severe and prolonged attack of influenza, she either jumped or fell from her second-story window in Venice. She is known to have suffered periods of acute depression, associated with the deaths of each of her parents and with the intellectually taxing nature of her writing. At the time of her death she had just completed *Horace Chase,* and, although conflicting accounts of her death exist, she may have been in a state of mental depression.

Woolson's correspondence reveals her preoccupation with what it meant to be a female writer. She saw herself as different from her contemporaries. In an 1875 letter to one of her literary advisers, poet Paul Hamilton Hayne, she wrote: "I have the idea that women run too much into mere beauty at the expense of power; and the result is, I fear, that I have gone too far the other way; too rude; too abrupt." She felt that the heroes in fiction by other women writers (such as Frances Christine Fisher, Augusta Jane Evans Wilson, and Mrs. Catherine Ann Ware Warfield) were too " 'knightly,'–for the real life of today." Woolson was also critical of the lack of discrimination evidenced by the general reading public: "Names that to me are the brightest stars in the horizon, are known not at all; names that I have never heard, take their place." Her own favorite authors included Ivan Turgenev ("in my estimation the greatest of modern novelists"), George Eliot, George Sand, Charles Reade, Charlotte Brontë, and Alexandre Dumas *père*; her favorite novel in the 1870s was Eliot's *The Mill on the Floss* (1860). She wondered what would result from her own artistic theories: "I generally throw half across the room all the new novels of the day. Now *these* novels the *Public* like! Moral: will they not be likely to throw mine *entirely* across the room? I fear so."

Another of Woolson's literary advisers was poet and critic E. C. Stedman, who, along with Hayne, encouraged her literary aspirations and provided valuable literary advice. After the publication of *Anne*, Stedman predicted that Woolson would "become our foremost writer of imaginative prose." In another letter he referred to her as "a woman of taste, industry, insight, *plus* genius. . . . " Woolson's notebooks, however, reveal that she may have had some reservations about Stedman's conception of woman's genius; commenting on Stedman's *Victorian Poets* (1876), she had written, "Mrs. Browning. Mr. Stedman does not really believe in woman's genius. His disbelief peeps through every line of the criticism below, whose essence is–'She did wonderfully well for a woman.' " In this passage and in similar comments in her review of James's *The Europeans* ("The Contributors' Club," *Atlantic Monthly*, 1878), Woolson appears as one of America's earliest feminist critics. In her notebooks she also states her preference to write stories about women: "To have, above all things, a sympathetic heroine." She valued Henrik Ibsen's portrayals of Nora and Hedda and worked to present relationships between men and women which were true to nature and not seen through "a mist of romantic illusion." Because she cared "only for motives," she created "analytical" fiction. In one of her last stories, "In Sloane Street" (*Harper's Bazar*, June 1892), Woolson defends writers and readers who are "interested in the study of character. . . . "

Nine of Woolson's twenty-three stories set in and around the Great Lakes region are collected in *Castle Nowhere: Lake-Country Sketches*. Eight had appeared previously in magazines: "Peter the Parson" (*Scribner's Monthly*, September 1874), "Jeannette" (*Scribner's Monthly*, December 1874), "Solomon" (*Atlantic Monthly*, October 1873), "The Lady of Little Fishing" (*Atlantic Monthly*, September, 1874), "Wilhelmina" (*Atlantic Monthly*, January 1875), "Misery Landing" (*Harper's New Monthly*, May 1874), "St. Clair Flats" (*Appletons' Journal*, 4 October 1873), and "The Old Agency" (*Galaxy*, 1874). The title story, "Castle Nowhere," was written especially to begin the volume. Interesting individuals inhabit the Great Lakes shores, some reminiscent of characters in Cooper's frontier tales. Contrasts between past and present and "natural" and "civilized" characters as well as between a "natural" moral code and more orthodox religious and moral standards also seem related to themes from Cooper's work. A more obvious literary influence on the volume, however, is Bret Harte. In "Misery Landing," the rehabilitation of John Jay is tied to his reading of Harte's fiction: "After all; as long as I can read Harte's pages, I cannot be so bad as I seem, since, to my idea there is more of goodness and generosity and courage in his words than in many a sermon." The influence of the writer Woolson called one of "the brightest stars on the horizon" is clearly seen in "The Lady of Little Fishing," which nineteenth- and twentieth-century critics have called Woolson's best early story. Some, in fact, have argued that Woolson's artistry surpasses Harte's. For example, W. D. Howells's review of *Castle Nowhere* (*Atlantic Monthly*, June 1875) contends that Woolson's fiction rests on a "solid basis . . . a high truth to human nature never once weakened by any vagueness of the moral ideal in the author, as happens with Mr. Harte's sketches. . . . "

In "The Lady of Little Fishing," set in 1850, Miss Woolson uses a frame-narrative technique. The first-person narrator, a young city gentleman on vacation (camping, hunting, and fishing, "close to the great heart of nature"), discovers a deserted town. After settling down among the ruins for the night, he is visited by a specter from the past. The deerskin-clad visitor is a flesh and blood former inhabitant of the town of Little Fishing, which now lies in shambles around them, and he recounts the manner of its demise. Thirty

Woolson, circa 1890

seems to reflect Woolson's own realistic views about relationships. As Mitchell concludes, "Love is not made to order."

As Kern has indicated, "Just as she had been a pioneer in revealing the peculiar atmosphere and charm of the lake region, so she became a pioneer in exploring the state of the prostrate South during the period of Reconstruction." Of Woolson's fourteen stories based on her southern experiences, ten are collected in *Rodman the Keeper: Southern Sketches*: "Rodman the Keeper" (*Atlantic Monthly*, March 1877), "Sister St. Luke" (*Galaxy*, April 1877), "Miss Elisabetha" (*Appletons' Journal*, 13 March 1875), "Old Gardiston" (*Harper's New Monthly*, April 1876), "The South Devil" (*Atlantic Monthly*, February 1880), "In the Cotton Country" (*Appletons' Journal*, 29 April 1876), "Felipa" (*Lippincott's Magazine*, June 1876), "Bro' " (*Appletons' Journal*, 1878), "King David" (*Scribner's Monthly*, April 1878), and "Up in the Blue Ridge" (*Appletons' Journal*, August 1878). As Henry James said of Woolson's southern tales, "Miss Woolson has done nothing better than the best pages in this succession of careful, strenuous studies of certain aspects of life after the war, in Florida, Georgia and the Carolinas. As the fruit of a remarkable minuteness of observation and tenderness of feeling on the part of one who evidently did not glance and pass, but lingered and analyzed, they have a high value" (*Harper's Weekly*, 1887). In "Old Gardiston," "Rodman the Keeper," and "King David"–often singled out as Woolson's best stories of this period–Northern characters go south after the Civil War and are confronted with effects of the war and Reconstruction on Southern attitudes. In "Old Gardiston" two Northern officers, Captain Newell and Lieutenant Saxton, attempt to befriend the young Miss Gardis Duke, the last survivor of a proud South Carolina family. A company of federal troops is quartered near Old Gardiston, the manor house, which stands impoverished and isolated, filled with remnants of old furniture, china, silks, and laces, "reduced now to shadows." Although Gardis views the Northerners as enemies, vandals, and despots, she becomes obligated to them when they save the plantation from pillaging marauders. In acknowledgment of this aid Gardis gives a dinner for Captain Newell and Lieutenant Saxton. Both men fall in love with her and wish to rescue her from her destitute situation; but Gardis declares that she could never marry a Northerner, who could never understand the heart of a Southern

years earlier Little Fishing had been a station for the Northwest and Hudson Bay Companies, inhabited by forty rough hunters and trappers, men of all nationalities and classes, with only one characteristic in common–"badness." Yet, this community of drinking, gambling, violent wild men was transformed by the arrival of the "lady" of Little Fishing–a tall, slender, pale-faced, golden-haired woman, a "lily lady," dressed in dove-colored robes. Out of devotion to this beautiful Scottish missionary, the men built new houses and a meetinghouse, attended worship services, and, in general, reformed. Only one man, Mitchell, remained unmoved by the lady's presence, and, ironically, she fell in love with him. On learning that their idol is "but common flesh and blood," the other men became disillusioned and reverted to their wild ways. Mitchell, steadfastly refusing to love the lady, fled the camp, and the lady died of a broken heart. The camp disintegrated; any semblance of civilization disappeared. As the story returns to the present, the reader learns that the specter from the past is Mitchell himself, returned to visit the lady's grave. The story woman. Lieutenant Saxton returns to the North, but Captain Newell remains. Gardis, reduced to selling her old home to a Northern contractor's wife, accidentally sets the place on fire and is forced to watch as it burns to the ground. At this point Newell finally convinces Gardis that her false pride is unfounded. Old Gardiston is gone, but a new union of North and South rises from its ashes.

Both "King David" and "Rodman the Keeper" also juxtapose well-meaning Northerners and proud Southerners, struggling toward resolutions to war-related problems. In "King David" a Yankee schoolmaster, David King, goes south to educate the newly freed slaves. His work is hampered by resistance and hatred from patrician planters who remain in the area, and by unscrupulous Northerners who sell cheap liquor to the freedmen and buy their votes. King's scholars misunderstand his good intentions, abandon his school, and turn Jubilee Town into a dangerous place. Unable to comprehend their motives, King returns to the North in defeat. Woolson also portrays the complexities of the regional differences and the "problem of emancipation" in "Rodman the Keeper," the story of Civil War veteran Colonel Rodman, a Northerner who returns to the South to serve as keeper of a national cemetery. He presides over the graves of fourteen thousand U.S. soldiers and views the cemetery as "part of a great problem now working itself out. . . ." Rodman is contrasted with Ward de Rosset, a severely wounded Confederate officer, who has returned to his deserted and ruined plantation house. Despite their differences, Rodman begins to tend the poverty-stricken Confederate, providing him with medicine and food, and finally sheltering him in his own quarters at the cemetery. While Rodman and de Rosset come to understand each other, de Rosset's cousin, Miss Bettina, is outraged that de Rosset accepts Rodman's help. As the story concludes, de Rosset dies, and the old plantation house is sold and razed; but—wrapped in her "armor of pride"—Bettina continues to scorn any idea of reconciliation between North and South. She refuses Rodman's offer of aid and friendship and sets out alone and in despair to become a teacher in another state. Rodman understands why she cannot change and mourns her fate.

The Front Yard and Other Italian Stories contains six stories—"The Front Yard" (*Harper's New Monthly*, December 1888), "Neptune's Shore" (*Harper's New Monthly*, October 1888), "A Pink Villa"

(*Harper's New Monthly*, November 1888), "The Street of the Hyacinth" (*Century Magazine*, May 1882), "A Christmas Party" (*Harper's New Monthly*, December 1892), and "In Venice" (*Atlantic Monthly*, April 1882)—while the five stories in *Dorothy and Other Italian Stories* are "Dorothy" (*Harper's New Monthly*, March 1892), "A Transplanted Boy" (*Harper's New Monthly*, February 1894), "A Florentine Experiment" (*Atlantic Monthly*, October 1880), "A Waitress" (*Harper's New Monthly*, June 1894), and "At the Chateau of Corinne" (*Harper's New Monthly*, October 1887). In "The Front Yard" a New England woman, who has come to Italy as companion to a distant cousin, remains at Perugia after the cousin's death in order to marry a good-natured Italian reprobate. A "plain, simple-hearted spinster," Prudence devotes her savings and her "wonderful strength and energy" to Tonio, who enjoys a year of "paradisiacal opulence" at her expense. At the end of those twelve months he succumbs to a fever, and his widow is left to support his eight children, grandmother, and old uncle on the remaining eighty-five of her original six-hundred-dollar savings. Prudence, who never complains or has regrets no matter how much they take advantage of her, toils for sixteen years on behalf of her thankless and heartless stepchildren and in-laws. Her one dream is to replace the cow shed in her front yard with a New-England style flower garden, complete with white picket fence and swinging gate, but each time she seems to have saved enough to achieve her goal, some member of the family begs or steals her hard-earned savings. Exhausted and near death, Prudence is discovered by an American woman who accomplishes the task for her. Kern calls Prudence "one of Miss Woolson's finest creations. . . . In all of the best of Miss Woolson's short stories and novels there is at least one woman whose character is a miracle of self-abnegation, but in none of them does the writer achieve a finer example of feminine idealism."

"A Transplanted Boy" is an investigation of another sort. While Prudence preserves her honest New England character in Italy, Thomas Ross Coe becomes Tommasco (or Maso) after spending his developmental years there. The boy's widowed mother, who transplanted him to Italy when he was two, failed to give him a sense of his American heritage. As he approaches adolescence, he realizes that he has become alienated from Italians and Americans. As the story concludes, the boy's mother realizes that she has acted selfishly by keeping her son away from his homeland for so long. Yet, when his uncle at home hears of her plan to return, he comments that she "thinks it will be better for the boy. But I'm afraid it's too late for that."

Each of these posthumously published collections contains a story about a woman artist, and in addition to "The Street of the Hyacinth" and "At the Chateau of Corrine," Woolson wrote two uncollected stories that deal with the question of art and artists: "Miss Grief" (*Lippincott's Magazine*, May 1880) and "In Sloane Street" (*Harper's Bazar*, June 1892), in which independent women resist society's efforts to force them into stereotypical molds. The heroines of "The Street of the Hyacinth" and "At the Chateau of Corrine" succumb to society's pressures, give up their art, and marry. The protagonists in "Miss Grief" and "In Sloane Street" seem most like Constance Woolson, proud, independent, and committed to their work, yet sometimes lonely and unsure of their aesthetic in a culture which discouraged serious women artists. Woolson's correspondence often comments on the strenuous nature of her literary life and emphasizes the psychic energy required by her work. Commenting on her final novel, *Horace Chase*, she wrote: "But we must all do as we can, and the only way I can write at all, is to do my very best. Something in me makes me take these enormous pains."

Henry James's 1887 statement about Woolson's creation of a character in *East Angels* may be applied to Woolson's work in general: "The care, the ingenuity, the precautions the author has exhibited, to make us accept Mrs. Harold in her integrity, are perceptible on every page, and they leave us finally no alternative but to accept her; she remains exalted, but she remains at the same time thoroughly sound." Woolson's contribution to American literature is her gallery of "distinct personages" inextricably involved with the settings in which they are placed.

Letters:

Jay B. Hubbell, ed., "Some New Letters of Constance Fenimore Woolson," *New England Quarterly*, 14 (1941): 715-735.

References:

Leon Edel, *Henry James: The Conquest of London, 1870-1881* (Philadelphia & New York: Lippincott, 1962);

Edel, *Henry James: The Middle Years, 1882-1885* (Philadelphia & New York: Lippincott, 1962);

Evelyn Helmick, "Constance Fenimore Woolson: First Novelist of Florida," in *Feminist Criticism: Essays on Theory, Poetry, and Prose*, edited by Cheryl L. Brown and Karen Olson (Metuchen, N.J.: Scarecrow Press, 1978);

Henry James, "Miss Constance Fenimore Woolson," *Harper's Weekly*, 31 (12 February 1887): 114-115; republished in his *Partial Portraits* (London & New York: Macmillan, 1888);

John Dwight Kern, *Constance Fenimore Woolson: Literary Pioneer* (Philadelphia: University of Pennsylvania Press, 1934);

Rayburn S. Moore, *Constance Fenimore Woolson* (New York: Twayne, 1963);

Moore, "The Full Light of a Higher Criticism: Edel's Biography and Other Recent Studies of Henry James," *South Atlantic Quarterly*, 63 (1964): 104-114;

Moore, "The Strange Irregular Rhythm of Life: James's Late Tales," *South Atlantic Bulletin*, 41 (1976): 86-93;

Fred Lewis Pattee, *The Development of the American Short Story* (New York: Harper, 1923);

Arthur Hobson Quinn, *American Fiction: An Historical and Critical Survey* (New York: Appleton-Century, 1936);

Lyon N. Richardson, "Constance Fenimore Woolson: 'Novelist Laureate' of America," *South Atlantic Quarterly*, 39 (1940): 18-36;

Anne Rowe, *The Enchanted Country: Northern Writers in the South, 1865-1910* (Baton Rouge: Louisiana State University Press, 1979);

Ann Douglas Wood, "The Literature of Impoverishment: The Women Local Colorists in America, 1865-1914," *Women's Studies*, 1 (1972): 3-46.

Papers:

Woolson's letters to Henry James are at the Houghton Library, Harvard University. Other significant collections are at the Beinecke Library, Yale University; the Pierpont Morgan Library; the William R. Perkins Library, Duke University; the John Hay Library, Brown University; the Western Reserve Historical Society, Cleveland, Ohio; and the Alderman Library, University of Virginia.

Books for Further Reading

Canby, Henry S. *The Short Story in English*. New York: Holt, 1909.

Charvat, William. *Literary Publishing in America, 1790-1850*. Philadelphia: University of Pennsylvania Press, 1959.

Charvat. *The Profession of Authorship in America, 1800-1870: The Papers of William Charvat*, edited by Matthew J. Bruccoli. Columbus: Ohio State University Press, 1968.

Current-García, Eugene. *The American Short Story Before 1850: A Critical History*. Boston: G. K. Hall, 1985.

Douglas, Ann. *The Feminization of American Culture*. New York: Knopf, 1977.

Hoffman, Daniel. *Form and Fable in American Fiction*. New York: Oxford University Press, 1961.

Klinkowitz, Jerome. *The Practice of Fiction in America: Writers from Hawthorne to the Present*. Ames: Iowa State University Press, 1980.

Martin, Terence. *The Instructed Vision: Scottish Common Sense Philosophy and the Origins of American Fiction*. Bloomington: Indiana University Press, 1961.

Matthews, Brander. *The Philosophy of the Short-Story*. New York & London: Longmans, Green, 1901.

May, Charles E., ed. *Short Story Theories*. Athens: Ohio University Press, 1976.

Moore, Jack B. *Native Elements in American Magazine Short Fiction, 1741-1800*. Chapel Hill: University of North Carolina Press, 1963.

Mott, Frank Luther. *A History of American Magazines*, 5 volumes. Cambridge, Mass.: Harvard University Press, 1938-1968.

O'Brien, Edward J. *The Advance of the American Short Story*, revised edition. New York: Dodd, Mead, 1931.

Pattee, Fred Lewis. *The Development of the American Short Story: An Historical Survey*. New York & London: Harper, 1923.

Slotkin, Richard. *Regeneration Through Violence: The Mythology of the American Frontier, 1600-1860*. Middletown, Conn.: Wesleyan University Press, 1973.

Spencer, Benjamin T. *The Quest for Nationality: An American Literary Campaign*. Syracuse, N.Y.: Syracuse University Press, 1957.

Thompson, G. R., and Virgil L. Lokke, eds. *Ruined Eden of the Present: Hawthorne, Melville, Poe*. West Lafayette, Ind.: Purdue University Press, 1981.

Voss, Arthur. *The American Short Story: A Critical Survey*. Norman: University of Oklahoma Press, 1973.

Contributors

David D. Anderson ....*Michigan State University*
Samuel I. Bellman ....*California State Polytechnic University, Pomona*
Laurie Buchanan ....*Central Michigan University*
Eric W. Carlson ....*University of Connecticut*
Jean Ferguson Carr ....*University of Pittsburgh*
Cathy N. Davidson ....*Michigan State University*
William V. DeTora ....*Temple University*
Josephine Donovan ....*University of Maine*
Mary P. Edwards ....*Randolph-Macon College*
Bernard F. Engel ....*Michigan State University*
Paul J. Ferlazzo ....*Northern Arizona University*
Joseph M. Flora ....*University of North Carolina at Chapel Hill*
Robert L. Gale ....*University of Pittsburgh*
Miriam S. Gogol ....*Fashion Institute of Technology, State University of New York*
Henry L. Golemba ....*Wayne State University*
William E. Grant ....*Bowling Green State University*
Alan Gribben ....*University of Texas at Austin*
Doty Hale ....*California State University, Los Angeles*
Dean G. Hall ....*Kansas State University*
Wade Hall ....*Bellarmine College*
Bert Hitchcock ....*Auburn University*
Gary Hoppenstand ....*Michigan State University*
Theodore R. Hovet ....*University of Northern Iowa*
Nancy Huse ....*Augustana College, Rock Island, Illinois*
Laura Ingram ....*Columbia, South Carolina*
Carolyn L. Karcher ....*Temple University*
A. Robert Lee ....*University of Kent at Canterbury*
George C. Longest ....*Virginia Commonwealth University*
Richard D. Rust ....*University of North Carolina at Chapel Hill*
Thelma J. Shinn ....*Arizona State University*
Philip G. Terrie ....*Bowling Green State University*
Laura M. Zaidman ....*University of South Carolina, Sumter*

Cumulative Index

Dictionary of Literary Biography, Volumes 1-74
Dictionary of Literary Biography Yearbook, 1980-1987
Dictionary of Literary Biography Documentary Series, Volumes 1-4

Cumulative Index

DLB before number: *Dictionary of Literary Biography*, Volumes 1-74
Y before number: *Dictionary of Literary Biography Yearbook*, 1980-1987
DS before number: *Dictionary of Literary Biography Documentary Series*, Volumes 1-4

A

C

D

E

H

I

K

M

Cumulative Index

N

Q

R

S

T

U

V

W

Z

Dictionary of Literary Biography

1: *The American Renaissance in New England,* edited by Joel Myerson (1978)

2: *American Novelists Since World War II,* edited by Jeffrey Helterman and Richard Layman (1978)

3: *Antebellum Writers in New York and the South,* edited by Joel Myerson (1979)

4: *American Writers in Paris, 1920-1939,* edited by Karen Lane Rood (1980)

5: *American Poets Since World War II,* 2 parts, edited by Donald J. Greiner (1980)

6: *American Novelists Since World War II,* Second Series, edited by James E. Kibler, Jr. (1980)

7: *Twentieth-Century American Dramatists,* 2 parts, edited by John MacNicholas (1981)

8: *Twentieth-Century American Science-Fiction Writers,* 2 parts, edited by David Cowart and Thomas L. Wymer (1981)

9: *American Novelists, 1910-1945,* 3 parts, edited by James J. Martine (1981)

10: *Modern British Dramatists, 1900-1945,* 2 parts, edited by Stanley Weintraub (1982)

11: *American Humorists, 1800-1950,* 2 parts, edited by Stanley Trachtenberg (1982)

12: *American Realists and Naturalists,* edited by Donald Pizer and Earl N. Harbert (1982)

13: *British Dramatists Since World War II,* 2 parts, edited by Stanley Weintraub (1982)

14: *British Novelists Since 1960,* 2 parts, edited by Jay L. Halio (1983)

15: *British Novelists, 1930-1959,* 2 parts, edited by Bernard Oldsey (1983)

16: *The Beats: Literary Bohemians in Postwar America,* 2 parts, edited by Ann Charters (1983)

17: *Twentieth-Century American Historians,* edited by Clyde N. Wilson (1983)

18: *Victorian Novelists After 1885,* edited by Ira B. Nadel and William E. Fredeman (1983)

19: *British Poets, 1880-1914,* edited by Donald E. Stanford (1983)

20: *British Poets, 1914-1945,* edited by Donald E. Stanford (1983)

21: *Victorian Novelists Before 1885,* edited by Ira B. Nadel and William E. Fredeman (1983)

22: *American Writers for Children, 1900-1960,* edited by John Cech (1983)

23: *American Newspaper Journalists, 1873-1900,* edited by Perry J. Ashley (1983)

24: *American Colonial Writers, 1606-1734,* edited by Emory Elliott (1984)

25: *American Newspaper Journalists, 1901-1925,* edited by Perry J. Ashley (1984)

26: *American Screenwriters,* edited by Robert E. Morsberger, Stephen O. Lesser, and Randall Clark (1984)

27: *Poets of Great Britain and Ireland, 1945-1960,* edited by Vincent B. Sherry, Jr. (1984)

28: *Twentieth-Century American-Jewish Fiction Writers,* edited by Daniel Walden (1984)

29: *American Newspaper Journalists, 1926-1950,* edited by Perry J. Ashley (1984)

30: *American Historians, 1607-1865,* edited by Clyde N. Wilson (1984)

31: *American Colonial Writers, 1735-1781,* edited by Emory Elliott (1984)

32: *Victorian Poets Before 1850,* edited by William E. Fredeman and Ira B. Nadel (1984)

33: *Afro-American Fiction Writers After 1955,* edited by Thadious M. Davis and Trudier Harris (1984)

34: *British Novelists, 1890-1929: Traditionalists,* edited by Thomas F. Staley (1985)

35: *Victorian Poets After 1850,* edited by William E. Fredeman and Ira B. Nadel (1985)

36: *British Novelists, 1890-1929: Modernists,* edited by Thomas F. Staley (1985)

37: *American Writers of the Early Republic,* edited by Emory Elliott (1985)

38: *Afro-American Writers After 1955: Dramatists and Prose Writers,* edited by Thadious M. Davis and Trudier Harris (1985)

39: *British Novelists, 1660-1800,* 2 parts, edited by Martin C. Battestin (1985)

40: *Poets of Great Britain and Ireland Since 1960,* 2 parts, edited by Vincent B. Sherry, Jr. (1985)

41: *Afro-American Poets Since 1955,* edited by Trudier Harris and Thadious M. Davis (1985)

42: *American Writers for Children Before 1900,* edited by Glenn E. Estes (1985)

43: *American Newspaper Journalists, 1690-1872,* edited by Perry J. Ashley (1986)

44: *American Screenwriters,* Second Series, edited by Randall Clark, Robert E. Morsberger, and Stephen O. Lesser (1986)

45: *American Poets, 1880-1945,* First Series, edited by Peter Quartermain (1986)

46: *American Literary Publishing Houses, 1900-1980: Trade and Paperback,* edited by Peter Dzwonkoski (1986)

47: *American Historians, 1866-1912,* edited by Clyde N. Wilson (1986)